G000299085

STREE

North

Hampshire

First published in 1994 by

Philip's, a division of
Octopus Publishing Group Ltd
2-4 Heron Quays, London E14 4JP

Third colour edition 2006
First impression 2006
NHACA

ISBN-10   0-540-08769-6 (pocket)
ISBN-13   978-0-540-08769-3 (pocket)

© Philip's 2006

Ordnance Survey®

This product includes mapping data licensed from
Ordnance Survey® with the permission of the
Controller of Her Majesty's Stationery Office.
© Crown copyright 2006. All rights reserved.
Licence number 100011710.

Printed by Toppan, China

Contents

III	**Key to map symbols**
IV	**Key to map pages**
VI	**Route planning**
VIII	**Administrative and Postcode boundaries**
1	**Street maps** at 2⅔ inches to 1 mile
210	**Index** of towns and villages
212	**Index** of streets, hospitals, industrial estates, railway stations, schools, shopping centres, universities and places of interest

Digital Data

The exceptionally high-quality mapping found in this atlas is available as digital data in TIFF format, which is easily convertible to other bitmapped (raster) image formats.

The index is also available in digital form as a standard database table. It contains all the details found in the printed index together with the National Grid reference for the map square in which each entry is named.

For further information and to discuss your requirements, please contact Philip's on 020 7644 6932 or james.mann@philips-maps.co.uk

Key to map symbols

III

(22a)	**Motorway** with junction number
	Primary route – dual/single carriageway
	A road – dual/single carriageway
	B road – dual/single carriageway
	Minor road – dual/single carriageway
	Other minor road – dual/single carriageway
	Road under construction
	Tunnel, covered road
	Rural track, private road or narrow road in urban area
	Gate or obstruction to traffic (restrictions may not apply at all times or to all vehicles)
	Path, bridleway, byway open to all traffic, road used as a public path
	Pedestrianised area
DY7	**Postcode boundaries**
	County and unitary authority boundaries
	Railway, tunnel, railway under construction
	Tramway, tramway under construction
	Miniature railway
⌖ Walsall	**Railway station**
(railway symbol)	**Private railway station**
South Shields	**Metro station**
	Tram stop, tram stop under construction
	Bus, coach station

◆	**Ambulance station**
◆	**Coastguard station**
◆	**Fire station**
◆	**Police station**
✚	**Accident and Emergency entrance to hospital**
H	**Hospital**
✛	**Place of worship**
i	**Information Centre** (open all year)
🛒	**Shopping Centre**
P P&R	**Parking, Park and Ride**
PO	**Post Office**
Å	**Camping site**
🚐	**Caravan site**
▶	**Golf course**
✕	**Picnic site**
Prim Sch	**Important buildings, schools, colleges, universities and hospitals**
	Built up area
	Woods
River Medway	**Water name**
	River, weir, stream
	Canal, lock, tunnel
	Water
	Tidal water
Church	**Non-Roman antiquity**
ROMAN FORT	**Roman antiquity**
87	**Adjoining page indicators and overlap bands**
24	

Abbr	Full	Abbr	Full	Abbr	Full
Acad	**Academy**	Inst	**Institute**	Recn Gd	**Recreation Ground**
Allot Gdns	**Allotments**	Ct	**Law Court**		
Cemy	**Cemetery**	L Ctr	**Leisure Centre**	Resr	**Reservoir**
C Ctr	**Civic Centre**	LC	**Level Crossing**	Ret Pk	**Retail Park**
CH	**Club House**	Liby	**Library**	Sch	**School**
Coll	**College**	Mkt	**Market**	Sh Ctr	**Shopping Centre**
Crem	**Crematorium**	Meml	**Memorial**	TH	**Town Hall/House**
Ent	**Enterprise**	Mon	**Monument**	Trad Est	**Trading Estate**
Ex H	**Exhibition Hall**	Mus	**Museum**	Univ	**University**
Ind Est	**Industrial Estate**	Obsy	**Observatory**	W Twr	**Water Tower**
IRB Sta	**Inshore Rescue**	Pal	**Royal Palace**	Wks	**Works**
	Boat Station	PH	**Public House**	YH	**Youth Hostel**

■ The small numbers around the edges of the maps identify the 1 kilometre National Grid lines

■ The dark grey border on the inside edge of some pages indicates that the mapping does not continue onto the adjacent page

The scale of the maps on the pages numbered in blue is 4.2 cm to 1 km • 2⅔ inches to 1 mile • 1: 23810

0	¼	½	¾	1 mile
0	250m	500m	750m	1 kilometre

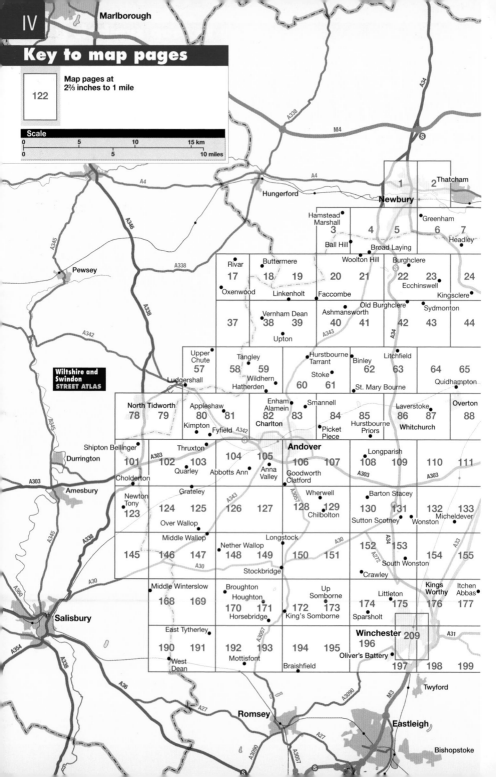

IV

Key to map pages

Map pages at
2⅔ inches to 1 mile

122

Scale

| 0 | 5 | 10 | 15 km |

| 0 | 5 | 10 miles |

Marlborough

Hungerford

Newbury

1 2 Thatcham

Hamstead Marshall
3   4   5   6   7 Headley
Greenham

Ball Hill   Broad Laying
Woolton Hill   Burghclere

Rivar   Buttermere
17   18   19   20   21   22   23   24
Oxenwood   Linkenholt   Faccombe   Ecchinswell
Kingsclere

Pewsey

Vernham Dean   Ashmansworth   Old Burghclere   Sydmonton
37   38   39   40   41   42   43   44
Upton

Wiltshire and Swindon STREET ATLAS

Upper Chute   Tangley   Hurstbourne Tarrant   Binley   Litchfield
57   58   59   60   61   62   63   64   65
Wildhern   Stoke   Quidhampton
Ludgershall   Hatherden   St. Mary Bourne

North Tidworth   Appleshaw   Enham Alamein   Smannell   Laverstoke   Overton
78   79   80   81   82   83   84   85   86   87   88
Kimpton   Fyfield   Charlton   Picket Piece   Hurstbourne Priors   Whitchurch

Shipton Bellinger   Thruxton   Andover   Longparish
Durrington   101   102   103   104   105   106   107   108   109   110   111
Cholderton   Quarley   Abbotts Ann   Anna Valley   Goodworth Clatford
Amesbury

Newton Tony   Grateley   Wherwell   Barton Stacey
123   124   125   126   127   128   129   130   131   132   133
Over Wallop   Chilbolton   Sutton Scotney   Wonston   Micheldever

Middle Wallop   Longstock
145   146   147   148   149   150   151   152   153   154   155
Nether Wallop   South Wonston
Stockbridge   Crawley

Middle Winterslow   Broughton   Up Somborne   Kings Worthy   Itchen Abbas
168   169   170   171   172   173   174   175   176   177
Houghton   King's Somborne   Littleton
Horsebridge   Sparsholt

East Tytherley   Winchester 209
190   191   192   193   194   195   196   197   198   199
West Dean   Mottisfont   Braishfield   Oliver's Battery

Salisbury

Romsey

Twyford

Eastleigh

Bishopstoke

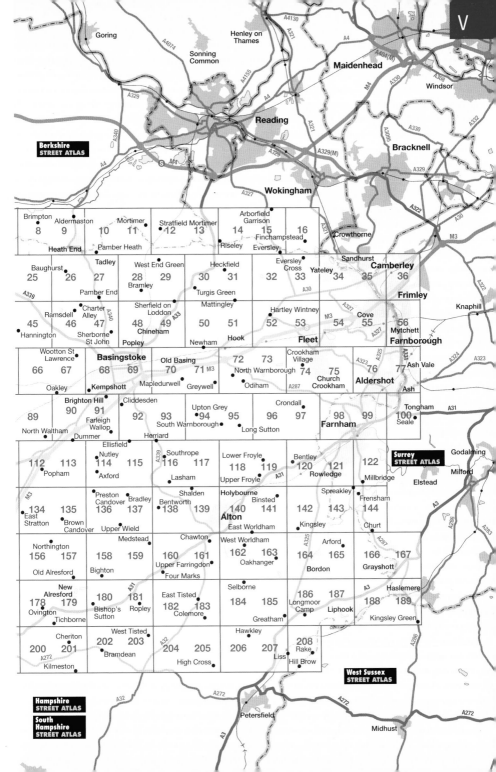

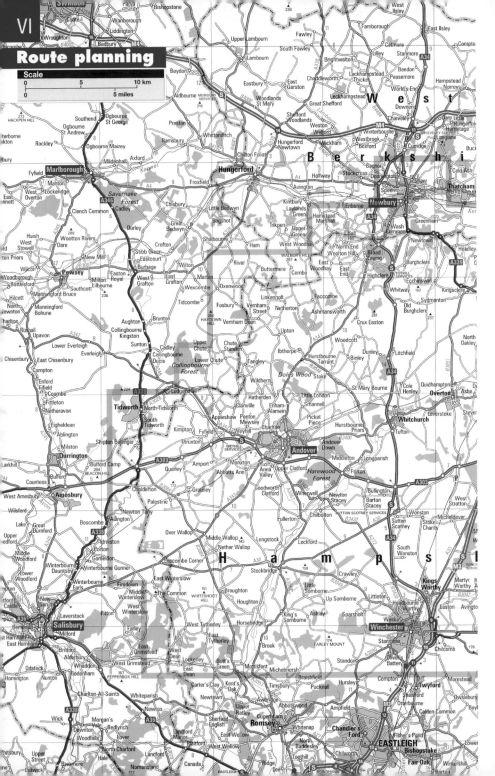

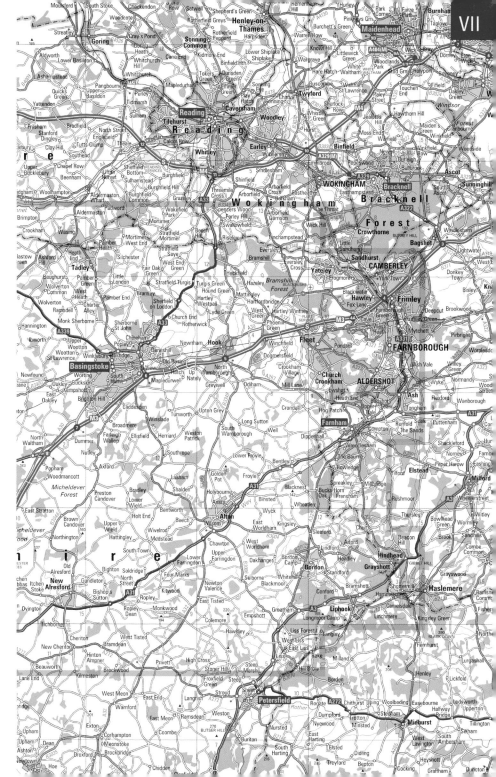

Major administrative and Postcode boundaries

County and unitary authority boundaries
District boundaries
Postcode boundaries

Scale

0   5   10   15 km
0   5   10 miles

Bracknell Forest

Wokingham

West Berkshire

Newbury

Mortimer

Surrey

Camberley
Frimley
Camberley
GU15
GU16
GU14
GU17
GU51
GU11
GU12
Aldershot
Farnham
Blackwater
GU46
GU52
GU29
Yateley
RG40
RG27
Hook
Odiham
Fleet
GU9
GU10
Bentley
GU35
Bordon
Grayshott
Haslemere
GU26
Liphook
GU30
GU27
GU33
Liss
GU31

RG7
Tadley
Bramley
Chineham
RG24
Basingstoke
RG23
RG21
RG22
Ellisfield
RG25
Alton
GU34
Medstead
Bentworth
New
Alresford
SO24
East Hampshire
West
Meon
GU32
Petersfield
P08
Horndean
P09
P010
Thorney Island
P018
West Sussex

RG19
RG14
RG20
Kingsclere
Burghclere
RG28
Whitchurch
North
Waltham
South
Wonston
Micheldever
SO21
Itchen
Abbas
SO23
Winchester
SO22
Twyford
SO53
Hampshire
SO50
Meonstoke
Bishop's
Waltham
SO32
Wickham
P017
P07
P016
Fareham
Fareham
P014
P015
P013
Gosport
P012
Gosport
P01
P02
P03
P04
P05
City of Portsmouth
Portsmouth
P06
P011
Havant
P010
Havant

SN8
RG17
Vernham
Dean
SP11
SP10
Andover
Thruxton
Tangley
St Mary Bourne
Wherwell
Test Valley
Broughton
SO20
SO51
Over Wallop
Mottisfont
West Wellow
SO52
Romsey
Eastleigh
West End
SO31
SO30
Eastleigh
SO19
SO18
SO16
SO17
Netley
Hythe
Fawley
SO45

SP9
SP4
West Dean
SP5
Cadnam
SO43
Lyndhurst
New Forest
Totton
SO40
SO15
SO14
City of Southampton
Southampton
SO42
Beaulieu
SO41
Sway
Lymington
Barton on Sea

SP6
Fordingbridge
Martin
Croucheston
Ibsley
BH24
Ringwood
Burley
Brockenhurst
BH25
BH23
Christchurch
Bournemouth
BH6
BH5
BH1
BH2
BH7
BH4
BH8

Wiltshire

Dorset

Verwood
BH31
BH21
Wimborne Minster
BH22
Ferndown
BH10
BH3
BH9
BH22
BH18
BH17
BH16
BH15
Poole
BH14
BH13
BH12
BH11
BH1
Bournemouth
BH2
Poole

Isle of Wight

ST SU

ST SU

SY SZ

SU SZ

SY SZ

ST

SU

SY

SZ

500
90
80
70
60
50
40
30
20
10
100
90

70
60
50
40
30
20
10
100
90

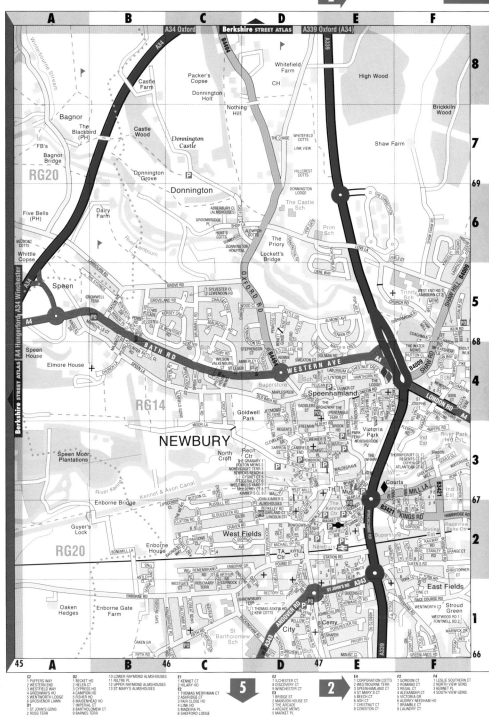

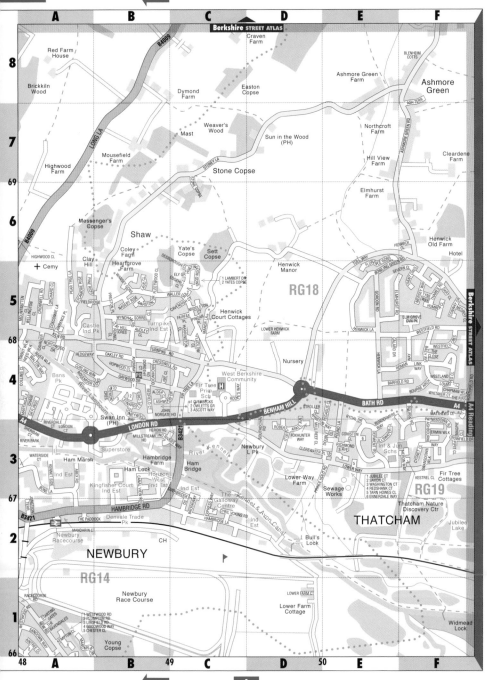

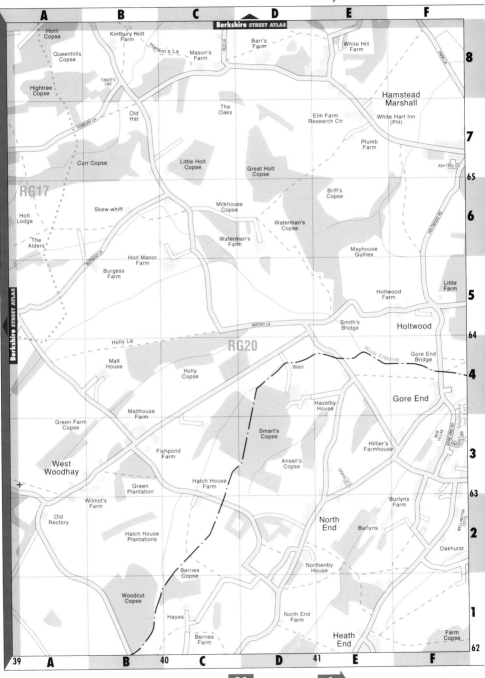

Berkshire STREET ATLAS

| A | B | C | D | E | F |

8

Horn Copse

Queenhills Copse

Kintbury Holt Farm

Hankin's La.

Mason's Farm

Barr's Farm

White Hill Farm

PARK LA

Hightree Copse

TINKER'S CNR.

OLD LA

Hamstead Marshall

Old Hat

FORBURY LA.

The Oaks

Elm Farm Research Ctr

White Hart Inn (PH)

7

Plumb Farm

Curr Copse

Little Holt Copse

Great Holt Copse

ASH TREE GR

65

RG17

Skew-whiff

Milkhouse Copse

Briff's Copse

6

HOLTWOOD RD

Holt Lodge

Waterman's Copse

Waterman's Farm

The Alders

BURGESS LA.

Holt Manor Farm

Mayhouse Gullies

Burgess Farm

Holtwood Farm

Little Farm

5

WATERY LA.

Smith's Bridge

Holtwood

64

Holly La.

RG20

River Enborne

Gore End Bridge

4

Malt House

Holly Copse

Weir

Gore End

Green Farm Copse

Malthouse Farm

Smart's Copse

Hazelby House

Hillier's Farmhouse

NEW VILLAS

GORE END RD

Studlands Ind Est

KNIGHTS LA

3

West Woodhay

Fishpond Farm

Hatch House Farm

Ansell's Copse

GRANGE LA

Burlyns Farm

63

Wilmot's Farm

Green Plantation

North End

Burlyns

WELLINGTON COTTS

2

Old Rectory

Hatch House Plantations

Northenby House

Oakhurst

Berries Copse

Woodcut Copse

Hayes

North End Farm

Heath End

Farm Copse

1

Berries Farm

62

| 39 | A | B | 40 | C | D | 41 | E | F |

Berkshire STREET ATLAS

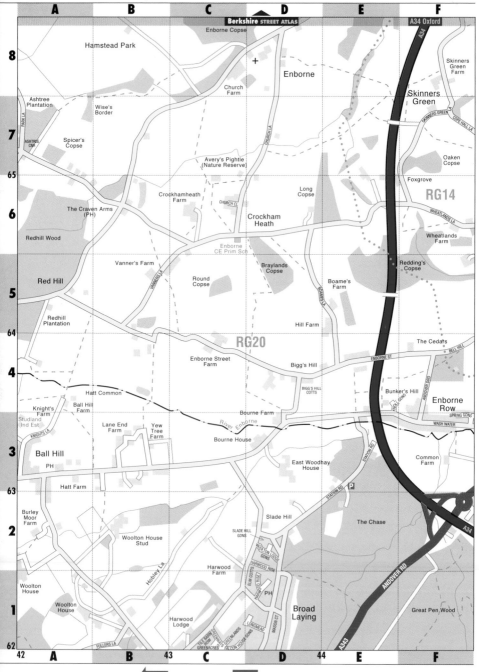

A34 Oxford

Hamstead Park

Enborne Copse

Enborne

Church Farm

Skinners Green Farm

Skinners Green

Ashtree Plantation

Wise's Border

Ashtree Cnr

SKINNERS GREEN LA

CVR HALL LA

PARK LA

Spicer's Copse

Oaken Copse

Avery's Pightle (Nature Reserve)

Foxgrove

CHURCH LA

RG14

Crockhamheath Farm

Long Copse

WHEATLANDS LA

The Craven Arms (PH)

CHURCH CL

Crockham Heath

Wheatlands Farm

Redhill Wood

Enborne CE Prim Sch

Braylands Copse

Redding's Copse

Vanner's Farm

Round Copse

Boame's Farm

Red Hill

VANNERS LA

BOAME'S LA

Redhill Plantation

Hill Farm

The Cedars

RG20

BELL HILL

Enborne Street Farm

Bigg's Hill

ENBORNE ST

Bunker's Hill

ANDOVER DRO

Enborne Row

Hatt Common

BIGG'S HILL COTTS

Knight's Farm

Ball Hill Farm

Bourne Farm

RIL GDNS

SPRING GDNS

Studland Ind Est

River Enborne

WASH WATER

KNIGHTS LA

Lane End Farm

Yew Tree Farm

Bourne House

Ball Hill

East Woodhay House

STATION RD

Common Farm

PH

Hatt Farm

P

Burley Moor Farm

Woolton House Stud

Slade Hill

SLADE HILL GDNS

The Chase

HOBLEY LA

Harwood Farm

WOOLTON LODGE GDNS

Woolton House

Woolton House

Harwood Lodge

HARWOOD RISE

ELM COTTS

PH

LONGMEAD

MASON CT

Broad Laying

Great Pen Wood

ANDOVER RD

A34

FULLERS LA

ELLE BARN ROW

GREENACRES

GREENLANDS

TALTON HOSEROAD

A343

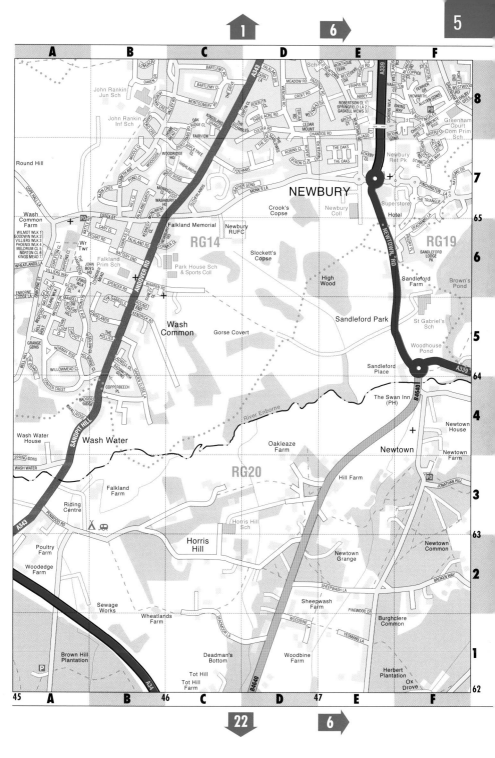

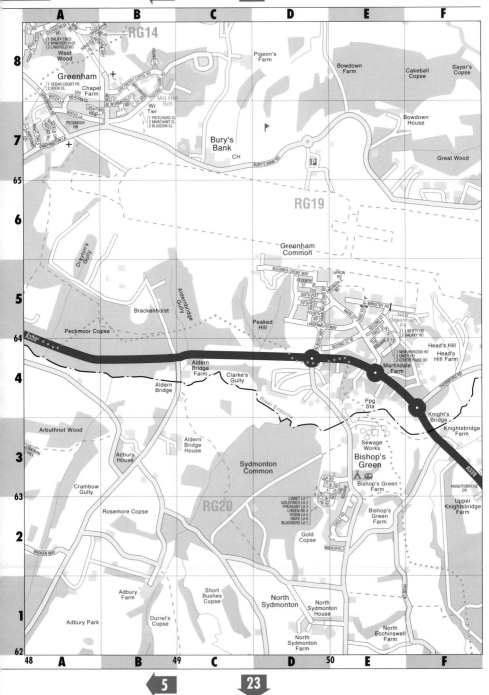

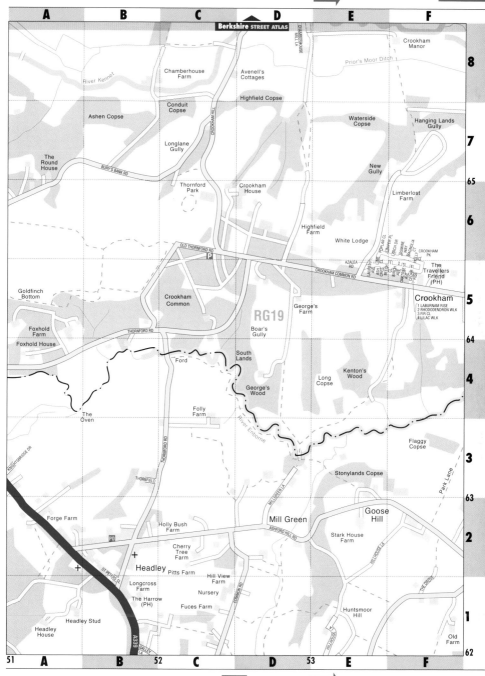

Berkshire STREET ATLAS

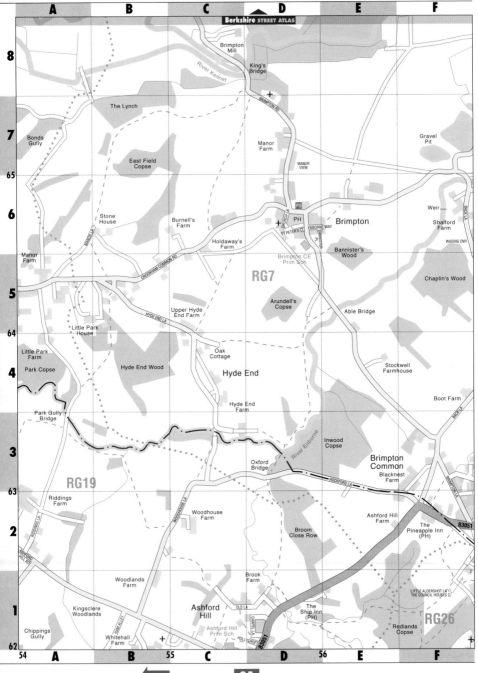

Berkshire STREET ATLAS

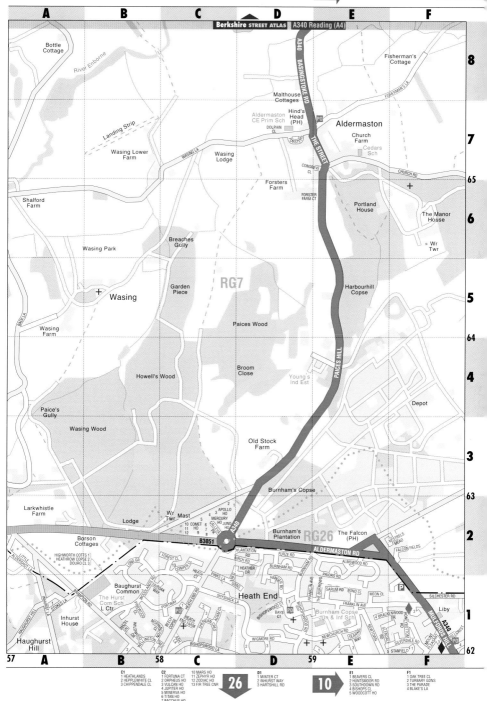

Berkshire STREET ATLAS | A340 Reading (A4)

C1	C2		E1	F1
1 HEATHLANDS	1 FORTUNA CT	10 MARS HO	1 BEAVERS CL	1 OAK TREE CL
2 HEPPLEWHITE CL	2 ORPHEUS HO	11 ZEPHYR HO	2 HUNTSMOOR RD	2 TURBARY GDNS
3 CHIPPENDALE CL	3 VULCAN HO	12 ZODIAC HO	3 SOUTHDOWN RD	3 THE PARADE
	4 JUPITER HO	13 FIR TREE CNR	4 BISHOPS CL	4 BLAKE'S LA
	5 MINERVA HO		5 WOODCOTT HO	
	6 TITAN HO			
	7 BACCHUS HO	D1		
	8 MIDAS HO	1 MINTER CT		
	9 SATURN HO	2 INHURST WAY		
		3 HARTSHILL RD		

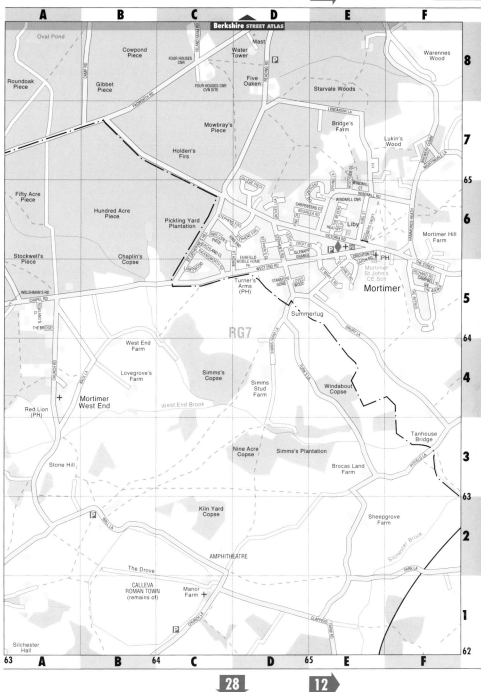

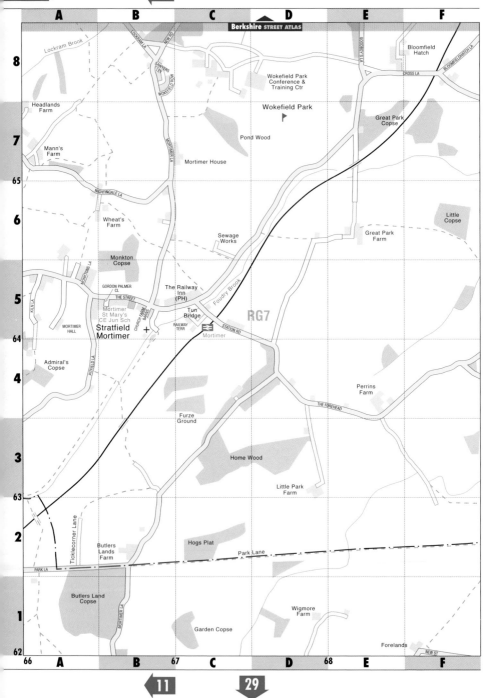

11

Berkshire STREET ATLAS

Lockram Brook

Headlands Farm

Mann's Farm

Wokefield Park Conference & Training Ctr

Bloomfield Hatch

CROSS LA

Wokefield Park

Great Park Copse

Pond Wood

NIGHTINGALE LA

Mortimer House

Little Copse

Wheat's Farm

Sewage Works

Great Park Farm

Monkton Copse

KILN LA

GORDON PALMER CL

THE STREET

The Railway Inn (PH)

Foudry Brook

RG7

Mortimer St Mary's CE Jun Sch

Tun Bridge

MORTIMER HALL

Stratfield Mortimer

RAILWAY TERR

STATION RD

Mortimer

Admiral's Copse

Perrins Farm

THE FOREHEAD

Furze Ground

Home Wood

Little Park Farm

Ticklecorner Lane

Butlers Lands Farm

Hogs Plat

Park Lane

PARK LA

Butlers Land Copse

Wigmore Farm

Garden Copse

Forelands

NEW ST

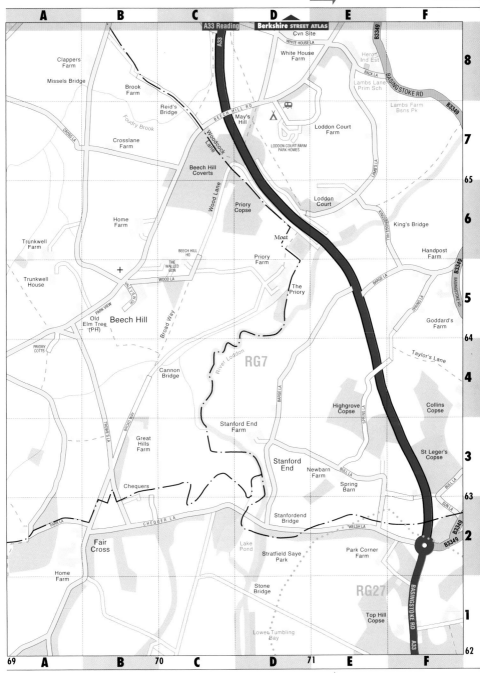

A33 Reading
Berkshire STREET ATLAS
A33

Cvn Site
WHITE HOUSE LA
White House Farm
Heron Ind Est
BACK LA
Lambs Lane Prim Sch
BASINGSTOKE RD
B3349

Clappers Farm
Missels Bridge
Brook Farm
Reid's Bridge
BEECH HILL RD
May's Hill
Lambs Farm Bsns Pk

Foudry Brook
Woodcock Lane
Loddon Court Farm
LAMBS LA

Crosslane Farm
Beech Hill Coverts
LODDON COURT FARM PARK HOMES

CROSS LA
Priory Copse
Loddon Court
KINGSBRIDGE HILL

Home Farm
Wood Lane
Moat
King's Bridge

Trunkwell Farm
BEECH HILL HO
Priory Farm
Handpost Farm
B3349

Trunkwell House
THE WALLED GDN
WOOD LA
The Priory
BARGE LA
BASINGSTOKE RD

VALLEY LE
PARK VIEW
Broad Way
Goddard's Farm
SPRING LA

Old Elm Tree (PH)
Beech Hill
River Loddon
RG7
Taylor's Lane

PRIORY COTTS
Cannon Bridge
BARGE LA

THORNE LA
Stanford End Farm
Highgrove Copse
Collins Copse
LONG LA

Great Hills Farm
BROAD WAY
Stanford End
St Leger's Copse
BULL LA

Chequers
Newbarn Farm
BULL LA
Spring Barn
SUN LA

CHEQUER LA
Stanfordend Bridge
WELSH LA
B3349

Fair Cross
Lake Pond
Stratfield Saye Park
Park Corner Farm
B3349
BASINGSTOKE RD

Home Farm
Stone Bridge
RG27

PARK LA
Top Hill Copse
A33

Lowes Tumbling Bay

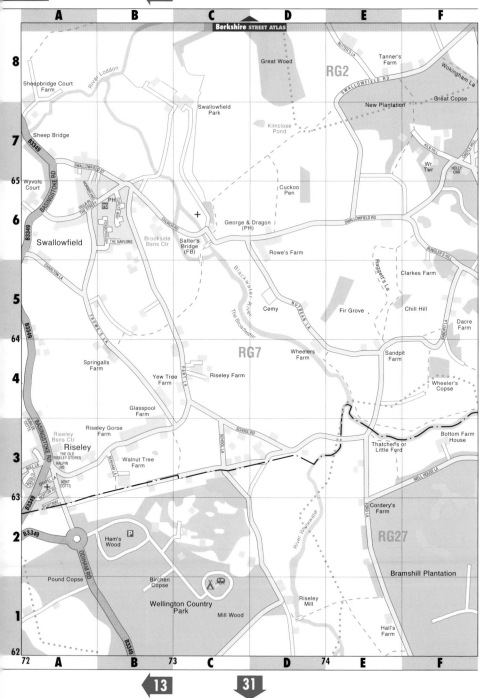

13

Berkshire STREET ATLAS

RG2

Tanner's Farm

Wokingham La

Sheepbridge Court Farm

River Loddon

Great Wood

New Plantation

Great Copse

Swallowfield Park

Kilnclose Pond

SWALLOWFIELD RD

NUTTER'S LA

KILN HILL

CASTLE HILL

Sheep Bridge

Wr Twr

HOLLY CNR

SWALLOWFIELD ST

Wyvols Court

WYVOLS DRIVE

PH

THE STREET

Cuckoo Pen

CHURCH RD

George & Dragon (PH)

SWALLOWFIELD RD

Swallowfield

BASINGSTOKE RD

B3349

VILLA PL

CHILD'S WAY

THE NAYLORS

Brookside Bsns Ctr

Salter's Bridge (FB)

Rowe's Farm

Raggett's La

Clarkes Farm

BUNGLER'S HILL

CHARLTON LA

TROWE'S LA

Cemy

NUTBEAN LA

Fir Grove

Chill Hill

Dacre Farm

SANDPIT LA

The Broadwater

Blackwater River

RG7

Wheelers Farm

Sandpit Farm

Springalls Farm

Yew Tree Farm

Riseley Farm

PART LA

Wheeler's Copse

Glasspool Farm

Riseley Gorse Farm

Riseley Bsns Ctr

SCHOOL LA

SCHOOL RD

Thatchers or Little Ford

Bottom Farm House

Riseley

THE OLD RISELEY STORES

HALPIN HO

Walnut Tree Farm

BULL LA

CHAPEL LA

KENT COTTS

NORTOH RD

TWIG LA

BENHAM LA

FORD LA

Cordery's Farm

WELL HOUSE LA

B3349

BASINGSTOKE RD

WHITEWATER COTTS

NORTHWAY

River Whitewater

RG27

B3349

ODIHAM RD

Ham's Wood

P

Pound Copse

Birchen Copse

Bramshill Plantation

Wellington Country Park

Mill Wood

Riseley Mill

Hall's Farm

B3349

13   31

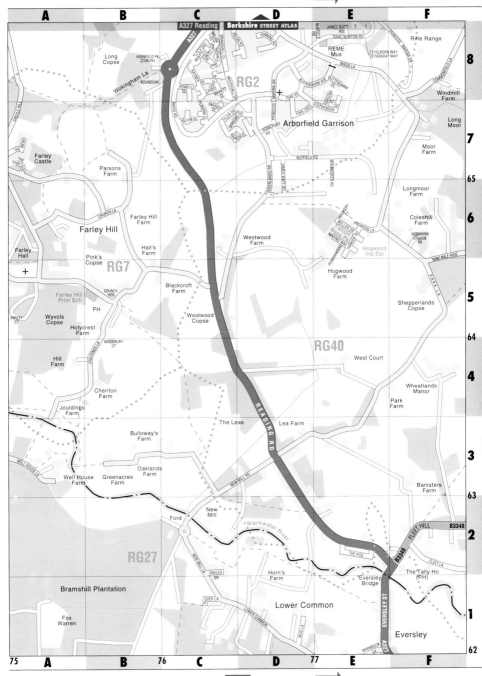

A327 Reading **Berkshire** STREET ATLAS

A **B** **C** **D** **E** **F**

Rifle Range

JAMES WATT RD
ISAAC NEWTON RD
REME Mus

1 HILBORN WAY
2 FARADAY WAY

PRINCESS MARINA DR
COMPWELL LA

Windmill Farm

8

Long Copse

HIGHFIELD PK (CVN PK)

Wokingham La
BOUNDOAK

RG2

BIGGS LA

Long Moor

7

Farley Castle
THE CHASE

Parsons Farm

BUTTENSHAW AV
BUTTENSHAW

Arborfield Garrison

TOPE RD
TOPE CRES
STEPHENSON

Moor Farm

65

CHURCH LA

Farley Hill Farm

NUFFIELD RD

JAMES WATT RD

WHITWORTH RD

Longmoor Farm

6

Farley Hill

Hall's Farm

Westwood Farm

HOGWOOD LA
WELLER DR

Hogwood Ind Est

Coleshill Farm

ROBINSON CRUSOE PK

Pink's Copse

RG7

Blackcroft Farm

Hogwood Farm

NINE MILE RIDE

Farley Hall

COUNCIL HOS
PH

Westwood Copse

Shepperlands Copse

PARK LA

5

FARLEY CT

Wyvols Copse
Holycrest Farm

WOODBURY CT

RG40

West Court

64

Hill Farm

Cheriton Farm

Wheatlands Manor

Park Farm

4

Jouldings Farm

The Leas

Lea Farm

3

WELL HOUSE LA

Bulloway's Farm

Oaklands Farm

NEW MILL RD

READING RD

Banisters Farm

63

Well House Farm

Greenacres Farm

Ford

New Mill

Blackwater River

FLEET HILL

B3348

2

RG27

NEW MILL LA
OAKLEA

OAKLEA DR

Horn's Farm

THE RISE
Eversley Bridge

B3348
FLEET LA
The Tally Ho (PH)

EVERSLEY ST

Bramshill Plantation

OVER LA

LOWER COMMON

Lower Common

1

Fox Warren

MUD LA

Eversley

WARBROCK LA

62

75 **A** **B** 76 **C** **D** 77 **E** **F**

15

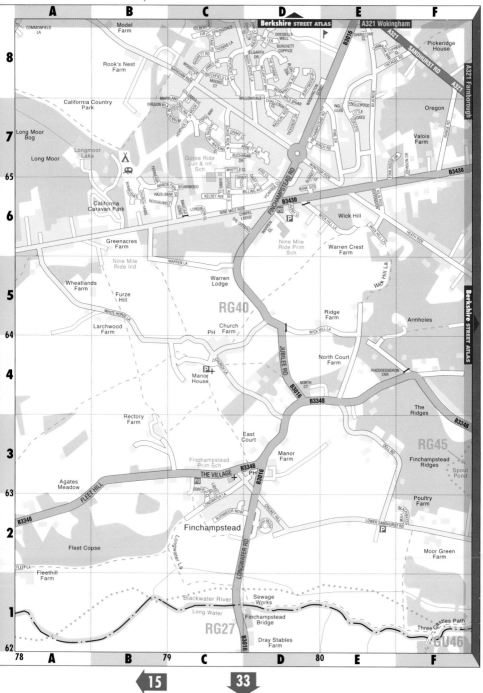

33

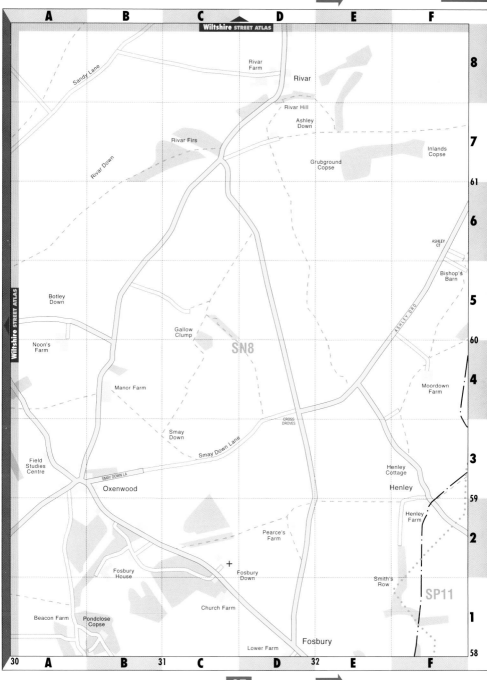

Wiltshire STREET ATLAS

Wiltshire STREET ATLAS

Sandy Lane

Rivar Farm

Rivar

Rivar Hill

Ashley Down

Rivar Firs

Inlands Copse

Rivar Down

Grubground Copse

ASHLEY CT

Botley Down

Bishop's Barn

Gallow Clump

SN8

Noon's Farm

Moordown Farm

ASHLEY DRO

Manor Farm

Smay Down

CROSS DROVES

Field Studies Centre

Smay Down Lane

Henley Cottage

SMAY DOWN LA

Henley

Oxenwood

Henley Farm

Pearce's Farm

Fosbury House

Smith's Row

SP11

Fosbury Down

Church Farm

Beacon Farm

Pondclose Copse

Fosbury

Lower Farm

8
7
61
6
5
60
4
3
59
2
1
58

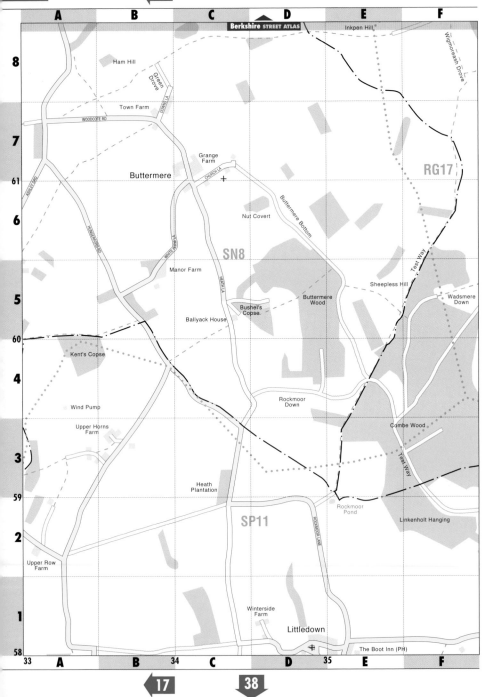

Berkshire STREET ATLAS

18

17

Ham Hill

Green Drove

Town Farm

WOODCOTE RD

Grange Farm

CHURCH LA

Buttermere

Nut Covert

Buttermere Bottom

SN8

Manor Farm

HEATH LA

Sheepless Hill

Wadsmere Down

Bushel's Copse

Buttermere Wood

Ballyack House

Kent's Copse

Rockmoor Down

Combe Wood

Wind Pump

Test Way

Upper Horns Farm

Heath Plantation

Rockmoor Pond

Linkenholt Hanging

SP11

ROCKMOOR LANE

Upper Row Farm

Winterside Farm

Littledown

The Boot Inn (PH)

Inkpen Hill

Wigmoreash Drove

RG17

Test Way

HUNGERFORD RD

WHITE LA

ASHLEY LA

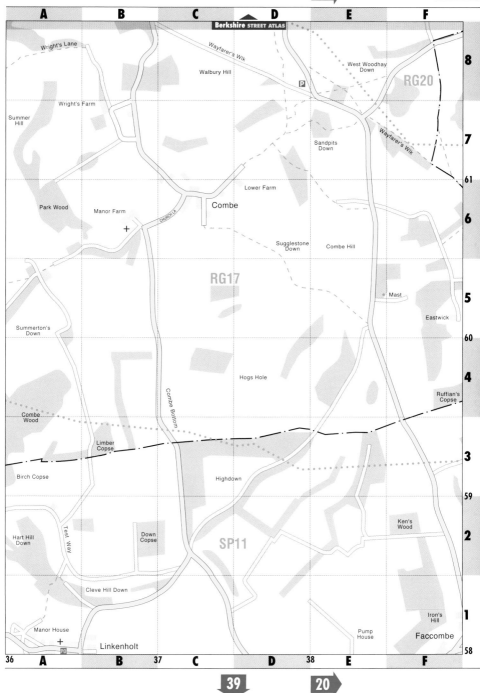

Berkshire STREET ATLAS

Wright's Lane

Wayfarer's Wlk

Walbury Hill

West Woodhay Down

RG20

Wright's Farm

Summer Hill

Sandpits Down

Wayfarer's Wlk

61

Park Wood

Manor Farm

CHURCH LA

Combe

Lower Farm

Sugglestone Down

Combe Hill

RG17

Mast

Eastwick

Summerton's Down

60

Hogs Hole

Ruffian's Copse

Combe Wood

Combe Bottom

Limber Copse

Birch Copse

Highdown

59

Ken's Wood

Hart Hill Down

Test Way

Down Copse

SP11

Cleve Hill Down

Iron's Hill

Manor House

Pump House

Faccombe

Linkenholt

58

36   A   B   37   C   D   38   E   F

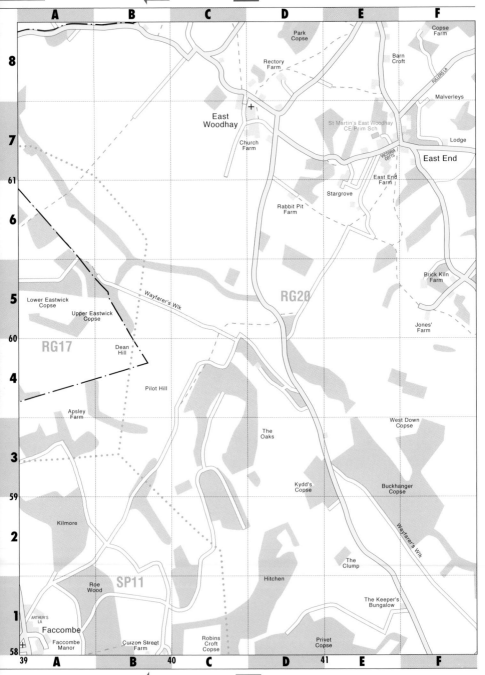

A   **B**   **C**   **D**   **E**   **F**

8

7

61

6

5

60

4

3

59

2

1

58

Copse Farm

Park Copse

Rectory Farm

Barn Croft

Malverleys

East Woodhay

St Martin's East Woodhay CE Prim Sch

Lodge

Church Farm

VICTORIA COTTS

East End

East End Farm

Stargrove

Rabbit Pit Farm

Brick Kiln Farm

RG20

Lower Eastwick Copse

Upper Eastwick Copse

Wayfarer's Wlk

Jones' Farm

RG17

Dean Hill

Pilot Hill

Apsley Farm

The Oaks

West Down Copse

Kydd's Copse

Buckhanger Copse

Kilmore

Wayfarer's Wlk

Roe Wood

SP11

Hitchen

The Clump

The Keeper's Bungalow

ARTHUR'S LA

Faccombe

Faccombe Manor

Curzon Street Farm

Robins Croft Copse

Privet Copse

39   **A**   40   **B**   **C**   **D**   41   **E**   **F**

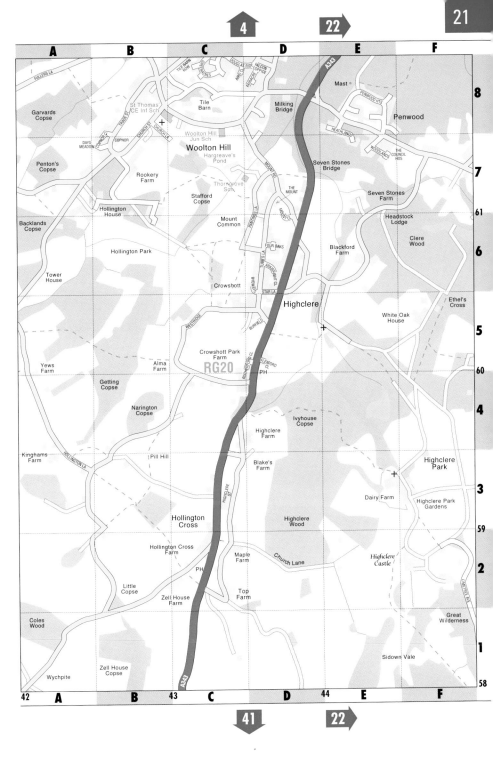

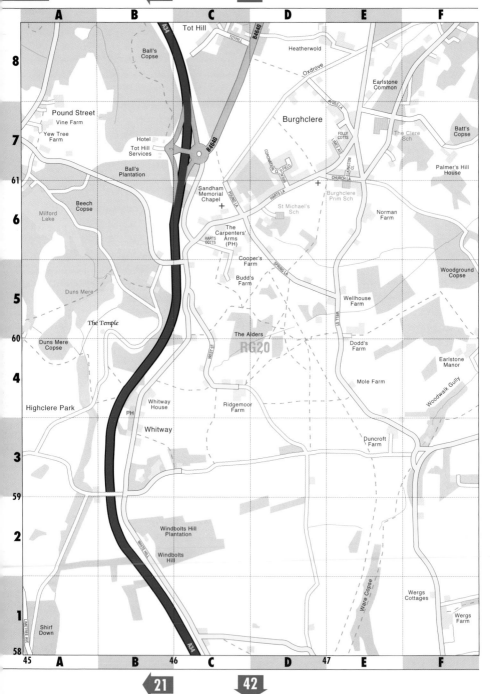

21

5

Tot Hill

Heatherwold

Oxdrove

Earlstone
Common

Pound Street

Vine Farm

Yew Tree
Farm

Burghclere

The Clere
Sch

Batt's
Copse

Ball's
Copse

Hotel
Tot Hill
Services

Ball's
Plantation

Sandham
Memorial
Chapel

FOLLY
COTTS

Palmer's Hill
House

Burghclere
Prim Sch

CHURCH LA

HARTS LA

St Michael's
Sch

Norman
Farm

Beech
Copse

Milford
Lake

The
Carpenters'
Arms
(PH)

HARTS
COTTS

Cooper's
Farm

Duns Mere

Budd's
Farm

SPRING LA

Woodground
Copse

Wellhouse
Farm

The Temple

WELL ST

Duns Mere
Copse

The Alders

RG20

Dodd's
Farm

Earlstone
Manor

Highclere Park

WEST ST

PH

Whitway
House

Ridgemoor
Farm

Mole Farm

Woodwalk Gully

Whitway

Duncroft
Farm

Windbolts Hill
Plantation

WHITE HILL

Windbolts
Hill

Ware Copse

Wergs
Cottages

Shirf
Down

LIME TREE AVE

Wergs
Farm

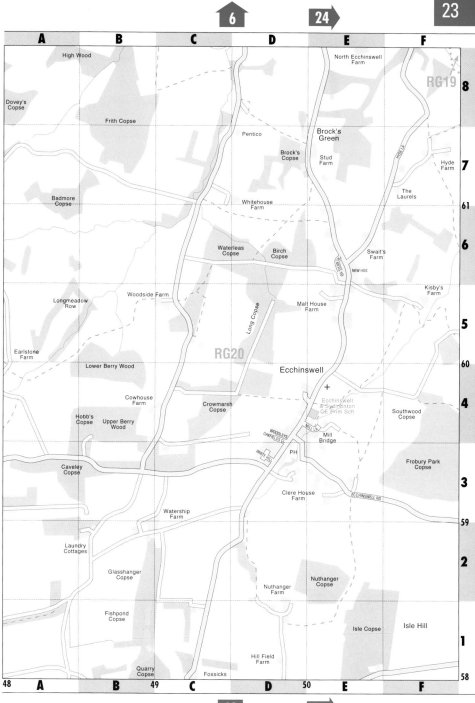

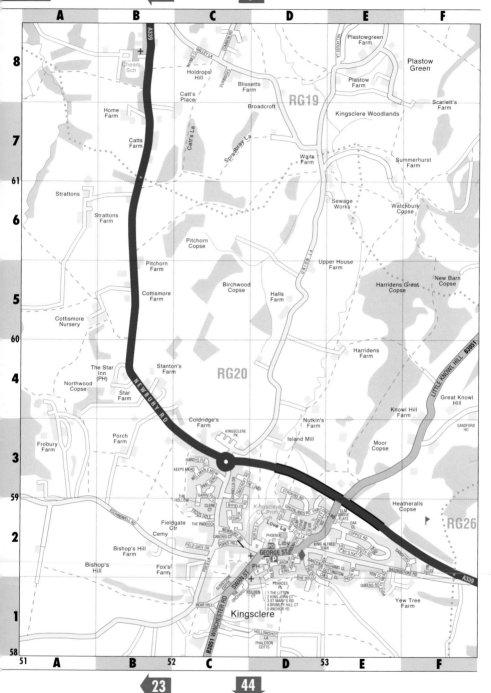

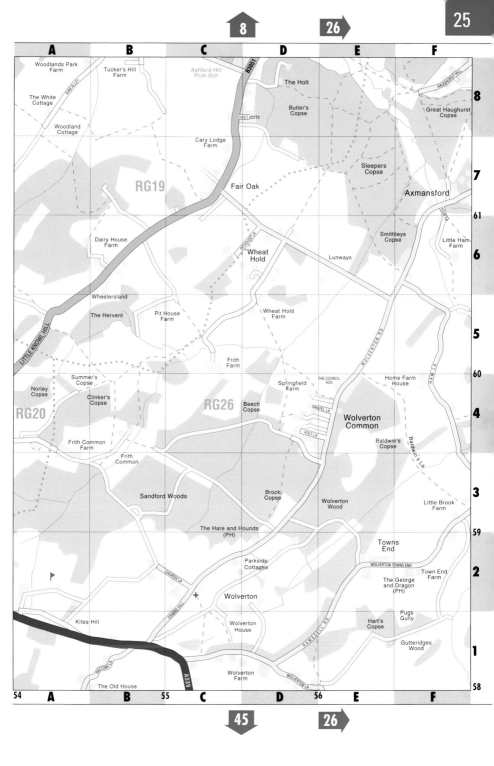

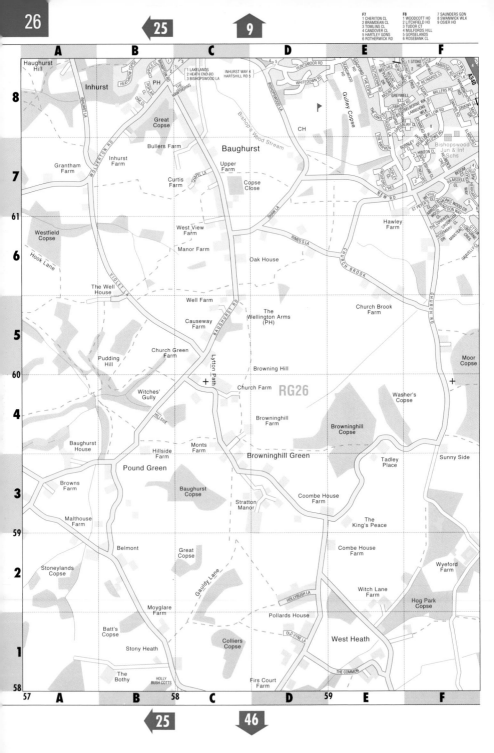

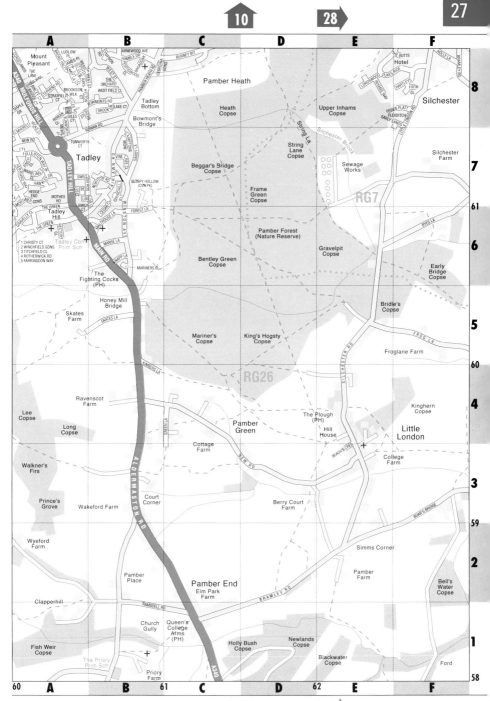

27
11

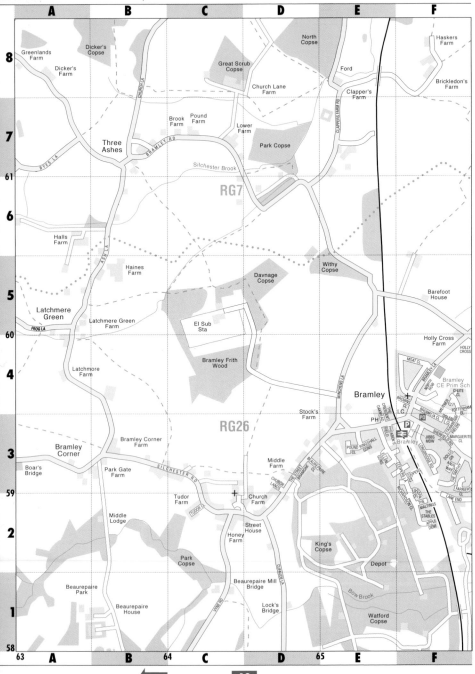

27
48

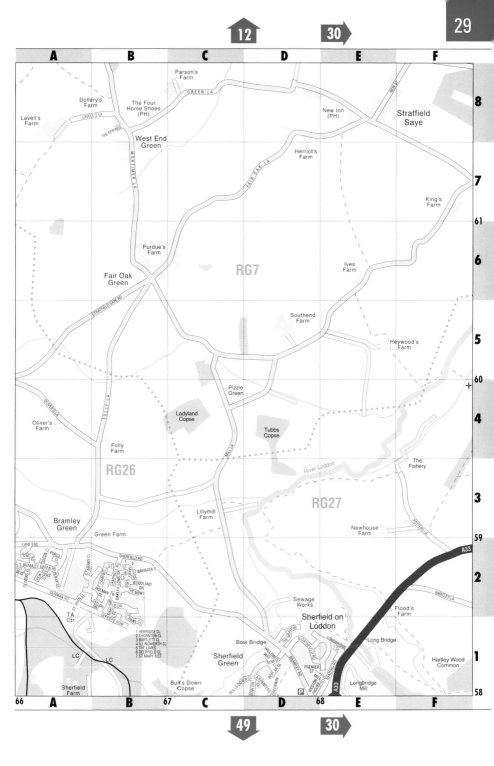

A   B   C   D   E   F

Lavell's Farm

Dollery's Farm

LAVELL'S LA

THE SPRINGS

The Four Horse Shoes (PH)

Parson's Farm

GREEN LA

West End Green

New Inn (PH)

Stratfield Saye

8

Herriot's Farm

NEW ST

TAIR OAK LA

7

King's Farm

61

MORTIMER LA

Purdue's Farm

RG7

Ives Farm

6

Fair Oak Green

STRATFIELD SAYE RD

Southend Farm

Heywood's Farm

5

60

Oliver's Farm

OLIVER'S LA

FOLLY LA

Pizzie Green

Ladyland Copse

Tubbs Copse

The Fishery

4

Folly Farm

RG26

MILL LA

River Loddon

RG27

POTTERS LA

3

Lillymill Farm

Newhouse Farm

A33

59

Bramley Green

Green Farm

LANE END

UND

BRAMLEY GREEN RD

BECK

SEXON

FORGE

DELLY CL

SHERFIELD RD

ST. BARBARA'S CL

THE LIMES

WOODLAND DR

THE MEWS

Sewage Works

Flood's Farm

HARTLEY LA

2

GERMAN RD

ST. JAMES CL

CAMPBELL

HOLMAN

OAKLEY

JAMES DR

OFFICERS ROW

1 HERRIDGE CL
2 THORNTON CL
3 BARTLETT CL
4 ILLINGWORTH CL
5 THE LIMES
6 DEERFIELD CL
7 ST MARY'S CT

Sherfield on Loddon

Long Bridge

TA Ctr

LC

LC

Bull's Down Copse

Bow Bridge

Sherfield Green

BULL'S DOWN CL

BOW DR

CARPENTERS

GREENWAY

WESTON MILL

WELLINGTON WAY

BRAMLEY RD

N. CASTLE RD

PREMIER CT

MORGAN

POPLAR CL

WESTERN

LONGBRIDGE

READING RD

A33

Hartley Wood Common

Longbridge Mill

1

Sherfield Farm

58

66   A   B   67   C   D   68   E   F

29
13

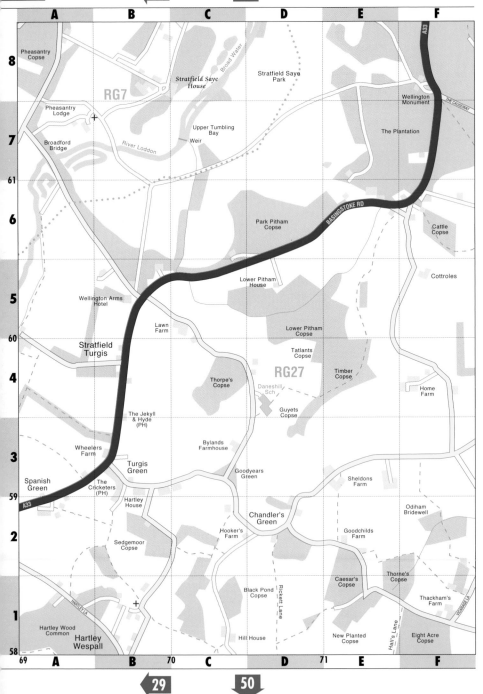

29
50

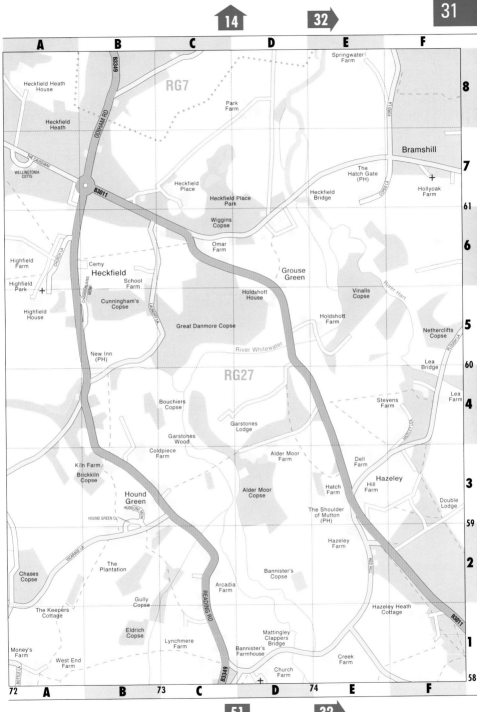

A **B** **C** **D** **E** **F**

8

Springwater Farm

Heckfield Heath House

RG7

Park Farm

Heckfield Heath

Bramshill

THE CAUSEWAY

WELLINGTONIA COTTS

The Hatch Gate (PH)

7

Hollyoak Farm

ODIHAM RD

B3349

B3011

Heckfield Place

Heckfield Bridge

61

Wiggins Copse

6

CHURCH LA

Omar Farm

Heckfield Place Park

Highfield Farm

Cemy

Heckfield

Grouse Green

River Hart

Highfield Park

School Farm

CHAMBERLAINS MDW

Cunningham's Copse

Holdshott House

Vinalls Copse

Highfield House

LANER LA

Great Danmore Copse

Holdshott Farm

Netherclifts Copse

5

New Inn (PH)

River Whitewater

Lea Bridge

60

FORD LA

RG27

Bouchiers Copse

Stevens Farm

Lea Farm

4

Garstones Lodge

HAZELEY LA

Garstones Wood

Coldpiece Farm

Alder Moor Farm

Dell Farm

Hazeley

Kiln Farm

Brickkiln Copse

Alder Moor Copse

Hatch Farm

Hill Farm

3

Double Lodge

Hound Green

HUDSONS MDW

The Shoulder of Mutton (PH)

HOUND GREEN CL

RED HILL

59

VICARAGE LA

The Plantation

Hazeley Farm

2

Chases Copse

Bannister's Copse

Hazeley Heath Cottage

B3011

The Keepers Cottage

Gully Copse

READING RD

Arcadia Farm

1

Money's Farm

Eldrich Copse

Lynchmere Farm

Mattingley Clappers Bridge

Creek Farm

West End Farm

BOTTLE LA

Bannister's Farmhouse

Church Farm

B3349

58

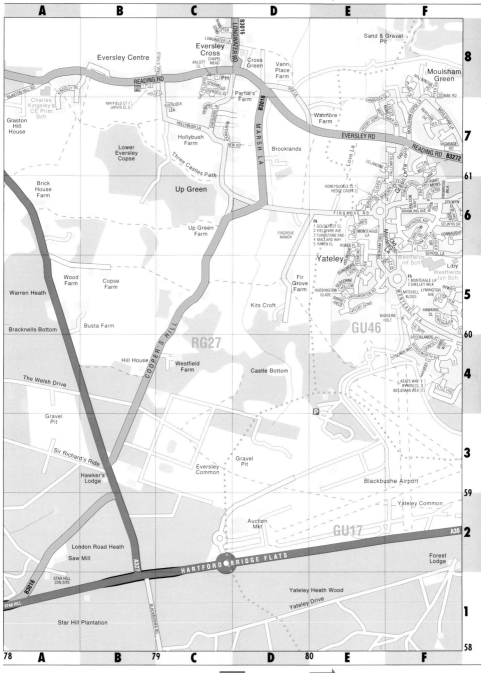

Sand & Gravel Pit

Moulsham Green

Eversley Centre

Eversley Cross

Cross Green

Vann Place Farm

READING RD

Charles Kingsley's CE Prim Sch

Glaston Hill House

Watmore Farm

EVERSLEY RD

READING RD

B3272

Parfitt's Farm

Hollybush Farm

Brooklands

Lower Eversley Copse

Three Castles Path

Up Green

HONEYSUCKLE CL 1
HEDGE CROFT 2

Brick House Farm

FIRGROVE RD

Up Green Farm

FIRGROVE MANOR

F6
1 GOLDCREST CL
2 FIELDFARE AVE
3 TURNSTONE END
4 MACLARD WAY
5 RAVEN CL

MONTEAGLE LA

Yateley

Wood Farm

Copse Farm

Fir Grove Farm

Kits Croft

HUDDINGTON GLADE

F5
1 MONTEAGLE LA
2 SHELLEY WLK

Westfields Inf Sch

Westfields Jun Sch

Liby Westfields

Warren Heath

Busta Farm

BADGERS HOLT

GU46

Brooklands

Bracknells Bottom

RG27

Hill House

Westfield Farm

Castle Bottom

KEATS WAY 1
BYRON CL 2
BETJEMAN WLK 3

LITTLE VIGO

COOPER'S HILL

The Welsh Drive

Gravel Pit

Sir Richard's Ride

Eversley Common

Gravel Pit

Blackbushe Airport

Hawker's Lodge

Yateley Common

London Road Heath

Saw Mill

STAR HILL CVN SITE

A327

BLACKBUSHES RD

HARTFORD BRIDGE FLATS

Auction Mkt

GU17

A30

Forest Lodge

B3016

STAR HILL

Star Hill Plantation

Yateley Heath Wood

Yateley Drive

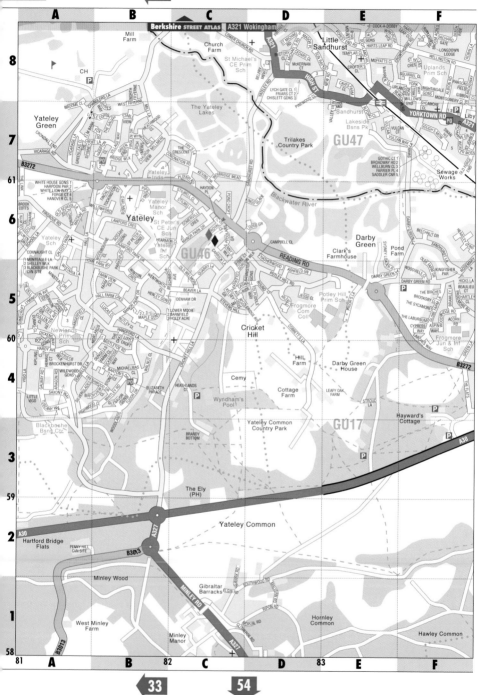

Berkshire STREET ATLAS A321 Wokingham

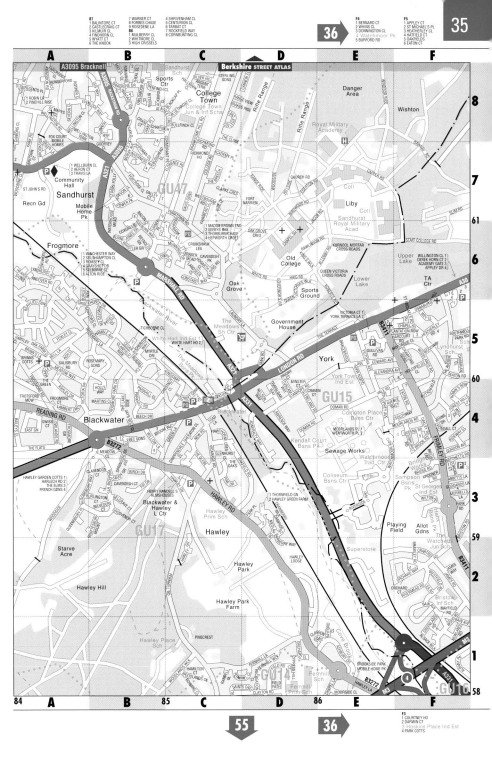

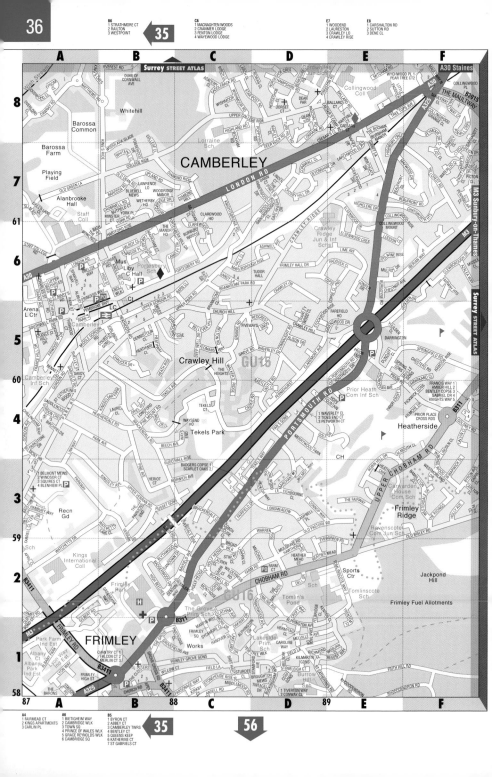

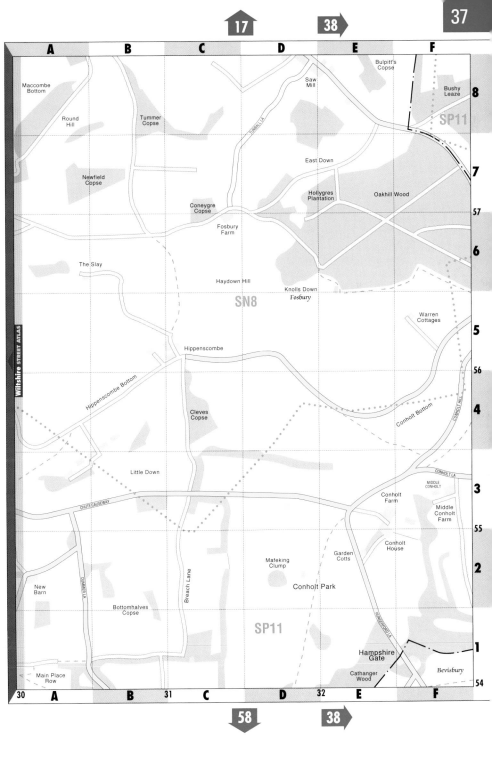

Wiltshire STREET ATLAS

A **B** **C** **D** **E** **F**

8

Maccombe
Bottom

Round
Hill

Tummer
Copse

Saw
Mill

Bulpitt's
Copse

Bushy
Leaze

SP11

Newfield
Copse

East Down

7

TUMBALL LA

Coneygre
Copse

Hollygres
Plantation

Oakhill Wood

57

Fosbury
Farm

6

The Slay

Haydown Hill

Knolls Down
Fosbury

SN8

Warren
Cottages

5

Hippenscombe

56

Hippenscombe Bottom

Cleves
Copse

Conholt Bottom

CONHOLT HILL

4

Little Down

Conholt
Farm

CONHOLT LA

MIDDLE
CONHOLT

3

CHUTE CAUSEWAY

Middle
Conholt
Farm

55

Mafeking
Clump

Garden
Cotts

Conholt
House

New
Barn

DIMMER LA

Bottomhalves
Copse

Breach Lane

Conholt Park

SP11

HINGERSDELL LA

2

Hampshire
Gate

Bevisbury

1

Main Place
Row

Cathanger
Wood

54

30 **A** **B** 31 **C** **D** 32 **E** **F**

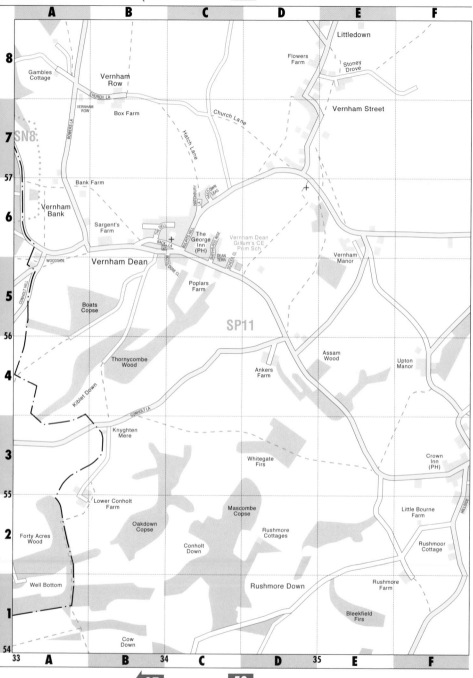

A **B** **C** **D** **E** **F**

Littledown

8

Gambles
Cottage

Flowers
Farm

Stoney
Drove

Vernham
Row

Vernham Street

CHURCH LA

VERNHAM
ROW

Box Farm

Church Lane

7

SN8

Hatch Lane

57

Bank Farm

HATCHBURY LT

CROWN
THE LEAS

Vernham
Bank

6

Sargent's
Farm

THE DELL

The George
Inn
(PH)

Vernham Dean
Gillum's CE
Prim Sch

Vernham
Manor

BACK LA

ST PETERS RD

DEAN
TERR

SCHOOL CT

WOODSIDE

Vernham Dean

BUTTS BOURNE CL

CONHOLT HILL

5

Poplars
Farm

SP11

Boats
Copse

56

Thornycombe
Wood

Assam
Wood

Upton
Manor

4

Ankers
Farm

Kidlet Down

CONHOLT LA

Knyghten
Mere

3

Whitegate
Firs

Crown
Inn
(PH)

55

Lower Conholt
Farm

Little Bourne
Farm

FALL EDGE

2

Forty Acres
Wood

Oakdown
Copse

Mascombe
Copse

Rushmore
Cottages

Rushmoor
Cottage

Conholt
Down

Well Bottom

Rushmore
Farm

1

Rushmore Down

Bleekfield
Firs

Cow
Down

54

33 **A** **B** 34 **C** **D** 35 **E** **F**

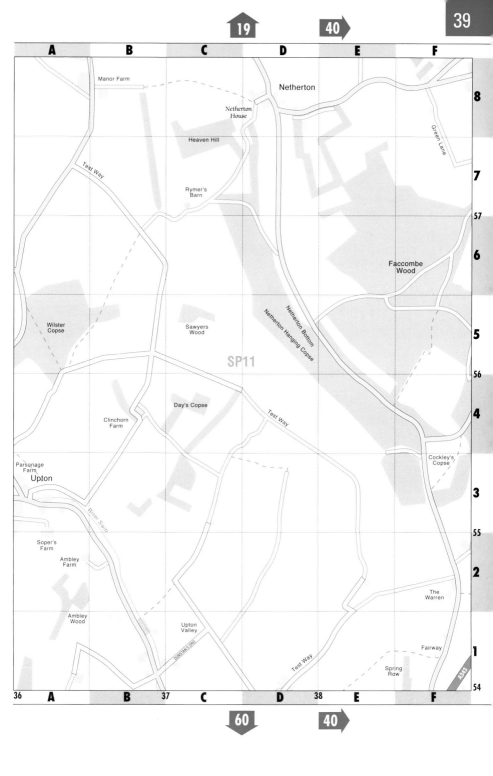

19   40

Manor Farm

Netherton

Netherton House

Heaven Hill

Green Lane

Test Way

Rymer's Barn

Faccombe Wood

Wilster Copse

Sawyers Wood

Netherton Bottom

Netherton Hanging Copse

SP11

Day's Copse

Clinchorn Farm

Test Way

Cockley's Copse

Parsonage Farm

Upton

Soper's Farm

Ambley Farm

River Swift

The Warren

Ambley Wood

Upton Valley

DUNSTAN'S DRO

Fairway

Test Way

Spring Row

A343

8

7

57

6

5

56

4

3

55

2

1

54

36   A   B   37   C   D   38   E   F

60   40

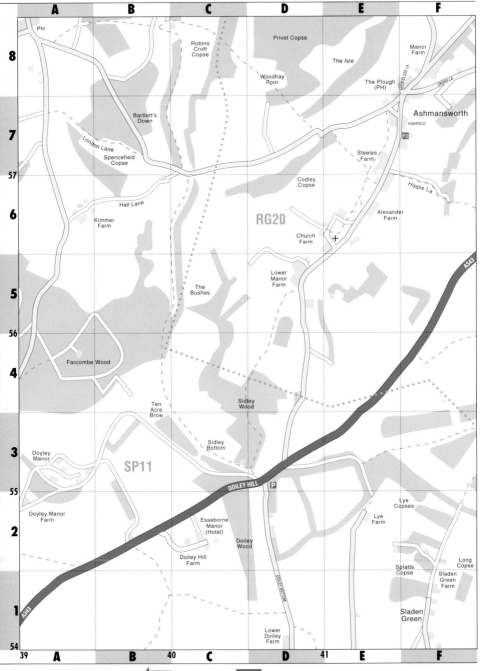

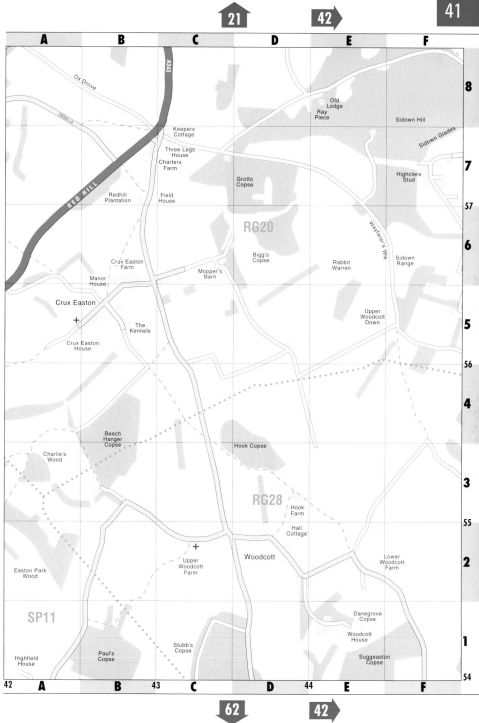

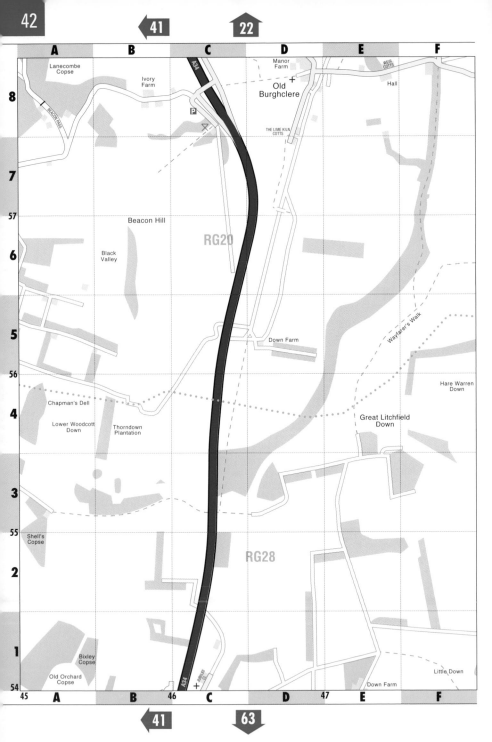

A   B   C   D   E   F

Lanecombe
Copse

Ivory
Farm

Manor
Farm

Old
Burghclere

Hall

WEIR
COTTS

P

THE LIME KILN
COTTS

BEACON PASS

8

7

57

Beacon Hill

RG20

Black
Valley

6

5

Down Farm

Wayfarer's Walk

Hare Warren
Down

56

Chapman's Dell

Great Litchfield
Down

4

Lower Woodcott
Down

Thorndown
Plantation

3

55

Shell's
Copse

RG28

2

1

Bixley
Copse

Old Orchard
Copse

Down Farm

Little Down

54

45   A   B   46   C   D   47   E   F

A34

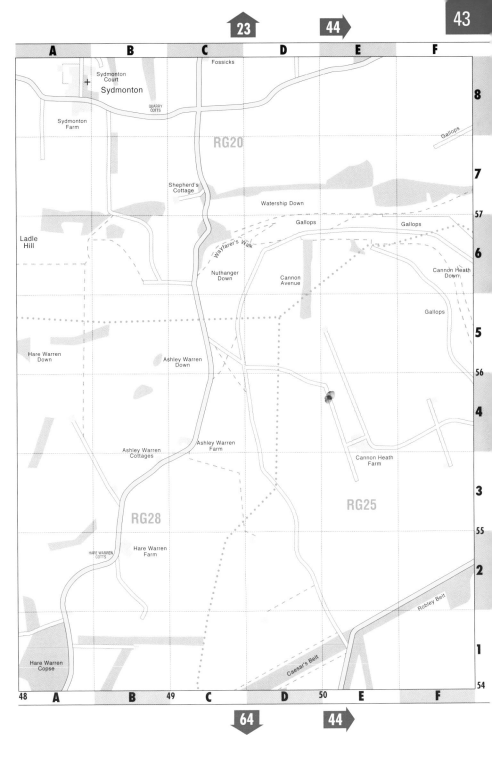

43
24

A B C D E F

8

Gallop

Wells Head
(springs)

Sainfoin

PARK HOUSE
COTTS

Park House
Stables

Hollowshot Lane

RG20

Field Barn
Farm

Gallops

WINCHESTER RD

B3051

7

57

Freemantle Park Down

Combe
Hole

Wireless
Station

Mast

6

The Warren

WHITE HILL

Cottington's Hill

RG26

Stubbington
Down

Cannon Heath
Down

Freemantle Park
Farm

Hannington
Scrubs

5

Gallops

Meadham Copse

56

MEADHAM LA

Wayfarer's Wlk

Siddon
Cottage

4

Cannon
Heath
Cottages

Hannington

Walkeridge
Farm

For Down

Manor
Farm

Hannington
Farm

3

RG25

Polhampton Lodge
Plantation

55

Scotland
Cottages

2

Polhampton
Lodge
Stud

Tidgrove Warren
Farm

The Manor
Farm

1

North
Oakley

54

B3051

51 A   B   52   C   D   53   E   F

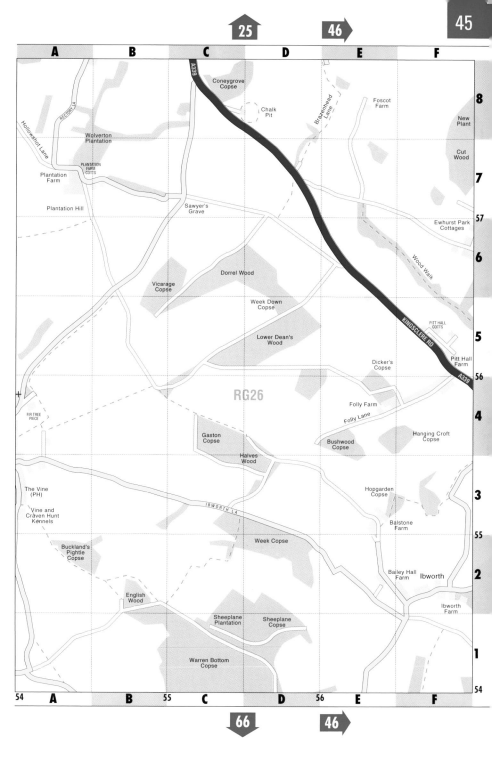

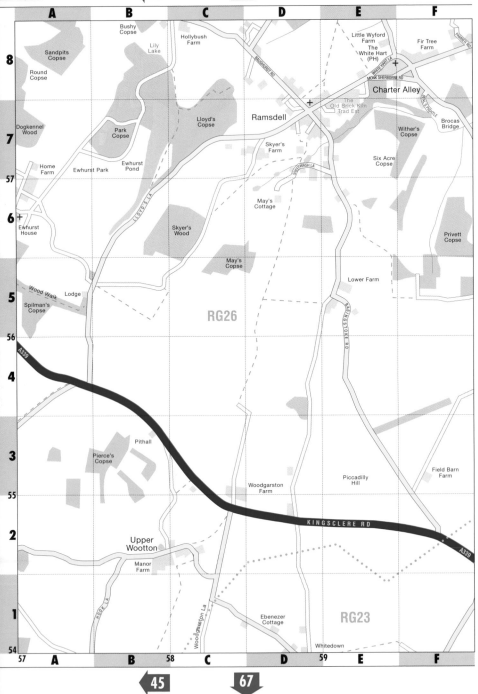

45

26

8

Sandpits
Copse

Round
Copse

Bushy
Copse

Lily
Lake

Hollybush
Farm

BAUGHURST RD

Little Wyford
Farm
The
White Hart
(PH)

WHITE HART LA

MONK SHERBORNE RD

Fir Tree
Farm

FRIMLEY RD

Charter Alley

YEW TREE LA

7

Dogkennel
Wood

Park
Copse

Lloyd's
Copse

Ramsdell

The
Old Brick Kiln
Trad Est

Wither's
Copse

Brocas
Bridge

57

Home
Farm

Ewhurst Park

Ewhurst
Pond

Skyer's
Farm

LLOYD'S LA

SAND WASH LA

Six Acre
Copse

6

Ewhurst
House

Skyer's
Wood

May's
Cottage

Privett
Copse

May's
Copse

Lower Farm

5

Wood Walk

Spilman's
Copse

Lodge

RG26

BASINGSTOKE RD

56

A339

4

3

Pierce's
Copse

Pithall

Woodgarston
Farm

Piccadilly
Hill

Field Barn
Farm

55

2

Upper
Wootton

Manor
Farm

KINGSCLERE RD

A339

HOOK LA

1

Woodgarston La

Ebenezer
Cottage

Whitedown

RG23

54

57 **A** **B** 58 **C** **D** 59 **E** **F**

45

67

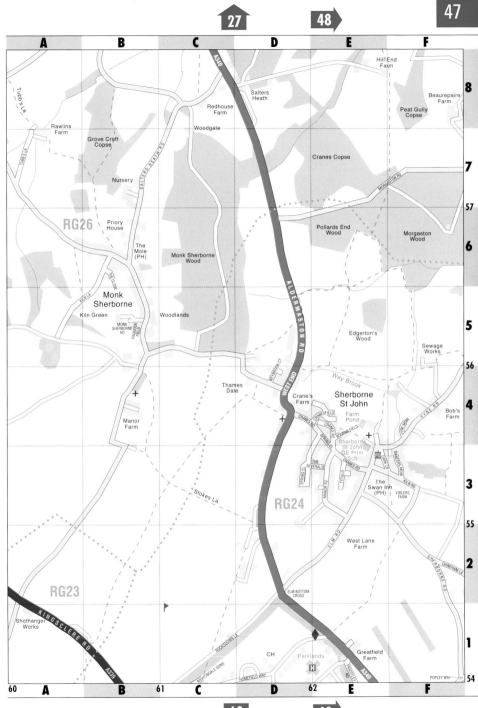

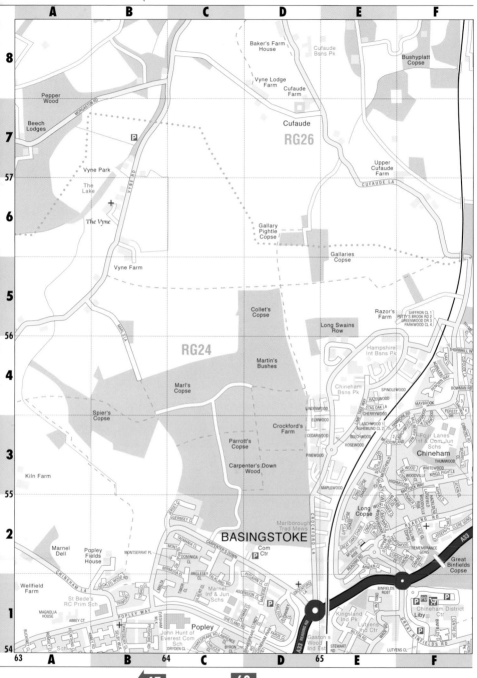

Baker's Farm House
Cufaude Bsns Pk
Bushyplatt Copse

Pepper Wood

Vyne Lodge Farm
Cufaude Farm

Beech Lodges

Cufaude
RG26

Vyne Park
Upper Cufaude Farm

The Lake
CUFAUDE LA

The Vyne

Gallary Pightle Copse

Vyne Farm
Gallaries Copse

Collet's Copse
Razor's Farm

SAFFRON CL 1
PETTY'S BROOK RD 2
GREENWOOD DR 3
PARKWOOD CL 4

Long Swains Row

RG24
Hampshire Int Bsns Pk

Martin's Bushes
THORNHILL W

Chineham Bsns Pk
HAZELWOOD
SPINDLEWOOD
Marl's Copse
STAG OAK LA
CHERRYWOOD
MAYBROOK

Spier's Copse
LINDENWOOD
LARCHWOOD 1
AGHEMUND CL 2
Four Lanes Inf & Com Jun Schs

Crockford's Farm
ELMWOOD
BEECHWOOD
Chineham
THUMWOOD

CEDARWOOD
ROSEWOOD
WHITEWOOD
WOODVILLE
KINGS PIGHTLE

Parrott's Copse
PINEWOOD
HIGHWOODS
MATTOCK WAY

Carpenter's Down Wood

Kiln Farm
MAPLEWOOD
Long Copse

55

Marlborough Trad Mews
BASINGSTOKE

2
Marnel Dell
Popley Fields House
TASMANIA CL
CARPENTER'S DOWN
Com Ctr
Great Binfields Copse

MONTSERRAT PL
MONTG
DOMINICA CL
ANGLESEY PL
ISLAND RD
BINFIELDS RDBT

Wellfield Farm
BERMUDA CL
Marnel Inf & Jun Schs
PITCAIRN CL
Chineham District Liby

CHINEHAM LA
MALTA
TOBAGO
ASCENSION CL
Kingsland Ind Ctr
Chineham District Ctr

Magnolia House
St Bede's RC Prim Sch
POPLEY WAY
SHETLAND RD
FARDE CL
Lutyens Ind Ctr

ABBEY CT
SELBY WLK
Popley
GREAT BINFIELDS RD

John Hunt of Everest Com Sch
DRYDEN CL
BYRON CL
Gaston's Wood Ind Est
STEWART RD

LUTYENS CL

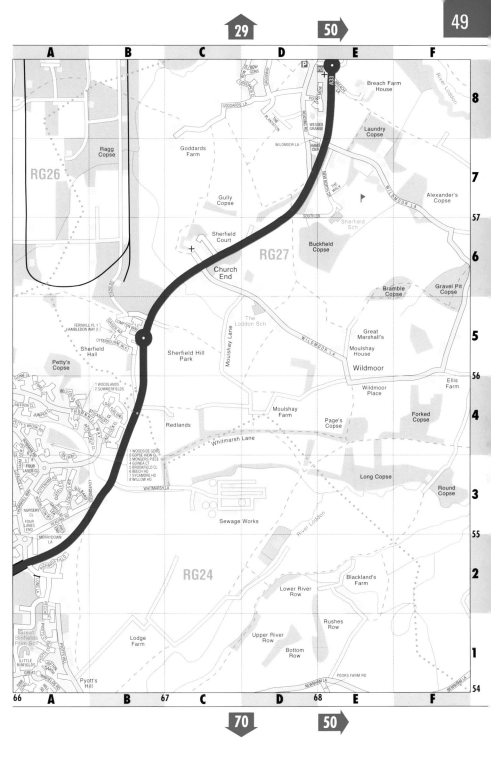

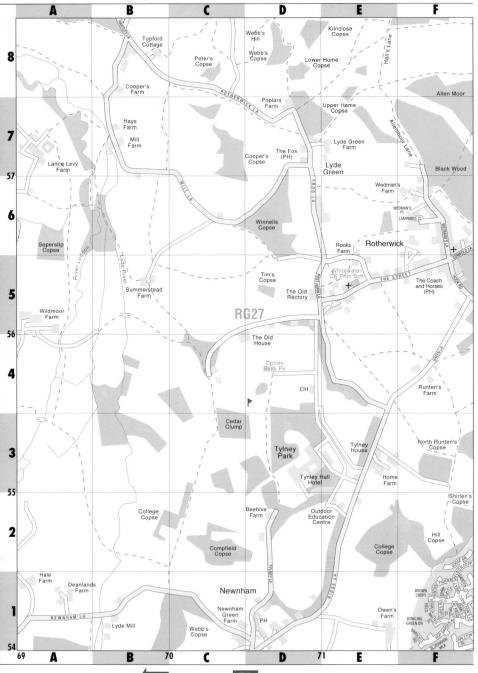

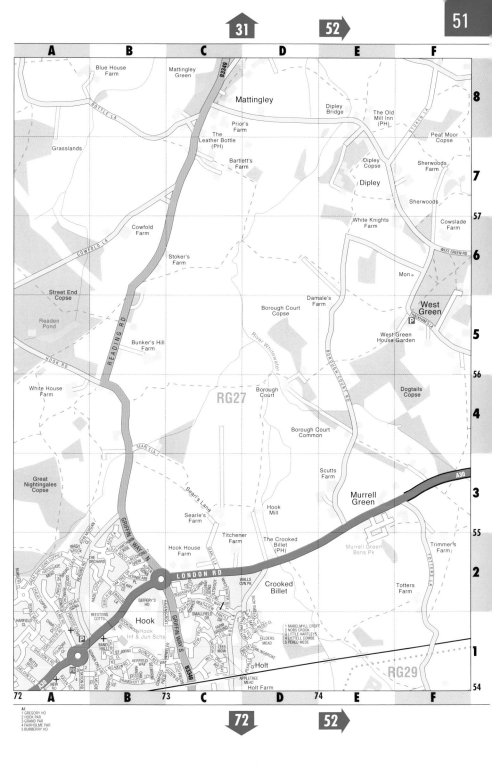

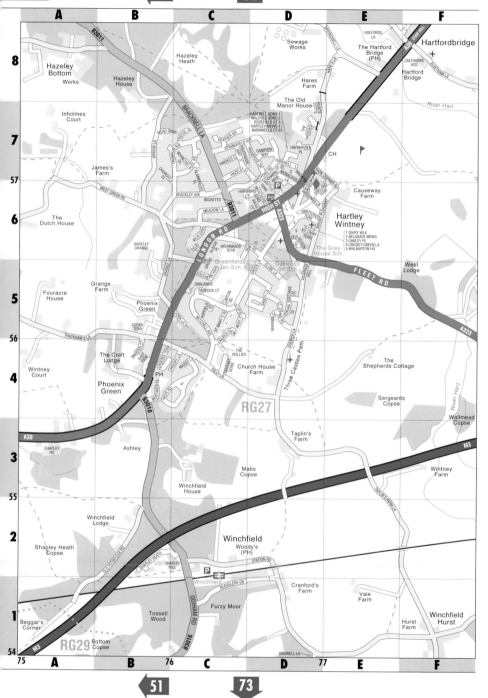

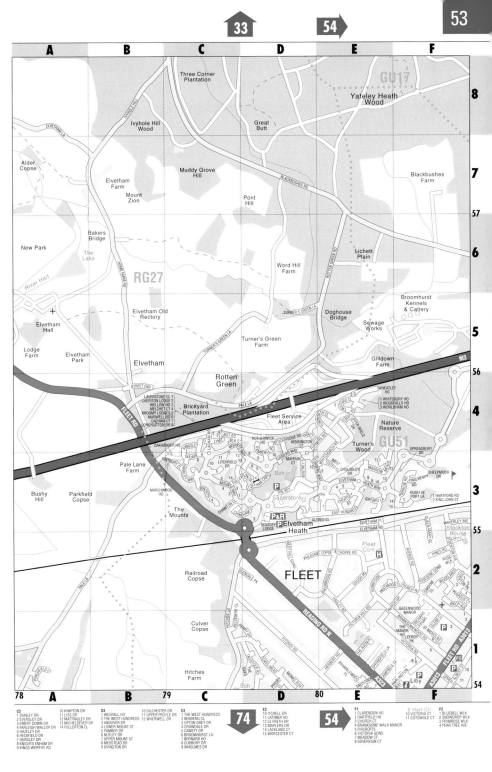

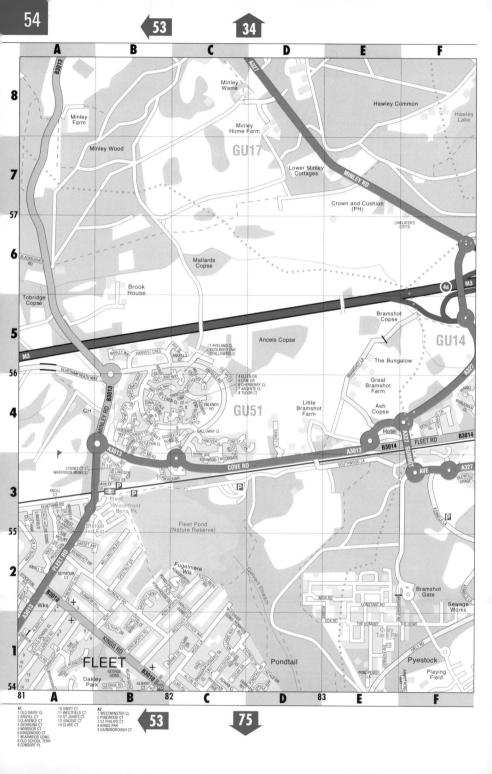

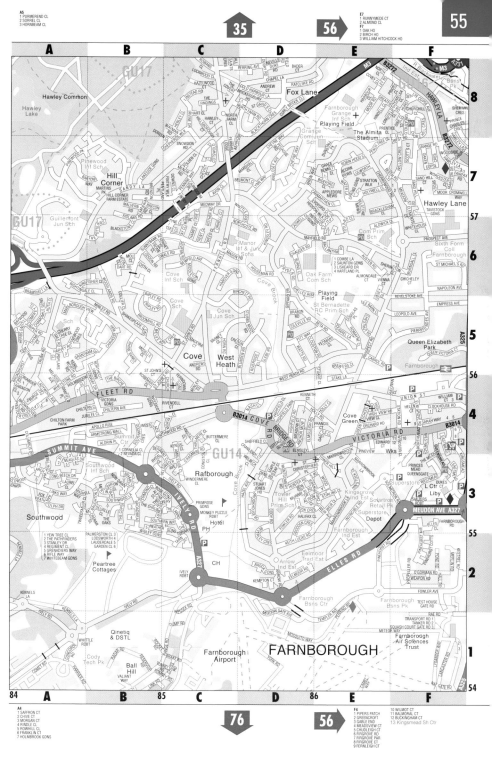

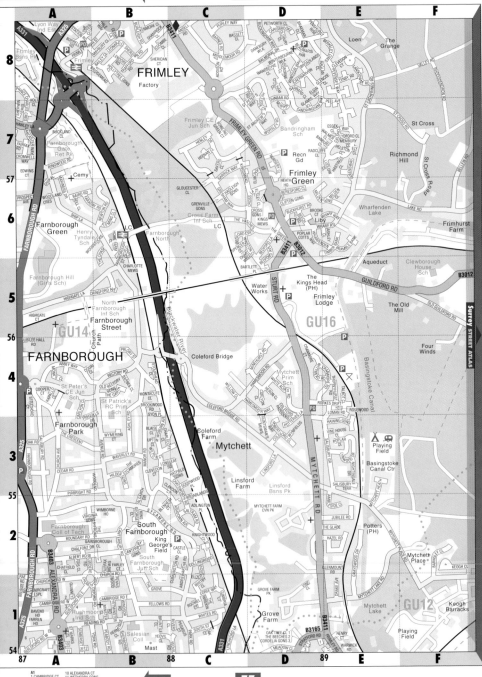

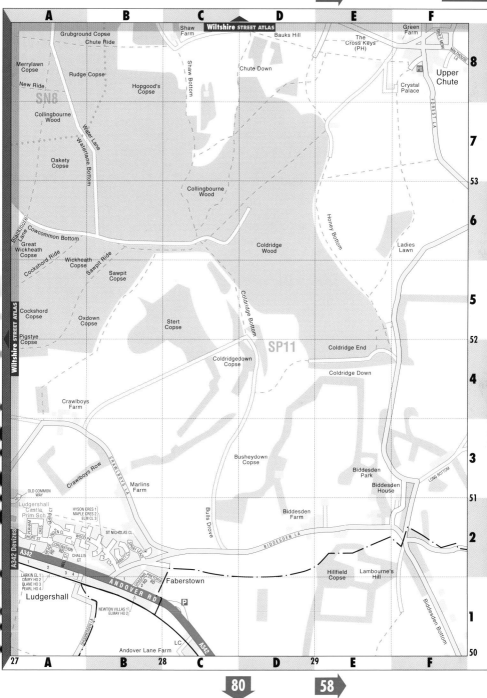

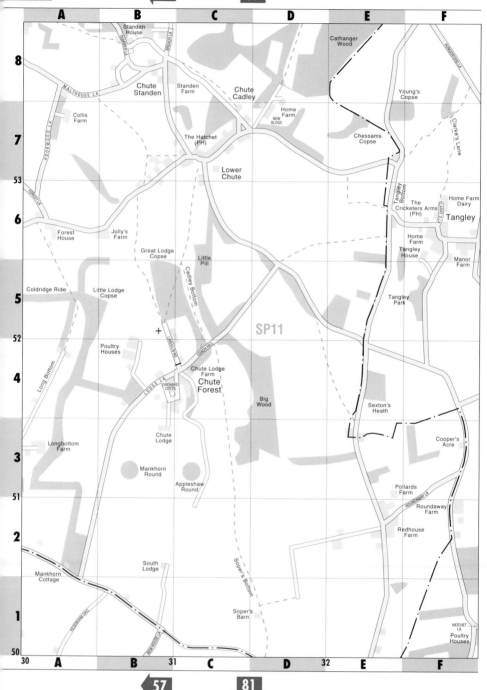

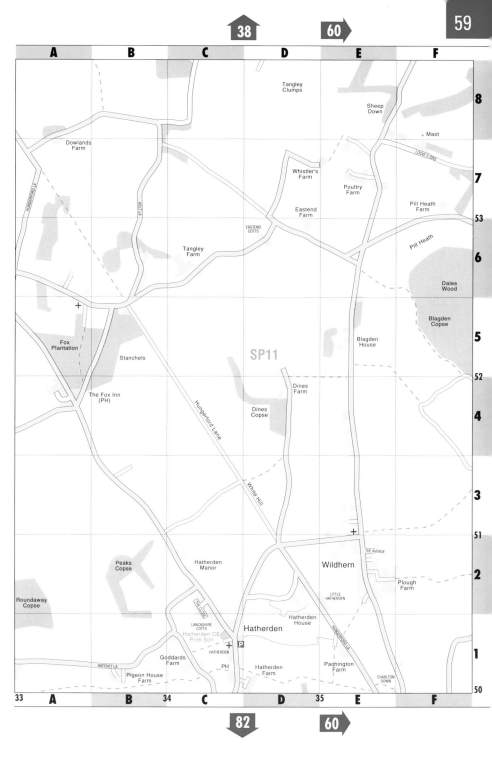

A B C D E F

8

Ibthorpe

Upper
Ibthorpe
Farm

Prosperous
Farm

HORSESHOE LA

Yewtree
Farm

Ibthorpe Manor
Farm

A343

Test Way

Hurstbourne
Tarrant

The
Dene

Locke's
Barn

LOCKE'S DRO

Adams
Farm

THE RANK

7

WINDMILL LA

LOCKMANS LA

DINES CL

PO

THE DRSSETS

DEAN RISE

Windmill Hill
Down

Dolomans La

The George
and Dragon
(PH)

Parsonage
Farm

53

Windmills Farm

LOCKS DRO

B3048 CHURCH ST

STOKE RD

Windmills

VICTORIA
PL

River Swift

B3048

Windmill
Hill

Hurstbourne
Tarrant
CE Prim Sch

Lower
Farm

6

Hurstbourne
Hill

Bourne Rivulet

Blagden
Copse

Hurstbourne
Common

5

SP11

Doles
Wood

Doles
Copse

52

Test Way

4

Doles
Farm

Doles
House

Bourne
Park

3

Frenches
Farm

Rag
Wood

Lee's
Wood

51

2

GREEN DRO

Rag
Copse

Frenche's
Lodge

Straits
Copse

Long
Copse

1

A343 NEWBURY RD

Great
Stubbage

Ridges
Copse

50

36 A B 37 C D 38 E F

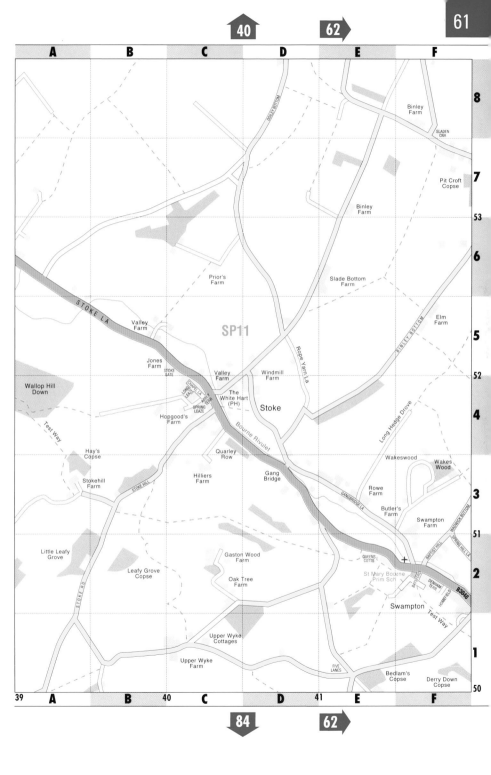

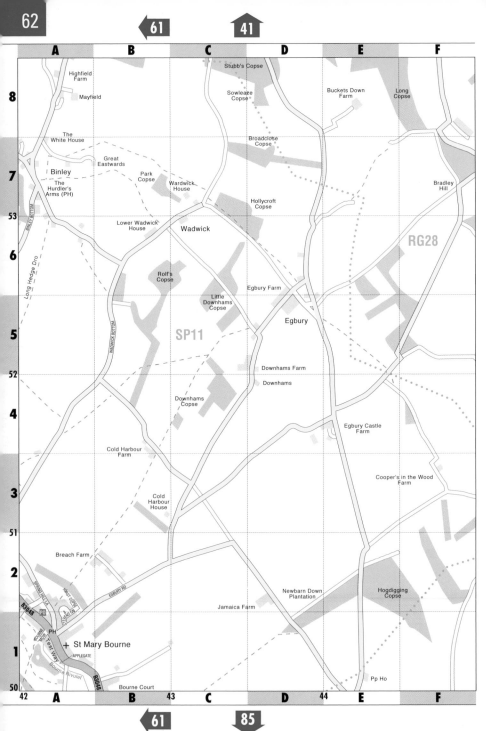

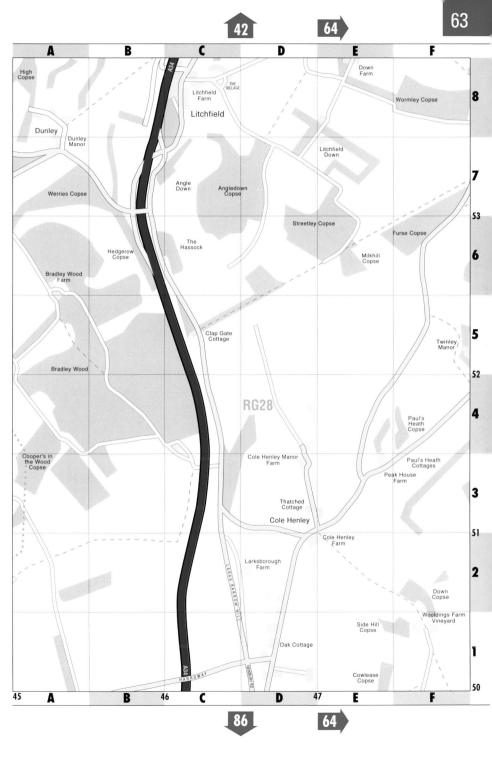

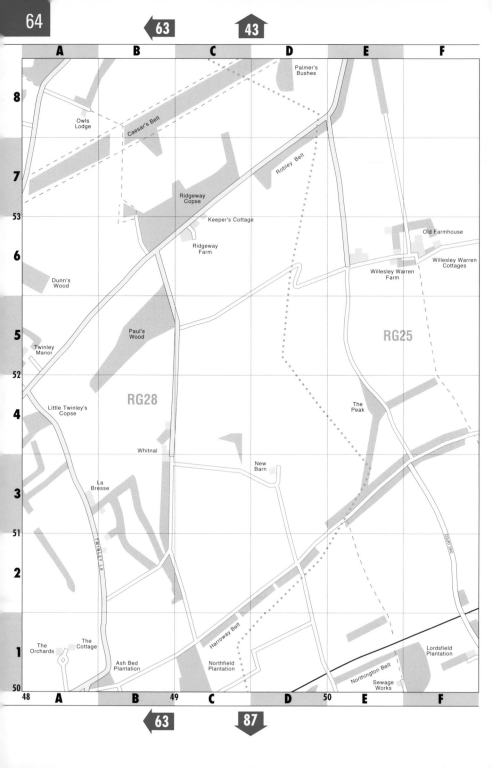

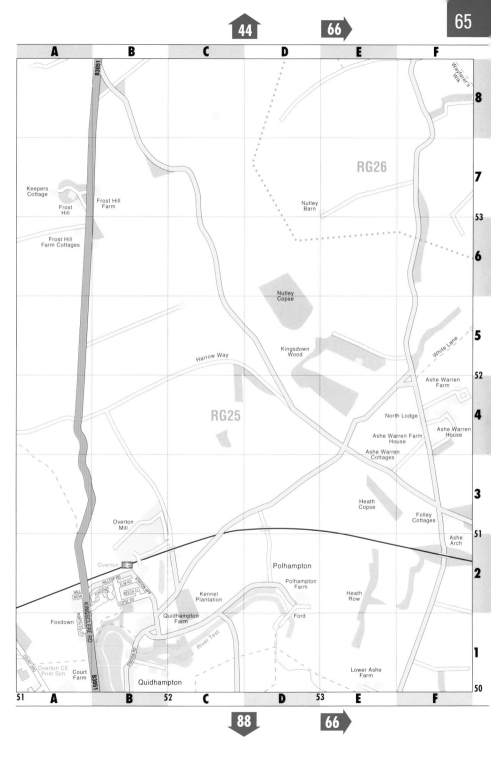

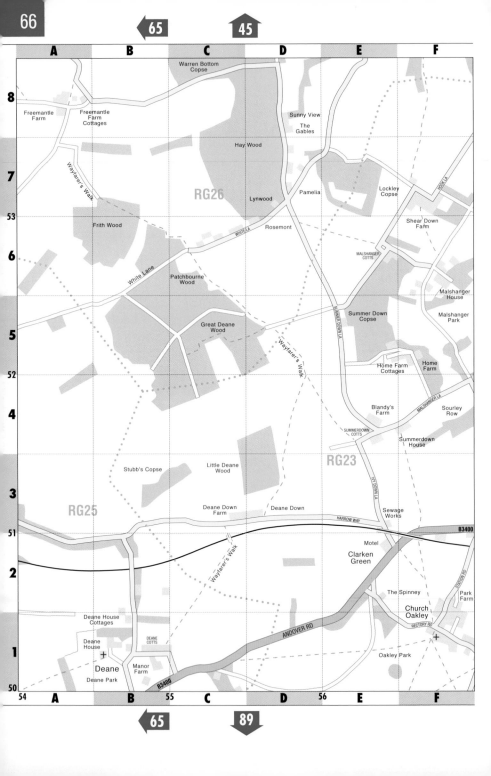

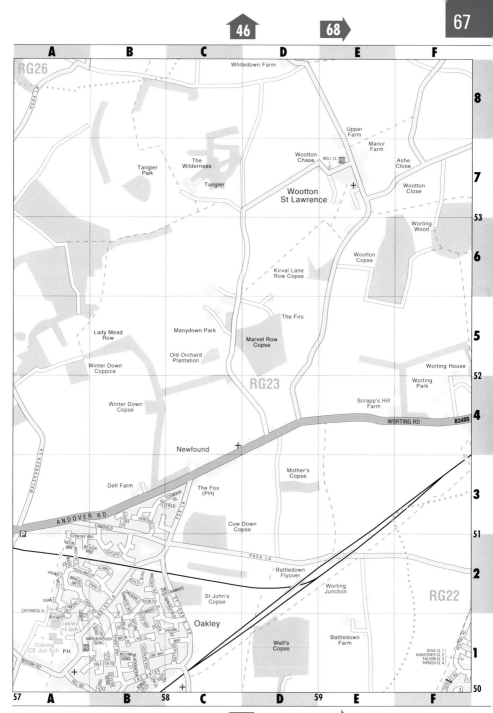

A   B   C   D   E   F

RG26

HOOK LA

Whitedown Farm

8

Upper
Farm

Manor
Farm

Tangier
Park

The
Wilderness

Wootton
Chase

WELL CL
RD

Ashe
Close

7

Tangier

Wootton
St Lawrence

Wootton
Close

53

Worting
Wood

6

Kirval Lane
Row Copse

Wootton
Copse

Lady Mead
Row

Manydown Park

The Firs

5

Marvel Row
Copse

Old Orchard
Plantation

Winter Down
Coppice

RG23

Worting House

52

Worting
Park

Winter Down
Copse

Scrapp's Hill
Farm

4

WORTING RD

B3400

Newfound

MALSHANGER LA

Dell Farm

Mother's
Copse

3

The Fox
(PH)

LOGMOOR
CL

LFIELD

FOX LA

HUNTERS CL

ANDOVER RD

Cow Down
Copse

LONGFIELD

P

TURNPIKE WAY

PACK LA

51

BOON
WAY

LUTHER
RISE

LIGHTSFIELD

Battledown
Flyover

2

HIGHLAND DR

GLAMIS

MEDWAY CT

Worting
Junction

RG22

ARRAN CL

OBAN CL

CACKAMT

AVON RD

ADLER

St John's
Copse

CAITHNESS CL

AVIEMORE

THE GREENAWAYS

FROME CL

Oakley
Inf Sch

MARLBOROUGH
GDNS

Oakley

1

Oakley
CE Jun Sch

PH

PO

KENNET WAY

LYDE CL

LINK WAY

WAY

Well's
Copse

Battledown
Farm

DOVE CL 1
KINGFISHER CL 2
FALCON CL 3
THRUSH CL 4

RECTORY RD

HILL RD

THE DRIVE

KINGS
CIRCLE

50

57   A   58   B   C   58   D   59   E   F

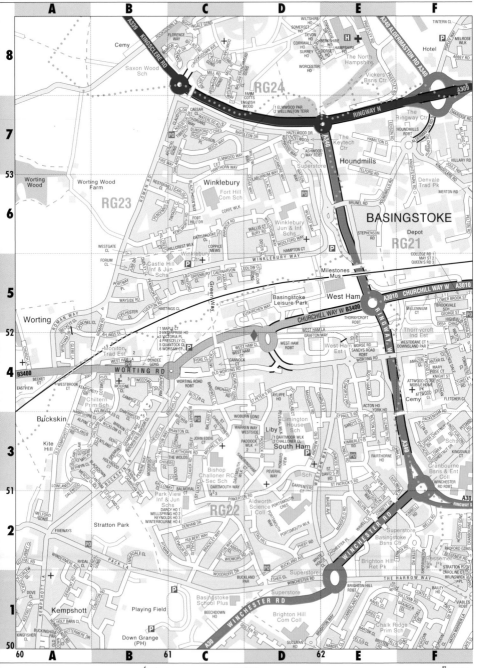

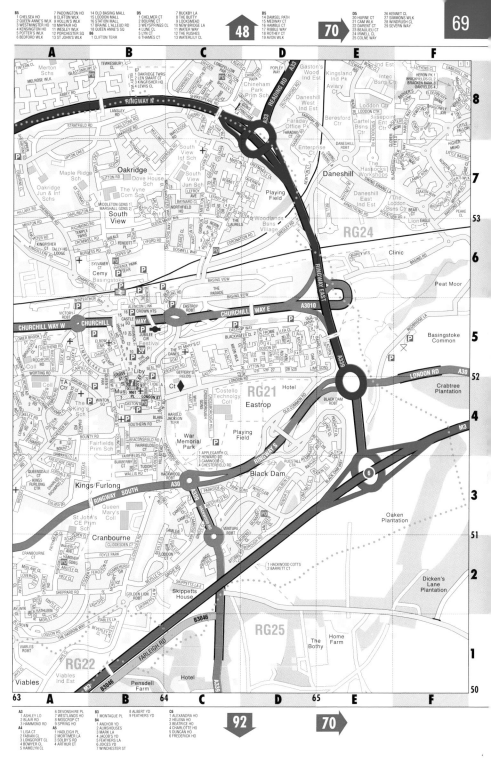

69 49

A B C D E F

8

NEWNHAM LA

Lower Mill
Lower Mill Farm
NEWNHAM LA
Bain's Wood
Elliot's Copse
Poors Farm
POORS FARM RD
POT LA
Gold's Farm
WATER END LA

Oliver's Battery
Motte & Baileys
Wildwood Farm
Round Copse

POTTS HILL
RIVER LODDON
PADDOCK CLOSE

POPPY FIELDS
1 POPPY FIELDS
2 GREAT BINFIELDS CRES
3 AMPORT CL
4 BRICKFIELDS CL
5 CHARLDON GN
6 TRELLIS GR
7 CAVEL CT
8 COPSE FIELD
9 BEDDINGTON CT

BARR GDNS
PRIVETT RD
RIPPEN LONG
GREAT BINFIELDS RD
BARTONS LA

LITTLE FALLOW
LITTLE BASING
MILL PATH

7

Barton's Mill
River Loddon
RILEY LA
Cemy
1 CHESTNUT BANK
2 CHAPEL CL
3 POWER RD

Bushy Lease Copse
Hodd's Copse
Virnell's Copse
ASHMOOR LA

53

MOOR VIEW
BUNTON'S GDNS
PRIORY CLOSE
THE CRUN

Grange Farm
CROWN CRES
BELMONT WAY
Brown's Farm
St Mary's CE Jun Sch
St Mary's
RG24
Old Basing
Hodd's Farm
Hodd's Hill

6

The Crown (PH)
MUSIC
CROWN LA
Old Basing Inf Sch
PARK LA
PH
BRAMBLE
BELLE VUE RD
CAVALIER RD

RG27
Priory Farm
Lyde River
Andwell Moor
A30
M3

Basing House (remains of)
BEDDINGTON
PARK LA
APPLE WEST
LINDEN AVE
HATCH LA
Swannill Nursery
East Moor

5

Basingstoke Common
LINDEN CT
PARK AVE
PELHAM
Basingfield
RAINBOW CL
Hatch
BACHELOR
LONDON RD
PH
GREYWELL RD

OAK TREE COTTS
GREYWELL RD
COB TREE COTTS

52

A30
CRAB
OLIVER
BASIN
FIELD CL
M3

Crabtree Plantation
P
DICKENS LA
KEMBERS LA
LUNDBOROUGH RD

4

M3

New Park
Huish Farm
Webb's Farm
Mapledurwell
The Gamekeepers (PH)

3

Dicken's Lane Plantation
Huish House
HUISH LA
Moorhams Cottage
RG25
Nunnery Hill
Manor Farm

Moorhams Copse
Sheetlands Copse

51

2

Gray's Farm
LUNDBOROUGH RD

1

Blackdown Farm
POLECAT CNR
Ragmore

50

66 A B 67 C D 68 E F

69 93

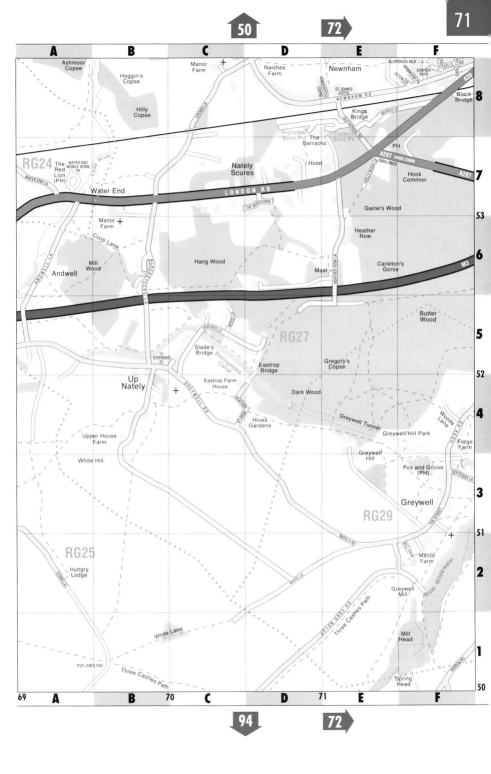

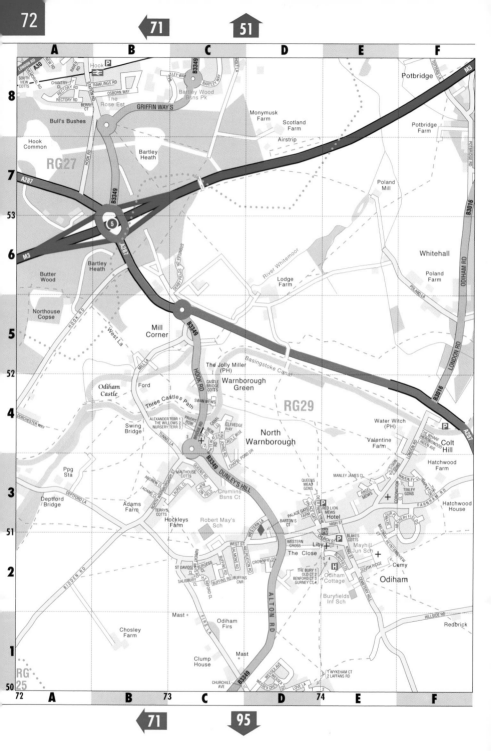

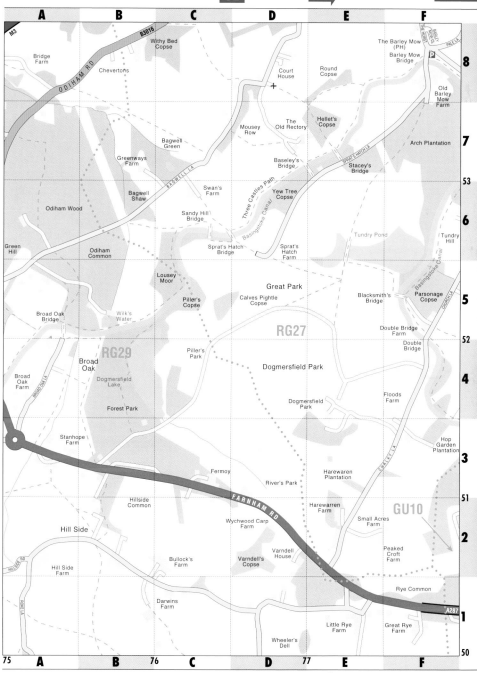

73 53

Hungerford Farm
Pale La
Gunner's Copse
Hitches Farm
Calthorpe Park Sch
L Ctr
SHALDON WAY 2
PRIORY CL 1
COPSE END 3
THE CROFT
DUKES MEAD
CHANTERS
Calthorpe Park
DORKHA SQ 1
WOODMAN CT 2
JAMESON HO 3
OSBORNE CT 4
RESENT CT 5
KINGFISHER CT 6
FRAYNES CROFT
ST JAMES
READING RD S
A323 B3013

8

Jack Reid's Copse
Tavistock Inf Sch
THE SPINNEY
FIELDWAY
HEATHFIELD CT
BADGERS
GLEN RD
LAWRENCE

Burnbake Copse
All Saints CE Jun Sch
NEW BARN CL
LEA WOOD RD
FRERE AVE
THE LEA
GRAMPLET

MEADOWILK
LARMER CL

7

Chatter Alley
Pilcot Farm
Norman's Green
Cemy
RICHARD CT
CEMETERY RD
GRENVILLE CT
SPRING WOODS
LITTLE CL
Court Moor Sch

53

Dogmersfield CE Prim Sch
Pilcot
GU51
NETHERHOUSE CT
LINKWAY PARK

Dogmersfield
PH

6

Pilcot Bridge
Daegmarsfield Farm
CHURCH LA
Brook Meadow Farm
PILCOT RD
Netherhouse Copse
KILN WORKSHOPS
The Black Horse (PH)
Grove Farm
WICKHAM PL
WICKHAM CT
GU52

RG27

Peatmoor Copse
HILLSIDE CL
Brook Hill
Crookham Village
THE STREET
MALTHOUSE BRIDGE COTTS
TALL PINES
FREELANDS
Grange Estate
SILVER BIRCH

5

Ormersfield Farm
STROUD LA
52
Whitlow Alders
Zebon Copse
Crookham CE Inf Sch

4

Cunningham's Row
P
Bridge House
Chequers Bridge
CROOKHAM LA
Poulter's Bridge
CHRISTCHURCH CT
ATTLEE GDNS
COTTRELL CL

Coxmoor Wood

3

Hancock's Farm
BOWENHURST LA
Two Ponds
Garden Ctr
Stables
Stillers Farm

51

Coxmoor Farm
Falkner's Copse
Redfield Rows
Redfields Pk
Blackmoor Copse

2

Coxmoor Wood
Oakes Copse
Fusney Copse
St Nicholas Sch
Redfields Cottage Farm

Finns Ind Pk
GU10
Bowenhurst La
CH
Triggs

Mill Lane
Bowenhurst Farm
AQUARIUS CL
DARE'S LA
Seymour Farm

1

A287
FARNHAM RD
The Horns (PH)
Downsland House
Marsh Farm Bsns Ctr
Goddards Farm
DARES FARM
A287

50

73 97

E4
1 WOODLAND CT
2 ANNETTES CROFT
3 HOUSE PLAT CT
4 HORNES FIELD CT
5 NICOTIANA CT
6 RYE CROFT
7 MELLERSH CL
8 SEPEN MEADE
9 TWISELL THORNE
10 FRENCHMANS CREEK
11 CONSTANTIUS CT

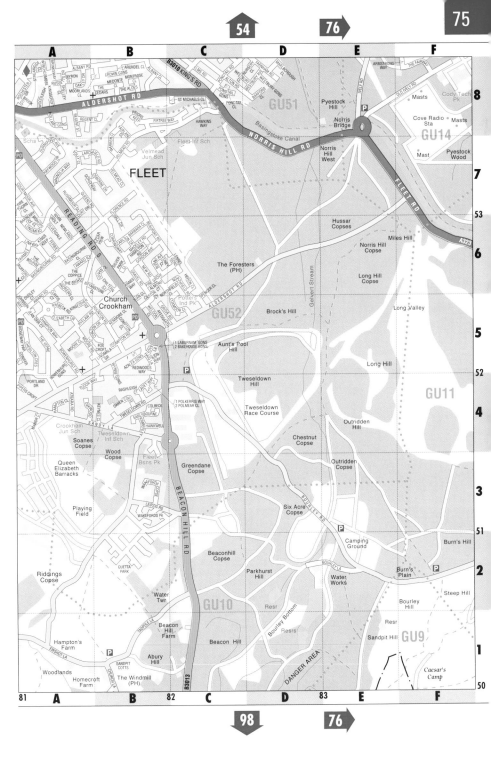

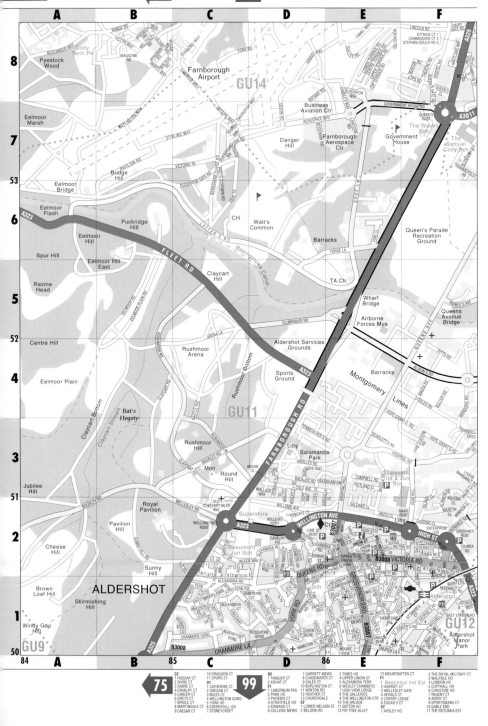

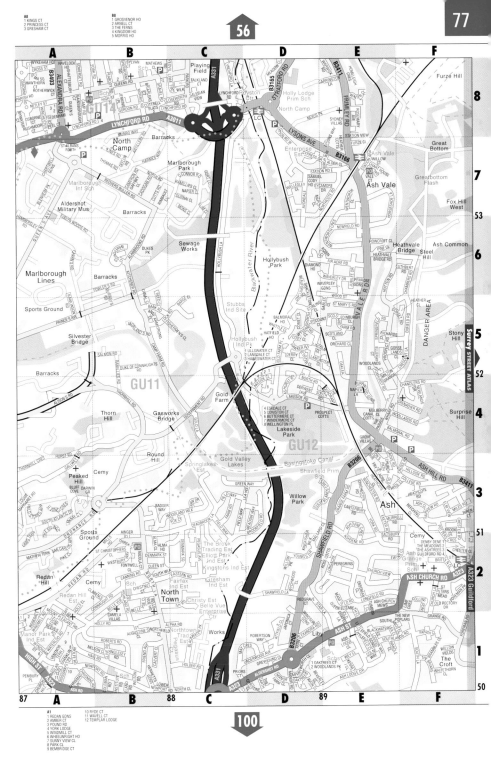

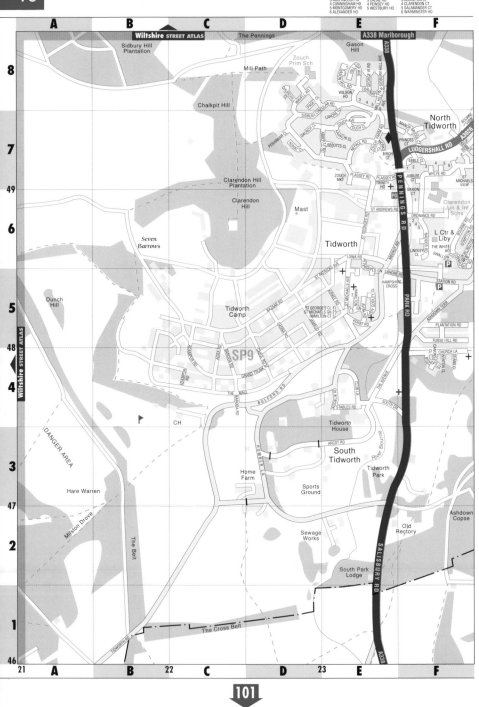

Wiltshire STREET ATLAS

The Pennings

A338 Marlborough

Sidbury Hill
Plantation

Gason
Hill

North
Tidworth

Mill Path

Chalkpit Hill

Clarendon Hill
Plantation

Clarendon
Hill

LUDGERSHALL RD

Mast

Seven
Barrows

Tidworth

Dunch
Hill

Tidworth
Camp

SP9

Clarendon
Jun & Inf
Schs

L Ctr &
Liby

THE WHITE
HO

STATION RD

Hampshire
Cross

PARK RD

PLANTATION RD

FURSE HILL RD

THE
MALL

BULFORD RD

CH

Tidworth
House

South
Tidworth

Tidworth
Park

DANGER AREA

Home
Farm

Sports
Ground

Hare Warren

Sewage
Works

Old
Rectory

Ashdown
Copse

Milston Drove

The Belt

South Park
Lodge

SALISBURY RD

The Cross Belt

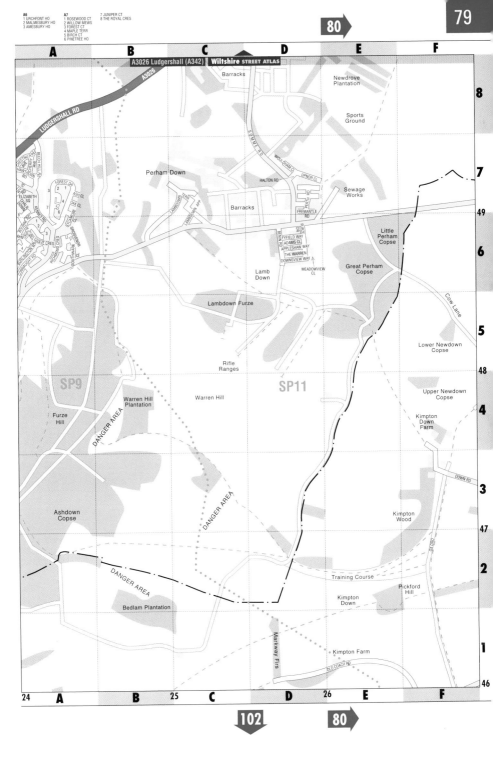

A6
1 URCHFONT HO
2 MALMESBURY HO
3 AMESBURY HO

A7
1 ROSEWOOD CT
2 WILLOW MEWS
3 FOREST CT
4 MAPLE TERR
5 BIRCH CT
6 PINETREE HO

7 JUNIPER CT
8 THE ROYAL CRES

A3026 Ludgershall (A342) **Wiltshire** STREET ATLAS

A3026

LUDGERSHALL RD

Barracks

Newdrove
Plantation

8

Sports
Ground

Perham Down

HALTON RD

7

Sewage
Works

49

Barracks

Little
Perham
Copse

6

Lamb
Down

MEADOWVIEW
CL

Great Perham
Copse

FYFIELD WAY
ADAMS CL
APPLESHAW WAY
THE WARREN
DOWNSVIEW WAY

Lambdown Furze

Cow Lane

5

Lower Newdown
Copse

48

Rifle
Ranges

SP9

SP11

Upper Newdown
Copse

Warren Hill

Warren Hill
Plantation

DANGER AREA

Furze
Hill

Kimpton
Down
Farm

4

DOWN RD

DANGER AREA

3

Ashdown
Copse

Kimpton
Wood

47

DANGER AREA

Training Course

2

Pickford
Hill

Bedlam Plantation

Kimpton
Down

Markway Firs

Kimpton Farm

1

OLD COACH RD

46

24

25

26

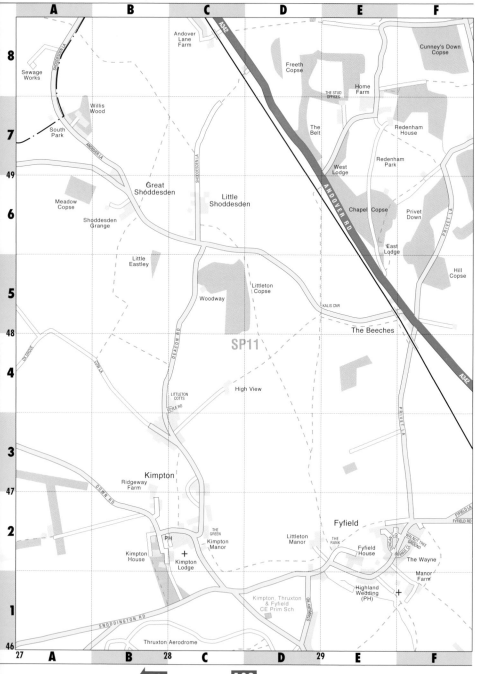

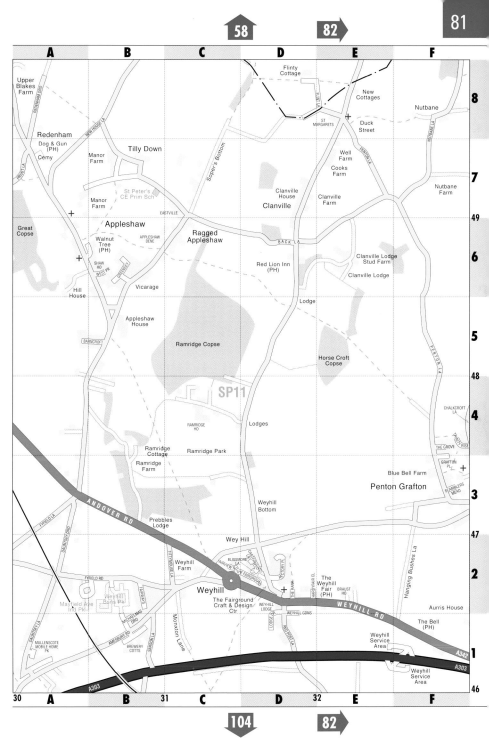

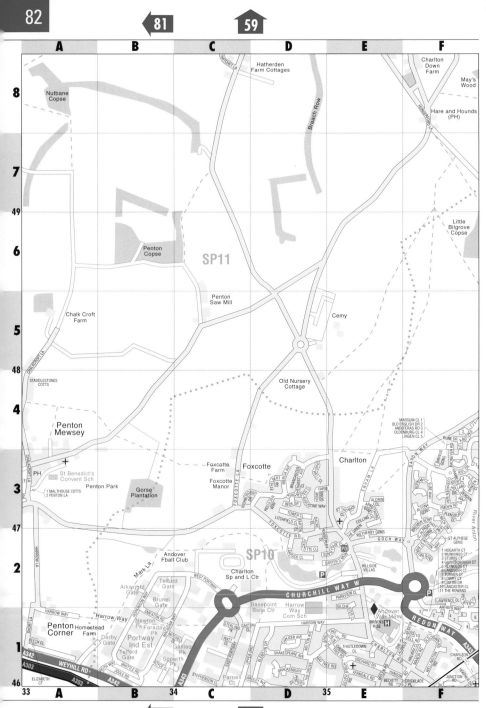

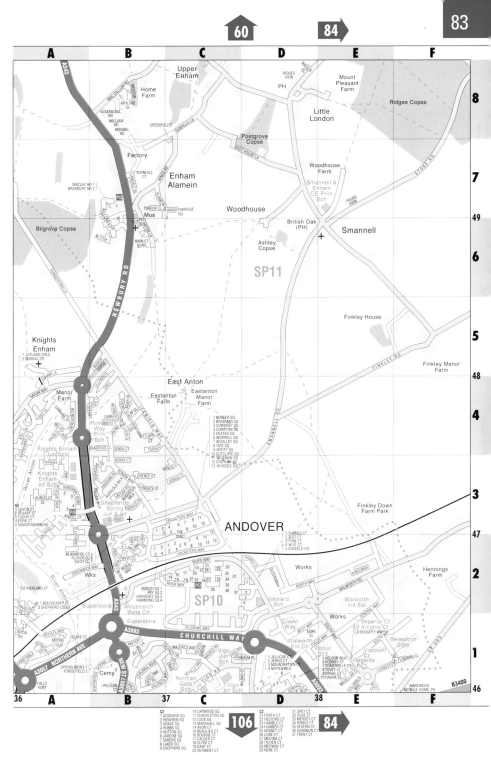

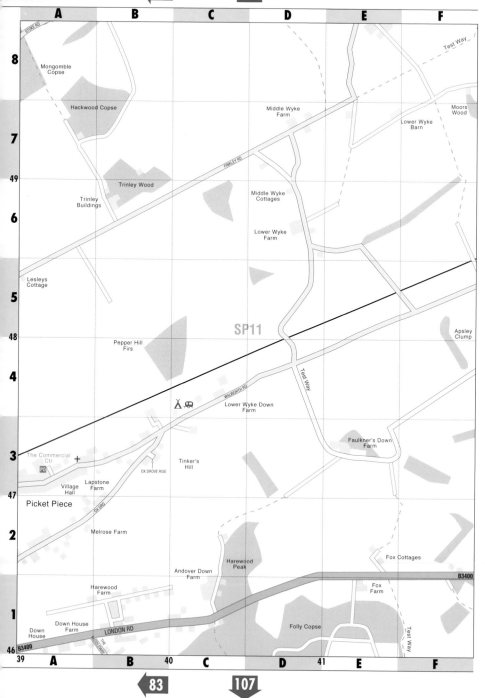

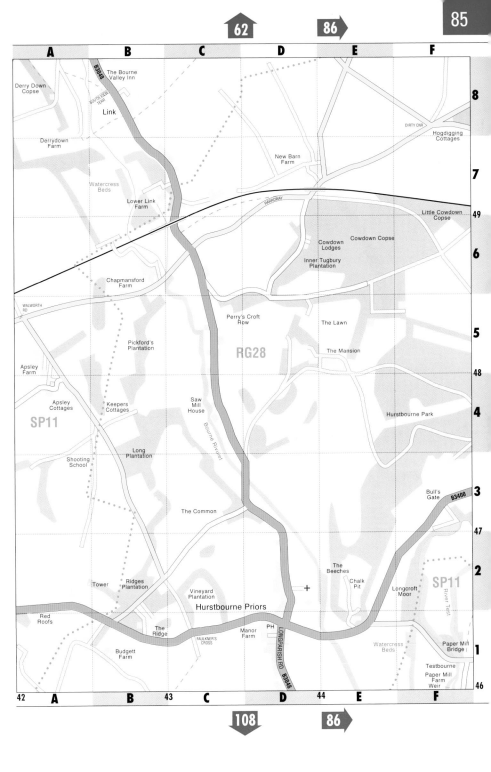

85
63

	A	B	C	D	E	F

8

Down Farm

Sheepcrook
Cottages

HARROWAY

7

Bere Hill
Farm

Winterhill
Plantation

49

Whitchurch

GREENWOODS
CROSSWAYS

Water
Twr

STATION RD
NEWBURY RD

6

Whitchurch

Wells-in-the-Field
Farm

BERE HILL

Skylark RISE

BRADBURY
CL

Evingar
Ind Est

BICESTER

RG28

B3400

5

Manor
Farm

MEADOW DR

BLUEWOOD DR

OAKLAND CT

LONDON ST

LONDON RD

KINGS WLK

LYNCH HILL PK

Lynch Hill

THE GREEN

POUND
MDW

HILLSIDE

THE
GABLES

48

WARWICK
CL

SEEVIOUR'S
CT

Liby TOWN HALL
PH

CHURCH ST

WELLS LA

FAIRCLOSE

FAIRCLOSE
TERR

TOWN MILLS

TEST RD

1 WATERLOO CT
2 MULBERRY MEAD
3 KINGFISHER CL
4 CHATTER LA
5 LORD DENNING CT

River Test

Whitchurch
CE Prim Sch

4

Hurstbourne Park

Cemy

CLARK
MEWS

Whitchurch
Silk Mill

Great
Town
Bridge

PAGES
YD

HIDES

THE KNOWLINGS

WHEELER CL

BRIDGES CL

NEW
WAY

Coombedown
Hanger

3

B3400

Fulling
Mill

THE WEIR

MILLERS FARM CL

CHARLCOT CL

Testbourne
Com Sch

CHIMMEY DECK

MICHELDEVER RD

Southfield
Farm

47

2

RIVERSIDE
COTTS

Manor Farm

Manor
House

Tufton

Sewage
Works

Knowle
Clump

SP11

1

A34

Buftons

46

45	A	B	46	C	D	47	E	F

85
109

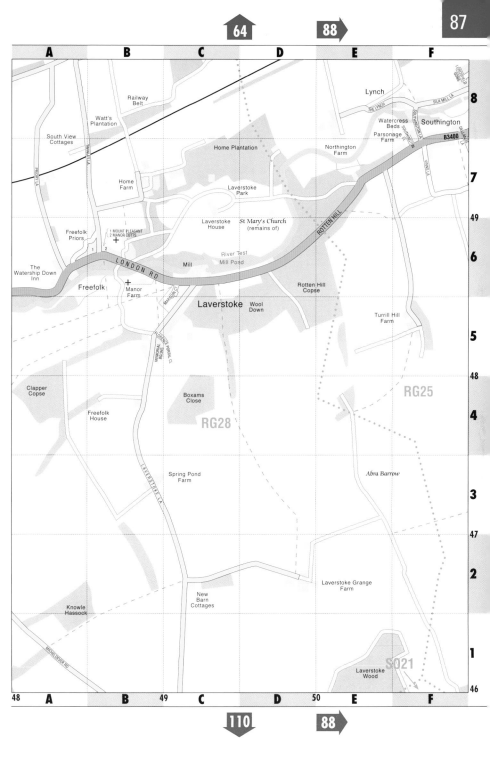

8

Lynch

Railway
Belt

Watt's
Plantation

Watercress
Beds

Southington

Parsonage
Farm

South View
Cottages

Home Plantation

Northington
Farm

B3400

7

Home
Farm

Laverstoke
Park

49

ROTTEN HILL

Laverstoke
House

St Mary's Church
(remains of)

Freefolk
Priors

1 MOUNT PLEASANT
2 MANOR COTTS

6

The
Watership
Down
Inn

LONDON RD

Mill

River Test
Mill Pond

Rotten Hill
Copse

Freefolk

Manor
Farm

Laverstoke

Wool
Down

Turrill Hill
Farm

5

48

Clapper
Copse

Boxams
Close

RG25

RG28

4

Freefolk
House

Abra Barrow

Spring Pond
Farm

3

47

2

Laverstoke Grange
Farm

New
Barn
Cottages

Knowle
Hassock

1

MICHELDEVER RD

Laverstoke
Wood

SO21

46

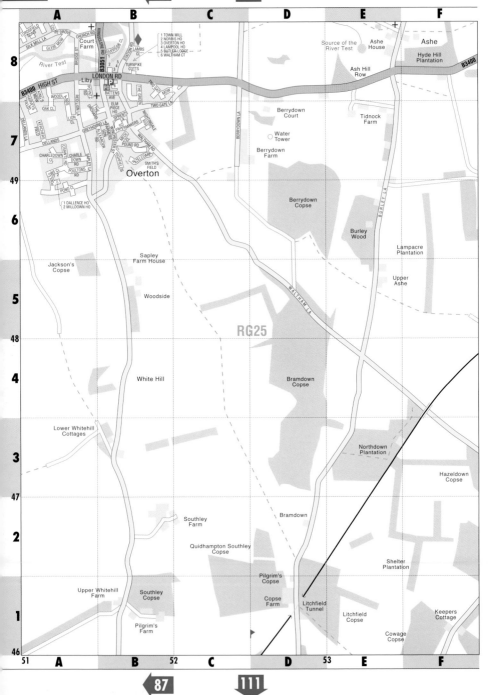

River Test

Court Farm

1 TOWN MILL
2 NORRIS HO
3 OVERTON HO
4 LAMPOOL HO
5 BUTLER LODGE
6 WALTHAM CT

LONDON RD

B3051

Libry

HIGH ST

B3400

TURNPIKE COTTS

Source of the River Test

Ashe House

Ashe

Hyde Hill Plantation

B3400

Ash Hill Row

Berrydown Court

Tidnock Farm

Water Tower

Berrydown Farm

Overton

Berrydown Copse

Burley Wood

Lampacre Plantation

Upper Ashe

BURLEY LA

1 DALLENCE HO
2 MILLDOWN HO

Sapley Farm House

Jackson's Copse

Woodside

WALTHAM LA

RG25

White Hill

Bramdown Copse

Lower Whitehill Cottages

Northdown Plantation

Hazeldown Copse

Southley Farm

Bramdown

Quidhampton Southley Copse

Shelter Plantation

Pilgrim's Copse

Upper Whitehill Farm

Southley Copse

Copse Farm

Litchfield Tunnel

Litchfield Copse

Keepers Cottage

Pilgrim's Farm

Cowage Copse

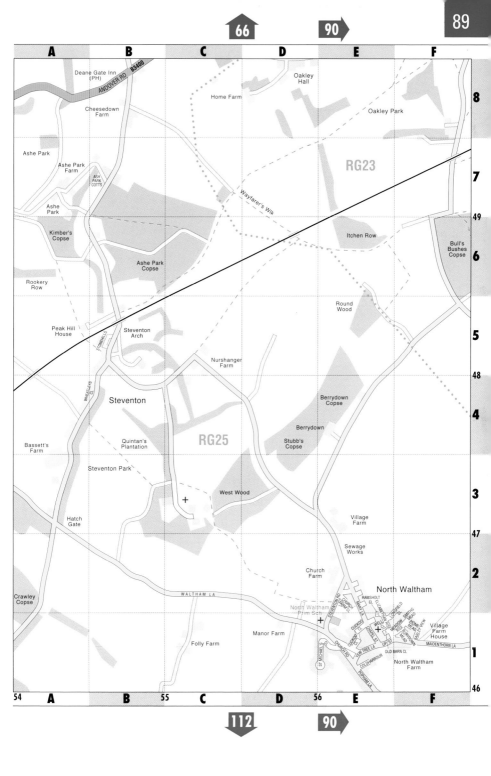

89
67

A **B** **C** **D** **E** **F**

8

WESTBROOK CL

BEECH TREE CL
ASH TREE CL

KINGS ORCH
ST JOHN'S PIECE
ST JOHN'S RD

Breach
Farm

Breach
Cottages

Jeffery's
Copse

OSPREY
RD
THRUSH
CL

LARK
CL
STARLING CL
PHEASANT
CL
EAGLE
WOODPECKER
CL
BLACKBIRD
SEAGULL
CORMORANT

HUMMING BIRD
CT

SANDPIPER WAY

BRAMBLING CL

SWINNY MEAD

Bakers Yd

Sewage
Works

7

Pardown

RG22

CRES
TEAL

BIRCH
FERN

WOODMERE
CROFT

MALLARD CL
REDWING RD

MARTINGALE CT

LAPWING CL

SKYLARK
NUTHATCH
YELLOWHAMMER
TERN

49

Pardown
Copse

Small's
Copse

FIRECREST RD

GOLDFINCH GDNS 1
PUFFIN CL 2
MERLIN MEAD 3

Bull's Bushes
Copse

6

Bull's
Bushes Farm

RG23

SHORTWOOD
COPSE LA

A30

5

Little Stubbs
Copse

South
Wood

Great Stubbs
Copse

WINCHESTER RD

CH

BROADMERE
RD

48

Dean Heath
Copse

Wayfarer's Wlk

4

Southwood
Farm

Kempshott
Park

Kempshott
Park
Ind Est

M3

Ganderdown
Copse

The
Cedars

3

Cvn
Site

Peak Copse

THE CEDARS

Oakdown
Farm

A30

47

7

Wayfarer's Wlk

CH

2

RG25

CH

Rowley
Copse

The Sun Inn
(PH)

MAIDENTHORN LA

Mast

1

Dummer

CHAPEL
GLEBE CL
POST OFFICE
DOWN ST
DEANSFIELD
UP ST

The Queen
(PH)

FARLEIGH LA
NUTLEY LA
Clump
Farm

Dummer
Clump

Cemy

46

57 **A** **B** 58 **C** **D** 59 **E** **F**

A30

M3

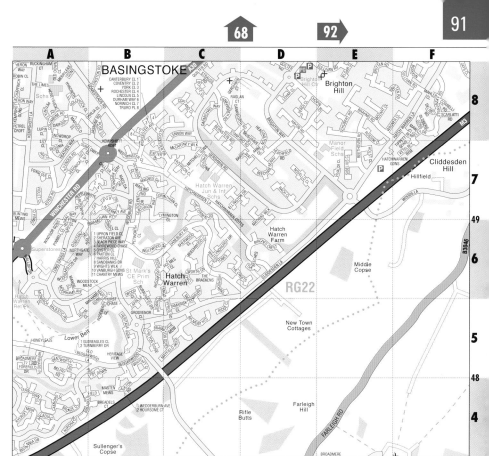

91
69

A   B   C   D   E   F

RG22

M3

AYE CL

B3046

FARLEIGH RD

SOUTHDEN

8

Pensdell Farm

Audleys Wood

The Basin

Spring Wood

Broad Walk

Hackwood House

The Cubs

Hackwood Park

7

PH

WOODS LA

Cliddesden

49

B3046

RECTORY ROW

CHURCH LA

HOOPERS MEAD

CENTURY CL

STATION RD

Poultry Farm

HACKWOOD LA

Swallick Wood

Manor Farm

6

Cliddesden Nurseries

Lodge Plantation

Winslade Farm

Cliddesden Prim Sch

5

Pidden Hill

Swallick Cottages

Winslade

48

Swallick Farm

Buckshorn Copse

Little Hen Wood

4

White Hill

RG25

Eight Acre Dell

West Field Beeches

Poor Hill

3

Kingsmore Copse

Whinkney's Copse

Round Copse

The Avenue

Doper's Copse

White Hill Dell

Fryingdown Copse

Forfield Plantation

47

Allwood Copse

Three Castles Path

Winslade La

Quidliz Round

Herriard Park

2

Northgate Farm

Little Bushywarren Copse

A339

GRAMMARSHAM LA

HOOPSIDE LA

Webb's Copse

Great Bushywarren Copse

Alley Lane

1

Hallowed Litten

OXLEASE Lane

46

GREEN LA

CHURCH LA

BUSHYWARREN LA

63   A   B   64   C   D   65   E   F

91
115

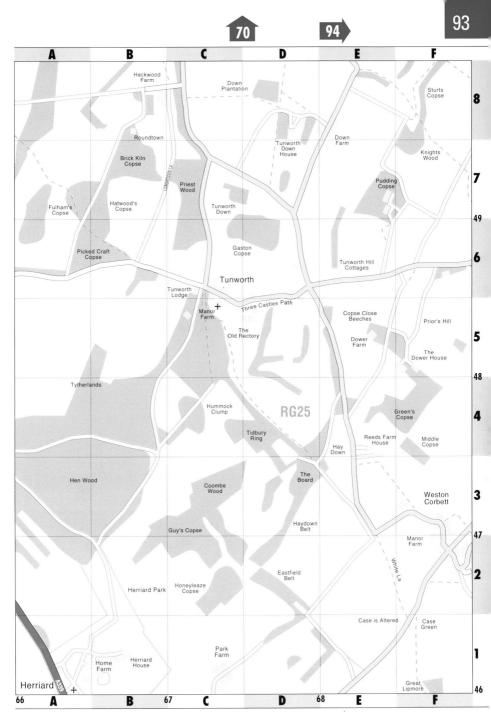

A   B   C   D   E   F

8

Hackwood Farm

Down Plantation

Sturts Copse

Roundtown

Tunworth Down House

Down Farm

Knights Wood

7

Brick Kiln Copse

Pudding Copse

49

Priest Wood

Fulham's Copse

Hatwood's Copse

Tunworth Down

Picked Craft Copse

Gaston Copse

Tunworth Hill Cottages

6

Tunworth

Tunworth Lodge

Three Castles Path

Manor Farm

Copse Close Beeches

Prior's Hill

5

The Old Rectory

Dower Farm

The Dower House

48

Tytherlands

Hummock Clump

RG25

Green's Copse

4

Tidbury Ring

Reeds Farm House

Middle Copse

Hen Wood

Coombe Wood

Hay Down

The Board

Weston Corbett

3

Guy's Copse

Haydown Belt

Manor Farm

47

White La

Herriard Park

Honeyleaze Copse

Eastfield Belt

2

Case is Altered

Case Green

Park Farm

Home Farm

Herriard House

1

Herriard

A303

Great Lipmore

46

93
71

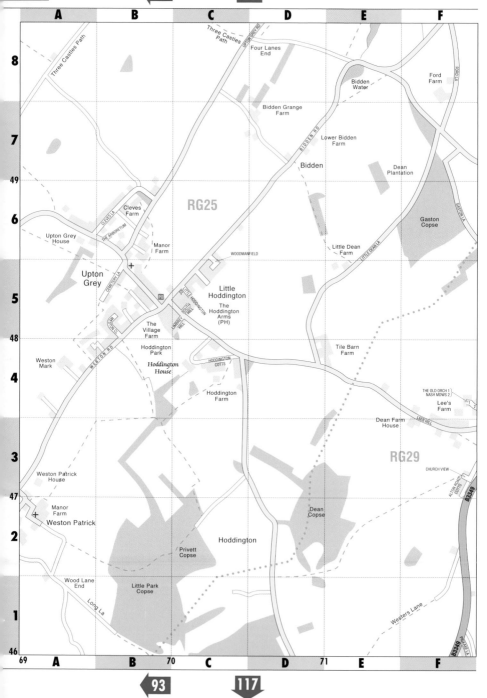

93
117

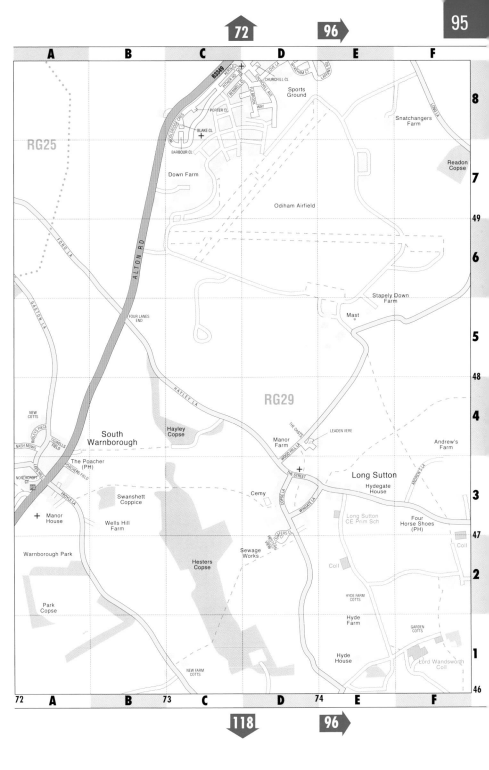

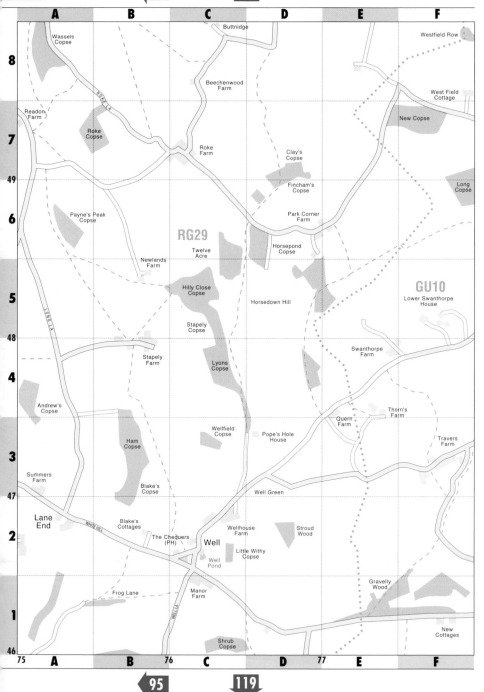

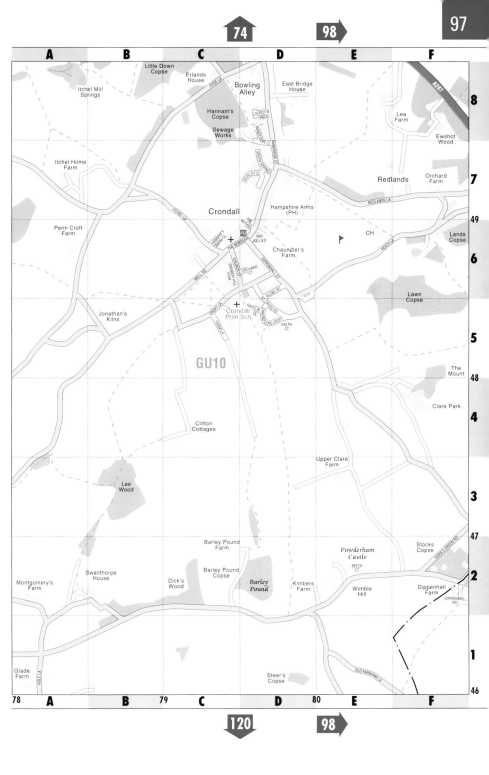

A B C D E F

8

Little Down
Copse
Erlands
House
Bowling
Alley
East Bridge
House
Lea
Farm
Ewshot
Wood

Itchel Mill
Springs
Hannam's
Copse
LEFROY'S
FIELD
Sewage
Works

7

Itchel Home
Farm
GREEN SPRINGS
ITCHEL LA
Redlands
Orchard
Farm
REDLANDS LA

49

Crondall
Hampshire Arms
(PH)
Penn Croft
Farm
HANNAM'S
FARM CL
THE WITHIES
THE BOROUGH
PO
THE
JOLLIES
CH
Lands
Copse
HEATH LA

6

WELL RD
CHURCH HILL TERR
CHURCH ST
ORCHARD
CT
Chaundler's
Farm
DIPPENHALL ST
GLEBE RD
ST DRO'S RD
Lawn
Copse

Jonathan's
Kilns
CROFT LA
TINKLE LA
Crondall
Prim Sch
RAVELIN
CL
PLOVERS CROFT
RALPH
CT

5

GU10

The
Mount

48

Clare Park

Clifton
Cottages

4

Upper Clare
Farm

Lee
Wood

3

47

Barley Pound
Farm
Powderham
Castle
Stocks
Copse
DORA'S GREEN RD

Montgomery's
Farm
Swanthorpe
House
Dick's
Wood
Barley Pound
Copse
Barley
Pound
Kimbers
Farm
BEECH
CT
Wimble
Hill
Dippenhall
Farm
DIPPENHALL
RD

2

Glade
Farm
HYDE LA
Steer's
Copse
OLD FARNHAM LA

1

46

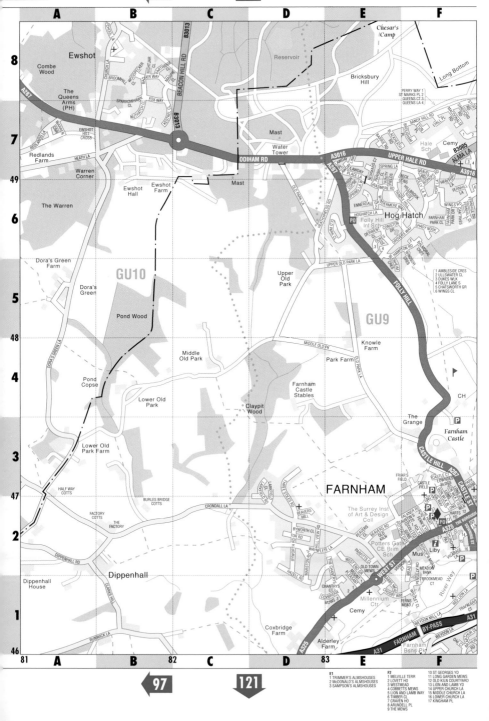

E1
1 TRIMMER'S ALMSHOUSES
2 McDONALD'S ALMSHOUSES
3 SAMPSON'S ALMSHOUSES

F2
1 MELVILLE TERR
2 LOVETT HO
3 WESTMEAD
4 COBBETTS MEWS
5 LION AND LAMB WAY
6 TIMBER CL
7 CRAVEN HO
8 ARUNDELL PL
9 THE MEWS

10 ST GEORGES YD
11 LONG GARDEN MEWS
12 OLD KILN COURTYARD
13 LION AND LAMB YD
14 UPPER CHURCH LA
15 MIDDLE CHURCH LA
16 LOWER CHURCH LA
17 KINGHAM PL

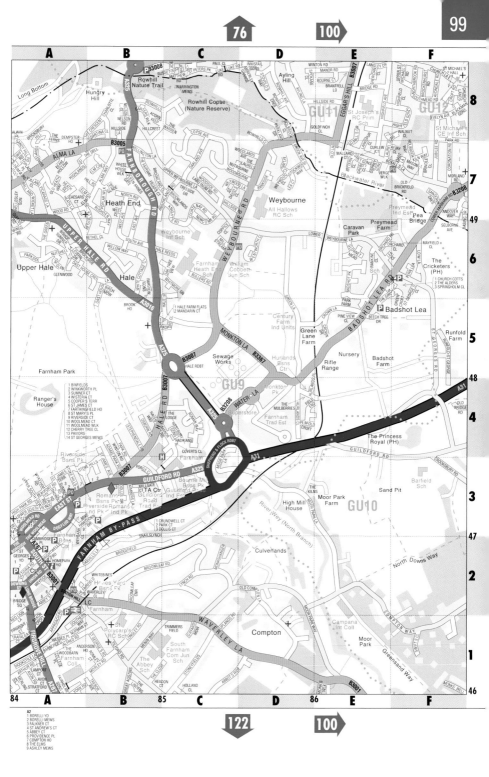

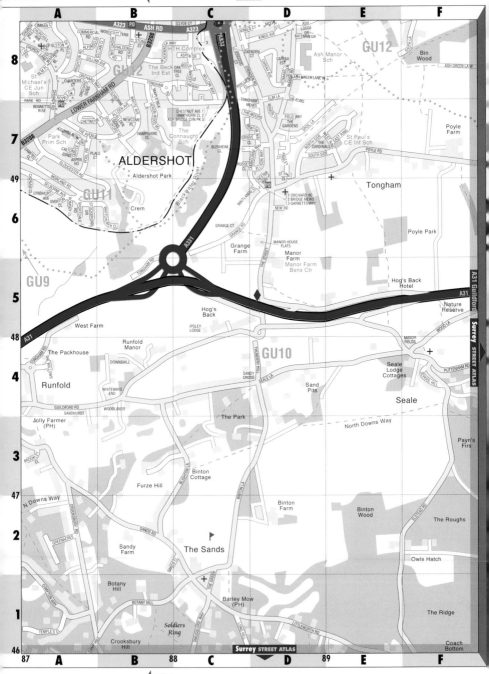

Surrey STREET ATLAS

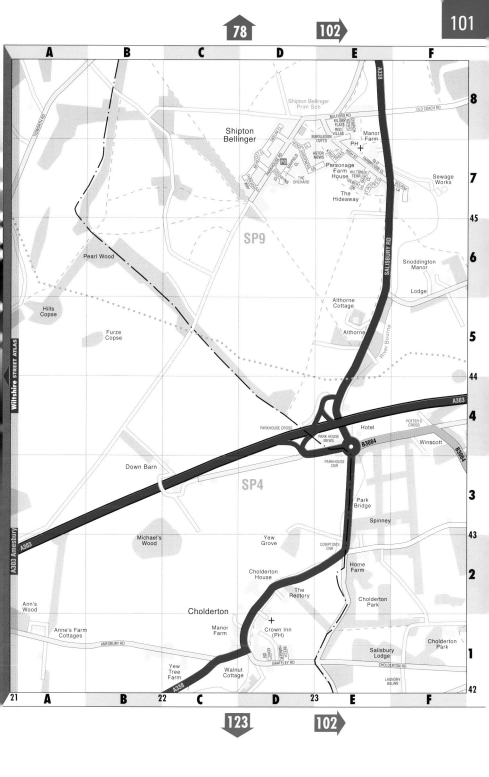

101
79

	A	B	C	D	E	F

8

Shipton Plantation

OLD COACH RD

OLD COACH RD

SNODDINGTON RD

Shipton Wood

7

SP9

45

Snoddington Down Farm

6

Racedown Farm

RACEDOWN COTTS

A303

Snoddington Hill

Thruxton Down House

5

SP11

44

A303

Thimble Hall

Middlecot House

4

Thruxton Farm

Thruxton Hill

Hugh's Settlement

3

SP4

Fairhaven

Cholderton Hill

CHOLDERTON RD

43

Victoria Copse

Horseshoe Meadow Farm

Curlews

2

B3084

Windy Dido

Cholderton Park

Coronation Belt

Lodge

1

Quarley Hill

42

B3084

GRATELEY DRO

24	A	B	25	C	D	26	E	F

101
124

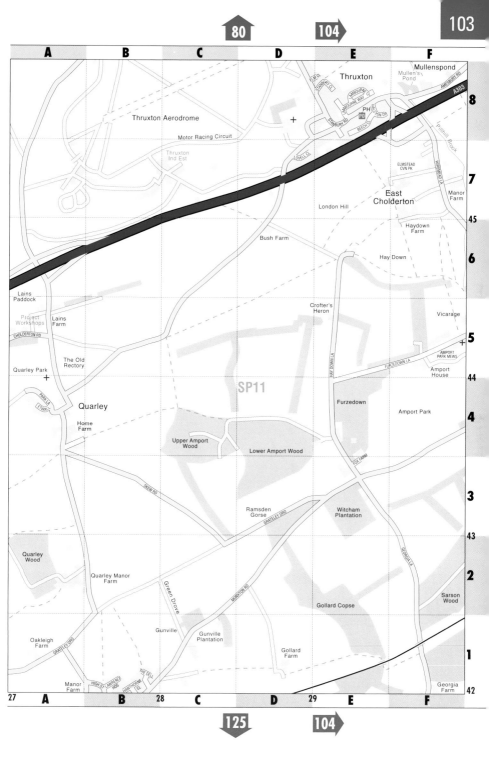

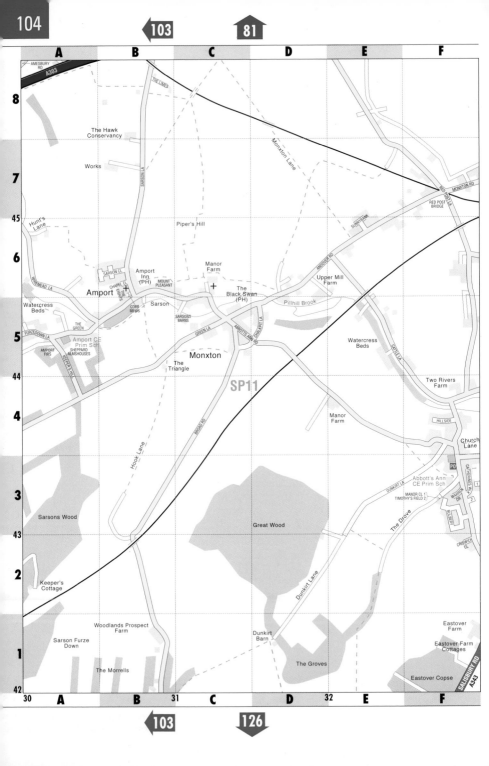

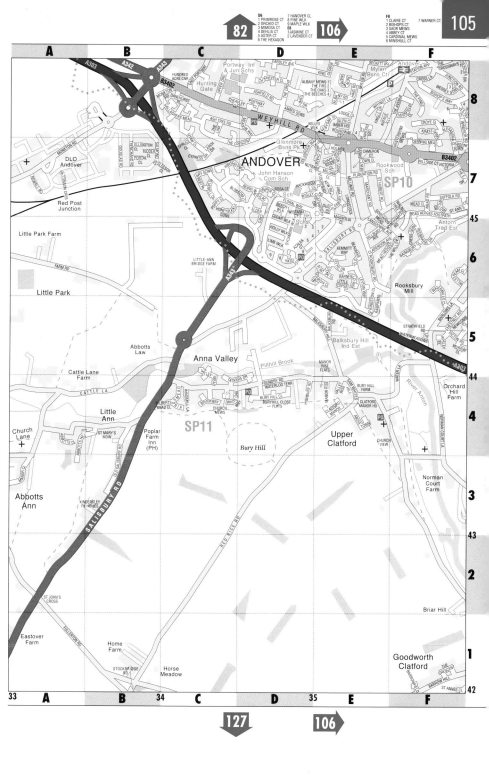

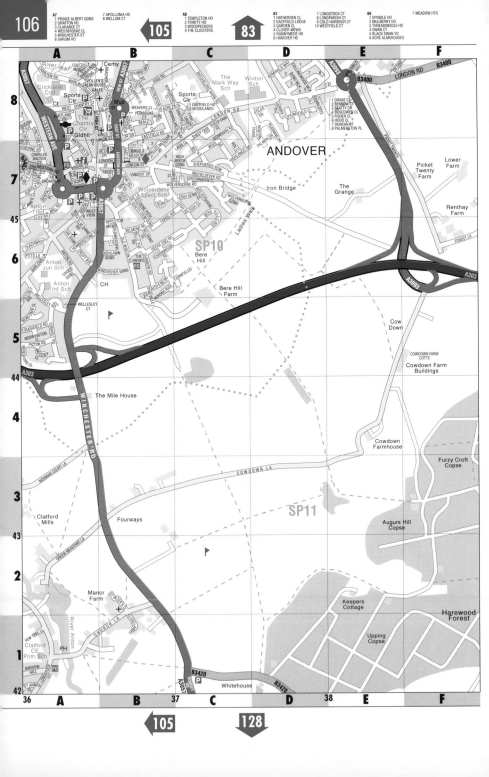

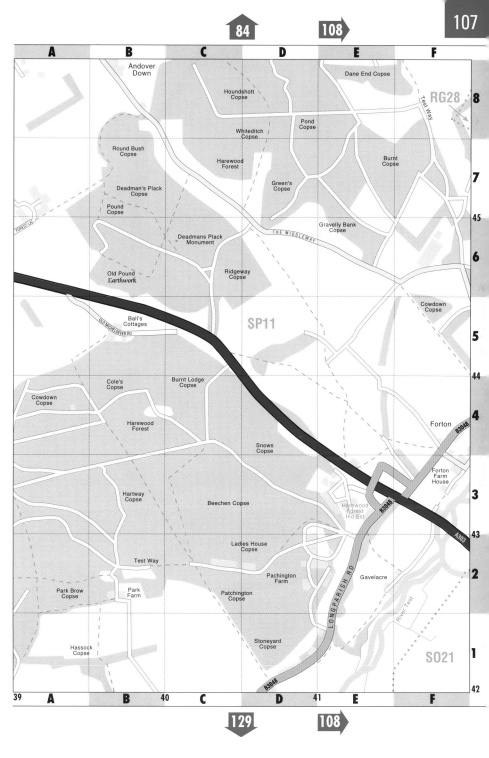

A B C D E F

Andover Down

Dane End Copse

Houndshott Copse

RG28 8

Test Way

Whiteditch Copse

Pond Copse

Round Bush Copse

Burnt Copse

7

Harewood Forest

Green's Copse

Deadman's Plack Copse

45

Pound Copse

THE MIDDLEWAY

Gravelly Bank Copse

Deadmans Plack Monument

FOREST LA.

6

Old Pound Earthwork

Ridgeway Copse

OLD MICHELDEVER RD

Ball's Cottages

SP11

Cowdown Copse

5

44

Cole's Copse

Burnt Lodge Copse

Forton

B3048

4

Cowdown Copse

Harewood Forest

Snows Copse

Forton Farm House

Hartway Copse

Beechen Copse

Harewood Forest Ind Est

B3048

3

Ladies House Copse

A303

43

Test Way

Pachington Farm

Gavelacre

LONGPARISH RD

2

Park Brow Copse

Park Farm

Patchington Copse

River Test

Hassock Copse

Stoneyard Copse

SO21

1

B3048

42

39 A B 40 C D 41 E F

107
85

RG28

Three Halve Copse

Bourne Rivulet

Watercress Beds

Tracy's Dell

Paul's Dell

Wood Walk Plantation

DRURY LN · LONGPARISH RD · B3048

East Aston

Mill House

45

NORTH SIDE

Longparish House

Cricketers Inn

River Test

Watercress Beds

Larkwhistle Farm

SP11

Longparish

6

Lower Farm

Lower Mill

Vale Farm

Big Firs

5

THE BRIDGE WAY

GLADSTONE TERR

The Plough Inn

MILL LA

Middleton Park

Middleton

THE WITHIES · SOUTHSIDE RD

THE COMMON

44

Middleton House

+

Longparish CE Prim Sch

Southside Farm

4

B3048

Drayton

PRIORY · WILLIAMS RD · THE AVENUE

3

43

Lodge Farm

A303

Drayton Down

2

DRAYTON PK

Bransbury Manor Farm

SO21

Playing Field

A303

1

THE BARRACKS

Bransbury

River Dever

Sewage Works

42

Weir

Bransbury Hill

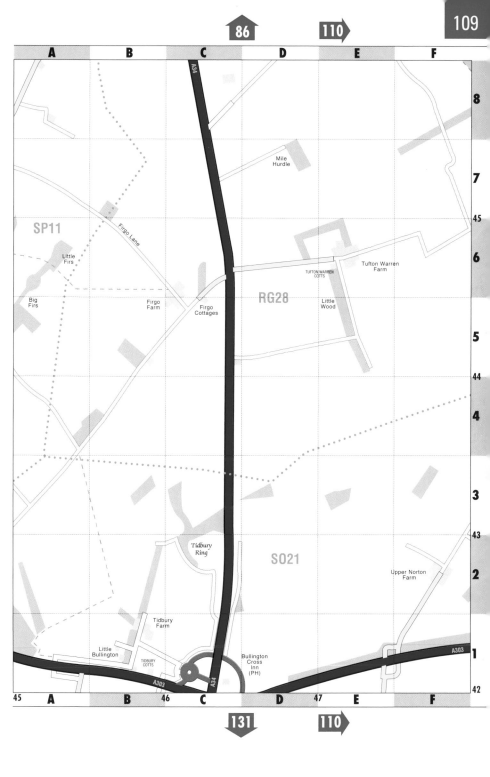

A B C D E F

8
7
45
6
5
44
4
3
43
2
1
42

SP11

Firgo Lane

Little
Firs

Big
Firs

Firgo
Farm

Firgo
Cottages

A34

Mile
Hurdle

TUFTON WARREN
COTTS

Tufton Warren
Farm

RG28

Little
Wood

Tidbury
Ring

SO21

Upper Norton
Farm

Tidbury
Farm

Little
Bullington

TIDBURY
COTTS

Bullington
Cross
Inn
(PH)

A303

A34

A303

45 A B 46 C D 47 E F

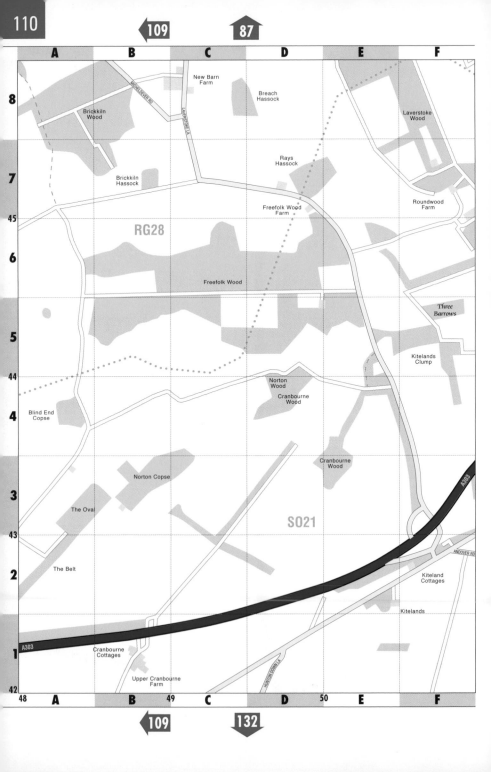

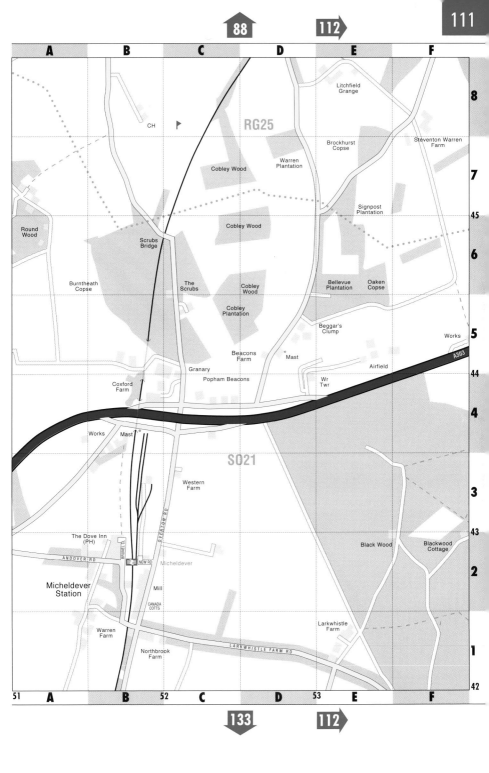

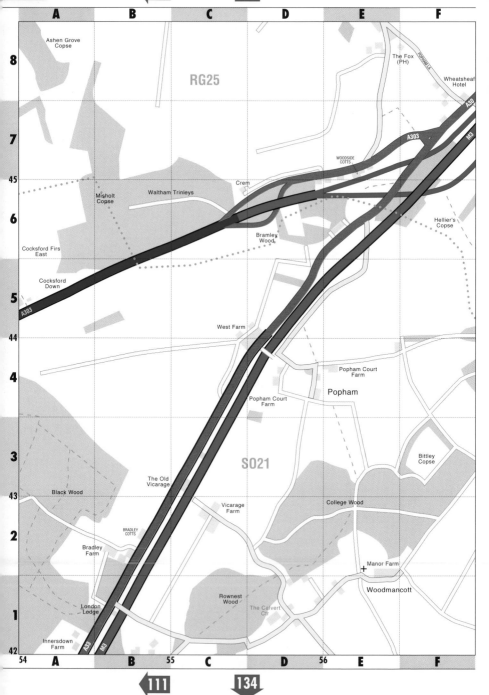

A **B** **C** **D** **E** **F**

8

Ashen Grove
Copse

RG25

The Fox
(PH)

Wheatsheaf
Hotel

7

A303

M3

WOODSIDE
COTTS

45

Misholt
Copse

Waltham Trinleys

Crem

Hellier's
Copse

6

Bramley
Wood

Cocksford Firs
East

Cocksford
Down

5

A303

West Farm

44

Popham Court
Farm

4

Popham

Popham Court
Farm

3

SO21

Bittley
Copse

Black Wood

The Old
Vicarage

43

Vicarage
Farm

College Wood

2

BRADLEY
COTTS

Bradley
Farm

Manor Farm

Woodmancott

1

London
Lodge

Rownest
Wood

The Calvert
Ctr

42

Innersdown
Farm

A33

M3

54 **A** **B** 55 **C** **D** 56 **E** **F**

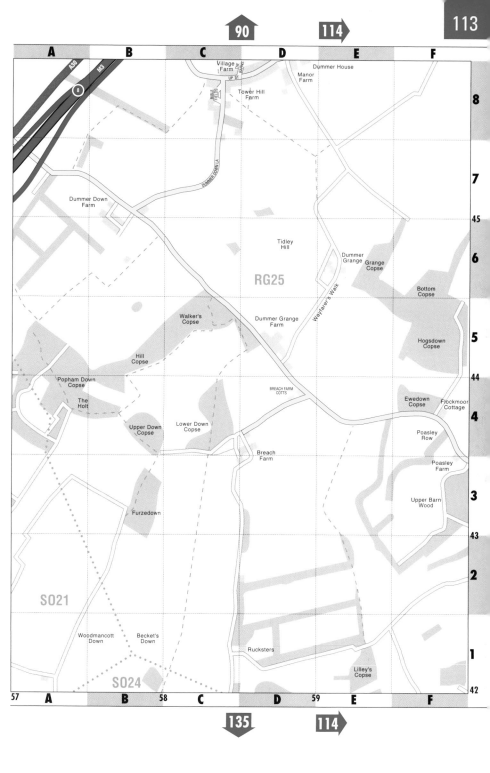

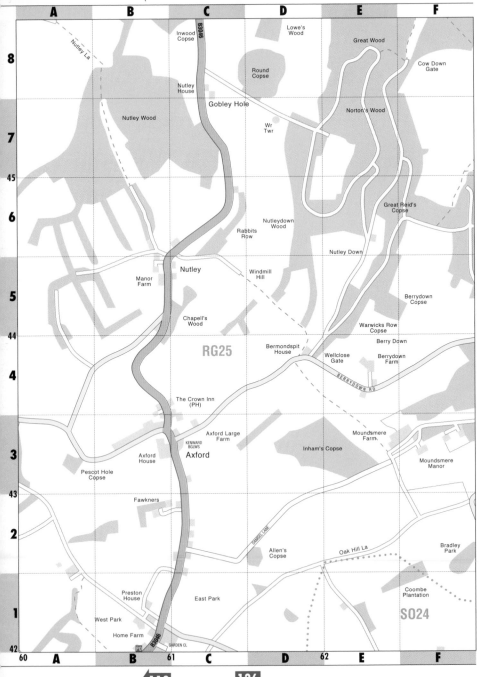

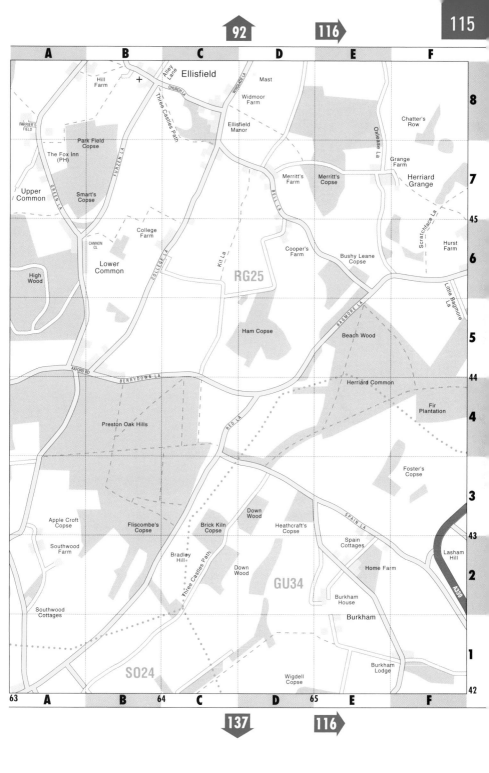

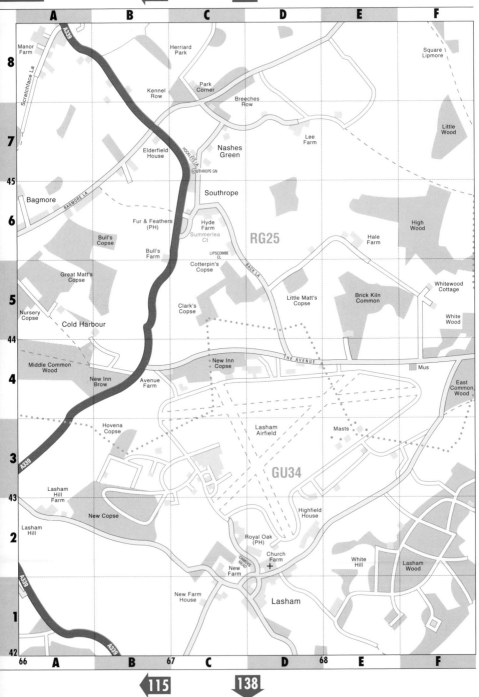

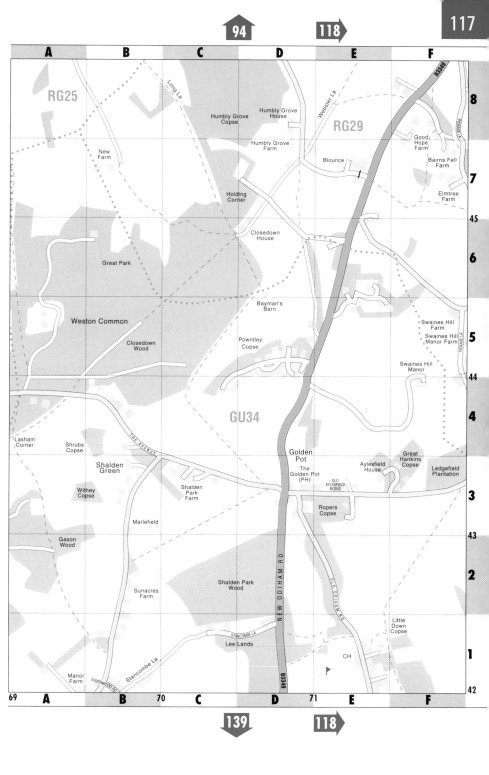

A **B** **C** **D** **E** **F**

8

New Farm

Vinney Copse

Sheephouse Copse

Pickaxe Copse

White House Farm

Sutton Common

Highham Copse

7

45

RG29

Great Wood

Gaston Copse

6

West View

Broadlands Copse

Little Wood

5

Yarnhams Farm

Hawkins Wood

44

Beech Hangers La

Mast

Liddenfield Copse

Stowell Copse

4

Dicket's Plantation

Yarnhams Cottages

Stowell Cottage

Fielders Copse

Ham Wood

Shrub Croft Copse

3

GU34

Masts

43

Spollycombe Copse

2

Peakham Copse

Holybourne Down

Brockham Hill Farm Cottages

Brockham Hill Barn

New La

1

Round Wood

Howard's La

42

72 **A** **B** 73 **C** **D** 74 **E** **F**

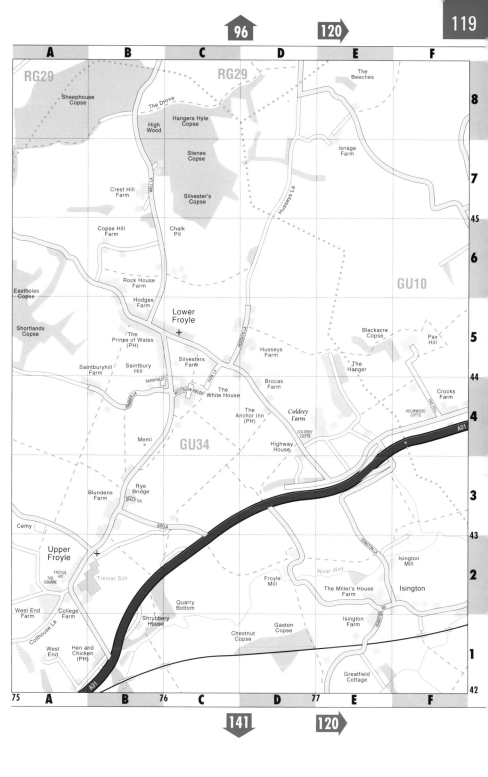

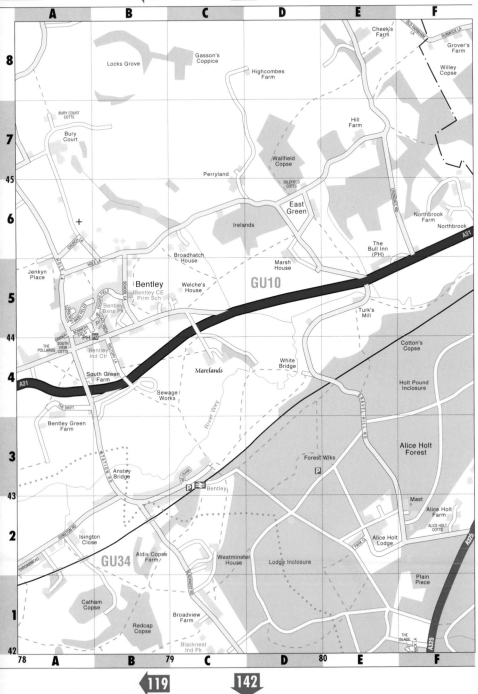

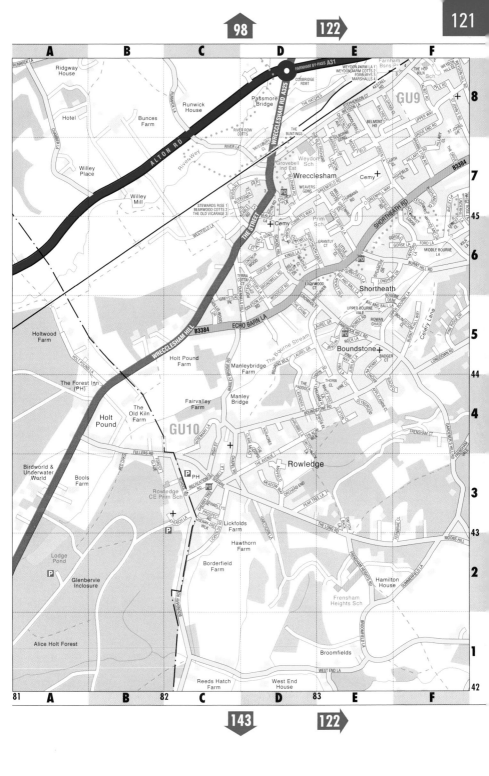

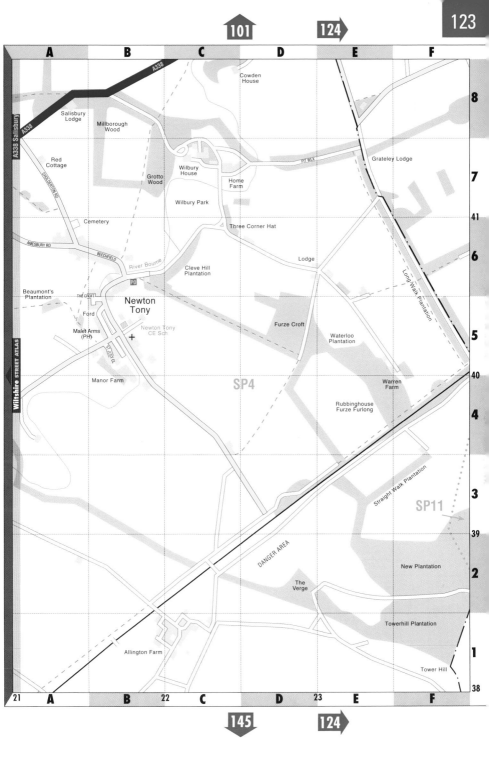

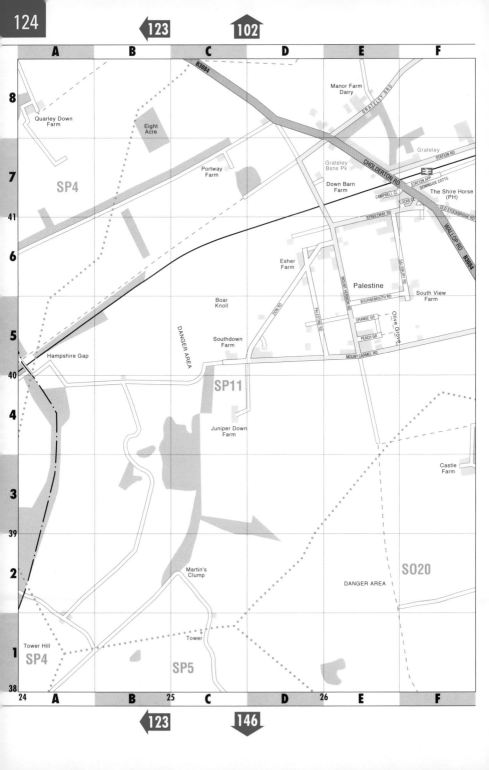

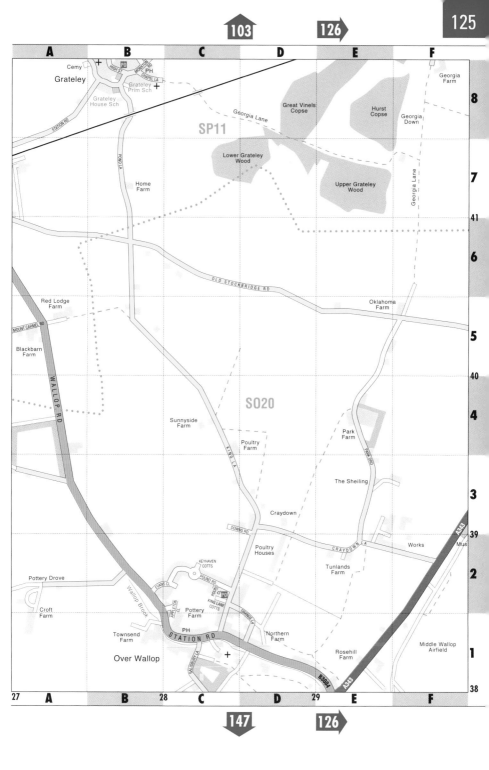

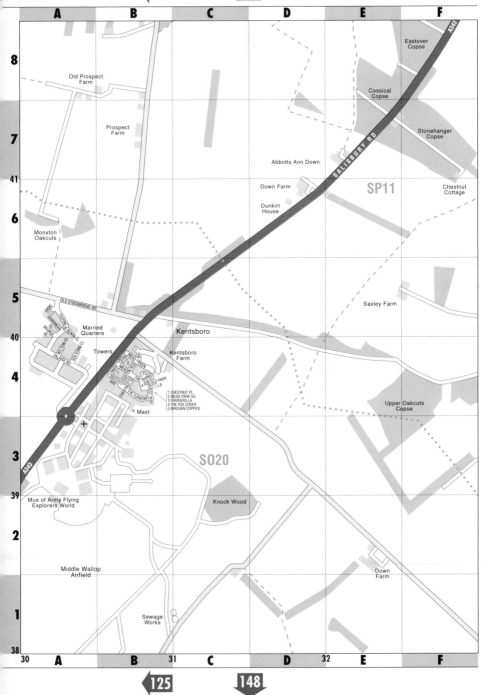

125
104

A **B** **C** **D** **E** **F**

8

Old Prospect Farm

Prospect Farm

Eastover Copse

Cossical Copse

Stonehanger Copse

7

Abbotts Ann Down

SALISBURY RD

41

Down Farm

SP11

Chestnut Cottage

Dunkirt House

6

Monxton Oakcuts

5

OLD STOCKBRIDGE RD

Saxley Farm

Married Quarters

40

Kentsboro

Towers

Kentsboro Farm

Upper Oakcuts Copse

4

THE GREEN
MEAD MEADS
THE AVENUE
MEAD PARK LA

1 CHESTNUT PL
2 MEAD PARK SQ
3 FARRIERS LA
4 THE FOX COVER
5 BIRCHEN COPPICE

Mast

3

SO20

A343

39

Mus of Army Flying Explorers World

Knock Wood

2

Middle Wallop Airfield

Down Farm

1

Sewage Works

38

A **B** **C** **D** **E** **F**

30   31   32

125
148

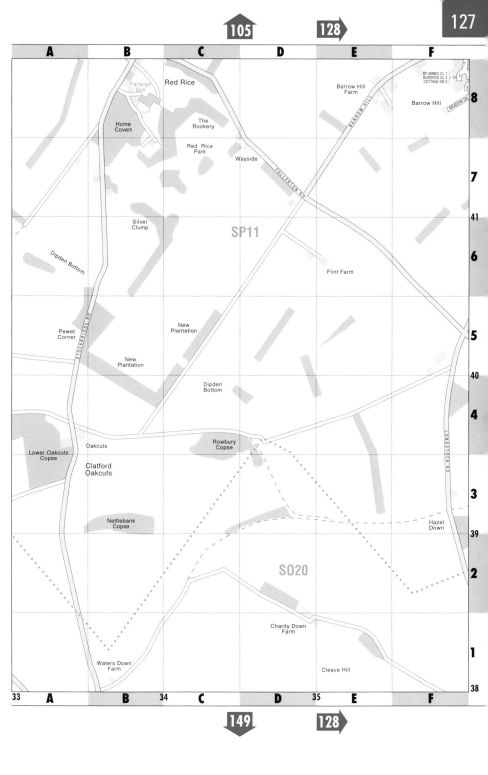

A   B   C   D   E   F

ST ANNES CL 1
BURDOCK CL 2
COTTAGE GN 3

Barrow Hill
Farm

Barrow Hill

8

Farleigh
Sch

Red Rice

Home
Covert

The
Rookery

Red Rice
Park

Wayside

7

41

Silver
Clump

SP11

Dipden Bottom

6

Flint Farm

Pewet
Corner

New
Plantation

5

New
Plantation

40

Dipden
Bottom

4

Oakcuts

Lower Oakcuts
Copse

Clatford
Oakcuts

Rowbury
Copse

Hazel
Down

3

Nettlebank
Copse

39

SO20

2

Charity Down
Farm

1

Waters Down
Farm

Cleave Hill

38

33   A   B   34   C   D   35   E   F

STOCKBRIDGE RD

FULLERTON RD

BARROW HILL

LONGSTOCK RD

MEADOW DR

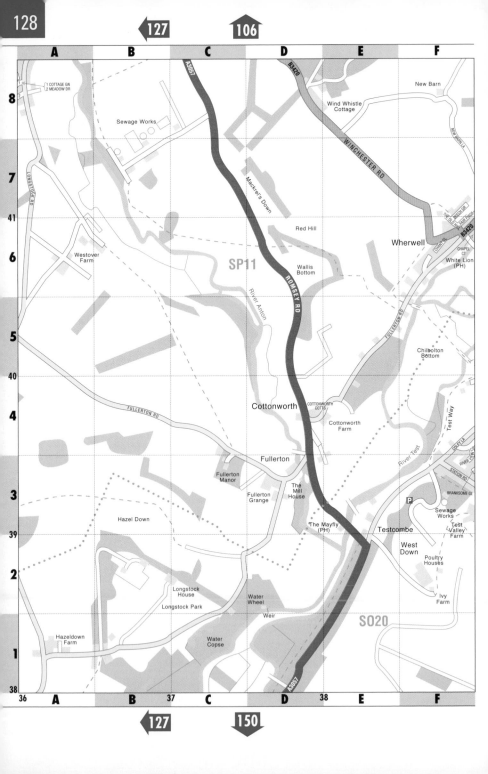

127
106

1 COTTAGE GN
2 MEADOW DR

New Barn

Wind Whistle
Cottage

WINCHESTER RD

Sewage Works

Mackrel's Down

Red Hill

Wherwell

CHAPEL
CT
White Lion
(PH)

SP11

Westover
Farm

Wallis
Bottom

ROMSEY RD

River Anton

Chilbolton
Bottom

FULLERTON RD

FULLERTON RD

Cottonworth

COTTONWORTH
COTTS

Test Way

Cottonworth
Farm

River Test

Fullerton

Fullerton
Manor

Fullerton
Grange

The
Mill
House

STATION RD

BRANSOME CL

P

Sewage
Works

Hazel Down

The Mayfly
(PH)

Testcombe

Test
Valley
Farm

West
Down

Longstock
House

Poultry
Houses

Longstock Park

Water
Wheel

Weir

SO20

Ivy
Farm

Hazeldown
Farm

Water
Copse

LONGSTOCK RD

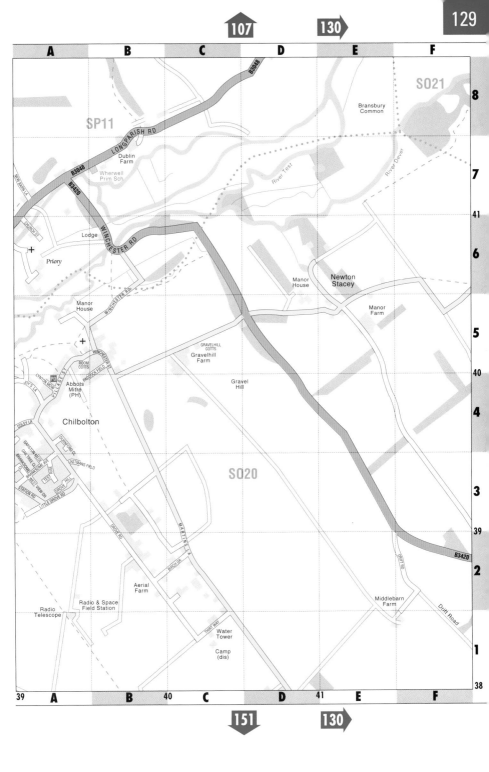

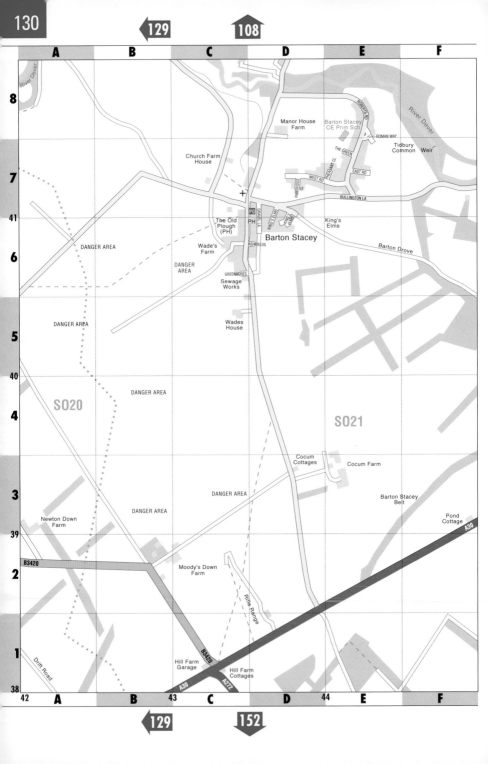

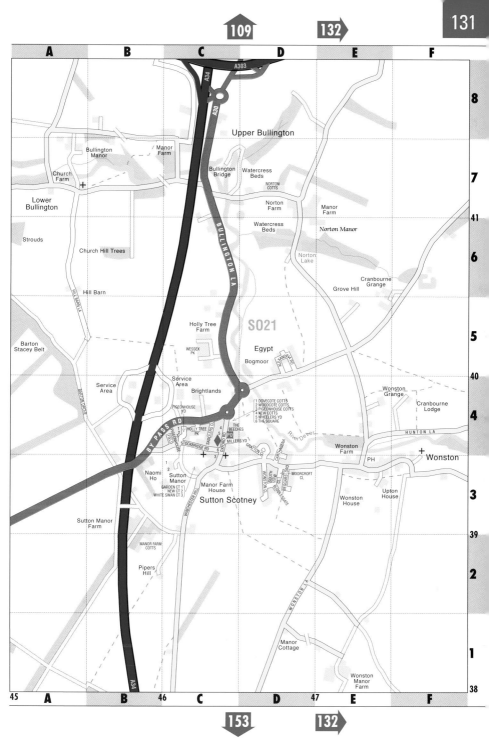

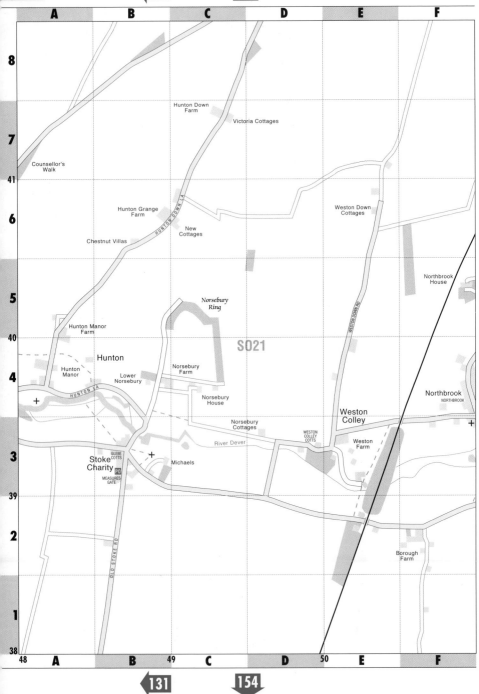

111
134

A B C D E F

8 Black Wood
Works
7
41 Parkhill Farm PARKHILL FARM COTTS
A33
M3
6 Middle Lodge
THE CLOCKHOUSE
Shepherd's Close
Stratton Park
West Stratton
5 West Stratton Farm
Stratton End
The Bothy
40 Winchester Lodge
CHURCH BANK RD
SO21
4 Chapel Ave
Highways Cottages
Cowdown Wood
Micheldever
3 WATERLOO COTTS
DEVER CL
SOUTHBROOK
ROOK LA
1 LANE END BGLWS
2 MEADOW VIEW
3 SOUTHBROOK COTTS
Cowdown Farm
Highways
New Farm
NEW FARM RD
Manor Farm
CHURCH CL
Micheldever CE Prim Sch
DUKE ST
2 3
1
Highways Nursery
South Down La
39 Half Moon & Spread Eagle (PH)
South Down
2 WITCHESTER RD
Cole's Barn
Dodsley Wood
SO24
1 Micheldever Wood
A33
M3
Butcher's Copse
Folly Wood
38

51 A B 52 C D 53 E F

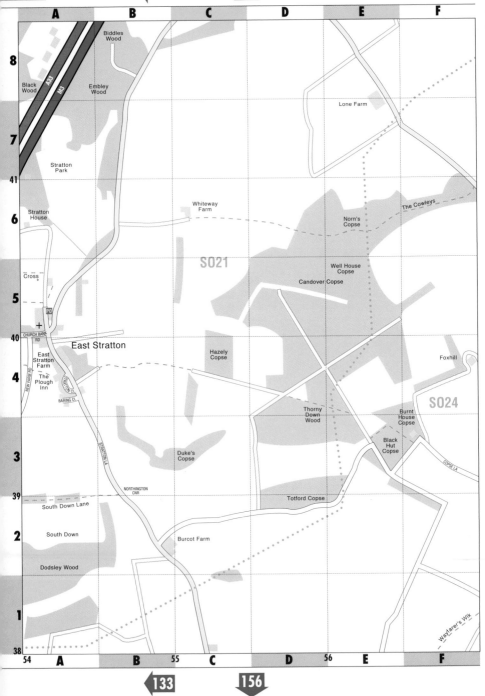

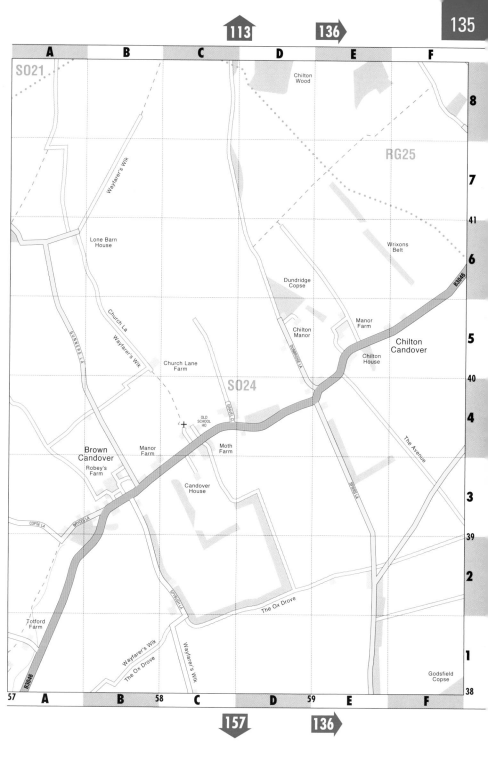

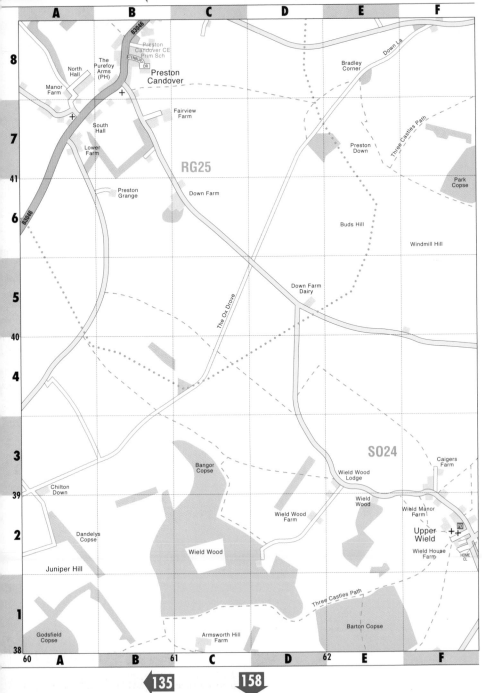

135
114

A **B** **C** **D** **E** **F**

8

North
Hall

Manor
Farm

The Purefoy
Arms (PH)

B3046

Preston
Candover CE
Prim Sch

STENBURG
DR

Preston
Candover

Bradley
Corner

Down La

7

South
Hall

Lower
Farm

Fairview
Farm

Preston
Down

Three Castles Path

RG25

41

Preston
Grange

Down Farm

Park
Copse

6

B3046

Buds Hill

Windmill Hill

5

The Ox Drove

Down Farm
Dairy

40

4

3

Bangor
Copse

Wield Wood
Lodge

SO24

Caigers
Farm

39

Chilton
Down

Wield Wood
Farm

Wield
Wood

Wield Manor
Farm

2

Dandelys
Copse

Wield Wood

Upper
Wield

Wield House
Farm

RD

HOME
CL

Juniper Hill

1

Godsfield
Copse

Armsworth Hill
Farm

Three Castles Path

Barton Copse

38

60 **A** **B** 61 **C** **D** 62 **E** **F**

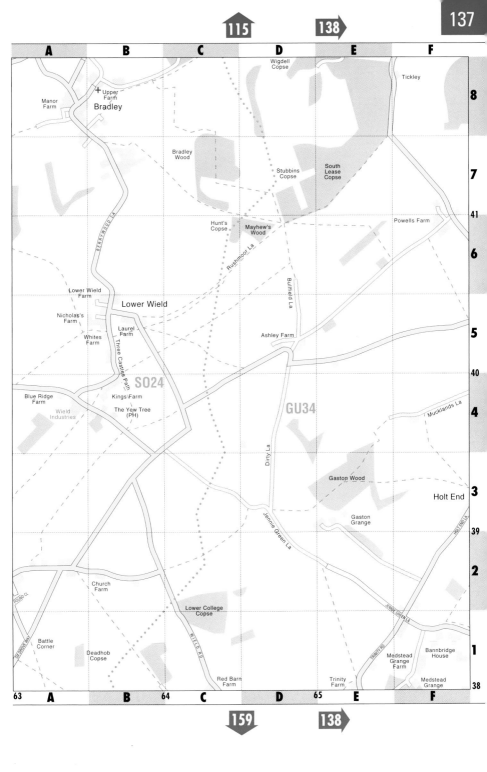

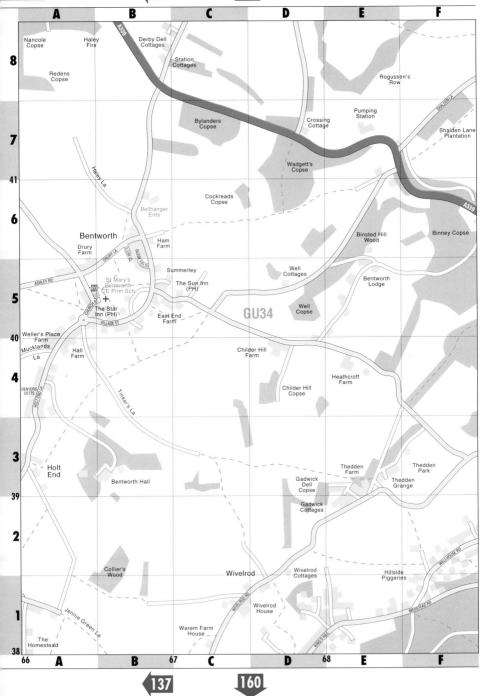

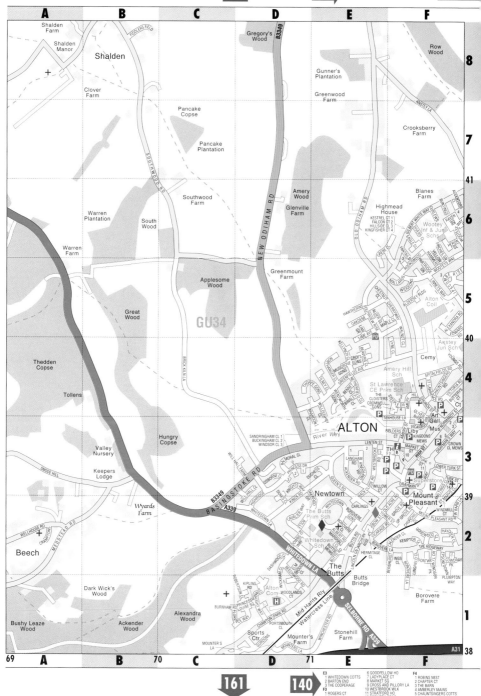

117 140

161 140

E3
1 WHITEDOWN COTTS
2 BARTON END
3 THE COOPERAGE
F3
1 ROGERS CT
2 SAXON HO
3 SAXON MEWS
4 MANOR PARK COTTS
5 INWOOD CT

6 GOODFELLOW HO
7 LADYPLACE CT
8 MARKET SQ
9 CROSS AND PILLORY LA
10 WESTBROOK WLK
11 STRATFORD HO
12 BREWERY GDNS
13 LINDEN HO
14 THE WINDMILLS

F4
1 ROBINS NEST
2 CHAPTER CT
3 THE BARN
4 AMBERLEY MAINS
5 CHAUNTSINGERS COTTS
6 GEALE'S ALMSHOUSES
7 NETHER ST

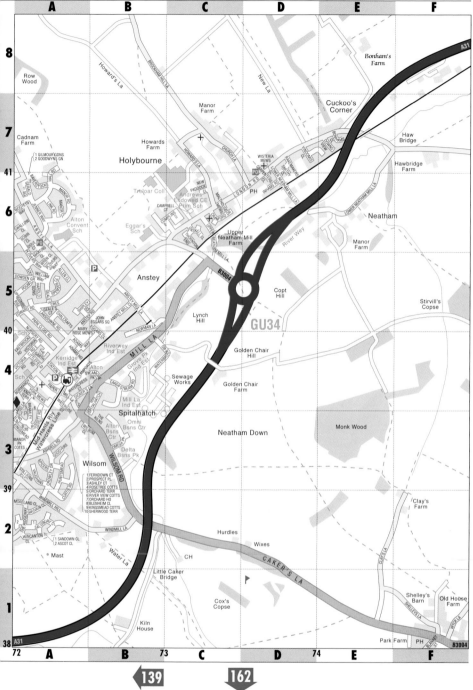

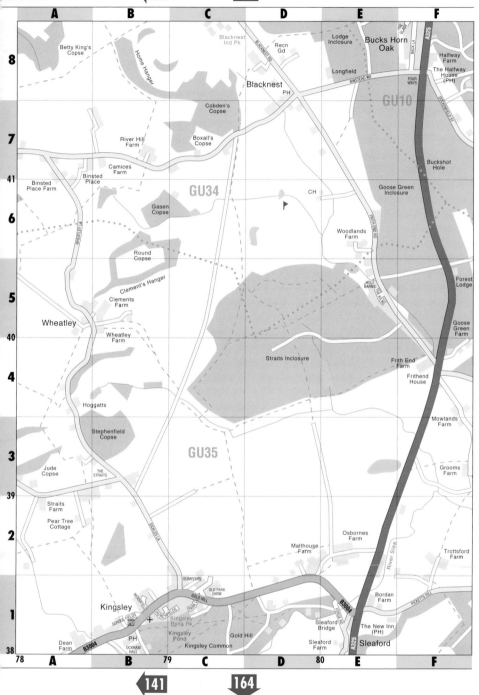

A B C D E F

8

Betty King's Copse

Home Hanger

Blacknest Ind Pk

Blacknest Rd

Recn Gd

Lodge Inclosure

Bucks Horn Oak

Halfway Farm

The Halfway House (PH)

Longfield

Binstead Rd

Four Ways

Blacknest

PH

GU10

Back La

The Glade

A325

7

Cobden's Copse

River Hill Farm

Boxall's Copse

Buckshot Hole

41

Camices Farm

Binsted Place

Binsted Place Farm

GU34

CH

Goose Green Inclosure

6

Gasen Copse

Woodlands Farm

Frith End Rd

Round Copse

Wheatley La

Clement's Hanger

Clements Farm

WOLF BARNS

Forest Lodge

5

Wheatley

Straits Inclosure

Goose Green Farm

40

Wheatley Farm

Frith End Farm

Frithend House

4

Hoggatts

Mowlands Farm

Stephenfield Copse

GU35

Grooms Farm

3

Jude Copse

THE STRAITS

Sickle La

39

Straits Farm

Pear Tree Cottage

Osbornes Farm

Malthouse Farm

River Slea

Trottsford Farm

2

Sunnyside

Old Park Farm

Gold Hill

Bordan Farm

Pickett's Hill

1

Kingsley

Woolmer La

School Fields Rd

Kingsley Barns Pk

Kingsley Hall

Kingsley Pond

Gold Hill

Sleaford Bridge

B3004

The New Inn (PH)

38

Dean Farm

B3004

PH

OCKHAM HALL

Kingsley Common

Sleaford Farm

A325

Sleaford

78 A B 79 C D 80 E F

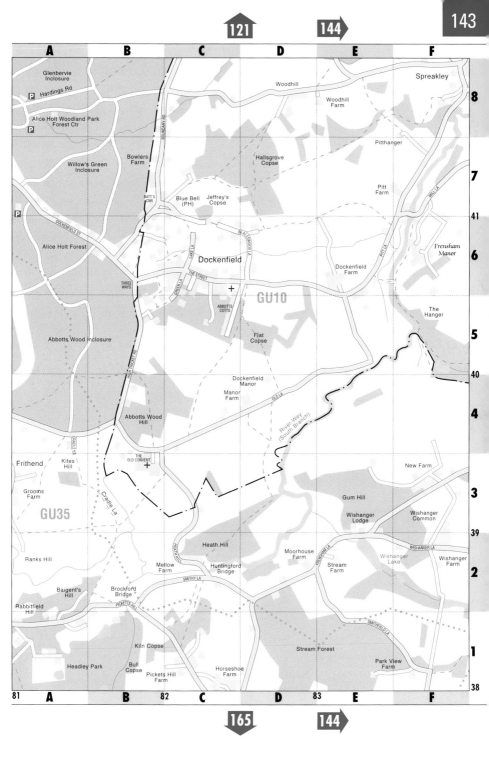

143
122

Spreakley

Millbridge

A287

River Wey

Chuter's Cottage

PRIORY LA

P

Lane End

St Mary's CE Inf Sch

River Wey South Branch

Frensham Little Pond

GRANGE RD

ST MARY'S COTTS

THE STREET

THE GRANGE

Rushmoor

THE STREET

COVERS LA

PEASEFIELD

MILL LA

Frensham

DE LISLE PARK

CARLISLE RD

41

Frensham Common

WELLESLEY RD

LOWICKS RD

6

Lowicks

Gray Walls

SANDY LA

P

P

Frensham Country Park

Lowicks House

Frensham Great Pond

Mon

The Flashes

5

GU10

40

Crosswater Farm

Hotel

POND LA

4

Crosswater

The Devil's Jumps

Stony Jump

Churt House

Churt Common

FARNHAM RD

Hales Copse

Furze Hill

FRENSHAM LA

BACON LA

CROSSWATER LA

OLD KILN RD

3

THE CHASE

Buttermilk Hill

JUMPS RD

Churt Lea

39

WAYSIDE COTTS

STAR HILL DRI

STAR HILL

CRABTREE LA

WIDMANGER LA

Symondstone Farm

Silverbeck Farm

Old Kiln Farm

2

SYMONDSTONE LA

OLD KILN LA

HALE HOUSE LA

GREEN CROSS LA

Avalon

OLD BARN LA

LAMPARD LA

HALE HOUSE

Churt

GU35

CHURT RD

Hale House

Green Cross Farm

Green Cross

HILL HOUSE

1

Park La

THE MEADOWS

QUINNETTES

PO

A287

EDDYSTONE CT

PH

St John's CE Inf Sch

KITTELS CNR

CROSSWAYS

CHURT RD

HACKHURST FIELDS

HAZEL GROVE

BRIAR LA

GREEN LA

38

143
166

Surrey STREET ATLAS

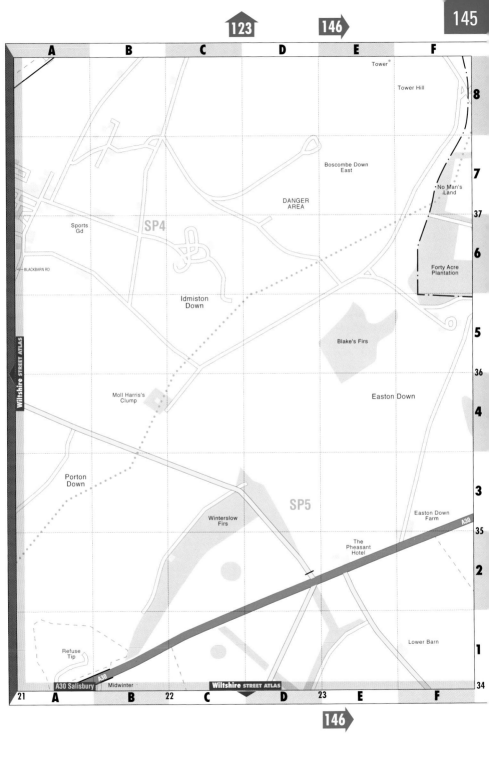

Tower

Tower Hill

8

Boscombe Down
East

7

No Man's
Land

37

DANGER
AREA

6

Forty Acre
Plantation

Sports
Gd

SP4

BLACKBARN RD

Idmiston
Down

Blake's Firs

5

36

Easton Down

Moll Harris's
Clump

4

Porton
Down

3

Winterslow
Firs

SP5

Easton Down
Farm

A30

35

The
Pheasant
Hotel

2

Lower Barn

1

Refuse
Tip

A30

Wiltshire STREET ATLAS

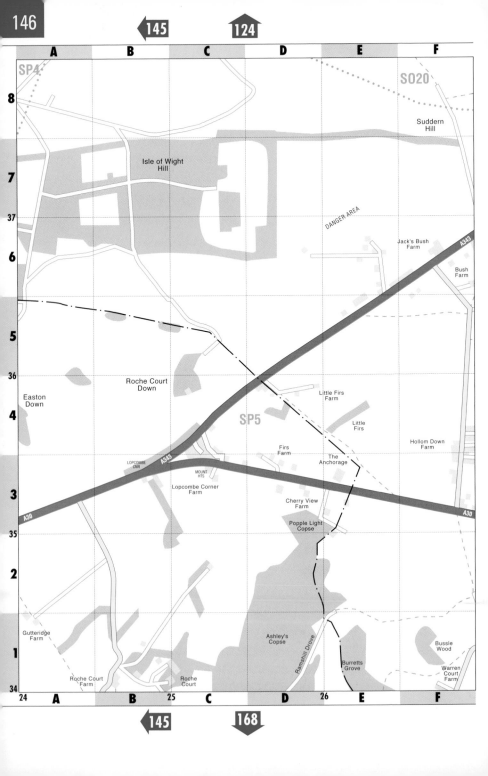

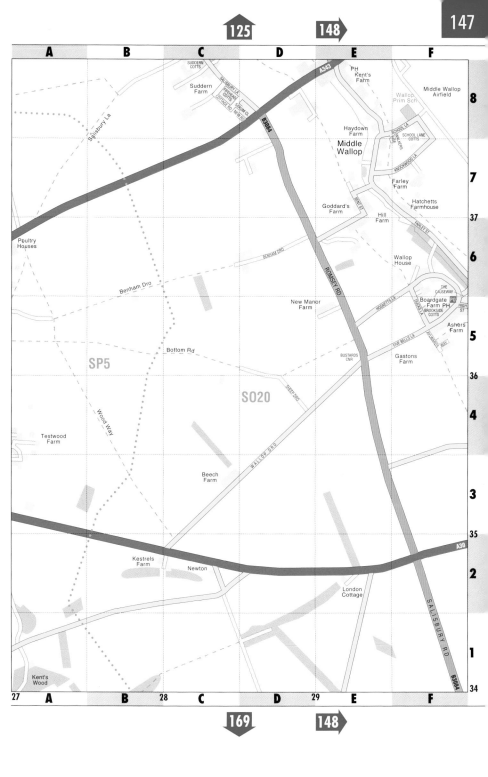

125
148

A B C D E F

SUDDERN
COTTS

Suddern
Farm

SALISBURY LA

SUDDERN
COTTS

COTTAGE RD

SUSUM CL

NEW RD

A343

PH
Kent's
Farm

Middle Wallop
Airfield

Wallop
Prim Sch

8

Salisbury La

B3084

Haydown
Farm

Middle
Wallop

SCHOOL LA

SCHOOL LANE
COTTS

THE
WEAVERS

KNOCKWOOL LA

7

Goddard's
Farm

BELL ST

Hill
Farm

Farley
Farm

Hatchetts
Farmhouse

FARLEY ST

37

Poultry
Houses

BENHAM DRO

Wallop
House

6

Benham Dro

New Manor
Farm

THE CAUSEWAY

Boardgate PO
Farm PH
BROOKSIDE
COTTS

HIGH
ST

HOSKETTS LA

DOCKS

ROOKSMOOR

Ashers
Farm

Bottom Rd

FIVE BELLS LA

RICKMANS WAY

Gastons
Farm

5

SP5

BUSTARDS
CNR

36

SO20

SHEEP DRO

Wood Way

4

Testwood
Farm

WALLOP DRO

Beech
Farm

3

35

A30

Kestrels
Farm

Newton

London
Cottage

2

SALISBURY RD

Kent's
Wood

B3084

1

34

27 A B 28 C D 29 E F

169
148

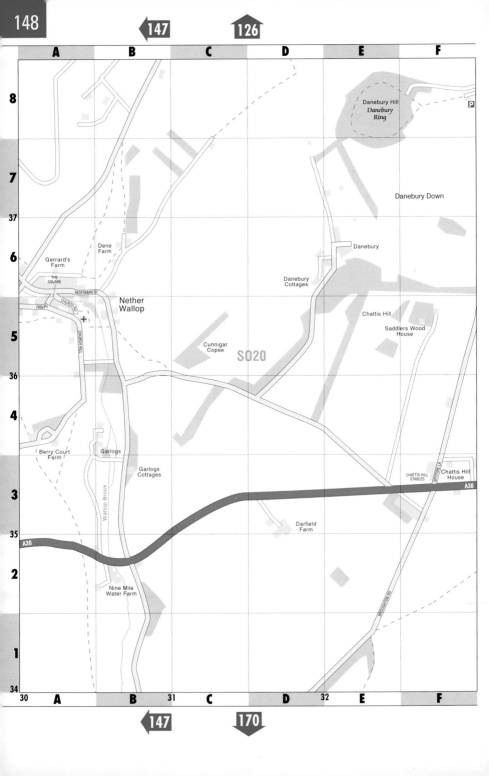

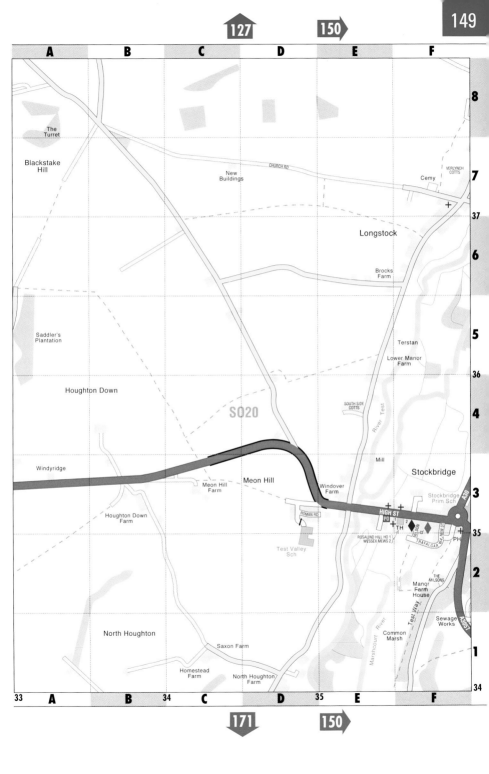

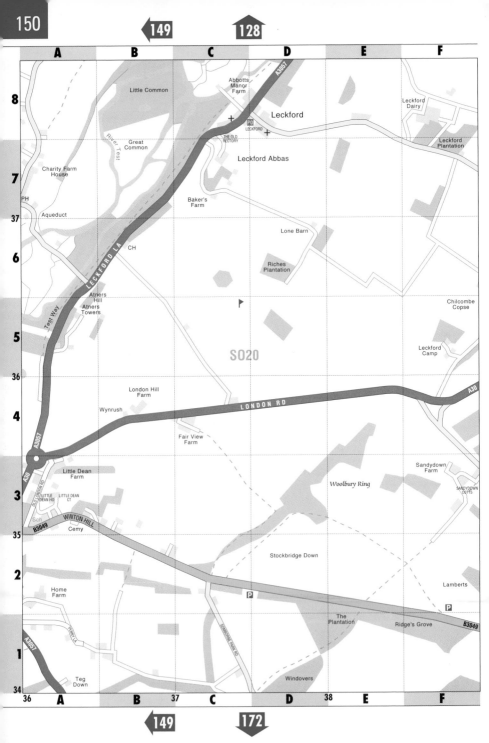

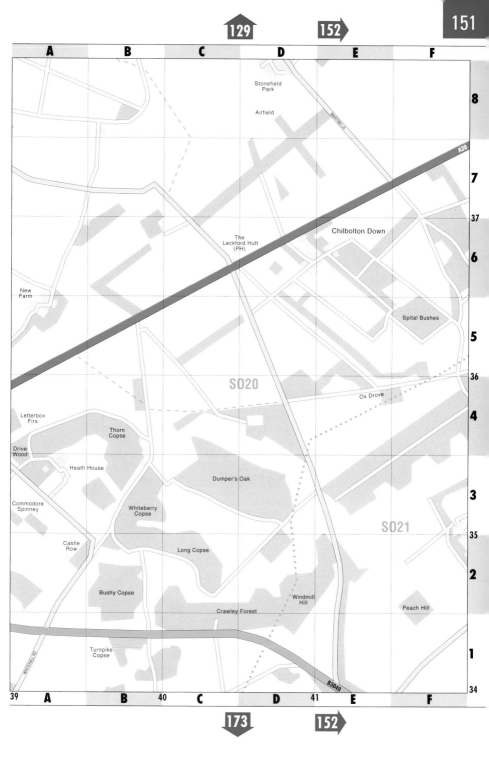

129
152
173
152

Stonefield
Park

Airfield

MARTINS LA

A30

The
Leckford Hutt
(PH)

Chilbolton Down

New
Farm

Spital Bushes

SO20

Ox Drove

Letterbox
Firs

Thorn
Copse

Drive
Wood

Heath House

Dumper's Oak

Commodore
Spinney

Whiteberry
Copse

SO21

Castle
Row

Long Copse

Bushy Copse

Windmill
Hill

Peach Hill

Crawley Forest

WHITEHALL RD

Turnpike
Copse

B3049

A B C D E F

8 7 37 6 5 36 4 3 35 2 1 34

39 40 41

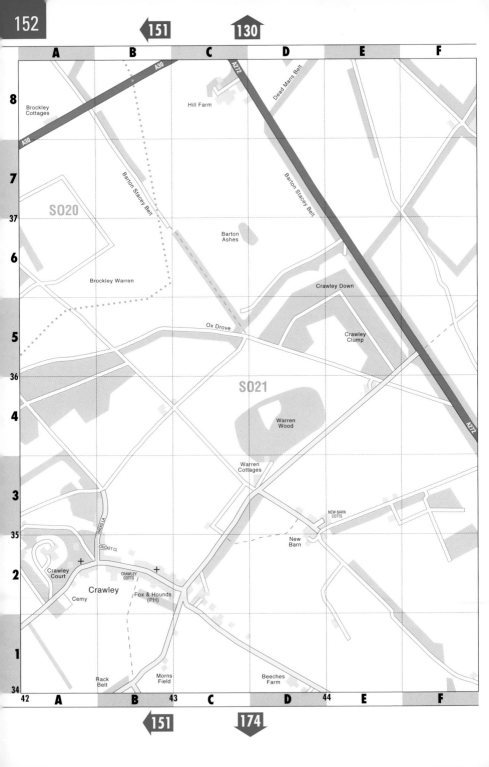

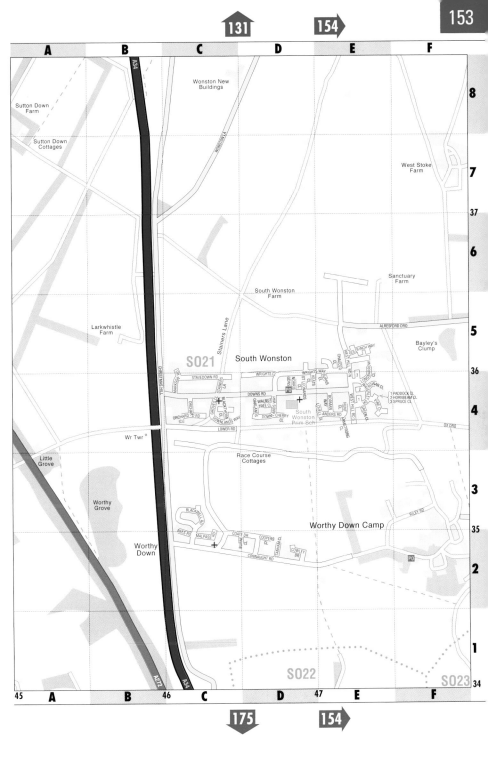

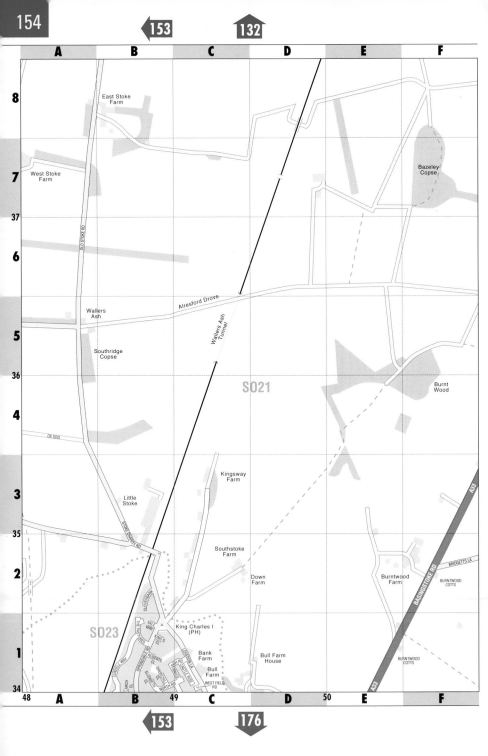

153
132

8

7

37

6

5

36

4

3

35

2

1

34

A B C D E F

East Stoke
Farm

West Stoke
Farm

Bazeley
Copse

OLD STOKE RD

Alresford Drove

Wallers
Ash

Wallers Ash
Tunnel

Southridge
Copse

SO21

Burnt
Wood

OX DRO

Kingsway
Farm

Little
Stoke

Burntwood
Farm

BRIDGETTS LA

BURNTWOOD
COTTS

STOKE CHARITY RD

Southstoke
Farm

Down
Farm

BASINGSTOKE RD

A33

SO23

THE PASTURES

CLIFTON PARK

VALE
WAY

KING'S
CLE

King Charles I
(PH)

Bank
Farm

Bull Farm
House

BURNTWOOD
COTTS

CURZON WAY

LARCH WAY

SPRINGVALE RD

ROBERTS
CL

ELIZABETH RD

CHINOOK

OAKEN RD

CASTLE ST

NORTH RD

Bull
Farm

WEST FIELD
RD

48 A 49 B C 50 D E F

153
176

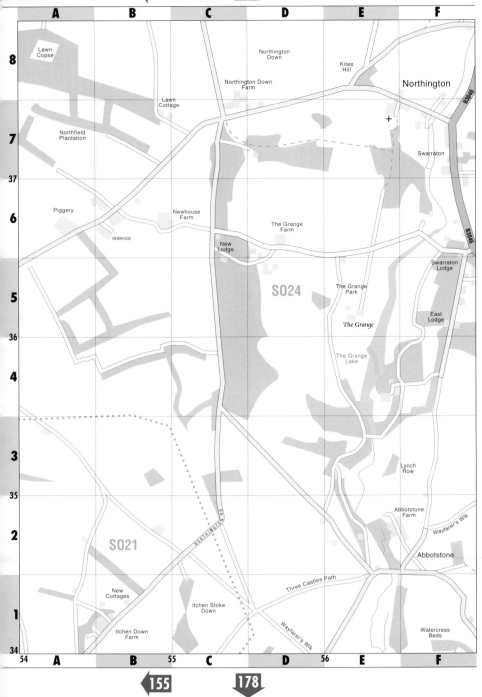

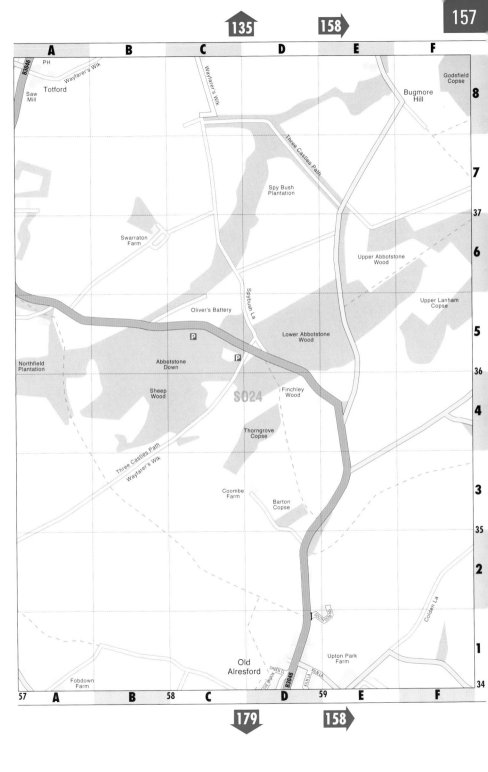

Godsfield
Copse

Three Castles Path

8

Long
Plantation

Armsworth
House

7

Armsworth Park

Armsworth
Park
Farm

Park
House

Hoggs
Lodge

UPPER LENHAM LA

Barton Copse

Barton
Ind Est

Barton
House

Newmen
Farm

OF GROVE WAY

FERNEY LA

Godsfield
Farm

+

Upper
Abbotstone
Wood

37

Upper Lanham
Farm

Woodridden
Wood

GU
34

6

Lower Lanham
Copse

Upper
Lanham
Copse

The
Border

Bighton
Wood

SO24

5

Marks
Wood

Lower Lanham
Farm

Lucys
Wood

SO24

36

Scrivens
Copse

Bighton
Wood

Breach
Farm

4

The
Plantation

Nettlebeds
Farm

Bighton
House

Nettlebeds
Farm
Stables

COSENS LA

Gardeners
Cottage

Inner
Lodge

3

NETTLEBEDS LA

35

High
Dell
Farm

2

Cricket
Ground

The
Three
Horse Shoes
(PH)

Bighton
Manor

+

BARNETTS WOOD
LA

1

Bighton

MALTHOUSE LA

BIGHTON LA

Manor Farm

BIGHTON DEAN LA

34

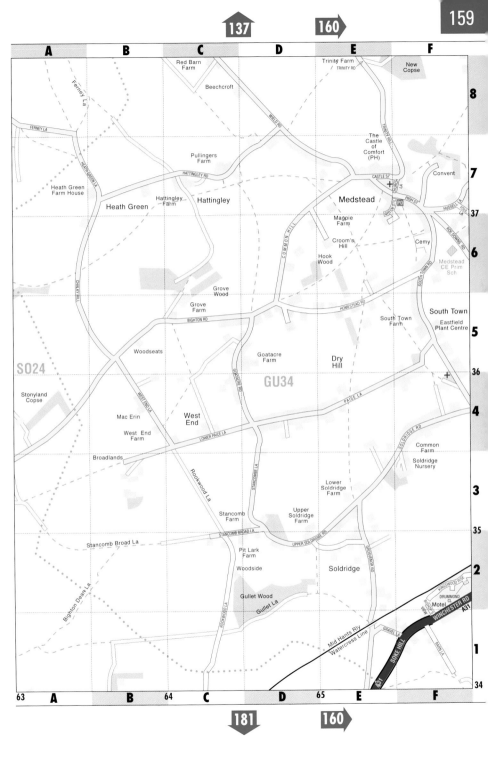

159 138

A B C D E F

8

Meadow View Farm
Redwood Farm
Bushy Leaze Wood
Mast
Alton Abbey
Cemy
Old Park Farm

Redwood
Redwood Poultry Farm

JENNIE GREEN LA
WIVELROD RD
ABBEY RD
KING'S HILL

HUSSELL LA

7

The Oaks
Spruce Copse
The Hassock
Lodge Hill

Foul La

37

Down Copse

6

Chawton Park Wood
Chawton Park Bungalow

Roe Downs Farm
High Wood
Brickiln Farm

ROE DOWNS RD

BRICKILN LA

A31

Roedowns Cottage
Redhill Copse
Park Dale

5

Red Hill Farm
Wr Twr
Mast
Gibbet Copse
Mid Hants Rly
Watercress Line

36

RED HILL
THE CRESCENT
WINDSOR RD
BOYNESWOOD CL
Eighteen Acre Plantation
Firtree Copse

FIVE ASH RD
BEECHLANDS RD
FRIARS OAK
Fourteen Acre Plantation
THE SHRAVE

4

Beverley Farm
Estevan Farm
BOYNESWOOD LA
Houghton's Piece
New Copse

STONY LA
CHAWTON RD
WEATHERMORE LA
ST SWITHIN'S WAY

Medstead & Four Marks
Woodlea Farm
Works
FARMHOUSE
Weathermore Copse
Dell Piece

LYMINGTON BOTTOM RD
STATION APP
STATION RD
WINCHESTER RD
PH
MULBERRY CT

3

Mansfield Bsns Pk
ARTHUR CL
OAKGREEN PAR
BLACKBERRY
WELLHOUSE RD

Lymington Farm Ind Est
WINSTON RISE
ELDON RD
THORNE LA
BLACKBERRY LA

35

DAIRY GR
LYMINGTON CL
MERLIN COURT FLATS
WATERWORKS RD

PENROSE WAY
BRIDGE FIELD
BOXMOOR CL
FERNHAMS CL

2

A31
BLUNDEN CL
ST BARTS CL
BRIGHTSTONE LA
Semaphore Farm
Pies Farm

Four Marks
Battles Copse

VISTIS CL
TIMBERCROFT LA
ALTON LA
ST SWITHIN'S WAY
WILLS LA
BRIGHTSTONE LA

1

Greenways Farm
Garden Ctr
Kitcombe La

LYE CROSS LA
BRISCAMBLE LA
Willis Farmhouse
CH

34

Crofters Farm

66 A 67 B C 68 D E F

GU34

Mansfield Bsns Pk

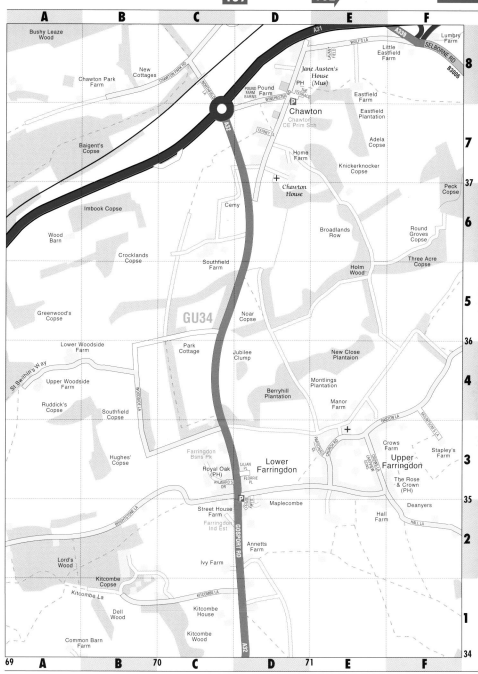

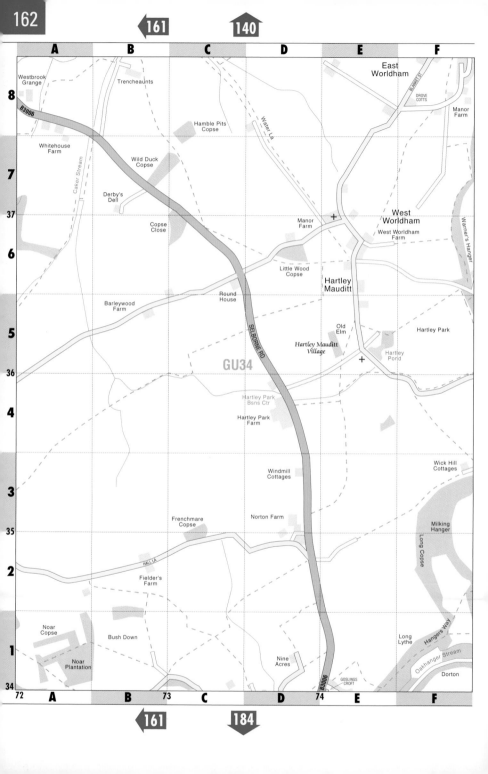

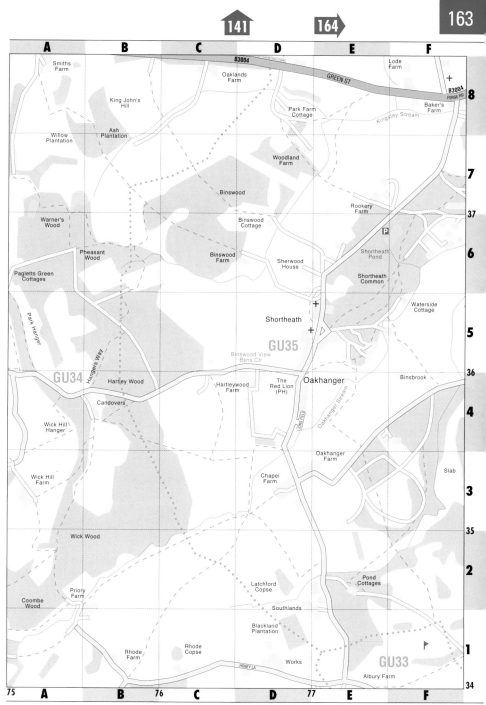

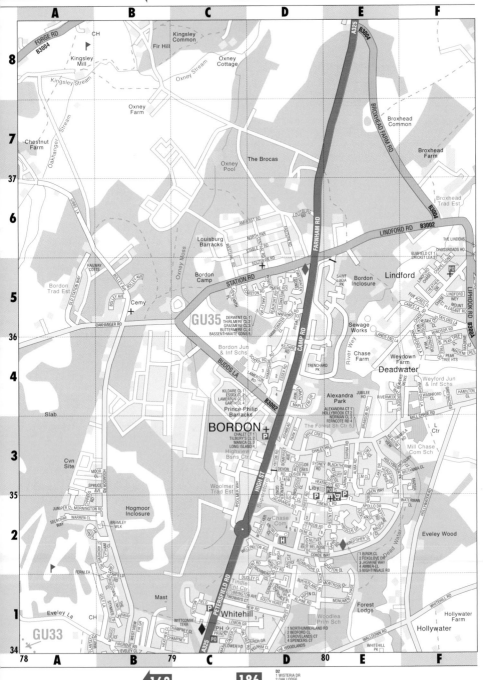

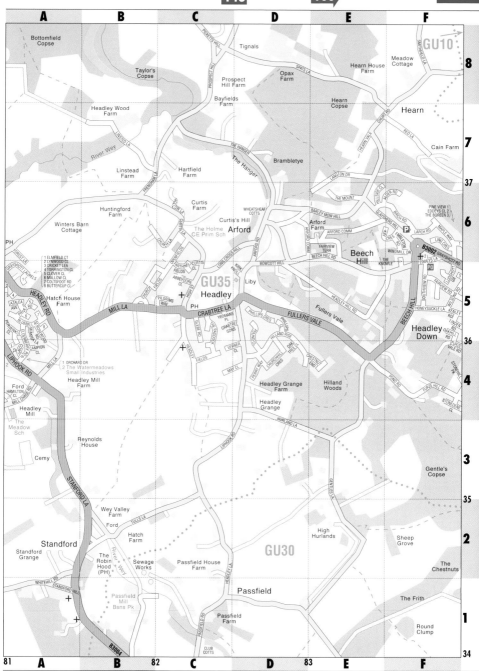

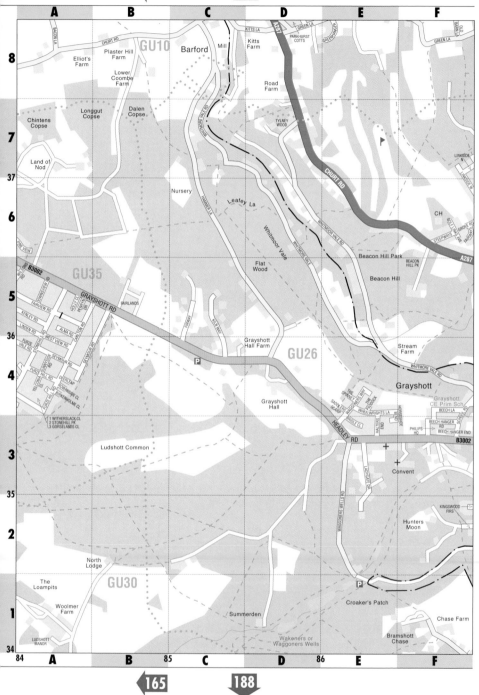

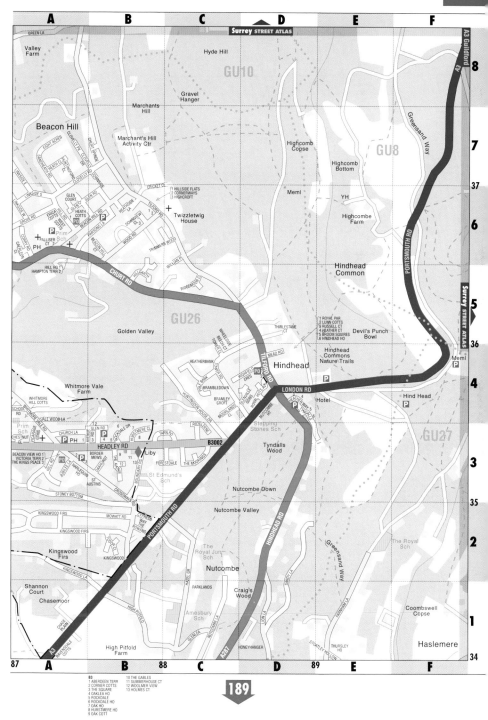

Surrey STREET ATLAS

A B C D E F

GREEN LA

Valley
Farm

GU10

Hyde Hill

Gravel
Hanger

Beacon Hill

Marchants
Hill

Marchant's Hill
Activity Ctr

Highcomb
Copse

GU8

Highcomb
Bottom

8

7

37

Meml

YH

Highcombe
Farm

6

1 HILLSIDE FLATS
2 CORNERWAYS
3 HIGHCROFT

Twizzletwig
House

CHURT RD

GU26

Golden Valley

Hindhead
Common

Hindhead
Commons
Nature Trails

Devil's
Punch
Bowl

1 ROYAL PAR
2 LUNN COTTS
3 RUSSELL CT
4 HEATHER CT
5 BROOM SQUIRES
6 HINDHEAD HO

5

36

Meml

HEATHERBANK

THIRLESTANE
CT

Hindhead

LONDON RD

TILFORD RD

MEAD RD

Whitmore Vale
Farm

Hotel

Hind Head

4

GU27

HEADLEY RD

Liby

B3002

Stepping
Stones Sch

St Edmund's
Sch

Tyndalls
Wood

3

35

Nutcombe Down

Nutcombe Valley

PORTSMOUTH RD

HINDHEAD RD

2

The Royal
Sch

Greensand Way

Kingswood
Firs

The
Royal Jun
Sch

Nutcombe

Craig's
Wood

Coombswell
Copse

Shannon
Court

Chasemoor

Parklands

Amesbury
Sch

Haslemere

1

High Pitfold
Farm

A3

A287

Honeyhanger

THURSLEY
HO

34

A 87 B 88 C A287 D 89 E F

B3
1 ABERDEEN TERR
2 CORNER COTTS
3 THE SQUARE
4 OAKLEA HO
5 ROCKDALE
6 ROCKDALE HO
7 OAK HO
8 HURSTMERE HO
9 OAK COTT
10 THE GABLES
11 SUMMERHOUSE CT
12 WOOLMER VIEW
13 HOLMES CT

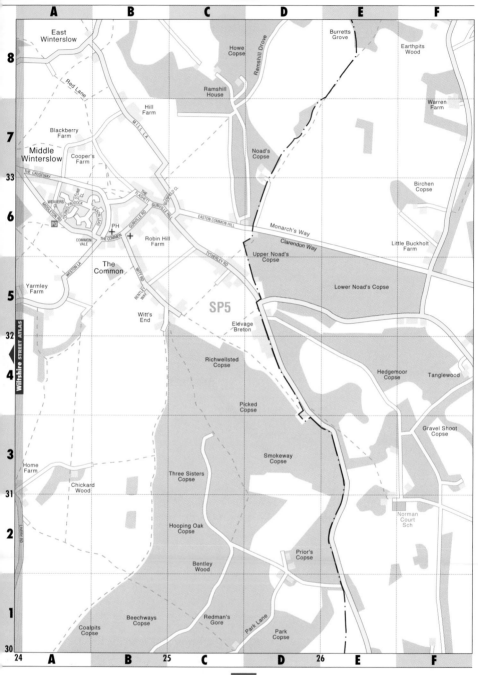

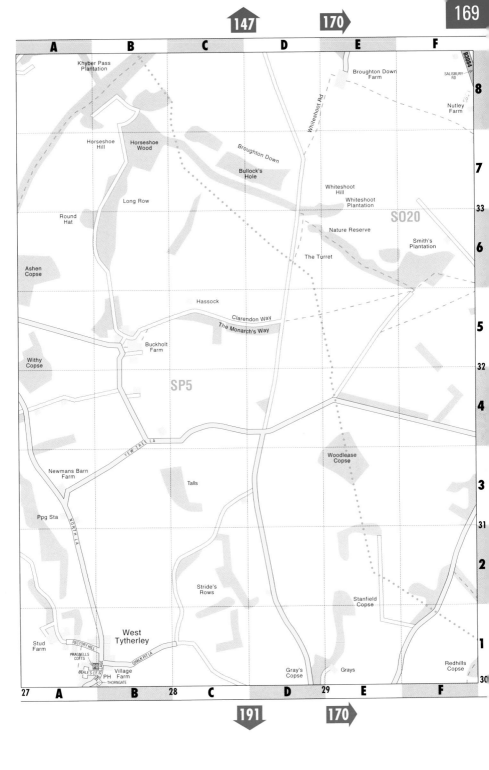

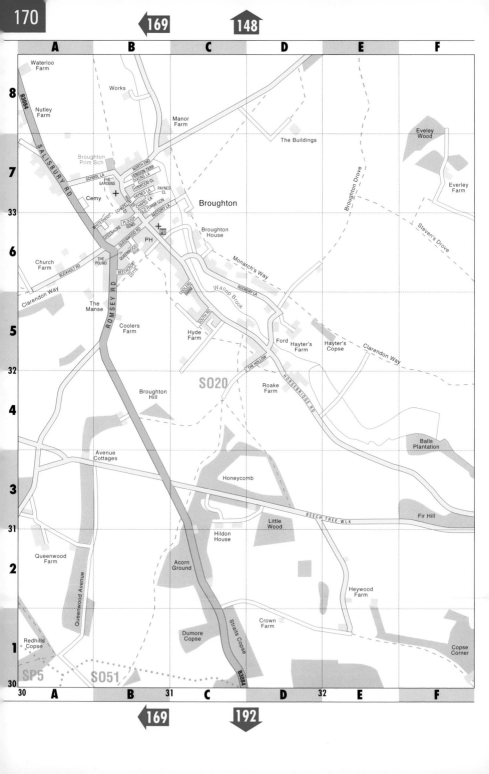

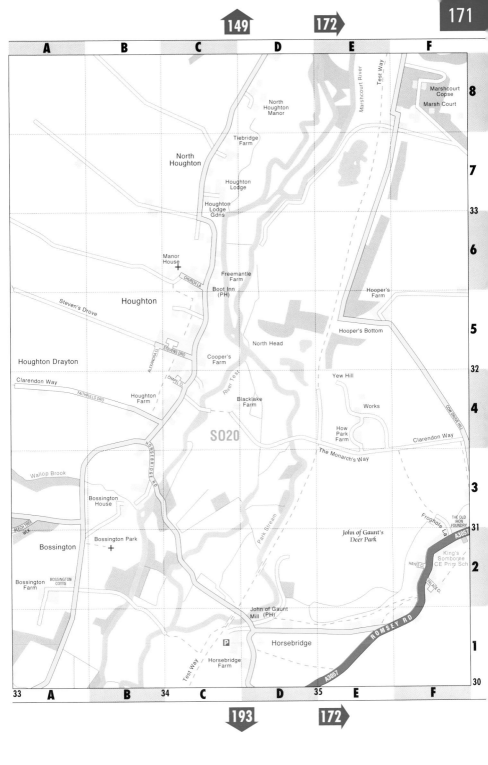

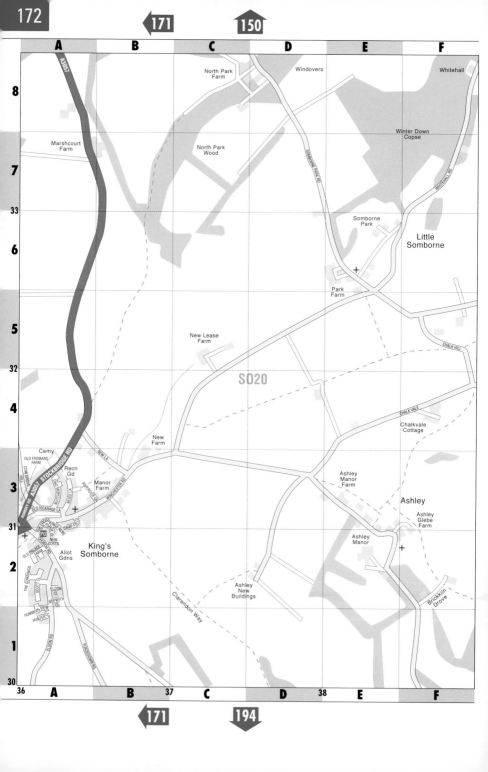

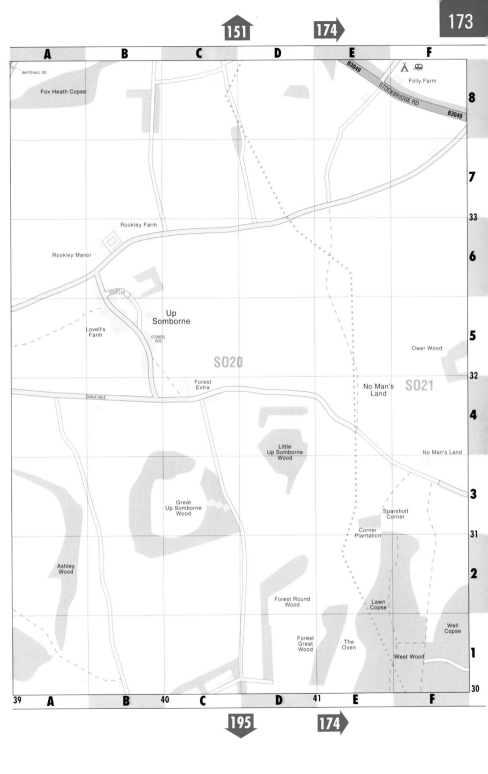

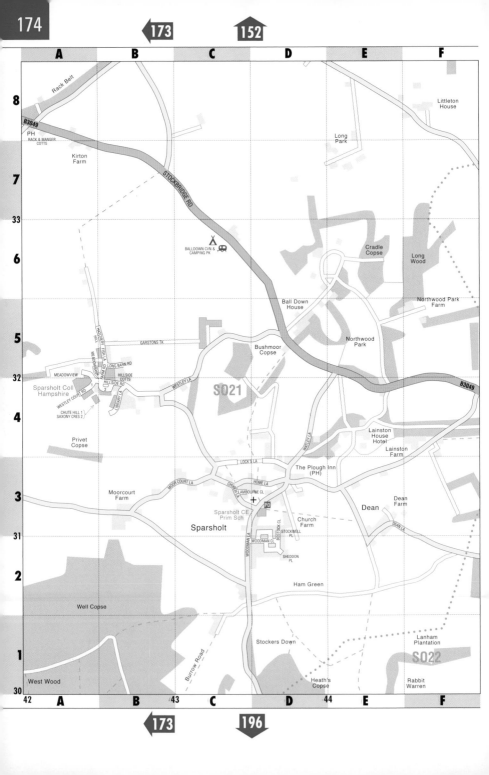

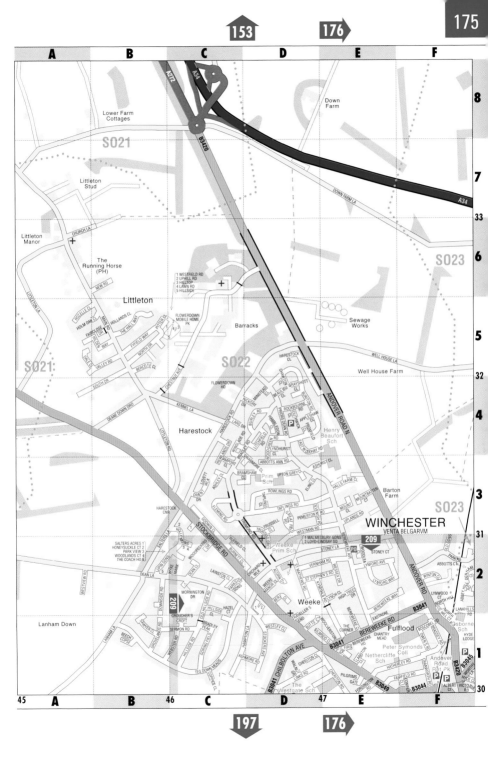

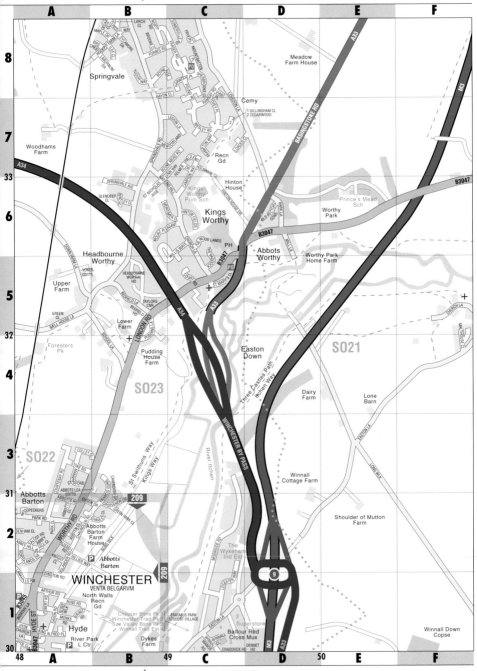

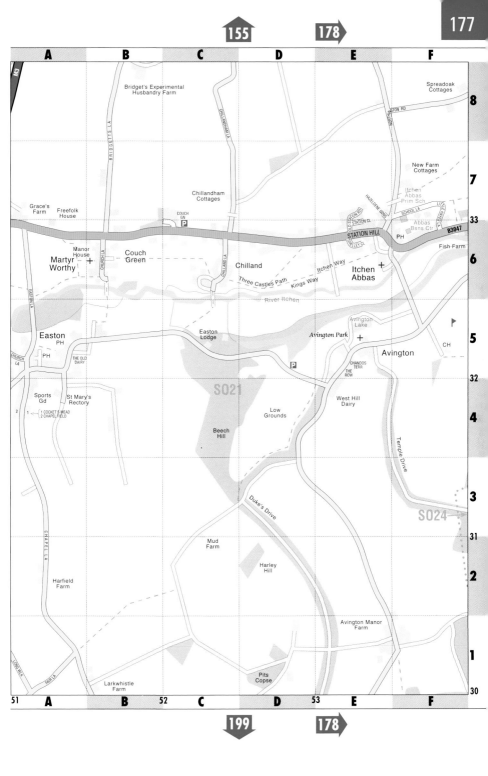

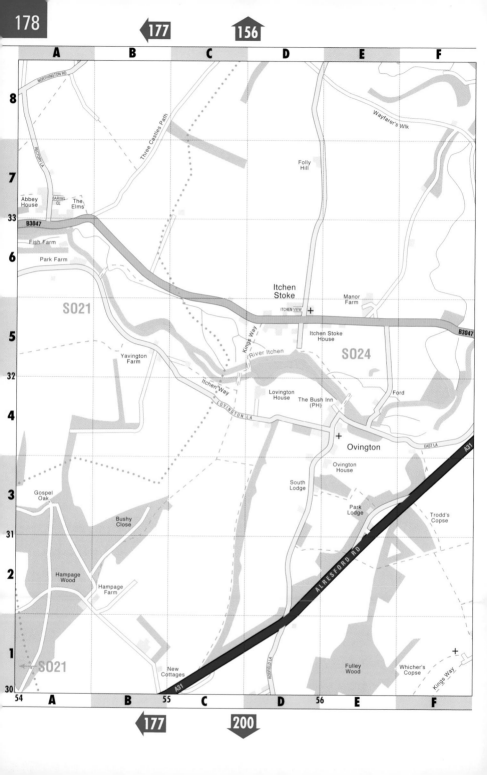

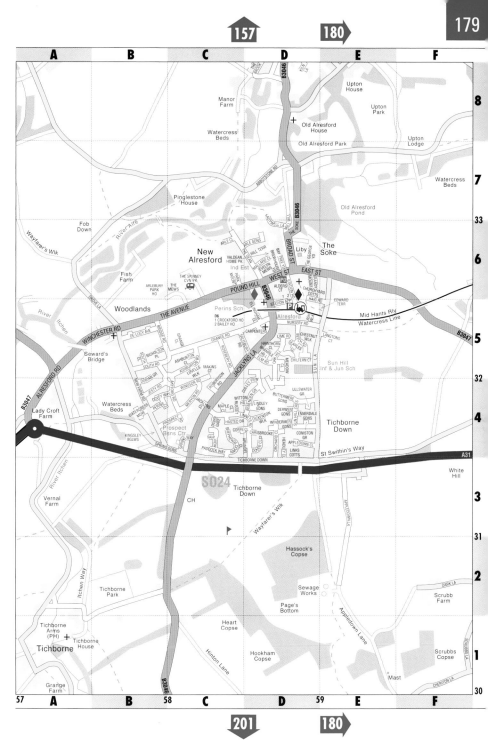

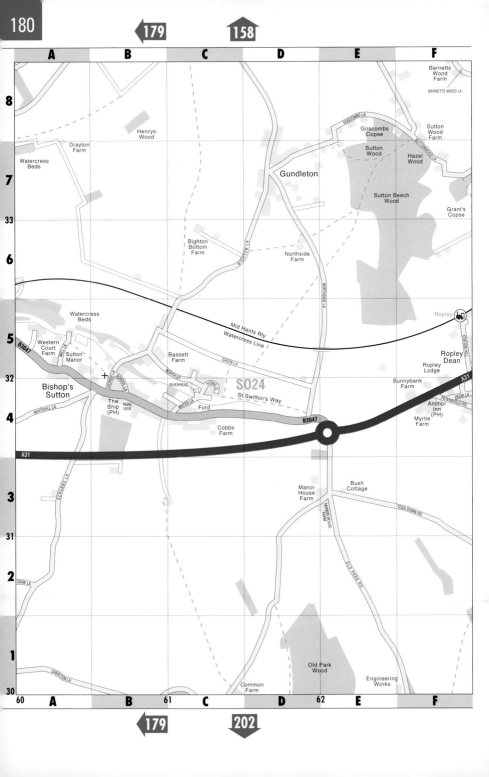

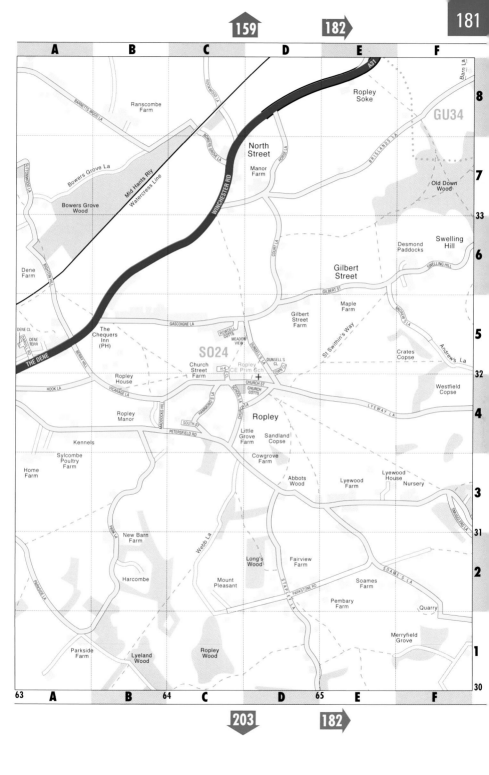

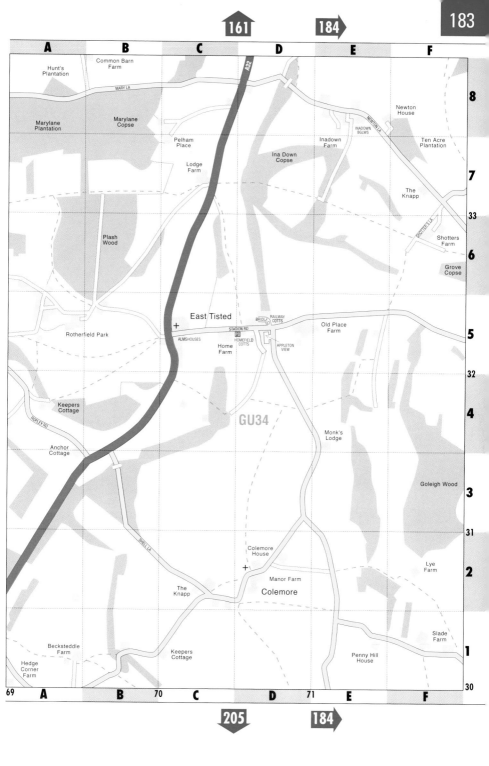

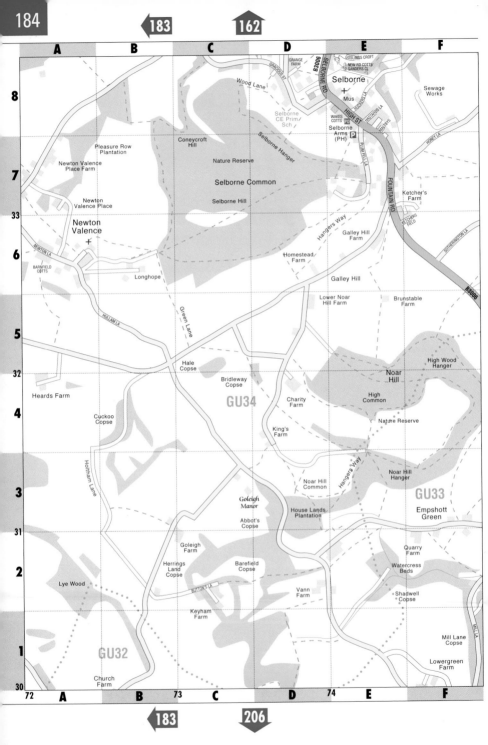

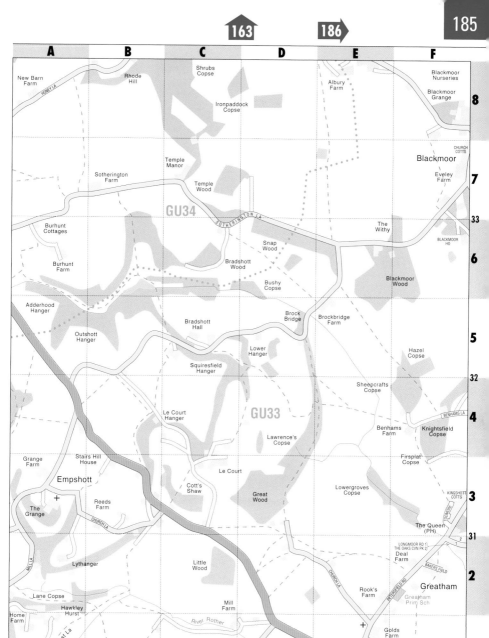

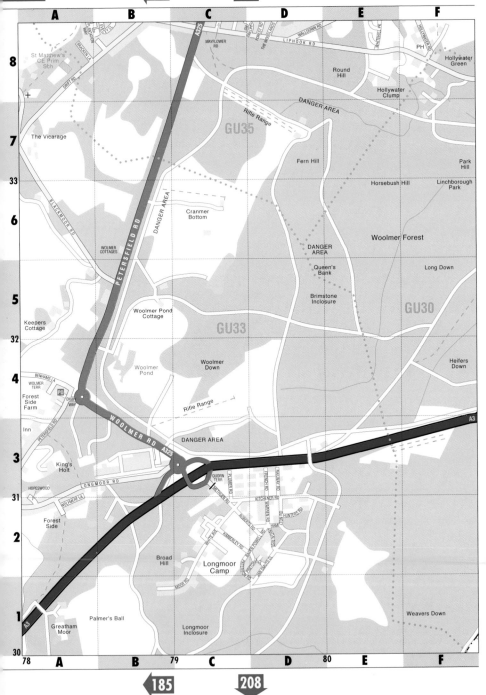

185
164

St Matthew's
CE Prim
Sch

MAYFLOWER
RD

Round
Hill

PH

Hollywater
Green

Hollywater
Clump

+

The Vicarage

DANGER AREA

Rifle Range

GU35

Fern Hill

Park
Hill

Horsebush Hill

Linchborough
Park

DANGER AREA

Cranmer
Bottom

Woolmer Forest

WOLMER
COTTAGES

DANGER
AREA

Queen's
Bank

Long Down

Brimstone
Inclosure

GU30

Keepers
Cottage

Woolmer Pond
Cottage

GU33

Heifers
Down

Woolmer
Pond

Woolmer
Down

BENHAMS LA

WOLMER
TERR

Rifle Range

A3

Forest
Side
Farm

PO

DIGBY
WAY

Inn

WOOLMER   RD

A325

DANGER AREA

King's
Holt

LONGMOOR RD

QUORN
TERR

HOPESWOOD

WOLMERE LA

Forest
Side

Broad
Hill

Longmoor
Camp

A3

Greatham
Moor

Palmer's Ball

Longmoor
Inclosure

Weavers Down

185
208

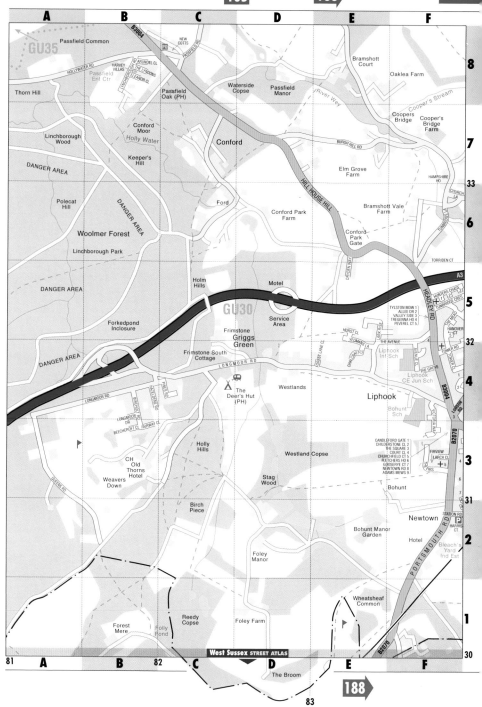

	A	B	C	D	E	F

The Hanger

Spring Pond Hanger

Cooper's Stream

Spring Pond

Coach House Copse

Downlands Farm

Downlands House

P

P

Kent's Hill

Bramshott Common

Bramshott Chase

GU26

A3

8

Glebe House Farm

RECTORY LA

The Spaniard Inn (Hotel)

7

LIMES CL

33

CHURCH RD

CHURCH LA

Bramshott

PORTSMOUTH RD

6

B2171

A3

Woodlands

Cold Ash Hill

Old Barn Farm

Hewshott Farm

Prince of Wales (PH)

HAMMER LA

LONDON RD

Penally Farm

Hewshott Lodge

HEWSHOTT LA

HEWSHOTT CR

River Wey

Hammer Bottom

Gillham's Moor

5

LUNDHURST DR

WELLANDS

PADDOCK WAY
2 GREENFIELD CL
3 TOWER RD

MEADOW END

HEWSHOTT LA

GILLHAM'S LA

GU30

Hewshott House

Gillham's Farm

GU27

B2131

32

MEADOW

CALVECROFT

WEY LODGE

LOCKE RD

THE MALTINGS

HAWKSHAW CL

Bridge

LIPHOOK RD

Linchmere Common

4

B2171

P

Liby

MALTHOUSE CT

ERLES

HASLEMERE RD

MANOR FIELDS

HAZELBANK CL

COLLIERS CRES

Bridge Lodge

P

P

B2131

P

LITTLE MANOR

GRENVILLE

ONSLOW

HAZELBANK MEWS

MONTREAL WLK

CANFIELD

WILLOW CLOSE

CHESTNUT CL

Lower Brookham

DANLEY LA

LINCHMERE RD

Super store

Liphook

Brookham Plantation

Danley Farm

3

Beaver Ind Est

SHEPHERDS WAY

MIDHURST RD

CHILTLEE MANOR

CHILTLEY WAY

CHILTLEE LA

LONGMOOR RD

Brookham Sch

Highfield Sch

Poison Copse

Linchmere Church Farm

THE COURTYARD

31

STATION RD

Liphook

HEATHERLEY MEWS

BUNNS O FARM

HOLLYCOMBE CL

OAKE CRES

SOUTH RD

Churcher's Coll Jun Sch

Ash Copse

2

Bleach's Yard Ind Est

Sussex Border Path

Stanley Common

Golden Valley

1

North Lodge Ind.Pk

Hazel Piece

Hilly Field Copse

30

84	A		B	85	C		D	86	E		F

A2
1 ADAMS MEWS
A3
1 SHIPLEY CT
2 COURT CL
A4
1 CHILDERSTONE CL
2 LINCOLN CT

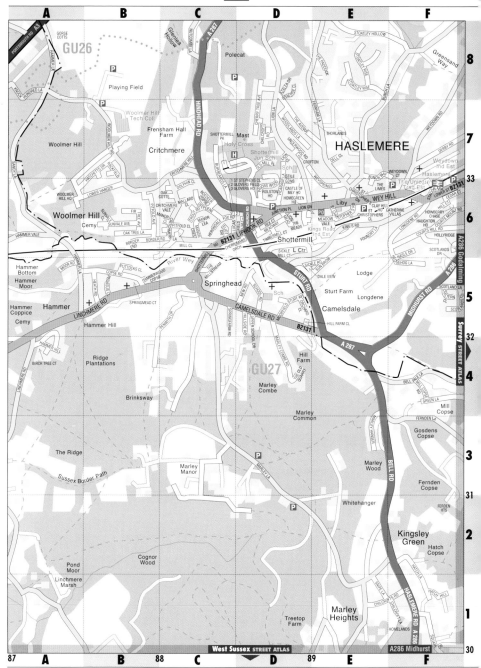

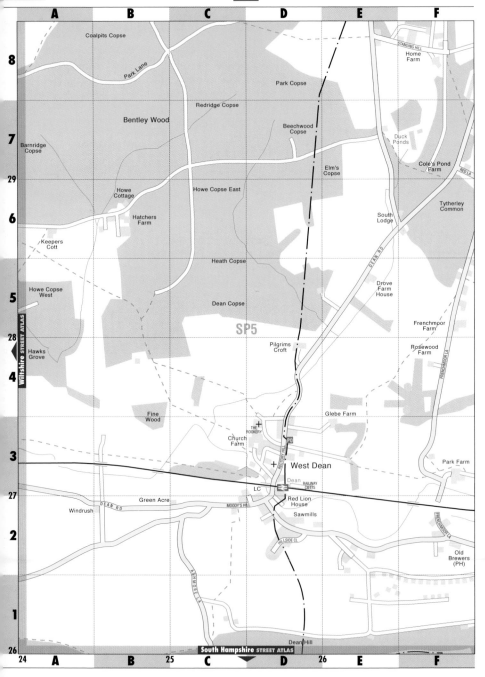

Coalpits Copse

Park Lane

Park Copse

Redridge Copse

Bentley Wood

Beechwood Copse

Barnridge Copse

Duck Ponds

Cole's Pond Farm

RED LA

Elm's Copse

Howe Cottage

Howe Copse East

Tytherley Common

Hatchers Farm

South Lodge

Keepers Cott

Heath Copse

Drove Farm House

Howe Copse West

Dean Copse

SP5

Frenchmoor Farm

Hawks Grove

Pilgrims Croft

Rosewood Farm

FRENCHMOOR LA

DEAN RD

Fine Wood

Glebe Farm

Park Farm

THE ROOKERY

Church Farm

West Dean

Dean RAILWAY COTTS

LC

Green Acre

Red Lion House

Windrush

DEAN RD

MOODY'S HILL

Sawmills

FRENCHMOOR LA

HILLSIDE CL

Old Brewers (PH)

ASHMORE LA

BISHOPS HILL

Dean Hill

Wiltshire STREET ATLAS

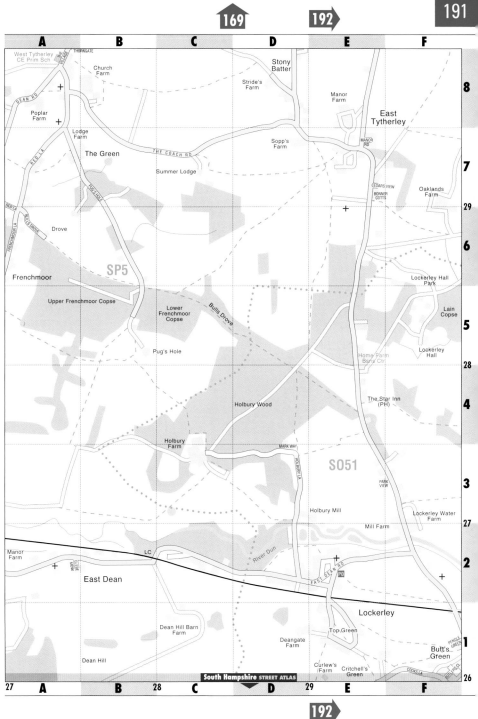

A B C D E F

8

West Tytherley
CE Prim Sch
THORNGATE
Church
Farm
Stride's
Farm
Stony
Batter
Manor
Farm
East
Tytherley

DEAN RD
Poplar
Farm
Sopp's
Farm
MANOR RD

Lodge
Farm
THE COACH RD

7

The Green
RED LA
Summer Lodge
CEDARS VIEW
BONNER
COTTS
Oaklands
Farm

29

PUG'S HOLE
BULL'S DROVE
BERT LA
Drove

6

FRENCHMOOR LA
Frenchmoor
SP5
Lockerley Hall
Park

Upper Frenchmoor Copse
Lower
Frenchmoor
Copse
Bulls Drove
Lain
Copse

5

Pug's Hole
Home Farm
Bsns Ctr
Lockerley
Hall

28

Holbury Wood
The Star Inn
(PH)

4

Holbury
Farm
MARK WAY
SO51
HOLBURY LA

3

PARK
VIEW
Holbury Mill
Lockerley Water
Farm

27

Mill Farm
Manor
Farm
GLEBE MDW
LC
River Dun
EAST DEAN RD
PO

2

East Dean
Lockerley

Dean Hill Barn
Farm
Top Green
PENDLE GREEN

1

Deangate
Farm
Butt's
Green

Dean Hill
Curlew's
Farm
Critchell's
Green
COOKS LA
BUTTS LA

26

27 A B 28 C D 29 E F

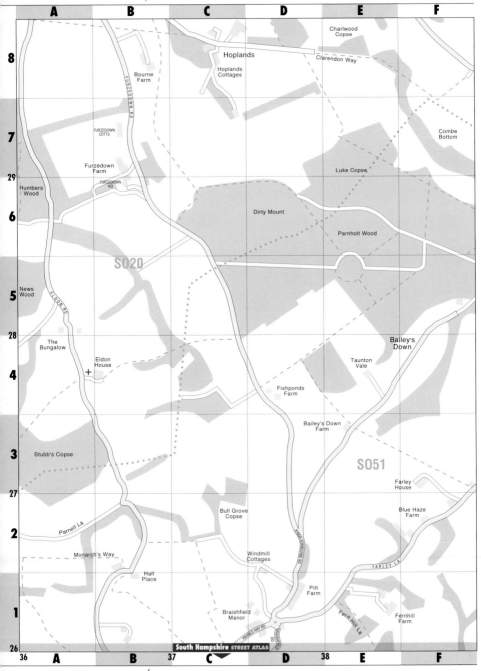

8

7

29

6

5

28

4

3

27

2

1

26

A   B   C   D   E   F

Charlwood
Copse

Hoplands

Clarendon Way

Combe
Bottom

Hoplands
Cottages

Bourne
Farm

FURZEDOWN
COTTS

Furzedown
Farm

Luke Copse

PURZEDOWN
HO

Humbers
Wood

Dirty Mount

Parnholt Wood

SO20

News
Wood

ELDON RD

Bailey's
Down

The
Bungalow

Eldon
House

Taunton
Vale

Fishponds
Farm

Bailey's Down
Farm

Stubb's Copse

SO51

Farley
House

Bull Grove
Copse

Blue Haze
Farm

Parnell La

Monarch's Way

Windmill
Cottages

FARLEY LA

Hall
Place

KINGS SOMBORNE RD

Pitt
Farm

Fern Hill La

Fernhill
Farm

Braishfield
Manor

PAYNES HAY RD

36   A   B   37   C   D   38   E   F

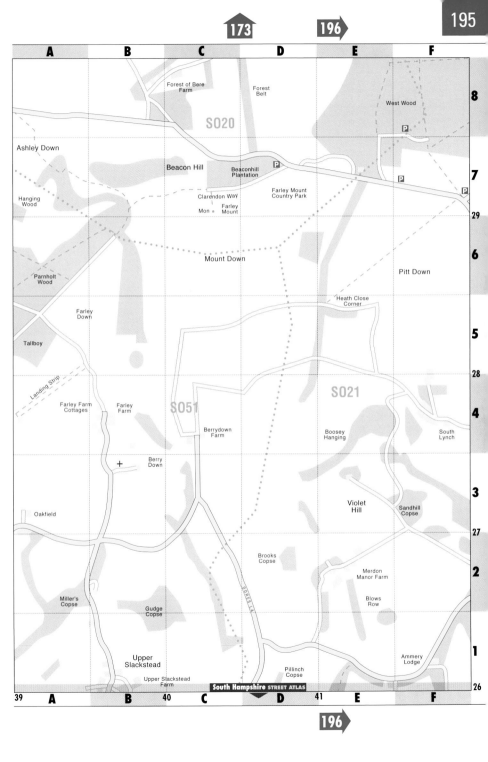

173
196

A   B   C   D   E   F

8

Forest of Bere
Farm

Forest
Belt

West Wood

SO20

P

Ashley Down

7

Beacon Hill

Beaconhill
Plantation

P

P

P

Hanging
Wood

Clarendon Way

Farley Mount
Country Park

29

Mon

Farley
Mount

6

Mount Down

Pitt Down

Parnholt
Wood

Heath Close
Corner

5

Farley
Down

Tallboy

28

Landing Strip

SO21

4

Farley Farm
Cottages

Farley
Farm

SO51

Berrydown
Farm

Boosey
Hanging

South
Lynch

3

Berry
Down

Violet
Hill

Sandhill
Copse

Oakfield

27

Brooks
Copse

2

Miller's
Copse

Gudge
Copse

Merdon
Manor Farm

Blows
Row

1

Upper
Slackstead

Ammery
Lodge

Upper Slackstead
Farm

Pillinch
Copse

39   A   B   40   C   D   41   E   F

26

196

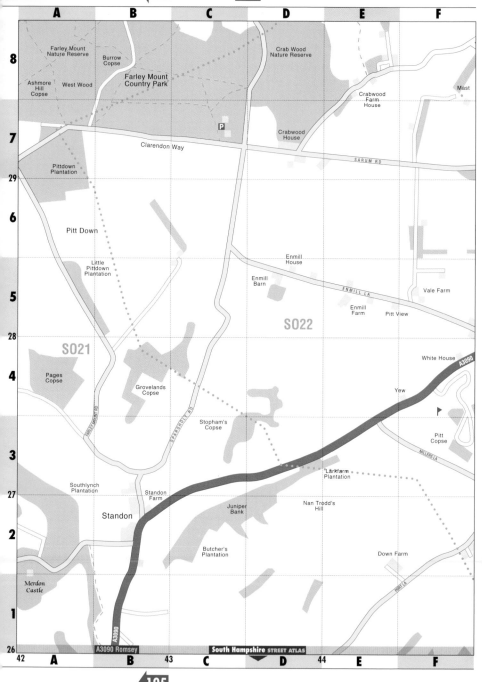

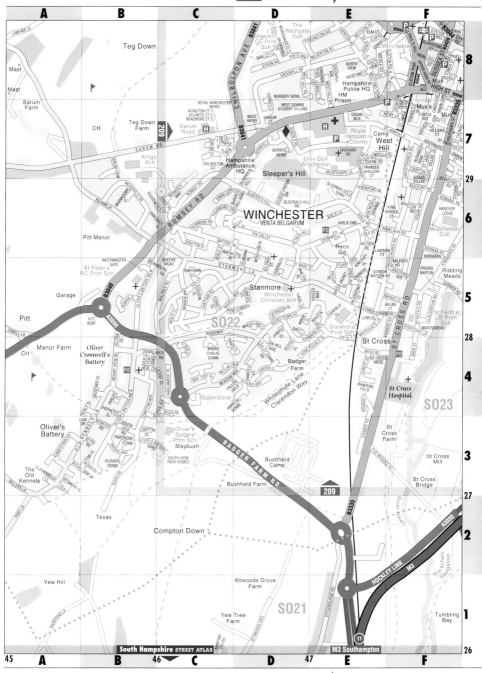

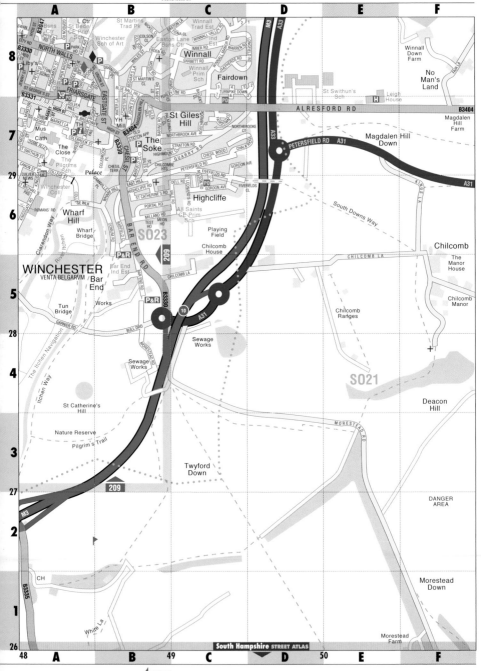

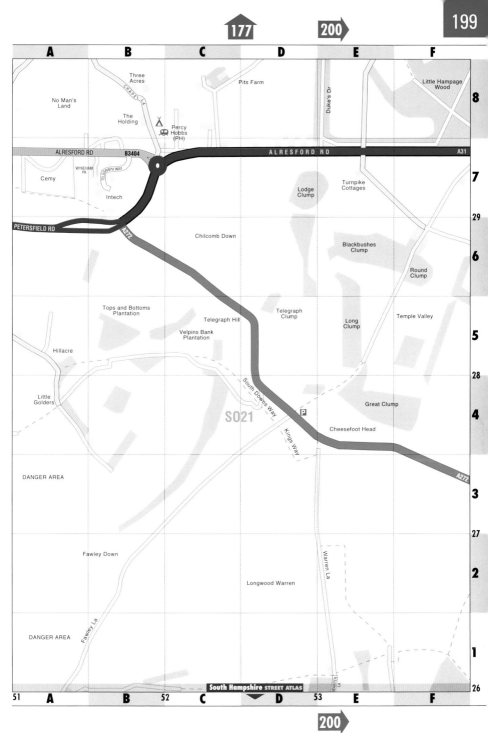

A B C D E F

8

Little Hampage Wood

Three Acres

Pits Farm

Duke's Dr

No Man's Land

The Holding

Percy Hobbs (PH)

ALRESFORD RD B3404

ALRESFORD RD A31

7

Cemy

WYKEHAM PK

TELEGRAPH WAY

Intech

Lodge Clump

Turnpike Cottages

29

PETERSFIELD RD

A272

Chilcomb Down

Blackbushes Clump

6

Round Clump

Tops and Bottoms Plantation

Telegraph Hill

Telegraph Clump

Long Clump

Temple Valley

5

Velpins Bank Plantation

Hillacre

South Downs Way

28

Little Golders

SO21

P

Great Clump

4

Kings Way

Cheesefoot Head

A272

DANGER AREA

3

27

Fawley Down

Warren La

2

Longwood Warren

Fawley La

DANGER AREA

1

WARREN LA

South Hampshire STREET ATLAS

26

51 A B 52 C D 53 E F

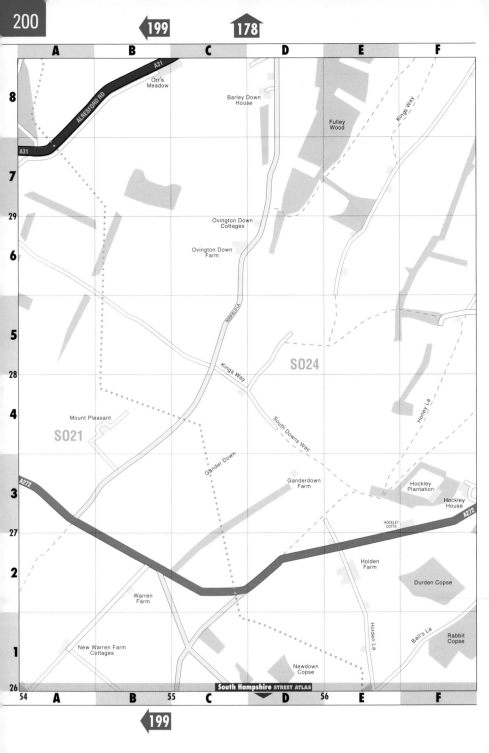

199

178

A31
ALRESFORD RD
Orr's Meadow
Barley Down House
Fulley Wood
Kings Way
A31
Ovington Down Cottages
Ovington Down Farm
MOOR LA LA
Kings Way
SO24
Honey La
Mount Pleasant
SO21
South Downs Way
A272
Ganderdown Farm
Gander Down
Hockley Plantation
Hockley House
A272
HOCKLEY COTTS
Holden Farm
Durden Copse
Warren Farm
Holden La
Ball's La
Rabbit Copse
New Warren Farm Cottages
Newdown Copse

199

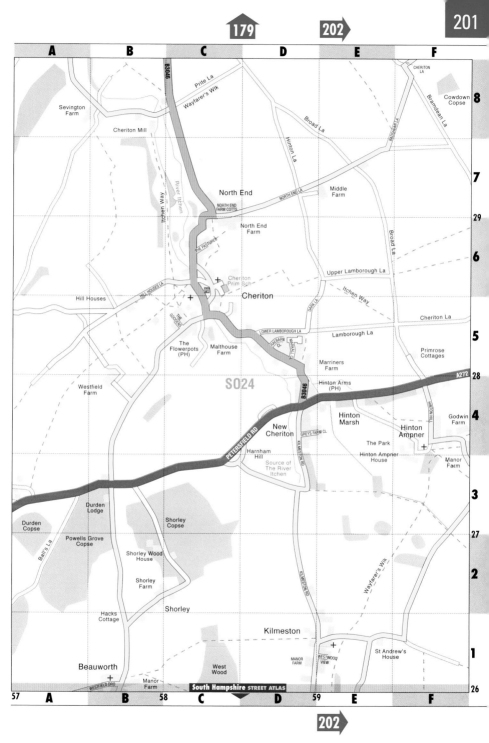

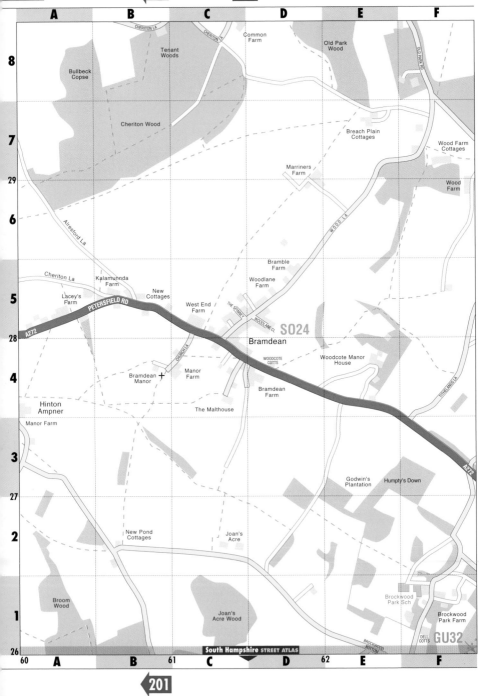

A **B** **C** **D** **E** **F**

8

CHERITON LA

Tenant
Woods

Common
Farm

Old Park
Wood

OLD PARK RD

Bullbeck
Copse

CHERITON

7

Cheriton Wood

Breach Plain
Cottages

Wood Farm
Cottages

29

Marriners
Farm

Wood
Farm

6

Alresford La

WOOD LA

Bramble
Farm

Cheriton La

Kalamunnda
Farm

New
Cottages

Woodlane
Farm

5

Lacey's
Farm

PETERSFIELD RD

West End
Farm

THE SPINNEY

WOODLANE CL

SO24

A272

28

Bramdean

WOODCOTE
COTTS

Woodcote Manor
House

4

Bramdean
Manor

CHURCH LA

Manor
Farm

Bramdean
Farm

TITHE LANDS LA

Hinton
Ampner

The Malthouse

Manor Farm

3

27

Godwin's
Plantation

Humpty's Down

A272

2

New Pond
Cottages

Joan's
Acre

1

Broom
Wood

Joan's
Acre Wood

Brockwood
Park Sch

Brockwood
Park Farm

BROCKWOOD
BOTTOM

DELL
COTTS

GU32

26

A **B** 61 **C** **D** 62 **E** **F**
60

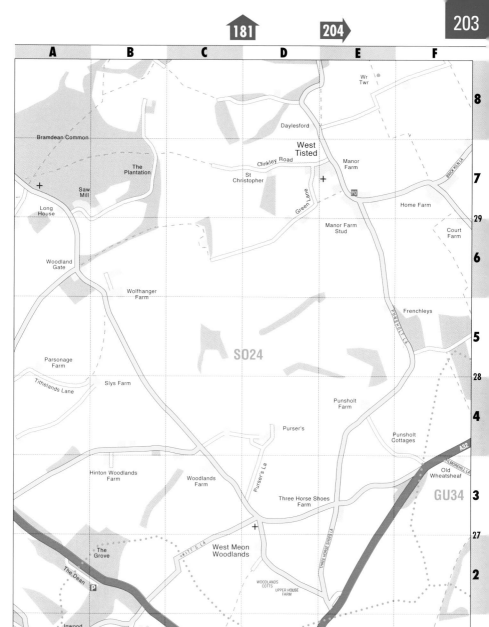

A   B   C   D   E   F

8

Wr
Twr

Daylesford

West
Tisted

Clinkley Road

St
Christopher

Manor
Farm

Bramdean Common

The
Plantation

Green Lane

PO

7

BRICK KILN LA

Home Farm

29

Long
House

Saw
Mill

Manor Farm
Stud

Court
Farm

Woodland
Gate

6

Wolfhanger
Farm

Frenchleys

PUNSHOLT LA

SO24

5

28

Parsonage
Farm

Tithelands Lane

Slys Farm

Punsholt
Farm

Punsholt
Cottages

4

A32

Purser's

Purser's La

Hinton Woodlands
Farm

Woodlands
Farm

Three Horse Shoes
Farm

Old
Wheatsheaf

ST MOREHILL LA

GU34

3

27

SKITT'S LA

West Meon
Woodlands

WOODLANDS
COTTS
UPPER HOUSE
FARM

THREE HORSE SHOES LA

The Grove

The Dean

P

2

Inwood
Copse

The West Meon Hut
(PH)

1

Shutt's
Copse

GU32

PEST HOS

Garage

A32

Martin's Wood

A272

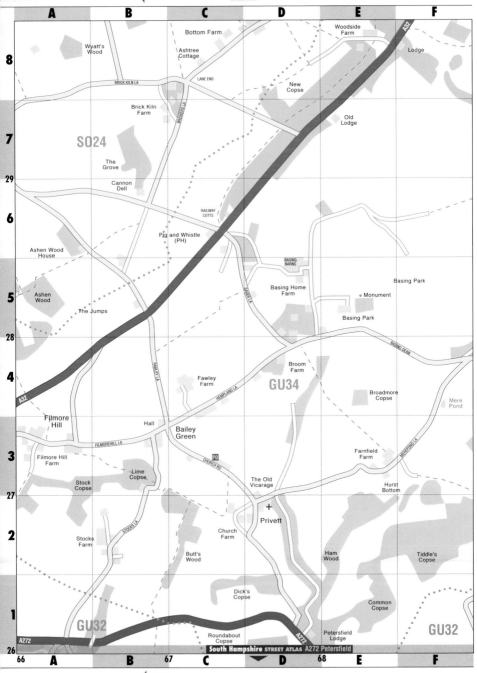

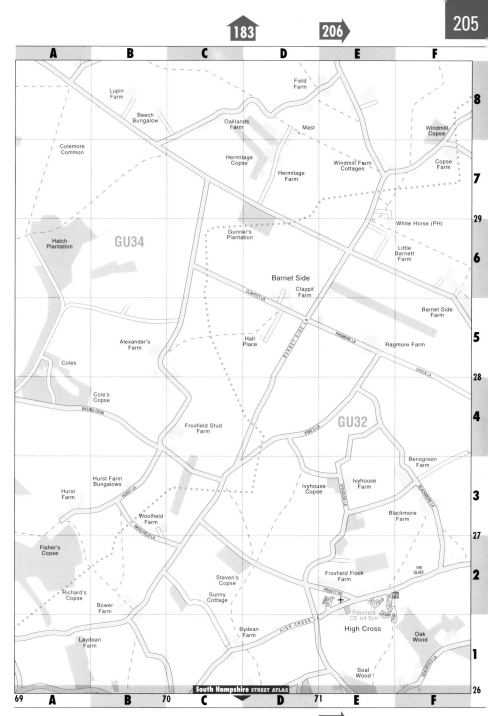

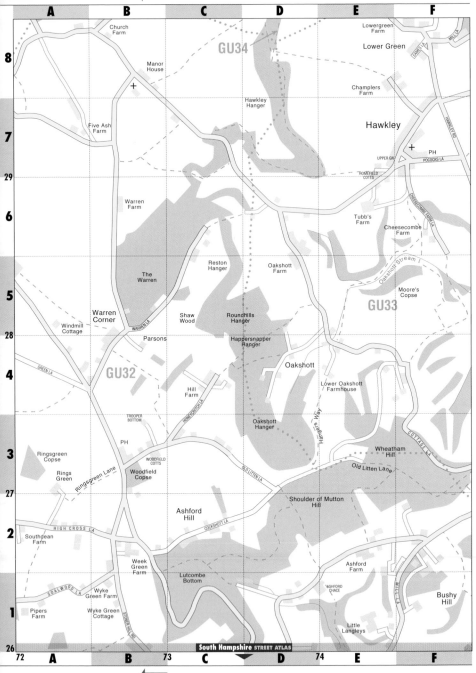

A   **B**   **C**   **D**   **E**   **F**

Church
Farm

Lowergreen
Farm

GU34

Lower Green

8

Manor
House

Champlers
Farm

Hawkley
Hanger

Five Ash
Farm

Hawkley

7

PH

UPPER GN

29

ROMEFIELD
COTTS

Warren
Farm

6

Tubb's
Farm

Cheesecombe
Farm

Oakshott Stream

Reston
Hanger

Oakshott
Farm

Moore's
Copse

The
Warren

GU33

5

Windmill
Cottage

Warren
Corner

Shaw
Wood

Roundhills
Hanger

WARREN LA

28

Parsons

Happersnapper
Hanger

GREEN LA

GU32

Oakshott

4

Hill
Farm

Lower Oakshott
Farmhouse

HANGERS LA

Hangers Way

TROOPER
BOTTOM

Oakshott
Hanger

COTTAGE LA

PH

Wheatham
Hill

3

Ringsgreen
Copse

WOODFIELD
COTTS

Old Litten Lane

Rings
Green

Ringsgreen Lane

Woodfield
Copse

OLD LITTEN LA

27

Shoulder of Mutton
Hill

Ashford
Hill

2

HIGH CROSS LA

COCKSHOTT LA

Southdean
Farm

Ashford
Farm

MILL LA

Week
Green
Farm

ASHFORD
CHACE

Bushy
Hill

1

SOALWOOD LA

Wyke
Green Farm

Lutcombe
Bottom

Pipers
Farm

Wyke Green
Cottage

STONER RD

Little
Langleys

26

72   **A**   **B**   73   **C**   **D**   74   **E**   **F**

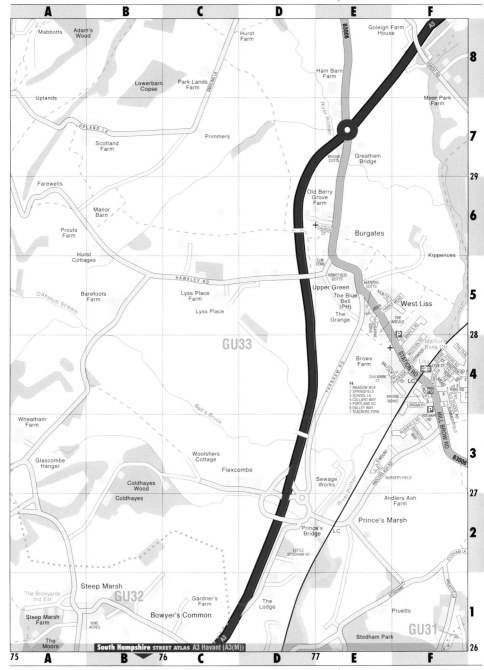

GU30

A B C D E F

8

Longmoor
Inclosure

Little Dean
Bottom

7

The
Wylds

Warren
Hill

Wylds
Farm

Langley

The Lake

WARREN RD

29

SHERWOOD CL

Langley Bridge
Farm

PO

PINE WLK

TEMPLE RD

6

The
Temple
Inn
(PH)

Liss
Forest

The
Mint

MINT RD

Mangers

REEDS LA

Reeds

Brewells
Farm

Little
Langley
Farm

ROTHERBANK
FARM LA

FOREST RISE

Whangerei Nursery
Palmers Farm

Home
Farm

Palmers

Newlands

BREWELLS LA

West Sussex STREET ATLAS

LC

Rake CE
Fst Sch

5

DUDLEY
TERR

WYLDE GREEN LA

Ciddy
Hall

ST PATRICK'S LA

Rake
Bsns Pk

B2070

28

Wyld Green
Farm

MILLBROOK

ROCKPIT
COTTS

GU33

St Patrick's
Copse

The
Flying Bull
(PH)

Coldharbour Park
Farm

East Liss

SILVER BIRCH

OAK TREE DR

Liss

YEW TREE

RAKE RD

CHURCH RD

PENINSULA LA

FIR TREE
COTTS

Rake

4

MEADOW
WLK

PATRICK

COPSE

CHASE

LITTLE BARN

HIGHFIELD GDNS

High Firs
House

HATCH LA

PO

BULL HILL

WILLOW
RD

WOOD RD

MOSS CL

VINSON RD

THE
RIDINGS

Highfield
Farm

Highfield
Wood

SANDY LA

Sussex Border Path

CARLYLE LA

East
Hill

Liss
Inf & Jun
Schs

HUNTSBOTTOM LA

Pot
Well

3

B3006

27

HILL BROW RD

Hill
Side

Black
Pond

STODHAM LA

HILLSIDE
COTTS

EDGEWOOD
CT

MALVERN RD

Rake
Common

GU31

2

Hill
Brow

CHATSWORTH

B3006

Rake
Hanger

Hambledon
Piece

B2070 LONDON RD

COMBE RD

BORDER CL

PH

ANTHILL MDW

1

Farther
Commons

Clayton
Court

Combe
Hill

Harting
Combe

26

GU31

West Sussex STREET ATLAS

78 A B 79 C D 80 E F

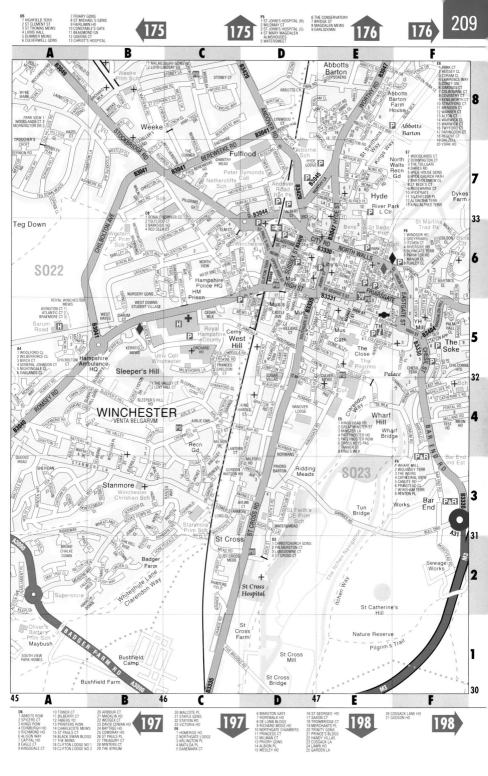

Index

Place name May be abbreviated on the map

Location number Present when a number indicates the place's position in a crowded area of mapping

Locality, town or village Shown when more than one place has the same name

Postcode district District for the indexed place

Page and grid square Page number and grid reference for the standard mapping

Church Rd 6 Beckenham BR2.........53 C6

Public and commercial buildings are highlighted in magenta   Places of interest are highlighted in blue with a star★

Abbreviations used in the index

Acad	**Academy**	Comm	**Common**	Gd	**Ground**	L	**Leisure**	Prom	**Promenade**
App	**Approach**	Cott	**Cottage**	Gdn	**Garden**	La	**Lane**	Rd	**Road**
Arc	**Arcade**	Cres	**Crescent**	Gn	**Green**	Liby	**Library**	Recn	**Recreation**
Ave	**Avenue**	Cswy	**Causeway**	Gr	**Grove**	Mdw	**Meadow**	Ret	**Retail**
Bglw	**Bungalow**	Ct	**Court**	H	**Hall**	Meml	**Memorial**	Sh	**Shopping**
Bldg	**Building**	Ctr	**Centre**	Ho	**House**	Mkt	**Market**	Sq	**Square**
Bsns, Bus	**Business**	Ctry	**Country**	Hospl	**Hospital**	Mus	**Museum**	St	**Street**
Bvd	**Boulevard**	Cty	**County**	HQ	**Headquarters**	Orch	**Orchard**	Sta	**Station**
Cath	**Cathedral**	Dr	**Drive**	Hts	**Heights**	Pal	**Palace**	Terr	**Terrace**
Cir	**Circus**	Dro	**Drove**	Ind	**Industrial**	Par	**Parade**	TH	**Town Hall**
Cl	**Close**	Ed	**Education**	Inst	**Institute**	Pas	**Passage**	Univ	**University**
Cnr	**Corner**	Emb	**Embankment**	Int	**International**	Pk	**Park**	Wk, Wlk	**Walk**
Coll	**College**	Est	**Estate**	Intc	**Interchange**	Pl	**Place**	Wr	**Water**
Com	**Community**	Ex	**Exhibition**	Junc	**Junction**	Prec	**Precinct**	Yd	**Yard**

Index of localities, towns and villages

A

Abbotstone..............156 F2
Abbots Worthy..........176 D6
Abbotts Ann............105 A3
Abbotts Barton.........209 E8
Aldermaston..............9 E7
Aldermaston Soke......10 D3
Aldershot...............76 B1
Alton.................139 E3
Amport................104 B6
Andover...............106 D7
Andwell.................41 A6
Anna Valley...........105 C5
Anstey................140 B5
Appleshaw..............81 B6
Arborfield Garrison....15 D7
Arford................165 D6
Ash.....................77 E3
Ashe...................88 F8
Ashford Hill
  Hawkley.............206 C2
  Thatcham...............8 C1
Ashmansworth...........40 F7
Ashmore Green...........2 F8
Ash Vale...............77 E7
Avington..............177 E5
Axford................114 C3
Axmansford.............25 F7

B

Badshot Lea............99 F5
Bagmore...............116 A6
Bagnor..................1 A7
Bailey Green..........204 C3
Ball Hill...............4 A3
Bar End...............209 F3
Barford...............166 C8
Barnet Side...........205 D6
Barton Stacey.........130 D6
Basingstoke............68 E6
Baughurst..............26 C7
Beacon Hill...........167 A7
Beauworth.............201 B1
Beech.................139 A2
Beech Hill
  Bordon..............165 E6
  Mortimer.............13 B5
Bentley...............120 B5
Bentworth.............138 A6
Bidden.................94 D7
Bighton...............158 B1
Binsted...............141 E6
Bishop's Green..........6 E3
Bishop's Sutton.......180 A4
Black Dam..............69 D3

C

Camberley..............36 A6
Camelsdale............189 E5
Chandler's Green.......30 D2
Charlton...............82 E3
Charter Alley..........46 E8
Chatter Alley..........74 A7
Chawton...............161 D7
Cheriton..............201 D5
Chilbolton............129 A4
Chilcomb..............198 F6
Chilland..............177 D6
Chilton Candover......135 F5
Cholderton............101 C2
Church Crookham........75 B5
Church End.............49 C6
Church Oakley..........66 F1
Churt................144 D1
Chute Cadley...........58 C8
Chute Forest..........58 C4
Chute Standen.........58 B8
City....................1 D1
Clanville..............81 D7
Clarken Green..........66 E2

D

Daneshill..............69 E7
Darby Green............34 E6
Deadwater............164 E4
Dean.................174 E3
Dibley.................51 E7
Dippenhall.............98 B1
Dockenfield...........143 C6
Dogmersfield...........74 A6
Donnington.............90 D1
Dummer.................90 D1
Dunbridge.............192 D1
Dunley.................63 A8

E

East Anton.............83 C4
East Aston............108 E7
East Cholderton......103 F7
East Dean............191 B2
East End...............20 F7
East Fields.............1 F1
East Green...........120 D6

Clatford Oakcuts......127 B3
Cliddesden.............92 A7
Cliddesden Hill........91 F7
Cold Harbour.........116 A5
Cole Henley............63 D3
Colemore...............183 D2
College Town...........35 C8
Colt Hill..............72 F4
Combe..................19 C6
Compton
  Farnham..............99 D1
  King's Somborne.....193 D7
Conford...............187 C7
Cottonworth..........128 D4
Couch Green...........177 B6
Cove...................55 C5
Cove Green.............55 E4
Cranbourne............69 B2
Crawley...............152 B2
Crawley Hill...........36 C5
Cricket Hill...........34 D5
Critchmere............189 C7
Crockham Heath..........4 D6
Crondall...............97 C7
Crooked Billet.........51 D2
Crookham...............7 F5
Crookham Village......74 C5
Crosswater...........144 C4
Crux Easton............41 A5
Cuckoo's Corner......140 E7
Cufaude................48 D7

East Hill..............208 A3
East Liss.............208 B4
Easton................177 A5
Eastrop................69 D4
East Stratton........134 A4
East Tisted..........183 C5
East Tytherley........191 E8
East Winterslow......168 A8
East Woodhay...........20 C7
East Worldham........141 A1
Ecchinswell............23 D4
Edgeborough..........122 A3
Egbury.................62 D5
Egypt.................131 D5
Ellisfield............115 C8
Elvetham...............53 B5
Elvetham Heath.........53 D3
Empshott.............185 A3
Empshott Green.......184 F3
Enborne................4 F4
Enborne Row............4 F4
Enham Alamein..........83 C7
Eversley...............15 F1
Eversley Centre........33 B8
Eversley Cross.........33 C8
Ewshot.................98 A8

F

Faberstown............57 C6
Faccombe..............20 A1
Fair Cross.............13 B2
Fair Oak...............25 C7
Fair Oak Green.........29 B6
Farleigh Wallop........91 E2
Farley Hill............15 B6
Farnborough............55 D1
Farnborough Green......56 A6
Farnborough Park.......56 A3
Farnborough Street.....56 B5
Farnham................98 E3
Filmore Hill.........204 A3
Finchampstead.........16 C2
Fleet..................54 B1
Forton...............107 F4
Foscombe...............82 D3
Fox Lane...............55 D8
Freefolk...............87 B6
Frenchmoor...........191 A6
Frensham.............144 A7
Frimley................36 B1
Frimley Green..........56 D7
Frimley Ridge..........36 F3
Frithend..............143 A3
Frogmore...............35 A6
Fulflood.............209 D7

Fullerton............128 D3
Fyfield................80 E2

G

Gilbert Street.......181 E6
Gobley Hole..........114 C7
Golden Pot...........117 D3
Gong Hill............122 B4
Goodworth Clatford...105 F1
Goose Hill..............7 E2
Gore End................3 F4
Grateley.............125 B8
Grayshott............166 F4
Greatham.............185 F2
Great Shoddesden......80 B6
Green Cross..........144 F1
Greenham................6 A3
Greywell...............71 F3
Grouse Green...........31 D6

H

Hale...................99 F6
Hammer................189 A5
Hampshire Gate.........37 C3
Hamstead Marshall.......3 F8
Hannington............44 F4
Harestock............175 C4
Hartfordbridge........52 F8
Hartley Mauditt......162 E6
Hartley Wespall........30 A1
Hartley Wintney........52 E6
Haslemere............189 E7
Hatch Warren...........91 C6
Hatherden.............59 D1
Hatt Hill..............93 D5
Hattingley...........159 C7
Hawkley..............184 D1
Hawley.................35 C3
Hawley Lane............55 F7
Hawthorn.............182 D8
Hazeley................31 E3
Hazeley Bottom.........52 A8
Headbourne Worthy....176 B5
Headley
  Bordon..............165 C5
  Kingsclere............7 B2
Headley Down.........165 F5
Head's Hill.............6 F4
Hearn................165 F7
Heath End
  Farnham..............99 B7
  Tadley................9 D1
  Woolton Hill..........3 E1
Heatherside...........36 F4
Heath Green..........159 B7

B

Blackmoor............185 F7
Blacknest............142 D8
Blackwater............35 B4
Bordon...............164 C3
Bossington...........171 A2
Boundstone...........121 E5
Bowling Alley.........97 D8
Bradley..............137 B8
Bramdean............202 D4
Bramley...............28 E4
Bramley Corner........28 A3
Bramley Green.........29 A3
Bramshill..............31 F7
Bramshott............188 A6
Bransbury............108 A1
Brighton Hill.........91 E8
Brimpton...............8 E6
Brimpton Common........8 E3
Broad Laying...........4 D1
Broad Oak..............73 B4
Brock's Green.........23 E7
Broughton............170 C7
Brown Candover.......135 B3
Browninghall Green....26 D3
Bucks Horn Oak.......142 E8
Buckskin...............68 A3
Burgates.............207 E6
Burghclere............22 D7
Burkham..............115 E1
Buttermere............18 B7
Butt's Green.........191 F1

Heckfield 31 B6
Henley 17 F3
Herriard 93 A1
Highclere 21 D5
High Cross 205 E1
Highways 133 D3
Hill Brow 208 B2
Hindhead 167 D4
Hinton 201 E4
Hinton Ampner 201 F4
Hog Hatch 98 E6
Hollington Cross 21 C3
Hollywater 164 F1
Holt 51 D1
Holt End 138 A3
Holt Pound 121 B4
Holtwood 3 F5
Holybourne 140 B7
Hook 51 B1
Hoplands 194 C8
Horris Hill 5 C2
Horsebridge 171 D1
Houghton 171 B5
Hound Green 31 B3
Houndmills 68 E7
Hunton 132 B4
Hurstbourne Priors . . . 85 C2
Hurstbourne Tarrant . . 60 E8
Hyde 209 E7
Hyde End 8 C4

I

Ibthorpe 60 D8
Ibworth 45 F2
Idmiston Down 146 C5
Inhurst 26 A8
Islington 119 F2
Itchen Abbas 177 E6
Itchen Stoke 178 D6

K

Kempshott 68 A1
Kentsboro 126 C5
Kilmeston 201 D1
Kimpton 80 B3
Kingsclere 24 C1
Kings Furlong 69 A3
Kingsley 142 B1
Kingsley Green 189 F2
King's Somborne 172 B2
Kings Worthy 176 C6
Kitwood 182 A7
Knights Enham 83 A5

L

Langley 208 F7
Lasham 116 D1
Latchmere Green 28 A5
Laverstoke 87 C5
Leckford 150 D8
Leckford Abbas 150 D7
Linchmere 188 F2
Lindford 164 F5
Link 85 B8
Liphook 188 B3
Liss 208 B4
Liss Forest 208 B6
Litchfield 63 C8
Little Ann 105 B4
Littledown 18 D1
Little Hoddington 94 C5
Little London
  Andover 83 E8
  Tadley 27 F4
Little Sandhurst 34 E8
Little Shoddesden 80 C6
Little Somborne 172 F6
Littleton 175 B5
Lockerley 191 E1
Longparish 108 C5
Longstock 149 E6
Long Sutton 95 E3
Lower Bourne 122 C6
Lower Brook 193 C4

Lower Bullington 131 A7
Lower Chute 58 C7
Lower Common
  Basingstoke 115 B6
  Sandhurst 15 D1
Lower Farringdon . . . 161 D3
Lower Froyle 119 C5
Lower Green 206 E8
Lower Wield 137 B5
Ludgershall 57 A1
Lyde Green 50 E7
Lynch 87 E8

M

Mapledurwell 70 E3
Marley Heights 189 E1
Martyr Worthy 177 A6
Mattingley 51 D8
Medstead 159 E7
Micheldever 133 A3
Michelmersh 193 D1
Middle Bourne 122 A7
Middleton 108 A5
Middle Wallop 147 E7
Middle Winterslow . . . 168 A7
Millbridge 122 C1
Mill Corner 72 B5
Mill Green 7 D2
Mill Lane 74 B1
Monk Sherborne 47 B5
Monkwood 182 B2
Monxton 104 C5
Mortimer 11 E5
Mortimer West End . . . 11 B4
Mottisfont 192 E2
Moulsham Green 33 F8
Mount Pleasant 139 F2
Mullenspond 103 F8
Murrell Green 51 E3
Mytchett 56 C3

N

Nashes Green 116 C7
Nately Scures 71 C7
Neatham 140 E6
Netherton 39 D8
Nether Wallop 148 B5
Newbury 1 C3
New Cheriton 201 D4
Newfound 67 C4
Newnham 50 C1
Newton Stacey 129 E6
Newton Tony 123 B5
Newton Valence 184 A6
Newtown
  Alton 139 E3
  Liphook 187 F2
  Newbury 5 F4
No Man's Land 198 F8
Northbrook 132 F4
North Camp 77 B7
North End
  New Alresford 201 C7
  Woolton Hill 3 E2
North Houghton 171 C7
Northington 156 F8
North Oakley 44 F1
North Street 181 D7
North Sydmonton 6 D1
North Tidworth 78 F7
North Town 77 B2
North Waltham 89 F2
North Warnborough . . 72 A4
Nutcombe 167 C2
Nutley 114 C3

O

Oakhanger 163 E6
Oakley 67 C1
Oakridge 69 B7
Oakshott 206 D4
Odiham 72 E2
Old Alresford 157 C1

Old Basing 70 C6
Old Burghclere 42 D8
Oliver's Battery 197 A3
Overton 88 B7
Over Wallop 125 B1
Ovington 178 E4
Oxenwood 17 B3

P

Padworth 10 E8
Padworth Common . . . 10 E6
Palestine 124 E6
Pamber End 27 C2
Pamber Green 27 D4
Pamber Heath 10 D1
Pardown 90 B7
Passfield 165 D1
Penton Corner 82 A1
Penton Grafton 81 F3
Penton Mewsey 82 A4
Penwood 21 F8
Phoenix Green 52 B4
Picket Piece 84 A2
Pilcot 74 B6
Polhampton 65 D2
Pondtail 54 D1
Popham 112 E4
Popley 48 C1
Porton Down 145 A3
Potbridge 72 F8
Pound Green 26 B3
Pound Street 22 A7
Preston Candover . . . 136 B8
Prince's Marsh 207 E2
Privett 204 D2
Pyestock 54 F1

Q

Quarley 103 B4
Quidhampton 65 B1

R

Rafborough 55 C3
Ragged Appleshaw . . . 81 C6
Rake 208 F4
Ramsdell 46 D7
Redenham 81 A8
Redlands 97 F7
Red Rice 127 C8
Redwood 160 A8
Riseley 14 A3
Rivar 17 D8
Ropley 181 D4
Ropley Dean 180 F5
Ropley Soke 181 E8
Rotherwick 50 E6
Rotten Green 53 C4
Rowledge 121 D3
Runfold 100 A4
Rushmoor 144 F7

S

St Cross 209 C2
St Giles' Hill 198 C7
St Mary Bourne 62 A1
Sandhurst 35 A7
Seale 100 F4
Selborne 184 E8
Shalden 139 B8
Shalden Green 117 B3
Shaw 2 B6
Sherborne St John 47 E4
Sherfield Green 29 C1
Sherfield on Loddon . . . 29 D1
Shipton Bellinger 101 D8
Shorley 201 C2
Shortfield Common . . . 122 A1
Shortheath
  Bordon 163 D5
  Wrecclesham 121 E6
Shottermill 189 D6
Silchester 10 F1

Skinners Green 4 F7
Slade Hill 4 D2
Sladen Green 40 F1
Sleaford 142 E1
Sleeper's Hill 209 B5
Smannell 83 E6
Soldridge 159 E2
South Farnborough . . . 56 B2
South Ham 68 D3
Southington 87 F8
Southrope 116 C6
South Tidworth 78 E3
South Town 159 F5
South View 69 B7
South Warnborough . . . 95 B4
South Wonston 153 D5
Southwood 55 A3
Spanish Green 30 A3
Sparsholt 174 C3
Spearywell 192 D3
Speen 1 A5
Speenhamland 1 E4
Spitalhatch 140 B3
Spreakley 144 A8
Springhead 189 C5
Springvale 176 B8
Standford 165 A2
Standon 196 B2
Stanford End 13 D3
Stanmore 209 B8
Steep Marsh 207 B1
Steventon 89 B4
Stockbridge 149 F3
Stoke 61 D4
Stoke Charity 132 B3
Stone Copse 2 C7
Stony Batter 191 D8
Stonymarsh 193 B1
Stratfield Mortimer . . . 12 B5
Stratfield Saye 29 F8
Stratfield Turgis 30 B4
Stratton Turgis 30 B4
Sutton Scotney 131 C3
Swallowfield 14 A6
Swampton 61 F2
Swelling Hill 181 F6
Sydmonton 43 B8

T

Tadley 27 A7
Tangley 58 F6
Testcombe 128 C3
Thatcham 2 E2
The Beeches 80 E5
The Bourne 122 B6
The Butts 139 E2
The Common 168 B5
The Green 191 B7
The Sands 100 C2
The Soke
  New Alresford 179 E6
  Winchester 209 F5
The Straits 142 B3
Three Ashes 28 B7
Thruxton 103 E8
Tichborne Down 179 E4
Tidworth 78 E6
Tilford 122 F4
Tilford Reeds 122 E3
Tilly Down 62 D8
Tongham 100 E6
Totford 157 A8
Tot Hill 22 C8
Towns End 25 E2
Tufton 84 F8
Tunworth 93 C6
Turgis Green 30 B3

U

Up Green 33 C6
Up Nately 71 B4
Upper Bullington 131 D8
Upper Chute 57 F8
Upper Clatford 105 E4
Upper Common 115 A7
Upper Enham 83 C8

Upper Farringdon . . . 161 F3
Upper Froyle 119 A2
Upper Hale 99 A6
Upper Slackstead . . . 195 B1
Upper Wield 136 F2
Upper Wootton 46 B2
Up Sombourne 173 C5
Upton 39 A3
Upton Grey 94 A5

V

Vernham Bank 38 A6
Vernham Dean 38 B5
Vernham Row 38 B8
Vernham Street 38 E7
Viables 69 A1

W

Wadwick 62 C6
Warnborough Green . . 72 C4
Warren Corner 206 B5
Wash Common 5 C5
Wash Water 5 B4
Wasing 9 B5
Water End 71 B7
Weeke 209 B8
West Dean 190 D3
West End 159 C4
West End Green 29 B8
West Fields 1 D2
West Green 51 F5
West Ham 68 E5
West Heath
  Farnborough 55 C5
  Tadley 26 C1
West Hill 209 C6
West Liss 207 F5
West Meon Woodlands 203 C2
Weston Colley 132 E4
Weston Corbett 93 F3
Weston Patrick 94 A2
West Stratton 133 E5
West Tisted 203 D7
West Tytherley 169 B1
West Woodhay 3 A3
West Worldham 162 E6
Weybourne 99 D7
Weyhill 81 C2
Wharf Hill 209 E4
Wheat Hold 25 D6
Wheatley 142 A5
Wherwell 128 F6
Whitchurch 86 D6
Whitehall 72 F6
Whitehill 164 C1
Whitway 22 B3
Wildhern 59 E2
Wildmoor 49 E5
Wilsom 140 B3
Winchester 209 B4
Winchfield 52 C2
Winchfield Hurst 52 F1
Winklebury 68 C6
Winnall 198 C8
Winslade 92 F5
Wivelrod 138 C2
Wolverton 25 C2
Wolverton Common . . . 25 E4
Woodcott 43 D2
Woodhouse 83 D7
Woodlands 179 B5
Woodmancott 112 E1
Woolmer Hill 189 A6
Woolton Hill 21 C7
Wootton St Lawrence . . 67 D7
Worthy Down Camp . . 153 E3
Worting 68 A5
Wrecclesham 121 D7
Wyck 141 B4

Y

Yateley 34 B6
Yateley Green 34 A7
York Town 35 E5

212 Abb – Ass

A

Abbas Bsns Ctr SO21 ....177 F6
Abbatt Cl SP11 ....57 B2
Abberbury Cl (Almshouses) RG14 ....1 C6
Abbetts La GU15 ....35 F3
Abbey Bsns Pk GU9 ....122 E8
Abbey Cl RG14 ....5 E8
Abbey Ct
4 Andover SP10 ....105 F8
Basingstoke RG24 ....48 A1
2 Camberley GU15 ....36 B5
5 Farnham GU9 ....99 A2
Abbey Hill Cl SO23 ....209 E8
Abbey Hill Rd SO23 ....209 E8
Abbey Pas SO23 ....209 E5
Abbey Rd
Basingstoke RG24 ....69 A8
Medstead GU34 ....160 C8
Abbey Sch The GU9 ....99 B1
Abbey St GU9 ....99 A2
Abbey Terr SP11 ....61 C4
Abbey Way GU14 ....56 A4
Abbeydore Cl GU35 ....165 C5
Abbot's Ride GU9 ....99 C1
Abbots Cl GU51 ....54 A1
Abbots Lea Cotts SO23 ....176 B3
Abbots Rd RG14 ....1 E1
Abbots Row 1 SO22 ....209 D6
Abbotstone Rd SO24 ....179 D7
Abbotswood Cl RG26 ....26 F7
Abbott Cl RG22 ....68 C2
Abbott's Ann CE Prim Sch SP11 ....104 F3
Abbotts Ann Rd
Monxton SP11 ....104 C5
Winchester SO22 ....175 D3
Abbotts Cl
Abbotts Ann SP11 ....105 A4
North Tidworth SP9 ....78 E7
Winchester SO23 ....209 E8
Abbotts Cotts GU10 ....143 C5
Abbotts Ct SO22 ....209 D8
Abbotts Hill SP11 ....105 A4
Abbotts Rd
North Tidworth SP9 ....78 E7
Winchester SO23 ....209 E8
Aberdeen Terr 1 GU26 ....167 B3
Abex Rd RG14 ....2 A3
Abingdon Rd GU47 ....35 A8
Above Town SP11 ....105 E4
Academy Cl GU15 ....36 C8
Academy Gate GU15 ....35 F6
Academy Pl GU47 ....35 C7
Accentors Cl GU34 ....139 F6
Acheulian Cl GU9 ....122 A7
Achilles Cl RG24 ....48 F4
Ackender Rd GU34 ....139 E3
Acorn Cl Basingstoke RG21 ....69 E5
Winchester SO22 ....209 B8
Acorn Keep GU9 ....99 B8
Acorn Mews GU14 ....55 E7
Acorn Rd GU17 ....34 F5
Acre Almshouses 6 SP10 ....106 B8
Acre Ct SP10 ....106 A7
Acre Path SP10 ....106 C8
Acton Ho RG22 ....68 E4
Adam Cl RG26 ....9 C1
Adampur Rd SP9 ....78 C4
Adams Cl
North Tidworth SP11 ....79 D6
North Warnborough RG29 ....72 B3
Adams Dr GU51 ....54 C1
Adams Ho GU34 ....140 A4
Adams Mews 1 GU30 ....188 A2
Adams Park Rd GU9 ....99 B3
Adams Way GU34 ....140 A4
Addison Cl SO22 ....209 A3
Addison Gdns RG29 ....72 E3
Addison Rd GU16 ....56 C8
Adelaide Rd SP10 ....106 B8
Adey's Cl RG14 ....1 F2
Adlington Pl GU14 ....56 C2
Admers Cres GU30 ....188 A2
Admirals Way SP10 ....106 D8
Admiralty Way GU15 ....35 D4
Adrian Cl RG27 ....52 D5
Aerospace Bvd GU14 ....76 D7
Aghemund Cl RG24 ....48 E3
Agra Rd SP9 ....78 C4
Agricola Wlk SP10 ....83 A3
Ainger Cl GU12 ....77 B3
Aintree Cl RG14 ....2 A1
Airborne Forces Mus* GU11 ....76 E5
Aircraft Espl GU14 ....56 A1
Aird Cl RG20 ....21 C8
Airlie Cnr SO22 ....209 C4
Airlie La SO22 ....209 C4
Airlie Rd SO22 ....209 C4
Ajax Cl RG24 ....48 F4
Alamein Rd
Aldershot GU11 ....76 F2
Enham Alamein SP11 ....83 B7
Alanbrooke Cl RG27 ....52 C6
Alanbrooke Rd GU11 ....77 B6
Albany Cl GU51 ....75 B8
Albany Ct Fleet GU51 ....54 B1
Frimley GU16 ....36 A1
Albany Mews SP10 ....105 E8
Albany Park Ind Est GU16 ....36 A1
Albany Pk Camberley GU16 ....35 F1
Frimley GU16 ....36 A1
Albany Rd Andover SP10 ....105 E8
Fleet GU51 ....75 A8
Albert Ct SO23 ....209 D7
Albert Rd Aldershot GU11 ....76 F2
Alton GU34 ....139 E2
Camberley GU15 ....36 A5
Farnborough GU14 ....56 A2
Newbury RG14 ....1 E3
Albert St GU51 ....53 F1
Albert Yd 8 RG21 ....69 B4
Albion Pl
Hartley Wintney RG27 ....52 C6
14 Winchester SO23 ....209 E6
Albion Rd GU47 ....34 F8
Albury Way RG19 ....6 D4
Alder Cl Alton GU34 ....139 E5
Ash Vale GU12 ....77 E7
Newbury RG14 ....2 B4
Alder Gr GU46 ....34 A5
Alder Rd GU35 ....165 F6
Alder Wood Dr RG27 ....51 B2
Aldermaston CE Prim Sch RG7 ....9 D7
Aldermaston Rd
Basingstoke RG24 ....68 F8
Pamber End RG26 ....27 B3
Pamber Heath RG26 ....9 E2
Sherborne St John RG24, RG26 ....47 D5
Aldermaston Rd S RG21 ....68 F7
Alderney Ave RG22 ....91 B7
Alders Ct SO24 ....179 D6
Alders The GU9 ....99 F6
Aldersey Flds GU34 ....139 F5
Aldershot Military Mus* GU11 ....77 A7
Aldershot Rd Ash GU12 ....77 D1
Fleet GU51 ....75 B8
Fleet,Church Crookham GU52 ....75 C5
Aldershot Sta GU11 ....76 F1
Alderwood RG24 ....48 F3
Aldrin Cl SP10 ....82 E3
Aldrin Pl GU14 ....55 B4
Aldwick Cl GU14 ....55 E6
Aldworth Cres RG22 ....68 E4
Aldworth Science Coll RG22 ....68 D2
Aldwych Cotts RG14 ....1 D6
Alencon Link RG21 ....69 B5
Alexander Cl SO20 ....171 B5
Alexander Ct 4 RG14 ....1 F2
Alexander Ho 6 SP9 ....78 E8
Alexander Rd RG25 ....88 B7
Alexander Terr RG29 ....72 C4
Alexandra Ave GU15 ....35 E5
Alexandra Ct
Aldershot GU11 ....76 C1
Bordon GU35 ....164 E3
10 Farnborough GU14 ....56 A1
Alexandra Ho
1 Basingstoke RG21 ....69 C6
Enham Alamein SP11 ....83 B8
Alexandra Rd
Aldershot GU11 ....76 C1
Alton GU34 ....139 F5
Andover SP10 ....105 F8
Ash GU12 ....77 D1
Basingstoke RG21 ....68 F5
Farnborough GU14 ....56 A1
Alexandra Terr
5 Aldershot GU11 ....76 E2
Winchester SO23 ....209 D5
Alexandria Rd SO21 ....131 D5
Alfonso Cl GU12 ....100 A8
Alford Cl GU47 ....34 E7
Alfred Cl GU51 ....53 D3
Alfred Gdns SP10 ....82 F2
Alfred Rd GU9 ....99 A1
Alice Holt Cotts GU10 ....120 F2
Alice Holt Woodland Park Forest Ctr* GU10 ....143 A8
Alice Rd GU11 ....76 F2
Alison Cl GU14 ....55 D3
Alison Dr GU15 ....36 D5
Alison Way
Aldershot GU11 ....76 D2
6 Winchester SO22 ....209 D6
Alison's Rd GU11 ....76 F4
All Hallows RC Sch GU9 ....99 D7
All Saints CE Jun Sch GU51 ....74 D8
All Saints CE Prim Sch SO23 ....209 F4
All Saints Cres GU14 ....35 C1
Allden Ave GU12 ....100 B7
Allden Gdns GU12 ....100 B7
Allee Dr GU30 ....187 F5
Allen Cl Alton GU34 ....140 A5
Basingstoke RG21 ....68 F3
Allen Gallery* GU34 ....139 F3
Allenby Rd GU15 ....35 E6
Alliston Way
Basingstoke RG22 ....68 B3
Whitchurch RG28 ....86 D4
Allnutt Ave RG21 ....69 C5
Alma Cl GU12 ....77 B2
Alma Ho GU12 ....77 B2
Alma La GU9 ....99 A7
Alma Rd Bordon GU35 ....164 E3
Headley GU35 ....166 A5
Alma Sq GU14 ....77 A8
Alma Way GU9 ....99 B7
Almond Ave RG14 ....1 E5
Almond Cl
2 Farnborough GU14 ....55 E7
Old Basing RG24 ....70 A6
Almond Ct GU52 ....75 B6
Almondale Ct GU14 ....55 E6
Almshouses
2 Basingstoke RG21 ....69 B4
East Tisted GU34 ....183 C5
Almswood Rd RG26 ....9 E2
Aloes The GU51 ....75 B8
Alpha Rd GU12 ....77 B1
Alphington Ave GU16 ....36 D1
Alphington Gn GU16 ....36 D1
Alpine Cl GU14 ....55 B3
Alpine Ct RG22 ....68 B3
Alpine Rd GU35 ....164 D1
Alresford Dro SO21 ....153 F5
Alresford Rd
Chilcomb SO21 ....199 D7
Ovington SO24 ....178 E2
Winchester SO23 ....198 D7
Alresford Sta* SO24 ....179 D5
Alsace Wlk GU15 ....35 F1
Alswitha Terr 12 SO23 ....209 E7
Alton Bsns Ctr GU34 ....140 B3
Alton Coll GU34 ....139 F5
Alton Com Hospl GU34 ....139 D1
Alton Convent Sch GU34 ....140 A6
Alton Ct 13 SO23 ....209 E8
Alton Inf Sch GU34 ....140 A4
Alton La GU34 ....160 C1
Alton Rd Farnham GU10 ....121 C7
Fleet GU51 ....75 C8
Odiham RG29 ....95 B6
Alton Ride GU17 ....35 A6
Alton Road Cotts RG29 ....94 F3
Alton Sta GU34 ....140 A4
Altona Gdns SP10 ....82 F3
Alverstoke Gdns GU11 ....76 C1
Alwin Pl GU9 ....99 A7
Amazon Cl RG21 ....68 F4
Amber Cl GU35 ....164 E2
Amber Ct 2 GU12 ....77 A1
Amber Gdns SP10 ....105 D8
Amber Hill GU15 ....36 F4
Amberley Cl RG14 ....1 D4
Amberley Grange GU11 ....99 D8
Amberley Mains 4 GU34 ....139 F4
Amberwood Dr GU15 ....36 D7
Ambleside Cl
Farnborough GU14 ....55 C3
Mytchett GU16 ....56 E2
Ambleside Cres GU9 ....98 E6
Ambrose Rd RG26 ....26 F8
Amery Hill GU34 ....139 F4
Amery Hill Sch GU34 ....139 F4
Amery St GU34 ....139 F3
Amesbury Ho 3 SP9 ....79 A6
Amesbury Rd
Cholderton SP4 ....101 B1
Newton Tony SP4 ....123 A6
Weyhill SP11 ....81 B1
Amesbury Sch GU26 ....167 C1
Amherst Rd GU35 ....164 D6
Ampere Rd RG14 ....1 F3
Amport CE Prim Sch SP11 ....104 A5
Amport Cl
Old Basing RG24 ....70 A8
Winchester SO22 ....175 C3
Amport Firs SP11 ....104 A5
Amport Park Mews SP11 ....103 F5
Ancells Ct GU51 ....54 C5
Ancells Rd GU51 ....54 C5
Anchor Mdw GU14 ....55 D4
Anchor Rd RG20 ....24 D2
Anchor Yd
1 Basingstoke RG21 ....69 B4
Kingsclere RG20 ....24 D2
Andeferas Rd SP10 ....82 F3
Anders Rd SO21 ....153 E4
Anderson Ho GU9 ....99 B1
Andlers Ash Rd GU33 ....207 E3
Andover CE Prim Sch SP10 ....106 B7
Andover Dr 3 GU51 ....53 D3
Andover Dro RG20 ....4 F4
Andover La SP11 ....80 A7
Andover Rd
Blackwater GU17 ....35 A6
Fyfield SP11 ....80 E6
Ludgershall SP11 ....57 B1
Micheldever SO21 ....111 A2
Monxton SP11 ....104 D6
Newbury RG20 ....5 B6
Oakley RG23,RG25 ....66 D1
Wash Water RG20 ....4 E1
Winchester SO23 ....209 D8
Andover Road N SO22 ....175 E4
Andover Road Ret Pk SO23 ....209 D7
Andover Sta SP10 ....105 F8
Andover War Meml Hospl SP10 ....82 E1
Andover Way GU11 ....99 F7
Andrew Cl RG29 ....72 B3
Andrew Ct GU14 ....55 D8
Andrew's La
Gilbert Street SO24 ....181 F5
Long Sutton RG29 ....95 F3
Andrewartha Rd GU14 ....56 C2
Andrews Cl GU52 ....75 A6
Andrews Endowed CE Prim Sch GU34 ....140 C6
Andrews Rd GU14 ....55 C5
Andwell La RG24,RG27 ....71 A6
Angel Ct RG14 ....1 E4
Angel Mdws RG29 ....72 E3
Anglesey Ave GU14 ....55 D7
Anglesey Cl
Andover SP10 ....106 A5
Basingstoke RG24 ....48 C2
Anglesey Rd GU12 ....77 B1
Angora Way GU51 ....54 B4
Annandale Dr GU10 ....122 B6
Anne Armstrong Cl GU11 ....77 B5
Annes Way GU52 ....75 B6
Annettes Croft 2 GU52 ....74 E4
Ansell Rd GU16 ....36 C1
Anson Cl GU11 ....76 D3
Anstey Cl RG21 ....69 A2
Anstey Jun Sch GU34 ....139 F4
Anstey La GU34 ....140 A6
Anstey Mill Cl GU34 ....140 B5
Anstey Mill La GU34 ....140 B5
Anstey Rd GU34 ....140 A5
Antar Cl RG21 ....68 F4
Anton Cl RG23 ....67 B1
Anton Inf Sch SP10 ....106 A6
Anton Jun Sch SP10 ....106 A6
Anton La SP11 ....83 B6
Anton Mill Rd SP10 ....106 A7
Anton Rd SP10 ....106 A6
Anton Trad Est SP10 ....106 A7
Antrim Cl RG22 ....68 B3
Anvil Way RG26 ....28 F3
Anzio Cl GU11 ....76 E2
Apex Dr GU16 ....36 B1
Apollo Dr GU35 ....164 E2
Apollo Ho RG7 ....9 C2
Apollo Rise GU14 ....55 B4
Apollonia Ho 7 SP10 ....106 A7
Apple Dene RG26 ....28 F2
Apple Tree Cl RG14 ....5 C7
Apple Tree Gr SP10 ....82 E1
Apple Way RG24 ....70 B5
Appledore Mews GU14 ....55 E7
Appledown Cl SO24 ....179 D4
Appledown La SO24 ....179 E3
Applegarth Cl RG21 ....69 C3
Applegate SP11 ....62 A1
Applelands Cl GU10 ....121 E4
Appleshaw Cl Tadley RG26 ....26 F7
Winchester SO22 ....175 D4
Appleshaw Dene SP11 ....81 B6
Appleshaw Way SP11 ....79 D6
Appleton Cl SO20 ....125 C2
Appleton Mews SP10 ....106 B6
Appleton View GU34 ....183 D5
Appletree Cl RG23 ....90 B8
Appletree Mead RG27 ....51 C1
Appley Ct 1 GU15 ....35 F5
Appley Dr GU15 ....35 F6
Approach Rd GU9 ....99 A1
April Cl GU15 ....36 A2
Apron Rd RG19 ....6 E5
Apsley Cl SP10 ....105 F5
Apsley Ho 1 GU11 ....76 F2
Aquarius Cl GU10 ....74 B1
Aragon Rd GU46 ....34 A4
Arbery Way RG2 ....15 C8
Arboretum The RG25 ....94 B6
Arbour Ct 20 SO22 ....209 D6
Arcade Mews 4 RG14 ....1 E3
Arcade The
10 Aldershot GU11 ....76 E2
Liss GU33 ....207 E5
3 Newbury RG14 ....1 E3
Arcadia Cl RG22 ....91 A4
Archery Fields RG29 ....72 F3
Archery La SO23 ....209 D5
Archery Rise GU34 ....139 E2
Arcot Rd SP9 ....78 E3
Ardglen Rd RG28 ....86 C6
Ardrossan Ave GU15 ....36 E5
Arena L Ctr GU15 ....36 A5
Arena La GU11 ....76 C5
Arford Comm
Headley GU35 ....165 D6
Headley GU35 ....165 E6
Arford Rd GU35 ....165 D5
Argent Terr GU47 ....35 C8
Argente Cl GU51 ....54 B4
Argyle Cl GU35 ....164 D2
Argyle Rd RG14 ....1 D2
Argyll Ct 2 GU51 ....54 A1
Arkle Ave RG19 ....2 D3
Arkwright Cl RG20 ....21 D6
Arkwright Gate SP10 ....82 B2
Arle Cl SO24 ....179 C6
Arle Gdns SO24 ....179 D6
Arlebury Park Ho SO24 ....179 B6
Arlington Pl 3 SO23 ....209 E6
Arlington Terr GU11 ....76 D1
Arlott Cl RG27 ....33 C8
Arlott Dr RG21 ....69 B7
Armitage Dr GU16 ....36 D1
Armstrong Cl SO21 ....153 E4
Armstrong Mall GU14 ....55 B4
Armstrong Rd RG24 ....69 E7
Armstrong Rise SP10 ....82 E3
Armstrong Way GU14 ....75 F8
Arne Cl RG22 ....91 D7
Arnell Ct 2 GU14 ....77 B8
Arnett Ave RG40 ....16 D7
Arnewood Ave RG26 ....27 B8
Arnhem Cl GU11 ....76 F2
Arnhem Rd RG14 ....1 F3
Arran Cl RG23 ....67 A2
Arrow Ind Est GU14 ....55 D2
Arrow La RG27 ....52 B7
Arrow Rd GU14 ....55 D2
Artemis Ho RG14 ....1 F4
Arthur Cl GU9 ....98 F1
Arthur Ct
4 Basingstoke RG21 ....69 A5
Four Marks GU34 ....160 B3
Arthur Rd Farnham GU9 ....99 A1
Newbury RG14 ....1 C2
Winchester SO23 ....209 E7
Arthur St GU11 ....76 F2
Arthur's La SP11 ....20 A1
Artillery Rd
Aldershot GU11 ....76 F2
Farnborough GU11 ....77 B7
Artists Way SP10 ....83 A1
Arun Ct RG21 ....69 D5
Arundel Cl Fleet GU51 ....75 B8
Liphook GU30 ....187 B8
New Alresford SO24 ....179 D4
Arundel Gdns RG23 ....68 B7
Arundell Pl 8 GU9 ....98 F2
Ascension Cl RG24 ....48 D1
Ascot Cl Alton GU34 ....140 A2
Newbury RG14 ....6 A8
Ascot Ct GU11 ....76 E1
Ascott Way RG14 ....2 B4
Ash Bridge Cvn Pk GU12 ....100 C8
Ash Church Mews GU12 ....77 E2
Ash Church Rd GU12 ....77 F2
Ash Cl Ash GU12 ....77 F3
Blackwater GU17 ....35 A5
North Tidworth SP9 ....79 A7
Ash Cres RG19 ....7 E5
Ash Ct 6 RG14 ....1 E4
Ash Gr Kingsclere RG20 ....24 D2
Liphook GU30 ....188 B3
Old Basing RG24 ....70 C6
Ash Grange Prim Sch GU12 ....77 F2
Ash Green La W GU10, GU12 ....100 D8
Ash Hill Rd GU12 ....77 F3
Ash La Bramley RG7,RG26 ....28 B6
Pamber Heath RG26 ....9 C1
Ash Lodge Cl GU12 ....77 E1
Ash Lodge Dr GU12 ....77 E1
Ash Manor Sch GU12 ....100 D8
Ash Park Cotts RG25 ....89 B7
Ash Rd Aldershot GU12 ....100 B8
Bishop's Green RG20 ....6 D3
Ash St GU12 ....77 E1
Ash Sta GU12 ....77 F2
Ash Terr RG18 ....2 F8
Ash Tree Cl
Farnborough GU14 ....55 A3
Oakley RG23 ....90 A8
Ash Tree Gr RG20 ....3 F7
Ash Tree Rd SP10 ....105 C8
Ash Vale Sta GU12 ....77 E7
Ash Wlk SO24 ....179 D5
Ashbarn Cres SO22 ....209 C3
Ashbourne Way RG19 ....2 F3
Ashburton Cl SO24 ....179 C5
Ashburton Rd SO24 ....179 C5
Ashbury Dr GU17 ....35 E1
Ashbury Rd GU35 ....164 D2
Ashdell Rd GU34 ....140 A3
Ashdene Cres GU12 ....77 E3
Ashdene Rd GU12 ....77 E2
Ashdown Ave GU14 ....56 C2
Ashdown Terr SP9 ....78 F5
Ashfield RG24 ....48 F3
Ashfield Gn GU46 ....34 D5
Ashfield Rd SP10 ....105 D8
Ashfields SO21 ....130 D6
Ashford Chace GU32 ....206 E1
Ashford Hill Prim Sch RG19 ....8 C1
Ashford Hill Rd RG19 ....7 D2
Ashlawn Gdns SP10 ....106 B6
Ashlea RG27 ....51 B2
Ashley Cl Camberley GU16 ....56 E6
Crondall GU10 ....97 D7
Winchester SO22 ....175 C3
Ashley Ct Alton GU34 ....140 A4
Buttermere SN8 ....17 F6
Ashley Dr GU17 ....35 A4
Ashley Dro SN8 ....17 F5
Ashley Gdns RG23 ....67 B2
Ashley Ho 4 GU35 ....164 D2
Ashley Lodge 9 RG21 ....69 A3
Ashley Mews 9 GU9 ....99 A2
Ashley Rd
Bentworth GU34 ....138 A5
Farnborough GU14 ....56 B3
Ashmead GU35 ....164 D3
Ashmoor La RG24 ....70 E7
Ashmore Green Rd RG18 ....2 F7
Ashmore La SP5 ....190 C1
Ashmore Rd SO22 ....209 B7
Ashridge GU14 ....55 C7
Ashridge Ct 2 RG14 ....1 E2
Ashton Rd RG14 ....1 F2
Ashtree Cnr RG20 ....4 A7
Ashtrees The GU12 ....77 F2
Ashurst Cl Tadley RG26 ....26 E8
Winchester SO22 ....175 D3
Ashurst Rd GU12 ....77 D4
Ashwell Ave GU15 ....36 D6
Ashwood Dr RG14 ....2 B4
Ashwood Way RG23 ....68 D7
Ashwood Way Rdbt RG23 ....68 D7
Aspen Cl GU35 ....164 D1
Aspen Gdns RG27 ....51 B2
Aspen Gr GU12 ....100 C8
Aspen Ho GU11 ....100 A7
Aspin Way GU17 ....34 F5
Assheton Ct 3 SP9 ....78 F7

Aster Ct 5 SP10 105 D6
Aster Rd RG22 91 A7
Astley Cl RG14 1 B2
Astor Mews SP9 101 E7
Atbara Rd GU52 75 A4
Athlone Cl SP11 83 B8
Atholl Ct SP10 83 A3
Atholl Rd GU35 164 D1
Atlantean Ct RG14 1 F3
Atlantic Ct SO22 209 A5
Atrium The
Basingstoke RG21 69 B5
29 Winchester SO23 209 D6
Attenborough Cl GU51 54 B3
Attfield Cl GU12 77 D1
Attlee Gdns GU52 74 F4
Attwood Cl RG21 68 F4
Attwood Close Mobile Home Pk RG21 68 F4
Attwood Cl RG2 15 C8
Attwoods Dro SO21 197 D1
Auchinleck Ho 3 SP9 78 E8
Auchinleck Way GU11 76 C2
Audley Cl RG14 2 B5
Audley Ho GU9 122 B7
Audrey Needham Ho 6 RG14 1 F2
Augustine Way SP10 82 D3
Augustus Dr RG23 68 C7
Augustus Wlk SP10 83 B3
Auklet Cl RG22 90 F7
Aurora Dr RG22 91 A4
Austen Ave SO22 209 A2
Austen Cl SO23 209 E8
Austen Gdns RG14 5 F8
Austen Gr RG22 68 E2
Austen Rd GU14 55 E6
Austin's Cotts GU9 98 E1
Aveley La GU9 122 A7
Avenue Cl Andover SP10 105 E8
Liphook GU30 187 F4
Avenue Rd
Farnborough GU14 56 B3
Fleet GU51 53 F2
Grayshott GU26 167 A3
Winchester SO22 209 C6
Avenue Sucy GU15 35 E4
Avenue The
Aldershot GU12 100 A7
Andover SP10 105 F8
Barton Stacey SP11 108 C3
Camberley GU15 35 F5
Farleigh Wallop RG22 91 D2
Fleet GU51 53 E1
Golden Pot GU34 117 B4
Grayshott GU26 167 B3
Haslemere GU27 189 D7
Hatherden SP11 59 E2
Liphook GU30 187 F4
Middle Wallop SO20 126 B4
Mortimer RG7 11 F5
New Alresford SO24 179 C5
Rowledge GU10 121 D3
South Tidworth SP9 78 E4
Southrope RG25,GU34 116 D4
Avery Cl RG40 16 D6
Avery Ct 6 GU11 76 F2
Aviary Ct RG24 69 E8
Aviemore Dr RG23 67 A1
Avington Ct SO22 209 A5
Avington Pk* SO21 177 E5
Avlan Ct SO23 209 D3
Avocet Cres GU47 35 C8
Avon Cl Ash GU12 77 D1
Farnborough GU14 55 C7
Avon Ct 14 Andover SP10 83 C2
Farnham GU9 99 A1
Avon Rd Farnham GU9 99 A1
Oakley RG23 67 B2
South Tidworth SP9 78 E5
Avon Wlk 19 RG21 69 D5
Avondale GU12 77 D7
Avondale Rd
Aldershot GU11 99 F8
Fleet GU51 54 B2
Avonway RG14 2 B4
Award Rd GU52 75 A5
Axford Rd RG25 115 A5
Ayesgarth GU52 75 B5
Ayjay Cl GU11 99 F7
Aylesham Way GU46 33 F6
Ayliffe Ho RG22 68 D4
Ayling Ct GU9 99 D7
Ayling Hill GU11 76 D1
Ayling La GU11 99 D8
Aylings Cl RG22 68 B3
Aylward's Dr GU34 161 C3
Aylwards Way SO20 147 F5
Aylwin Cl RG21 69 A2
Ayres La RG20 22 E8
Ayrshire Gdns GU51 54 B4
Azalea Ave GU35 165 A5
Azalea Ct SP10 105 D6
Azalea Dr GU27 189 D8
Azalea Gdns GU52 75 B5
Azalea Rd RG19 7 E5
Azalea Way GU15 36 F6

B

Babbs Mead GU9 98 E1
Babs Fields GU10 120 A5
Bacchus Ho 7 RG7 9 C2
Bach Cl RG22 91 D7
Back La Appleshaw SP11 81 D6
Brimpton RG7 9 A5
Bucks Horn Oak GU10 142 F8
Back La *continued*
Mottisfont SO51 192 E5
Silchester RG7 11 B4
Southrope RG25,GU34 116 D5
Swallowfield RG7 13 E8
Vernham Dean SP11 38 C6
Back St SO23 209 D2
Bacon Cl GU47 35 B6
Bacon La GU10 144 A3
Badajos Rd GU11 76 D3
Baden Powell Rd GU33 186 D2
Bader Ct GU14 55 D8
Badger Cl GU34 160 C3
Badger Ct GU10 121 E5
Badger Farm Rd SO22 209 B1
Badger Way
Aldershot GU12 77 B3
Ewshot GU10 98 B8
Badger's Bank RG24 69 F8
Badgers Cl GU52 74 F8
Badgers Copse GU15 36 C4
Badgers Croft RG7 11 E6
Badgers Holt GU46 33 F5
Badgers Ridge RG20 5 B4
Badgerwood Dr GU16 36 B2
Badshear La SO24 201 F8
Badshot Lea Rd GU9 99 E5
Badshot Lea Village Inf Sch GU9 99 E6
Badshot Pk GU9 99 E6
Badsworth Gdns RG14 5 B5
Bagmore La
Ellisfield RG25 115 E5
Herriard RG25 116 A6
Bagnols Way RG14 1 C2
Bagwell La RG27,RG29 73 C7
Baigent Cl SO23 198 C8
Bailey Cl Camberley GU16 56 B8
Winchester SO22 209 B4
Bailey Ho
Basingstoke RG21 68 F1
2 New Alresford SO24 179 D6
Baileys Cl GU17 35 A4
Baily Ave RG18 2 F4
Bain Ave GU15 35 F2
Baird Ave RG22 68 E2
Baird Rd
Arborfield Garrison RG2 15 C7
Farnborough GU14 56 A6
Bakehouse Gdns GU52 75 B5
Bakers Field GU33 185 F2
Bakers Yd RG23 90 B8
Baldreys GU9 121 E8
Balfour Cres RG14 5 A6
Balfour Dr GU33 207 F4
Balfour Red Cross Mus* SO23 176 C1
Balintore Ct 1 GU47 35 B7
Balksbury Hill SP11 105 E5
Balksbury Hill Ind Est SP11 105 E5
Balksbury Inf Sch SP10 105 D7
Balksbury Jun Sch SP10 105 D6
Balksbury Rd SP11 105 E5
Ball & Wicket La GU9 99 A7
Ballantyne Rd GU14 55 E6
Ballard Cl RG22 68 C3
Ballard Ct GU15 36 E8
Ballard Rd GU15 36 E8
Balldown Cvn & Camping Pk SO21 174 C6
Balmoral Cl GU34 139 D3
Balmoral Cres GU9 98 F6
Balmoral Ct
Basingstoke RG22 68 C3
11 Farnborough GU14 55 F4
Balmoral Dr GU16 56 D8
Balmoral Ho GU12 77 D5
Balmoral Rd
Andover SP10 106 A8
Ash Vale GU12 77 E4
Balmoral Way RG25 91 A6
Balsan Cl RG24 68 C8
Bamber La GU34 119 B4
Banbury Cl GU16 56 E7
Band Hall Pl RG27 51 A1
Bank Rd GU11 77 B5
Bank Side RG40 16 D6
Banks Cl SP10 105 E7
Bankside GU9 99 D7
Bankside Ho 3 SO22 209 C6
Bannister Gdns
Eversley Cross RG27 33 C8
Yateley GU46 34 D5
Bannister Pl RG7 8 D6
Baptist Hill SP11 61 F2
Bar End Ind Est SO23 209 F3
Bar End Rd SO23 209 F4
Barbara Cl GU52 75 B6
Barbel Ave RG21 69 E5
Barberry Cl GU52 75 A6
Barberry Way GU17 35 D2
Barbour Cl RG29 95 C8
Barcelona Cl SP10 83 B1
Bardsley Dr GU9 121 E7
Bardwell Cl RG22 68 C4
Baredown The RG27 71 D7
Barfield Cl SO23 209 F4
Barfield Rd RG18 2 E4
Barfield Sch GU10 99 F3
Barford Cl GU51 75 D8
Barge Cl GU11 77 C5
Barge La Swallowfield RG7 13 E5
Swallowfield,Stanford End RG7 13 D4
Baring Cl
East Stratton SO21 134 A4
Baring Cl *continued*
Itchen Abbas SO21 178 A7
Baring Rd SO23 209 F5
Barker Cl RG2 15 C7
Barkham Ride RG40 16 C8
Barley Down Dr SO22 209 B2
Barley Mow Cl RG27 73 F8
Barley Mow Hill GU35 165 E6
Barley View RG25 89 F1
Barley Way GU51 54 B5
Barlows La SP10 105 F5
Barlows Rd RG26 26 F7
Barn Cl GU15 36 C6
Barn Close La RG20 40 F8
Barn Cres RG14 5 B7
Barn La Four Marks GU34 159 F1
Oakley RG23 90 A8
Barn Meadow Cl GU52 74 E3
Barn The 3 GU34 139 F4
Barnard Cl GU16 56 D8
Barnard Way GU11 76 D3
Barncroft Appleshaw SP11 81 B5
Farnham GU9 99 A1
Barnes Cl
Farnborough GU14 56 B4
Winchester SO23 209 D3
Barnes Rd GU16 56 C8
Barnes Terr 9 RG14 1 D2
Barnet Side La GU32, GU34 205 D5
Barnetts Wood La SO24 181 A8
Barnfield GU46 34 B5
Barnfield Cl GU34 119 C4
Barnfield Cotts GU34 184 A6
Barnfield Rise SP10 105 E6
Barns The RG25 113 C8
Barnside Way GU33 207 F3
Barnsley Cl GU12 56 F2
Barnwells Ct RG27 52 D7
Baroda Rd SP9 78 C4
Barons The GU16 36 A1
Barossa Rd GU15 36 B7
Barra Cl RG23 67 A2
Barrack Rd GU11 76 E2
Barracks The SO21 108 A1
Barracuda Rd GU11 76 C7
Barrett Ct RG21 69 C2
Barrie Rd GU9 98 E7
Barron Pl RG24 68 C8
Barrow Hill SP11 127 E8
Barrowfield SP11 105 F1
Barry Way RG22 91 D7
Bartholomew Cl 7 SO23 209 E7
Bartholomew Ct 8 RG14 1 D2
Bartholomew St RG14 1 D2
Bartlemy Cl RG14 5 C8
Bartlemy Rd RG14 5 C8
Bartlett Cl RG26 29 B2
Bartlett Pl GU16 56 D5
Bartley Way RG27 72 C8
Bartley Wood Bsns Pk RG27 72 C8
Bartok Cl RG22 68 E1
Barton Cl Aldershot GU11 76 C1
Andover SP10 82 D3
Barton Ct 2 GU14 56 A1
Barton Dro SO21 131 A4
Barton End 2 GU34 139 E3
Barton Ind Est SO24 158 F8
Barton Stacey CE Prim Sch SO21 130 E8
Barton's Ct RG29 72 D3
Barton's Dr GU46 34 B4
Bartons La RG24 70 A7
Bartons Way GU14 55 B7
Basepoint Bsns Ctr SP10 82 D2
Basepoint Ent Ctr RG24 69 E8
Basing Barns GU34 204 D5
Basing Dean GU34 204 E4
Basing Dr GU11 99 F7
Basing Ho* RG24 70 A6
Basing Rd RG24 69 F6
Basing View RG21 69 C6
Basingbourne Cl GU52 75 A6
Basingbourne Rd GU52 75 A6
Basingfield Cl RG24 70 C4
Basingstoke Bsns Ctr RG22 68 E2
Basingstoke Canal Ctr* GU16 56 E3
Basingstoke Coll of Tech RG21 69 A4
Basingstoke Rd
Aldermaston RG7 9 D8
Alton GU34 139 C2
Itchen Abbas SO21 155 A4
Kings Worthy SO21,SO23 176 D7
Kingsclere RG20 24 E2
Ramsdell RG26 46 E5
Riseley RG7 14 A3
Stratfield Turgis RG27 30 E6
Swallowfield RG7 14 A6
Basingstoke School Plus RG22 68 C1
Basingstoke Sta RG21 69 B6
Bassenthwaite Gdns GU35 164 D5
Bassett Cl GU16 56 C8
Bat & Ball La GU10 121 E6
Batchelor Dr RG24 70 C5
Batchelors Barn Rd SP10 106 C8
Bateman Gr GU12 100 D8
Bath Rd Camberley GU15 36 B6
Newbury RG14 1 B4
Thatcham RG18 2 E4
Batsford SP11 61 F2
Batt's Cnr GU10 143 B7
Battens Ave RG25 88 B8
Battery End RG14 5 B6
Battery Hill SO22 209 A4
Battle Cl RG14 1 B4
Battle Rd RG14 5 A6
Baughurst Rd
Baughurst RG26 26 C5
Padworth RG7 10 E6
Ramsdell RG26 46 D8
Baveno Ho GU14 56 A1
Baverstocks GU34 140 A6
Baxendales The RG14 2 A1
Bay Tree Yd SO24 179 D6
Bayfield Ave GU16 36 C2
Bayford Cl GU17 35 E1
Baynard Cl RG21 69 C7
Bays Ct RG26 9 D1
Baytree Ho 24 SO23 209 D6
Baywood Cl GU14 55 A5
Bazaar Rd SP9 78 D5
Beach Piece Way RG22 91 B7
Beach's Cres RG26 27 E3
Beacon Cl GU10 121 E5
Beacon Hill Com Prim Sch GU26 167 A6
Beacon Hill Ct GU26 167 B6
Beacon Hill Rd
Beacon Hill GU26 167 B6
Ewshot GU10 98 C8
Fleet GU10,GU52 75 C3
Beacon Pass RG20 42 A8
Beacon Rd GU14 76 F8
Beacon View Ho GU26 167 A3
Beaconsfield Rd RG21 69 B4
Beal's Pightle RG26 46 F8
Beale's Cl SP10 106 B8
Beale's Ct SP5 169 A1
Beales La GU10 121 D7
Bealeswood La GU10 143 D6
Beam Hollow GU9 99 A7
Bear Ct RG24 69 F7
Bear Hill RG20 24 C1
Bear La Farnham GU9 99 A3
Newbury RG14 1 E3
Beard Ct SP11 57 A2
Bearwood Cotts GU10 121 D7
Bearwood Gdns 7 GU51 54 A1
Beatrice Ho 3 RG21 69 C6
Beatty Ct SP10 106 C7
Beauclerk Gn RG27 52 C1
Beaufort Rd
Ash Vale GU12 77 D6
Bordon GU35 164 D5
Farnham GU9 99 A3
Fleet GU52 75 B6
Winchester SO23 209 D4
Beaufront Cl GU15 36 E7
Beaufront Rd GU15 36 F7
Beaulieu Cl SO22 175 D4
Beaulieu Ct
15 Andover SP10 83 C2
23 Basingstoke RG21 69 D5
Blackwater GU17 34 F5
Beaulieu Gdns GU17 35 A5
Beaumaris Cl SP10 105 E6
Beaumaris Par GU16 56 D8
Beaumond Gn 11 SO23 209 D5
Beaumont Gr GU11 76 C2
Beaumont Jun Sch GU11 76 D2
Beaurepaire Cl RG26 28 D3
Beaver Ind Est GU30 188 A3
Beaver La GU46 34 C5
Beavers Cl Alton GU34 139 E4
Farnham GU9 98 E2
1 Pamber Heath RG26 9 E1
Beavers Hill GU9 98 D2
Beavers Mews GU35 164 E3
Beavers Rd GU9 98 E2
Bechin Cl GU52 74 D3
Beck Gdns GU9 98 E6
Beck Ind Est The GU12 100 B8
Becket Ct RG23 68 A4
Becket Ho 1 RG14 1 D2
Beckett Cl RG23 68 A5
Beckett Rd SP10 105 E8
Becketts RG27 52 C6
Beddington Ct RG24 70 A8
Bede Dr SP10 82 D3
Bedfield Ho SO23 176 B5
Bedfield La SO23 176 B5
Bedford Ave GU16 56 D5
Bedford Cl Bordon GU35 164 D1
Newbury RG14 5 A5
Bedford Cres GU16 56 D6
Bedford La GU16 56 D6
Bedford Wlk 6 RG21 69 B5
Bedser Sq SP10 83 B3
Beech Ave
Camberley GU15 36 B4
Farnham GU10 122 A5
Middle Wallop SO20 126 B4
Beech Cl Aldershot GU12 100 C8
Bramley RG26 29 A2
Overton RG25 65 B2
Penton Corner SP11 82 A1
Thatcham RG19 7 F5
Thruxton SP11 103 E8
Winchester SO22 197 B3
Beech Copse
Pamber Heath RG26 9 C1
Winchester SO22 175 B1
Beech Ct Crondall GU10 97 E2
Hindhead GU26 167 C4
5 Newbury RG14 1 E4
Whitchurch RG28 86 C6
Beech Dr GU17 35 B4
Beech Gr
Upper Froyle GU34 119 B3
Wherwell SP11 128 F7
Beech Hanger SP4 101 D1
Beech Hanger End GU26 166 F3
Beech Hanger Rd GU26 166 F3
Beech Hill GU35 165 F5
Beech Hill Ho RG7 13 C6
Beech Hill Rd
Headley GU35 165 E6
North Tidworth SP9 79 A7
Swallowfield RG7 13 C7
Beech Ho RG24 49 A4
Beech La GU26 166 F4
Beech Rd
Bishop's Green RG20 6 E3
Camberley GU16 56 D6
Farnborough GU14 55 E7
New Alresford SO24 179 D5
Beech Ride Fleet GU52 74 F7
Sandhurst GU47 34 F8
Beech Tree Cl RG23 90 A8
Beech Tree Dr GU9 99 E5
Beech Tree Wlk SO20 170 D3
Beech Way RG23 68 C7
Beech Wlk SP10 105 D7
Beecham Berry RG22 91 D7
Beechbrook Ave GU46 34 C5
Beechcrest View RG27 51 B2
Beechcroft Cl
Andover SP10 83 A1
Liphook GU30 187 B3
Beechcroft Cotts SO20 170 B6
Beechdown Ho RG22 68 C1
Beeches The
Andover SP10 105 E8
Ash Vale GU12 56 D1
Basingstoke RG22 91 D6
Sutton Scotney SO21 131 C4
Tadley RG26 26 E8
Beechfield SP4 123 B6
Beeching Cl GU12 77 F3
Beechlands Rd GU34 160 B4
Beechnut Dr GU17 34 F6
Beechnut Ind Est 1 GU11 76 F1
Beechnut Rd GU12 76 F1
Beechwood RG24 48 E3
Beechwood Cl
Basingstoke RG22 91 C6
Fleet GU51 74 E6
Beechwood Ct GU33 208 A6
Beechwood Rd GU34 139 D2
Beestons Cotts RG27 51 A1
Beethoven Rd RG22 91 E7
Beeton's Ave GU12 77 E4
Beggar's La SO23 209 F6
Beggars Dro SO21 131 D3
Beggarwood La RG22 91 B5
Begonia Cl RG22 91 A7
Belaga Cl SO20 126 A5
Beldham Rd GU9 121 D7
Belfry Mews GU47 34 D8
Belfry Sq RG22 91 A5
Belgrave Cres SP9 79 A6
Belgrave Ct GU17 35 B3
Belgrave Mews RG27 52 D6
Bell Cl GU14 56 A6
Bell Hill RG14,RG20 4 F4
Bell Holt RG14 5 A5
Bell La Blackwater GU17 35 A5
Ellisfield RG25 115 D7
Rowledge GU10 121 C3
Bell Meadow Rd RG27 51 B1
Bell Rd Andover SP10 106 C7
Basingstoke RG24 69 E7
Haslemere GU27 189 F3
Bell St Ludgershall SP11 57 A2
Whitchurch RG28 86 C5
Bell Vale La GU27 189 F4
Bell Yd RG28 86 C5
Belland Dr GU11 76 C1
Belle Vue Cl GU12 77 B2
Belle Vue Ent Ctr GU12 77 C2
Belle Vue Ho GU12 77 B2
Belle Vue Inf Sch GU12 77 B2
Belle Vue Rd
Aldershot GU12 77 B2
Andover SP10 106 B6
Old Basing RG24 70 C6
Bellever Hill GU15 36 C5
Bellevue RG28 86 C5
Bellew Rd GU16 56 F7
Bellhanger Ents GU34 138 B6
Belmont Cl Andover SP10 106 B6
Farnborough GU14 55 D7
Belmont Cotts RG20 1 A6
Belmont Ho GU9 121 E8
Belmont Hts RG22 91 C5
Belmont Mews GU15 36 A3
Belmont Rd
Andover SP10 106 B6
Camberley GU15 36 A4
Belsize Rd GU14 56 A1
Belstone Mews GU14 55 E7
Belton Rd GU15 36 C5
Belvedere Cl GU51 53 C1
Belvedere Ct GU17 35 B3
Belvedere Dr RG14 5 E8
Belvedere Gdns RG24 49 A4
Belvedere Rd GU14 56 A2
Belvoir Cl GU16 36 D1
Bembridge Ct 9 GU12 77 A1
Benbow Ct SP10 106 C7

Bendeng Cl 2 GU51 ...53 E3
Benenden Gn SO24 ...179 D4
Benett Cl RG14 ...1 D5
Benett Gdns RG14 ...1 D5
Benford Ct RG29 ...72 E2
Benger's La SO51 ...192 E2
Benham Dro SO20 ...147 D6
Benham Hill RG18 ...2 D4
Benham La RG7 ...14 B3
Benhams La GU33 ...186 A4
Benin Rd SP11 ...79 D6
Bennet Cl Alton GU34 ...139 E4
Basingstoke RG21 ...69 C7
Bennett Ct GU15 ...36 A5
Bennetts Rise GU11 ...100 A8
Bent St SO20 ...147 E7
Benta Cl SO20 ...126 A5
Bental Pl SP10 ...106 A7
Bentley Bsns Pk GU10 ...120 B5
Bentley CE Prim Sch
GU10 ...120 B5
Bentley Cl SO23 ...176 B6
Bentley Copse GU15 ...36 F4
Bentley Ct 4 GU15 ...36 B5
Bentley Dr RG2 ...15 C8
Bentley Ind Ctr GU10 ...120 B4
Bentley Lodge GU51 ...53 D3
Bentley Sta GU10 ...120 C3
Bentley Way SP5 ...168 B5
Benwell Cl RG29 ...95 C8
Bercote Cl SO22 ...175 B5
Bere Cl SO22 ...209 B8
Bere Hill RG28 ...86 D6
Bere Hill Cl RG28 ...86 D6
Bere Hill Cres SP10 ...106 C7
Bere Hill Cvn Site RG28 ...86 D6
Berehurst GU34 ...139 F2
Beresford Cl
Andover SP10 ...106 A5
Camberley GU16 ...56 D6
Beresford Ctr RG24 ...69 E8
Beresford Gate SP10 ...83 F1
Bereweeke Ave SO22 ...209 C8
Bereweeke Cl SO22 ...209 C7
Bereweeke Ho SO22 ...209 C7
Bereweeke Rd SO22 ...209 C7
Bereweeke Way SO22 ...209 C8
Berewyk Cl RG22 ...91 A7
Berkeley Cl GU51 ...54 B1
Berkeley Cres GU16 ...56 E8
Berkeley Dr RG22 ...91 F8
Berkeley Rd RG14 ...1 D2
Berkshire Bsns Pk RG7 ...10 C4
Berkshire Copse Rd
GU11 ...76 C7
Berkshire Ho RG24 ...68 E8
Berkshire Rd GU15 ...36 D8
Bermuda Cl RG24 ...48 C2
Bernard Ave GU34 ...160 B2
Bernard Ct 1 GU15 ...35 F4
Bernard Ho 7 GU51 ...53 E3
Bernstein Rd RG22 ...91 C8
Berry Ct RG27 ...72 A8
Berry Hill SO24 ...181 A5
Berry Way SP10 ...105 D7
Berrybank GU47 ...35 C6
Berrydown La
Axford RG25 ...114 E4
Ellisfield RG25 ...115 B4
Overton RG25 ...88 C7
Berrylands GU33 ...208 A7
Berrywood La SO24 ...137 B6
Berwyn Cl RG22 ...68 A3
Besom Ct RG26 ...26 F7
Bessemer Pk RG21 ...68 F2
Bessemer Rd RG21 ...68 F2
Beta Rd GU14 ...55 E5
Bethel Cl GU9 ...99 B6
Bethel La GU9 ...99 B6
Betjeman Wlk GU46 ...33 F4
Beveren Cl GU51 ...54 B4
Beverley Cl Ash GU12 ...77 D1
Basingstoke RG22 ...69 B1
Beverley Cres GU14 ...55 D2
Bevers The RG7 ...11 E6
Bewicks Reach RG14 ...1 D3
Bexmoor RG24 ...70 A6
Bexmoor Way RG24 ...70 A6
Beyne Rd SO22 ...197 B3
Bible Fields RG25 ...113 C8
Bicester Cl RG28 ...86 C5
Bicknell Rd GU16 ...36 C2
Bidden Rd Odiham RG29 ...72 A2
Upton Grey RG25 ...94 D7
Biddesden La SP11 ...57 D2
Bideford Cl GU14 ...55 E7
Bietigheim Way 1 GU15 ...36 A6
Bigg's Hill Cotts RG20 ...4 D4
Biggs La RG2 ...15 E8
Bighton Dean La SO24 ...158 E1
Bighton Hill SO24 ...181 A6
Bighton La SO24 ...180 D6
Bighton Rd GU34 ...159 C5
Bilbao Ct SP10 ...83 D1
Bilberry Ct 11 SO22 ...209 D6
Billing Ave RG40 ...16 D6
Bilton Rd RG24 ...48 E1
Binfields GU9 ...99 A3
Binfields Cl RG24 ...48 F1
Binfields Rdbt RG24 ...48 E1
Bingley Cl Alton GU34 ...139 E4
Basingstoke RG21 ...69 C7
Binley Bottom SP11 ...61 F5
Binley Ct RG26 ...27 A8
Binstead Rd GU34,GU10 ...142 E8
Binsted CE Prim Sch
GU34 ...141 E7
Binsted Dr GU17 ...35 B5
Binswood View Bsns Ctr
GU35 ...163 D5
Binton La GU10 ...100 C3
Birch Ave Fleet GU51 ...53 F1
Thatcham RG19 ...7 F5
Birch Cl Bordon GU35 ...164 E2
Camberley GU15 ...36 C8
Liss GU33 ...208 A4
Rowledge GU10 ...121 E4
Birch Ct
5 North Tidworth SP9 ...79 A7
Tidworth SP9 ...78 E7
3 Winchester SO22 ...209 A4
Birch Dr GU17 ...35 B3
Birch Gr Bordon GU35 ...164 D1
Chilbolton SO20 ...129 C2
Hook RG27 ...51 B2
Birch Ho 2 GU14 ...55 F7
Birch La RG7 ...11 D6
Birch Mdw GU9 ...99 B6
Birch Rd
Finchampstead RG40 ...16 E7
Headley GU35 ...165 F6
Pamber Heath RG26 ...9 D2
Birch Tree Ct GU27 ...189 A4
Birch Way GU12 ...77 E7
Birchen Coppice SO20 ...126 B4
Birches Crest RG22 ...91 D6
Birches The
Blackwater GU17 ...34 F5
Farnborough GU14 ...55 B4
Birchett Rd
Aldershot GU11 ...76 E2
Farnborough GU14 ...55 D6
Birchfields GU15 ...36 A4
Birchland Cl RG7 ...11 C6
Bircholt Rd GU30 ...187 B4
Birchview Cl GU46 ...34 B4
Birchwood RG24 ...48 F3
Birchwood Rd RG14 ...2 B4
Birdhaven GU10 ...121 E6
Birdwood Rd GU15 ...35 D7
Birdworld & Underwater
World* GU10 ...121 A3
Birinus Rd SO23 ...209 E7
Birkenholme Cl GU35 ...166 A4
Bishearne Gdns GU33 ...207 E5
Bishop Challoner RC Sec Sch
RG22 ...68 C3
Bishop Sumner Dr GU9 ...99 A6
Bishop's Mead GU9 ...98 F2
Bishop's View GU34 ...159 F1
Bishop's Way SP10 ...105 F8
Bishops Cl Fleet GU52 ...75 A6
4 Pamber Heath RG26 ...9 E1
South Tidworth SP9 ...78 F4
Bishops Ct 2 SP10 ...105 F8
Bishops Rd GU9 ...98 F7
Bishopswood Ct RG26 ...9 D1
Bishopswood Jun Sch
RG26 ...26 F7
Bishopswood La
Baughurst RG26 ...26 C8
Pamber Heath RG26 ...9 C1
Bishopswood Rd RG26 ...9 D1
Bishopwood Inf Sch
RG26 ...26 F8
Bittern Cl Aldershot GU11 ...99 E7
Basingstoke RG22 ...90 F8
Sandhurst GU47 ...35 B8
Black Dam Rdbt RG21 ...69 E4
Black Dam Way RG21 ...69 E3
Black Pond La GU10 ...122 A6
Black Swan Bldgs 16
SO22 ...209 D6
Black Swan Yd 5 SP10 ...106 B8
Blackbarn Rd SP4 ...145 A6
Blackberry Cl GU34 ...160 C3
Blackberry La GU34 ...160 C2
Blackberry Wlk RG24 ...69 F7
Blackbird Cl
Basingstoke RG22 ...90 F8
Sandhurst GU47 ...35 B8
Blackbird Ct SP10 ...83 B2
Blackbird La RG20 ...6 E3
Blackbushe Bsns Ctr
GU46 ...34 A4
Blackbushe Park Cvn Site
GU46 ...34 A5
Blackbushes Rd RG27 ...53 D7
Blackcap Pl GU47 ...35 C8
Blackdown Cl RG22 ...68 B3
Blackheath Rd GU9 ...98 E7
Blackman Gdns GU11 ...99 F8
Blackmoor Ho GU33 ...185 F6
Blackmoor Rd GU33 ...186 A6
Blackmore La GU32 ...205 F3
Blacknest Ind Pk GU34 ...142 C8
Blacknest Rd GU34 ...120 C1
Blackstocks La RG27 ...71 B6
Blackstone Cl GU14 ...55 B6
Blackthorn Cl SO21 ...153 C4
Blackthorn Cres GU14 ...55 D8
Blackthorn Way RG23 ...68 C6
Blackthorne Cl GU35 ...164 E3
Blackwater Cl Ash GU12 ...77 E1
Basingstoke RG21 ...69 C5
Oakley RG23 ...67 B1
Blackwater Pk GU12 ...77 C1
Blackwater Sta GU17 ...35 C4
Blackwater View RG40 ...16 F2
Blackwater Way GU12 ...100 B8
Blackwell Rd SO21 ...153 C3
Blagdon Cl RG19 ...6 B7
Blair Rd 2 RG21 ...69 A3
Blaire Pk GU46 ...33 F8
Blaise Cl GU14 ...56 B3
Blake Cl RG29 ...95 C8
Blake Ct Andover SP10 ...83 A1
Basingstoke RG21 ...69 B4
Blake's La
4 Pamber Heath RG26 ...9 F1
Tadley RG26 ...10 A1
Blakes Cotts RG29 ...72 E2
Blakes Ride GU46 ...33 F6
Blanket St GU34 ...162 F8
Bleach's Yard Ind Est
GU30 ...188 A2
Bledlow Cl RG14 ...5 A5
Blendon Dr SP10 ...82 D1
Blenheim Cl Alton GU34 ...140 A3
Four Marks GU34 ...160 B3
Tongham GU10 ...100 C7
Blenheim Cotts RG18 ...2 F8
Blenheim Cres GU9 ...98 E5
Blenheim Ct GU14 ...56 B2
Blenheim Pk GU11 ...77 A7
Blenheim Rd
Farnborough GU11 ...76 F7
Newbury RG14 ...1 D2
Old Basing RG24 ...70 C5
Blenhiem Pl GU15 ...36 A3
Blighton La GU10 ...100 C3
Bliss Cl RG22 ...68 E1
Blissmore La SP11 ...81 D2
Block Cotts RG7 ...10 F6
Bloomfieldhatch La RG7 ...12 F8
Bloomsbury Way GU17 ...35 B3
Blossom Cl SP10 ...105 D7
Bloswood Dr RG28 ...86 B5
Bloswood La RG28 ...86 A6
Blue Ball Hill SO23 ...209 F6
Blue Hayes Cl SP10 ...106 A7
Blue Pryor Ct 12 GU52 ...74 E3
Blue Timbers Cl 8
GU35 ...164 D2
Bluebell Cl SP10 ...105 C7
Bluebell Mews GU15 ...36 B7
Bluebell Rd GU35 ...165 A5
Bluebell Wlk 1 GU51 ...53 F2
Blueberry Gdns SP10 ...105 C7
Bluehaven Wlk RG27 ...50 F1
Bluethroat Cl GU47 ...35 C8
Bluff Cove GU11 ...77 A3
Blunden Cl RG21 ...69 A1
Blunden Rd GU14 ...55 D5
Blunt Rd RG22 ...90 F4
Blythe Cl SP11 ...83 B6
Blythwood Dr GU16 ...36 B2
Boames La RG20 ...4 E5
Boar's Bridge RG26 ...27 F3
Bodin Gdns RG14 ...5 F8
Bodmin Cl RG22 ...68 B3
Bofors Rd GU14 ...76 E8
Bogmoor Cl GU34 ...160 B2
Bohunt Sch GU30 ...187 F4
Bolle Rd GU34 ...139 D2
Bolley Ave GU35 ...164 B5
Bolton Cres RG22 ...68 E3
Bond Cl Basingstoke RG24 ...69 E8
Pamber Heath RG26 ...9 E1
Bone La RG14 ...2 A3
Bonemill La RG20 ...1 B2
Bonhams Cl GU34 ...140 E7
Bonner Cotts SP5 ...191 E7
Bonners Field GU10 ...120 A5
Boon Way RG23 ...67 A2
Borden Gates SP10 ...106 A7
Border Cl GU33 ...208 B1
Border End GU27 ...189 B6
Border Mews GU26 ...167 B3
Border Rd GU27 ...189 B6
Borderside GU46 ...33 E6
Bordon Cl RG26 ...26 E8
Bordon Jun & Inf Schs
GU35 ...164 C4
Bordon Trad Est GU35 ...164 A5
Boreen The GU35 ...165 F5
Borelli Mews 2 GU9 ...99 A2
Borelli Yd 1 GU9 ...99 A2
Borkum Cl SP10 ...82 F3
Borman Way SO21 ...153 E4
Borodin Cl RG22 ...91 F8
Borough Court Rd RG27 ...51 E5
Borough The
Crondall GU10 ...97 C6
Farnham GU9 ...98 F2
Borovere Cl GU34 ...139 E2
Borovere Gdns GU34 ...139 E2
Borovere La GU34 ...139 E2
Borsberry Cl SP10 ...106 B8
Boscobel Rd SO22 ...209 D7
Boscowen Cl SP10 ...106 C7
Bostock Cl SO21 ...174 D3
Botany Hill GU10 ...100 B1
Botisdone Cl SP11 ...38 C5
Bottle La RG27 ...51 B8
Boulters Rd GU11 ...76 F1
Boundary Rd
Dockenfield GU10 ...143 B8
Farnborough GU14 ...56 A2
Grayshott GU26 ...167 B3
Newbury RG14 ...1 F2
Rowledge GU10 ...121 C2
Boundoak RG2 ...15 B8
Boundstone Cl GU10 ...121 F5
Boundstone Rd GU10 ...121 E4
Bounty Rd RG21 ...69 A4
Bounty Rise RG21 ...69 A4
Bourley La GU10 ...75 E2
Bourley Rd
Aldershot GU11 ...76 C3
Fleet GU9,GU10,GU11,GU52 ...75 D3
Bourne Arch RG18 ...2 F4
Bourne Ct Aldershot GU11 ...99 E8
16 Andover SP10 ...83 C2
2 Basingstoke RG21 ...69 D5
Bourne Dene GU10 ...121 E5
Bourne Field RG24 ...47 E4
Bourne Firs GU10 ...122 B5
Bourne Gr GU10 ...122 C7
Bourne Grove Cl GU10 ...122 C7
Bourne Grove Dr GU10 ...122 C7
Bourne Hts GU9 ...122 A8
Bourne Inf Sch The
GU10 ...122 B6
Bourne La SP9 ...101 F7
Bourne Mdw SP11 ...62 A1
Bourne Mill Bsns Pk GU9 ...99 C3
Bourne Rd
North Tidworth SP9 ...78 F6
Thatcham RG19 ...2 F4
Bourne The GU52 ...75 A6
Bourne View SP9 ...78 F7
Bournemouth Rd SP11 ...124 E5
Bournewood Pk GU10 ...122 C7
Bow Dr RG27 ...49 D8
Bow Field RG27 ...51 C1
Bow Gdns RG27 ...49 D8
Bow Gr RG27 ...29 D1
Bow St GU34 ...139 E2
Bowcott Hill GU35 ...165 D5
Bowdown Ct RG14 ...1 D2
Bowenhurst Gdns GU52 ...75 A5
Bowenhurst La GU51 ...74 C3
Bowenhurst Rd GU52 ...75 A5
Bower Rd GU10 ...121 E5
Bowers Grove La SO24 ...181 C8
Bowers La SP11 ...38 A7
Bowling Green Ct GU16 ...56 C7
Bowling Green Dr RG27 ...50 F1
Bowling Green Rd RG18 ...2 E5
Bowlings The GU15 ...36 A6
Bowman Rd RG24 ...49 A4
Bowmonts Rd RG26 ...27 B8
Bowyer Cl 4 RG21 ...69 A4
Boxall's Gr GU11 ...99 E8
Boxall's La GU11 ...99 F7
Boyce Cl RG22 ...91 C8
Boyne Mead Rd SO23 ...176 C7
Boyne Rise SO23 ...176 B8
Boyneswood Cl GU34 ...160 C4
Boyneswood La GU34 ...160 B4
Boyneswood Rd GU34 ...160 C4
Brabon Rd GU14 ...55 D5
Bracebridge GU15 ...35 E5
Bracher Cl SP10 ...106 B8
Bracken Bank RG24 ...69 F8
Bracken La Bordon GU35 ...186 A8
Yateley GU46 ...33 F6
Brackenbury SP10 ...82 D2
Brackendale Cl GU15 ...36 C3
Brackendale Rd GU15 ...36 B4
Brackens The RG22 ...91 C6
Brackenwood Dr RG26 ...9 E1
Brecklesham Cl GU14 ...55 E7
Brackley Ave RG27 ...52 C6
Brackley Way RG22 ...68 C2
Bracknell La RG27 ...52 C7
Bradbury Cl RG28 ...86 B5
Bradbury Ho SP11 ...83 B6
Bradley Cotts SO21 ...112 B2
Bradley Peak SO22 ...209 A7
Bradley Rd SO22 ...175 C4
Bradman Sq SP10 ...83 B3
Bradwell Cl SP10 ...82 D3
Braemar Cl GU16 ...56 D8
Braemar Dr RG23 ...67 A2
Braemore Ct SO22 ...209 A5
Braeside Cl
Haslemere GU27 ...189 D8
Winchester SO22 ...197 B4
Brahms Rd RG22 ...91 E8
Braine L'Alleud Rd 17
RG21 ...69 B5
Braishfield Rd SO51 ...194 D1
Brake Rd GU14 ...55 C1
Brakes Rise GU47 ...35 C8
Bramble Bank GU16 ...56 E6
Bramble Ct 7 RG14 ...1 F2
Bramble Hill SO24 ...179 D5
Bramble Way RG24 ...70 C6
Brambledown GU26 ...167 C4
Brambles Cl Ash GU12 ...77 F1
Four Marks GU34 ...160 B2
Brambles The RG14 ...5 C8
Brambleton Ave GU9 ...121 F7
Bramblewood Pl GU51 ...53 E1
Brambling Cl RG22 ...90 F7
Bramblys Cl RG21 ...69 A4
Bramblys Dr RG21 ...69 A4
Bramdean Cl 2 RG26 ...26 F7
Bramdown Hts RG22 ...91 B7
Bramley CE Prim Sch
RG26 ...28 F4
Bramley Cl GU34 ...140 A3
Bramley Croft GU26 ...167 C4
Bramley Green Rd RG26 ...29 A2
Bramley La
Blackwater GU17 ...34 F5
Bramley RG26 ...28 F4
Bramley Rd
Camberley GU15 ...35 F2
Pamber End RG26 ...27 D2
Sherfield on L RG27 ...29 D1
Silchester RG7 ...10 F1
Three Ashes RG7 ...28 B7
Bramley Sta RG26 ...28 F3
Bramley Wlk GU35 ...164 B2
Bramling Ave GU46 ...33 F6
Bramoak RG26 ...28 D3
Brampton Gdns RG22 ...91 C5
Bramshaw Cl SO22 ...175 C3
Bramshill Cl RG2 ...15 C8
Bramshill Ho (Police Coll)
RG27 ...32 B4
Bramshot Dr GU51 ...54 A2
Bramshot La
Farnborough GU14 ...55 A6
Farnborough GU51 ...54 E5
Bramshott Dr RG27 ...51 B1
Bramshott Rd GU51 ...54 E2
Brancaster Ave SP10 ...82 D3
Brandon Cl GU34 ...139 E4
Brandon Rd GU52 ...74 E4
Brandy Bottom GU46 ...34 C3
Brandy Mount SO24 ...179 D6
Branksome Ave SO20 ...129 A3
Branksome Cl
Camberley GU15 ...36 C6
Chilbolton SO20 ...129 A3
Winchester SO22 ...197 B6
Branksome Hill Rd GU47 ...35 C8
Branksome Park Rd
GU15 ...36 C6
Branksome Walk Manor 4
GU51 ...53 F1
Branksomewood Rd
GU51 ...53 F1
Branson Rd GU35 ...164 E3
Brantfell Lo GU11 ...99 E8
Branton Cl RG22 ...68 C3
Brassey Rd SO22 ...209 D7
Braunfels Wlk RG14 ...1 C2
Braust Ho SP11 ...81 E2
Braxton Ho 1 SO23 ...198 C8
Breach Farm Cotts
RG25 ...113 D4
Breach La
Sherfield on L RG27 ...49 E8
Upper Chute SP11 ...58 B8
Breachfield RG20 ...22 D7
Breadels Ct RG22 ...91 B4
Breadels Field RG22 ...91 A4
Brecon Cl GU14 ...55 B7
Breech The GU47 ...35 C7
Bremen Gdns SP10 ...82 F3
Brendon Rd GU14 ...55 B7
Bret Harte Rd GU16 ...36 C1
Brew House La RG27 ...52 D6
Brewells La GU33 ...208 E5
Brewer Cl RG22 ...68 C3
Brewers Cl GU14 ...55 E5
Brewers La SO24 ...204 C7
Brewery Comm RG7 ...11 F7
Brewery Cotts SP11 ...81 B1
Brewery Gdns 12 GU34 ...139 F3
Brewhouse Yd SO24 ...179 D6
Briar La GU34 ...160 C3
Briar Way RG26 ...27 A8
Briar Wood GU33 ...208 A7
Briarlea Rd RG7 ...11 E6
Briarleas Ct GU14 ...77 B8
Briars Cl GU14 ...55 B3
Briars The Ash GU12 ...77 F1
Fleet GU52 ...75 A6
Briarwood RG40 ...16 C6
Brick Kiln Ind Est RG26 ...10 A1
Brick Kiln La Alton GU34 ...139 C4
West Tisted SO24 ...204 B8
Brick La GU51 ...54 A2
Brickersbury Ho GU14 ...55 D8
Brickfields Cl RG24 ...70 A8
Brickiln La GU34 ...160 F6
Bricksbury Hill GU9 ...99 A8
Brickyards Ind Est The
GU32 ...207 A1
Bridge Cotts GU33 ...207 E7
Bridge Ct RG26 ...27 A8
Bridge End GU15 ...35 F4
Bridge Mdws GU33 ...207 F4
Bridge Mews GU10 ...100 D7
Bridge Rd Aldershot GU11 ...99 E8
Camberley GU15 ...35 F3
Farnborough GU14 ...55 D4
New Alresford SO24 ...179 B5
North Warnborough RG29 ...72 C4
Bridge Sq GU9 ...99 A2
Bridge St Andover SP10 ...106 A7
1 Newbury RG14 ...1 E3
Overton RG25 ...88 A8
7 Winchester SO23 ...209 F5
Bridge Wlk GU46 ...34 B7
Bridge Works GU15 ...35 F3
Bridgefield GU9 ...99 B2
Bridgemead GU16 ...56 B8
Bridges The RG7 ...11 A5
Bridgetts La SO21 ...155 B2
Bridle Cl
East Tisted GU34 ...183 D5
Grayshott GU26 ...166 E3
Bridle Ct 7 GU11 ...76 C2
Brighton Hill Com Coll
RG22 ...68 D1
Brighton Hill Ctr RG22 ...91 D8
Brighton Hill Rdbt RG22 ...68 E1
Brighton Hill Ret Pk
RG22 ...68 E2
Brighton Rd GU12 ...100 A8
Brighton Way RG22 ...91 D8
Brightstone La GU34 ...161 B2
Brightwells Rd GU9 ...99 A2
Brimley Hill Ct RG20 ...24 D2
Brimpton CE Prim Sch
RG7 ...8 D6
Brimpton La RG7 ...8 F3
Brimpton Rd
Baughurst RG26 ...26 B8
Brimpton RG7 ...8 D7

Brimpton Rd *continued*
  Pamber Heath RG26 . . . . .9 A1
Brindle Cl GU11 . . . . .99 F7
Brinksway GU51 . . . . .75 A8
Brinn's La GU17 . . . . .35 A5
Brinns Cotts GU17 . . . . .35 A5
Brislands La GU34 . . . . .181 E7
Bristow Inf Sch GU15 . . . . . . .35 F2
Bristow Rd GU15 . . . . .36 A3
Britannia Cl GU35 . . . . .164 F3
Britannia Dr RG22 . . . . .91 A4
Brittain Ct GU47 . . . . .35 A7
Britten Rd RG22 . . . . .91 E8
Broad Chalke Down
  SO22 . . . . .209 A2
Broad Ha'penny GU10 . . . . .121 E5
Broad Leaze RG27 . . . . .51 A2
Broad Oak La RG29 . . . . .73 A4
Broad Rd SP11 . . . . .104 C4
Broad St SO24 . . . . .179 D6
Broad View La SO22 . . . . . . .197 A3
Broad Way RG7 . . . . .13 B3
Broad Wlk GU16 . . . . .36 C2
Broadacres GU51 . . . . .74 D8
Broadhalfpenny La RG26 . .10 A1
Broadhurst GU14 . . . . .55 A4
Broadhurst Gr RG24 . . . . . . .69 F7
Broadlands
  Camberley GU16 . . . . .56 D8
  Farnborough GU14 . . . . . . .56 C2
Broadlands Cl GU10 . . . . . .120 B5
Broadmere RG25 . . . . .91 E4
Broadmere Rd RG22 . . . . . . .91 A5
Broadoak RG26 . . . . .27 B8
Broadview Cl GU34 . . . . . . .141 E7
Broadway RG28 . . . . .86 D4
Broadway Ho GU47 . . . . .34 F7
Broadway The
  Andover SP10 . . . . .106 A7
  Newbury RG14 . . . . .1 E4
  Sandhurst GU47 . . . . .34 F8
  Winchester SO23 . . . . .209 E5
Broadwell Rd GU10 . . . . . . .121 D6
Brocas Dr RG21 . . . . .69 C7
Brockenhurst Dr GU46 . . . . .34 B5
Brockenhurst Rd GU11 . . . . .99 F8
Brockham Hill La GU34 . . . .118 A2
Brockhurst Lodge GU27 . . .121 F7
Brocklands GU46 . . . . .33 F4
Brockwood Bottom
  SO24 . . . . .202 E1
Brockwood Park Sch
  SO24 . . . . .202 F1
Broken Way RG20 . . . . .5 F2
Brokle Cl GU52 . . . . .74 E8
Bromelia Cl RG26 . . . . .28 F4
Bronte Rise RG14 . . . . .5 F8
Bronze Cl RG22 . . . . .91 A4
Brook Ave GU9 . . . . .99 D7
Brook Cl Ash GU12 . . . . .77 F3
  Fleet GU51 . . . . .75 A8
Brook Cotts
  King's Somborne SO20 . . . .193 C6
  Yateley GU46 . . . . .34 A6
Brook Gdns GU14 . . . . .55 D2
Brook Gn RG26 . . . . .27 B8
Brook Ho Farnham GU9 . . . . .99 B6
  Newbury RG14 . . . . .1 E3
Brook Rd GU15 . . . . .35 F4
Brook The SO24 . . . . .179 D6
Brook Trad Est The
  GU12 . . . . .77 C2
Brooke Cl SO23 . . . . .176 B8
Brooke Ct GU16 . . . . .56 D6
Brookfield Cl RG24 . . . . .49 A3
Brookfield Rd GU12 . . . . .77 D3
Brookham Sch GU30 . . . . . .188 C2
Brookhouse Rd GU14 . . . . . .55 D3
Brooklands GU11 . . . . .76 A3
Brooklands Cl GU9 . . . . .99 B7
Brooklands Rd GU9 . . . . .99 C7
Brooklands Way GU9 . . . . . . .99 C7
Brookley Cl GU10 . . . . .100 A3
Brookly Gdns GU51 . . . . .54 B2
Brookmead Ct GU9 . . . . .98 F1
Brooks Cl RG28 . . . . .86 D4
Brooks Rise SP10 . . . . .82 E1
Brooks Sh Ctr The SO23 . . .209 E6
Brooksby Cl GU17 . . . . .34 F5
Brookside Farnham GU9 . . . .99 B6
  Sandhurst GU47 . . . . .35 A7
Brookside Bsns Ctr RG7 . . .14 B6
Brookside Cotts SO21 . . . . .147 F5
Brookside Park Mobile Home
  Pk GU14 . . . . .55 C2
Brookside Wlk RG26 . . . . . . .27 A8
Brookvale Cl RG21 . . . . .69 A5
Brookvale Sch RG21 . . . . . . .68 F5
Brookway
  Anna Valley SP11 . . . . .105 C4
  Newbury RG14 . . . . .2 C2
Brookwood Rd GU14 . . . . . . .54 F6
Broom Acres Fleet GU52 . . . .74 F6
  Sandhurst GU47 . . . . .34 F8
Broom Squires GU26 . . . . . .167 D4
Broom Way GU17 . . . . .35 C4
Broome Cl GU46 . . . . .34 A7
Broomfield La GU10 . . . . . . .121 E1
Broomfield Rd GU35 . . . . . .164 B2
Broomhill GU10 . . . . .98 B8
Broomhill Rd GU14 . . . . .55 B5
Broomhurst La **5** GU45 . . . . .53 E3
Broomleaf Cnr GU9 . . . . .99 B2
Broomleaf Rd GU9 . . . . .99 B2
Broomrigg Rd GU51 . . . . .53 E2
Broomwood Way GU10 . . . .122 A6

Broomy Lodges GU51 . . . . .53 C4
Brougham Pl GU9 . . . . .98 F7
Broughton Mews GU16 . . . .36 D1
Broughton Prim Sch
  SO20 . . . . .170 B7
Broughton Rd SO20 . . . . . .148 E2
Brown Croft RG27 . . . . .50 F1
Browning Cl RG24 . . . . .69 C8
Browning Dr SO22 . . . . . . .209 B6
Browning Rd GU52 . . . . .74 E3
Browns Cl RG26 . . . . .28 F4
Browns Wlk GU10 . . . . .121 F6
Brownsover Rd GU14 . . . . . .55 A4
Broxhead Farm Rd
  GU35 . . . . .164 E7
Broxhead Trad Est
  GU35 . . . . .164 F6
Bruan Rd RG14 . . . . .5 D8
Brummell Rd RG14 . . . . .1 C5
Brunel Cl SO21 . . . . .111 B2
Brunel Gate SP10 . . . . .82 E2
Brunel Rd RG21 . . . . .68 E6
Brunswick Pl RG21 . . . . .68 F1
Bruntile Cl GU14 . . . . .56 B1
Bryanstone Cl GU52 . . . . . . .75 A6
Bryce Gdns GU11 . . . . .100 A7
Bryces La SO24 . . . . .135 A3
Bryn Rd GU10 . . . . .121 D2
Buccaneer Way GU14 . . . . . .76 A7
Buchan The GU31 . . . . .145 F4
Buchanan Dr RG40 . . . . .16 C7
Buckby La **7** RG21 . . . . .69 F5
Buckfast Cl RG24 . . . . .48 A1
Buckholt Rd SO20 . . . . .170 A6
Buckhurst Rd GU16 . . . . .56 D6
Buckingham Cl GU34 . . . . . .139 D3
Buckingham Dr
  Basingstoke RG22 . . . . .91 A8
  12 Farnborough GU14 . . . .55 F4
Buckingham Par RG22 . . . . .68 A1
Buckingham Rd RG14 . . . . . .1 D1
Buckingham Way GU16 . . . .56 D8
Buckland Ave RG22 . . . . .68 D2
Buckland Cl GU14 . . . . .56 A7
Buckland Par RG22 . . . . .68 A1
Buckner-Croke Way RG19 . .6 D5
Buckskin La RG22 . . . . .68 B3
Budd's Cl RG21 . . . . .69 A4
Buddesgate SO21 . . . . .131 D3
Budds La GU35 . . . . .164 C4
Buffbeards La GU27 . . . . . .189 C7
Buffins Cnr RG29 . . . . .72 C2
Buffins Rd RG29 . . . . .72 C2
Bufton Field RG29 . . . . .72 C3
Bulbery SP11 . . . . .104 F3
Bulford Rd
  Shipton Bellinger SP9 . . . .101 E8
  South Tidworth SP9 . . . . . . .78 D4
Bull Dro SO23 . . . . .209 F3
Bull Hill GU33 . . . . .208 E4
Bull La RG7 . . . . .13 E3
Buller Ct **8** GU14 . . . . .56 A1
Buller Rd GU11 . . . . .76 F4
Bullers Rd GU9 . . . . .99 C6
Bullfinch Cl GU47 . . . . .35 C8
Bullington La
  Barton Stacey SO21 . . . . . .130 E7
  Upper Bullington SO21 . . . .131 C6
Bulls Down Cl RG27 . . . . . . .29 D1
Bulls Dro SP5 . . . . .191 A6
Bulpits Hill SP11 . . . . .38 C6
Bunch La GU27 . . . . .189 E8
Bunch Way GU27 . . . . .189 E7
Bungler's Hill RG7 . . . . .14 F6
Bunkers Hill RG14 . . . . .5 A5
Bunnian Pl RG21 . . . . .69 B6
Bunting Mews GU14 . . . . . . .91 A7
Buntings GU34 . . . . .139 F6
Buntings The GU9 . . . . .121 D7
Burberry Cl RG21 . . . . .69 C8
Burbery Rd **3** RG27 . . . . .51 A1
Burbury Woods GU15 . . . . . .36 C6
Burchell Rd RG14 . . . . .1 C5
Burchett Coppice RG40 . . . .16 D8
Burdock Cl SP11 . . . . .127 F8
Burfield RG20 . . . . .21 D5
Burford Rd **5** GU15 . . . . .35 F4
Burgage Field RG28 . . . . . . .86 D6
Burge Cl GU14 . . . . .55 A4
Burgess Cl RG29 . . . . .72 C2
Burgess La GU20 . . . . .3 B6
Burgess Rd RG21 . . . . .44 A4
Burgh Hill Rd GU30 . . . . . . .187 E7
Burghclere Prim Sch
  RG20 . . . . .22 E6
Burghead Cl GU47 . . . . .35 B7
Burgoyne Rd GU15 . . . . .36 E6
Buriton Rd SO20 . . . . .175 D4
Burkal Dr SP10 . . . . .83 A4
Burleigh Rd GU16 . . . . .56 B8
Burles Bridge Cotts
  GU10 . . . . .98 A1
Burley La RG25 . . . . .88 E6
Burley Rd SO22 . . . . .175 D4
Burlington Ct
  10 Aldershot GU11 . . . . . . .76 E1
  Blackwater GU17 . . . . .64 D5
Burnaby Cl GU34 . . . . .139 C3
Burne Cl SO21 . . . . .153 C2
Burne-Jones Dr GU47 . . . . . .35 B6
Burnet Cl SO22 . . . . .209 D8
Burney Rd RG26 . . . . .27 C8
Burnham Copse Jun & Inf
  Sch RG26 . . . . .9 F1
Burnham Manor GU15 . . . . .36 E8
Burnham Rd Alton GU34 . . .139 C1

Burnham Rd *continued*
  Pamber Heath RG26 . . . . .9 D2
Burnhams Cl SP10 . . . . .83 A4
Burnley Cl RG26 . . . . .26 F7
Burnmoor Mdw RG40 . . . . . .16 C2
Burns Ave GU52 . . . . .75 B6
Burns Cl Basingstoke RG24 . .69 C8
  Farnborough GU14 . . . . . . .55 D6
  South Wonston SO21 . . . . .153 E4
Burnsall Cl GU14 . . . . .55 F6
Burnside GU51 . . . . .54 A1
Burnt Hill Rd GU10 . . . . . . .121 F6
Burnt Hill Way GU10 . . . . . .121 F5
Burnt Oak GU46 . . . . .16 D8
Burntwood Cotts SO21 . . . .154 F2
Burrell Rd GU16 . . . . .56 A8
Burrow Hill Sch GU16 . . . . .36 D1
Burrowfields RG22 . . . . .91 B5
Burrows The RG26 . . . . .9 E1
Burrwood Gdns GU12 . . . . . .77 E4
Bursledon Cotts SP9 . . . . . .101 E8
Burton's Gdns RG24 . . . . . . .70 B7
Bury Court Cotts GU10 . . . .120 A7
Bury Hill Cl SP11 . . . . .105 C4
Bury Hill Farm SP11 . . . . . .105 E4
Bury The RG29 . . . . .72 E2
Bury's Bank Rd RG19 . . . . . . .6 D7
Burydown Mead RG25 . . . . .89 F1
Buryfields RG29 . . . . .72 E2
Buryfields Inf Sch RG29 . . .72 E2
Buryhill Close Flats
  SP11 . . . . .105 C4
Bushell Way RG21 . . . . .15 C8
Bushnells Dr RG20 . . . . .24 C3
Bushywarren La RG25 . . . . . .92 E1
Busk Cres GU14 . . . . .55 D3
Busket La SO23 . . . . .209 E6
Bustards Cnr SO20 . . . . . . .147 E5
Butler Cl RG22 . . . . .68 C4
Butler Lodge RG25 . . . . .88 B8
Butler's Cl SP51 . . . . .191 F1
Butson Cl RG14 . . . . .1 C5
Buttenshaw Ave RG22 . . . . . .91 A5
Buttenshaw Cl RG2 . . . . .15 E8
Buttercup Cl GU35 . . . . .165 A5
Butterfield GU15 . . . . .35 F4
Buttermer Cl GU10 . . . . . . .121 D7
Buttermere
  Bordon GU35 . . . . .164 D5
  Farnborough GU14 . . . . . . .55 A8
Buttermere Cl GU12 . . . . . . .77 D4
Buttermere Dr RG22 . . . . . . .91 A8
Buttermere Gdns SO24 . . .179 D4
Butterys Ct GU34 . . . . .139 F4
Button's La GU34 . . . . .184 C2
Butts Mdw RG27 . . . . .51 A1
Butts Mews GU34 . . . . .139 C2
Butts Prim Sch The
  GU34 . . . . .139 C2
Butts Rd GU34 . . . . .139 E2
Butts The RG7 . . . . .27 F8
Butts The **6** RG21 . . . . .69 B5
By Pass Rd SO21 . . . . .131 B4
Byes La RG27 . . . . .27 F6
Byeways RG20 . . . . .21 D6
Byfield Rd RG20 . . . . .24 C2
Byfleet Ave RG24 . . . . .70 B5
Byfrons The GU14 . . . . .56 A2
Byng Wlk SP10 . . . . .106 D8
Byron Ave Frimley GU15 . . . .36 F3
  Winchester SO22 . . . . .209 B6
Byron Cl Basingstoke RG24 . .48 D1
  Fleet GU51 . . . . .75 A8
  Newbury RG14 . . . . .5 D7
  Yateley GU46 . . . . .33 F4
Byron Ct **1** GU15 . . . . .36 B5
Bywater Cl GU14 . . . . .75 C8
Byways GU46 . . . . .33 F5
Byworth Cl GU10 . . . . .98 D2
Byworth Rd GU9 . . . . .98 D2

C

Cabrol Rd GU14 . . . . .55 C5
Cabul Rd SP9 . . . . .78 D4
Cadet Way GU52 . . . . .75 B4
Cadham Cl GU11 . . . . .53 C4
Cadnam Cl
  Aldershot GU11 . . . . .100 A6
  Oakley RG23 . . . . .67 B2
Cadogan Rd GU11 . . . . .77 B7
Caerleon Cl GU26 . . . . .167 A6
Caerleon Dr SP10 . . . . .83 A4
Caernarvon Cl GU16 . . . . . . .56 D8
Caernarvon Cl RG23 . . . . . . .68 C5
Caesar Cl SO23 . . . . .68 C7
Caesar Ct **9** GU11 . . . . .76 C2
Caesar Rd SP10 . . . . .83 B3
Caesar's Camp Rd GU15 . . .36 E8
Caesar's Cl GU34 . . . . .139 E8
Caesar's Way RG28 . . . . .86 E6
Caesars Ct
  Camberley GU15 . . . . .36 E8
  Farnham GU9 . . . . .99 A7
Cairn Cl GU15 . . . . .36 F3
Cairngorm Cl RG22 . . . . .68 A4
Cairngorm Pl GU14 . . . . .55 C7
Caithness Cl RG23 . . . . .67 A2
Caker Stream Rd GU34 . . . .140 B4
Caker's La GU34 . . . . .140 D1
Calard Dr RG18 . . . . .1 D8
Calcott Pk GU46 . . . . .34 A6
Calder Cl **17** SP10 . . . . .83 C5
Calender Cl GU34 . . . . .139 F2

California Ctry Pk*
  RG40 . . . . .16 A7
Calleva Cl RG22 . . . . .91 B7
Calleva Mus* RG7 . . . . .10 F1
Calleva Pk RG7 . . . . .9 C2
Calleva Roman Town*
  RG7 . . . . .11 B1
Calne Ho **3** SP9 . . . . .78 F6
Calshot Way GU16 . . . . .56 E7
Calthorpe Hos RG27 . . . . . . .52 F8
Calthorpe Park Sch
  GU51 . . . . .74 C8
Calthorpe Rd GU51 . . . . .53 E2
Calton Gdns GU11 . . . . .100 A7
Calvecroft GU30 . . . . .188 A4
Calvert Cl GU12 . . . . .77 B1
Calvert Ctr The SO21 . . . . . .112 D1
Calvin Ho **5** GU11 . . . . .76 D2
Cam Wlk **3** RG21 . . . . .69 C8
Camberlet Twrs **3** GU15 . . . .36 B5
Camberley Inf Sch GU15 . . .36 A5
Camberley Sta GU15 . . . . . . .36 B5
Camberley Twrs GU15 . . . . .36 A5
Camberry Cl RG21 . . . . .69 C3
Cambrian Cl GU15 . . . . .35 F5
Cambrian Rd GU14 . . . . .55 B7
Cambrian Way
  Basingstoke RG22 . . . . .68 B3
  Finchampstead RG40 . . . . . .16 E8
Cambridge Cl **1** GU14 . . . . .56 A1
Cambridge Pl GU9 . . . . .99 A2
Cambridge Rd GU11 . . . . . . .76 D2
Cambridge Rd E GU14 . . . . .56 B1
Cambridge Rd W GU14 . . . . .56 A1
Cambridge Sq **8** GU15 . . . . .36 A5
Cambridge Wlk **2** GU15 . . . .36 A6
Camden Wlk GU51 . . . . .54 C1
Camel Way GU14 . . . . .55 E1
Camela Villas GU12 . . . . .77 B1
Camelot Cl SP10 . . . . .83 A2
Camelsdale Fst Sch
  GU27 . . . . .189 D5
Camelsdale Rd GU27 . . . . .189 D5
Cameron Cl SP10 . . . . .105 E7
Cameron Ct RG22 . . . . .77 B7
Camfield Cl RG21 . . . . .69 C3
Camford Cl RG22 . . . . .91 A4
Camlea Cl RG21 . . . . .69 C2
Camoys Mead GU34 . . . . . .116 C2
Camp Farm Rd GU11 . . . . . .77 B5
Camp Field SO20 . . . . .172 A3
Camp Rd Bordon GU35 . . . .164 D4
  Farnborough GU14 . . . . . . .77 A8
  Padworth RG7 . . . . .11 B8
Campana Int Coll GU11 . . . .99 E2
Campbell Cl
  Aldershot GU11 . . . . .100 A7
  Fleet GU51 . . . . .53 E1
  Grateley SP11 . . . . .124 E7
  Yateley GU46 . . . . .34 D6
Campbell Ct
  Bramley RG26 . . . . .29 B2
  Holybourne GU34 . . . . . . .140 C6
Campbell Fields GU11 . . . . .76 F1
Campbell Pl GU16 . . . . .36 D3
Campbell Rd
  Aldershot GU11 . . . . .76 E3
  Bramley RG26 . . . . .29 B2
Campbell's Gn RG7 . . . . .11 F5
Campion Cl
  Blackwater GU17 . . . . .35 D3
  Lindford GU35 . . . . .165 A4
Campion Ho **4** RG14 . . . . . . .1 D2
Campion Way
  Hartley Wintney RG27 . . . . .52 D7
  Kings Worthy SO23 . . . . . .176 C2
Campsie Cl RG22 . . . . .68 B4
Camrose Way RG21 . . . . .69 C3
Camus Cl GU52 . . . . .74 D5
Camwood Cl RG21 . . . . .69 C3
Canada Cotts SO21 . . . . . . .111 B2
Canada Way
  Bordon GU35 . . . . .164 D4
  Liphook GU30 . . . . .188 A3
Canal Cl
  Farnborough GU11 . . . . . . .77 B5
  North Warnborough RG29 . .72 C5
Canal Cotts GU12 . . . . .77 E4
Canal View Rd RG14 . . . . .2 B3
Canberra Cl GU46 . . . . .33 E7
Canberra Rd RG22 . . . . .91 A4
Candleford Gate GU30 . . . .187 F4
Candover Cl **4** RG26 . . . . . . .27 F7
Canes La GU35 . . . . .164 F5
Canhouse La GU31,GU33 . .208 F3
Canning Rd GU12 . . . . .77 B2
Cannock Ct RG22 . . . . .68 B3
Cannon Cl Elisfield RG25 . .115 B6
  Sandhurst GU47 . . . . .35 D8
Canon St SO23 . . . . .209 E5
Canon's Ct RG20 . . . . .24 C2
Canons St RG20 . . . . .78 F4
Canons Ct RG20 . . . . .24 C2
Cansfield End RG41 . . . . .1 D3
Canterbury Ct RG22 . . . . .91 B8
Canterbury Rd Ash GU12 . . .77 B2
  Farnborough GU14 . . . . . . .56 B2
Canute Rd **5** SO23 . . . . . . .209 F4
Capital Ho **7** SO22 . . . . . . .209 D6
Capper Rd GU15 . . . . .35 E4
Carbonel Cl RG28 . . . . .86 D5
Cardew Rd GU12 . . . . .208 A3
Cardinal Mews **6** SP10 . . .105 F8
Cardinals The GU15 . . . . . . .36 D4
Carfax Ave GU10 . . . . .100 D8
Carfax Est GU10 . . . . .100 D8

Cargate Ave GU11 . . . . .76 E1
Cargate Gr GU11 . . . . .76 E1
Cargate Hill GU11 . . . . .76 D1
Cargate Terr GU11 . . . . .76 D1
Carisbrooke GU16 . . . . .56 D8
Carisbrooke Cl
  Basingstoke RG23 . . . . .68 C6
  New Alresford SO24 . . . . . .179 D4
Carleton Cl RG27 . . . . .50 F1
Carlin Pl **3** GU15 . . . . .36 A4
Carlings GU34 . . . . .139 E2
Carlinwark Dr GU15 . . . . . . .36 D7
Carlisle Cl RG23 . . . . .68 C6
Carlisle Rd GU10 . . . . .144 F7
Carlton Cl GU15 . . . . .36 F3
Carlton Cres GU52 . . . . .75 B6
Carlton Rd GU35 . . . . .166 A5
Carlyon Cl
  Farnborough GU14 . . . . . . .56 A4
  Mytchett GU16 . . . . .56 D4
Carmarthen Cl GU14 . . . . . . .55 E7
Carmichael Way RG22 . . . . .91 C8
Carnegie Rd RG14 . . . . .1 E2
Carolina Pl RG40 . . . . .16 C2
Caroline Ct RG21 . . . . .68 F1
Caroline Way GU16 . . . . .36 D1
Carpenter's Down RG24 . . .48 C2
Carpenters Ct
  Alton GU34 . . . . .140 D6
  Sherfield on L RG27 . . . . . . .29 D1
Carpenters Ct
  Basingstoke RG22 . . . . .68 D3
  Mortimer RG7 . . . . .11 E6
Carrick La GU46 . . . . .34 C6
Carrington Cres RG26 . . . . . .26 F8
Carrington La GU12 . . . . .77 E8
Carshalton Rd **1** GU15 . . . . .36 E8
Cartel Bsns Ctr RG24 . . . . . .69 E8
Carter's Mdw SP10 . . . . .82 E2
Carters Wlk GU9 . . . . .99 B8
Carthagena SO21 . . . . .131 D4
Carthona Dr GU52 . . . . .74 F7
Carwarden House Com Sch
  GU15 . . . . .36 F3
Cary Cl RG14 . . . . .5 B6
Cassino Cl GU11 . . . . .76 C3
Casterbridge La SP11 . . . . . .81 D2
Castle Ave SO23 . . . . .209 D6
Castle Bridge Cotts RG29 . .72 C4
Castle Cl Camberley GU15 . .36 D4
  Farnham GU9 . . . . .99 B3
  Camberley GU15 . . . . .69 B3
Castle Rise
  Kings Worthy SO23 . . . . . .154 C1
  North Warnborough RG29 . .72 C4
Castle Sch The RG14 . . . . . . .1 D6
Castle Sq RG21 . . . . .69 B5
Castle St Farnham GU9 . . . . .98 F2
  Fleet GU52 . . . . .74 F7
  Medstead GU34 . . . . .159 E7
Castlecraig **2** GU47 . . . . . . .35 B7
Caston's Yd RG21 . . . . .69 B4
Castor Ct Fleet GU52 . . . . . . .75 B5
  Yateley GU46 . . . . .33 F7
Caswall Ride GU46 . . . . .34 D5
Caswell Cl GU14 . . . . .55 C6
Catesby Gdns GU46 . . . . . . .33 E5
Cathedral View **4** SO23 . .209 F4
Catherine Cl **1** GU11 . . . . . .76 D1
Catherine Rd RG14 . . . . .1 E2
Catherine Villas GU27 . . . .189 F6
Catherines Wlk SP11 . . . . .104 F3
Catkin Cl RG24 . . . . .48 F3
Cattle La SP11 . . . . .104 E5
Caunter Rd RG14 . . . . .5 C1
Causeway The
  Heckfield RG27 . . . . .31 A7
  Middle Winterslow SP5 . . .168 A7
  Nether Wallop SO20 . . . . . .147 F6
Causton Rd RG22 . . . . .91 B4
Cavalier Cl Newbury RG14 . . .2 A5
  Old Basing RG24 . . . . .70 C6
Cavalier Rd RG24 . . . . .70 C6
Cavalier Way GU34 . . . . . . .139 D2
Cavalry Ct **4** GU11 . . . . .76 C2
Cavalry Ho GU11 . . . . .76 D2
Cavan's Rd GU11 . . . . .77 A6
Cavel Ct RG24 . . . . .70 A8
Cavendish Cl
  Blackwater GU17 . . . . .35 B3
  Fleet GU52 . . . . .2 C5
Cavendish Gdns SO22 . . . . .74 E4
Cavendish Gr SO23 . . . . . .176 B3
Cavendish Mews GU11 . . . . .76 E1
Cavendish Pk GU47 . . . . .35 C6
Cavendish Rd
  Aldershot GU11 . . . . .76 E1
  Fleet GU52 . . . . .74 F4
Caves Farm Cl GU47 . . . . . . .34 E8
Cawett Dr **5** GU52 . . . . .53 E3
Caxton Cl SP10 . . . . .82 C1
Cayman Cl RG24 . . . . .48 D1

Cedar Ave GU17 ....35 B5
Cedar Cl Aldershot GU12 ..100 C8
Kings Worthy SO23 ......176 B8
Tadley RG26 ....27 B7
Cedar Court Pk RG19 ....6 A7
Cedar Ct GU27 ....189 F6
Cedar Dr Fleet GU51 ......54 C1
Kingsclere RG20 ....24 C2
Cedar La GU16 ....56 B8
Cedar Mount RG14 ....5 D8
Cedar Rd GU14 ....56 A3
Cedar Rise RG19 ....7 F5
Cedar Terr RG27 ....52 B5
Cedar Tree Cl RG23 ......90 A8
Cedar View GU22 ....75 B6
Cedar Way RG23 ....68 D6
Cedar Wlk Andover SP10 .105 D6
Winchester SO22 ....209 C5
Cedars Cl GU47 ....34 D8
Cedars Sch RG7 ....9 E7
Cedars The Fleet GU51 ...75 B8
Greenham RG19 ....6 A7
Cedars View SP5 ....191 E7
Cedarways GU9 ....121 F7
Cedarwood
Chineham RG24 ....48 E3
Kings Worthy SO23 ......176 C7
Celandine Ct GU46 ....33 F7
Celtic Dr GU10 ....105 E6
Cemetery Hill RG29 ......72 E2
Cemetery La RG25 ....94 B5
Cemetery Rd GU51 ....74 E7
Central Rd GU35 ....164 D6
Central Way SP10 ....83 E2
Centre Dr RG24 ....48 E1
Centre Terrace Rd GU14 ..76 E8
Centreprise Ho RG19 ......6 E4
Centurion Cl 5 GU47 ....35 B8
Centurion Way RG22 ......91 B7
Century Cl RG25 ....92 A7
Century Farm Ind Units
GU9 ....99 D5
Chaffers Cl RG29 ....95 D3
Chaffinch Cl
Basingstoke RG22 ....91 A8
Sandhurst GU47 ....35 B8
Chalcraft Cl GU30 ......187 E4
Chalcrafts GU34 ....140 A5
Chalet Ct GU35 ....164 D3
Chalet Hill GU35 ....164 D3
Chalfont Dr GU14 ....56 A2
Chalford Rd RG14 ....1 C2
Chalk Cl GU34 ....160 B2
Chalk Down SP9 ....79 A7
Chalk Hill SO20 ....172 F5
Chalk Pit La SP5 ....169 B1
Chalk Ridge SO23 ....198 D2
Chalk Ridge Prim Sch
RG22 ....68 F1
Chalk Vale
King's Somborne SO20 ..172 F4
Old Basing RG24 ....70 C5
Chalkcroft La
Penton Grafton SP11 ....81 F4
Penton Mewsey SP11 .....82 A4
Chalkpit La SP11 ....104 D5
Chalky Hill GU34 ....159 A6
Chalky La RG27 ....73 E3
Challenor Cl RG40 ....16 D7
Challis Cl RG22 ....68 C2
Challis Ct SP11 ....57 A2
Challoner Cl RG22 ....68 D3
Chamber La GU10 ....121 A7
Chamberhouse Mill La
RG19 ....7 D8
Chamberlains Mdw RG27 .31 B5
Chambers Rd GU12 ....77 F6
Champion Way GU52 .....55 A5
Champneys Cl GU35 .....164 C1
Chandler Rd RG21 ....69 A2
Chandlers La GU46 ......34 B7
Chandlers Rd GU12 ......77 F4
Chandos Rd RG14 ....5 D8
Chandos Terr SO21 .....177 E5
Chant Cl SP11 ....128 D6
Chantreys GU51 ....54 A1
Chantry Cl RG27 ....72 A8
Chantry Ct GU16 ....36 B1
Chantry Ctr The SP10 ..106 A8
Chantry Mead SO22 .....209 C7
Chantry Mews RG22 ......91 B7
Chantry St SP10 ....106 A8
Chantrys The GU9 ....98 E1
Chapel Cl Amport SP11 .104 B6
Dummer RG25 ....90 D1
Houghton SO20 ....171 C4
Old Basing RG24 ....70 B7
Chapel Ct
Broughton SO20 ....170 B7
Wherwell SP11 ....128 F6
Chapel Field SO21 .....177 A4
Chapel Gdns GU35 ......164 F5
Chapel Hill RG21 ....69 B6
Chapel La
Aldermaston RG7 ....10 D5
Ashford Hill RG19 ....8 D1
Baughurst RG26 ....26 C7
Enham Alamein SP11 ....105 E6
Farnborough GU14 ....55 D8
Grateley SP11 ....125 B8
Itchen Abbas SO21 .....177 A2

Chapel La continued
Riseley RG7 ....14 A3
Stoke SP11 ....61 C4
Wolverton Common RG26 .25 E4
Chapel Lodge RG40 ......16 C6
Chapel Mead RG27 ....33 C8
Chapel Pond Dr RG29 ....72 C3
Chapel Rd
Camberley GU15 ....35 F5
Rowledge GU10 ....121 C3
Silchester RG7 ....11 A5
Chapel River Cl SP10 ...105 E7
Chapel Row RG27 ....52 D7
Chapel Sq GU15 ....35 D6
Chapel St
Farnborough GU14 ....56 B6
North Waltham RG25 .....89 E1
Chapman Wlk RG18 ....2 A4
Chappell Cl GU30 ......188 A4
Chapter Ct 2 GU34 ....139 F4
Chapter Terr RG27 ......52 D6
Charfield Cl SO22 .....209 C3
Charlcot Cl RG28 ....86 C3
Charldon Gn RG24 ....70 A8
Charlecote Cl GU14 .....56 B3
Charlecote Mews 14
SO22 ....209 D6
Charledown Cl RG25 .....88 A7
Charledown Rd RG25 .....88 A7
Charles Cl Hook RG27 ...51 A1
Winchester SO23 ....209 F8
Charles Dalton Ct SP10 106 A7
Charles Kingsley's CE Prim
Sch RG21 ....33 A8
Charles Richards Cl
RG21 ....69 A3
Charles St
Basingstoke RG22 ....68 E4
Camberley GU15 ....36 A6
Newbury RG14 ....5 B6
Charlotte Cl
Andover SP10 ....106 D8
Farnborough GU14 ....99 B8
Charlotte Ho 4 RG21 ...69 C6
Charlotte Mews GU14 ....56 B5
Charlton Cl RG40 ....16 D8
Charlton Down SO21 .....59 E1
Charlton La RG7 ....14 A5
Charlton Pl RG14 ....1 E4
Charlton Rd
Andover SP10 ....106 A8
Andover SP10 ....82 E1
Charlton Sp & L Ctr SP10 .82 C1
Charlwood La SO24 .....182 D4
Charmwood Cl RG14 ......1 D5
Charnwood Cl
Andover SP10 ....106 B6
Basingstoke RG22 ....68 B3
Chart House Rd GU12 ....77 E7
Charter Rd RG14 ....5 D7
Charters Ct GU12 ......100 A8
Chartwell Camberley GU16 56 D6
Farnham GU9 ....121 D6
Chartwell Gdns GU11 ....77 A7
Chase Com Hospl GU15 .164 D2
Chase Cl GU35 ....164 F5
Chase Field GU35 ......161 D2
Chase Plain GU26 ......167 A1
Chase The Churt GU10 ..144 C3
Donnington RG14 ....1 D7
Farnborough GU14 ....56 B6
Chasewater Ct 8 GU11 ..76 E1
Chatfield Cl GU14 ......56 A2
Chatham Rd SO22 ......209 A3
Chatsworth GU33 ....208 B1
Chatsworth Dr SP10 ....105 E7
Chatsworth Gn RG22 ....91 C6
Chatsworth Gr GU9 .....98 F6
Chatsworth Hts GU15 ...36 F7
Chatsworth Rd GU35 ...164 A1
Chatter La RG26 ....86 C5
Chatters The RG7 ....15 A7
Chattis Hill Stables
SO20 ....148 F3
Chaucer Ave SP10 ....82 D1
Chaucer Bsns Pk SO23 .176 C1
Chaucer Cl
Basingstoke RG24 ....48 C1
South Wonston SO21 ...153 E5
Chaucer Cres RG14 ....1 C5
Chaucer Gr GU15 ....36 B5
Chaucer Rd GU14 ....55 D6
Chaundler Rd SO23 ....209 E8
Chaundlers Cotts 9
GU34 ....139 F4
Chauntsingers Rd GU34 139 F4
Chavasse Way GU14 .....55 B5
Chawton CE Prim Sch
GU34 ....161 D7
Chawton Cl Fleet GU51 .53 F3
Winchester SO22 ......175 D4
Chawton End Cl GU34 ..160 C3
Chawton Park Rd GU34 .139 D1
Cheam Sch RG19 ....24 B8
Cheap St RG14 ....1 E2
Cheavley Cl SP10 ......105 C8
Cheesecombe Farm La
GU33 ....206 F6
Chelsea Cl RG24 ....69 D5
Chelsea Ho RG21 ....69 B5
Chequer La RG27 ....13 C2
Chequers La RG27 ......33 C7
Chequers Rd RG21 ......69 C5

Cherberry Cl GU51 ......54 B4
Cheriton Cl Newbury RG14 .5 F8
7 Tadley RG26 ....26 F7
Winchester SO22 ......209 B7
Cheriton La SO24 ......180 A1
Cheriton Lodge GU51 ...53 C4
Cheriton Prim Sch
SO24 ....201 C6
Cheriton Rd SO22 .....209 C6
Cheriton Way GU17 .....54 C4
Cherrimans Orch GU27 .189 D6
Cherry Cl Hook RG27 ...51 B2
Newbury RG14 ....1 D4
South Wonston SO21 ...153 D4
Cherry Lodge 5 GU12 ..76 F1
Cherry Orch RG28 ....86 D3
Cherry Tree Ave
Haslemere GU27 ....189 D7
North Tidworth SP9 .....79 A7
Cherry Tree Cl
Farnborough GU14 ......55 A5
Farnham GU9 ....99 A3
Cherry Tree Rd
Andover SP10 ....82 E1
Rowledge GU10 ....121 C3
Cherry Tree Wlk
Basingstoke RG22 ......69 C8
Rowledge GU10 ....121 C3
Cherryhill Gr 6 GU11 ..76 D1
Cherryway GU34 ....139 F5
Cherrywood RG24 ....48 E3
Cherrywood Com Prim Sch
GU14 ....55 E6
Cherrywood Rd GU14 ...55 E7
Chertsey St GU51 ....53 E3
Chesil St SO23 ....209 F5
Chesil Terr SO23 ......209 F5
Chesil Wood SO23 .....198 C2
Chesilton Cres GU52 ...75 A5
Chester Cl Ash GU12 ....77 F2
Newbury RG14 ....2 A1
Chester Pl RG21 ....69 A6
Chester Rd Ash GU12 ...77 F3
Winchester SO23 ......209 F6
Chester Way GU10 .....100 D6
Chesterfield Rd
Basingstoke RG22 ......69 C3
Newbury RG14 ....1 C4
Chesters Rd GU15 ......36 F5
Chestnut Ave
Aldershot GU12 ....100 C8
Andover SP10 ....105 F5
Camberley GU15 ....36 A4
Farnham GU9 ....121 E8
Littleton SO22 ....175 C4
North Tidworth SP9 .....79 A7
Chestnut Bank RG24 ....79 B7
Chestnut Cl Alton GU34 139 E5
Blackwater GU17 ....35 C4
Fleet GU51 ....54 C4
Grayshott GU26 ....167 A3
Liphook GU30 ....188 B3
Chestnut Cres RG14 .....1 E4
Chestnut Ct
Aldershot GU12 ....77 B2
Bordon GU35 ....164 E2
7 Newbury RG14 ....5 B6
Chestnut End GU35 ....165 E4
Chestnut Gr GU51 ......54 B2
Chestnut Pl SO20 .....126 B4
Chestnut Rd GU14 .....55 E5
Chestnut Sq SO20 .....126 B4
Chestnut Wlk SO24 ...179 D5
Cheswell Gdns GU51 ...74 E6
Chetwode Pl GU12 .....100 A7
Chetwode Terr GU11 ....76 C1
Cheviot Cl
Basingstoke RG22 ......68 B3
Farnborough GU14 ......55 C7
Newbury RG14 ....5 A5
Cheviot Dr GU51 ....54 B4
Cheyne Way GU14 ......55 D7
Chicheley Cl GU14 .....55 F6
Chichester Cl SP10 ...105 D8
Chichester Pl RG22 ....68 E2
Chichester Rd GU12 ....77 E3
Chilbolton Ave SO22 ..209 B6
Chilbolton Cl GU51 ...209 A6
Chilcomb La
Chilcomb SO21 ....198 E5
Winchester SO23 ......198 C5
Chilcombe Hts SO23 ..209 F7
Chilcroft Cl GU27 ....189 F1
Chilcroft Rd GU27 ....189 D7
Chilcrofts Rd GU27 ...189 E1
Childerstone Cl GU30 .187 F4
Chilham Cl GU14 ....56 D8
Chillandham La
Itchen Abbas SO21 ....155 C2
Itchen Abbas SO21 ....155 C2
Chillingham Way GU15 .36 A4
Chilmark Ct GU33 .....207 F4
Chiltern Ave GU15 .....55 B4
Chiltern Cl
Farnborough GU14 ......55 B4
Fleet GU52 ....75 B6
Haslemere GU27 ....189 F5
Newbury RG14 ....5 A5
Chiltern Cl SO23 .....179 D5
Chiltern Prim Sch RG22 .68 B4
Chiltern Way RG22 .....68 B3
Chiltley Gn GU30 .....188 A3
Chiltley La GU30 .....188 A2
Chiltley Way GU30 ....188 A2
Chilton Farm Pk GU14 .55 A4
Chilton Ridge RG22 ....91 B5

Chine The GU10 ....121 D5
Chineham Bsns Pk RG24 .48 E4
Chineham Cl GU51 ......53 D3
Chineham District Ctr
RG24 ....48 F1
Chineham La
Basingstoke RG24 ......69 D8
Sherborne St John RG24 ..48 A1
Chineham Park Cl GU51 .53 D3
Chineham Park Prim Sch
RG24 ....69 D8
Chingford Ave GU14 ....56 B5
Chinnock Cl GU52 ......74 F7
Chippendale Cl
Blackwater GU17 ....35 C4
3 Hartley Wintney RG26 ..9 C1
Chislett Gdns GU47 ....34 D8
Chiswick Ho RG21 ......69 B5
Chive Ct 2 GU14 ....56 A4
Chivers Cl RG22 ....68 C3
Chivers Dr RG40 ....16 C7
Chobham Rd GU16 ......36 D2
Cholderton Rd
Grateley SP11 ....124 E7
Newton Tony SP4 ......123 A7
Shipton Bellinger SP11 .102 D3
Cholseley Dr GU15 .....53 E3
Chopin Rd RG22 ....91 D8
Chrismas Ave GU12 .....77 A1
Chrismas Pl GU12 ......77 A1
Christ's Hospl 13 SO23 209 D5
Christchurch Cl 2 GU47 ..35 B5
Christchurch Dr GU47 ..35 B5
Christchurch Rd 1
SO23 ....209 D3
Christchurch Rd
Winchester SO23 ......209 D4
Winchester SO23 ......209 D5
Christie Hts RG14 ......5 F8
Christie Wlk GU46 ......34 A4
Christine Cl GU12 ......77 D1
Christine Ho 8 GU11 ...76 F2
Christmas Hill SO23 ..153 B4
Christopher Ct RG14 ....1 F2
Christy Ct RG26 ....27 A7
Christy Est GU12 ......77 C2
Chudleigh Ct 5 GU14 ..55 F4
Church Ave GU14 ....56 A4
Church Bank Rd SO21 .133 F4
Church Brook RG26 .....26 E6
Church Circ GU14 ......56 A1
Church Cl Andover SP10 106 A8
Enborne RG20 ....4 C6
Church Cotts
Blackmoor GU33 ....185 F7
Farnham GU9 ....99 E6
Ropley SO24 ....181 D4
Church Ct 5 ....53 F1
Church Farm Barns RG27 12 B5
Church Farm Cl RG25 ..89 E2
Church Fields GU51 ...165 B5
Church Gr GU51 ....53 E2
Church Hams RG40 .....16 B6
Church Hill
Camberley GU15 ....36 C5
Headley GU35 ....148 A5
Church Hill Terr GU10 ..90 C6
Church La Alton GU34 .140 C7
Ash GU12 ....77 F2
Basingstoke RG21 ......69 B5
Basingstoke, Worting RG23 .68 A4
Bentley GU10 ....120 A6
Bishop's Sutton SO24 .180 B4
Bramdean SO24 ....202 C4
Bramshott GU30 ......188 A6
Brimpton RG7 ....8 A4
Burghclere RG20 ....22 E7
Buttermere SN8 ....31 C7
Cliddesden RG25 ....92 A7
Combe RG17 ....19 C6
Dogmersfield RG27 ....74 A6
Ellisfield RG25 ....115 C8
Empshott GU33 ....185 B3
Enborne RG20 ....4 D7
Ewshot GU10 ....98 B8
Farley Hill RG7 ....15 B6
Farnborough GU14 .....121 D7
Finchampstead RG40 ..116 C4
Goodworth Clatford SP11 .106 D4
Grayshott GU26 ....167 A3
Greatham GU33 ....185 E2
Hartley Wintney RG27 ..52 D5
Headley GU35 ....31 A6
Heckfield RG27 ....31 F4
Houghton SO20 ....171 C6
Kingsclere RG20 ....24 A4
Littleton SO22 ....175 A6
Martyr Worthy SO21 ..177 A6
Medstead GU34 ....159 F7
Mottisfont SO51 ......192 F2
Newbury RG14 ....1 B4
Old Basing RG24 ....70 B6
Ropley SO24 ....181 C3
Rowledge GU10 ....121 C3
Silchester RG7 ....22 B8
South Tidworth SP9 ....78 F7
Sparsholt SO21 ....153 C1
Vernham Dean SP11 ....38 B8
Wolverton RG26 ....25 A6
Woolton Hill RG20 .....21 B8

Church Pas GU9 ....98 E1
Church Path Ash GU12 ..77 E3
Hook RG27 ....71 F8
Church Rd Aldermaston RG7 ..9 F7
Aldershot GU11 ....100 A8
Bramshott GU30 ......188 A6
Fleet GU51 ....53 F2
Fleet GU51 ....54 A1
Frimley GU16 ....36 B1
Haslemere GU27 ....189 D6
King's Somborne SO20 172 A2
Longstock SO20 ....149 D7
Michelmersh SO51 ....193 D2
Nether Wallop SO20 ..148 A5
Overton RG25 ....84 A8
Pamber Heath RG26 ....10 C1
Privett GU34 ....204 C3
Sandhurst GU35 ....35 D7
Silchester RG7 ....11 A4
Swallowfield RG7 ......14 B6
Tadley RG26 ....26 F5
Upper Farringdon GU34 161 E3
Church Rd E GU14 .....56 B2
Church Rd W GU14 ....56 A1
Church Sq RG21 ....69 B5
Church St Aldershot GU11 .76 D1
Alton GU34 ....139 F4
Basingstoke RG21 ......69 B4
Basingstoke RG25 ......69 B5
Bentworth GU34 ......138 A5
Crondall GU10 ....97 C6
Hurstbourne Tarrant SP11 60 E6
Liss GU33 ....207 E6
Micheldever SO21 ....133 A3
Odiham RG29 ....72 E2
Ropley SO24 ....181 D4
Wherwell SP11 ....129 A6
Whitchurch RG28 ....86 C4
Woolton Hill RG20 .....21 B8
Church View Ash GU12 ..77 F2
Hartley Wintney RG27 ..52 C5
Hook RG27 ....51 B1
South Warnborough RG29 94 F3
Upper Clatford SP11 ..105 E4
Yateley GU46 ....34 B7
Churchdale 3 GU11 ....76 E1
Churcher's Coll Jun Sch
GU30 ....188 B2
Churchfield Ct GU30 ..187 F3
Churchfields GU34 ....142 B1
Churchill Ave
Aldershot GU12 ....100 A8
Odiham RG29 ....95 D8
Churchill Cl Alton GU34 139 F2
Farnborough GU14 .....55 F6
Four Marks GU34 ......160 B3
Hartley Wintney RG27 ..52 B7
Kings Worthy SO23 ...154 B1
North Tidworth SP9 ....78 D8
Odiham RG29 ....95 D8
Tadley RG26 ....27 B7
Churchill Cres
Farnborough GU14 .....55 F8
Headley GU35 ....165 D4
Churchill Way
Andover SP10 ....83 C1
Basingstoke RG21 ......69 B5
Churchill Way E RG21 ..69 C5
Churchill Way W
Andover SP10 ....82 D2
Basingstoke RG21 ......68 E5
Churchlands GU11 ......99 F8
Churchyard Cotts SO24 179 D6
Churn Cl RG24 ....70 B7
Churt Rd Barford GU10 166 B8
Beacon Hill GU26 ....166 F7
Headley GU35 ....165 F7
Churt Wynde GU26 ....167 B7
Chute Cl RG26 ....29 A8
Chute Cswy SP11 ....37 B3
Chute Hill SP11 ......174 A4
Cibbons Rd RG24 ....48 F3
City Bsns Ctr SO23 ...209 E6
City Rd SO23 ....209 E6
Claire Ct 1 SP10 .....105 F8
Clandon Ct GU14 ....56 B3
Clanfield Ride GU17 ...35 B5
Clappers Farm Rd RG7 .11 E1
Clapps Gate Rd RG26 ..10 C1
Clarance Ct 3 SP10 ..106 A7
Clare Ct 14 GU51 ......54 A1
Clare Mead GU10 ....71 E4
Clare Wlk RG14 ....5 A5
Claremont Ave GU15 ...36 D6
Claremont Cres RG14 ...2 B4
Clarence Cl GU12 ......77 D3
Clarence Ct GU51 ......54 A1
Clarence Dr GU15 ......36 F7
Clarence Rd GU15 ......54 A1
Clarendon Ave SP10 ..105 E6
Clarendon Ct
Blackwater GU17 ....35 B3
North Tidworth SP9 ....78 F7
Clarendon Gdns RG14 ...1 E4
Clarendon Ho 1 GU51 ..53 F1
Clarendon Jun & Inf Schs
SP9 ....78 F6
Clarewood Ct 5 GU15 ..36 C6
Clarewood Ho GU15 ...36 C7
Clark Mews RG28 ......86 C4
Clarke Cres GU15 ......54 A3
Clarke's La GU34 ......58 F6
Clarks Hill GU10 ....98 B1
Clatford CE Prim Sch
SP11 ....106 A1
Clatford Manor SP11 ..105 E4

Clatford Manor Ho
SP11 ....105 E4
Claudius Ct SP10 ....83 B4
Claudius Dr RG23 ....68 C7
Clausentum Rd SO23 ....209 D3
Clay Hill Cres RG14 ....2 B5
Clay Hill Ho GU27 ....189 E6
Clay's La Binsted GU34 ...141 A6
East Worldham GU34 ....140 E2
Claycart Rd
Aldershot GU11 ....76 B4
Aldershot GU11 ....76 C3
Claydon Gdns GU17 ....35 E1
Claypitt La GU32 ....205 D6
Claythorpe Rd RG22 ....68 C3
Clayton Cl RG22 ....52 C5
Clayton Rd GU14 ....35 D1
Cleaver Rd RG22 ....68 C3
Clem's Way SO51 ....192 A1
Clements Cl GU34 ....141 E7
Clements Gdns RG28 .....86 C5
Clere Ct RG20 ....24 C2
Clere Gdns RG14 ....48 F2
Clere Sch The RG20 ....22 E7
Clerewater Pl RG19 ....2 D3
Clevedge Way RG29 ....72 C4
Clevedon Ct
Camberley GU16 ....56 E8
Farnborough GU14 ....56 B3
Cleveland Cl RG22 ....68 B2
Cleveland Gr RG14 ....1 D3
Cleves La RG25 ....94 B6
Clewborough Dr GU15 ...36 F6
Clewborough House Sch
GU16 ....56 F5
Cliddesden Ct RG21 ....69 B2
Cliddesden La RG22 ....91 D6
Cliddesden Prim Sch
RG25 ....92 A5
Cliddesden Rd
Basingstoke,Cranbourne
RG21 ....69 B2
Basingstoke,Kings Furlong
RG21 ....69 B3
Clifton Cl GU10 ....121 E4
Clifton Gdns GU16 ....56 D6
Clifton Hill SO22 ....209 D6
Clifton Lodge No 1 18
SO22 ....209 D6
Clifton Lodge No 2 19
SO22 ....209 D6
Clifton Rd Newbury RG14 ...1 C2
Winchester SO22 ....209 D6
Clifton Terr
 1 Basingstoke RG21 ......69 B6
Winchester SO22 ....209 D6
Clifton Wlk RG21 ....69 B5
Clitheroe Rd GU17 ....34 D1
Clive Rd GU12 ....77 B1
Clockhouse Rd GU14 .....55 F4
Clockhouse The SO21 ...133 F6
Cloisters The Alton GU34 .139 E4
 4 Andover SP10 ....106 A8
Frimley GU16 ....36 B1
Close The Camberley GU15 ...54 A8
Farnham GU9 ....99 B1
Hatherden SP11 ....59 C2
Liphook GU30 ....188 A2
Monk Sherborne RG26 ....47 B6
Sandhurst GU47 ....35 C8
Thatcham RG18 ....2 F4
Closeworth Rd GU14 .....77 C8
Clouston Rd GU14 ....35 D5
Clovelly Dr GU26 ....167 A7
Clovelly Pk GU26 ....167 A7
Clovelly Rd GU26 ....167 A7
Clover Cl GU35 ....165 A5
Clover Field RG24 ....69 F7
Clover La GU46 ....33 E6
Clover Leaf Way RG24 ...70 B4
Clover Mews 4 SP10 ...106 B7
Cloverbank SO23 ....154 B2
Club Cotts GU30 ....165 C1
Club La SP9 ....78 E4
Clubhouse Rd GU11 ....76 D5
Clumps Rd GU10 ....122 C4
Clyde Ct Aldershot GU12 .100 C8
 18 Andover SP10 ....83 C2
Coach Hill SP11 ....58 C4
Coach Ho The SO22 .....175 B2
Coach House Cl GU16 ...36 C3
Coach House Gdns GU15 .54 A3
Coach Rd The SP5 ....191 C7
Coachman's Ct RG14 ....1 F5
Coachmans Gr GU47 .....34 F7
Coachways SP10 ....106 A6
Coate Dr SO21 ....153 C2
Coates Cl RG22 ....68 F1
Cob Tree Cotts RG25 .....70 E4
Cobb Mews SP11 ....104 B6
Cobbett Cl SO22 ....209 A3
Cobbett Gn RG22 ....68 E2
Cobbett's La GU46,GU17 .34 D5
Cobbetts Mews 4 GU9 ...98 F2
Cobbetts Way GU10 .....121 D6
Cock-A-Dobby GU47 .....34 E8
Cocket's Mead SO21 ...177 A4
Cockshott La GU32 ....206 C2
Cody Cl GU12 ....77 D5
Cody Rd GU14 ....55 D3
Cody Tech Pk
Farnborough GU14 ....55 B1
Farnborough GU51 ....54 E1
Coe Ct GU11 ....76 E1
Cokenor Wood GU10 .....122 A4
Coker Ct SO22 ....209 C6
Colbeck GU52 ....75 B4
Colbourne Ct 7 SO23 ..209 E8

Colbred Cnr GU51 ....54 C4
Cold Harbour Ct 9
SP10 ....106 B7
Cold Harbour La GU14 ...55 D8
Colden La SO24 ....158 A3
Coldharbour RG25 ....89 E1
Coldrey Cotts GU34 .....119 D4
Cole Ave GU11 ....76 D3
Cole Cl SP10 ....83 A4
Colebrook Pl SO23 ....209 E5
Colebrook St SO23 ....209 E5
Colebrook Way NO SP10 .105 D7
Coleford Bridge Rd
GU16 ....56 C4
Coleford Cl GU16 ....56 D3
Coleford Paddocks GU16 .54 D2
Coleman Cl RG21 ....69 C7
Coleman Rd GU12 ....77 B1
Colenzo Dr SP10 ....83 C1
Coleridge Ave GU46 ......34 C5
Coleson Hill Rd GU10 ...121 D5
Coleville Rd GU14 ....55 D5
Coley La SO20 ....128 F4
Coliseum Bsns Ctr GU15 .35 E3
Colindale Way 4 GU33 .207 F4
College Cl GU15 ....36 B7
College Cres GU47 ....35 C8
College Gdns GU9 ....98 F2
College La RG25 ....115 B6
College Mews SP10 .....106 A8
College Piece RG7 ....11 D6
College Pl GU9 ....99 A1
College Rd Ash GU12 ....77 F3
Basingstoke RG21 ....69 B7
Sandhurst GU47 ....35 C7
College Ride GU15 ....36 B7
College St SO23 ....209 C6
College Town Jun & Inf Schs
GU47 ....35 C8
Colley Cl SO23 ....176 A3
Colley Ct GU14 ....55 B5
Collingwood GU14 ....56 C2
Collingwood Coll GU15 .36 E8
Collingwood Grange Cl
GU15 ....36 F8
Collingwood Pl GU15 .....36 E6
Collingwood Rise GU15 .36 E7
Collingwood Wlk SP10 .106 D8
Collins Cl Andover SP10 .82 E3
Newbury RG14 ....2 A4
Collins Ct 1 SP9 ....78 E8
Collins Gdns GU12 ....77 F2
Collyers Cres GU30 .....188 C4
Colne Way Ash GU12 ......77 E1
 6 Basingstoke RG21 ......69 D5
Colson Cl SO23 ....209 F6
Colson Rd SO23 ....209 F6
Coltsfoot Pl RG27 ....51 C2
Coltsfoot Rd GU35 ....165 A5
Columbia Ct RG40 ....16 C8
Columbine Rd RG22 ......91 A8
Columbus Dr GU14 ....55 A4
Colunbus Way SP10 ....83 E1
Colvin Cl SP10 ....106 B7
Colwyn Cl GU46 ....34 A6
Colyer Cl RG22 ....68 C3
Combe La GU14 ....55 E6
Combe Rd GU33 ....208 B1
Combe Rise GU33 ....122 B5
Comet Cl RG27 ....77 D5
Comet Ho RG7 ....9 C2
Comet Rd GU14 ....55 A1
Comfrey Cl GU14 ....55 A5
Commercial Ctr The
SP11 ....84 A3
Commercial Rd GU12 ...100 A8
Commodore Ct GU14 .....76 F8
Common Hill GU34 ....159 D6
Common Rd
Headley RG19 ....24 C8
Headley, Nr Greenham RG19 ..7 D1
Common The
Longparish SP11 ....108 C4
Middle Winterslow SP5 ...168 B6
Ramsdell RG26 ....26 E1
Common Vale SP5 ....168 A6
Commonfield La RG40 ...15 F8
Communications Rd RG19 .6 D5
Compass Field RG27 .....51 B1
Complins GU34 ....140 C6
Compton Cl Fleet GU52 .75 B5
Hook RG27 ....51 B1
Winchester SO22 ....197 B3
Compton Cotts SO20 ...193 D7
Compton Ho 7 GU9 ......99 A2
Compton Place Bsns Ctr
GU15 ....35 E4
Compton Rd Fleet GU52 .75 B5
North Tidworth SP9 ....78 F6
Winchester SO23 ....209 D5
Compton Sq SP10 ....83 C3
Compton Way
Farnham GU10 ....99 F1
Sherfield on L RG27 ....49 F8
Winchester SO22 ....197 B3
Compton's Cnr SP4 .....101 E2
Concorde Rd GU14 ....55 A1
Conde Way GU35 ....164 D2
Coney Gn 5 SO23 ....209 F8
Congreve Cl RG7 ....9 E7
Conholt Hill SP11 ....37 F4
Conholt La SP11 ....38 B4
Conholt Rd SP10 ....106 A5
Conifer Cl Bordon GU35 .164 C1
Fleet GU52 ....74 F5

Conifer Cl continued
Pamber Heath RG26 ....9 C2
Winchester SO22 ....209 D7
Conifer Crest RG14 ....5 A4
Conifer Dr GU15 ....36 E6
Coniston Cl
Farnborough GU14 ....55 C3
Thatcham RG19 ....2 E3
Coniston Ct
Ash Vale GU12 ....77 D4
 8 Newbury RG14 ....1 E4
Coniston Dr GU9 ....98 F6
Coniston Gr SO24 ....179 D4
Coniston Rd
Basingstoke RG22 ....68 B1
Bordon GU35 ....164 D5
Coniston Way GU52 ......74 E5
Connaught Cl
 7 Bordon GU35 ....164 D2
Yateley GU46 ....34 A6
Connaught Rd
Aldershot GU12 ....77 B2
Camberley GU15 ....56 A8
Fleet GU51 ....54 A1
Newbury RG14 ....1 F3
North Tidworth SP9 ....79 A6
Worthy Down Camp SO21 .153 D2
Connaught Sch The
GU12 ....100 C7
Connaught Way GU34 ...139 D1
Connection The RG14 ......1 E6
Connop Way GU51 ....56 D3
Conservatory The 6
SO23 ....209 C5
Consort Pl 9 GU51 ....54 A1
Constable Cl RG21 ....69 D3
Constable Ct SP10 ....83 A1
Constable Way GU47 .....35 C6
Constable's Gate 10
SO23 ....209 D5
Constant Rd GU14 ....54 E2
Constantine Way RG22 ...91 A6
Constantius Ct 11 GU52 ..74 E1
Conway Cl GU16 ....36 D1
Conway Dr
Farnborough GU14 ....55 D4
Thatcham RG18 ....2 F5
Cooks La SO51 ....191 F1
Coolarne Rise GU16 ......36 E6
Coolers Farm SO20 .....170 C6
Coombe Cl GU14 ....56 B8
Coombe Dr GU51 ....54 C1
Coombe Rd GU14 ....33 D8
Coombehurst Dr RG21 ...69 B2
Cooper Ct GU14 ....56 A4
Cooper Ho 5 GU35 .....164 D2
Cooper's Hill GU47 ....77 A1
Cooper's Terr GU9 ....99 A3
Cooperage The 2 GU34 .139 E3
Coopers Cl SO21 ....153 D2
Coopers Ct RG26 ....28 F3
Coopers La RG26 ....28 F3
Cope Hall La RG14 ....5 A7
Copes La RG27 ....31 F7
Copland Cl RG22 ....91 C8
Copner RG22 ....21 B7
Copner Cl RG22 ....21 B7
Copperbeech Pl RG14 ...5 A7
Coppice Cl
Baughurst RG26 ....26 B8
Farnham GU9 ....99 C6
Newbury RG14 ....5 F8
Winchester SO22 ....209 A7
Coppice Gdns GU46 ......34 A5
Coppice Mews RG23 .....68 C6
Coppice Rd RG24 ....24 E2
Coppice The GU52 ....75 A6
Copse Ave GU9 ....99 C8
Copse Cl Camberley GU15 .36 E6
Liss SO23 ....208 A4
Copse End
Camberley GU15 ....36 E6
Fleet GU51 ....54 D8
Copse Field RG24 ....70 A8
Copse La
Brown Candover SO24 ...134 F3
Crookham Village GU52 ...74 F7
Long Sutton RG29 ....95 D3
Copse Rd
Haslemere GU27 ....189 B5
Overton RG25 ....65 B2
Copse The
Basingstoke RG23 ....90 D3
Farnborough RG40 ....53 B3
Rowledge GU10 ....121 D4
Tadley RG26 ....26 E8
Copse View GU14 ....49 A4
Copse Way
Farnham GU10 ....121 D6
Finchampstead RG40 ......16 C7
Copthall Ho 5 GU51 ....54 A1
Coram Ct 3 SO23 ....209 E8
Cordale Rd RG21 ....69 A3
Cordelia Gdns GU11 .....56 D1
Cordwalles Jun Sch
GU15 ....36 C5
Corfe Cl SO24 ....179 D4
Corfe Gdns GU16 ....56 C6
Corfe Way GU14 ....56 C1
Corfe Wlk RG23 ....68 C6
Corfield Rd RG40 ....16 C3
Coriander Ct GU14 ....55 A5
Corinthian Cl
Basingstoke SO20 ....83 B4
Basingstoke RG22 ....91 C7
Crabtree Gdns GU35 ....165 D5
Crabtree La Churt GU10 .144 E2
Headley GU35 ....165 C5
Crabtree Rd GU15 ....35 F2

Cornelia Cl GU14 ....55 B3
Corner Cotts 2 GU26 ...167 B3
Corner The SO22 ....209 C7
Cornerways GU26 ....167 B6
Cornes Cl SO22 ....209 B5
Cornfields Andover SP10 .106 C6
Yateley GU46 ....33 F4
Cornfields The RG22 .....91 C7
Cornish Cl RG22 ....68 C3
Cornish Cl GU15 ....36 D7
Cornwall Ho RG24 ....68 D8
Cornwall Rd GU35 ....164 D1
Coronation Cl
Burghclere RG20 ....22 D7
Odiham RG29 ....72 F3
Coronation Rd
Aldershot GU11 ....99 F7
Basingstoke RG21 ....69 C6
Ludgershall SP11 ....57 A2
Winchester SO22 ....197 A6
Yateley GU46 ....34 C7
Corporation Cotts 1
RG14 ....1 E4
Correlli Rd RG22 ....91 F8
Corringway GU52 ....75 B6
Corry Rd GU26 ....167 A6
Coruuna Main SP10 ....83 B1
Cossack La 28 SO23 ....209 E6
Cossack Lane Ho 28
SO23 ....209 E6
Cossaton Rise SO20 ....126 B4
Costello Technology Coll
RG21 ....69 C4
Coster Ct RG14 ....1 B5
Cotswold Cl
Basingstoke RG22 ....68 B4
Farnborough GU14 ....55 C7
Cotswold The 11 GU51 ..53 F1
Cottage Gdns RG14 ....1 B5
Cottage Gn
Goodworth Clatford SP11 .128 A8
Hartley Wintney RG27 .....52 D5
Cottage Ho GU32 ,GU33 .205 C3
Cottington Cl RG22 ....24 E2
Cottle Cl RG21 ....69 A2
Cotton Cl GU14 ....76 D3
Cottonworth Cotts
SP11 ....128 C4
Cottrell Cl GU52 ....74 F4
Cottrell Flats GU14 ....77 B8
Couch Gn SO21 ....177 C7
Council Hos
Farley Hill RG7 ....15 B5
Up Sombourne SO20 .....173 B5
Council Hos The
Penwood RG20 ....21 E7
Wolverton Common RG26 .25 E4
Council Houses The RG20 .20 A1
Court Cl GU11 ....99 B4
Court Ct GU34 ....188 A3
Court Dr GU52 ....75 A7
Court Dro RG25 ....64 F2
Court Farm RG7 ....10 B6
Court Gdns GU15 ....36 B5
Court La
Gilbert Street SO24 ....181 D6
Up Sombourne SO20 .....173 B6
Court Moor Sch GU52 ....74 F7
Court Rd Aldershot GU11 .76 E2
Kings Worthy SO23 ....176 C5
Courtenay Rd
Farnham GU9 ....99 C7
Winchester SO22 ....176 A3
Courtlands Rd GU14 ......1 F1
Courtmoor Ave GU52 .....75 A7
Courtney Ho 1 GU15 .....35 F3
Courts Hill Rd GU27 .....189 F6
Courts Mount RG21 .....189 F6
Courtyard The GU27 ....188 F2
Cove Inf Sch GU14 ....55 C6
Cove Jun Sch GU14 ......55 C5
Cove Rd
Farnborough GU14 ....55 D4
Fleet GU51 ....54 C3
Cove Sch GU14 ....55 C5
Coventry Cl RG22 ....91 B8
Coventry Ct 8 SO23 .....209 E8
Covert The GU14 ....55 C8
Coverts Rd GU14 ....99 C4
Coverts The RG26 ....26 F6
Covey Cl GU14 ....55 E8
Covey Way SO24 ....179 B4
Cow Drove Hill SO20 ...172 A3
Cow La SP11 ....80 B4
Cowdown Farm Cotts
SP11 ....106 F5
Cowdown La SO21 ....128 A2
Cowdrey Ho 22 SO23 ...209 D6
Cowdrey Pk GU34 ....139 F2
Cowdrey Hts RG24 ....69 E6
Cowdrey Sq SP10 ....83 B3
Cowfold La RG27 ....51 B6
Cowley Dr SO21 ....153 D2
Cowslade GU14 ....55 C8
Cowslip Bank RG24 ......69 F8
Cowslip Cl GU35 ....165 A4
Cowslip Cl RG26 ....26 B8
Coxbridge Mews GU9 ...98 E1
Coxbridge Rdbt GU9 .....121 D8
Coxeter Rd RG14 ....1 B2
Coxgreen GU47 ....35 B6
Coxheath Rd GU51,GU52 .74 F4
Coxmoor Cl GU52 ....75 C5
Crabbs Hill RG26 ....26 B8
Cracknore La GU35 ......165 D5
Crabtree Ct SO23 ....209 C4

Crabtree Way RG24 ....70 B4
Craddock Ho 2 SO23 ...198 C8
Cradle La GU35 ....143 A4
Crake Pl GU47 ....35 B8
Cramptons GU34 ....139 A2
Cranberry Wlk GU17 .....35 D3
Cranbourne Bsns & Ent Coll
RG21 ....68 F3
Cranbourne Ct RG21 ....69 A2
Cranbourne La RG21 ....69 A2
Cranbrook Ct GU51 ......54 A3
Crane Cl GU47 ....35 B8
Cranes Rd RG24 ....47 D4
Cranesfield RG24 ....47 E4
Cranford Ave GU52 ....74 F5
Cranford Dr GU34 ....140 C6
Cranford Park Dr GU46 ..34 B6
Cranleigh Ct GU14 ....56 A6
Cranmer Lodge 2 GU15 .36 C6
Cranmore Cl GU11 ....76 C1
Cranmore Cl GU16 ....56 D4
Cranmore Gdns GU11 ...76 C1
Cranmore La GU11 ....76 C1
Cranmore La GU34 ....56 D4
Cranworth Rd SO22 .....209 D7
Craven Cl GU10 ....122 A6
Craven Ct GU15 ....35 D4
Craven Dene RG14 ....1 F4
Craven Ho 7 GU9 ....98 F2
Craven Rd RG14 ....1 C2
Crawford Gdns GU15 ....35 F5
Crawford Pl RG14 ....1 D3
Crawlboys La SP11 ....57 B3
Crawley Cotts SO21 .....152 B2
Crawley Dr GU15 ....36 D6
Crawley Hill GU15 ....36 D5
Crawley Lo GU15 ....36 E5
Crawley Ridge GU15 .....36 D6
Crawley Ridge Jun Sch
GU15 ....36 D7
Crawley Ridgel Inf Sch
GU15 ....36 D7
Crawley Rise 4 GU15 ...36 D6
Crawley Wood Cl GU15 ..36 D6
Crawts Rd RG25 ....88 A7
Craydown La SO20 ......125 E2
Credon Cl GU14 ....55 D5
Crerar Cl GU14 ....55 B3
Crescent Cl SO22 ....197 B4
Crescent La GU12 ....77 F5
Crescent The
Andover SP10 ....105 C7
Basingstoke RG24 ....68 D8
Bramley RG26 ....28 E3
Crookham Village GU51 ..74 C6
Farnborough GU14 ....56 A2
Farnham GU9 ....99 B8
Four Marks GU34 ....160 B4
Goodworth Clatford SP11 .105 F1
Hurstbourne Tarrant SP11 .60 E7
Mortimer RG7 ....11 D6
Yateley GU46 ....34 B7
Cress Gdns SP10 ....105 F6
Cresswell Rd RG14 ....2 B4
Creswell RG27 ....51 D1
Crichton Ct RG7 ....11 E6
Cricket Cl
Beacon Hill GU26 ....167 B6
Crawley SO21 ....152 B2
Cricket Green La RG27 ..52 D6
Cricket Hill RG40 ....16 D2
Cricket Hill La GU46 ......34 C4
Cricket La GU10 ....122 B6
Cricket Lea GU35 ....165 C5
Cricketers Way SP10 .....83 C2
Cricklade Coll SP10 .....106 A8
Cricklade Pl SP10 ....82 F1
Crimea Rd GU11 ....76 F2
Cripley Rd GU14 ....55 B5
Crispstead La SO23 .....209 F3
Criswick Cl SP11 ....104 F2
Critchmere Hill GU27 ...189 C7
Critchmere La GU27 .....189 C6
Critchmere Vale GU27 ..189 C6
Crockford Ho 1 SO24 ..179 D6
Crockford La
Basingstoke RG24 ....48 D1
Basingstoke RG24 ....48 D2
Croft Ave SP10 ....106 A6
Croft Gdns Alton GU34 ..139 E4
Andover SP10 ....106 A6
Croft La Crondall GU10 ...97 C5
Newbury RG14 ....1 C4
Yateley GU46 ....34 B7
Croft Rd Aldershot GU11 .99 F8
Mortimer RG7 ....11 D6
Newbury RG14 ....5 D8
Oakley RG23 ....67 B2
Croft The Fleet GU51 .....74 D8
Newton Tony SP4 ....123 B5
Croft Way SP10 ....106 A6
Crofter's Cl GU47 ....34 E8
Crofters Mdw RG24 ......69 D7
Crofton Cl GU27 ....189 D7
Crofts The RG22 ....91 C6
Cromwell Cl RG24 ....70 B6
Cromwell Gdns GU14 ...139 F4
Cromwell Pl RG14 ....1 E3
Cromwell Rd
Basingstoke RG21 ....69 A6
Camberley GU15 ....54 A4
Newbury RG14 ....2 A4
Winchester SO22 ....209 C4
Cromwell Terr RG14 ....1 B5
Cromwell Way GU14 .....55 F7

Crondall Ct GU15 . . . . .35 F4
Crondall End GU46 . . . . .34 A7
Crondall La GU9,GU10 . . . . .98 C2
Crondall Prim Sch GU10 .97 D6
Crondall Rd
  Bentley GU10 . . . . .120 E6
  Crookham Village GU10,
  GU51 . . . . .74 C3
Crookham CE Inf Sch
  GU52 . . . . .74 F4
Crookham Ct RG26 . . . . .26 F6
Crookham Common Rd
  Brimpton RG7 . . . . .8 B5
  Thatcham RG19 . . . . .7 E5
Crookham Hill RG12 . . . . . . .7 C7
Crookham Pk RG19 . . . . .7 F6
Crookham Rd GU51,GU52 .74 E5
Crookham Reach GU52 . . . .74 E5
Crooksbury Rd GU10 . . . . .100 A2
Cropmark Way RG22 . . . . . .91 B7
Crosby Gdns GU46 . . . . .33 E7
Crosby Hill Dr GU15 . . . . . .36 D7
Crosby Way GU9 . . . . .98 E1
Cross & Pillory La **9**
  GU34 . . . . .139 F3
Cross Droves SN8 . . . . .17 D3
Cross Farm Inf Sch GU16 .56 C6
Cross Gdns GU16 . . . . .56 A6
Cross Keys Pas **6** SO23 .209 E5
Cross La Andover SP10 . . .105 F8
  Ashmansworth RG20 . . . . . .41 A8
  Beech Hill RG7 . . . . .13 A7
  Camberley GU16 . . . . .56 D6
  Stratfield Mortimer RG7 . . .12 F8
Cross Rd Ash GU12 . . . . . . .77 F3
  Farnborough GU14 . . . . .55 C1
Cross St Aldershot GU11 . .76 E2
  Basingstoke RG25 . . . . .69 B5
  Farnborough GU14 . . . . .77 A8
  Winchester SO23 . . . . .209 D6
Cross The SO20 . . . . .172 A3
Crossborough Gdns
  RG21 . . . . .69 C4
Crossborough Hill RG21 .69 C4
Crossroads GU35 . . . . .164 F6
Crosswater La GU10 . . . . .144 D4
Crossways Aldershot GU12 .77 A1
  Churt GU10 . . . . .144 C1
  Crookham Village GU51 . . .74 C6
  Whitchurch RG28 . . . . .86 C6
Crossways Rd GU26 . . . . . .167 B3
Crossways The SP10 . . . . .105 F8
Croucher's Croft SO22 . . .209 A7
Crowdale Dr **4** GU15 . . . .53 E3
Crowder Terr SO22 . . . . . .209 D5
Crowfield Dr RG19 . . . . .2 F3
Crowley Dr GU34 . . . . .140 A3
Crown Cl Mews GU34 . . . .139 F3
Crown Cres RG24 . . . . .70 A6
Crown Dr GU9 . . . . .99 E5
Crown Gdns GU51 . . . . .75 B8
Crown Hts RG21 . . . . .69 B5
Crown La Farnham GU9 . . .99 E5
  Newnham RG27 . . . . .70 B6
  Old Basing RG24 . . . . .70 B6
Crown Way SP10 . . . . .83 D1
Crownfields RG29 . . . . .72 D2
Crows La GU34 . . . . .161 E3
Crowthorne Rd GU47 . . . . .34 F8
Croyde Cl GU14 . . . . .55 E6
Croye Cl SP10 . . . . .105 F8
Cruikshank Lea GU47 . . . .35 C6
Crumbles Bsns Ct RG29 . .72 C3
Crundwell Ct GU9 . . . . .99 B3
Cuckoo Cl RG26 . . . . .89 E1
Cudbury Dr **6** GU51 . . . .53 E3
Cufaude Bsns Pk RG26 . . .48 D8
Cufaude La Bramley RG26 .28 D1
  Cufaude RG26 . . . . .48 E6
Cuffelle Cl RG24 . . . . .49 A3
Cullen Cl GU46 . . . . .34 A5
Cullens Mews **6** GU11 . .76 E1
Culley View SO24 . . . . . . .179 D4
Culver Mews SO23 . . . . . .209 E5
Culver Rd
  Basingstoke RG21 . . . . .69 A3
  Newbury RG14 . . . . .5 D8
  Winchester SO23 . . . . .209 D4
Culverlands Cres GU12 . . .77 E3
Culverwell Gdns **6**
  SO23 . . . . .209 D5
Cumberland Ave RG22 . . .68 E1
Cumbria Ct GU14 . . . . .56 C1
Cummins Cl SP10 . . . . .106 C7
Cundell Way SO23 . . . . . . .154 B1
Cunningham Ho **4** SP9 .78 E8
Cunnington Rd GU14 . . . . .56 C2
Curlew Cl RG22 . . . . .68 A1
Curlew Ct GU11 . . . . .99 E7
Curlews GU34 . . . . .139 F6
Curling Way RG14 . . . . .2 A4
Curly Bridge Cl GU14 . . . .55 D8
Curlys Way RG7 . . . . .14 B6
Curnock Ct RG14 . . . . .1 C1
Curtis Cl GU35 . . . . .165 C5
Curtis Ct GU35 . . . . .75 A6
Curtis La GU35 . . . . .165 C6
Curtis Mus* GU34 . . . . . . .139 F3
Curtis Rd GU34 . . . . .140 A2
Curzon Dr GU52 . . . . .74 F5
Cuthbert Rd GU12 . . . . .77 F6
Cutts Rd GU11 . . . . .95 B7

Cuxham Way SP10 . . . . . . .82 F3
Cygnet Cl RG14 . . . . .2 F3
Cygnet Ct Fleet GU51 . . . .54 B3
  Newbury RG14 . . . . .1 D3
Cypress Cl RG40 . . . . .16 E8
Cypress Dr GU51 . . . . .54 D1
Cypress Gr Andover SP10 .105 C7
  Ash Vale GU12 . . . . .77 D7
Cypress Hill Ct GU14 . . . . .35 D1
Cypress Ho **3** RG14 . . . . .1 D2
Cypress Rd GU15 . . . . .164 A2
Cypress Way
  Blackwater GU17 . . . . .34 F5
  Grayshott GU26 . . . . .167 B2
Cyprus Rd RG22 . . . . .91 C5
Cyril Vokins Rd RG14 . . . . .2 C2

D

Dacre Cl SP10 . . . . .82 D3
Daffodil Cl RG22 . . . . .91 A8
Dahlia Cl RG22 . . . . .91 B8
Dairy Gate Rd GU14 . . . . . .76 F8
Dairy Ho SP11 . . . . .57 A2
Dairy Wlk RG27 . . . . .52 D6
Dalby Cres RG14 . . . . .6 A8
Dale Cl Farnham GU10 . . .121 D7
  Littleton SO22 . . . . .175 A5
Dale Gdns GU47 . . . . .34 E8
Dale View GU27 . . . . .189 D5
Dalewood RG22 . . . . .68 A3
Dallence Rd RG25 . . . . .88 A7
Dalley Ct GU47 . . . . .35 B7
Dalley Way **3** GU33 . . . .207 F4
Dalzell **10** SO23 . . . . . . .209 E8
Damask La RG25 . . . . .114 D2
Damsel Path **11** RG21 . .69 D5
Damsel Path **12** RG21 . .69 D5
Dancers Mdw RG24 . . . . . .47 F3
Dances Cl SP10 . . . . .83 B1
Dances La RG20 . . . . .86 D6
Danebury Rd RG22 . . . . . . .91 C6
Danebury Ring* SO20 . . .148 E8
Danebury Wlk GU10 . . . . . .56 D8
Dangerfield Cl SP10 . . . . . .83 B4
Danehurst Pl SP10 . . . . . .105 C8
Danemark Ct **3** SO23 . .209 E6
Danes Rd **4** SO23 . . . . . .209 E7
Danes The RG21 . . . . .69 C5
Daneshill Br RG24 . . . . .70 A8
Daneshill East Ind Est
  RG24 . . . . .69 E7
Daneshill Rdbt RG24 . . . . .69 E7
Daneshill Sch RG27 . . . . . .30 D4
Daneshill West Ind Est
  RG24 . . . . .69 D8
Daniel Rd RG28 . . . . .86 D4
Dankworth Rd RG22 . . . . .91 C8
Danley La GU27 . . . . .188 E3
Danvers Dr GU52 . . . . .74 E4
Darby Green La GU17 . . . . .34 F6
Darby Green Rd GU17 . . . .34 F5
Darcy Cl RG21 . . . . .69 C7
Darcy Ho RG22 . . . . .68 C2
Dare's La GU10 . . . . .74 F1
Darent Ct **22** RG21 . . . . . .69 D5
Dares Farm GU10 . . . . .74 F1
Dark La Cheriton SO24 . . .201 D5
  New Alresford SO24 . . . . . .179 F2
  Sherborne St John RG24 . . .47 E3
Darlington Rd RG21 . . . . . .69 A7
Darracott Cl GU15 . . . . .36 F8
Darrington GU15 . . . . .36 E5
Darset Ave GU51 . . . . .54 A5
Dart Cl
  Finchampstead RG40 . . . . . .16 D6
  Thatcham RG18 . . . . .2 F5
Dart Ct **11** SP10 . . . . .83 C2
Dart Rd GU14 . . . . .55 B6
Dartmoor Wlk RG22 . . . . .68 D3
Dartmouth Way RG22 . . .68 C3
Dartmouth Wlk RG22 . . . .68 C3
Darvill Rd SO24 . . . . .181 A5
Darvills La GU9 . . . . .99 B2
Darwin Cl **2** GU15 . . . . . .35 F3
Darwin Gr GU11 . . . . .77 A3
Dashwood Cl GU34 . . . . . .139 D2
Dasna Rd SP9 . . . . .78 D5
Dauntless Dro SP11 . . . . . .81 A2
Dauntsey La SP11 . . . . .81 A1
David Cowan Ho **25**
  SO23 . . . . .209 D6
Davis Gdns GU47 . . . . .35 C7
Davy Cl RG22 . . . . .68 E4
Dawn Cl GU15 . . . . .36 D8
Dawn Gdns RG22 . . . . . . .209 A4
Dawnay Rd
  Camberley GU15 . . . . .36 A8
  Sandhurst GU47 . . . . .35 F7
Days Mdw RG20 . . . . .21 A7
De Lunn Bldgs **8** SO23 .209 E6
De Montfort Rd RG14 . . . . .1 C5
De-Lucy Ave SO24 . . . . . .179 B5
Deacon Rd SP11 . . . . .80 C4
Deadbrook La GU12 . . . . . .77 C3
Deadmans La RG14,RG19 . .5 F6
Dean Cl RG20 . . . . .5 C1
Dean Cl SO22 . . . . .209 A8
Dean La SP10 . . . . .175 B2
Dean Par GU15 . . . . .36 E5
Dean Rd West Dean SP5 . .190 B3
  West Tytherley SP5 . . . . . .190 E5
Dean Rise SP11 . . . . .60 F7
Dean Side SP5 . . . . .190 D3
Dean Terr SP11 . . . . .38 C5

Dean The SO24 . . . . .179 D6
Deane Cotts RG25 . . . . . . .66 B1
Deane Down Dro SO22 . .175 B4
Deanes Cl RG21 . . . . .69 C6
Deans Cl SP9 . . . . .78 F4
Deans Dell GU32 . . . . .205 E1
Deanswood Rd RG26 . . . . .26 E8
Decouttere Cl GU52 . . . . . .74 E4
Deedman Cl GU12 . . . . .77 E2
Deep La RG21 . . . . .68 F5
Deep Well Dr GU15 . . . . . . .35 A5
Deepdene Farnham GU10 .122 B7
  Haslemere GU27 . . . . .189 C6
Deer Park View RG29 . . . .72 D3
Deer Rock Rd GU15 . . . . . .36 B2
Deerfield Cl RG26 . . . . .29 B2
Deerleap GU35 . . . . .166 A4
Defiant Rd GU14 . . . . .76 D8
Dehlia Cl **4** SP10 . . . . . .105 D6
Delibes Rd RG22 . . . . .91 F8
Delius Cl RG22 . . . . .68 E1
Dell Cl GU27 . . . . .189 E7
Dell Cotts SO24 . . . . .202 F1
Dell Gr RG22 . . . . .36 D2
Dell Rd Andover SP10 . . . .82 F1
  Finchampstead RG40 . . . . . .16 E3
  Winchester SO23 . . . . .188 A8
Dell The Farnham GU9 . . . .99 B7
  Grateley SP11 . . . . .103 B1
  Kingsclere RG20 . . . . .24 D2
  Old Basing RG24 . . . . .70 C5
  Vernham Dean SP11 . . . . . . .38 B6
  Yateley GU46 . . . . .34 A5
Dellands RG25 . . . . .88 A7
Dellands La RG25 . . . . .88 A7
Dellfield High Cross GU32 .205 E2
  Oakley RG23 . . . . .67 B3
Delta Bsns Pk GU34 . . . . .140 B3
Delville Cl GU14 . . . . .55 B3
Dempster Ho GU9 . . . . .99 B8
Denby Ct RG14 . . . . .56 A1
Denby Dene GU12 . . . . .77 F2
Dene Cl Bordon GU35 . . . .164 D2
  3 Camberley GU15 . . . . . .36 E8
  Ropley SO24 . . . . .181 A5
Dene Ct SP10 . . . . .106 B7
Dene La GU10 . . . . .122 C6
Dene La W GU10 . . . . .122 C5
Dene Path SP10 . . . . .106 B7
Dene Rd Andover SP10 . . .106 B7
  Farnborough GU14 . . . . .55 D3
Dene Terr SO24 . . . . .181 A5
Dene The SO24 . . . . .181 A5
Dene Way RG14 . . . . .1 E5
Dene Wlk GU10 . . . . .122 B6
Denham Cl SO23 . . . . .209 D8
Denham Dr
  Basingstoke RG22 . . . . .68 C2
  Yateley GU46 . . . . .34 B5
Denham Terr SP11 . . . . .61 F2
Denman Cl GU51 . . . . .54 C1
Denmark Rd RG14 . . . . .1 E3
Denmark Sq GU12 . . . . . . .77 F2
Denmead Rd RG26 . . . . . . .26 F8
Dennet Ho SO23 . . . . .176 D1
Denning Cl GU51 . . . . .74 C6
Denning Mead SP10 . . . .105 F7
Dennis Way GU14 . . . . .208 A3
Dennistoun Cl GU15 . . . . .36 B5
Denton Way GU16 . . . . .36 B2
Denvale Trad Pk RG21 . . . .68 F6
Denvale Trade Pk RG14 . . .2 B2
Denyers Cotts GU34 . . . . .138 A4
Deptford La RG29 . . . . .72 A3
Derby Fields GU34 . . . . . . .72 A3
Derby Gate RG27 . . . . .82 B1
Derby Rd
  Haslemere GU27 . . . . .189 F7
  Newbury RG14 . . . . .1 D1
Derek Horn Ct GU15 . . . . .35 F6
Derry Cl GU12 . . . . .77 D5
Derry Rd GU14 . . . . .55 D8
Derwent Ave GU12 . . . . . . .77 D4
Derwent Cl Bordon GU35 .164 D5
  Farnborough GU14 . . . . .55 A3
  Farnham GU9 . . . . .98 E6
Derwent Ct **20** SP10 . . .83 C2
Derwent Gdns SO24 . . . . .179 D4
Derwent Rd
  Basingstoke RG22 . . . . .68 A1
  Haslemere GU27 . . . . .2 E3
Desborough Cl RG14 . . . . .2 C5
Devenish Rd SO22 . . . . . .175 D3
Dever Cl SO21 . . . . .133 A3
Dever Way RG23 . . . . .67 B1
Devils La GU30 . . . . .188 C3
Devizes Cl **7** SP9 . . . . . .78 F7
Devon Cl Fleet GU51 . . . . .54 B4
  Sandhurst GU47 . . . . .35 B7
Devon Ho RG24 . . . . .68 D8
Devon Rd Bordon GU35 . .164 D5
  Farnborough GU14 . . . . .76 D7
Devonshire Dr GU15 . . . . .36 D1
Devonshire Pl
  Aldershot GU11 . . . . .77 A4
  6 Basingstoke RG21 . . . . .69 A4
Dewpond Wlk RG26 . . . . . .29 B2
Dexter Sq SP10 . . . . .83 C3
Dexter Way GU51 . . . . .54 B4
Diamond Hill GU15 . . . . . . .36 C7
Diamond Rd GU12 . . . . .77 D6
Diamond Ridge GU15 . . . .36 B7
Diamond Way GU14 . . . . . .76 C8
Diana Cl GU12 . . . . .77 D5
Dibley Cl RG22 . . . . .68 C3
Dickens La RG24 . . . . .70 A4

Dickens Way GU46 . . . . . . .34 A5
Dickens Wlk **1** RG14 . . . . .5 E8
Dickenson Wlk SO24 . . . .179 D4
Dicker's La GU34 . . . . .140 A4
Digby Rd RG14 . . . . .1 C4
Digby Way GU33 . . . . .186 A4
Dilly La RG27 . . . . .52 C4
Dines Cl SP11 . . . . .60 E7
Dingley Way GU14 . . . . . . .76 E8
Dinorben Ave GU52 . . . . . .74 F7
Dinorben Beeches GU51 . .74 F7
Dinorben Cl GU52 . . . . .74 F7
Dinwoodie Dr RG24 . . . . . .68 E8
Dippenhall Rd GU10 . . . . .98 A2
Dippenhall St GU10 . . . . . .97 D6
Dirty Cnr RG20 . . . . .85 F8
Discovery Ct **8** RG14 . . . .1 E2
Ditchfield La RG40 . . . . . . .16 C8
Dittons The RG40 . . . . .16 C8
Divers Cl GU34 . . . . .139 F6
Dixon Rd RG27 . . . . .49 B6
Dixons La SO20 . . . . .170 B7
Dockenfield St GU10 . . . .143 A6
Doctors Acre RG27 . . . . . .51 D1
Doctors Dro SP11 . . . . .60 D7
Dodsells Well RG40 . . . . . .16 D8
Dogflud Way GU9 . . . . .99 D8
Dogmersfield CE Prim Sch
  RG27 . . . . .74 A7
Doiley Bottom SP11 . . . . . .40 D3
Doiley Hill SP11 . . . . .40 C3
Dollis Cl GU9 . . . . .99 B3
Dollis Dr GU9 . . . . .99 B3
Dollis Rd RG26 . . . . .28 F3
Dolman Rd RG14 . . . . .1 E4
Dolomans La SP11 . . . . . . .60 E8
Dolphin Cl
  Haslemere RG7 . . . . .9 D7
  Haslemere GU27 . . . . .189 C6
Dolton Mews RG14 . . . . . . .1 D3
Doman Rd GU15 . . . . .35 E4
Dome Alley SO23 . . . . . . .209 E5
Dominica Cl RG24 . . . . .48 C2
Domitian Gdns RG24 . . . . .68 C8
Domum Rd SO23 . . . . .209 E5
Donaldson Way RG14 . . . . .1 C6
Donnington Castle* RG14 . .1 C7
Donnington Cl **3** GU15 .36 E8
Donnington Ct **2** SO23 .209 E7
Donnington Hospl RG14 . .1 C6
Donnington Lodge RG14 . .1 D6
Donnington Pk RG14 . . . . .1 D5
Donnington Sq RG14 . . . . .1 D5
Dora's Green La
  Dippenhall GU10 . . . . .98 A3
  Ewshot GU10 . . . . .98 A3
Doras Green La GU10 . . . .98 A2
Dorcas Ct GU15 . . . . .35 F3
Dorchester Cl RG23 . . . . . .68 B5
Dorchester Rd RG27 . . . . .51 A1
Dorchester Way RG24 . . . .72 A4
Dores La SO21,SO51 . . . .195 D2
Doria Gr SO24 . . . . .179 B4
Dormer Cl RG14 . . . . .5 B6
Dorneywood Way RG14 . . .1 B6
Dorothy Ct RG14 . . . . .2 A4
Dorrel Cl RG22 . . . . .91 B6
Dorset Cl GU15 . . . . .36 D8
Dorset Ho RG24 . . . . .68 D8
Dorset Rd GU12 . . . . .77 F5
Dosswell Way RG21 . . . . . .69 C6
Douai Cl GU14 . . . . .56 A4
Doublet Cl RG19 . . . . .3 C3
Doughty Way SP10 . . . . . . .83 E1
Douglas Gr GU10 . . . . . . .122 A5
Douglas Pl GU14 . . . . .55 E5
Douglas Rd SP11 . . . . .105 B7
Douglas Ride RG20 . . . . . .21 C8
Dove Cl Andover SP10 . . . .83 B2
  Basingstoke RG22 . . . . .67 F1
Dove Ct GU34 . . . . .140 A6
Dove House Sch RG14 . . . .69 B7
Dovecote Cotts SO21 . . . .131 C4
Dover Cl Basingstoke RG23 .68 D6
Dover Rd Basingstoke RG24 .179 D4
Doveton Way RG14 . . . . . . .1 C4
Dowden Gr GU34 . . . . . . .140 A5
Down Farm La SO22 . . . . .175 A2
Down Gate SO24 . . . . .179 C4
Down La RG25 . . . . .70 F3
Down Rd SP11 . . . . .80 B2
Down St GU46 . . . . .90 D1
Downing St GU9 . . . . .98 F2
Downlands Rd SO22 . . . .197 B4
Downlands Way
  South Wonston SO21 . . . . .153 C4
  Winchester SO23 . . . . .153 D4
Downs Cl GU14 . . . . .55 C7
Downs La SN8 . . . . .18 B7
Downs Rd
  Over Wallop SO20 . . . . .125 D3
  South Wonston SO21 . . . . .153 D4
Downs View GU34 . . . . . . .140 E7
Downs Way SO34 . . . . .139 D2
Downshill SO22 . . . . .100 B4
Downside RG26 . . . . .167 B7
Downside Cotts SO23 . . . .124 F7
Downsland Par RG21 . . . . .68 E7
Downsland Rd RG21 . . . . . .69 A4
Downsview Rd SO22 . . . . . .79 D6
Downview Ct GU26 . . . . . .167 B6
Doyen Ct RG14 . . . . .1 F3
Doyle Gdns GU46 . . . . .34 A5
Dragonfly Dr RG24 . . . . . . .69 F8
Dragoon Ct **10** GU11 . . .76 C2

Drake Ave GU16 . . . . .56 E5
Drake Cl RG40 . . . . .16 C7
Drake Ct SP10 . . . . .83 D1
Drayman's Way GU34 . . .139 F3
Drayton Pk SO21 . . . . .108 D2
Drayton St SO22 . . . . .209 A4
Draytons View RG19 . . . . . .6 B7
Drift Rd
  Bordon GU33,GU35 . . . . .186 A8
  Chilbolton SO20 . . . . .129 F2
Drift The GU10 . . . . .120 A4
Driftway Rd RG27 . . . . .51 C1
Drive The Farnham GU9 . .121 F7
  Newbury RG14 . . . . .5 C8
  Quarley RG3 . . . . .67 B1
Drive Cl GU34 . . . . .162 F8
Drove Hill SO20 . . . . .129 A3
Drove La SO24 . . . . .179 B5
Drove Rd SP11 . . . . .129 B3
Drove The Andover SP10 .105 D8
  Headley, Nr Greenham RG19 .7 F8
Drovers End GU51 . . . . . . .54 C4
Drovers Way GU9 . . . . .98 E6
Droxford Cres RG26 . . . . . .26 E7
Drummond Cl
  Four Marks GU34 . . . . .159 F2
  Winchester SO22 . . . . .209 C3
Drury Cl La Bentworth GU34 .138 B6
  Mortimer RG7 . . . . .11 E5
Dryden Cl RG24 . . . . .49 C4
Dryden Rd GU14 . . . . .55 D6
Dryden Way GU30 . . . . . . .187 E5
Du Maurier Cl GU52 . . . . . .74 E3
Duchess Cl GU34 . . . . .139 E3
Ducklands GU35 . . . . .164 E2
Duckmead La GU33 . . . . . .208 B5
Ducks La SO20 . . . . .147 F5
Duddon Way RG21 . . . . . . .69 D5
Dudley Cl
  Basingstoke RG23 . . . . .68 B5
  Bordon GU35 . . . . .164 D1
Dudley Ct GU52 . . . . .75 A5
Dudley Terr GU31 . . . . . . .208 A5
Duke Cl SP10 . . . . .83 D1
Duke of Connaughts Rd
  GU11 . . . . .77 B5
Duke of Cornwall Ave
  GU15 . . . . .36 B8
Duke St SO21 . . . . .133 B3
Dukes Cl Alton GU34 . . . .139 D2
  Farnham GU9 . . . . .98 E6
Dukes Ct GU14 . . . . .55 D3
Dukes Mead GU51 . . . . . . .53 D1
Dukes Pk GU11 . . . . .77 B6
Dukes Ride RG27 . . . . .27 E8
Dukes Wlk GU9 . . . . .98 E6
Dumas Cl GU46 . . . . .34 A5
Dummer Down La RG25 .113 C7
Dummer La SP11 . . . . .37 A2
Dummer Mews **5** SO23 .209 D5
Dump Rd GU14 . . . . .55 C1
Dunbar Rd GU16 . . . . .56 D7
Dunbridge La
  Chilton Candover SO24 . . .135 D5
  Dunbridge SO51 . . . . .192 D1
Duncan St SP10 . . . . .106 C7
Duncan Ho **3** RG21 . . . . .69 D6
Duncan's Ct SP11 . . . . .80 E2
Dundaff Cl GU15 . . . . .36 E5
Dundee Gdns RG22 . . . . . .68 B4
Dungells Farm Cl GU46 . .34 A4
Dungells La GU46 . . . . .34 A4
Dunhills La SP11 . . . . .83 C8
Dunkirt La SP11 . . . . .104 E3
Dunley Dr **1** GU51 . . . . . .53 D1
Dunley's Hill RG29 . . . . . . .72 C3
Dunmow Hill GU51 . . . . . . .54 A2
Dunmow Rd SP10 . . . . . . .106 B6
Dunsell's Cl SO24 . . . . . . .181 D5
Dunsell's La SO24 . . . . . . .181 D5
Dunsford Cres RG23 . . . . .68 C7
Dunsmore Gdns GU46 . . .33 E5
Dunston Dro SP11 . . . . .39 C1
Durbidges RG19 . . . . .24 C8
Durham Way RG22 . . . . . . .91 B8
Durley Cl SP10 . . . . .105 E2
Durnford Cl SO20 . . . . . . .129 A4
Durngate PI SO23 . . . . . . .209 F6
Durngate Terr **6** SO23 .209 F6
Durnsford Ave GU52 . . . . .75 A7
Dyson Dr SO23 . . . . .209 E8
Dytche St RG14 . . . . .1 C3

E

Eagle Cl Alton GU34 . . . . .139 F6
  Basingstoke RG22 . . . . .69 F6
Eagle Ct Basingstoke RG24 .69 F6
  8 Winchester SO23 . . . .209 D6
Eagle Rd RG20 . . . . .6 E2
Eames La GU33 . . . . .206 F8
Eardley Ave SP10 . . . . .82 D1
Earle Ho **1** SO23 . . . . . .198 D8
Earls Gr GU15 . . . . .36 C6
Earlsbourne GU52 . . . . . . .75 B4
Earlsdown **9** SO23 . . . . .209 F5
Early Lands RG7 . . . . .27 F8
East Acre GU9 . . . . .99 B6
East Dean Rd SO51 . . . . . .191 E2
East Gn GU17 . . . . .35 A4
East Hill GU33 . . . . .209 F4
East Hill Dr GU33 . . . . . . .208 A3
East Hundreds GU51 . . . . .53 E3
East La SO24 . . . . .178 F4

East Portway SP10 ....82 C1
East Rd SO21 ....130 E7
East Ring GU10 ....100 E7
East St Andover SP10 ....106 B7
　Andover SP10 ....106 B8
　Farnham GU9 ....99 A3
　New Alresford SO24 ....179 D6
East Station Rd GU12 .....76 F1
East View RG27 ....52 B4
East Woodhay Rd GU34 ..175 D4
Eastacre SO22 ....209 C7
Eastbrooke Rd GU34 .....140 A4
Eastend Cotts SP11 ....59 D6
Eastern Ave SP10 ....106 B7
Eastern Rd
　Aldershot GU12 ....77 C2
　Bordon GU35 ....164 D6
Eastfield Ave RG21 ....69 C5
Eastfield Cl SP10 ....106 C8
Eastfield Ho SP10 ....106 C7
Eastfield Lodge ❷ SP10 106 B7
Eastgate St SO23 ....209 F5
Eastlyn Rd RG26 ....10 C1
Eastmans Field SO20 ....129 A3
Eastmead
　Farnborough GU14 ......55 F3
　Farnborough GU14 ......55 F4
Easton Common Hill
　SP5 ....168 C6
Easton La Easton SO21 ..176 E3
　Easton SO21 ....177 A5
　Winchester SO23 ......176 C1
Easton Lane Bsns Ctr
　SO23 ....209 F6
Eastrop La RG21 ....69 C5
Eastrop Rdbt RG21 ....69 C5
Eastrop Way RG21 ....69 C5
Eastview RG23 ....68 A4
Eastview Gdns GU34 ....161 E3
Eastville SP11 ....81 C7
Eaton Ct ❻ GU15 ....35 F5
Eaton Rd GU15 ....35 F4
Ebble Cl SP9 ....78 F7
Ebden Rd SO23 ....209 F6
Ecchinswell & Sydmonton CE
　Prim Sch RG20 ....23 E4
Ecchinswell Rd
　Ecchinswell RG20 ....23 E3
　Kingsclere RG20 ....24 B2
Echo Barn La GU10 .....121 D5
Eddeys Cl GU35 ....165 F6
Eddeys La GU35 ....165 F5
Eddy Rd GU12 ....77 A1
Eddystone Ct GU10 .....144 D1
Edgar Cl SP10 ....83 B4
Edgar Rd SO23 ....209 D4
Edgar Villas SO23 ....209 D4
Edgeborough Sch GU10 122 A3
Edgecombe La RG14 ......2 A5
Edgehill Cl
　Basingstoke RG22 ......68 C4
　Newbury RG14 ....2 C5
Edgewood Ct GU33 .....208 B2
Edinburgh Cl GU12 ......77 D2
Edinburgh Ho ❹ SO22 .209 D6
Edinburgh Rd SO23 .....154 C1
Edington Rd SO23 ....209 E7
Edison Rd RG21 ....68 E7
Edney Cl GU52 ....74 A6
Edric's Gn SP4 ....101 D1
Edrich Sq SP17 ....83 B2
Edward Ave GU15 ....35 E5
Edward Ct
　❺ Aldershot GU11 ......76 E1
　Farnborough GU14 ......55 E4
Edward Rd Alton GU34 .140 A5
　Farnham GU9 ....122 D7
　Winchester SO23 ......209 D3
Edward St GU11 ....76 D2
Edward Terr SO24 ....179 E5
Edwins Ct GU14 ....56 A7
Eeklo Pl RG14 ....1 E1
Eelmoor Plain Rd GU11 .76 B5
Eelmoor Rd
　Aldershot GU14 ....76 B5
　Farnborough GU14 ......55 D2
Eelmoor Trad Est GU14 ..55 D2
Egbert Rd SO23 ....209 E7
Egbury Rd SP11 ....62 B2
Egerton Rd GU15 ....35 D7
Eggar's Ct ❻ GU12 ......76 F1
Eggar's Hill GU11 ....99 E8
Eggar's Sch GU34 ......140 B6
Eggars Cl GU34 ....140 B4
Eggars Field GU10 ......120 B5
Eggleton Cl GU52 ....74 E5
Eglinton Rd GU14 ....144 F6
Egret Gdns GU11 ....99 E2
Eight Acres GU26 ....167 A4
Eight Bells RG14 ....1 D2
Eights The SP11 ....104 B6
Eland Rd GU12 ....104 F8
Elane Ho SP11 ....57 A2
Elbe Way SP10 ....82 F3
Elbow Cnr RG21 ....69 B5
Elder Cl SO22 ....209 A2
Elder Cres SP10 ....105 D7
Elderberry Bank RG24 ...69 F8
Elderfield Rd GU35 .....165 A5
Eldergrove GU14 ....56 C2
Eldon Cl SO20 ....172 A2
Eldon Dr GU10 ....122 B5
Eldon Rd SO20 ....194 A5
Eleanor Cl GU30 ....187 B8
Elgar Cl RG22 ....91 E8
Elgarth Dr RG40 ....16 D8
Elgin Rd GU17 ....34 C1

Elgin Way GU16 ....56 D8
Eling Cl SO22 ....175 D3
Eliot Cl GU15 ....36 F7
Eliot Dr GU27 ....189 C6
Elizabeth Ave RG14 ......5 B7
Elizabeth Ct SO23 ......154 B1
Elizabeth Ct SP11 ....82 A1
Elizabeth Dr GU52 ....75 A5
Elizabeth Par GU46 ......34 B4
Elizabeth Rd RG22 ....68 E3
Elizabeth Sq SP9 ....79 A7
Elizabethan Rise RG25 ..89 E1
Elkington Cl RG20 ....22 E7
Ellen Dr GU51 ....54 B4
Ellen Gdns RG26 ....28 E3
Elleray Ct GU12 ....77 E5
Elles Cl GU14 ....55 F3
Elles Rd GU14 ....55 E2
Ellingham Cl SO24 .....179 D5
Ellington Cl SP11 ....105 B7
Ellington Dr RG22 ....91 C7
Elliott Park Ind Est GU12 77 D7
Ellison Way GU10 ......100 D7
Elm Bank GU46 ....34 A7
Elm Bank Rd SP10 .....106 A6
Elm Bottom Cross RG24 ..47 D2
Elm Cl Bordon GU35 ...164 E3
　Ludgershall SP11 ....57 B2
　Thruxton SP11 ....103 D8
Elm Cres RG20 ....4 D1
Elm Cres GU9 ....99 B7
Elm Ct Andover SP10 ...106 A7
　Winchester SO22 ......209 C6
Elm Gr Farnham GU9 ....99 A7
　Kingsclere RG20 ....24 D2
Elm Grove Cvn Pk RG18 ..2 F5
Elm Grove Flats RG20 ...24 D2
Elm Grove Fm RG20 .....24 D2
Elm Grove Rd GU14 .....55 F4
Elm La GU10 ....100 D8
Elm Piece Ho RG25 ......88 B7
Elm Pl GU11 ....100 A8
Elm Rd Farnham GU9 ....99 B7
　New Alresford SO24 ...179 D5
　Overton RG25 ....65 B2
　Sherborne St John RG24 ..47 D2
　Winchester SO22 ......209 C6
Elm Terr GU33 ....207 E5
Elm View GU12 ....77 F3
Elmay Ho SP11 ....57 B1
Elmcroft Cl GU16 ....56 D7
Elmfield GU35 ....165 A5
Elmfield Ct GU35 ....164 F5
Elmfield Gdns RG14 ......1 C4
Elmhurst RG26 ....27 A7
Elmhurst Rd RG18 ....2 E5
Elms Aldershot GU11 ....76 E1
　Fleet GU51 ....75 C8
　Hook RG27 ....51 A1
Elms The Andover SP10 ..105 F7
　Blackwater GU17 ....35 B4
　❽ Farnham GU9 ....99 B2
　Tongham GU10 ....100 D8
Elmsleigh Rd GU14 ......55 D4
Elmsley Ct GU14 ....55 D4
Elmstead Cvn Pk SP11 .103 F7
Elmwood RG24 ....48 E3
Elmwood Cl GU34 ....139 D2
Elmwood Par RG23 ......68 C7
Elmwood Way RG23 ......68 C7
Elsenwood Cres GU15 ...36 E6
Elsenwood Dr GU15 .....36 E7
Elsley Cl GU16 ....56 D6
Elstead Rd GU10 ....100 F2
Elston Pl GU12 ....100 A8
Elston Rd GU12 ....100 A8
Elvetham Cl GU51 ....54 A3
Elvetham Cres GU51 .....54 A3
Elvetham Heath Prim Sch
　GU51 ....53 D3
Elvetham Heath Way
　GU51 ....53 E3
Elvetham La RG27 ....53 A8
Elvetham Pl GU51 ....53 D3
Elvetham Rd GU51 ....53 E3
Ely Cl GU14 ....56 B2
Ely Gr RG14 ....2 C5
Embleton Rd GU35 .....165 F6
Emden Rd SP10 ....82 F3
Emery Down Dr ❸ GU51 53 C3
Emily Ct RG26 ....27 A6
Empress Ave GU14 ......55 F5
Enborne CE Prim Sch
　RG20 ....4 C6
Enborne Gate RG14 ......1 B1
Enborne Gr RG14 ....1 C2
Enborne Lodge La RG14 ..1 A6
Enborne Rd RG14 ....1 C1
Enborne St Enborne RG20 ..4 E4
　Newtown RG20 ....5 A6
Enborne Way RG7 ....8 D6
Enfield Rd GU12 ....77 F5
Engineer's Rd RG19 ......6 E5
English Wood RG24 ......68 C7
Enham Alamein Mus*
　SP11 ....83 B7
Enham La
　Andover,Charlton SP10 ..82 E3
　Andover,Knights Enham
　SP10 ....83 A3
Enmill La GU22 ....196 E5
Ennerdale Cl RG22 ....68 B2
Ennerdale Gdns SO24 ..179 D4
Ennerdale Gr GU35 .....164 D5
Ennerdale Way RG19 .....2 E3
Enterprise Ct RG24 ......69 D7

Enterprise Est GU12 .....77 D7
Enterprise Ho
　Aldershot GU11 ....76 F2
　Basingstoke RG22 ......68 B4
Epsom Cl GU15 ....36 A8
Epsom Cres RG14 ....1 F1
Epsom Down GU34 .....139 F2
Equine Way GU14 ....5 F7
Erasmus Park Student Village
　SO23 ....176 C1
Erica Cotts GU26 ....167 A6
Erleigh Dene RG14 ....1 D1
Erles Rd GU30 ....188 A4
Ermin Wlk RG19 ....2 F3
Ernest Cl GU10 ....121 F6
Erskine Cl RG26 ....10 D1
Erskine Rd SO22 ....209 C5
Esher Cl RG22 ....68 D1
Eskdale Ct GU12 ....77 D4
Essex Cl Bordon GU35 ..164 D4
　Camberley GU15 ....36 E7
Essex Rd
　Basingstoke RG21 ......69 A5
　Bordon GU35 ....164 D4
Essex St RG14 ....5 B7
Ethelbert Dr SP10 ....82 D3
Eton Cl RG22 ....91 A6
Eton Pl GU9 ....98 F7
Etps Rd GU14 ....76 F8
Ettrick Ct GU14 ....36 C3
Etwall SP11 ....103 A4
Europa Cl RG26 ....28 F3
Euskirchen Way RG22 ...68 D5
Evans Cl SO20 ....125 B2
Eveley Cl GU35 ....165 A6
Evelyn Ave GU11 ....99 F8
Evelyn Mews GU34 ......179 D6
Evelyn Woods Rd GU11 ..77 A6
Evenlode Way GU47 .....35 B8
Everest Rd GU15 ....36 B8
Evergreen Rd GU34 .....126 E3
Eversfield Cl SP10 .....105 F8
Eversley Dr ❷ GU51 .....53 C3
Eversley Pl SO22 ......209 B3
Eversley Rd RG27,GU46 ..33 F7
Eversley St RG27 ....15 E1
Evingar Gdns RG28 ......86 C6
Evingar Ind Est RG28 ....86 C5
Ewing Way RG14 ....5 F8
Ewins Cl GU12 ....105 A8
Ewshot Hill Cross GU10 ..98 A7
Ewshot La GU10,GU52 ...74 A2
Exbury Way SP10 ....105 E7
Exeter Cl RG27 ....91 A7
Exeter Gdns GU46 ....33 F7
Exeter Rd GU12 ....77 F5
Exmoor Cl RG22 ....68 B3
Express Way RG14 ....2 C2

F

Fabers Yd ❶❷ SO22 ...209 D6
Fabian Cl ❷ RG21 ....69 A4
Factory Cotts GU10 ......98 A1
Factory The GU10 ....98 B2
Fair Close Ho ❸ RG14 ....1 E2
Fair La Chilcomb SO21 ...199 F8
　Itchen Abbas SO21 ....177 A1
Fair Oak La RG7 ....29 D7
Fair Piece SP11 ....128 F6
Fair View SO24 ....179 C4
Fairacre RG20 ....21 D8
Fairacres GU10 ....121 D4
Fairclose RG28 ....86 C4
Fairclose Dr SO22 ......175 B5
Fairclose Terr RG28 .....86 C4
Fairdown Cl SO23 ......154 B1
Fairfax Cl SO22 ....197 B5
Fairfax Ind Est GU12 ....77 C2
Fairfax Mews GU14 ......2 B2
Fairfax Pl RG14 ....2 C5
Fairfax Rd GU14 ....56 A7
Fairfield RG28 ....86 C3
Fairfield Gn GU34 ......160 C3
Fairfield Mobile Home Pk
　RG7 ....11 D5
Fairfield Rd SO22 ......209 D7
Fairfield The GU9 ....99 A2
Fairfields Ct RG21 ....69 B4
Fairfields Prim Sch RG21 .69 B4
Fairfolds Rd RG21 ....69 B5
Fairground Craft & Design
　Ctr The* SP11 ....81 B2
Fairground The SP11 ....81 D2
Fairholme Gdns GU9 ....99 A1
Fairholme Par ❹ RG27 ..51 A1
Fairland Cl SO22 ....55 B8
Fairlands GU35 ....166 B5
Fairlawn Ho ❸ SO22 ...209 D5
Fairlawn Rd SO22 ....27 B7
Fairlight Gdns GU34 ...160 C3
Fairmead Cl GU47 ....35 C7
Fairmead Ct ❶ GU15 ....36 A4
Fairmile SO22 ....75 A6
Fairoak Way RG26 ....9 F8
Fairthorne Rd RG25 ......68 E3
Fairthorne Rise RG22 ...91 C7
Fairview RG14 ....5 C8
Fairview Gdns GU34 .....99 B6
Fairview Mdw RG23 ......90 B8
Fairview Rd Ash GU12 ...77 F3
　Headley GU35 ....166 A5
　Penton Grafton SP11 ...81 C1
Fairview Terr GU35 .....165 E6
Fairway Cl GU30 ....187 B3

Fairway Hts GU15 ....36 F6
Fairway The
　Bordon GU35 ....164 B1
　Farnborough GU51 ......54 E1
　Farnham GU9 ....99 B7
　Fleet GU14 ....75 F8
　Frimley GU15 ....36 E3
Fairways
　Beacon Hill GU26 .....166 F6
　Weyhill SP11 ....81 B2
Faithfulls Dro SO20 ....171 B4
Falaise Cl GU11 ....76 F2
Falaise Rd SO20 ....126 A4
Falcon Bsns Pk RG40 ...15 E6
Falcon Cl RG14 ....5 F8
Falcon Coppice RG20 ...21 D8
Falcon Ct Alton GU34 ..139 F6
　Frimley GU16 ....36 B1
Falcon Fields RG20 ....5 F8
Falcon House Gdns RG20 ..4 C1
Falcon View GU52 ......209 A2
Falcon Way GU46 ....33 F6
Falkland Ct GU14 ....77 C8
Falkland Dr RG14 ....5 D8
Falkland Garth RG14 .....5 B7
Falkland Prim Sch RG14 ..5 B6
Falkland Rd
　Basingstoke RG24 ......48 C1
　Newbury RG14 ....5 B6
Falkner Ct ❽ GU9 ....99 A2
Falkner Ho GU51 ....54 A2
Falkner Rd GU9 ....98 F2
Falkners Cl GU51 ....54 C4
Fallow Field SO22 ......209 B2
Fallowfield Fleet GU51 ...54 C4
　Yateley GU46 ....33 F7
Falmouth Cl GU15 ....36 E4
Fantails GU34 ....139 F6
Faraday Cl RG2 ....15 C7
Faraday Ct RG24 ....69 D8
Faraday Office Pk RG24 ..69 D8
Faraday Pk SP10 ....82 B1
Faraday Rd
　Basingstoke RG24 ......69 D8
　Farnborough GU14 ......56 A6
　Newbury RG14 ....2 B1
Faraday Way RG22 ....15 C8
Farcrosse Cl GU47 ....35 A8
Farefield Ho GU15 ....36 E5
Fareham Dr GU46 ....33 F7
Faringdon Ct ❶❼ SO23 ..209 E8
Farleigh La RG21 ....91 B2
Farleigh Rd RG25 ....92 A7
Farleigh Rise RG22 ......69 C2
Farleigh Sch SP11 ......127 B8
Farleigh Wallop Dr ❹
　GU51 ....53 C3
Farley Cl SO22 ....197 B4
Farley Ct Farley Hill RG7 ..15 B1
Farley Hill Prim Sch RG7 .15 B1
Farley La SO22 ....56 B2
Farley Mount Ctry Pk*
　SO21 ....196 B8
Farley Mount Rd SO21 .196 A3
Farley St SO20 ....147 F6
Farm Cl GU46 ....34 B5
Farm Cotts GU34 ....68 D8
Farm Ct GU16 ....36 D2
Farm Dr GU51 ....54 B4
Farm Ground Cl RG27 ...51 C1
Farm La GU10 ....97 C5
Farm Rd
　Abbotts Ann SP11 .....105 A6
　Aldershot GU12 ....77 C3
　Frimley GU16 ....56 D2
　Sparsholt SO21 ....174 B5
Farm View GU46 ....34 B5
Farm View Dr RG24 .....49 A4
Farmers Gdn RG25 ....88 B7
Farmhouse Way GU52 ...74 E5
Farnborough Air Sciences
　Trust (Mus)* GU14 ......55 F1
Farnborough Airport
　GU14 ....55 D2
Farnborough Bsns Ctr
　GU14 ....55 D2
Farnborough Bsns Pk
　GU14 ....55 F2
Farnborough Coll of Tech
　GU14 ....56 A2
Farnborough Gate Ret Pk
　GU14 ....56 A7
Farnborough Hill (Girls Sch)
　GU14 ....56 A5
Farnborough Ind Est
　GU14 ....55 E3
Farnborough North Sta
　GU14 ....56 B6
Farnborough Rd
　Aldershot GU11 ....76 D3
　Farnborough,Frnboro Gn
　GU14 ....56 A6
　Farnborough GU14 ......56 A6
Farnborough St GU14 ...56 B6
Farnborough Bsns Ctr GU9 ..98 F1
Farnham By-Pass GU9 ...98 B3
Farnham Castle* GU9 ....98 D1
Farnham Coll GU9 ....99 A1
Farnham Heath End Sch
　GU9 ....99 C3
Farnham Hospl GU9 .....99 C3
Farnham La GU27 ......189 E7
Farnham Mus* GU9 .....98 E1

Farnham Park Cl GU9 ....98 F6
Farnham Park Dr GU9 ...98 F6
Farnham Rd
　Bordon GU35 ....164 D6
　Churt GU10 ....144 B3
　Crondall GU10 ....74 A1
　Fleet GU51 ....75 D8
　Liss GU33 ....207 E4
　Odiham RG29,RG27,GU10 ..73 D2
Farnham Sta GU9 ....99 A2
Farnham Trad Est GU9 ...99 D4
Faroe Cl RG24 ....48 D1
Farrell Cl GU15 ....36 A3
Farren Ho GU14 ....56 A1
Farrier Pl GU47 ....34 F7
Farrier's Field RG25 ....115 A8
Farriers Cl Bramley RG26 ..28 F3
　Crookham Village GU52 ..74 E3
Farriers La SO20 ....126 B4
Farringdon Bsns Pk
　GU34 ....161 C3
Farringdon Ind Est
　GU34 ....161 C2
Farringdon Way RG26 ...26 F7
Farrs Ave GU11 ....106 B7
Farthing Fields GU35 ...165 C5
Farthingfield Ho GU9 ...99 A3
Farwalters' Cross RG28 ..85 C1
Fawconer Rd RG20 ....24 D2
Fawley La GU34 ....204 B4
Fawn Dr GU12 ....77 C3
Fayrewood Chase RG22 ..91 B7
Feathers La ❺ RG21 .....69 B4
Feathers Yd ❾ RG21 .....69 B4
Feilden Cl RG20 ....21 D8
Felbridge Cl GU16 ....36 D1
Feld Way RG24 ....70 A8
Felders Mead RG27 ......51 D1
Fellows Rd GU14 ....56 B1
Felmer Dr SO23 ....176 C1
Feltre Pl ❶❶ RG14 ....1 D2
Fencott Pl RG21 ....69 B6
Fen's Yd GU9 ....98 E1
Fennel Cl Chineham RG24 ..49 A4
　Farnborough GU14 ......2 B5
　Newbury RG14 ....2 B5
Fenton Lodge ❸ GU15 ..36 C8
Ferbies GU52 ....75 A6
Ferden Hts GU27 ....189 F7
Ferguson Cl RG21 ....69 B2
Fermor Dr GU11 ....76 D3
Fern Cl GU12 ....77 D1
Fern Ct GU12 ....77 D1
Fern Dr GU51 ....74 E6
Fern Lea GU9 ....99 F6
Fernbank RG40 ....16 B6
Fernbrae Cl GU10 ......121 F3
Ferncote Rd GU35 ......164 E3
Ferndale Gdns RG27 .....51 E3
Ferndale Rd Andover SP10 ..82 E1
　Fleet GU51 ....75 C8
Ferndon La GU27 ....189 F3
Ferndown Cl RG22 ......91 A4
Ferndown Ct Alton GU34 ..140 A4
　Fleet GU14 ....122 B5
Ferndown Gdns GU14 ...55 C4
Ferney Cl GU34 ....161 D7
Fernhill Cl
　Farnborough GU17 ......35 D1
　Fleet GU51 ....98 F6
Fernhill Dr GU9 ....98 F6
Fernhill La
　Farnborough GU17 ......35 D1
　Fleet GU51 ....98 F6
Fernhill Lodge GU14 ....35 D1
Fernhill Pk RG27 ....48 B3
Fernhill Prim Sch GU14 .35 D1
Fernhill Rd
　Farnborough,Cove GU14 ..55 C6
　Farnborough,Hawley GU14 ..35 D1
Fernhill St GU34 ....35 D1
Fernhill Wlk GU17 ......35 D1
Ferniehurst GU15 ....36 D4
Fernlea GU15 ....164 B1
Fernleigh Ct ❾ GU14 ....55 F4
Ferns Mead GU9 ....98 E1
Ferns The
　❸ Farnborough GU14 ...77 B8
　Farnham GU9 ....99 A7
Ferrell Field RG27 ....50 F1
Ferrier Gr RG14 ....5 F8
Festival Pl RG21 ....69 B5
Fiddlers Field GU34 ....139 B8
Field End Farnham GU9 ..99 D4
　Kings Worthy SO23 ....176 C7
Field Gate Dr RG20 .....24 C2
Field La GU16 ....36 C1
Field Path GU14 ....35 D1
Field Pl GU30 ....188 A3
Field Rd GU14 ....55 D1
Field Stores App GU11 ..77 A3
Field Way Aldershot GU12 ..77 C3
　Tongham GU10 ....100 D7
Fielders Ct GU34 ....139 F3
Fielders The RG27 ....25 C2
Fieldfare Ave ❷ GU46 ..33 F6
Fieldgate Ctr RG20 .....24 C2
Fielding Rd GU47 ....34 C6
Fieldridge RG14 ....2 B5
Fieldway GU51 ....74 D8
Fifehead Cotts SO20 ...147 C8
Fifield La GU10 ....122 B2
Fifth Rd RG14 ....1 C1
Fifth St RG19 ....6 D5
Filmorehill La GU34 ....204 B3

220 Fin – Gle

Finch Cl RG26 .....27 A7
Finchampstead Prim Sch RG40 .....16 C3
Finchampstead Rd RG40 .16 D6
Finches Gn GU34 .....139 F6
Findhorn Cl 4 GU47 .....35 B7
Findings The GU14 .....55 C8
Fingle Dr SP10 .....105 E8
Finkley Down Farm Pk* SP11 .....83 E3
Finkley Rd SP11 .....84 C7
Finns Ind Pk GU10 .....74 B2
Fintry Pl GU14 .....55 C7
Fintry Wlk GU14 .....55 C7
Fiona Cl SO23 .....198 C8
Fir Acre Rd GU12 .....77 E6
Fir Cl Fleet GU51 .....74 F8
Thatcham RG19 .....7 F5
Fir Cottage Rd RG40 .....16 C8
Fir Dr GU17 .....35 B3
Fir Gr GU35 .....164 B1
Fir Tree Alley 12 GU11 .....76 E2
Fir Tree Ave GU27 .....189 B6
Fir Tree Cnr 13 RG26 .....9 C2
Fir Tree Cotts GU33 .....208 E4
Fir Tree La RG14 .....2 C4
Fir Tree Piece RG26 .....45 A4
Fir Tree Prim Sch RG14 .....2 C4
Fircrofts 5 GU51 .....53 F1
Fire Station Rd GU11 .....76 F3
Fire Thorn Cl GU52 .....75 A7
Firecrest Rd RG22 .....90 F6
Firfield Rd GU9 .....121 E7
Firglen Dr GU46 .....34 B7
Firgrove Ct
8 Farnborough GU14 .....55 F4
Farnham GU9 .....99 A1
Firgrove Hill GU9 .....99 A1
Firgrove Manor RG27 .....33 D6
Firgrove Par 7 GU14 .....55 F4
Firgrove Rd
Bordon GU35 .....164 B1
6 Farnborough GU14 .....55 F4
Yateley RG27,GU46 .....33 E6
Firlands Ave GU15 .....36 B5
Firmstone Rd SO23 .....198 C8
Firs Cl Farnborough GU14 .56 A2
Finchampstead RG40 .....16 D7
Firs Cres SO23 .....176 B8
Firs End RG7 .....11 D6
Firs La RG29 .....72 C1
Firs The Andover SP10 .....105 E8
Liphook GU30 .....187 F3
Thatcham RG18 .....2 F4
Winchester SO22 .....209 C7
Firs Way RG23 .....68 B7
First Ave RG7 .....10 B2
First St RG19 .....6 E5
Firsway RG28 .....86 C5
Firth Cl RG7 .....27 F8
Firtree Cl GU47 .....34 D8
Firtree Way GU52 .....75 B8
Firview GU30 .....187 F3
Firway GU26 .....166 C5
Firwood Ct GU15 .....36 A5
Firwood Dr GU15 .....36 A5
Fish La SO21 .....174 B5
Fisher Cl SP10 .....106 C7
Fisher Ho 5 RG14 .....1 D2
Fisherman's La RG7 .....9 F8
Fishermen's Cl GU11 .....77 C5
Fiske Cl RG22 .....68 C4
Fiske Ct GU46 .....34 C6
Fitzgerald Ct RG14 .....1 D3
Fitzroy Rd GU51 .....53 D1
Five Acres Cl GU35 .....164 F5
Five Ash Rd GU34 .....160 A4
Five Bells La SO20 .....147 F5
Five Bridges Rd SO23 .....209 C1
Five Lanes SP11 .....61 E1
Five Lanes End RG25 .....71 B1
Fivefields Cl SO23 .....198 C6
Fivefields Rd SO23 .....198 C7
Fiveways
Basingstoke RG22 .....68 A2
Camberley GU15 .....36 C5
Flashett The SP5 .....168 B6
Flats The GU17 .....34 F4
Flaxfield Ct RG21 .....69 A5
Flaxfield Rd RG21 .....69 A5
Fleet Bsns Pk GU52 .....75 B3
Fleet Com Hospl GU51 .....53 E2
Fleet Hill RG40 .....16 B3
Fleet Inf Sch GU52 .....75 C7
Fleet La RG40 .....15 F2
Fleet Pond (Nature Reserve)* GU51 .....54 C3
Fleet Rd Aldershot GU11 .....76 C6
Farnborough GU14 .....55 B4
Fleet GU51 .....54 A2
Hartley Wintney RG27 .....52 E5
Fleet Sta GU51 .....54 B3
Fleetwood Cl RG14 .....2 B5
Fleming Cl
Arborfield Garrison RG2 .....15 C7
Farnborough GU14 .....56 B6
Fleming Rd Newbury RG14 ..1 F3
Winchester SO22 .....175 C3
Flensburg Cl SP10 .....82 F3
Fletcher Cl RG21 .....68 F4
Fletchers Field GU30 .....188 A3
Fletchers Ho GU30 .....187 F3
Flexditch RG7 .....27 F8
Flexford Cl RG20 .....21 D5
Flinders Cl SP10 .....83 F1
Flint Cl SP10 .....105 E6
Flint La SP11 .....81 E8
Floral Way SP10 .....105 D7
Floreat Gdns RG14 .....1 C1
Florence Cl GU46 .....34 A6
Florence Ct SP10 .....83 B3
Florence Gdns RG18 .....2 E5
Florence Portal Cl RG28 .87 B5
Florence Rd Fleet GU52 ..75 B7
Sandhurst GU47 .....35 C7
Florence Way
Alton GU34 .....139 D1
Sherborne St John RG24 .....68 C8
Florrie Pl GU34 .....161 D3
Flowerdew Ct SP10 .....106 A5
Flowerdown Ho SO22 .....175 C4
Flowerdown Mobile Home Pk SO22 .....175 C5
Focus 303 SP10 .....83 E1
Focus Way SP10 .....83 E1
Foden Rd GU11 .....76 E1
Folly Cl GU52 .....75 A7
Folly Cotts RG20 .....22 E7
Folly Hill GU9 .....98 F5
Folly Hill Inf Sch GU9 .....98 E6
Folly La RG26 .....29 B4
Folly La N GU9 .....98 F6
Folly La S GU9 .....98 E5
Folly Rdbt SP10 .....83 A1
Folly The RG14 .....1 F1
Fontwell Cl GU12 .....77 B2
Fontwell Dr GU34 .....139 F2
Fontwell Rd RG14 .....1 F1
Forbes Chase 8 GU47 .....35 B7
Forbes Rd SO23 .....176 B8
Forbury La RG20 .....3 A7
Forburys GU9 .....121 F8
Ford La Farnham GU10 .....121 F6
Lower Common RG27 .....14 E2
Odiham RG29 .....95 A6
South Warnborough RG29 .....94 F8
Fordington Ave SO22 .....209 C6
Fordington Rd SO22 .....209 C7
Forefield Dr RG22 .....91 A5
Forehead The RG7 .....12 D4
Foreman Pk GU12 .....77 F2
Foreman Rd GU12 .....77 F1
Forest Cl RG26 .....9 C2
Forest Cnr GU33 .....208 A7
Forest Ct 3 SP9 .....79 A7
Forest Dean GU51 .....54 C4
Forest Dr Chineham RG24 ..48 F4
Gong Hill GU10 .....122 A4
North Tidworth SP9 .....79 A7
Forest End GU52 .....74 F6
Forest End Rd GU47 .....34 E8
Forest Glade GU10 .....121 B3
Forest Hills GU15 .....35 F4
Forest La Andover SP11 ..106 F6
Lindford GU35 .....165 A6
Tadley RG26 .....27 B6
Upper Chute SP11 .....57 F7
Forest Lane Cl GU30 .....187 E4
Forest Rd Bordon GU35 ..164 D2
Bordon,Whitehill GU35 .....164 D1
Greatham GU33 .....185 F1
Liss GU33 .....208 A6
Forest Rise GU33 .....208 A6
Forest Sh Ctr The GU35 .164 E3
Forestdale GU26 .....167 C3
Foresters Pk SO23 .....176 A4
Forge Cl Bramley RG26 .....29 A2
Farnham GU9 .....99 B3
King's Somborne SO20 .....172 A2
Forge Ct GU46 .....34 B7
Forge Field SP10 .....83 B1
Forge La GU11 .....76 E6
Forge Rd Kingsley GU35 ..164 A8
Sleaford GU35 .....142 E1
Forsters RG7 .....9 D7
Forsters Farm Ct RG7 .....9 D6
Forsythia Wlk RG21 .....69 C8
Fort Hill Com Sch RG23 ..68 C6
Fort Hill Dr RG23 .....68 C6
Fort Narrien GU15 .....35 D7
Forth Cl GU14 .....55 B6
Forth Ct 21 SP10 .....83 C2
Fortrose Cl GU47 .....35 B7
Fortuna Ct 1 RG7 .....9 C2
Forum Cl RG23 .....68 B5
Fossewood Dr GU15 .....36 B7
Fosters Bsns Pk RG27 .....71 E8
Foul La GU34 .....159 F7
Foundry Cl RG27 .....51 A1
Foundry La GU27 .....189 E6
Foundry Rd SP11 .....105 D4
Fountain Rd GU34 .....184 E7
Fountains Cl RG24 .....48 A1
Four Acre Coppice RG27 .51 C2
Four Houses Cnr RG7 .....11 C8
Four Houses Cnr Cvn Site RG7 .....11 C8
Four Lanes Cl RG24 .....49 A3
Four Lanes End
Chineham RG24 .....49 A3
Odiham RG29 .....95 B5
Four Lanes Inf & Com Jun Schs RG24 .....48 F3
Four Marks CE Prim Sch GU34 .....182 B8
Four Oaks RG20 .....21 D6
Four Ways GU10 .....142 F8
Fourth St RG19 .....6 D5
Fowler Ave GU14 .....55 F2
Fowler Rd GU14 .....55 D3
Fowler's Rd GU11 .....77 B6
Fox Court Mobile Homes GU47 .....35 A8
Fox Cover The SO20 .....126 B4
Fox Croft GU52 .....75 A5
Fox Ct GU12 .....77 C3
Fox Dr GU46 .....34 B7
Fox Farm SP11 .....103 E3
Fox Heath GU14 .....55 A3
Fox La Eversley Cross RG27 .33 D8
Oakley RG23 .....67 C3
Winchester SO22 .....209 A3
Fox Rd Farnham GU10 .....122 A7
Haslemere GU27 .....189 C6
Fox Way GU10 .....98 B8
Fox Yd GU9 .....98 F2
Fox's La RG20 .....24 C2
Foxborough RG7 .....14 B6
Foxcote RG40 .....16 E7
Foxcotte Cl SP10 .....82 D2
Foxcotte La SP10 .....82 C3
Foxcotte Rd SP10 .....82 D2
Foxdown RG25 .....65 B2
Foxdown Cl GU15 .....36 A5
Foxglove Cl RG22 .....91 A7
Foxglove Dr GU35 .....164 E2
Foxhill Cres GU15 .....36 F8
Foxhunter Way RG19 .....2 D3
Foxhurst Rd GU12 .....77 E4
Foxley Cl GU17 .....35 A5
Foxmoor Cl RG23 .....67 C3
Foxs Furlong RG24 .....49 B4
Foxwood GU51 .....54 C3
Foye La GU52 .....75 B5
Foyle Pk RG21 .....69 B2
Foyle Rd SP11 .....80 C4
Frampton Way SO23 .....176 C7
France Hill Dr GU15 .....36 A5
Frances Rd RG21 .....69 A4
Frances Sheldon Ct SO22 .....209 C5
Francis Ct GU14 .....55 D4
Francis Gdns SO23 .....176 B3
Francis Way GU15 .....36 F4
Franklin Ave
Hartley Wintney RG27 .....52 C7
Pamber Heath RG26 .....9 E1
Franklin Ct 6 GU14 .....55 A4
Fraser Cl RG24 .....70 B6
Fraser Mead GU47 .....35 C6
Fraser Rd SO23 .....176 C8
Fraynes Croft GU51 .....74 F8
Frederick Ho 6 RG21 .....69 C6
Frederick St GU11 .....76 E2
Freelands Dr GU52 .....74 E5
Freeman Ct RG14 .....1 D3
Freemantle Cl RG21 .....69 D7
Fremantle Rd SP11 .....79 D7
French Gdns GU17 .....35 B4
French Rd GU33 .....186 D3
Frenchmans Creek 10 GU52 .....74 E4
Frenchmoor La
East Dean SP5 .....190 F2
West Tytherley SP5 .....190 F4
Frensham Ave GU51 .....54 C1
Frensham Cl GU46 .....33 F6
Frensham Country Pk* GU10 .....144 C5
Frensham Ct GU10 .....121 F4
Frensham Heights Rd GU10 .....121 E2
Frensham Heights Sch GU10 .....121 E2
Frensham La
Headley GU10 .....143 E2
Lindford GU35 .....165 B6
Frensham Rd GU9,GU10 ..122 B5
Frensham Vale GU10 .....122 A4
Frere Ave GU51 .....74 E7
Frescade Cres RG21 .....69 A3
Freshwood Dr GU46 .....34 B4
Friar's Field GU9 .....98 E3
Friars Ct Farnham GU9 .....99 B7
Sandhurst GU47 .....34 D8
Friars Oak GU34 .....160 C4
Friars Rd RG14 .....5 E8
Friarsgate SO23 .....209 E6
Friary Gdns 7 SO23 .....209 D5
Friend Ave GU12 .....77 B1
Friesian Cl GU51 .....54 B4
Frimley Bsns Pk
Camberley GU16 .....56 A8
Frimley GU16 .....55 F8
Frimley CE Jun Sch GU16 .....56 C7
Frimley Green Rd GU16 ..56 C7
Frimley Grove Gdns GU16 .....36 C1
Frimley Hall Dr GU15 .....36 D6
Frimley High St
Camberley GU16 .....56 A8
Frimley GU16 .....36 B1
Frimley Park Hospl GU16 .36 B2
Frimley Rd Ash Vale GU12 ..77 E8
Camberley GU15 .....35 F4
Frimley GU16 .....36 A1
Frimley Sq GU16 .....36 C1
Frimley Sta GU16 .....56 A8
Frith End Rd GU35,GU34 .142 E6
Frith Hill Rd GU16 .....36 E1
Frithmead Cl RG21 .....69 A2
Frog La Bramley RG26 .....28 A5
Little London RG26 .....27 F5
Mapledurwell RG25 .....70 F4
Rotherwick RG27 .....50 D6
Froghole La SO20 .....171 F2
Frogmore Com Coll GU46 .....34 D5
Frogmore Ct GU17 .....35 A4
Frogmore Gr GU17 .....35 A4
Frogmore Jun & Inf Schs GU17 .....34 F5
Frogmore Park Dr GU17 ..35 B4
Frogmore Rd GU17 .....35 A4
Frogs Hole RG20 .....24 C2
Frome Cl
Basingstoke RG21 .....69 D5
Farnborough GU14 .....55 B6
Oakley RG23 .....67 C1
Fromond Rd SO22 .....175 D3
Froome Pl RG24 .....48 E2
Frouds Cl RG27 .....71 F8
Froxfield CE Inf Sch GU32 .....205 E2
Froxfield Cl SO22 .....175 D4
Froyle Ho GU34 .....119 A2
Froyle La RG29 .....95 A3
Fry Sq SP10 .....83 B2
Fry's Acre GU12 .....77 E3
Fry's La GU46 .....34 C7
Fryers Cl SO23 .....176 C8
Fugelmere Rd GU51 .....54 C2
Fulbrook Way RG29 .....95 D8
Fulflood Ct 2 SO22 .....209 C6
Fullers La RG20 .....21 A8
Fullers Rd GU10 .....121 B4
Fullers Vale GU35 .....165 D5
Fullerton Cl 14 GU51 .....53 C3
Fullerton Rd
Goodworth Clatford SP11 ..127 D7
Wherwell SP11 .....128 E5
Fullerton Way RG26 .....27 A7
Fulmar Cl RG22 .....90 F7
Furley Cl 8 SO23 .....209 F6
Furrows The SO20 .....126 B4
Furse Hill Rd SP9 .....78 F5
Further Vel-Mead GU52 ..74 E4
Further Vell-Mead GU52 ..74 E4
Furze Cl GU12 .....77 E7
Furze Dr SP11 .....79 D6
Furze Hill Rd GU35 .....166 A4
Furze Rd RG26 .....9 D2
Furze Vale Rd GU35 .....166 A4
Furzedown Cotts SO20 ..194 B7
Furzedown Ho SO20 .....194 B6
Furzedown La SP11 .....103 F5
Furzedown Rd SO20 .....194 B8
Furzen La RG25 .....115 B7
Fuzzy Dro RG22 .....90 F8
Fyfield Cl GU17 .....35 B5
Fyfield La SP11 .....81 A3
Fyfield Rd SP11 .....81 B2
Fyfield Way
Littleton SO22 .....175 B5
North Tidworth SP11 .....79 D6
Fylingdales Cl RG22 .....68 B3

G

Gable End
10 Aldershot GU11 .....76 F2
3 Farnborough GU14 .....55 F4
Gables Cl Ash Vale GU12 ..77 E5
Farnborough GU14 .....55 E4
Gables Rd GU52 .....74 F4
Gables The
10 Grayshott GU26 .....167 B3
Whitchurch RG28 .....86 E5
Gabriel Dr GU15 .....36 F4
Gabriels The RG14 .....5 B5
Gaffney Cl GU11 .....77 B7
Gage Cl RG24 .....69 F7
Gaiger Ave RG27 .....49 B5
Gainsborough Cl
Camberley GU15 .....36 D7
Farnborough GU14 .....56 B2
Gainsborough Ct
Andover SP10 .....82 F1
Farnborough GU14 .....77 A8
5 Fleet GU51 .....54 A2
Gainsborough Rd RG21 ..69 C2
Galahad Cl SP10 .....83 A3
Galaxy Ho RG19 .....6 E5
Gales Ct SP10 .....106 A7
Galileo Pk SP10 .....82 C1
Gallaghers Mead SP10 ..105 C8
Galleries The 8 GU11 .....76 E2
Galley La RG19 .....24 C8
Gallop The GU46 .....34 B7
Galloway Cl
Basingstoke RG22 .....68 B3
Fleet GU51 .....54 C4
Galloway Ctr The RG14 .....2 C2
Gallwey Rd GU11 .....77 A3
Gally Hill Rd GU52 .....74 E5
Galway Rd GU46 .....34 A4
Gander Dr RG24 .....68 C8
Ganders Cl GU34 .....184 E8
Gangbridge La SP11 .....61 E3
Gannet Cl RG22 .....90 F8
Gar St SO23 .....209 D5
Garbett Rd SO23 .....198 C8
Garbetts Way GU10 .....100 D6
Garden Cl
3 Andover SP10 .....106 B7
Axford RG25 .....114 B1
Farnborough GU14 .....55 C3
Hook RG27 .....50 F1
Kingsclere RG20 .....24 D2
Garden Close La RG14 .....5 B4
Garden Cotts RG29 .....95 F1
Garden Ct SO21 .....131 C3
Garden La 25 SO23 .....209 E6
Gardener's Hill Rd GU10 121 F4
Gardeners Gn SP9 .....101 D7
Gardens The
Broughton SO20 .....170 B7
Gardens The *continued*
Tongham GU10 .....100 D7
Garfield Rd GU15 .....36 A5
Garford Cres RG14 .....5 B8
Garland Ct RG14 .....1 D2
Garnet Field GU46 .....33 E5
Garnet Rd GU35 .....164 E2
Garnier Rd SO23 .....209 E3
Garrett Cl RG20 .....24 C3
Garrett Mews 7 GU11 .....76 E1
Garrett Rd RG40 .....16 C8
Garrick Way GU16 .....56 C7
Garston Mede SO20 .....129 A3
Garstons Tk SO21 .....174 B5
Garth Cl Bordon GU35 .....164 D4
Farnham GU9 .....121 E7
Garth Rd RG7 .....11 E5
Garth The Alton GU34 .....140 A4
Ash GU12 .....77 D1
Farnborough GU14 .....56 B4
Gascoigne La SO24 .....181 C5
Gaskell Cl GU34 .....140 C6
Gaskell Mews RG14 .....5 F8
Gason Hill Rd SP9 .....78 E8
Gaston La
South Warnborough RG29 ..95 A5
Upper Farringdon GU34 ..161 F4
Gaston's Wood Ind Est RG24 .....69 D8
Gatekeeper Cl 7 SO23 ..198 C8
Gates The GU51 .....54 C4
Gauvain Cl GU34 .....140 A2
Gawaine Cl SP10 .....83 A4
Gaywood Dr RG14 .....2 B4
Geale's Almshouses 6 GU34 .....139 F4
Geale's Cres GU34 .....140 A5
Geale's Ct GU34 .....140 A5
Geffery's Fields RG21 .....69 C5
Geffery's Ho RG27 .....51 B2
General Johnson Ct 4 SO22 .....209 A4
Genoa Ct Andover SP10 .....83 B3
Andover SP10 .....83 B4
Gentles La GU30 .....165 E3
George Eyston Dr SO22 .209 B4
George Gdns
Aldershot GU11,GU12 .....100 A7
Fleet GU51 .....54 B1
George Rd GU51 .....54 B1
George St
Basingstoke RG21 .....68 F5
Kingsclere RG20 .....24 D2
George VI Rd SP9 .....78 E8
George Yd SP10 .....106 B7
George Yd The SO24 .....179 D6
Georgia Cl SP10 .....105 E6
Georgia La SP11 .....103 F2
Georgian Cl GU15 .....36 C7
Georgina Ct 4 GU51 .....54 A1
Georgina Gdns RG26 .....27 B8
Gerald Sq GU34 .....140 A6
German Rd RG26 .....29 A2
Gerring Rd RG2 .....15 D7
Gershwin Ct RG22 .....91 C8
Gershwin Rd RG22 .....91 C7
Gibbet La GU15 .....36 E7
Gibbons Cl GU47 .....35 A8
Gibbs Cl RG40 .....16 C6
Gibbs Way GU46 .....33 F4
Gibbs' La GU35 .....164 A6
Gid La GU34 .....119 B3
Giffard Dr GU14 .....55 D5
Giffard La GU51 .....53 E3
Giffards Mdw GU9 .....99 C1
Gilbard Ct RG24 .....49 A3
Gilbert Cl RG24 .....48 C1
Gilbert Rd GU16 .....36 A2
Gilbert St SO24 .....181 E6
Gilbert Way RG40 .....16 C8
Gilbert White Way GU34 .....139 F6
Gilbert's Gn SP9 .....101 E7
Gilberts Mead Cl SP11 ..105 C4
Giles Cl RG14 .....1 C2
Giles Ct RG26 .....27 A8
Giles Rd RG26 .....27 A8
Gillham's La GU27 .....188 E5
Gillian Ave GU12 .....100 B8
Gillian Cl GU12 .....100 B8
Gillies Dr RG24 .....68 C8
Gillingham Cl SO23 .....176 C7
Gilmour Gdns GU34 .....140 A6
Gilroy Cl RG14 .....5 A6
Glade Cl RG24 .....48 F2
Glade The Binsted GU10 ..120 F1
Farnham GU9 .....99 B7
Mytchett GU16 .....56 E2
Newbury RG14 .....5 D7
Gladiator Way GU14 .....76 E8
Gladstone St SO23 .....209 D6
Gladstone Terr SP11 .....108 B5
Glamis Cl Camberley GU16 .56 D7
Oakley RG23 .....67 B2
Glaston Hill Rd RG27 .....33 A8
Glastonbury Cl RG24 .....69 A8
Glayshers Hill GU35 .....165 F6
Glebe Cl Bentworth GU34 .138 B6
Dummer RG25 .....90 D1
Tadley RG26 .....27 A7
Glebe Cotts SO21 .....132 B3
Glebe Ct GU51 .....53 F1
Glebe Fields GU34 .....138 B5
Glebe La Basingstoke RG23 .68 A4
Hartley Wintney RG27 .....52 D5
Glebe Mdw
East Dean SP5 .....191 A2
Overton RG25 .....88 A8

Glebe Rd Crondall GU10 . . .97 D6
Farnborough GU14 . . . . . . .55 D5
Headley GU35 . . . . .165 C5
Glebe The GU17 . . . . .35 C4
Glebefields RG14 . . . . .1 F5
Gleland Rd GU15 . . . . .35 D4
Gleblands SP11 . . . . .106 B1
Glen Cl Andover SP10 . . . .105 E8
Beacon Hill GU10 . . . . . .167 A6
Glen Ct GU20 . . . . .167 A6
Glen Rd Beacon Hill GU10 .167 B6
Fleet GU51 . . . . .74 F8
Grayshott GU26 . . . . .167 B3
Glen The Farnham GU9 . . .99 A6
Pamber Heath RG26 . . . . . .10 C1
Glenagp Grange RG7 . . . . .11 D6
Glenavon Gdns GU46 . . . . .34 B4
Glencoe Cl GU16 . . . . .56 E8
Glendale Ave RG14 . . . . . . .5 A5
Glendale Pk GU51 . . . . . . .53 D2
Glendale Rd RG26 . . . . .9 E1
Glendeep Cl SO23 . . . . . .176 B6
Gleneagles Cl RG12 . . . . . .91 A5
Gleneagles Dr GU14 . . . . . .55 A3
Glenfield Cl SP5 . . . . . . .168 B6
Glenhurst Cl GU17 . . . . . . .35 C4
Glenlea GU26 . . . . .167 C1
Glenmore Bsns Pk
SP10 . . . . .105 D7
Glenmound Pl GU14 . . . . . .55 A4
Glenville Gdns GU26 . . . . .167 D4
Glenwood GU9 . . . . .99 A6
Globe Farm La GU47 . . . . .34 F5
Glorney Mead GU9 . . . . . . .99 E6
Gloster Cl GU12 . . . . .77 D5
Gloucester Cl
Camberley GU15 . . . . .56 C6
Four Marks GU34 . . . . . .160 A2
Gloucester Dr RG22 . . . . . .91 B8
Gloucester Rd
Aldershot GU11 . . . . . . .100 A7
Newbury RG14 . . . . .1 C2
Glovers Field GU27 . . . . .189 D6
Glovers Ho GU27 . . . . . .189 D6
Glynswood Frimley GU15 . .36 D3
Rowledge GU10 . . . . .121 E4
Goat La RG21 . . . . .69 C5
Goatacre Rd GU14 . . . . . . .55 A4
Goch Way SP10 . . . . .82 E2
Goddard Sq ■ SP10 . . . . . .83 C2
Goddards Cl RG27 . . . . . . .49 D8
Goddards Firs RG23 . . . . . .90 C8
Goddards La
Camberley GU15 . . . . .35 F3
Sherfield on L RG27 . . . . . .49 C8
Goddards Mead SP10 . . . .105 E7
Godfrey Cl GU47 . . . . .35 B7
Godson Ho ② SO23 . . . . .209 E6
Godwin Cl GU47 . . . . . . .175 C3
Gold Hill RG35 . . . . .142 C1
Gold La GU11 . . . . .77 C4
Goldcrest Cl ■ GU46 . . . . .33 F6
Golden Lion Rdbt RG21 . . .69 B2
Goldenfields GU30 . . . . . .188 B3
Goldenfields Cl GU30 . . . .188 B3
Goldfields Cl GU11 . . . . . . .99 E8
Goldfinch Gdns RG22 . . . . .90 F6
Goldfinch La RG20 . . . . .6 E3
Goldfinch Way SO21 . . . . .153 E5
Goldhill GU10 . . . . .122 B6
Goldney Rd GU14 . . . . .1 D3
Goldwell Dr RG14 . . . . .1 D3
Golf Dr GU15 . . . . .36 D4
Golf La GU35 . . . . .164 B1
Golf Links Ave GU26 . . . . .166 F6
Gondreville Gdns GU52 . . .74 E4
Gong Hill GU10 . . . . .122 B4
Gong Hill Dr GU10 . . . . . .122 B4
Goodboy's La RG7 . . . . . . .12 E8
Goodden Cres GU14 . . . . . .55 D3
Goodens The SO24 . . . . . .201 C5
Goodfellow Ho ⑥ GU34 . .139 F3
Goodman Cl RG21 . . . . . . .68 F4
Goodwin Wlk RG14 . . . . . . .5 A6
Goodwood Cl Alton GU34 .139 E2
Camberley GU15 . . . . .36 A8
Goodwood Pl GU14 . . . . . .56 C3
Goodwood Way RG41 . . . . .2 A1
Goodwyns Cl SP9 . . . . . . .101 D7
Goodwyns Gn GU34 . . . . .140 A6
Goodyers GU34 . . . . .140 A3
Goose Gn RG27 . . . . .50 F2
Goose La RG27 . . . . .51 A2
Gooserye Ct GU30 . . . . . .187 F3
Gordon Ave
Camberley GU15 . . . . .35 F4
Fleet GU52 . . . . .75 B6
Winchester SO23 . . . . . . .198 C6
Winchester SO23 . . . . . . .198 C7
Gordon Cl RG21 . . . . .69 C6
Gordon Cres GU15 . . . . . . .36 A4
Gordon Cr ■ RG14 . . . . . . .1 F2
Gordon Palmer Cl RG2 . . .12 B5
Gordon Rd Aldershot GU11 .76 E1
Camberley GU15 . . . . .36 A5
Farnborough GU14 . . . . . . .77 B8
Newbury RG14 . . . . .1 F2
Thatcham RG18 . . . . .2 E5
Winchester SO23 . . . . . . .209 E6
Gordon Watson Ho
SO23 . . . . .209 D3
Gordon Wlk GU46 . . . . . . .34 D5
Gore End Rd RG20 . . . . .3 F3
Goring Field SO22 . . . . . .209 A7
Gorrings The SO20 . . . . . .172 A2
Gorse Cl GU10 . . . . .121 F6
Gorse Cotts
Haslemere GU27 . . . . . . .189 A8

Gorse Cotts continued
Shortfield Common GU10 .122 A1
Gorse La GU10 . . . . .121 F6
Gorse Rd GU16 . . . . .36 C2
Gorse Ride Jun & Inf Sch
RG40 . . . . .16 C2
Gorse Ride N GU40 . . . . . .16 C7
Gorse Ride S RG40 . . . . . .16 C6
Gorsedown Cl GU35 . . . . .164 B1
Gorselands Farnham GU9 . .99 A7
Newbury RG14 . . . . .5 B5
Pamber Heath RG26 . . . . . . .9 F1
Tadley RG26 . . . . .27 A8
Gorselands Cl
Ash Vale GU12 . . . . .77 E5
Headley GU35 . . . . .166 A4
Gorseway GU52 . . . . .75 A7
Gort Cl GU11 . . . . .77 C7
Goscombs La SO24 . . . . . .180 E8
Goslings Croft GU34 . . . . .184 E8
Gosport Rd GU34 . . . . . . .161 D2
Gothic Ct GU47 . . . . .34 F7
Gough Rd GU15 . . . . .53 E2
Gough's Mdw GU47 . . . . . .34 F7
Gould Cl RG14 . . . . .1 F3
Government House Rd
GU11,GU14 . . . . .76 F7
Government Rd GU11 . . . . .77 C4
Governor's Rd GU15 . . . . . .35 D6
Gower Cl RG21 . . . . .69 B7
Gower Cres RG27 . . . . .51 B1
Gower Pk GU47 . . . . .35 B7
Grace Bennett Cl GU14 . . . .55 E7
Grace Gdns GU51 . . . . . . .74 F8
Grace Reynolds Wlk ⑤
GU15 . . . . .36 A6
Grace Sq ⑧ SP10 . . . . . . .83 C2
Gracemere Cres RG22 . . . . .90 F7
Gracious St GU34 . . . . . . .182 F8
Gradwell La GU34 . . . . . . .182 A8
Grafton Cl GU35 . . . . .164 E2
Grafton Ho ② SP10 . . . . .106 A7
Grafton Pl SP11 . . . . .81 F3
Grafton Rd SO23 . . . . . . .209 D4
Grafton Way RG22 . . . . . . .68 D4
Grainger Cl RG22 . . . . .53 E2
Grammarsham La RG25 . . . .92 A2
Grampian Way RG22 . . . . . .68 B3
Granada Pl SP10 . . . . .83 D1
Granary The RG14 . . . . .1 D3
Grand Ave GU15 . . . . .36 A6
Grand Par ⑧ RG27 . . . . . . .51 A1
Grand Trunk Rd SP9 . . . . .101 D7
Grange Cl Fyfield SP11 . . . .80 F2
Farnborough GU14 . . . . . .179 C5
Winchester SO23 . . . . . . .209 C2
Grange Com Jun Sch
GU14 . . . . .55 F1
Grange Ct Newbury RG14 . . .1 F2
Tongham GU10 . . . . .100 C6
Grange Farm GU34 . . . . . .184 D8
Grange Farm Rd GU12 . . . .77 E3
Grange Gdns RG21 . . . . . . .5 A5
Grange La RG27 . . . . .52 B5
Grange Rd Ash GU12 . . . . .77 F1
Camberley GU15 . . . . .36 C5
Farnborough GU14 . . . . . . .55 D7
Fleet GU52 . . . . .74 F5
New Alresford SO24 . . . . .179 C5
Rushmoor GU10 . . . . .144 F8
Tongham GU10 . . . . .100 C6
Winchester SO23 . . . . . . .209 C1
Grange The
Frensham GU10 . . . . .144 B7
Newbury RG14 . . . . .5 A5
* Northington GU34 . . . . .156 E5
Grantham Dr GU14 . . . . . . .55 B5
Grantham Rd GU52 . . . . . .74 F7
Grantly Ct GU10 . . . . .121 D6
Granville Pl SO23 . . . . . . .209 F4
Grasmere Cl GU35 . . . . . .164 D5
Grasmere Rd
Farnborough GU14 . . . . . . .55 C4
Farnham GU9 . . . . .98 E6
Graspan Rd SP11 . . . . .57 B1
Grateley Bsns Pk SP11 . . .124 E7
Grateley Dro
Amport SP11 . . . . .103 D3
Grateley SP11 . . . . .103 A1
Grateley House Sch
SP11 . . . . .125 B8
Grateley Prim Sch SP11 . .125 B8
Grateley Rd SP4 . . . . .101 D1
Grateley Sta SP11 . . . . . . .125 B7
Gratton Cl SO21 . . . . .131 D4
Gravel Cl SO24 . . . . .135 C4
Gravel Hill Rd GU10 . . . . .120 E4
Gravel La
Barton Stacey SO21 . . . . .130 D7
Ropley SO24 . . . . .159 E1
Gravel Rd
Farnborough GU14 . . . . . . .77 B8
Farnham GU9 . . . . .98 F7
Fleet GU52 . . . . .75 B6
Gravelhill Cotts SO20 . . . .129 C5
Gravelly Cl Ball Hill RG20 . .3 E3
Tadley RG26 . . . . .27 A8
Graveney Sq SP10 . . . . . . .83 B2
Grayshot Dr GU17 . . . . . . .35 A3
Grayshott CE Prim Sch
GU26 . . . . .167 F8
Grayshott Cl SO22 . . . . . .175 D4
Grayshott Laurels GU35 . .165 A5
Grayshott Rd GU35 . . . . . .166 B5
Grayswood Dr GU16 . . . . . .56 E2
Great Austins GU9 . . . . . .122 B8
Great Austins Ho GU9 . . .122 C8

Great Binfields Cres
RG24 . . . . .70 A8
Great Binfields Prim Sch
RG24 . . . . .49 A1
Great Binfields Rd
Chineham RG24 . . . . .48 F1
Old Basing RG24 . . . . .49 A1
Great Field Rd SO22 . . . . .175 D3
Great La RG28 . . . . .86 C5
Great Marlow RG27 . . . . . .51 D5
Great Minster St ②
SO23 . . . . .209 E5
Great Oaks Chase RG24 . . .48 E2
Great Sheldons Coppice
RG27 . . . . .51 A2
Greatfield Cl GU14 . . . . . . .55 B8
Greatfield Rd GU14 . . . . . . .55 B8
Greatham Prim Sch
GU33 . . . . .185 F2
Grebe Cl Aldershot GU11 . . .99 E7
Alton GU34 . . . . .139 E6
Basingstoke RG22 . . . . . . .90 F7
Green Acres GU11 . . . . . . .76 D1
Green Acres SO21 . . . . . . .130 C6
Green Cl
Kings Worthy SO23 . . . . . .176 A5
Old Alresford SO24 . . . . . .157 D1
South Wonston SO21 . . . . .153 E4
Green Croft GU9 . . . . .99 F6
Green Cross La GU10 . . . . .144 E1
Green Dro SP11 . . . . .60 B1
Green End GU46 . . . . .34 B7
Green Glades GU52 . . . . . .74 F5
Green Jacket Cl SO22 . . . .209 C3
Green La
Beacon Hill GU10 . . . . . . .167 A8
Bishop's Sutton SO24 . . . .180 C5
Blackwater,Darby Green
GU17 . . . . .34 F4
Blackwater,Hawley GU17 . .35 C4
Churt GU10 . . . . .144 E1
Dockenfield GU10 . . . . . . .143 C6
Ellisfield RG25 . . . . .115 A7
Farnham,Weybourne GU9 . .99 D5
Farnham,Wrecclesham
GU9 . . . . .121 E7
Four Marks GU34 . . . . . . .182 A8
Hartley Wintney RG27 . . . .52 D5
Haslemere GU27 . . . . . . .189 F4
High Cross GU32 . . . . . . .205 F5
Monxton SP11 . . . . .104 C5
Newbury RG14 . . . . .1 C2
Pamber End RG26 . . . . . . .27 C4
Rotherwick RG27 . . . . .50 E5
Sandhurst GU47 . . . . .35 A7
Stratfield Saye RG7 . . . . . .29 C8
Yateley GU46 . . . . .33 F6
Green Lane Cl GU15 . . . . . .36 A7
Green Lane Cotts GU10 . .144 E1
Green Leys GU52 . . . . .74 F4
Green Meadows La
SP11 . . . . .106 A2
Green Park Cl SO23 . . . . .209 F8
Green Springs GU10 . . . . . .97 D7
Green St GU35 . . . . .163 E8
Green Stile GU34 . . . . . . .159 E7
Green The Amport SP11 . .104 A1
Andover SP10 . . . . .82 E2
Barton Stacey SO21 . . . . .130 E7
Blackwater GU17 . . . . .35 A4
Camberley GU15 . . . . .36 C5
Farnham,Badshot GU9 . . . .99 E6
Farnham,Upper Hale GU9 . .99 A6
Kimpton SP11 . . . . .80 C2
Liss GU33 . . . . .207 E5
Middle Wallop SO20 . . . . .126 B4
Overton RG25 . . . . .85 B8
Tadley RG26 . . . . .27 B6
The Sands GU10 . . . . . . .100 C1
Whitchurch RG28 . . . . .86 D5
Green Way GU12 . . . . .77 C3
Green's School La GU14 . . .55 E4
Greenacre
Broughton SO20 . . . . . . .170 B6
Kingsclere RG20 . . . . .24 D2
Greenacres Bordon GU35 .164 F4
Runfold GU10 . . . . .100 A2
Woolton Hill RG20 . . . . . . .8 E6
Greenaways The RG23 . . . . .67 C2
Greenbank Way GU16 . . . . .36 B2
Greenbirch Cl RG22 . . . . . .90 F7
Greenbury Cl RG23 . . . . . . .68 C5
Greencroft ② GU14 . . . . . .55 F4
Greenfield Cl GU30 . . . . . .188 A5
Greenfield Rd GU9 . . . . . .121 E7
Greenfields
Enham Alamein SP11 . . . . .83 C8
Liss GU33 . . . . .208 A4
Greenfields Ave GU34 . . . .139 E4
Greenfields Jun Sch
RG27 . . . . .50 E2
Greenfinch Cl GU47 . . . . . .35 B8
Greenham Cl RG19 . . . . .6 A8
Greenham Court Comm Prim
Sch RG14 . . . . .5 F8
Greenham Mill RG14 . . . . . .1 F3
Greenham Rd
Greenham RG14,RG19 . . . . .6 A7
Newbury RG14 . . . . .1 F3
Greenhanger GU10 . . . . . .166 E8
Greenhaven GU46 . . . . . . .33 F5
Greenhaven Cl SP10 . . . . .106 C7
Greenhill Ave SO22 . . . . . .209 C6
Greenhill Cl
Farnham GU9 . . . . .121 E7
Winchester SO22 . . . . . . .209 C6
Greenhill Rd
Farnham GU9 . . . . .122 B8

Greenhill Rd continued
Winchester SO22 . . . . . . .209 B6
Greenhill Terr SO22 . . . . .209 C6
Greenhill Way GU9 . . . . . .121 E7
Greenhills GU9 . . . . .122 C8
Greenlands Rd RG20 . . . . . .4 C1
Greenlands Rd
Camberley GU15 . . . . .35 F1
Kingsclere RG20 . . . . .24 D2
Newbury RG14 . . . . .1 F1
Greenleas GU16 . . . . .36 C2
Greenleas Cl GU46 . . . . . . .34 A7
Greenride Cl RG27 . . . . . . .32 B4
Greensey SP11 . . . . .81 B6
Greenways Fleet GU52 . . . .74 F6
Woolton Hill RG20 . . . . . . .4 C1
Greenways Ho ④ RG14 . . . .1 C2
Greenwich Way SO22 . . . . .83 A2
Greenwood Dr RG24 . . . . . .48 F4
Greenwood Manor SO21 . . .53 F2
Greenwoods RG28 . . . . . . .86 C6
Gregan Ct ② RG11 . . . . . .76 D7
Gregory Cl RG21 . . . . .69 C7
Gregory Ho ■ RG27 . . . . . .51 A1
Grenadier Rd GU12 . . . . . . .77 F4
Grenadiers Way GU14 . . . . .55 A3
Grensell Cl RG27 . . . . .33 C8
Grenville Cl GU30 . . . . . . .188 A4
Grenville Dr GU51 . . . . .74 E7
Grenville Gdns GU16 . . . . . .56 D8
Gresham Ct ⑧ GU14 . . . . .77 A8
Gresham Ind Est GU12 . . . .77 F2
Gresham Way GU16 . . . . . .56 C6
Gresley Rd RG21 . . . . .69 D6
Greville Cl RG21 . . . . .76 D2
Grey House Sch The
RG27 . . . . .52 D6
Greybberry Copse Rd RG19 .6 B8
Greyfriars ② SO23 . . . . . .209 F6
Greyhound Cl GU12 . . . . . .77 D1
Greyhound La RG25 . . . . . .88 A7
Greys Ct ⑥ GU14 . . . . . . .76 C2
Greys Farm Cl SO24 . . . . .201 D4
Greystead Pk GU14 . . . . . .121 C5
Greywell Cl RG26 . . . . .10 B3
Greywell Rd
Mapledurwell RG24,RG25 . .70 E5
Old Basing RG24 . . . . .70 D5
Up Nately RG27 . . . . .71 C4
Grieg Cl RG22 . . . . .68 E1
Grieve Cl GU10 . . . . .100 C7
Griffin Way N RG27 . . . . . .51 B2
Griffin Way S RG27 . . . . . . .72 B8
Griffon Cl GU14 . . . . .55 A3
Groombridge Pl RG14 . . . . .1 C6
Grosvenor Cl
Basingstoke RG22 . . . . . . .91 B5
North Tidworth SP9 . . . . . .79 A6
Grosvenor Ct GU17 . . . . . . .35 B3
Grosvenor Dr SO23 . . . . . .209 F8
Grosvenor Ho ■ GU14 . . . . .77 B8
Grosvenor Lawn ⑥ RG14 . . .1 C2
Grosvenor Rd
Aldershot GU11 . . . . .76 E1
Medstead GU34 . . . . .159 E2
Grove Cl RG21 . . . . .69 C3
Grove Cross Rd GU16 . . . . .36 B1
Grove Ct GU14 . . . . .5 E8
Grove End Rd GU9 . . . . . .121 F8
Grove Farm Pk GU16 . . . . .56 D1
Grove Park Ind Est
GU14 . . . . .140 B4
Grove Prim Sch The
GU16 . . . . .36 C2
Grove Rd Alton GU34 . . . . .139 F2
Ash GU12 . . . . .77 E3
Basingstoke RG21 . . . . . . .69 C3
Beacon Hill GU26 . . . . . . .167 A6
Camberley GU15 . . . . .36 D5
Fleet GU52 . . . . .75 B5
Newbury RG14 . . . . .1 C5
Grove The Aldershot GU11 . .76 E1
Frimley GU16 . . . . .36 B1
Hartley Wintney RG27 . . . .52 D7
Liphook GU30 . . . . .187 F4
Penton Grafton SP11 . . . . .81 F4
Grove Villas GU12 . . . . . . .77 E4
Grovebell Ind Est GU9 . . .121 D7
Grovefields Ave GU16 . . . . .36 B1
Groveland Rd RG14 . . . . . . .1 B5
Grovelands Cl GU10 . . . . .122 C7
Grovelands Cl GU35 . . . . .164 E1
Grovelands Rd GU35 . . . . .175 B1
Groves Cl SO21 . . . . .153 C4
Groves Lea RG7 . . . . .11 D6
Guernsey Cl RG24 . . . . . . .48 C2
Guernsey Dr GU51 . . . . . . .54 B4
Guildford Rd
Aldershot GU12 . . . . .100 B7
Ash GU12 . . . . .99 B3
Farnham,Badshot GU10 . . .99 E4
Fleet GU51 . . . . .54 C1
Mytchett GU16 . . . . .56 E5
Runfold GU10 . . . . .100 A4
Guildford Rd E GU14 . . . . .56 A1
Guildford Rd Ind Est
GU14 . . . . .56 A1
Guildford Rd W GU14 . . . . .56 A1
Guildford Road Trad Est
GU9 . . . . .99 B3
Guillemont Jun Sch
GU14 . . . . .55 A6
Guinea Ct RG24 . . . . .49 A4
Gulley Rd GU14 . . . . .76 E8

Gun Hill GU11 . . . . .76 F3
Gunners La GU34 . . . . . . .135 A5
Gunns Farm GU30 . . . . . . .188 A2
Gunville Hill SP5 . . . . . . .168 B6
Gunville Rd SP5 . . . . .168 B6
Gurdons GU34 . . . . .139 D1
Gurkha Mus The*
SO23 . . . . .209 D5
Gurkha Sq GU51 . . . . .74 F8
Gurney Cl RG29 . . . . .72 E2
Guttridge La RG26 . . . . . . .26 E8
Gwyn Cl RG14 . . . . .5 C8

H

H Jones Cres GU11 . . . . . . .77 A3
Haccupps La SO11 . . . . . .193 D1
Hacks La SO21 . . . . .152 B3
Hackwood Cl SP10 . . . . . .105 D7
Hackwood Cotts RG21 . . . .69 C2
Hackwood La RG25 . . . . . . .92 C6
Hackwood Rd RG21 . . . . . .69 C3
Hackwood Rdbt RG21 . . . . .69 C3
Hadleigh Gdns GU16 . . . . .56 C6
Hadleigh Pl ■ RG21 . . . . . .69 A5
Hadleys GU10 . . . . .121 C3
Hadrian Rd SP10 . . . . .83 E3
Hadrians Cl SP10 . . . . .99 C4
Hadrians Way RG23 . . . . . .68 C7
Hagley Rd GU51 . . . . .53 E2
Haig La GU52 . . . . .75 B5
Haig Rd Aldershot GU12 . . .77 A1
Andover SP10 . . . . .105 E8
New Alresford SO24 . . . . .179 D6
Sandhurst GU15 . . . . .56 E3
Hailstone Rd RG21 . . . . . . .69 B8
Haining Gdns GU16 . . . . . .56 E3
Halcyon Dr SP11 . . . . . . .103 E8
Hale Cl SO24 . . . . .181 C5
Hale Farm Flats GU9 . . . . .99 B5
Hale House Cl GU10 . . . . .144 D1
Hale House La GU10 . . . . .144 D1
Hale Pl GU9 . . . . .99 C5
Hale Rd GU9 . . . . .99 B4
Hale Reeds GU9 . . . . .99 C6
Hale Sch GU9 . . . . .98 F7
Hale Way GU16 . . . . .56 B8
Half Way Cotts GU10 . . . . .98 A3
Halifax Cl Andover SP10 . . .82 F1
Farnborough GU14 . . . . . . .55 D3
Halimote Rd GU11 . . . . . . .76 E1
Hall Cl GU15 . . . . .36 C6
Hall Dr GU52 . . . . .75 B6
Hall Farm Cres GU46 . . . . .34 B5
Hall La
Hartley Mauditt GU34 . . . .162 B2
Yateley GU46 . . . . .34 A6
Hall Rd Alton GU34 . . . . . .140 A6
Farnborough GU14 . . . . . . .55 F2
Hall Way The SO22 . . . . . .175 D3
Halliday Cl RG21 . . . . .69 A2
Hallmark Cl GU47 . . . . .35 C8
Halls Farm Cl SO22 . . . . .175 E3
Halpin Ho RG7 . . . . .14 A3
Halters End GU26 . . . . . . .166 E3
Halters The RG14 . . . . .5 F7
Halton Rd SP11 . . . . .79 D7
Ham La RG26 . . . . .25 F5
Hamble Ave GU17 . . . . .35 B5
Hamble Ct RG23 . . . . .67 B1
Hamble Ct
② Andover SP10 . . . . .83 C2
② ⑥ Basingstoke RG21 . . .69 D5
Hamble Dr RG26 . . . . .27 B8
Hambledon Cl SO22 . . . . .175 D4
Hambledon Way RG27 . . . .49 B5
Hambledon Cl GU16 . . . . . .36 F3
Hambridge La RG14 . . . . . . .2 C2
Hamburg Cl SP10 . . . . .82 F3
Hamelyn Cl ■ RG21 . . . . . .69 A5
Hamelyn Rd RG21 . . . . . . .69 A4
Hamesmoor Rd GU16 . . . . .56 D4
Hamesmoor Way GU16 . . . .56 D4
Hamilton Cl
Basingstoke RG21 . . . . . . .68 E7
Bordon GU35 . . . . .164 F4
Hamilton Ct
Basingstoke RG21 . . . . . . .35 C1
Newbury RG14 . . . . .5 F8
South Tidworth SP9 . . . . . .78 E5
Hamilton Gn SP9 . . . . .78 E5
Hamilton Pl GU11 . . . . . . .76 D1
Hamilton Rd Fleet GU52 . . .75 B6
Greatham GU33 . . . . .186 D2
Hamlash Cotts GU10 . . . .122 A2
Hamlash La GU10 . . . . . . .122 A2
Hamlet Gdns SP11 . . . . . . .83 B6
Hammer Hill GU27 . . . . . .189 A4
Hammer La
Bramshott GU27 . . . . . . .188 F6
Haslemere GU26 . . . . . . .189 A8
Haslemere GU27 . . . . . . .189 A5
Headley GU35 . . . . .166 C6
Hammer Vale GU27 . . . . . .188 E6
Hammersley Rd GU11 . . . . .77 A6
Hammerwood Copse
GU27 . . . . .189 B5
Hammond Rd ⑧ RG21 . . . .69 A3
Hammond Sq SP10 . . . . . . .83 B2
Hammond's La SO24 . . . . .181 C4
Hammonds Heath RG7 . . . .11 F6
Hampdens The RG14 . . . . . .5 A6

Hampshire Cl
Aldershot GU12 ....**100** B7
Basingstoke GU22 ....**68** A3
Hampshire Cross SP9 ...**78** E5
Hampshire Ho
Basingstoke RG24 ....**68** E8
Liphook GU30 ....**187** F7
Hampshire Int Bsns Pk
RG24 ....**48** E4
Hampshire Rd
Bordon GU35 ....**164** D4
Camberley GU15 ....**36** D8
Hampstead Ho RG21 ....**69** B5
Hampton Cl GU52 ....**75** A4
Hampton Ct RG23 ....**68** D6
Hampton La SO22 ....**209** A7
Hampton Rd Farnham GU9 ...**98** F6
Newbury RG14 ....**1** D1
Hampton Terr GU26 ....**167** A6
Hams Cnr RG27 ....**49** E7
Hanbury Way GU15 ....**36** A3
Handcroft Cl GU10 ....**97** D7
Handel Cl RG22 ....**68** E1
Handford La GU46 ....**34** B5
Handy Villas SO23 ....**209** E6
Hanger Rd RG26 ....**9** D1
Hanger The GU35 ....**165** D7
Hangerfield Cl GU46 ....**34** A5
Hanmore Rd RG24 ....**48** E3
Hannam's Farm Cl GU10 .**97** C6
Hanover Ct
7 Andover SP10 ....**105** D6
Frimley GU16 ....**36** C1
Yateley GU46 ....**34** B7
Hanover Ct GU30 ....**187** F5
Hanover Dr GU51 ....**54** C4
Hanover Gdns
Basingstoke RG21 ....**69** A2
Farnborough GU14 ....**55** C6
Hanover Ho 6 SP10 ....**106** B7
Hanover Lodge SO23 ....**209** D4
Hanover Mead RG14 ....**5** B6
Hanson Cl GU15 ....**36** F7
Hanson Rd SP10 ....**82** E1
Harbour Cl GU14 ....**55** E8
Harbury Ct RG14 ....**1** E2
Harcourt Rd GU15 ....**35** F5
Hardings La RG27 ....**52** D6
Hardy Ave GU46 ....**34** A4
Hardy La RG21 ....**69** A4
Hardyfair Cl SP11 ....**81** D2
Hardys Field RG20 ....**24** C6
Hare Warren Cotts RG28 ..**43** B2
Hare's La RG27 ....**52** E8
Harebell Cl RG27 ....**52** D7
Harebell Gdns RG27 ....**52** D7
Harestock Cl SO22 ....**175** D5
Harestock Cnr SO22 ....**175** C3
Harestock Prim Sch
SO22 ....**175** D3
Harestock Rd SO22 ....**175** C4
Harewood Forest Ind Est
SP11 ....**107** E3
Harewood Mobile Home Pk
SP11 ....**83** F1
Harfield Cl RG27 ....**51** A1
Harlech Cl RG23 ....**68** C5
Harlech Rd GU17 ....**35** B4
Harlequin Ho GU26 ....**167** A3
Harlington Way GU51 ....**53** F1
Harmes Way GU11 ....**77** B7
Harmsworth Rd RG26 ....**26** F8
Harold Gdns GU34 ....**140** A5
Harold Jackson Terr
RG21 ....**69** C4
Harpdon Par GU46 ....**34** B7
Harpton Cl GU46 ....**34** B7
Harrier Rd GU14 ....**55** A1
Harriet Ct 2 GU12 ....**76** F1
Harrington Cl RG14 ....**2** C5
Harris Ct GU30 ....**187** F2
Harris Hill RG22 ....**91** B7
Harrow Down SO22 ....**209** B2
Harrow La Fleet GU51 ....**53** F4
Penton Corner SP11 ....**82** A2
Harrow Way
Andover SP10 ....**82** D1
Oakley RG23 ....**66** E3
Penton Corner SP11 ....**82** A2
Harrow Way Com Sch
SP10 ....**82** D2
Harrow Way The RG21,
RG22 ....**69** A1
Harroway RG28 ....**85** D7
Hart Cl GU14 ....**55** C8
Hart Ctr 9 GU51 ....**53** F1
Hart Mews GU46 ....**33** F6
Hart The GU9 ....**98** F2
Hartfield Ho 2 GU51 ....**53** F1
Hartford Bridge Flats
RG27,GU17 ....**33** C2
Hartford Ct RG27 ....**52** C6
Hartford Rd Fleet GU51 ...**53** F3
Hartley Wintney RG27 ....**52** D7
Hartford Rise GU15 ....**36** B6
Hartford Terr RG27 ....**52** D6
Hartland Pl GU14 ....**55** E6
Hartley Cl GU17 ....**34** F5
Hartley Gdns 6 RG26 ....**26** F7
Hartley Grange RG27 ....**52** B6
Hartley La
Hartley Wespall RG27 ....**30** A1
Sherfield on L RG27 ....**29** F2
Hartley Mdw RG28 ....**86** B5
Hartley Mews RG27 ....**52** D7

Hartley Park Bsns Ctr
GU34 ....**162** D4
Hartleys RG7 ....**27** F8
Harts Cotts RG20 ....**22** C6
Harts Ct RG20 ....**22** D6
Harts Leap Cl GU47 ....**34** F8
Harts Leap Rd GU47 ....**34** E8
Harts Yd GU9 ....**98** F2
Hartshill Rd 8 RG26 ....**9** D1
Hartshull Cl GU51 ....**74** F8
Hartswood RG24 ....**48** F2
Hartvale Ct GU15 ....**36** E8
Harvest Cl
Winchester SO22 ....**209** B2
Yateley GU46 ....**33** F4
Harvest Cres GU51 ....**54** B5
Harvest Gn RG14 ....**1** C1
Harvest Way
Middle Wallop SO20 ....**126** B4
Old Basing RG24 ....**69** F8
Harvey Pl SP10 ....**106** D8
Harvey Rd GU14 ....**55** A5
Harvey Villas GU34 ....**187** B8
Harveys Field RG25 ....**88** A8
Harwood Pl SO23 ....**176** C8
Harwood Rise
Woolton Hill,Broad Laying
.........**4** D1
Woolton Hill,Slade Hill RG20 ..**4** D2
Hasle Dr GU47 ....**189** F6
Haslemere Rd
Liphook GU30 ....**188** B4
Marley Heights GU27 ....**189** F1
Haslemere Sta GU27 ....**189** F6
Hassocks Workshops The
RG24 ....**69** E7
Hastards La GU34 ....**184** E8
Hasted Dr SO24 ....**179** C4
Hastings Cl
Basingstoke RG23 ....**68** B5
Camberley GU16 ....**56** E7
Hatch Hill GU27 ....**189** F1
Hatch La
Kingsley Green GU27 ....**189** F2
Liss GU33 ....**208** C4
Old Basing RG24 ....**70** C5
Hatch Warren Inf Sch
RG22 ....**91** C7
Hatch Warren Jun Sch
RG22 ....**91** C7
Hatch Warren La RG22 ...**91** F8
Hatch Warren Ret Pk
RG22 ....**91** A6
Hatchbury La SP11 ....**38** C6
Hatchery Hill SO21 ....**174** B5
Hatches The
Basingstoke RG24 ....**56** D6
Farnham GU9 ....**121** D8
Hatchet La SP11 ....**59** B1
Hatchetts Dr GU27 ....**189** B7
Hatchgate Mead RG27 ....**51** A2
Hatchwarren Cotts RG22 ...**91** E7
Hatchwarren Gdns RG22 ...**91** E7
Hatchwarren La RG22 ....**91** C7
Hatfield Ct 4 GU47 ....**34** E8
Hatfield Gdns GU14 ....**56** C5
Hatfield Ho GU12 ....**77** D5
Hathaway Gdns RG24 ....**69** C8
Hatherden SP11 ....**59** C1
Hatherden CE Prim Sch
SP11 ....**59** C1
Hatherden Cl 1 GU34 ....**106** B7
Hatherley Rd SO22 ....**209** D7
Hatherwood GU46 ....**34** D5
Hatt La SO51 ....**192** E2
Hattem Pl SP10 ....**82** F3
Hattingley Rd GU34 ....**159** C7
Haughton Ho RG27 ....**189** F6
Haughurst Hill
Axmansford RG26 ....**25** F8
Pamber Heath RG26 ....**9** A1
Havelock Ho GU46 ....**77** A8
Haven Way GU9 ....**99** B4
Haweswater Cl GU35 ....**164** D5
Haweswater Ct GU12 ....**77** D5
Hawk Cl RG22 ....**90** F8
Hawk Conservancy The*
SP11 ....**104** B8
Hawke Cl SP10 ....**83** D1
Hawker Rd GU12 ....**77** D5
Hawkes Cl RG27 ....**52** C7
Hawkfield La RG21 ....**69** A3
Hawkins Cl GU46 ....**33** F5
Hawkins Gr GU51 ....**74** D6
Hawkins Way GU52 ....**75** C8
Hawkley Dr RG26 ....**27** A7
Hawkley Rd GU33 ....**207** C5
Hawkley Way GU51 ....**53** C3
Hawks Mead GU33 ....**207** E5
Hawkshaw Cl GU34 ....**188** B4
Hawkswood Ave GU46 ....**34** B5
Hawkwell GU52 ....**75** B4
Hawley Cl GU14 ....**55** C8
Hawley Garden Cotts
GU17 ....**35** B4
Hawley Gn GU17 ....**35** C2
Hawley Gr GU17 ....**35** C2
Hawley Green Farm
GU17 ....**35** D3
Hawley La GU14 ....**55** F8
Hawley Lane Ind Est
GU14 ....**55** F8
Hawley Lodge GU17 ....**35** D3
Hawley Place Sch GU17 ...**35** C1
Hawley Prim Sch GU17 ...**35** C3
Hawley Rd GU17 ....**35** C3
Hawthorn Cl
Aldershot GU11 ....**100** C8

Hawthorn Cl continued
Micheldever SO21 ....**133** B2
New Alresford SO24 ....**179** D5
Hawthorn Ct GU14 ....**77** A8
Hawthorn La
Four Marks GU34 ....**182** E8
Rowledge GU10 ....**121** D3
Hawthorn Rd
Four Marks GU34 ....**182** C8
Frimley GU16 ....**36** D2
Newbury RG14 ....**1** E4
North Tidworth SP9 ....**79** A7
Hawthorn Rise RG27 ....**51** B2
Hawthorn Way RG23 ....**68** C7
Hawthorne Cl SP11 ....**103** B1
Hawthorns Cl GU34 ....**35** C4
Hawthorns GU34 ....**139** C5
Hawthorns The RG26 ....**26** C8
Hay Down La SP11 ....**103** E5
Haydn Cl SO23 ....**176** B8
Haydn Rd RG22 ....**91** D8
Haydock Cl GU34 ....**139** F2
Haydon Pl GU46 ....**34** C6
Haydown Leas SP11 ....**38** C6
Hayes Cl SO20 ....**171** F2
Hayley La RG29 ....**95** C4
Haysoms Dr RG19 ....**5** F7
Haywarden Pl RG27 ....**52** D7
Haywood Dr GU52 ....**75** A7
Hazel Ave GU14 ....**55** D3
Hazel Cl Andover SP10 ....**105** D6
Oakley RG23 ....**67** B1
Hazel Coppice RG27 ....**51** B2
Hazel Ct SO22 ....**209** A8
Hazel Gn RG26 ....**9** B1
Hazel Gr
Haslemere GU27 ....**167** C2
Winchester SO22 ....**209** A8
Hazel Rd
Four Marks GU34 ....**160** C3
Mytchett GU16 ....**56** E2
Hazelbank RG40 ....**16** C6
Hazelbank La GU30 ....**188** B4
Hazelbank Mews GU30 ...**188** A4
Hazelcombe RG25 ....**88** B7
Hazeldene RG24 ....**48** F2
Hazeldene Gdns SO21 ....**177** E7
Hazeldene Rd GU34 ....**188** A4
Hazeley Ct RG27 ....**52** C7
Hazeley Dr 5 GU51 ....**53** C3
Hazeley Lea RG27 ....**31** F4
Hazell Rd GU9 ....**98** D1
Hazelwood RG24 ....**48** E4
Hazelwood Cl RG23 ....**68** D7
Hazelwood Ct GU14 ....**55** C8
Hazelwood Dr GU34 ....**68** D7
Headbourne Worthy Ho
SO23 ....**176** B5
Headington Cl RG22 ....**91** D7
Headley Cl GU34 ....**179** D4
Headley Fields GU35 ....**165** C4
Headley Hill Rd GU35 ....**165** C5
Headley La GU30 ....**165** C2
Headley Rd
Grayshott GU26 ....**166** E3
Lindford GU35 ....**165** A5
Liphook GU30 ....**187** F5
Headmore La GU34 ....**160** E1
Headon Ct GU9 ....**99** B1
Hearmon Cl GU46 ....**34** C6
Hearn Vale GU35 ....**165** E7
Hearsey Gdns GU17 ....**34** F6
Heath Cl
Beacon Hill GU26 ....**167** A7
Farnham GU9 ....**99** A7
Heath Cnr GU15 ....**36** E3
Heath Cotts
Beacon Hill GU26 ....**167** A6
Edgeborough GU10 ....**122** B3
Heath Ct RG26 ....**9** C1
Heath End Farm RG26 ....**9** C1
Heath End Rd RG26 ....**9** C1
Heath Green La GU34 ....**159** B7
Heath Hill GU10 ....**143** C2
Heath Ho GU16 ....**56** D6
Heath La Buttermere SN8 ..**18** C5
Crondall GU10 ....**97** C6
Ewshot GU10 ....**98** A7
Farnham GU9 ....**99** B8
Heath Rd
Haslemere GU27 ....**189** B5
Pamber Heath RG26 ....**10** C1
Heath Ride RG40 ....**16** F6
Heath Rise GU15 ....**36** B5
Heath Vale SP10 ....**105** D8
Heathcote Cl GU12 ....**77** E3
Heathcote Rd Ash GU12 ...**77** F3
Bordon GU35 ....**164** B3
Camberley GU15 ....**36** B5
Heather Cl Aldershot GU11 .**76** C1
Ash Vale GU12 ....**76** F3
Bordon GU35 ....**164** B1
Farnham GU9 ....**121** D6
Finchampstead RG40 ....**16** C7
Heather Cotts GU12 ....**77** E7
Heather Ct
12 Aldershot GU11 ....**76** E1
Hindhead GU26 ....**167** D4
Heather Dr Andover SP10 .**105** F8
Fleet GU52 ....**74** F5
Lindford GU35 ....**164** F5
Pamber Heath RG26 ....**9** D2
Heather Gdns
Farnborough GU14 ....**55** B3
Newbury RG14 ....**5** C7
Heather Gr RG27 ....**52** C7
Heather La RG27 ....**71** C5
Heather Mead GU16 ....**36** D2

Heather Mead Ct GU16 ...**36** D2
Heather Row La
Newnham RG27 ....**71** C4
Up Nately RG27 ....**71** E6
Heather Way
Basingstoke RG22 ....**91** A7
Hindhead GU26 ....**167** D4
Heatherbank GU26 ....**167** C4
Heatherdale Rd GU15 ....**36** B3
Heatherley Cl 3 GU35 ....**35** F5
Heatherley Mews GU30 ...**188** A2
Heatherley Rd GU15 ....**36** B3
Heatherside Jun & Inf Schs
GU51 ....**75** A8
Heathfield RG7 ....**11** E6
Heathfield Cl GU52 ....**74** E7
Heathfield Rd RG22 ....**91** D7
Heathland St GU11 ....**76** E2
Heathlands
1 Pamber Heath RG26 ....**9** C1
Penwood RG20 ....**21** E8
Heathlands Cl GU34 ....**34** C4
Heathman Copse RG26 ....**26** A8
Heathside Ct SP10 ....**167** B6
Heathside Way RG27 ....**52** C7
Heathvale Bridge Rd
GU12 ....**77** E6
Heathview RG27 ....**51** C2
Heathway GU15 ....**36** B5
Heathway Cl GU15 ....**36** B5
Heathwood Cl GU46 ....**34** B7
Heathyfields Rd GU9 ....**98** B3
Heckfield Dr 6 GU51 ....**53** C3
Heddon Wlk GU14 ....**55** E7
Hedge Croft GU46 ....**33** F6
Hedge End RG26 ....**27** A7
Hedge End Rd SP10 ....**106** B6
Hedgehog La GU27 ....**189** F5
Hedgerows The RG24 ....**70** A8
Hedges Cl SP9 ....**101** D7
Hedgeway RG14 ....**1** C1
Heenan Cl GU16 ....**56** C7
Heights The GU15 ....**36** C5
Hele Cl RG21 ....**69** A2
Helen Ct
Farnborough GU14 ....**55** F4
Newbury RG14 ....**1** D2
Helena Ho 2 RG21 ....**69** C6
Helford Ct 22 SP10 ....**83** C2
Helix Bsns Pk GU15 ....**35** F3
Helston Cl GU16 ....**56** E7
Hempland La GU34 ....**204** C4
Hendon Rd GU35 ....**164** D2
Hendren Sq 2 SP10 ....**83** C2
Hengest Gr SP10 ....**82** D3
Henley Cl GU14 ....**55** A4
Henley Dr GU16 ....**56** C1
Henley Gdns GU46 ....**34** B5
Henry Beaufort Sch
SO22 ....**175** E3
Henry Ct GU12 ....**56** E1
Henry Randell's Almshouses
GU17 ....**35** C3
Henry Tyndale Sch GU14 ...**56** B6
Henshaw Cres RG14 ....**5** B8
Henwick Cl GU14 ....**2** E4
Henwick La RG18 ....**2** E4
Hepplewhite Cl RG26 ....**9** C1
Hepplewhite Dr RG22 ....**91** A7
Hepworth Cl SP10 ....**83** A1
Hepworth Croft GU47 ....**35** C6
Herald Ct 4 GU12 ....**76** F1
Herbert Rd GU51 ....**54** A5
Herbs End GU14 ....**55** A5
Hereford Cl RG29 ....**72** C2
Hereford Ho GU11 ....**76** E1
Hereford La GU9 ....**99** B1
Hereford Mead GU51 ....**54** B4
Hereford Rd GU51 ....**68** C5
Herewood Cl RG14 ....**1** D4
Heriot Cl GU15 ....**36** B3
Heritage Pk RG22 ....**91** B5
Heritage View RG21 ....**91** B5
Hermes Cl GU51 ....**54** C1
Hermitage Cl Alton GU34 .**139** E2
Farnborough GU14 ....**56** B3
Frimley GU16 ....**36** D1
Heron Cl Alton GU34 ....**139** F6
Fleet GU52 ....**75** C6
Heron Ct GU47 ....**35** A7
Heron Ho RG14 ....**2** B3
Heron Ind Est RG27 ....**13** E8
Heron Pk Chineham RG24 .**48** F1
Old Basing RG24 ....**69** F8
Heron Way
Basingstoke RG22 ....**90** F8
Thatcham RG19 ....**2** F3
Heron Wood Rd GU12 ....**100** B7
Herondale GU27 ....**189** C6
Herons Rise SP10 ....**106** B6
Heronswood RG29 ....**72** F4
Herrett St GU12 ....**100** B8
Herretts Gdns GU12 ....**77** B1
Herriard Pl RG22 ....**91** A5
Herriard Way RG26 ....**27** A7
Herridge Cl RG26 ....**29** B2
Herriot Ct GU46 ....**34** A4
Hesters View RG20 ....**99** D2
Heswell La GU30 ....**188** C5
Hewshott La GU30 ....**188** C5
Hexagon The 6 SP10 ....**105** D6
Hibiscus Cres SP10 ....**105** C4
Hibiscus Gr SP10 ....**144** E2
Hickory Dr SO22 ....**175** C4
Hicks Cl RG26 ....**27** A7
Hicks La GU17 ....**34** F5

Hides Cl RG28 ....**86** C4
High Beech Gdns SP10 ...**106** C7
High Beeches GU16 ....**36** B2
High Copse GU9 ....**98** E5
High Crissels 3 GU47 ....**35** B8
High Cross GU34 ....**205** E2
High Cross La GU32 ....**205** D1
High Dr RG22 ....**68** D2
High Park Rd GU9 ....**99** A3
High Pitfold GU26 ....**167** B1
High St Aldershot GU11 ....**76** F2
Alton GU34 ....**139** F3
Andover SP10 ....**106** A8
Bordon GU35 ....**164** D3
Broughton SO20 ....**170** B7
Camberley GU15 ....**36** D6
Farnborough GU14 ....**77** B8
Grateley SP11 ....**125** B8
Hartley Wintney RG27 ....**52** D6
Headley GU35 ....**165** C5
Medstead GU34 ....**159** F7
Nether Wallop SO20 ....**49** A3
Odiham RG29 ....**72** E3
Overton RG25 ....**88** A8
Rowledge GU10 ....**121** C4
Sandhurst GU47 ....**34** D8
Selborne GU34 ....**184** E8
Shipton Bellinger SP9 ....**101** E7
Stockbridge SO20 ....**149** E3
Winchester SO23 ....**209** D6
Winchester,The Soke
SO23 ....**209** F5
High Thicket Rd GU10 ...**143** B5
High Trees Dr SO22 ....**209** C8
High View Cl GU14 ....**55** E4
High View Lodge 7
GU11 ....**76** E2
High View Rd GU14 ....**55** E4
Highams Cl RG20 ....**24** E2
Highbury Cres GU15 ....**36** E8
Highbury Rd GU15 ....**36** E8
Highclere Castle* RG20 ...**21** F2
Highclere Dr GU15 ....**36** E7
Highclere Rd GU12 ....**100** B8
Highclere St RG20 ....**21** C3
Highcliffe Rd SO23 ....**209** F4
Highcroft GU26 ....**167** B6
Highdown GU51 ....**54** A2
Highdowns RG22 ....**91** C6
Higher Mead RG24 ....**69** F7
Highfield RG20 ....**40** F7
Highfield Ave
Aldershot GU11 ....**99** E8
Newbury RG14 ....**1** E2
Highfield Chase RG21 ....**68** F5
Highfield Cl
Aldershot GU11 ....**99** F8
Farnham GU9 ....**121** F7
Highfield Cres GU26 ....**167** D4
Highfield Gdns
Aldershot GU11 ....**99** F8
Liss GU33 ....**208** A4
Highfield La GU30 ....**188** C3
Highfield Path GU14 ....**55** D4
Highfield Pk (Cvn Pk)
RG2 ....**15** B8
Highfield Rd
Farnborough GU14 ....**55** D4
Newbury RG14 ....**1** D1
Highfield Sch GU30 ....**188** B3
Highfield Terr 1 SO22 ...**209** D5
Highfields RG25 ....**88** B7
Highgate Cl GU14 ....**56** A5
Highgate La GU14 ....**56** A5
Highgrove GU14 ....**55** F7
Highland Dr Fleet GU51 ....**54** A4
Oakley RG23 ....**67** A2
Highland Rd
Aldershot GU12 ....**77** B2
Camberley GU15 ....**36** C8
Highlands RG14 ....**5** C7
Highlands Cl GU9 ....**121** F7
Highlands Rd
Andover SP10 ....**106** C7
Basingstoke RG22 ....**68** A3
Farnham GU9 ....**99** A7
Highmoors RG24 ....**48** F3
Highmount Cl SO23 ....**198** C2
Highpath Way RG24 ....**68** C8
Highridge GU34 ....**139** D2
Highview Bsns Ctr
GU35 ....**164** C3
Highview Bsns Pk RG27 ...**71** D8
Highwood Cl Newbury RG14 .**1** D7
Yateley GU46 ....**34** B4
Highwood Ridge RG22 ....**91** B6
Highworth Cotts RG26 ....**9** A1
Hilary Ho 2 RG14 ....**1** C1
Hilborn Way RG42 ....**15** E8
Hilden Way SO22 ....**175** B5
Hilder Gdns GU14 ....**56** B5
Hilfield GU46 ....**34** A3
Hill Barn La SO21 ....**131** A5
Hill Brow Rd GU33 ....**208** F5
Hill Cl RG14 ....**5** B7
Hill Corner Farm Est
GU14 ....**56** A6
Hill Crest Dr GU10 ....**121** D6
Hill Ct GU27 ....**189** F6
Hill Farm Cl GU27 ....**189** D5
Hill Farm Rd SO24,GU34 .**182** C2
Hill Ho GU26 ....**167** A6
Hill House Hill GU30 ....**187** E6
Hill Houses La SO24 ....**201** B6
Hill Mdw RG25 ....**116** A4
Hill Rd Beacon Hill GU26 ...**167** A6

Hill Rd continued
Farnham GU9 ....99 B7
Graysholt GU26 ....167 A3
Newbury RG14 ....1 C4
Oakley RG23 ....90 B8
Hill Sq RG24 ....49 A1
Hill Terr SO24 ....179 D6
Hill Top Ave SP9 ......78 E8
Hill View Rd
Basingstoke RG22 .....68 E3
Farnham GU9 ....98 D2
Hilland Rise GU35 ...165 D5
Hillary Cl GU14 .....121 F7
Hillary Rd
Basingstoke RG21 .....69 A7
Farnham GU9 ....121 F7
Hillbrook Rise GU9 ...98 F6
Hillbury Ave SP10 ...105 E6
Hillcrest Farnham GU9 .99 B8
Fleet GU51 ....54 A3
Pamber Heath RG26 ....9 F1
Hillcrest Cotts RG14 ..1 D7
Hillcrest Ct RG23 ....68 B6
Hillcrest Rd GU15 ....36 F7
Hillcrest Wlk RG23 ...46 E8
Hillgarth GU26 ......167 B5
Hillhouse La
Headley RG19 ....24 E8
Headley, Nr Greenham RG19 .7 E1
Headley,Goose Hill RG19 .7 E2
Hillier Way SO23 ....209 E8
Hillsborough Ct GU14 .55 C8
Hillside Abbotts Ann SP11 .104 F4
Baughurst RG26 ......26 B4
Littleton SO22 ......175 C5
Sandhurst GU15 ......35 D7
Upton SP11 ....38 F2
Whitchurch RG28 .....86 E5
Hillside Cl Alton GU34 .139 F5
Crookham Village GU51 .74 C6
Headley GU35 ....165 E6
West Dean SP5 ......190 D2
Winchester SO22 ....209 A8
Hillside Cotts
Hill Brow GU33 .....208 B2
Sparsholt SO21 .....174 B4
Hillside Cres GU16 ...56 D7
Hillside Ct SP10 ....105 F7
Hillside Flats GU26 ..167 B6
Hillside La GU9 ......99 C8
Hillside Rd Aldershot GU11 .99 E8
Ash GU12 ....77 F3
Edgeborough GU10 ...122 A3
Farnham,Weybourne GU9 .99 C7
Haslemere GU27 .....189 D5
Odiham RG29 ....72 F1
Sparsholt SO21 .....174 B4
Winchester SO22 ....209 A7
Hillside Villas SP10 ..82 E2
Hillstead Ct RG21 ....69 B3
Hilltop SO22 ....175 C5
Hilltop Rd RG25 .....65 B2
Hilltop View GU46 ....33 F5
Hinaidi Way GU14 ....76 D8
Hindell Cl GU14 .....55 E8
Hindhead Commons Nature
Trails* GU26 ....167 E4
Hindhead Ho GU26 ..167 D4
Hindhead Rd GU26 ..167 D2
Hinstock Cl GU14 ....55 E3
Hinton Ampner Ho*
SO24 ....201 E3
Hinton Cl RG26 ......29 D8
Hinton Fields SO23 .176 C6
Hinton Hill SO24 ....201 F4
Hinton House Dr SO23 .176 C6
Hinwood Cl SO20 ....170 B7
Hirst Copse SP11 ....62 A2
Hitches La GU51 .....74 C7
Hobbs Cl SO24 .....180 C4
Hobbs Sq [4] SP10 ...83 C2
Hockford La RG19 .....8 E3
Hockley Cotts SO24 .200 E3
Hockley Link SO21 ..197 E1
Hockleys La RG25 ...116 C7
Hoddington Cotts RG25 .94 C4
Hogarth Cl
Basingstoke RG21 ....69 E4
Sandhurst GU47 .....35 C6
Hogarth Ct SP10 .....82 F1
Hoghatch La GU9 ....99 A8
Hogmoor Rd GU35 ..164 B3
Hogwood Ind Est RG40 .15 E6
Hogwood La RG40 ...15 E6
Holbeche Cl GU46 ...33 E6
Holbein Cl RG22 ....69 D3
Holborne Cl RG14 ....5 A5
Holbrook Cl GU9 .....99 D8
Holbrook Way GU11 ..99 F7
Holbury La SO51 ....191 D3
Holdaway Cl SO23 ..176 C7
Holder Rd GU12 .....77 C1
Hole La GU10 ....120 A5
Holland Cl GU9 ......99 C1
Holland Dr GU9 ......82 F3
Holland Gdns GU51 ..75 A8
Hollands Cl SO22 ...175 B5
Hollies The
Hartley Wintney RG27 .52 C4
Newbury RG14 ....5 B5
Hollin's Wlk [9] RG21 .69 B5
Hollington La RG20 ..21 A3
Hollis Wood Dr GU10 .121 C5
Hollow La GU35 ....165 C6
Hollow The
Broughton SO20 .....170 D5
Hangsclere RG20 .....24 C2
Hollowshot La RG20 .24 C1

Holly Acre GU46 .....34 B5
Holly Ave GU16 ......36 F3
Holly Bush Cotts RG26 .26 B1
Holly Bush La RG27 ..71 E7
Holly Cl Aldershot GU12 .77 A2
Bramley RG26 ....29 A2
Eversley Centre RG27 .33 C8
Farnborough GU14 ....55 E4
Headley GU35 ....166 A5
Thatcham RG19 ....7 F6
Holly Cnr RG7 ....14 F7
Holly Cross RG26 ....28 F4
Holly Dr RG24 ....70 C6
Holly Hedge Cl GU16 .36 C2
Holly Hedge Rd GU16 .36 C2
Holly La RG7 ....17 D8
Holly Lodge Prim Sch
GU12 ....77 D8
Holly Mdws SO22 ...209 A8
Holly Rd Aldershot GU12 .77 B1
Farnborough GU14 ....55 E4
Holly Tree Pk SO21 .131 C4
Holly Way GU17 .....35 B4
Holly Wlk SP10 .....105 D6
Hollybrook Cl GU35 .164 E3
Hollybrook Pk GU35 .164 E3
Hollybush La
Eversley Cross RG27 .33 C7
Farnborough GU11 ...77 C6
Ramsdell RG26 ......26 D2
Hollycombe Cl GU30 .188 A2
Hollycroft RG19 ......8 D1
Hollyfields Cl GU15 .35 F5
Hollyhock Cl RG22 ..91 A8
Hollyridge GU27 ....189 C6
Hollytree Gdns GU16 .56 B8
Hollytrees GU51 ....74 E6
Hollywater Rd
Bordon GU35 ....164 F2
Liphook GU30 ......187 A8
Holm Oak Cl GU35 .175 B5
Holmbrook Cl GU14 ..77 E7
Holmbrook Ct GU14 ..55 A4
Holmbrook Gdns [7]
GU14 ....55 A4
Holme CE Prim Sch The
GU35 ....165 C6
Holmes Cl RG22 .....91 C6
Holmes Ct Andover SP10 .105 E7
[6] Graysholt GU26 ..167 B3
Holmwood Cotts GU10 .119 F4
Holmwood Terr RG27 .52 C6
Holst Cl RG22 ....91 E7
Holt Barns GU35 ....142 E5
Holt Cl GU14 ....56 A7
Holt Cotts RG19 .....25 D8
Holt End La GU34 ...138 A4
Holt La Hook RG27 ...51 C1
Tangley SP11 ....59 B7
Wolverton Common RG26 .25 D4
Holt Pound La GU10 .121 A5
Holt Way RG27 ......51 C2
Holtwood Rd RG20 ....3 F6
Holy Barn Cl RG22 ...68 A1
Holy Cross Hospl GU27 .189 C7
Holyrood Ct RG22 ...68 B3
Holywell Cl GU14 ...55 B3
Home Cl SO24 ......136 F2
Home Farm Bsns Ctr
SO51 ....191 E5
Home Farm Cl GU14 .56 B6
Home Farm Gdns GU10 .82 D3
Home Farm Rd GU14 .53 B6
Home La GU14 ....54 F1
Home Mead RG25 ....89 F1
Home Mead Rd RG14 .5 C8
Home Park Rd GU46 .34 B5
Homefield SP11 .....61 F2
Homefield Cotts
East Tisted GU34 ...183 D5
Hawkley GU33 ......206 E7
Lisle GU33 ....207 E5
Homefield Way RG24 .47 D1
Homegreen Ho GU27 .189 E6
Homelands GU27 ...189 F1
Homelea Cl GU14 ...77 F8
Homeleigh Cres GU12 .77 E8
Homepark Ho GU9 ...99 E8
Homerise Ho [1] SO23 .209 E6
Homestead Rd GU14 .159 E5
Homesteads Rd RG22 .91 B8
Hone Hill GU47 .....34 F8
Honey Yard Bsns Pk GU9 .99 B2
Honey Bottom Rd RG20 .9 F1
Honey La GU34 .....185 A8
Honeycritch La GU34 .206 C3
Honeyhanger GU26 ..167 D1
Honeyheaze RG22 ...91 A5
Honeysuckle Cl
Basingstoke RG22 ....91 A8
Winchester SO22 ....209 C2
Yateley GU46 ....34 A3
Honeysuckle Ct SO22 .175 C3
Honeysuckle Gdns
SP10 ....105 C7
Honeysuckle La GU35 .165 F5
Honister Gdns GU51 .54 C2
Hood Cl SP10 ......106 C7
Hook Cl RG19 ....6 A7
Hook Comm RG26 ...71 F7
Hook Inf Sch RG27 ..51 B1
Hook Jun Sch RG27 .51 B1
Hook La Axmansford RG26 .26 C8
Ropley SO24 ....181 A4
Wootton St Lawrence RG23,
RG26 ....67 A8
Hook Par [2] RG27 ..51 A1

Hook Rd Greywell RG29 .72 A5
Hook RG27 ....72 A7
Kingsclere RG20 ....24 E2
North Warnborough RG29 .72 C4
Rotherwick RG27 ....51 A5
Hook Sta RG27 .....72 B8
Hookpit Farm La SO23 .176 B8
Hookstile La GU9 ...99 A1
Hookwood La GU17 ..58 A7
Hoopers Way RG23 ..67 B1
Hooperslead RG25 ..92 A7
Hop Garden Rd RG27 .50 F1
Hop Gdn GU52 ....74 E4
Hop Kiln The GU9 ..121 F8
Hope Fountain GU15 .36 D4
Hope Grant's Rd GU11 .76 F3
Hope La GU9 ....98 F6
Hope Way GU11 .....76 D3
Hopeman Cl GU47 ...35 B7
Hopeswood GU34 ...186 A2
Hopfield Rd RG27 ...52 C5
Hopkinson Way SP10 .82 B1
Hopton Garth RG24 .49 A1
Hopwood Cl RG14 ....2 C4
Horizon West Ind Est
RG14 ....2 B3
Horizon West Ind Est
RG14 ....55 C5
Hornbeam Cl
[3] Farnborough GU14 .55 A5
South Wonston SO21 .153 E4
Hornbeam Pl RG27 ..51 B2
Hornbeams RG7 .....14 F7
Hornes Field Ct [4] GU52 .74 E4
Horris Hill Sch RG20 .5 C3
Horse La SO24 .....181 D7
Horsebridge Rd
Broughton SO20 .....170 D4
Houghton SO20 ....171 B3
Horseshoe Bend GU26 .166 F3
Horseshoe End RG14 .5 F7
Horseshoe Cres
Bordon GU35 ....164 E3
Horseshoe La GU15 .36 D8
Horseshoe La
Ash Vale GU12 ......77 A2
Hurstbourne Tarrant SP11 .60 D8
Horwood Gdns RG21 .68 F2
Hosketts La SO20 ..147 E5
Hoskins Place Ind Est [3]
GU35 ....165 C5
Hospital Hill GU11 ..76 E3
Hospital Rd GU11 ...76 E3
Hostel Rd GU14 ....76 E8
Houghton Lodge Gdns*
SO20 ....171 C7
Hound Green Cl RG27 .31 B3
Houndmills Rd RG21 .68 E6
Houndmills Rd RG21 .68 D7
Hoursome Ct RG22 ..91 C5
House Plat Ct [3] GU52 .74 E4
Houseman Rd GU11 ..54 C1
Howard Cl GU51 ....54 C1
Howard Cole Way GU11 .76 C2
Howard Dr GU14 ....54 F4
Howard Rd
Basingstoke RG21 ....69 C5
Newbury RG14 ....1 E1
Howard View RG22 ..68 D3
Howard's La GU34 .140 C7
Howarth Ct RG14 ....1 A7
Howberry Chase GU27 .189 F6
Howell Cl RG2 ......4 A2
Howes Gdns GU51 ..74 E6
HTH Complex GU12 .100 C8
Hubbard Rd RG21 ...68 F7
Hubert Rd RG23 ....209 C2
Huckers La GU34 ..184 E8
Huddington Glade GU46 .33 E5
Hudson Cl RG30 ...188 A3
Hudsons Mdw RG22 .31 B3
Hugh De Port La GU51 .53 F4
Hulbert Rd GU34 ...70 B3
Hulbert Way RG22 ..68 C2
Hulfords La RG27 ...32 E1
Hullam La GU34 ...184 B5
Humber Cl RG18 .....2 F5
Humber Ct [24] SP10 .83 C2
Humber Ct GU9 .....78 D3
Humber Way GU47 ..35 B8
Humbers View SO20 .172 E1
Humberstone Rd SP10 .106 A6
Humming Bird Ct RG22 .90 F8
Humphrey Pk GU52 .74 F1
Hundred Acre Cnr SP10 .105 C8
Hungerford Cl GU47 .35 A8
Hungerford La
Enham Alamein SP11 .82 F8
Hampshire Gate SP11 .37 E1
Hungerford Rd SN8 ..18 A8
Hunnels Cl GU52 ...74 E4
Hunt Cl SO21 ......153 E4
Hunt's Cotts RG14 ..1 C6
Hunter Cl SO20 ....172 A1
Hunter Rd GU14 ....76 A4
Hunters Chase GU30 .187 F5
Hunters Cl RG23 ...67 B3
Hunters Mews GU30 .76 D2
Hunters Rd GU33 ..186 D2
Hunting Gate RG24 .105 C8
Huntingdon Gdns RG22 .2 C5
Huntingdon House Dr
GU26 ....167 C4
Huntingdon Pl GU35 .167 A7
Hunton Down La GU34 .132 C6
Hunton La SO21 ...132 A4
Hunts Cl RG27 .....51 C1

Hunts Cotts RG27 ...52 D7
Huntsbottom La GU33 .208 B3
Huntsman's Mews SO23 .56 D3
Huntsmead GU34 ...54 E1
Huntsmoor Rd RG26 .26 D8
Hurland La GU35 ..165 D3
Hurlands Bsns Ctr GU9 .99 D4
Hurlands Cl GU9 ....99 D4
Hurlands Pl GU9 ....99 D4
Hurne Ct [20] RG21 .69 D5
Huron Dr GU30 ....188 B3
Hursley Dr [7] GU35 .53 C3
Hurst Cl GU30 .....187 E5
Hurst Com Sch The RG26 .9 B1
Hurst La GU34 .....205 B3
Hurst Rd Aldershot GU11 .77 A4
Farnborough GU14 ...55 F8
Hurst The RG27 ....32 E3
Hurstbourne Tarrant CE Prim
Sch SP11 ....60 E6
Hurstmere Cl GU30 .167 B3
Hurstmere Ho [8] GU30 .167 B3
Hussar Ct [1] GU11 .76 C2
Hussell La GU34 ...160 A7
Hussey Cl [2] SO23 .209 E8
Husseys La GU34 ..119 D5
Hutton Cl RG14 .....1 F4
Hutton Rd GU14 ....77 E6
Hutton Sq [5] SP10 .83 C2
Hyacinth Cl RG22 ..91 A8
Hyde Abbey Rd SO23 .209 E6
Hyde Church La SO23 .209 E7
Hyde Church Path [6]
SO23 ....209 E7
Hyde End La SO22 ...8 B5
Hyde Farm Cotts RG20 .95 E2
Hyde Gate [8] SO23 .209 E7
Hyde House Gdns [5]
SO23 ....209 E7
Hyde La
Bishop's Green RG20 .6 E1
Crondall GU10 ......74 F1
Ecchinswell RG20 ...23 F7
Hyde Lodge SO23 ..209 D7
Hyde St SO23 .....209 E7
Hydes Platt RG7 ...27 F8
Hylton Cl RG26 ....27 A8
Hyson Cres SP11 ..57 B2
Hythe Cl RG26 .....26 F7

Iberian Way GU15 ...36 F6
Ibworth La Fleet GU51 .53 C3
Hannington RG26 ....45 C3
Icknield Ho SP10 ...83 D2
Icknield Sch SP10 ..83 D2
Icknield Way SP10 ..83 B4
Iden Ct RG21 ....2 F4
Idlefield Cotts GU10 .120 D6
Ilchester Ct [7] RG14 .1 E2
Ilex Cl Kings Worthy SO23 .176 B8
Pamber Heath RG26 ..10 C1
Yateley GU46 ....33 F6
Illingworth Cl RG26 .68 C5
Imber Ho SP10 .....105 E8
Imber Rd SO23 ....198 C8
Imjin Cl GU11 ......76 F3
Imperial Ct Andover SP10 .83 E1
[7] Newbury RG14 ...1 A7
Imran Ct GU12 .....100 A8
Inadown Bglws GU34 .183 E8
Ingle Dell GU15 ....36 B4
Ingle Glen RG40 ....16 E2
Inglewood Dr RG22 ..91 B6
Ings Cl GU34 ......139 F2
Inhams Rd GU34 ...140 D6
Inhams Cl GU34 ...140 D6
Inhurst La Baughurst RG26 .26 A8
Pamber Heath RG26 ..9 A1
Inhurst Way [2] RG26 .9 A1
Inkpen Gdns RG24 ..70 A8
Innisfail Gdns GU11 .99 D8
Institute Rd GU12 ..77 B1
Intec Bsns Ctr RG24 .69 E8
Intech* SO21 ......199 B7
Inverness Way GU47 .35 B7
Invincible Rd GU14 ..55 E3
Inwood Ct [5] GU34 .139 F3
Inwood Rd GU30 ...208 A4
Ipoh Ct SO20 ......126 A5
Ipsley Lodge GU10 .121 C6
Iris Cl RG22 ....91 A7
Irvine Dr GU14 .....55 C8
Irwell Cl RG21 .....69 D5
Isaac Newton Rd RG2 .15 E8
Isington La GU34 ..119 E2
Isington Rd GU34 ..119 E1
Isis Way GU47 .....35 B8
Island Farm Rd GU14 .11 D8
Itchel La GU10 .....97 C7
Itchell Dr [10] GU51 .53 E3
Itchen Abbas Prim Sch
SO21 ....177 F6
Itchen Cl RG23 .....67 B1
Itchen Ct [28] Andover SP10 .83 C2
[3] Winchester SO23 .209 F6
Itchen Rd GU34 ...140 C6
Iterton Down La GU34 .178 D5
Ivanhoe Rd RG40 ...16 D5
Ivar Gdns RG24 ....49 A1
Ively Rd GU14 .....55 B3

Ively Rdbt GU14 ....55 C2
Ives Cl GU46 ....33 F7
Ivy Cl SO22 ....209 C3
Ivy Down La RG23 ..66 E3
Ivy La GU9 ....98 F2
Ivy Rd GU12 ....77 C2
Ivyhole Hill RG27 ...53 B8
Ivyhouse La GU32 ..205 E3

Jacaranda Rd GU35 .164 D2
Jack St RG14 ....1 E3
Jackdaw Cl RG22 ...90 F8
Jacklyns Cl SO24 ..179 C4
Jacklyns La SO24 ..179 C5
Jacob Rd GU15 ....35 D7
Jacob's Yd [4] RG21 .69 B4
Jagdalik Rd SP9 ....78 E4
Jago Ct RG14 ....5 E8
James Pl RG26 .....27 A8
James Rd GU15 ....35 F2
James Watt Rd
Arborfield Garrison RG2 .15 C7
Arborfield Garrison RG2 .15 E8
James Way GU15 ...35 F2
Jameson Ho GU51 ..74 F8
Jamrud Rd SP9 ....78 D5
Jan Smuts Rd GU33 .186 D2
Jane Austen's Ho (Mus)*
GU34 ....161 D8
Japonica Cl GU12 ..77 D1
Jardine Sq [6] SP10 .83 C2
Jarvis Cl RG27 .....33 B8
Jasmine Ct [1] SP10 .105 E6
Jasmine Rd GU35 ..91 B8
Jasmine Way
Bordon GU35 ....164 E2
Thatcham RG19 ....7 F6
Jays Cl RG22 ....69 A1
Jays Nest Cl GU17 .35 B4
Jean Orr Ct GU52 ..75 A5
Jefferson Rd RG21 .69 C7
Jellicoe Ct SP10 ...83 D1
Jenkins Pl GU14 ...77 B8
Jenner Way GU34 .140 A6
Jennie Green La
Bentworth GU34 ...137 F1
Medstead GU34 ...160 B8
Jenny's Wlk GU46 ..34 C6
Jenson Gdns SP10 .105 E7
Jerrymoor Hill RG40 .16 D8
Jersey Cl
Basingstoke RG24 ...48 C2
Fleet GU51 ....54 B4
Jervis Ct SP10 .....83 D1
Jesmond Dene RG14 .1 C4
Jesse Cl GU46 .....34 D5
Jessett Dr GU52 ...74 E4
Jesty Rd SO23 ....179 B4
Jewry St SO23 ....209 E6
Jibbs Mdw RG21 ...28 F3
Jobson Ct RG28 ....86 C5
John Boys Ho RG14 .5 A6
John Childs Cl RG14 .1 E1
John Ct GU11 ......99 C8
John Eddie Ct RG22 .68 C3
John Eggars Sq GU34 .140 B5
John Hanson Com Sch
SP10 ....105 D7
John Hunt of Everest Com
Sch RG24 ....48 C1
John Kimber's Almshouses
RG14 ....1 D2
John Morgan Ct RG27 .51 A2
John Norgate Ho RG14 .2 C3
John Pounds Ho [6]
GU35 ....164 D2
John Rankin Inf Sch RG14 .5 B8
John Rankin Jun Sch
RG14 ....5 B8
Johnson Dr RG40 ...16 F7
Johnson Way GU52 .75 A5
Joices Yd [6] RG21 .69 A5
Jollies The GU10 ...97 D6
Jonathan Hill RG20 ..5 F3
Jouldings La RG7 ..15 B4
Joule Rd Andover SP10 .82 B1
Basingstoke RG22 ...68 F7
Joy's La SO20 .....129 A4
Jubilee Cir GU35 ...69 B5
Jubilee Cl
Farnborough GU14 ..55 B4
Litchfield RG28 .....42 C1
Pamber Heath RG26 .10 C1
Jubilee Cotts RG27 .14 A3
Jubilee Ct
North Tidworth SP9 .78 F7
Thatcham RG19 ....7 E6
Jubilee Dr GU12 ...77 E6
Jubilee Hall Rd GU14 .56 A4
Jubilee Ho GU35 ..164 E4
Jubilee La
Farnham GU10 .....121 E5
Grayshott GU26 ...167 A3
Jubilee Rd Aldershot GU11 .99 F7
Basingstoke RG21 ...69 B4
Finchampstead RG40 .16 D4
Mytchett GU16 .....56 E2
Julius Cl RG24 .....68 C8
Jumps Rd GU10 ...144 E3
Junction Pl GU27 ..189 D6
Junction Rd SP10 ..106 A8

Junction Terr RG14 ....2 A2
June Dr RG23 ....68 B5
Juniper Cl Andover SP10 ...105 D7
　Bordon GU35 ....164 A2
　Chineham RG24 ....49 A4
　Winchester SO22 ....209 B3
Juniper Ct **7** SP9 ....79 A7
Juniper Pl RG19 ....1 F6
Juniper Rd GU14 ....55 A5
Juno Ho RG7 ....9 C2
Jupiter Ho **4** RG7 ....9 C2
Jutland Cres SP10 ....82 F4

K

Kalis Cnr SP11 ....80 E5
Karachi Cl SP9 ....78 E7
Kashmir Ct **7** GU14 .....56 A1
Katherine Ct **6** GU15 ...36 B5
Kathleen Cl RG21 ....69 A2
Kay Cres GU35 ....165 F6
Keable Rd GU10 ....121 D7
Keats Cl Basingstoke RG24 ..69 C8
　South Wonston SO21 ...153 D4
　Winchester SO22 ....209 A2
Keats Gdns GU51 ....54 B1
Keats Way GU46 ....33 F4
Keble St SO22 ....209 A4
Keenans Cotts GU33 ......207 E5
Keeper's Hill SP11 ....104 A5
Keepers La SO51 ....192 C2
Keeps Mead RG20 ....194 C3
Keith Lucas Rd GU14 .....55 D2
Kellynch Cl GU34 ....139 E4
Kellys Wlk SP10 ....105 E7
Kelsey Ave RG40 ....16 C6
Kelsey Cl GU33 ....208 A5
Kelsey Gr GU46 ....34 C5
Kelvin Cl RG2 ....15 C7
Kelvin Hill RG22 ....68 E2
Kelvin Rd RG14 ....1 A2
Kembers La RG25 ....70 E4
Kemmitt Way SP10 ....105 E6
Kempshott Gdns RG22 ....91 A8
Kempshott Int Sch RG22 ..91 A8
Kempshott Jun Sch
　RG22 ....91 A8
Kempshott La RG22 ....91 A8
Kempshott Park Ind Est
　RG23 ....90 F3
Kempshott Rdbt RG22 .....91 B7
Kempton Cl Alton GU34 ...139 F2
　Newbury RG14 ....2 A1
Kempton Ct GU14 ....55 D2
Kemys Gdns SP10 ....105 F8
Kendal Cl GU14 ....55 C4
Kendal Gdns RG22 ....68 B2
Kendall Court Bsns Pk
　GU15 ....35 D4
Kendrick Rd RG14 ....5 B5
Kenilworth Cres GU51 ....54 C2
Kenilworth Ct **8** SO23 .209 E8
Kenilworth Rd
　Basingstoke RG23 ......68 C6
　Farnborough GU14 ......55 A5
　Fleet GU51 ....54 B1
　Fleet GU51 ....54 C2
Kenley Rd GU35 ....166 A5
Kenmore Cl
　Camberley GU16 ....56 B8
　Fleet GU52 ....75 B5
Kennedy Cl RG14 ....5 B6
Kennel La Littleton SO22 .175 C4
　Shortfield Common GU10 .122 A2
Kennels La GU14 ....55 A2
Kennet Cl Ash GU12 ......77 E1
　26 Basingstoke RG21 ..69 D5
　Farnborough GU14 ......55 B6
Kennet Ct
　26 Andover SP10 ......83 C2
　1 Newbury RG14 ......1 E1
Kennet Ctr The RG14 ......1 E2
Kennet Pl **3** RG14 .....1 E2
Kennet Rd Newbury RG14 ..1 D2
　North Tidworth SP9 ......79 A7
Kennet Side RG14 ....2 A3
Kennet Way RG23 ....67 B1
Kenneth Ct GU14 ....55 D4
Kensington Ct GU51 ....53 D4
Kensington Ho **4** RG21 ..69 B5
Kent Cotts RG7 ....14 A3
Kent Rd Bordon GU35 .....164 D2
　Fleet GU51 ....54 B1
Kenton Cl GU16 ....36 D1
Kenward Bglws RG25 ....114 C3
Kenwith Ave GU51 ....54 C1
Kenyons Yd SP10 ....105 E8
Keogh Barracks GU12 .....56 F1
Keogh Cl GU12 ....56 F2
Kerchers Field RG25 ....88 A7
Kerfield Way RG27 ....51 B1
Kerrfield SO22 ....209 B5
Kerrfield Mews SO22 .....209 B5
Kerridge Ind Est GU34 ...140 A4
Kerry Cl GU51 ....54 B5
Kersey Cres RG14 ....1 C5
Kersley Cres RG29 ....95 C8
Kersten Cl GU34 ....6 A8
Kestrel Cl Ewshot GU10 ..98 B7
　Thatcham RG19 ....2 F3
　Winchester SO22 ......209 B2
Kestrel Ct GU34 ....139 F5
Kestrel Ho GU9 ....119 E8

Kestrel Rd
　Basingstoke RG22 ....67 F1
　Farnborough GU14 ......55 F2
Kestrels Mead RG26 ....9 F2
Ketchers Field GU34 .....184 F6
Ketelbey Rise RG22 ....91 F7
Kevin Cl RG20 ....24 F2
Kevins Dr GU46 ....34 C7
Kevins Gr GU51 ....54 B1
Kew Cotts RG14 ....1 C1
Kew Wlk GU35 ....165 E7
Key The GU51 ....53 D3
Keyhaven Cotts SO20 ....125 C2
Keynes Cl SO22 ....75 B4
Keytech Ctr The RG23 .....68 E7
Kiel Dr SP10 ....82 F3
Kildare Cl GU35 ....164 D4
Kildare Rd GU35 ....164 D4
Kilham La SO22 ....197 B6
Kilmarnock Gdns GU16 ...36 D1
Kilmeston Rd
　Cheriton SO24 ....201 D4
　Kilmeston SO24 ....201 D2
Kilmore Dr GU15 ....36 F4
Kilmuir Cl **3** GU47 ....35 B7
Kiln Field GU35 ....207 E5
Kiln Gdns RG27 ....52 C6
Kiln Hill RG7 ....14 F7
Kiln La Farnham GU10 ...122 A6
　Monk Sherborne RG26 ...47 B5
　Old Alresford SO24 .....157 D1
　Stratfield Mortimer RG7 ..12 A5
Kiln Rd Newbury RG14 .....2 A5
　Sherborne St John RG24 ..47 F3
Kiln Ride RG40 ....16 E8
Kiln Ride Extension RG40 .16 E6
Kiln Way Aldershot GU11 ..99 F7
　Grayshott GU26 ....166 C5
Kiln Workshops GU51 .....74 C6
Kilns The Alton GU34 ....140 B3
　Bucks Horn Oak GU35 ..142 E5
　Farnham GU9 ....119 E4
Kilsby Flats SP9 ....101 E8
Kimball Rd RG22 ....68 F2
Kimber Cl RG24 ....48 F2
Kimber's Cl RG14 ....1 D3
Kimber's La RG14 ....1 D3
Kimberley Cl GU52 ....75 B4
Kimberley Ct SP10 ....82 D2
Kimberley Rd
　Basingstoke RG22 ....68 E3
　Greatham GU33 ....186 C2
Kimbers Dr RG14 ....1 A5
Kimbers La Farnham GU9 ..99 B3
　Pamber End RG26 ....27 B5
Kimpton Dr **1** GU51 ...53 C3
Kimpton, Thruxton & Fyfield
　CE Prim Sch SP11 ....80 D1
Kindersley Pk Homes
　SP11 ....105 B3
King Alfred Pl SO23 .....209 E7
King Alfred Terr
　Kingsclere RG20 ....24 D2
　16 Winchester SO23 ..209 E7
King Arthur's Way SP10 ..83 A3
King George Cl GU14 .....56 B2
King George Rd SO10 ....105 E8
King Harold Ct SO23 .....209 D4
King Henry Rd GU51 .....53 F3
King John Ct RG20 ....24 D2
King John Rd RG20 ....24 D2
King John St GU51 ....53 F3
King Johns Rd RG29 .....72 C4
King La SO20 ....125 C3
King Lane Cotts SO20 ...125 C2
King St Mortimer RG7 ....11 E6
　Odiham RG29 ....72 E2
King's Somborne CE Prim
　Sch SO20 ....171 F2
King's Cl SO23 ....154 B1
King's Cres GU34 ....36 A8
King's Ct GU10 ....100 C8
King's Elms SO21 ....130 D7
King's Hill GU34 ....138 D1
King's La GU32 ....205 D4
King's Mdw RG25 ....88 A8
King's Rd
　Basingstoke RG22 ......68 E3
　Haslemere GU27 ....189 E6
　King's Ride GU15 ......35 E5
King's Royal Hussars Mus
　The* SO23 ....209 D5
King's Sch The RG21 .....69 A4
King's Wlk GU15 ....35 D6
King's Wlk **8** SO23 ...209 E5
King's Yd SP10 ....106 B8
Kingdom Ho **4** GU14 ..77 B8
Kingdons Mews GU34 ...139 F3
Kingfisher Cl
　Basingstoke RG22 ......67 F1
　Bordon GU35 ....164 E2
　Farnborough GU14 ......55 B6
　Fleet GU52 ....75 A5
　Whitchurch RG28 ......86 C5
Kingfisher Court Ind Est
　GU15 ....2 B3
Kingfisher Ct Alton GU34 .139 F6
　Basingstoke RG21 ......69 A6
　Fleet GU51 ....74 F8
Kingfisher Dr GU46 ......33 F6
Kingfisher Ho **3** RG21 ..69 C7
Kingfisher Par GU51 .....34 F5
Kingfisher Wlk GU12 .....77 D2
Kingfishers SP9 ....101 E7
Kings Acre SO20 ....172 A3
Kings Apartments **2**
　GU15 ....36 A4

Kings Ave
　Tongham GU10 ....100 D8
　Winchester SO22 ....209 C3
Kings Chase SP10 ....105 E7
Kings Ct **1** GU14 ......77 A8
Kings Furlong Ctr RG21 ..69 A3
Kings Furlong Dr RG21 ...68 F3
Kings Furlong Inf Sch
　RG21 ....68 F3
Kings Furlong Jun Sch
　RG21 ....68 F3
Kings Glade GU46 ....34 D6
Kings Head Yd **1** SO23 .209 E5
Kings Keep GU52 ....54 F4
Kings La Chilcomb SO21 ..198 F6
　Farnham GU10 ....121 D6
Kings Mdw Andover SP10 .106 B7
　Andover SP10 ....82 C1
Kings Mead RG14 ....1 A2
Kings Mews GU16 ....56 D6
Kings Orch RG23 ....90 B8
Kings Par **4** GU51 .....54 F4
Kings Peace The GU34 ...167 A3
Kings Pightle RG24 ......49 A2
Kings Rd Aldershot GU11 ..76 D1
　Alton GU34 ....139 D2
　Enham Alamein SP11 ....83 B7
　Fleet GU51 ....54 B1
　Newbury RG14 ....1 F2
　Silchester RG7 ....10 F2
　Winchester SO22 ......209 A4
Kings Rd W RG14 ....1 F2
Kings Road Ind Est
　GU27 ....189 E6
Kings Row **3** SO2 ....209 D6
Kings Somborne Rd
　SO51 ....194 D2
Kings Wlk RG28 ....86 C5
Kings Worthy Prim Sch
　SO23 ....176 C6
Kings Worthy Rd **8**
　GU51 ....53 C3
Kings Yd SP10 ....106 A7
Kings' Sch SO22 ....197 B7
Kingsbridge Copse RG27 .71 E8
Kingsbridge Hill RG7 .....13 E6
Kingsbridge Rd RG14 .....1 C1
Kingsclear Pk GU15 ....36 B4
Kingsclere CE Prim Sch
　RG20 ....24 D2
Kingsclere Rd
　Basingstoke RG21 ......68 F7
　Basingstoke RG24 ......69 A6
　Overton RG25 ....59 A3
　Upper Wootton RG26 ....46 E2
Kingscroft GU51 ....75 A8
Kingsdale Ct **9** SO22 ..209 D6
Kingsgate Rd SO23 .....209 D4
Kingsgate St SO23 ......209 E4
Kingsgrove Ind Est GU15 .55 E3
Kingsholt Cotts GU33 ....185 F3
Kingsland Grange RG14 ...5 C8
Kingsland Ind Pk RG24 ...48 E1
Kingsland Rd GU34 ......139 E3
Kingsley Ave GU15 ......36 B3
Kingsley Bglws SO24 ....179 B4
Kingsley Cl GU14 ....1 F6
Kingsley Pk RG28 ....86 C6
Kingsley Pl SO22 ....209 C3
Kingsley Rd
　Eversley Centre RG27 ....33 A8
　Farnborough GU14 ....55 D6
Kingsley Sq GU51 ....53 C4
Kingsmead Alton GU34 ...140 A3
　Anna Valley SP11 ......105 C4
　Camberley GU16 ....56 C7
　Farnborough GU14 ......55 F3
Kingsmead Cotts GU34 ...140 A3
Kingsmead Sh Ctr **10**
　GU14 ....55 F4
Kingsmill Rd RG21 ....69 A2
Kingston Cl SP10 ....105 E5
Kingston Rd GU15 ....36 D8
Kingstons Ind Est GU12 ..77 C2
Kingsvale Ct RG21 ....68 F3
Kingsway Aldershot GU11 ..76 C1
　Andover SP10 ....83 E2
　Blackwater GU17 ......35 C5
Kingsway Gdns SP10 .....83 A3
Kingswood Cl SO21 .....167 B2
Kingswood Ct **6** GU51 .54 A1
Kingswood Firs GU26 ....167 A2
Kingswood La GU26 .....167 A2
Kingswood Rise GU34 ...159 F7
Kintbury Ct GU51 ....53 C3
Kintyre Cl RG23 ....67 C2
Kipling Cl GU46 ....33 F4
Kipling Rd GU34 ....139 D1
Kipling Wlk RG21 ....68 F3
Kirk Knoll GU35 ....165 D5
Kirkby Ct GU16 ....36 C1
Kirke Rd SP9 ....78 E5
Kirtle Dr GU34 ....160 A2
Kitchener Rd
　Farnborough GU11 ......77 B6
　Greatham GU33 ....186 D2
Kitcombe La GU34 ......161 C1
Kitt's La GU32,SO24 ....203 C2
Kitts La GU10 ....166 D8
Kitwood La SO24,GU34 ..182 C7
Kitwood Rd GU34,GU34 ..182 C7
Knapp La RG26 ....27 B6
Knight Cl
　Crookham Village GU51 ..74 C6

Knight Cl continued
　Winchester SO22 ......209 E8
Knight St RG21 ....68 F4
Knights Ct SP10 ....83 E1
Knights Enham Dr **8**
　GU51 ....53 C3
Knights Enham Inf Sch
　SP10 ....83 A3
Knights Enham Jun Sch
　SP10 ....83 A3
Knights La RG20 ....4 A3
Knights Lea RG20 ....3 F3
Knights Park Rd RG21 ....68 F7
Knights Rd GU10 ....76 D3
Knights Way Alton GU34 ..139 D3
　Frimley GU15 ....36 F4
Knightsbridge Dr RG19 ....6 F4
Knightsbridge Rd
　Camberley GU15 ....36 C7
　Enham Alamein SP11 ....83 C7
Knightwood Cl GU34 .....56 C2
Knockhundred La GU26 ..189 A8
Knockwood La SO20 ....147 F7
Knoll Cl GU51 ....54 A2
Knoll Ct GU51 ....54 A3
Knoll Gdns RG20 ....4 E4
Knoll Rd Camberley GU15 .36 A8
　Fleet GU51 ....54 A2
Knoll Wlk GU15 ....36 B6
Knollys Rd Aldershot GU11 .76 D3
　Pamber Heath RG26 .....10 D1
Knook The **6** GU47 ....35 B7
Knowle Cres RG20 ....24 D2
Knowle Dr GU35 ....165 F6
Knowles Cl GU35 ....164 D2
Knowles Mdw GU33 ....208 B1
Knowlings The RG28 .....86 D4
Knox Cl GU52 ....74 E5
Knox Terr GU34 ....140 A4
Kohat Cl GU11 ....78 D7
Kohat Ct **2** GU11 .....76 D2
Kohat Rd SP9 ....78 E5
Kohima Cl GU11 ....76 F2
Krooner Rd GU15 ....35 A6
Kurnool Mortar Cross Roads
　GU15 ....35 E6
Kyftle Ct RG14 ....1 D2
Kynegils Rd SO22 ......209 B8

L

Laburnam Gdns GU52 .....75 B5
Laburnam Rise RG19 ......7 F5
Laburnum Cl GU11 ....76 E1
Laburnum Dr SO23 ......176 B8
Laburnum Gr RG14 ....1 E4
Laburnum Pas **1** GU11 ..76 E1
Laburnum Rd
　Aldershot GU11 ....76 E1
　Farnham GU9 ....99 C7
Laburnum Way RG20 ....24 D2
Laburnums The GU17 ....34 F5
Lackland Ct **14** GU51 ..53 E3
Ladwell Cl RG14 ....5 C8
Lady Godley Cl GU11 .....78 E5
Ladygate Dr GU26 ......166 E3
Ladyplace Ct **7** GU34 ..139 F3
Ladysmith Pl GU35 .....164 C5
Ladywell La SO24 ......179 D6
Ladywood Ave GU11 .....54 A4
Ladywood Ct GU10 .....121 D6
Laffan's Rd GU11 ....76 C6
Laffans Rd RG29 ....95 E8
Lahore Cl SP9 ....78 E7
Lahore Rd SP9 ....78 E7
Lainston Cl SO22 ....209 A8
Lake Ct RG26 ....27 B8
Lake Dr Bordon GU35 ...164 E3
　Winchester SO22 ......197 B3
Lake La GU10 ....143 C6
Lake Rd GU16 ....56 F6
Lake Side The GU17 .....34 E7
Lakeland Dr GU16 ....36 C1
Lakelands RG26 ....26 B8
Laker Sq **8** SP10 .....83 C2
Lakeside Bsns Pk GU47 ..34 E7
Lakeside Cl Andover SP10 .82 D2
　Ash Vale GU12 ....77 D4
Lakeside Ct GU51 ....54 B3
Lakeside Dr RG27 ....32 B4
Lakeside Gdns GU14 .....54 D6
Lakeside Prim Sch GU16 .36 D1
Lakeside Rd
　Ash Vale GU12 ....77 D4
　Farnborough GU14 .....76 E7
Lamb Cl SP10 ....106 C8
Lamb's La RG7 ....13 E7
Lambdens Wlk RG26 .....26 F8
Lambdon App SP11 ......79 C6
Lambdon Terr SP11 .....79 C7
Lambert Cres GU17 ......35 A4
Lambert Dr RG14 ....2 C5
Lambourn Ct RG14 ....1 F5
Lambourn Rd RG20 ....1 B5
Lambourne Cl
　Sparsholt SO21 ....174 C3
　Thruxton SP11 ....103 E8
Lambourne Way
　Thruxton SP11 ....103 E8
　Tongham GU10 ....100 D7
Lambs Cl RG25 ....88 B8
Lambs Farm Bsns Pk
　RG7 ....13 C8
Lambs Lane Prim Sch
　RG7 ....13 D8
Lambs Lease GU33 ......208 A3
Lambs Row GU24 ....69 F7

Lamerton Cl GU35 ......164 D4
Lamerton Rd GU35 .....164 D4
Lamiarra Way RG14 ......6 B8
Lampacres RG14 ....1 F5
Lampard La GU10 ....144 C2
Lampards Cl RG27 ....50 F6
Lampool Ho RG25 ....88 B8
Lamport Cl GU9 ....99 A1
Lanark Cl GU16 ....36 C2
Lancashire Cotts GU51 ...59 C1
Lancaster Ave GU10 ....122 B8
Lancaster Cl Andover SP10 .82 F1
　Ash Vale GU12 ....77 D5
Lancaster Dr GU15 ......36 B6
Lancaster Rd
　Basingstoke RG21 ......69 A6
　Farnborough GU14 ......55 F1
Lancaster Way GU14 .....56 A7
Lancer Ct **6** GU11 .....76 C2
Landale Cl SP11 ....83 B7
Lands End La GU35 .....164 E4
Landseer Cl
　Basingstoke RG21 ......69 D3
　Sandhurst GU47 ....35 C6
Landseer Ct SP10 ....82 F1
Lane End Bramley RG26 ..29 A2
　West Tisted SO24 .....204 C8
Lane End Bglws SO21 ...133 B3
Lane The RG26 ....27 A8
Lanes End RG24 ....49 A3
Laneswood RG7 ....11 C5
Langdale Cl GU14 ....55 C4
Langdale Ct GU12 ....77 D5
Langham Ct GU9 ....122 A7
Langham Rd GU34 .....139 E3
Langley Cl **1** GU52 ...74 F4
Langley Dr Aldershot GU11 ..99 E8
　Camberley GU15 ....36 B6
Langton Cl SO22 ....209 C7
Langton Dr GU35 ....165 E7
Langtons Ct SO24 ......179 E5
Lanham La SO22 ....175 B1
Lankhills Rd SO23 .....209 E7
Lansdowne Ave
　Andover SP10 ....105 E6
　Winchester SO22 ......209 D3
Lansdowne Ct **3** SO23 .209 E7
Lansdowne Rd
　Aldershot GU11 ....76 E1
　Alton GU34 ....140 A5
　Camberley GU16 ....56 E8
Lansley Rd RG21 ....69 B8
Lantarra Way RG14,RG19 ..6 A8
Lantern Ct SO23 ....209 C4
Lapin La RG22 ....91 B5
Lapwing Ct RG22 ....90 F7
Lapwing Rise RG28 .....86 B5
Larch Cl Camberley GU15 .36 C8
　Kings Worthy SO23 ...154 B1
　Liphook SO23 ....187 F3
　Newbury RG14 ....1 B5
Larch Dr Andover SP10 ..105 C7
　Kingsclere RG20 ....24 D2
Larch Rd GU35 ....165 F6
Larch Way GU14 ....55 A3
Larches Way GU17 ......34 F5
Larchfield Rd GU52 ......75 B7
Larchwood RG24 ....48 E3
Larchwood Glade GU15 ..36 E7
Larg Dr SO22 ....175 C4
Lark Hill Rise SO22 ....209 B2
Lark Rise GU30 ....187 E5
Larkfield RG24 ....48 F3
Larkfield Cl GU9 ....98 D2
Larkfield Rd GU9 ....98 D2
Larkin Cl SP11 ....57 A2
Larks Barrow Hill RG28 ..63 C2
Larkspur Cl GU11 ....99 E7
Larkwhistle Farm Rd
　SO21 ....111 D1
Larmer Cl GU51 ....74 D7
Larwood Sq **10** SP10 ..83 C2
Lasham Rd GU51 ....53 C4
Latchwood La GU10 ....122 B5
Latham Ave GU16 ....36 D2
Latimer Ho **11** GU51 ..53 E3
Laud Cl RG14 ....2 B5
Lauder Cl GU14 ....54 A3
Lauderdale GU51 ....55 B3
Launcelot Cl SP10 ....83 A3
Laundry Bglws SP4 .....101 F1
Laundry Ct **8** RG14 ....1 E4
Laundry La Heckfield RG27 .31 C5
　Sandhurst GU47 ....35 C5
Laundry Rd RG26 ....86 C5
Laurel Ave RG19 ....7 E5
Laurel Cl Camberley GU15 .55 A3
　Farnborough GU14 ......55 A3
　North Warnborough RG29 .72 C3
　Oakley RG23 ....91 E7
Laurel Dr GU10 ....121 D6
Laurel Gr GU10 ....121 D5
Laurels The Andover SP10 .82 E1
　Basingstoke RG21 ......69 C6
　Farnham GU9 ....99 D3
　Fleet GU51 ....54 A1
Laureston **2** GU15 ....36 C4
Lavant Field GU34 .....161 E8
Lavell's La RG7 ....27 B8
Lavender Cl **2** SP10 ..105 E6
Lavender Gdns GU35 ...164 D3
Lavender La GU10 ......121 D4
Lavender Rd RG22 ....91 A7
Laverstoke Cl GU51 .....53 C4

Laverstoke La RG28 ....87 B3
Lawday Link GU9 ....98 E7
Lawday Pl GU9 ....98 E7
Lawday Place La GU9 .....98 E7
Lawford Cres GU46 ....34 B6
Lawn Ho 4 SO23 ....209 E6
Lawn Rd RG22 ....175 C5
Lawn St SO23 ....209 E6
Lawns The GU14 ....55 C3
Lawrence Cl Andover SP10 .82 F2
Basingstoke RG24 ....48 C1
Lawrence Dale Ct RG21 ...68 F4
Lawrence Hos SP11 ......103 B1
Lawrence Lo GU15 ....36 B7
Lawrence Pl RG14 ....2 A5
Lawrence Rd GU52 ....74 F8
Lawrence Way
  Camberley GU15 ....35 D4
  4 Winchester SO23 .....209 E8
Laws Terr GU11 ....77 A2
Lay Field RG21 ....50 F1
Le Borowe GU52 ....74 E4
Le Freth Dr 12 GU51 .....53 C3
Le Marchant Rd GU16 ....36 D3
Lea Cl Ash GU12 ....77 E1
Basingstoke RG21 ....69 D5
Farnham GU9 ....99 E6
Lea Ct GU9 ....99 D7
Lea Rd GU15 ....35 F2
Lea Springs GU51 ....74 D7
Lea The
  Finchampstead RG40 .....16 D8
  Fleet GU51 ....74 E7
Lea Way GU12 ....77 D3
Lea Wood Rd GU51 ....74 E7
Leaden Vere RG29 ....95 D4
Leafy Oak Farm GU17 ....34 E4
Leckford SO20 ....150 D8
Leckford La SO20 ....150 B6
Lee Ct GU11 ....100 A8
Lee Rd GU11 ....76 C2
Lees Hill RG29 ....94 E4
Lees Mdw RG27 ....51 C1
Lefroy Ave RG21 ....69 C7
Lefroy Pk GU51 ....53 F1
Lefroy's Field GU10 .....97 D8
Leger Cl GU52 ....74 E5
Legge Cres GU11 ....77 A2
Legion La SO23 ....176 C7
Lehar Cl RG22 ....91 D8
Leicester Pl SP10 ......106 A7
Leicester Way SO23 .....176 C1
Leigh Cl SP10 ....106 C7
Leigh Cl SP10 ....106 C7
Leigh Field RG21 ....91 B7
Leigh Field RG7 ....11 D6
Leigh Gdns SP10 ....106 C7
Leigh House Hospl
  SO21 ....198 E7
Leigh La GU9 ....122 C8
Leigh Rd SP10 ....106 C7
Leipzig Rd GU52 ....75 B3
Leith Dr GU11 ....76 D3
Lemon Gr GU35 ....164 C1
Len Smart Ct 2 RG21 ....69 C7
Lendore Rd GU16 ....56 B8
Lennel Gdns GU52 ....75 C6
Lennon Way RG22 ....91 C8
Lennox Rd RG22 ....68 F2
Lent Hill Ct SO22 ......209 B4
Lenten St GU14 ....139 E3
Leonard Cl GU16 ....56 B8
Leonardslee Cres RG14 ...2 B4
Leopold Ave GU14 ....55 F5
Leslie Southern Ct 1
  RG14 ....54 C1
Lestock Way GU51 ....54 C1
Levern Dr GU9 ....99 A6
Levignen Cl GU52 ....74 D5
Lewendon Rd RG14 ....1 C5
Lewis Cl 3 RG21 ....69 C7
Lewis Wlk RG14 ....5 A6
Ley Rd GU14 ....55 E8
Leys Gdns RG14 ....1 D4
Leyton Way SP10 ....105 E6
Liberty Ho RG19 ....6 E5
Library La SO21 ....174 B4
Lickfolds Rd GU10 ......121 C3
Liddell Cl RG40 ....16 C3
Lightfoot Gr RG21 ....69 B2
Lightsfield RG23 ....67 B2
Lilac Cl Andover SP10 ..105 D7
  Bordon GU35 ....164 D2
Lilac Way RG23 ....68 D6
Lilac Wlk RG19 ....7 F5
Lilian Pl GU34 ....161 D3
Lillywhite Cres SP10 ....83 B8
Lily Cl RG22 ....91 A7
Limbrey Hill RG25 ....94 C5
Lime Ave Alton GU34 ...139 C5
  Camberley GU15 ....36 E6
Lime Cl Newbury RG14 ....2 B4
  Thatcham RG19 ....7 F3
Lime Cres GU12 ....77 F2
Lime Gdns GU51 ....54 B4
Lime Gdns RG21 ....69 E5
Lime Gr GU34 ....139 E5
Lime Kiln Cotts The
  RG20 ....42 D8
Lime Rd SO24 ....179 D5
Lime St GU11 ....76 D2
Lime St Rdbt GU11 ......76 D2
Lime Tree Way RG24 .....48 E4
Lime Tree Wlk GU14 .....77 C8
Lime Wlk SP10 ....105 D6
Limecroft GU46 ....34 A5
Limekiln Rd SP11 ....58 B4
Limes Ave RG20 ....22 E7
Limes Cl Bramshott GU30 .188 A7
  Liss GU33 ....207 F4

Limes Rd GU14 ....55 A5
Limes The Amport SP11 ..104 B8
Basingstoke RG22 ....91 A8
Bramley RG26 ....29 B2
Haslemere GU27 ....189 C6
Limetree Ave RG20 ....21 F2
Limetree Wlk 3 SO23 ...198 D8
Limington House Sch
  RG22 ....68 D3
Linchmere Rd
  Haslemere GU27 ....189 B5
  Linchmere GU27 ....189 A4
Lincoln Cl Ash Vale GU12 .77 D5
  Basingstoke RG22 ....91 B8
  Frimley GU15 ....36 F4
Lincoln Ct
  2 Liphook GU30 ....188 A4
  Newbury RG14 ....1 D2
Lincoln Gn GU14 ....139 E2
Lincoln Rd GU14 ....76 F8
Linden Ave Odiham RG29 .72 F4
  Old Basing RG24 ....70 B5
Linden Cl Ludgershall SP11 .57 A2
  Newbury RG14 ....1 D4
Linden Ct Camberley GU15 .36 D7
  Old Basing RG24 ....70 B5
Linden Dr GU33 ....207 F4
Linden Ho 10 GU34 ....139 F3
Linden Rd
  Bishop's Green RG19 .....6 D3
  Headley GU35 ....166 A5
Lindenmuth way RG19 ....6 D5
Lindens The Farnham GU9 .99 B1
  Lindford GU35 ....164 F6
Lindenwood RG24 ....48 E4
Lindford Chase GU35 ...164 F5
Lindford Rd GU35 ......164 F5
Lindford Wey GU35 ....164 F5
Lindley Cl SP9 ....78 F6
Lindley Gdns SO24 .....179 D4
Lindum Dene GU11 ....76 E1
Lines End GU52 ....75 D2
Lines The RG20 ....24 D3
Ling Cres GU35 ....165 F6
Lingen Cl SP10 ....82 F3
Lingfield GU51 ....54 A3
Lingfield Cl Alton GU34 ..139 F2
  Basingstoke RG24 ....70 C5
Lingfield Rd RG14 ....6 A8
Lingmala Gr GU52 ....75 B5
Link Ho 4 RG14 ....1 E2
Link Rd Alton GU34 ....140 A6
  Farnborough GU14 ......55 B1
  Kingsclere RG20 ....24 E2
Link The Andover SP10 ..105 C8
  Yateley GU46 ....34 A7
Link View RG14 ....1 D7
Link Way Oakley RG23 ...67 B1
  Thatcham RG19 ....7 A3
Linklater's Cotts GU17 ..54 F5
Links Cotts SO24 ......179 D4
Links Rd SO22 ....209 B7
Links The GU35 ....164 B1
Links Way GU14 ....55 A3
Linkside E GU26 ....167 A7
Linkside N GU26 ....166 F7
Linkside S GU26 ....167 A6
Linkside W
  Beacon Hill GU26 .....167 A6
  Hindhead GU26 ....166 F6
Linkway Camberley GU15 .36 A4
  Fleet GU52 ....75 A6
Linkway Par GU52 ....74 F6
Linnet Cl RG22 ....68 A2
Linnet La SO21 ....189 A4
Linnets Rd SO24 ....179 D4
Linnets Way GU14 ....55 D3
Linsford Bsns Pk GU16 ..56 D3
Linsford La GU16 ....56 D3
Linstead Rd GU14 ....55 C8
Linsted La GU35 ....165 B7
Linton Cl RG22 ....91 B8
Linton Dr SP10 ....83 A1
Lion & Lamb Way 5 GU9 .99 F2
Lion & Lamb Yd 13 GU9 .99 F2
Lion Cl Haslemere GU27 .189 D7
  Overton RG25 ....88 A7
Lion Ct RG24 ....69 F6
Lion Gn GU27 ....189 D7
Lion La GU27 ....189 D7
Lion Mead GU27 ....189 D7
Lion Way GU35 ....75 B5
Lions Field GU35 ......163 D4
Lions Hall 4 SO22 .....209 D5
Liphook CE Jun Sch
  GU30 ....189 A4
Liphook Inf Sch GU30 ..187 F4
Liphook Rd Bordon GU35 .186 D6
  Haslemere GU27 ....189 A6
  Headley GU35 ....165 D3
  Linchmere GU27 ....188 E4
  Lindford GU35 ....164 F5
  Liphook Sta GU30 .....188 A2
Lipscombe Cl
  Newbury RG14 ....1 C2
  Southrope RG25 ....116 C6
Lipscombe Rise GU34 ...139 F5
Lisa Ct 1 RG21 ....69 A4
Liskeard Dr GU14 ....55 E6
Lisle Cl 5 Newbury RG14 ..1 D5
  Winchester SO22 ......197 A3
Lisle Ct SO22 ....209 C4
Lismoyne Cl GU51 ....53 F2
Liss Inf & Jun Schs
  GU33 ....208 A3
Liss Sta GU33 ....207 F4

Lister Rd RG22 ....68 F2
Litchfield Cl SP10 ......82 D3
Litchfield Dr GU51 ......53 C3
Litchfield Ho 2 RG26 ...26 F8
Litchfield Rd SO22 ....175 D4
Litten The RG20 ....24 D2
Little Aldershot La
  Ashford Hill RG26 ....8 F2
  Pamber Heath RG26 ......9 A2
Little Austins Rd GU9 ..122 B8
Little Barn Pl GU33 ....208 B4
Little Basing GU34 ......70 A7
Little Binfields RG24 ...49 A1
Little Copse
  Andover SP10 ....105 E6
  Fleet GU52 ....74 F7
  Yateley GU46 ....34 B4
Little Copse Chase RG24 .48 E2
Little Croft GU46 ....34 B4
Little Dean Ct SO20 ...150 A3
Little Dean Ho SO20 ...150 A3
Little Dean La RG25 .....94 C6
Little Drove Rd SO20 ..129 A3
Little Fallow RG24 ......70 A8
Little Foxes RG40 ....16 C7
Little Green La GU9 ....121 E6
Little Hartleys RG27 ....51 D1
Little Hatherden SP11 ...59 E2
Little Hayes La SO21 ...177 F7
Little Hoddington Cl
  RG25 ....94 C5
Little Knowl Hill GU35 ..24 F4
Little London Rd RG7 ...27 F8
Little Minster St SO23 .209 E5
Little Paddock GU15 ....36 E8
Little Stodham Ho
  GU33 ....207 D2
Little Thurbans Cl GU12 .121 E6
Little Vigo GU46 ....33 F4
Little Wellington St
  GU11 ....76 E2
Little-Ann Bridge Farm
  SP11 ....105 C6
Littlefield Cl GU12 .....77 E1
Littlefield Gdns GU11 ...77 E1
Littlefield Rd GU34 ....140 A4
Littleton Cotts SP11 ....80 C4
Littleton La SO21,SO22 ..175 A5
Littleton Rd SO22 .....175 B4
Littleworth Rd GU10 ...100 D1
Litton Gdns RG21 ....67 B1
Livery Rd SP5 ....168 A2
Livia Cl SP10 ....83 B4
Livingstone Rd
  Andover SP10 ....83 E1
  Newbury RG14 ....1 A2
Lloyd's La RG26 ....46 B6
Loader Cl SO23 ....176 C7
Lock Rd GU11 ....77 B5
Lock Sq 12 SP10 ....83 C2
Lock's La SO21 ....174 C3
Locke Cl SP11 ....124 F7
Locke Rd GU30 ....188 B4
Locke's Dro SP11 ....60 B8
Lockerley CE Prim Sch
  SO51 ....192 A1
Lockerley Rd
  Dunbridge SO51 ....192 D1
  Lockerley SO51 ....192 A1
Lockram La RG7 ....12 B8
Locksmead 8 RG21 .....69 D5
Lockwood Ct GU14 ......55 C8
Loddon Bsns Ctr The
  RG24 ....69 E7
Loddon Cl GU15 ....36 E6
Loddon Court Farm Park
  Homes RG24 ....13 D7
Loddon Ct RG21 ....69 C2
Loddon Ctr RG24 ....69 E8
Loddon Dr RG21 ....69 B5
Loddon Mall 8 RG21 ....69 B5
Loddon Rd GU14 ....55 B6
Loddon Sch The RG27 ...49 B5
Loddon Way GU12 ....77 E1
Lodge Cl Aldershot GU11 .100 A8
  Andover SP10 ....105 E8
Lodge Dr SP11 ....81 D2
Lodge Gr GU34 ....139 F5
Lodge Hill Cl GU10 ....122 B6
Lodge La GU10 ....122 C6
Lodge La SP11 ....58 B4
Lodge The Farnham GU9 .99 C4
  Newbury RG14 ....1 E4
Lodsworth GU14 ....55 B3
Loggon Rd RG21 ....69 A1
Loman Rd GU16 ....56 F4
Lomond Cl RG22 ....67 A2
Londlandes GU52 ....74 E4
London Ct RG14 ....2 A3
London Ho 4 GU11 ......76 F7
London Rd Alton GU34 .140 D6
  Andover SP10 ....106 C8
  Basingstoke RG21 ......69 C4
  Camberley GU15 ....36 C6
  Hartley Wintney RG27 ...50 D7
  Hill Brow GU33 ....208 B1
  Hindhead GU26 ....167 D4
  Hook RG27 ....51 C2
  Kings Worthy SO23 ....176 B5
  Liphook GU30 ....188 A5
  Newbury RG14 ....1 E4
  Odiham RG29 ....72 D1
  Newbury,Speenhamland
    RG14 ....1 E4
  Odiham RG29 ....72 F5
  Odiham,Colt Hill RG29 ..72 F3
  Old Basing RG24,RG27 ...70 D5
  Overton RG25 ....88 B8

London Rd continued
  Picket Piece SP10 ......84 B1
  Sandhurst GU17,GU15 ...35 D5
  Stockbridge SO20 .....150 D4
  Whitchurch RG28 ....86 B6
London St Andover SP10 ..106 B7
  Basingstoke RG21 ......69 B4
  Whitchurch RG28 ....86 C5
Long Barn Rd SO21 ....174 B5
Long Beech Dr GU14 ....55 A3
Long Bottom SP11 ....57 F3
Long Bridge GU9 ....99 A2
Long Cl SO23 ....209 C3
Long Copse Chase RG24 .48 E3
Long Cross Hill GU35 ..165 C6
Long Cross La RG22 .....91 C6
Long Garden Mews 11
  GU9 ....98 F2
Long Garden Way GU9 ...98 F2
Long Garden Wlk GU9 ...98 F2
Long Garden Wlk E GU9 .98 F2
Long Garden Wlk W GU9 .98 F2
Long Gdn Way GU9 ......98 E1
Long Gdn Wlk GU9 ......98 E1
Long Gdn Wlk E GU9 ....98 E1
Long Gdn Wlk W GU9 ....98 E1
Long Gr RG26 ....9 B2
Long Gr GU10 ....100 C1
Long Island GU35 .....164 D3
Long La Long Sutton RG29 .96 A5
  Newbury RG14 ....2 B7
  Old Basing RG24 ....49 A2
Long Leaze SP11 ....61 C4
Long Rd The GU10 .....121 E3
Long Sutton CE Prim Sch
  RG29 ....95 E3
Long Sutton Dr GU51 ...53 C4
Long Wlk SO21 ....176 E3
Longacre Ash GU12 .....77 E2
Longacre Rise RG24 .....48 E2
Longbarrow Cl SO21 ...153 E4
Longbridge Cl RG27 ....29 E1
Longbridge Rd RG26 ....28 F3
Longcroft GU10 ....120 A5
Longcroft Cl 3 RG21 ....69 A4
Longcroft Rd RG20 .....24 C3
Longdene Rd GU27 .....189 F6
Longdon GU52 ....74 F6
Longdown GU10 ....122 A6
Longdown Lodge GU47 ..34 F8
Longdown Rd GU10 .....122 A5
Longfellow Par RG24 ...69 C8
Longfield RG27 ....67 B3
Longfield Cl
  Farnborough GU14 ......55 E8
  North Waltham RG25 ....89 E1
Longfield Rd Ash GU12 ..77 E2
  Winchester SO23 ......198 D8
Longford Cl GU15 ....36 B4
Longhope Dr GU10 .....121 E6
Longhouse Gn 6 SO23 ..198 C8
Longleat Sq GU14 ......56 B3
Longley Rd GU9 ....99 A5
Longmead Fleet GU52 ...75 A6
  Liss GU33 ....207 F4
Longmeadow GU16 ......36 D3
Longmoor Pk RG40 .....16 C6
Longmoor Dr GU30 ....187 B4
Longmoor La RG7 ....11 E7
Longmoor Rd
  Basingstoke RG21 ......69 A4
  Greatham GU33 ....186 A3
  Liphook GU30 ....187 D4
Longparish CE Prim Sch
  SP11 ....108 B4
Longparish Ct 8 SP10 ..106 B7
Longpraish Rd
  Hurstbourne Priors RG28 .85 D1
  Longparish SP11 ......107 E2
Longroden La RG25 .....93 C7
Longs Ct RG28 ....86 C5
Longstock Cl
  Andover SP10 ....105 E7
  Chineham RG24 ....49 B4
Longstock Ct SP10 ....106 B7
Longstock Rd SP11 ....127 F4
Longwater La
  Eversley Cross RG27 ....33 C8
  Finchampstead RG40 ...16 C2
Longwater Rd RG40 .....16 C2
Longwood Copse La
  RG23 ....90 F4
Lonscombe Carr SP5 ..146 B3
Lord Denning Ct RG28 ..86 C5
Lord Wandsworth Coll
  RG29 ....95 F1
Lordsfield Gdns RG25 ...88 A8
Lordswood RG7 ....27 E8
Lorraine Cl GU16 ....36 E8
Lorraine Sch GU15 ......36 C8
Louisburg Rd GU35 ....164 D6
Louise Margaret Rd
  GU11 ....76 F3
Loundyes Cl RG18 ....2 F1
Love La Andover SP10 ..106 B7
  Kingsclere RG20 ....24 D2
  Newbury RG14 ....1 E4
  Odiham RG29 ....72 D1
Lovedon La SO23 ......176 C7
Lovegroves RG24 ....49 B3
Lovell Cl
  South Wonston SO21 ..153 E4
  Thruxton SP11 ....103 D7
Lovells Wlk SO24 .....179 C5

Lav – Lyn 225

Loveridge Cl
  Andover SP10 ....83 B4
  Basingstoke RG21 ......69 A2
Lovers La GU10 ....144 A7
Loves Wood RG7 ....11 D5
Lovett Ho 1 SO22 ......175 A1
Lovett Wlk SO22 ......175 C3
Lovington La SO21,SO24 .178 C4
Low La GU9 ....99 F6
Lowa Rd SP9 ....78 E6
Lowden Cl SO22 ....209 B2
Lowe Cl GU11 ....76 D3
Lower Brook St
  Basingstoke RG21 ......68 F5
  Winchester SO23 ......209 E6
Lower Canes GU46 ......33 E6
Lower Charles St GU15 ..36 A6
Lower Chestnut Dr RG21 .68 F3
Lower Church La GU9 ...98 F2
Lower Church Rd GU47 ..34 C8
Lower Comm RG27 ......15 D1
Lower Evingar Rd RG28 ..86 C5
Lower Farm Ct RG18,RG19 .2 D1
Lower Farnham Rd
  GU11,GU12 ....100 A8
Lower Hanger GU27 ....189 B6
Lower Henwick Farm
  RG18 ....2 D5
Lower Lamborough La
  SO24 ....201 D5
Lower Mead SO20 ......126 B4
Lower Moor GU46 ....34 B5
Lower Mount St 4 GU51 .53 D3
Lower Neatham Mill La
  Alton GU34 ....140 D6
  Alton,Neatham GU34 ..140 E6
Lower Nelson St 1 GU11 .76 E2
Lower Newport Rd GU12 .77 D4
Lower Paice La GU34 ..159 C4
Lower Pool Rd RG27 ....32 B4
Lower Raymond Almshouses
  10 RG14 ....1 D2
Lower Rd SO21 ....153 C4
Lower Sandhurst Rd
  RG40 ....16 E2
Lower South View GU9 ..99 A3
Lower St GU27 ....189 F6
Lower Stanmore La
  SO23 ....209 C3
Lower Terrace Rd GU14 ..76 E8
Lower Turk St GU34 ...139 F3
Lower Way RG19 ....2 C3
Lower Weybourne La
  GU9 ....99 E6
Loveswater Gdns GU35 .164 D5
Lowicks Rd GU10 ......144 F6
Lowlands Rd
  Basingstoke RG22 ......68 A3
  Blackwater GU17 ....35 A4
Lowndes Bldgs GU9 ....98 E3
Lowry Cl GU47 ....35 B6
Lowry Ct SP10 ....62 E2
Loxwood Ave GU51 .....74 E7
Loyalty La RG24 ....70 C6
Loyd-Lindsay Sq SO22 .209 B4
Lubeck Dr SP10 ....82 F3
Lucas Cl GU46 ....34 B5
Lucas Field GU27 .....189 C6
Ludgershall Castle Prim Sch
  SP11 ....57 A2
Ludgershall Rd SP9 .....79 A8
Ludlow Cl
  Basingstoke RG22 ......68 C5
  Camberley GU16 ....36 E7
  Newbury RG14 ....2 C4
Ludlow Gdns RG23 ......69 B8
Ludlow Pl RG22 ....68 A7
Ludshott Gr GU35 .....165 F5
Ludshott Manor GU30 .166 A1
Luke Rd GU11 ....99 C8
Luke Rd E GU11 ....99 C8
Lulworth Cl GU14 ......55 B6
Lundy Cl RG24 ....48 D1
Lune Cl 4 RG21 ....69 D5
Lune Ct 25 SP10 ....83 C2
Lunn Cotts GU34 ......140 B3
Lupin Cl RG22 ....91 A8
Lupin Gdns SO22 ......175 B2
Lutyens Cl
  Basingstoke RG24 ......69 F8
  Chineham RG24 ....48 F1
Lutyens Ind Ctr RG24 ..48 E1
Lyall Pl GU9 ....98 F7
Lych Gate Cl GU47 .....34 D8
Lyde Cl RG23 ....67 D2
Lydford Cl
  Camberley GU16 ....56 E7
  Farnborough GU14 .....55 E7
Lye Copse Ave GU14 ....55 F8
Lyeway La SO24,GU34 .182 C4
Lyeway Rd SO24 ......182 B3
Lyford Rd RG21 ....69 B6
Lymington Ave GU46 ...34 A5
Lymington Bottom
  GU34 ....160 B1
Lymington Bottom Rd
  GU34 ....160 A3
Lymington Cl
  Basingstoke RG22 ......91 B7
  Four Marks GU34 .....160 B2
Lymington Farm Ind Est
  GU34 ....160 B1
Lymington Rise GU34 ..160 B2
Lyn Ct 5 RG21 ....69 D5
Lynams GU52 ....74 E3

Lynch Cl SO22 ....209 C8
Lynch Hill RG28 ....86 C5
Lynch Hill Pk RG28 ....86 D5
Lynch Rd GU9 ....99 C2
Lynch The Overton RG25 ..87 E8
Whitchurch RG28 ....86 D5
Lynchborough Rd GU30 .187 B8
Lynchford La GU14 ....77 C8
Lynchford Rd GU14 ....77 B8
Lyndale Dr GU51 ....54 D1
Lyndford Terr GU52 ....74 F7
Lyndhurst Ave
Aldershot GU11 ....100 A6
Blackwater GU17 ....35 A6
Lyndhurst Cl SO22 ....175 D4
Lyndhurst Dr RG22 ....91 C6
Lyndhurst Rd GU51 ....53 C4
Lyndhurst Sch GU15 ....35 F5
Lyndons The GU30 ....187 B8
Lyndsey Cl GU14 ....54 F4
Lynford Ave SO22 ....209 C8
Lynford Way SO22 ....209 C8
Lynn Way
Farnborough GU14 ....55 D7
Kings Worthy SO23 ....176 C7
Lynton Cl GU9 ....121 E7
Lynton Ct RG14 ....1 E4
Lynton Mdw SO20 ....129 A4
Lynton Rd GU35 ....164 D3
Lynwood Cl GU35 ....165 A5
Lynwood Ct SO22 ....209 C8
Lynwood Dr
Andover SP10 ....105 E8
Mytchett GU16 ....56 E3
Lynwood Gdns RG27 ....51 A1
Lyon Way GU16 ....36 A1
Lyon Way Ind Est GU16 ..36 A1
Lysander Way GU14 ....55 F1
Lyse Ct GU33 ....207 F4
Lysons Ave GU14 ....77 D8
Lysons Rd GU11 ....76 E1
Lysons Way GU11 ....77 E7
Lytham Ct GU35 ....164 B2
Lyttel Combe RG27 ....51 D1
Lytton Rd RG21 ....69 D5

M

Mabbs La RG27 ....52 C4
Mabelmyll Croft RG27 .....51 D2
Mabett Cl RG22 ....15 C8
Mac Callum Rd SP11 ....83 B8
Macadam Way SP10 ....82 B1
Macdonald Rd GU9 ....98 F7
Macklin Ho **21** SO22 .....209 D6
Maclay Ho SP11 ....83 B7
Macnaghten Woods 1
GU15 ....36 C6
Macrae Rd GU46 ....34 A6
Maddocks Hill SO24 ......181 B4
Madeira Cl RG24 ....48 D1
Madeira Ct GU15 ....55 C5
Madeira Pl **5** RG14 ....1 E2
Madeley Rd GU52 ....75 B6
Madox Brown End GU47 ..35 C6
Madrid Rd SP10 ....83 C1
Magazine Rd GU14 ....76 B8
Magdalen Hill SO22 ......209 F5
Magdalen Mews 8
SO23 ....209 F5
Magellan Cl SP10 ....83 E1
Magnolia Cl SP10 ....105 E7
Magnolia Ct RG19 ....7 F6
Magnolia Ho RG24 ....48 A1
Magnolia Way GU52 ....75 A7
Magnus Dr RG22 ....91 B7
Magpie Cl
Basingstoke RG22 ....90 F8
Bordon GU35 ....164 E2
Ewshot GU10 ....98 B8
Thatcham RG19 ....2 F3
Mahler Cl RG22 ....91 F8
Maida Rd GU11 ....76 F4
Maidenhead Ho **8** RG14 ..1 D2
Maidenthorn La RG25 .....90 A1
Main Rd Littleton SO22 ..175 B5
Tadley RG26 ....27 B6
Main St RG19 ....4 C5
Mainline Bsns Ctr GU33 .207 F4
Maitland Rd GU14 ....76 F8
Maitlands Cl GU10 ....100 D8
Majendie Cl RG14 ....1 B5
Majestic Rd RG22 ....91 A5
Majorca Ave SP10 ....83 C1
Makins Ct SO24 ....179 C5
Maldive Rd RG24 ....48 D1
Malham Gdns RG22 ....91 B5
Mall The Andover SP10 ..106 A7
South Tidworth SP9 ....78 F4
Mallard Cl Andover SP10 .83 B2
Ash GU12 ....77 D2
Basingstoke RG22 ....90 F7
Haslemere GU27 ....189 C6
New Alresford SO24 ......179 D6
Mallard Way **4** GU46 ....33 F6
Mallards GU34 ....139 F5
Mallards The GU16 ....36 D2
Mallow Cl GU35 ....165 A5
Malmesbury Gdns RG22 .209 B8
Malmesbury Ho **2** SP9 ...79 A6
Malmesbury Rd GU35 ....164 D2
Malpass Rd SO21 ....153 C2

Malshanger Cotts RG23 ..66 E6
Malshanger La RG23 ....67 A3
Malt House La SP11 ....83 D7
Malta Cl RG24 ....48 B1
Maltbys GU34 ....184 E8
Malthouse Bridge Cotts
GU51 ....74 D5
Malthouse Cl
Crookham Village GU52 ...74 E5
Itchen Abbas SO21 ....176 F4
Malthouse Cotts
North Warnborough RG29 .72 C3
Penton Mewsey SP11 ......82 A3
Malthouse Ct GU30 ......188 A4
Malthouse La
Bighton SO24 ....158 C1
Tadley RG26 ....27 B6
Upper Chute SP11 ....58 A8
Malthouse Mdws GU30 ..188 A4
Malthouse Mews GU34 ..140 C6
Maltings Cl GU34 ....139 F3
Maltings The
Bramley RG26 ....28 F2
Liphook GU30 ....188 B4
Malvern Cl RG22 ....68 A3
Malvern Ct RG14 ....1 D1
Malvern Rd
Farnborough GU14 ....55 B7
Hawley GU17 ....34 D1
Hill Brow GU33 ....208 B2
Mandarin Ct Farnham GU9 ..99 E5
Mandarin Rd RG24 ....2 A2
Mandarin Dr RG14 ....6 A8
Mandora Rd GU11 ....76 F4
Manfield Rd GU12 ....77 F2
Manica Cl GU35 ....164 D3
Manley Bridge Rd GU10 .121 C5
Manley James Cl RG29 ....72 E3
Mann Cl RG28 ....86 D4
Manningford Cl SO23 ....176 A3
Manor Bridge Ct SP9 ......78 F7
Manor Cl
Abbotts Ann SP11 ....105 A3
Alton GU34 ....140 A6
Basingstoke RG22 ....91 A6
Haslemere GU27 ....189 C6
Shipton Bellinger SP9 ....101 E7
Tongham GU10 ....100 D7
7 Winchester SO23 .....209 F6
Manor Copse SP10 ....83 B5
Manor Cotts RG28 ....87 B6
Manor Cres GU27 ....189 C5
Manor Ct GU52 ....53 C4
Manor Farm Bsns Ctr
GU10 ....100 D5
Manor Farm Cl GU12 ......77 D1
Manor Farm Cotts SO21 .131 B2
Manor Farm La SO51 ....193 E1
Manor Lea GU27 ....189 C6
Manor Parks Cotts GU34 .140 A3
Manor Park Dr
Finchampstead RG40 ......16 C6
Yateley GU46 ....34 B5
Yateley GU46 ....34 B5
Manor Park Ind Est GU12 .77 A1
Manor Pl RG14 ....1 B5
Manor Rd Aldershot GU11 .99 E8
Alton GU34 ....140 A6
Andover SP10 ....82 F1
East Tytherley SP5 ....191 E7
Farnborough GU14 ....56 B3
Farnham GU9 ....99 C4
Sherborne St John RG24 ..47 E3
Tongham GU10,GU12 ....100 D8
Manor Rise SP11 ....105 E4
Manor Rise Flats SP11 ...105 E4
Manor View RG21 ....8 D7
Manor Wlk GU12 ....76 F1
Manse La RG26 ....27 B6
Mansell Dr RG14 ....1 A5
Mansfield Bsns Pk
GU34 ....160 B3
Mansfield Rd RG22 ....68 E2
Mansion Dr RG27 ....32 B4
Mansion House St 2
RG14 ....1 E3
Maple Cl Alton GU34 .....139 F5
Ash Vale GU12 ....77 C1
Blackwater GU17 ....35 A5
New Alresford SO24 ......179 C4
Maple Cres
Basingstoke RG22 ....69 B7
Ludgershall SP11 ....57 F2
Newbury RG14 ....1 E4
Maple Ct RG22 ....68 B4
Maple Dr SO23 ....176 B8
Maple Gdns GU46 ....34 B5

Maple Gr RG26 ....26 F8
Maple Leaf Cl GU14 ....55 D3
Maple Leaf Dr GU14 ......164 D4
Maple Ridge Sch RG21 ....69 A7
Maple Terr **4** SP9 ....79 A7
Maple Way GU35 ....165 F6
Maple Wlk
Aldershot GU12 ....100 B8
2 Andover SP10 ....105 D6
Maplebank GU35 ....91 B6
Maplehurst Chase RG22 ..91 B6
Maplers Dr **16** SO21 .....53 E3
Maplespeen Ct RG14 ......1 D4
Mapletons The RG29 ......72 F3
Maplewood RG24 ....48 E3
March Cl SP10 ....83 B1
Marchant Cl RG19 ....6 B7
Marchant Rd SP10 ....105 E7
Marchwood Ho GU51 .....53 C3
Marconi Rd GU14 ....1 A5
Mareth Cl GU11 ....76 F2
Margaret Rd RG22 ....68 B8
Marguerite Cl RG26 ....28 F3
Marigold Cl RG22 ....91 A8
Mariners Cl RG26 ....27 B6
Mariners Dr GU14 ....56 A6
Marino Way RG40 ....15 E6
Marjoram Cl RG24 ....54 F4
Mark La **13** RG22 ....69 B4
Mark Way SO51 ....191 D3
Mark Way Sch The
SP10 ....106 C8
Markall Cl SO24 ....201 D5
Market La SO23 ....209 E5
Market Pl
Basingstoke RG22 ....69 B4
5 Newbury RG14 ....1 E3
Market Sq **8** GU34 ....139 F3
Market St Alton GU34 ....139 F3
Newbury RG14 ....1 E3
Winchester SO23 ....209 E5
Markham Ct GU15 ....36 B6
Markson Rd SO21 ....153 C4
Marl's La RG24 ....48 B4
Marlborough Cl **5** RG29 .75 D8
Marlborough Gdns RG23 .67 B2
Marlborough Inf Sch
GU11 ....77 A7
Marlborough Rise GU15 ..55 A5
Marlborough St SP10 ....106 A8
Marlborough Trad Mews
RG24 ....48 D2
Marley Combe Rd GU27 .189 D4
Marley Hanger GU27 ....189 D3
Marley La GU27 ....189 D3
Marlow Cl RG24 ....69 C8
Marlowes The RG14 ....1 C5
Marnel Inf & Jun Schs
RG24 ....48 C1
Marnhull Rise SO22 ......209 A5
Marrow Meade GU51 ......53 E3
Marrowbrook Cl GU14 ....55 E3
Marrowbrook La GU14 ....55 E3
Mars Ho **16** RG21 ....8 D7
Marsden Ct RG28 ....87 C6
Marsh Cl GU35 ....164 F3
Marsh Farm Bsns Ctr
GU10 ....74 D1
Marsh La
Eversley Cross RG27 ....33 D7
Newbury RG14 ....1 E3
Marshall Cl GU34 ....139 E2
Marshall Ct GU14 ....55 D7
Marshall Gdns RG21 ....69 B7
Marshall Rd GU47 ....35 C6
Marshall Sq **18** SP10 ....82 F1
Marshalls GU51 ....121 F8
Marshalls Ct RG14 ....1 B5
Marshcourt RG24 ....69 F8
Marston Dr
Farnborough GU14 ....55 F7
Newbury RG14 ....2 B5
Marston Gate **6** SO23 ..209 E6
Marston Rd GU9 ....98 D2
Marsum Cl SP10 ....82 F4
Martin Cl RG21 ....69 C7
Martin Way Andover SP10 .83 B2
Frimley GU16 ....36 C2
Martingale Chase RG14 ....2 A4
Martingale Ct **8** GU11 ..76 D2
Martins Cl Alton GU34 ...140 A5
Blackwater GU17 ....35 B4
Martins La SO20 ....129 C2
Martins Pk GU14 ....55 B7
Martins Wood RG24 ....48 F3
Marwell Rd GU51 ....53 C4
Mary La
Newton Valence GU34 ....183 B8
North Waltham RG25 ......89 E2
Mary Rose Cl SP10 ....105 E7
Mary Rose Mews GU34 ..140 A5
Maryland Cl GU14 ....55 E1
Masdar Gdns RG40 ....16 C6
Maskell Way GU14 ....55 A3
Mason Cl GU46 ....34 C5
Mason Ct RG20 ....4 D1
Mason Rd GU14 ....55 C6
Mason Way GU11 ....99 F7
Mather Terr GU11 ....77 A2
Mathews Cl GU14 ....77 B8
Mathias Wlk RG21 ....91 D7
Matilda Dr RG22 ....91 B7
Matilda Pl **4** SO23 ......209 E5
Matthew Rd GU11 ....99 C8
Matthews Cl **11** RG19 ....2 F1

Matthews Rd GU15 ....36 A8
Matthews Way RG23 ......67 C1
Mattingley Dr **12** GU51 ..53 C3
Mattock Way GU14 ....48 F3
Maultway Cl GU15 ....36 F8
Maultway Cres GU15 ......36 F8
Maultway N GU15 ....36 F8
Maultway The GU15 ....36 F8
Mavins Rd GU9 ....122 B8
Maw Cl RG22 ....91 F8
May Cl Headley GU35 ....165 D4
Old Basing RG24 ....70 C6
Sandhurst GU47 ....35 B8
May Cres GU12 ....77 C1
May Pl RG21 ....69 B4
May St RG21 ....68 F5
May Tree Cl SO22 ....209 A2
May Tree Rd SP10 ....82 D1
May's La RG7 ....10 E7
Maybrook RG24 ....48 F4
Maybury Cl GU16 ....56 B8
Mayfair Cl GU51 ....53 D4
Mayfair Dr RG14 ....1 C1
Mayfair Ho **10** RG21 .....69 B5
Mayfield GU11 ....121 D3
Mayfield Ave Ind Pk
SP11 ....81 A2
Mayfield Cl Farnham GU9 ..99 C1
Shipton Bellinger SP9 ....101 D7
Mayfield Ct RG27 ....33 B8
Mayfield Rd
Camberley GU15 ....35 F1
Farnborough GU14 ....55 D6
Mayfield Ridge RG22 ......91 C5
Mayflower Cl RG24 ....48 E2
Mayflower Dr GU46 ....33 F7
Mayhill Jun Sch RG29 ...72 C2
Maynard's Wood RG24 ....48 E2
Mayors La RG14 ....1 D2
Maywood Dr GU51 ....36 E7
McCarthy Way RG40 ......16 D8
McCartney Wlk RG22 .....91 C7
McDonald's Almshouses 2
GU9 ....98 E1
McFauld Way RG28 ....86 D4
McKay Cl GU11 ....77 A3
McKernan Ct GU47 ....34 D8
McNaughton Cl GU14 ....55 B3
Mead Cl SP10 ....105 F7
Mead Gdns RG24 ....52 B7
Mead Hedges SP10 ....105 E6
Mead Hedges Footpath
SP10 ....105 F7
Mead La GU9 ....98 F2
Mead Park Sq SO20 ......126 B4
Mead Rd Andover SP10 ..105 F7
Hindhead GU26 ....167 D4
Winchester SO23 ....209 C2
Mead The
Farnborough GU14 ....55 F3
Liphook GU30 ....187 F5
Liss GU33 ....207 F4
Meade Rd **11** RG21 ....57 A2
Meadham La RG26 ....44 E4
Meadow Bank GU9 ....98 E1
Meadow Cl Ash Vale GU12 .56 C1
Blackwater GU17 ....35 A4
Liphook GU30 ....188 A5
Meadow Court
7 Fleet GU51 ....53 F1
Meadow Dr SP11 ....127 F8
Meadow End GU10 ....188 A5
Meadow Gate Ave GU51 ..55 D2
Meadow Hts **7** SP10 ...106 B8
Meadow La RG27 ....52 C6
Meadow Rd
Basingstoke RG21 ....69 A1
Farnborough GU14 ....55 F7
Newbury RG14 ....5 D8
Meadow Rise RG25 ....89 F1
Meadow Sch The GU35 ..165 A4
Meadow The RG27 ....29 D1
Meadow Vale GU27 ....189 E6
Meadow View
Bordon GU35 ....164 E3
Crookham Village GU52 ..74 E5
Micheldever SO21 ....133 B3
Ropley SO24 ....181 C5
Whitchurch RG28 ....86 B5
Meadow Way
Aldershot GU12 ....77 D3
Old Basing RG24 ....105 D8
Blackwater GU17 ....35 A5
Liphook GU30 ....188 A5
Rowledge GU10 ....121 D3
Winchester SO22 ....209 A2
Meadow Wlk Fleet GU51 ..74 D7
1 Liss GU33 ....207 F4
Meadowbank SO21 ....174 A5
Meadowland
Chineham RG24 ....48 E3
Kings Worthy SO23 ......176 B7
Meadowridge RG22 ....91 D2
Meadows Bsns Pk The
GU17 ....35 C5
Meadows Sh Ctr The
GU17 ....35 C5
Meadows The Ash GU12 ..77 F2
Churt GU10 ....144 D1
Meadowview SO21 ....174 A5
Meadowview Cl SP11 .....79 D6
Meads The GU27 ....189 D6
Meadsview Ct **4** GU14 ..55 D2
Meadway Frimley GU16 ..36 D2

Meadway continued
Haslemere GU27 ....189 D6
Measures Cl SO21 ....132 B3
Mede Cl RG25 ....88 B7
Medina Ct **27** SP10 ....83 C2
Medina Gdns RG21 ....67 B1
Medlar Dr GU17 ....35 D3
Medonte Cl GU52 ....75 B8
Medstead & Four Marks Sta
GU34 ....160 B3
Medstead CE Prim Sch
GU34 ....159 F6
Medstead Dr **8** GU51 ....53 D3
Medstead Rd GU34 ....139 A2
Medway Ave RG23 ....67 B2
Medway Cl RG18 ....2 F5
Medway Ct
2 Andover SP10 ....83 C2
18 Basingstoke RG21 ....69 D5
Medway Dr GU14 ....55 C7
Meerut Rd SP9 ....78 E6
Meitner Cl RG26 ....28 F4
Melchet Ct GU51 ....53 C4
Meldrum Cl RG14 ....5 A6
Melford Gdns RG22 ....68 A2
Meliot Rise SP10 ....83 A4
Melksham Ho **1** SP9 .....78 F6
Mellersh Cl **7** GU52 ......74 E4
Melrose Ave GU14 ....55 A4
Melrose Cl GU35 ....164 D2
Melrose Rd GU14 ....69 A8
Melville Ave GU16 ....36 D1
Melville Terr **1** GU9 ......98 F2
Membury Cl RG24 ....56 E7
Memorial Bglws RG25 ....87 B5
Memorial Rd RG27 ....72 A8
Mendip Cl RG22 ....68 A3
Mendip Rd GU14 ....55 C7
Menin Way GU14 ....99 B1
Meon Cl
Farnborough GU14 ....55 B6
Pamber Heath RG26 ....9 E1
Meon Ho SO23 ....209 F4
Meon Rd RG23 ....67 B1
Meon Wlk RG23 ....69 C5
Mercer Cl RG22 ....68 C4
Merchants Pl **16** SO23 ..209 E6
Mercia Ave SP10 ....82 D3
Mercury Cl GU35 ....164 D3
Mercury Ho RG7 ....9 C2
Merepond La GU34 ....204 F3
Meriden Ct **11** SO23 .....209 E8
Merivale GU51 ....74 D8
Merlin Court Flats
GU34 ....160 B2
Merlin Cl GU16 ....36 B1
Merlin Mead RG22 ....90 F6
Merlin Rd
Farnborough GU14 ....55 F2
Four Marks GU34 ....160 B2
Merlin Way GU34 ....55 B3
Merlins Ct GU9 ....99 A1
Merriatt Cl RG21 ....69 B2
Merrileas Gdns RG22 .....91 A8
Merron Cl GU46 ....34 A5
Merrydown La
Chineham RG24 ....49 A3
Old Basing RG24 ....49 A2
Merryfield RG24 ....48 E3
Merryfield Pk GU15 ....36 C6
Merryworth Cl GU12 ......77 D1
Mersey Cl **13** SP10 ....83 C2
Mersey Way RG18 ....2 F5
Merton Inf Sch RG24 ......69 A8
Merton Jun Sch RG24 .....69 A8
Merton Rd RG21 ....69 A6
Meryon Rd SO24 ....179 C4
Mesh Rd SO51 ....193 B2
Meteor Way GU14 ....55 E1
Methuen Rd GU33 ....186 C6
Meudon Ave GU14 ....55 F3
Mews La SO22 ....209 D5
Mews The Andover SP10 .106 B6
Bramley RG26 ....29 B2
Farley Hill RG7 ....15 A7
9 Farnham GU9 ....98 F2
New Alresford SO24 ......179 C6
Meyrick Dr RG14 ....5 A5
Michael Ho SP11 ....83 B8
Michaelmas Cl GU46 ......34 B4
Michaelmas Dro SP11 ....81 B1
Micheldever CE Prim Sch
SO21 ....133 A3
Micheldever Dr RG28 .....86 D3
Micheldever Dr **18** GU51 .53 C3
Micheldever Gdns RG28 .86 D3
Micheldever Rd
Andover SP11 ....106 D7
Whitchurch RG28 ....86 E3
Micheldever Sta SO21 ...111 B2
Micheldever Wood
Archaeological Trail*
SO24 ....155 E5
Mid Hants Railway
Watercress Line*
GU34 ....160 D4
Mid Hants Rly Watercress
Line* SO24 ....179 E5
Midas Ho **8** RG7 ....9 C2
Middle Ave GU14 ....122 B8
Middle Bourne La GU10 ..122 A2
Middle Brook St SO23 ...209 E6
Middle Church La **18**
GU9 ....98 F2
Middle Cl Frimley GU15 ..35 F6
Newbury RG14 ....5 F3
Middle Conholt SP11 .....37 F3

Middle Gordon Rd GU15 ...36 B5
Middle Hill GU11 ....76 E3
Middle Mdw GU33 ....208 A4
Middle Mead RG27 ....51 A1
Middle Old Pk GU9 ....98 D4
Middle Rd SO22 ....209 C6
Middle Wallop Airfield
SO20 ....126 A2
Middlefield GU9 ....121 E7
Middlefield Ct GU14 .....121 E8
Middlemoor Rd
Camberley GU16 ....56 C8
Frimley GU16 ....36 C1
Middleton Ct RG14 ....2 C5
Middleton Gdns
Basingstoke RG21 ....69 B7
Farnborough GU14 ....55 C6
Middleton Rd
Camberley GU15 ....36 D7
Middle Winterslow SP5 ..168 A6
Middleway The SP11 .....107 D6
Midhurst Rd
Haslemere GU27 ....189 F5
Liphook GU30 ....188 A2
Midlane CI RG21 ....69 A2
Mike Hawthorn Dr GU9 ..99 A3
Milan Cl RG2 ....15 C8
Milden Cl GU16 ....56 E6
Milden Gdns GU16 ....56 D6
Mildmay Ct Odiham RG29 ..78 F3
2 Winchester SO22 ......209 F5
Mildmay St SO22 ....209 B3
Mildmay Terr RG27 ....52 D6
Miles Ct 3 GU11 ....76 D1
Miles Rd GU12 ....77 F3
Milestones Living History
Mus* RG22 ....68 E5
Milford Ho SO23 ....209 D3
Milkingpen La SO21 ......60 E4
Mill Chase Com Sch
GU35 ....164 F3
Mill Chase Rd GU35 .....164 F4
Mill Cl Haslemere GU27 ..189 C6
Sherfield on L RG27 ......29 E1
Mill Cnr GU51 ....54 C4
Mill Copse Rd GU27 .....189 F4
Mill Ct GU34 ....179 D6
Mill Hill Ave SP9 ....78 E8
Mill La Alton GU34 ....140 B4
Bishop's Sutton SO24 ....180 A5
Ecchinswell RG20 ....23 E4
Frensham GU10 ....143 F7
Hawkley GU33 ....184 F1
Headley GU35 ....165 B5
Kings Worthy SO21 ......176 D6
Lindford GU35 ....165 A4
Longparish SP11 ....108 C5
Middle Winterslow SP5 ..168 B7
Newbury RG14 ....1 F3
North Warnborough RG29 ..72 B5
Rotherwick RG27 ....50 C6
Steep Marsh GU32 ......206 F1
Stratfield Saye RG7,RG27,
RG26 ....29 C4
Mill Lane Ind Est GU34 ...34 B7
Mill Rd Basingstoke RG24 ..68 C8
Liss GU33 ....208 A5
Mill Reef Cl RG19 ....2 D3
Mill Rise SO51 ....192 D1
Mill Stream GU9 ....99 C6
Mill View RG29 ....71 F2
Milland Rd SO23 ....209 F6
Millard Cl RG21 ....68 F7
Millbridge Rd GU46 ....33 F8
Millbrook Cl GU33 ......208 A4
Milldown Ho RG25 ....88 A7
Millennium Ct RG21 ......68 F5
Millennium Ctr GU9 ....98 E1
Millers La SO22 ....196 F3
Millers Rd RG26 ....26 F8
Millers Yd SO21 ....131 C4
Millgate Ct GU9 ....99 B3
Millgreen La RG19 ....7 D3
Millmere GU46 ....34 B7
Mills Ho GU12 ....77 B2
Millstream Cl SP10 .....105 F6
Millstream Ho RG14 ....2 B3
Millstream The GU27 ...189 C5
Millway Cl SP10 ....105 E7
Millway Rd SP10 ....105 E7
Milman Ct 12 SO23 .....209 E6
Milner Pl SO22 ....209 C4
Milnthorpe La SO22 .....209 C5
Milsons The SO20 ....149 F2
Milton Ave SP10 ....82 D1
Milton Cl RG24 ....69 A5
Milton Grange GU12 ......77 E5
Milverton Rd SO22 .....209 C6
Mimosa Cl GU35 ....165 A5
Mimosa Ct 3 SP10 .....105 D6
Minchens La RG26 ....28 B8
Minden Cl Andover SP10 ..82 F3
Chineham RG24 ....48 E2
Minden Way SO22 ....209 A3
Minehurst Rd GU16 ....36 D4
Minerva Ho 5 RG47 ....9 C2
Ministry Rd RG19 ....6 E5
Minley Cl GU14 ....54 B4
Minley Gr GU51 ....54 B3
Minley Rd
Farnborough GU14 ....55 B8
Fleet GU51 ....54 B4
Hawley GU17 ....34 C1
Yateley GU14 ....54 E7
Minores Rd SP9 ....79 A6
Minshull Ct 6 SP10 .....105 F8

Minstead Cl Tadley RG26 ..26 F6
Winchester SO22 ....175 D4
Minstead Dr GU46 ....34 A5
Minster Cl GU14 ....56 B1
Minster Ct
Camberley GU15 ....36 B7
Camberley,York Town GU15 ..35 D4
Minster La 3 SO23 .....209 E5
Mint Rd GU33 ....208 B6
Minter Ct 7 RG26 ....9 D1
Minters Ct 28 SO23 ....209 D6
Mistletoe Rd GU46 ....34 B4
Mitcham Rd GU15 ....36 E8
Mitchell Ave RG27 ....52 C5
Mitchell Bldgs GU46 ......33 F5
Mitchell Cl SP10 ....82 C1
Mitchell Gdns RG22 ......91 C3
Mitford Rd SO24 ....179 C4
Moat Rd RG26 ....28 F4
Moffatts Cl GU47 ....34 E8
Mole Cl GU14 ....55 B6
Momford Rd SO22 ......197 B3
Monachus La RG27 ....52 D7
Monarch Cl RG22 ....91 A6
Monarch Way SO22 .....209 A4
Moneyer Rd SP10 ....82 F3
Mongers Piece RG24 ......49 A4
Monier Williams Rd
SP11 ....108 B3
Moniton Trad Est RG22 ...68 B4
Monk Sherborne Ho
RG26 ....47 B5
Monk Sherborne Rd
RG26 ....46 E8
Monk's La RG14 ....5 C7
Monks Cl SO23 ....209 E7
Monks Rise SO51 ....53 D1
Monks Wood Cres RG26 ..26 F7
Monks' Well GU10 ....99 F1
Monkswood Cl RG14 ......5 C7
Monkton La GU9 ....99 C5
Monkton Pk GU9 ....99 D4
Monktons La RG27 ....12 A5
Monmouth Sq 4 SO23 ...197 B5
Mons Cl GU11 ....77 C7
Mons The 17 SO23 .....209 D6
Montacute Cl GU14 ......56 B4
Montague Cl GU15 ....35 F5
Montague Pl 88 RG21 .....69 B3
Montague Terr RG14 ......5 E8
Monteagle La
Yateley GU46 ....33 E6
Yateley GU46 ....33 F5
Montgomery Cl
Sandhurst GU47 ....34 F8
Winchester SO22 ....209 C4
Montgomery Rd
Enham Alamein SP11 ......83 B6
Farnborough GU14 ....55 D3
Newbury RG14 ....5 C4
Montreal Wlk GU30 .....188 A3
Montrose Cl
Bordon GU35 ....164 E1
Fleet GU51 ....75 B8
Frimley GU16 ....36 C2
Montserrat Pl RG24 ......48 C2
Montserrat Rd RG24 .....48 C2
Monument Chase GU35 .164 E1
Monument Ct RG14 ....5 E8
Monxton Rd
Andover SP11 ....105 C8
Gratley SP11 ....103 D2
Monxton SP11 ....105 A7
Moody's Hill SP5 ....190 C2
Moons Hill GU10 ....122 A2
Moor Cl Bordon GU35 ...164 B3
Finchampstead RG40 .....16 C7
Moor Court La SO21 ....174 B3
Moor La RG14 ....1 C3
Moor Park La GU9 ....99 D3
Moor Park Way GU9 ......99 E3
Moor Place Farm RG27 ...32 A6
Moor Rd Camberley GU16 ..56 D8
Farnborough GU14 ....55 D8
Greatham GU33 ....186 C1
Haslemere GU27 ....189 A5
Moor View RG24 ....70 B7
Moorcroft Cl SO21 ......131 D3
Moore Cl Andover SP10 ...83 A1
Fleet GU52 ....75 A5
Tongham GU10 ....100 D3
Moore Rd GU52 ....75 A5
Moorfield SO22 ....189 D5
Moorfoot Gdns RG22 .....68 B3
Moorhams Ave RG22 .....91 A6
Moorings The
Basingstoke RG21 ....69 D5
Hindhead GU26 ....167 C3
Moorlands Cl Fleet GU51 ..75 B8
Hindhead GU26 ....167 C4
Moorlands Pl GU15 ....35 E4
Moorlands Rd GU15 ......35 F4
Moors Cl RG40 ....16 C8
Moors The GU10 ....100 D7
Moorside Cl GU14 ....35 E1
Moorside Rd SO23 ......176 C2
Moot Cl SP10 ....83 B4
Moray Ave GU47 ....35 B7
More House Sch GU10 ..122 A2

Moreland Cl GU34 ....140 A2
Morestead Rd
Winchester SO21 ....198 E3
Winchester SO23 ....209 F2
Moreton Cl Churt GU10 .144 C1
Fleet GU52 ....74 F4
Morgan Cl 3 GU14 ....55 A4
Morgaston Rd RG26 ......48 A7
Morland Rd GU11 ....100 A6
Morland's Rd GU11 ....77 B5
Morley Cl GU46 ....33 F5
Morley Rd
Basingstoke RG21 ....69 A1
Farnham GU9 ....99 B1
Mornington Ave RG40 ....16 D8
Mornington Cl
Andover SP10 ....106 A5
Pamber Heath RG26 ....9 C1
Mornington Dr SO22 ....209 A8
Mornington Rd GU35 ....164 A2
Morris Ho 5 GU46 ....77 B8
Morris Rd GU14 ....77 B8
Morris Rise RG24 ....48 E2
Morris St RG27 ....71 E8
Morse Rd RG22 ....68 E4
Mortimer Cl
Hartley Wintney RG27 ....52 B4
Kings Worthy SO23 .....176 C6
Mortimer Gdns RG26 .....27 A7
Mortimer Hall RG7 ....12 A5
Mortimer La
2 Basingstoke RG21 .....69 A5
Stratfield Mortimer RG7 ..12 B7
Stratfield Saye RG7 ....29 B7
Mortimer St John's CE Sch
RG7 ....11 E5
Mortimer Sta RG7 ....12 C5
Morton Cl GU14 ....56 D7
Morval Cl GU14 ....55 C4
Morval Rd GU17 ....34 B7
Moscrop Ct 8 RG21 ......69 A4
Moselle Cl GU14 ....55 B5
Mosquito Way GU14 ......55 D1
Moss Cl GU33 ....208 A4
Moss Rd SO23 ....209 F6
Mothes Ho RG26 ....9 C1
Mottisfont Abbey (NT)*
SO51 ....192 F3
Mottisfont Abbey Gdns*
SO51 ....192 F3
Moulsham Copse La
GU46 ....33 F7
Moulsham La GU46 ....33 F7
Mount Carmel Rd SP11 .124 E5
Mount Cl Highclere RG20 ..21 D6
Newbury RG14 ....2 A1
Winchester SO22 ....175 E3
Mount Hermon Rd SP11 .124 E6
Mount Hts SP5 ....146 C3
Mount Pleasant
Amport SP11 ....104 B6
Farnham GU9 ....98 E1
Hartley Wintney RG27 ....52 D6
Kings Worthy SO23 ......176 C6
Laverstoke RG28 ....87 B6
Tadley RG26 ....26 E8
Mount Pleasant Dr RG26 ..26 E8
Mount Pleasant Rd
Aldershot GU12 ....77 A7
Alton GU34 ....139 A1
Lindford GU35 ....164 F5
Mount Rd RG20 ....21 D7
Mount The Fleet GU51 ....54 A2
Headley GU35 ....165 E6
Highclere RG20 ....21 D7
Mount View GU11 ....76 E1
Mount View Rd SO22 ...197 B4
Mountbatten Cl RG14 .....2 A5
Mountbatten Ct
13 Aldershot GU11 ....76 E2
Andover SP10 ....83 D1
Winchester SO22 ....175 E3
Mountbatten Pl SO23 ...176 C8
Mounter's La GU34 .....139 D1
Mounters La GU34 .....139 D1
Mounts Way GU51 ....53 C3
Mountsom's La GU34 ...161 F3
Mourne Cl RG22 ....68 A4
Mowatt Rd GU26 ....167 B2
Mozart Cl RG22 ....91 E8
Mud La RG27 ....15 D1
Mulberries The GU9 ......99 D4
Mulberry Cl
Ash Vale GU12 ....77 E4
1 Sandhurst GU47 ....35 B8
Mulberry Ct
Four Marks GU34 ....160 C3
Newbury RG14 ....1 D3
Mulberry Ho 2 SP10 ....106 B8
Mulberry Mead RG28 .....86 C5
Mulberry Way GU34 ......48 F3

Murrell Green Bsns Pk
RG27 ....51 E2
Murrell Rd GU12 ....77 E3
Murrells La GU15 ....35 F3
Mus of Army Flying
Explorers' World*
SO20 ....126 A2
Muscott Cl SP9 ....101 D7
Museum of the Iron Age*
SP10 ....106 A7
Musgrave Cl RG22 ....91 D7
Musgrove Gdns GU34 ...139 E4
Musket Copse RG24 ......70 A6
Muss La SO20 ....172 A3
Mylen Bsns Ctr SP10 ...105 E8
Mylen Rd SP10 ....82 E1
Myllers Lond RG27 ....51 D1
Myrtle Dr GU17 ....35 B5
Mytchett Farm Cvn Pk
GU16 ....56 D2
Mytchett Heath GU16 ....56 E1
Mytchett Lake Rd GU16 ..56 E1
Mytchett Place Rd GU16 .56 D4
Mytchett Prim Sch GU16 .56 D4
Mytchett Rd GU16 ....56 D3

N

Naafi Rdbt GU11 ....76 F2
Nadder Rd SP9 ....78 F6
Nairn Cl GU14 ....36 C2
Napier Cl GU11 ....77 C7
Napier Dr GU15 ....36 E7
Napier La GU12 ....77 C8
Napier Wlk SP10 ....83 D1
Napoleon Ave GU14 ......55 A1
Napoleon Dr RG23 ....68 C7
Naseby Rise RG14 ....2 B5
Nash Cl Basingstoke RG22 ..91 C7
Farnborough GU14 ....55 D4
Nash Grove La RG40 .....16 D8
Nash Mdws RG29 ....95 A4
Nately Rd RG29 ....71 E2
Nations Hill SO23 ....176 B6
Naylors The RG7 ....14 B6
Neath Rd RG21 ....69 D5
Neelem Ct 3 GU14 ....56 A1
Nelson Cl Aldershot GU12 ..77 B1
Farnham GU9 ....99 B8
Stockbridge SO20 ....74 F4
Nelson Ho 2 GU11 ....76 E2
Nelson St GU11 ....76 E2
Nelson Way GU15 ....35 D4
Nelson Wlk SP10 ....83 D1
Nene Ct 50 SP10 ....82 F1
Nepaul Rd SP9 ....78 E7
Neptune Rd SO23 ....164 E2
Nestor Cl SP10 ....82 F1
Nether St 7 GU34 ......139 F4
Nether Vell-Mead GU52 ..74 E3
Nethercliffe Sch SO22 ..209 C7
Netherfield Cl GU34 ....139 E4
Netherhouse Ct GU51 ...74 D6
Netherhouse Moor GU51 ..74 D6
Netley St GU11 ....77 A8
Nettlebeds La SO24 .....158 B2
Neuvic Way RG28 ....86 D4
Nevada Cl GU14 ....55 B3
Neville Cl Andover SP10 .106 B6
Basingstoke RG21 ....69 B2
Neville Duke Rd GU14 ....55 D8
New Barn Cl GU51 ....74 D7
New Barn Cotts SO21 ...152 E3
New Barn La Alton GU34 .139 C2
Wherwell SP11 ....124 E3
New Bldgs SP11 ....58 D7
New Bridge Rd 10 RG29 ..69 D5
New Cotts
King's Somborne SO20 ..172 A3
Liphook GU30 ....187 C8
South Warnborough RG29 ..95 A4
Sutton Scotney SO21 ...131 C4
New Ct SO21 ....131 C3
New Dawn Cl GU14 ....55 C1
New Farm Cotts RG29 ....95 C1
New Farm Rd
East Stratton SO21 .....134 A4
New Alresford SO24 ....179 B4
New Greenham Pk RG19 ...6 E5
New Horizon Ho RG19 ....6 E4
New Hos RG20 ....23 E6
New House La SP11 ....81 B8
New La SO20 ....172 B3
New Mill La RG27 ....15 C2
New Mill Rd RG40 ....15 C3
New North Dr RG27 ......17 A8
New Odiham Rd GU34 ..139 D6
New Paddock Cl GU34 ...140 C6
New Poplars The GU12 ...77 E1
New Rd Basingstoke RG21 ..69 B7
Blackwater GU17 ....35 C4
Bordon GU35 ....164 D1
Eversley Cross RG27 ......33 C7
Fleet GU51 ....55 B6
Greenham RG19 ....6 D6
Hartley Wintney RG27 ....52 D6
Haslemere GU27 ....189 D5
Hook RG27 ....72 A8
Littleton SO22 ....175 B6
Micheldever SO21 ....111 B2
Newbury RG14 ....2 A1
North Warnborough RG29 ..72 C4
Over Wallop SO20 ....147 D3
Pamber End RG26 ....27 D3
Sandhurst GU47 ....34 E8

New Rd continued
Stratfield Mortimer RG7 ...12 B8
Tadley RG26 ....26 E7
Tongham GU10 ....100 D6
New Rd Cotts GU34 .....184 E8
New St Andover SP10 ...106 B8
Stockbridge SO20 ....149 F3
Stratfield Saye RG7 ....29 C8
New Villas RG20 ....3 F3
Newall Rd SP11 ....105 A7
Newark Rd GU17 ....34 C2
Newbold Rd RG14 ....1 B5
Newburgh St SO23 ......209 D6
Newbury Coll RG14 ....5 E7
Newbury Ho RG14 ....5 B6
Newbury Racecourse Sta
RG14 ....2 A2
Newbury Rd
Andover SP10,SP11 ....83 B5
Kingsclere RG20 ....24 B4
Whitchurch RG28 ....86 D7
Newbury Ret Pk RG14 ....5 F7
Newbury St
Andover SP10 ....106 B8
Whitchurch RG28 ....86 C5
Newbury Sta RG14 ....1 E2
Newchurch Rd RG26 ......9 E1
Newcomb Cl SP11 ......106 A5
Newcome Pl GU12 ......100 B7
Newcome Rd GU9 ....99 C6
Newfield Ave GU14 ....55 C6
Newfield Rd
Ash Vale GU12 ....77 E6
Liss GU33 ....208 A6
Newhouse Rd GU34 .....156 B6
Newlands GU52 ....75 A6
Newlands La GU46 ....34 B5
Newlands Dr GU12 ....77 D4
Newlands Prim Sch
GU46 ....34 A5
Newlands Rd GU15 ....35 F1
Newman La GU34 ....140 B5
Old Basing RG24,RG27 ....49 E1
Newnham Pk RG27 ....71 B8
Newnham Rd RG27 ....71 E8
Newport Cl RG14 ....1 F4
Newport Jun Sch GU12 ..77 B3
Newport Rd
Aldershot GU12 ....77 B1
Newton Cr RG24 ....69 D7
Newton La GU34 ....183 E8
Newton Pk SP10 ....82 B1
Newton Rd SP11 ....105 F7
Newton Toney CE Sch
SP4 ....123 B5
Newton Villas SP11 ....57 B1
Newton Way GU10 ......100 D7
Newtown RG26 ....9 E1
Newtown Cl SP10 ....105 E7
Newtown Rd
Liphook GU30 ....188 A3
Newbury RG14 ....5 E8
Newbury RG14,RG19,RG20 ..5 E6
Sandhurst GU47 ....34 E8
Nexus Pk GU12 ....77 D8
Nicholson Pl SO24 ......179 B5
Nickel Cl SO23 ....209 A8
Nicola Cr GU12 ....77 B2
Nicotiana Ct 6 GU52 .....74 E4
Night Owls RG6 ....6 A7
Nightingale Cl
Farnborough GU14 ....55 A6
8 Winchester SO22 .....209 A4
Nightingale Dr GU16 .....56 E3
Nightingale Gdns
Hook RG27 ....51 A2
Sandhurst GU47 ....34 F8
Sherborne St John RG24 ..68 C8
Nightingale La
Mortimer RG7 ....11 F7
Stratfield Mortimer RG7 ..12 A6
Nightingale Rd GU15 ...164 E2
Nightingale Rise RG25 ...88 B7
Nightingales The RG14 ....5 E8
Nightjar Cl GU10 ....98 B8
Nine Acres GU32 ....207 B1
Nine Mile Ride RG40 .....16 C6
Nine Mile Ride Ind RG40 .16 B5
Nine Mile Ride Prim Sch
RG40 ....16 D6
Ninfield Cl RG19 ....6 A7
Nobs Crook RG21 ....51 C1
Norden Cl RG21 ....69 B6
Norman Cl GU35 ....165 A5
Norman Court La
Goodworth Clatford SP11 .106 A3
Upper Clatford SP11 ....105 E2
Norman Court Sch SP5 ..168 F2
Norman Ct GU9 ....99 A1
Norman Gate Sch SP11 ..83 C1
Norman Rd SO23 ....209 D4
Normandy Dr GU34 .....140 A4
Normans SO23 ....209 B4
Normanton Rd RG21 .....69 B7
Normay Rise RG14 ....5 A5
Norn Hill RG21 ....69 C6
Norn Hill Cl RG21 ....69 C6
Norris Cl GU34 ....139 E4
Norris Gdns SO21 ......153 C4
Norris Hill Rd RG21 ......75 D7
Norris Ho RG25 ....88 B8

North Acre SP11 . . . . .108 C6
North Ave GU9 . . . . .99 B7
North Camp Sta GU12 . . . .77 D8
North Cl Aldershot GU12 . .77 C1
  Farnborough GU14 . . . . .55 E8
North Ct RG40 . . . . .16 D4
North Dr SO22 . . . . .175 B5
North End SO20 . . . . .170 B7
North End Farm Cotts
  SO24 . . . . .201 C7
North End La SO24 . . . . . . .201 D7
North Farm Cl GU14 . . . . . . .55 D8
North Farm Rd GU14 . . . . . .55 D8
North Farnborough Inf Sch
  GU14 . . . . .56 B5
North Field RG25 . . . . .65 A1
North Fryerne GU46 . . . . . . .34 B8
North Hampshire Hospl The
  RG24 . . . . .68 E8
North Hill Cl SO22 . . . . . . .209 D8
North Hill Ct SO22 . . . . . . .209 D7
North La Aldershot GU12 . . .77 B2
  West Tytherley SPS 169 A2
North Lodge Ind Pk
  GU30 . . . . .188 B1
North Par GU35 . . . . .164 D6
North Rd Ash Vale GU12 . . .77 D4
  Farnborough GU14 . . . . .77 B7
  Kings Worthy SO23 . . . . .154 B1
North Row RG26 . . . . .28 F4
North Side GU10 . . . . .100 D7
North St
  Bishop's Sutton SO24 . . . . . .180 C5
  Kingsclere RG20 . . . . .24 D2
North View SO22 . . . . .209 C6
North View Gdns 2 RG14 . .1 F4
North View Rd RG26 . . . . . . .27 B7
North Walls SO23 . . . . .209 E6
North Waltham Prim Sch
  RG25 .89 C1
North Warnborough St
  RG29 .72 B3
North Way GU10 . . . . .83 D2
Northanger Cl GU34 . . . . . .139 E4
Northbrook SO21 . . . . .132 F4
Northbrook Ave SO23 . . . . .198 C7
Northbrook Cl SO23 . . . . . .198 C7
Northbrook Pl RG14 . . . . .1 E3
Northbrook Rd GU11 . . . . . . .99 F8
Northbrook St RG14 . . . . .1 E3
Northbrooke SO23 . . . . . . .198 C7
Northcote Rd
  Ash Vale GU12 . . . . .77 E7
Farnborough GU14 . . . . .55 D6
Northcott Gdns GU14 . . . . . .55 B5
Northcroft Ct RG29 . . . . . . .95 A3
Northcroft La RG14 . . . . .1 D3
Northcroft Terr RG14 . . . . . . .1 D3
Northern Ave
  Andover SP10 . . . . .83 A1
  Donnington RG14 . . . . .1 E6
Northfield Cl
  Aldershot GU12 . . . . .77 B1
  Fleet GU52 . . . . .75 B6
Northfield Ho RG21 . . . . .69 C7
Northfield La GU34 . . . . . . .161 C8
Northfield Rd Fleet GU52 . .75 C6
  Sherfield on L RG27 . . . . .29 D1
  Thatcham RG18 . . . . .2 F4
Northgate Chambers 10
  SO23 . . . . .209 E6
Northgate Dr GU15 . . . . .36 E7
Northgate La RG25 . . . . .92 B1
Northgate Lodge 2
  SO23 . . . . .209 E6
Northgate Way RG22 . . . . . .91 A6
Northington Cnr SO21 . . . .134 B3
Northington Rd
  Itchen Abbas SO21 . . . . .177 F8
  Northington SO24 . . . . .156 C3
Northlands Dr SO23 . . . . . .209 E8
Northmead GU14 . . . . .55 F4
Northside La SO24 . . . . . . .180 E6
Northtown Trad Est
  GU12 .77 C1
Northumberland Rd
  GU35 . . . . .164 D1
Northway RG14 . . . . .1 F2
Northwick RG27 . . . . .33 C7
Northwood Dr RG14 . . . . .2 A4
Norton Cl RG14 . . . . .5 A6
Norton Cotts SO21 . . . . . . .131 D7
Norton Rd RG7 . . . . .14 A3
Norton Ride RG24 . . . . .69 F7
Norwich Ave GU15 . . . . .36 C3
Norwich Cl RG22 . . . . .91 B7
Novello Cl RG22 . . . . .91 D7
Nuffield Rd RG2 . . . . .15 E8
Nuns Rd SO23 . . . . .209 D7
Nuns Wlk SO23 . . . . .209 F8
Nursery Cl
  Camberley GU16 . . . . .56 D7
  Chineham RG24 . . . . .49 A3
  Fleet GU51 . . . . .75 D8
  Hook RG27 . . . . .51 A2
Nursery Field GU33 . . . . . .207 E3
Nursery Gdns SO22 . . . . . .209 B6
Nursery Rd Alton GU34 . . .140 A4
  New Alresford SO24 . . . . . . .179 D5
Nursery Terr RG29 . . . . .72 C4
Nutbane Cl SP10 . . . . .105 E7
Nutbane La SP11 . . . . .81 F8
Nutbean La RG7 . . . . .14 D5
Nutbourne GU9 . . . . .99 C7
Nutchers Dro SO20 . . . . . . .172 A3

Nutcombe Ht GU26 . . . . . . .167 D4
Nutcombe La GU26 . . . . . . .167 C1
Nutfield Ct GU15 . . . . .36 B7
Nuthatch Cl
  Basingstoke RG22 . . . . .90 F6
  Ewshot GU10 . . . . .98 B7
Nutley Cl Bordon GU35 . . .164 D1
  Yateley GU46 . . . . .34 B5
Nutley La RG25 . . . . .53 D3
Nutley Rd RG25 . . . . .90 F1
Nutmeg Cl GU14 . . . . .55 A5
Nutshell La GU9 . . . . .99 A6
Nutter's La RG2 . . . . .14 E8

O

O'bee Gdns RG26 . . . . .9 C1
O'connor Rd GU11 . . . . .77 C7
O'Gorman Ave GU14 . . . . . .55 F2
Oak Bank SP10 . . . . .106 A6
Oak Cl Basingstoke RG21 . . .69 D5
  Baughurst RG26 . . . . .26 B8
  Kingsclere RG20 . . . . .24 E2
  North Tidworth SP9 . . . . .79 F7
  Oakley RG23 . . . . .67 B1
  Overton RG25 . . . . .88 A7
Oak Cott 9 GU26 . . . . .167 B3
Oak Cotts GU27 . . . . .189 C6
Oak Ct Farnborough GU14 . .56 D7
  Farnham GU9 . . . . .98 F1
Oak Dr RG14 . . . . .1 D1
Oak Farm Cl GU17 . . . . .35 A5
Oak Farm Com Sch
  GU14 .55 D6
Oak Grove Cres GU15 . . . . . .35 D6
Oak Hanger Cl RG27 . . . . . . .51 B1
Oak Hill SO24 . . . . .179 D5
Oak Ho
  Farnborough GU14 . . . . .55 F7
  7 Grayshott GU26 . . . . .167 B3
Oak Lodge 2 GU35 . . . . . . .164 D2
Oak Rd GU14 . . . . .56 A3
Oak Ridge Cl RG14 . . . . .5 C8
Oak Tree Cl
  Aldershot RG12 . . . . .100 C8
  Ash Vale GU12 . . . . .56 D1
  Chilbolton SO20 . . . . .129 A3
  Headley GU35 . . . . .165 D4
Oak Tree Cotts RG25 . . . . . .70 F5
Oak Tree Dr Hook RG27 . . .51 B2
  Liss GU33 . . . . .208 A3
Oak Tree La GU34 . . . . .189 B6
Oak Tree Rd GU35 . . . . .164 C1
Oak Tree View GU9 . . . . .99 C6
Oakdene GU34 . . . . .139 E5
Oaken Copse La GU14 . . . . . .56 B4
Oaken Copse Cres GU14 . . .55 F7
Oaken Gr RG14 . . . . .5 B8
Oakfield Pl GU14 . . . . .55 A4
Oakfield Rd
  Blackwater GU17 . . . . .35 D3
  Pamber Heath RG26 . . . . .10 C1
Oakfields
  Basingstoke RG24 . . . . .69 F8
  8 Camberley GU15 . . . . .35 F5
Oakfields Cl RG20 . . . . .223 D4
Oakgreen Par GU34 . . . . . .160 D3
Oakhanger Ho GU51 . . . . . .53 C3
Oakhanger Rd GU35 . . . . . .164 B5
Oakhill Rd GU35 . . . . .165 F5
Oakhurst GU26 . . . . .167 B3
Oakland Ave GU9 . . . . .99 C7
Oakland Rd RG28 . . . . .86 C5
Oakland Terr RG27 . . . . .52 D6
Oaklands
  Hartley Wintney RG27 . . . . . . .52 C5
  Hook RG27 . . . . .71 E7
  South Wonston SO21 . . . . . .153 D4
  Yateley GU46 . . . . .34 B6
Oaklands Cl 6 SO22 . . . . .209 A4
Oaklands Way RG23 . . . . . . .68 C7
Oaklea GU12 . . . . .77 E5
Oaklea Dr RG27 . . . . .15 C2
Oaklea Gdns RG26 . . . . .29 B2
Oaklea Ho 4 GU26 . . . . . . .167 A5
Oakley CE Jun Sch RG23 . .67 A1
Oakley Inf Sch RG23 . . . . . .67 A1
Oakley La
  Mottisfont SO51 . . . . .192 F4
  Oakley RG23 . . . . .67 B2
Oakley Pl RG27 . . . . .52 D6
Oakley Rd Bordon GU35 . . .164 D5
  Camberley GU15 . . . . .35 F4
  Hannington RG26 . . . . .44 F7
  Mottisfont SO51 . . . . .192 E3
  Newbury RG14 . . . . .2 B4
Oakmead RG24 . . . . .28 E3
Oakridge Inf Sch RG21 . .69 A7
Oakridge Jun Sch RG21 . .69 A7
Oakridge Rd RG21 . . . . .69 B8
Oakridge Twrs 1 RG21 . . . .69 C7
Oaks Cvn Pk The GU33 . . .185 F2
Oaks The Andover SP10 . . . .105 E8
  Blackwater GU17 . . . . .35 C3
  Farnborough GU14 . . . . .55 B3
  Fleet GU51 . . . . .53 D1
  Medstead GU34 . . . . .160 A2
  Newbury RG14 . . . . .1 E7
  Tadley RG26 . . . . .26 E8
  Yateley GU46 . . . . .34 B6
Oaktree Ave RG19 . . . . .7 F5
Oaktrees Ash GU12 . . . . .77 D1
  Farnham GU9 . . . . .98 F6
Oakway Aldershot GU12 . . .100 C8
  Bentley GU10 . . . . .120 A5

Oakway Dr GU16 . . . . .36 C1
Oakwood Chineham RG24 . . .48 F3
  Fleet GU51 . . . . .75 A4
Oakwood Dr GU34 . . . . .139 E2
Oakwood Inf Sch RG27 . .52 D5
Oast House Cres GU9 . . . . . .99 B6
Oast House La GU9 . . . . .99 B6
Oast La GU11 . . . . .99 F7
Oasthouse Dr GU51 . . . . .54 C4
Oasts The RG29 . . . . .95 D4
Oates Mus, Gilbert White's
  Ho* GU34 . . . . .184 E8
Oban Ct RG23 . . . . .67 A2
Obelisk Way GU15 . . . . .36 A6
Oberursel Way GU11 . . . . . . .76 D2
Oceana Cres RG23 . . . . .90 F4
Ochil Cl RG22 . . . . .68 C2
Ockham Hall GU35 . . . . .142 B1
Octavia Hill SO22 . . . . .209 B4
Octavian Cl RG22 . . . . .91 B7
Oddfellows Rd RG14 . . . . .1 D2
Odette Gdns RG26 . . . . .10 A1
Odiham Cottage Hospl
  RG29 .72 B3
Odiham Rd Ewshot GU10 . . .98 B7
  Farnham GU10 . . . . .98 D7
  Heckfield RG7 . . . . .14 A2
  Odiham RG29 . . . . .72 F6
  Winchfield RG27,RG29 . . . . . .73 A8
Officers Row RG26 . . . . .29 B1
Oglander Rd SO23 . . . . .209 E8
Olaf Cl SP10 . . . . .83 B4
Old Acre Rd GU34 . . . . .139 F2
Old Ayrlesfield Bldgs
  GU34 . . . . .117 C3
Old Barn Cl RG25 . . . . .89 E1
Old Barn La GU10 . . . . .144 F1
Old Basing Inf Sch RG24 . .70 B6
Old Basing Mall 14 RG21 . .69 B5
Old Bath Rd RG14 . . . . .1 D4
Old Beggarwood La
  RG22 .91 A5
Old Bisley Rd GU16 . . . . .36 F3
Old Brick Kiln Trad Est The
  RG26 .46 E7
Old Brickfield Rd GU11 . . . .99 F7
Old Canal Pl RG21 . . . . .69 C5
Old Chapel La GU12 . . . . . . .77 E1
Old Church La GU9 . . . . . . .122 B7
Old Coach Rd
  Kimpton SP11 . . . . .79 E1
  Shipton Bellinger SP9 . . . . . .102 B8
Old College Rd RG14 . . . . . . .1 D4
Old Common Rd RG21 . . . . .69 D4
Old Common Way SP11 . . . .57 A2
Old Compton La GU9 . . . . . .99 D2
Old Contemptibles Ave
  GU11 .76 D2
Old Convent The GU10 . . . .143 B3
Old Cove Rd GU51 . . . . .54 B3
Old Ct RG29 . . . . .72 E2
Old Dairy Cl 1 GU51 . . . . . .54 A1
Old Dairy The SO21 . . . . . . .177 A5
Old Dean Rd GU15 . . . . .36 B7
Old Down Cl RG22 . . . . .68 A3
Old Down Rd SP10 . . . . .82 F1
Old English Dr SP10 . . . . . . .82 F4
Old Farm Pl
  Ash Vale GU12 . . . . .77 D5
  Ash Vale GU12 . . . . .77 D5
Old Farmhouse Cl SP9 . . . .101 E7
Old Farnham La
  Bentley GU10 . . . . .97 E1
  Farnham GU9 . . . . .122 A8
Old Forge End GU47 . . . . . . .34 F7
Old Forge Gdn SO20 . . . . . .170 B7
Old Forge Rd GU52 . . . . .74 E3
Old Frensham Rd GU10 . .122 C4
Old Fromans Farm
  SO20 . . . . .172 A3
Old Green La GU15 . . . . .36 A7
Old Guildford Rd GU16 . . . .56 F5
Old Heath Way GU9 . . . . . . .99 A7
Old Hill The SP11 . . . . .128 F5
Old Hillside Rd SO22 . . . . .209 A8
Old Iron Foundry The
  SO20 . . . . .171 F3
Old Ively Rd GU14,GU51 . . .75 F8
Old Kempshott La RG22 . . .68 A3
Old Kennels Cl SO22 . . . . . .197 A3
Old Kennels La SO22 . . . . . .197 B3
Old Kiln GU9 . . . . .98 E2
Old Kiln Cl GU10 . . . . .144 D2
Old Kiln Ctyd 12 RG27 . . . .51 A2
Old Kiln Rd GU10 . . . . .144 D2
Old La Aldershot GU11 . . . . . .99 E7
  Ashford Hill RG19 . . . . .8 D1
  Dockenfield GU10 . . . . .143 D4
  Hamstead Marshall RG20 . . . . .3 C8
Old Litten La GU32 . . . . . . .206 D3
Old London Rd SO20 . . . . . .150 A3
Old Micheldever Rd
  SO20 . . . . .107 B5
Old Mill Rd RG27 . . . . .189 D7
Old Monteagle La GU46 . . .33 F6
Old Newtown Rd RG14 . . . . .1 D1
Old Odiham Rd GU34 . . . . . .117 A5
Old Orch The RG29 . . . . .94 F4
Old Orchard The GU9 . . . . .122 A2
Old Park Cl GU9 . . . . .98 F1
Old Park Ct GU10 . . . . .175 C3
Old Park La Farnham GU9 . .98 E5
  Farnham,Hog Hatch GU10 . . .98 D5
  Middle Wallop SO20 . . . . . . .126 B4
Old Park Rd SO24 . . . . .180 E2
Old Pasture Rd GU16 . . . . . .36 F2

Old Pond Cl GU16 . . . . .36 A1
Old Portsmouth Rd GU15 . .36 E5
Old Potbridge Rd RG27 . . . .52 B2
Old Pumphouse Cl GU51 . . .54 B2
Old Quarry The GU27 . . . . .189 D4
Old Reading Rd RG21 . . . . . .69 C6
Old Rectory Dr GU12 . . . . . .77 F2
Old Rectory Gdns
  Farnham GU10 . . . . .56 B4
  Kings Worthy SO23 . . . . .176 D6
Old Rectory The SO20 . . . .150 C8
Old Riseley Stores The
  RG7 . . . . .14 A3
Old Salisbury Rd SP11 . . . .105 B3
Old School Cl Ash GU12 . . . .77 E3
  Fleet GU51 . . . . .54 A1
  Hartley Wintney RG27 . . . . . . .52 C6
Old School Ho SO24 . . . . . .135 C4
Old School La GU46 . . . . . . .34 A6
Old School Rd Liss GU33 . .207 F4
  Newnham RG27 . . . . .71 E8
Old School Terr 8 GU51 . . . .54 A1
Old Station App SO23 . . . . .209 F5
Old Station Rd SO21 . . . . . .177 E6
Old Station Way GU35 . . . .164 A5
Old Stockbridge Rd
  SO20 . . . . .125 C6
Old Stoke Rd SO21 . . . . . . .154 A6
Old Thornford Rd RG19 . . . . .7 C6
Old Town Mews GU9 . . . . . .98 E2
Old Vicarage La SO20 . . . . .172 A3
Old Vicarage The GU10 . . .121 D7
Old Vyne La RG26 . . . . .27 C5
Old Welmore SO23 . . . . .34 C5
Old Winton Rd SP10 . . . . . .106 B6
Old Worting Rd RG22 . . . . . .68 C4
Oldberg Gdns RG22 . . . . .91 F8
Oldbury Cl RG24 . . . . .56 D8
Oldcorne Hollow GU46 . . . . .33 E5
Olde Farm Dr GU17 . . . . .34 F5
Oldenburg Cl SP10 . . . . .83 C5
Oldfield View RG27 . . . . .52 C5
Oldwood Chase GU14 . . . . . .55 A3
Oliver Rise GU34 . . . . .139 F4
Oliver's Battery Cres
  SO22 . . . . .197 A4
Oliver's Battery Gdns
  SO22 . . . . .197 B3
Oliver's Battery Prim Sch
  SO22 . . . . .209 A1
Oliver's Battery Rd N
  SO22 . . . . .197 B5
Oliver's Battery Rd S
  SO22 . . . . .197 A4
Oliver's La RG26 . . . . .29 A4
Oliver's Wlk RG24 . . . . .69 F7
Omega Pk GU34 . . . . .140 B3
Omni Bsns Ctr GU34 . . . .140 B3
Onslow Cl RG24 . . . . .48 E1
Ontario Way GU30 . . . . .188 A3
Openfields GU35 . . . . .165 C6
Optrex Bsns Pk RG27 . . . . .50 D4
Orange Gr SP11 . . . . .124 E5
Orange La SO20 . . . . .123 F6
Orbit Cl RG40 . . . . .16 C6
Orchard Cl Ash Vale GU12 . .77 D5
  Farnborough GU17 . . . . .35 D1
  Farnham GU9 . . . . .99 E6
  Haslemere GU27 . . . . .189 D5
  New Alresford SO24 . . . . . . .179 D4
  Newbury RG14 . . . . .2 A5
  South Wonston SO21 . . . . . .153 C4
Orchard Cotts SP11 . . . . . . .58 B4
Orchard Ct
  Camberley GU15 . . . . .35 F2
  Crondall GU10 . . . . .97 D6
Orchard Dr GU35 . . . . .165 A4
Orchard End GU10 . . . . .121 D3
Orchard Fields GU51 . . . . . .53 F1
Orchard Gate GU47 . . . . .34 F8
Orchard La GU10 . . . . .100 A8
  Tongham GU10 . . . . .100 D7
  Winchester SO22 . . . . .209 C5
Orchard La GU34 . . . . .140 A3
Orchard Rd Andover SP10 . .82 E1
  Farnborough GU14 . . . . .55 E4
  Farnborough, Cove Green
  GU14 .55 E4
  Farnham GU9 . . . . .99 E6
  Mortimer RG7 . . . . .11 F5
  South Wonston SO21 . . . . . .153 C4
Orchard The Hook RG27 . . . .51 A2
  Kingsclere RG20 . . . . .24 C1
  Oakley RG25 . . . . .88 B7
  Shipton Bellinger SP9 . . . . . .101 D7
  Tadley RG26 . . . . .27 B8
Orchard Way
  Aldershot GU12 . . . . .100 A8
  Camberley GU15 . . . . .35 F2
Orchard Wlk SO23 . . . . .209 B8
Orchardene RG14 . . . . .1 F4
Orchid Cl 2 SP10 . . . . .105 D6
Ordnance Rd
  Aldershot GU11 . . . . .77 A3
  North Tidworth SP9 . . . . .78 F6
Ordnance Rdbt GU11 . . . . . .76 F2
Oregon Wlk RG40 . . . . .16 C7
Oriel Hill GU15 . . . . .36 B4
Orient Dr SO22 . . . . .209 C8
Orkney Cl RG24 . . . . .48 D1
Orpheus Ho 2 RG7 . . . . .12 E2
Orts Rd RG14 . . . . .1 F2
Orwell Cl GU14 . . . . .55 C6
Osborn Rd GU9 . . . . .99 B4
Osborn Way RG27 . . . . .72 B8

Osborne Cl Alton GU34 . . . .139 D3
  Basingstoke RG21 . . . . .69 A7
  Camberley GU16 . . . . .56 D8
Osborne Ct
  Farnborough GU14 . . . . .77 A8
  Fleet GU51 . . . . .74 F8
Osborne Dr GU52 . . . . .75 B7
Osborne Rd
  Andover SP10 . . . . .106 A7
  Farnborough GU14 . . . . .77 A8
Osborne Sch SO23 . . . . . . .209 D7
Osgood Cl GU10 . . . . .100 C8
Osier Ho 9 RG26 . . . . .26 F8
Osler Cl RG26 . . . . .28 F3
Osnaburgh Hill GU15 . . . . . .35 F5
Osprey Gdns GU11 . . . . .99 F2
Osprey Rd RG22 . . . . .67 F1
Ottawa Dr GU30 . . . . .188 A3
Otterbourne Cres RG26 . . . .26 F6
Otterbourne Rd SO21 . . . . .197 E1
Otterbourne Wlk RG27 . . . .49 B5
Ouse Cl 32 SP10 . . . . .83 C2
Oval Rd SO51 . . . . .192 A1
Oval The Andover SP10 . . . . .53 C2
  Liss GU33 . . . . .207 F4
Overbecks RG14 . . . . .2 B4
Overbridge Sq RG14 . . . . . . .2 C3
Overdale Pl GU35 . . . . .164 D1
Overdale Rise GU16 . . . . . . .36 C3
Overdale Wlk GU35 . . . . . . .164 D1
Overlord Cl GU15 . . . . .36 A8
Overton CE Prim Sch
  RG25 .65 A1
Overton Cl GU11 . . . . .100 A6
Overton Ho RG25 . . . . .88 B8
Overton Rd SO21 . . . . .111 C3
Overton Sta RG25 . . . . .65 B2
Ovington Dr 9 GU51 . . . . . .53 D3
Owen Rd RG14 . . . . .2 A4
Owen's Rd SO22 . . . . .209 D7
Owlets Gr RG14 . . . . .2 B4
Owlsmoor Rd GU47 . . . . . . .35 B8
Ox Dro Kimpton SP11 . . . . . .79 F2
  Picket Piece SP10,SP11 . . . . .83 F1
  South Wonston SO21 . . . . . .153 F4
Ox Drove Sta SP11 . . . . .84 B3
Ox Drove Way SO24 . . . . . .137 A1
Oxenden Cl GU10 . . . . .100 C8
Oxenden Rd GU10 . . . . .100 D8
Oxford Rd
  Farnborough GU14 . . . . .56 A1
  Newbury RG14 . . . . .1 D5
  Sutton Scotney SO21 . . . . . .131 C4
Oxford St RG14 . . . . .1 D4
Oyster Cl RG22 . . . . .91 B7

P

Pack La RG23 . . . . .67 D2
Packenham Rd RG21 . . . . . . .68 F3
Packway GU9,GU10 . . . . . . .122 C7
Paddington Ho 7 RG21 . . . . .69 B5
Paddock Cl
  Camberley GU15 . . . . .36 E6
  South Wonston SO21 . . . . . .153 E4
Paddock Ct RG27 . . . . .52 C5
Paddock Field
  Chilbolton SO20 . . . . .129 B5
  Monk Sherborne RG26 . . . . . .47 B5
Paddock Rd
  Basingstoke RG22 . . . . .68 D3
  Newbury RG14 . . . . .5 D8
Paddock The
  Farnham GU10 . . . . .121 D4
  Grayshott GU26 . . . . .166 E4
  Hartley Wintney RG27 . . . . . . .52 D7
  Haslemere GU27 . . . . .189 E8
  Headley GU35 . . . . .165 C5
  Kings Worthy SO23 . . . . .176 C5
  Kingsclere RG20 . . . . .24 C2
Paddock Way
  Liphook GU30 . . . . .188 A5
  New Alresford SO24 . . . . . . .179 C4
Paddock Wlk RG22 . . . . .68 D3
Paddockfields RG24 . . . . . . .70 B8
Padwick Cl RG21 . . . . .69 A4
Padworth Rd RG7 . . . . .11 B8
Pages Yd RG28 . . . . .86 C4
Paget Cl Camberley GU15 . . .36 F7
  North Tidworth SP9 . . . . .78 D8
Paice La GU34 . . . . .159 E4
Paices Hill RG7 . . . . .9 E4
Painters Field SO23 . . . . . .209 C2
Painters Pightle RG27 . . . . .50 F1
Pakenham Dr GU11 . . . . .76 D3
Palace Cl SO31 . . . . .171 F2
Palace Gate RG29 . . . . .72 D3
Palace Gate Farm RG29 . . .72 D3
Pale La Fleet RG27 . . . . .53 A2
  Hartley Wintney RG27 . . . . . . .53 D4
Palestine Rd SP11 . . . . .124 D5
Pallier Cl GU26 . . . . .167 A6
Palm Hall Cl SO23 . . . . .209 F5
Palmer Dr SP10 . . . . .106 D8
Palmerston Cl GU14 . . . . . . .55 B3
Palmerston Ct 2 SO23 . . . .209 D3
Palmerston Pl SP10 . . . . . . .106 E7
Pamber Dr 5 GU51 . . . . .53 D3
Pamber Heath Rd RG26 . . .10 C1
Pamber Rd
  Charter Alley RG26 . . . . .46 F8
  Silchester RG7 . . . . .10 F1
Pan's Gdns GU15 . . . . .36 D4
Pankridge St GU10 . . . . .97 D7
Pannells GU10 . . . . .122 B5

Pantile Dr RG27 ....51 C1
Pantings La RG20 ....21 D7
Paper Mill La GU34 ....140 A4
Papermakers RG25 ......88 B7
Parade The Ash Vale GU12 .77 E4
  Basingstoke RG21 ....69 C6
  3 Pamber Heath RG26 .....9 F1
Parchment St SO23 ....209 E6
Parfitts Cl GU9 ....98 E2
Parish Cl Ash GU12 .....77 F1
  Farnham GU9 ....98 E6
Parish Rd GU14 ....77 A8
Park Ave Camberley GU15 .36 B4
  Old Basing RG24 ....70 B5
  Winchester SO23 ......209 E6
Park Cl **8** Aldershot GU12 .77 A1
  Binsted GU10 ....120 E2
  Kingsley GU35 ....142 C1
  Oakley RG23 ....67 B2
  Winchester SO23 ......209 E8
Park Close Rd GU34 ...140 A5
Park Cotts GU15 ....35 F3
Park Ct Farnham GU9 ....99 B3
  1 Winchester SO23 ...209 E8
Park Dro SO20 ....125 E3
Park End RG14 ....1 E4
Park Farm GU9 ....98 E6
Park Farm Ind Est GU16 .36 A1
Park Gdns RG21 ....69 C3
Park Hill GU52 ....74 F5
Park Ho **2** Aldershot GU11 .76 E1
  Winchester SO23 ......209 E8
Park House Cotts RG20 .44 C8
Park House Mews SP4 ..101 E4
Park House Sch & Sports Coll
  RG14 ....5 C1
Park La
  Arborfield Garrison RG40 ...15 F3
  Camberley GU15 ....36 A5
  Hamstead Marshall RG20 ...3 E8
  Kings Worthy SO23 ....176 D6
  Lower Froyle GU34 ....119 C5
  Newbury RG14 ....1 E4
  Old Basing RG24 ....70 B5
  Quarley SP11 ....103 A4
  Ropley SO24 ....181 B3
  Silchester RG7 ....12 A2
  Stratfield Saye RG7 ...13 A2
  West Dean SP5 ....190 B8
Park Mount SO24 ....179 C6
Park Par SP4 ....74 F5
  Fleet GU52 ....74 F5
Park Prim Sch GU11 ...100 A8
Park Rd Aldershot GU11 .100 A8
  Camberley GU14 ....36 A4
  Farnborough GU14 ....77 C8
  Farnham GU9 ....99 B4
  Sandhurst GU47 ....35 A8
  South Tidworth SP9 ....78 F5
  Winchester SO22,SO23 .209 D8
Park Row GU9 ....98 F3
Park St Bordon GU35 ...164 D3
  Camberley GU15 ....36 A5
  Newbury RG14 ....1 E4
Park Terr RG14 ....1 E4
Park View Beech Hill RG7 .13 B5
  Bishop's Sutton SO24 ..180 B4
  Lockerley SO51 ....191 E3
  Winchester SO22 ......209 A8
Park View Inf Sch RG22 .68 C2
Park View Jun Sch RG22 .68 C2
Park Way RG14 ....1 E3
Parkfields GU46 ....34 B6
Parkhill Cl GU17 ....35 B4
Parkhill Farm Cotts
  SO21 ....133 F7
Parkhill Rd GU17 ....35 B4
Parkhouse Cnr SP4 ....101 D4
Parkhouse Rd SP9 .....101 D1
Parkhurst Cotts GU10 .166 D8
Parkhurst Fields GU10 .144 D1
Parkland Gr GU9 ....99 D8
Parklands GU26 ....167 C1
Parklands Hospl RG24 ..47 E1
Parkside GU9 ....99 A6
Parkside Gdns SO22 ...209 A8
Parkside La GU35 ......181 A2
Parkside Rd RG21 ......69 C3
Parkstone Dr GU15 .....36 A4
Parkstone Rd SO24 ....181 D2
Parkview Cl SP10 ....82 E2
Parkway GU15 ....36 A3
Parkwood Cl RG24 ......48 F4
Parliament Pl SO22 ...209 A2
Parmiter Ho **5** SO23 ...209 E8
Parnell Ct SP10 ....82 C1
Parsonage Cl GU34 ...161 E3
Parsonage Farm Inf Sch
  GU14 ....55 A5
Parsonage Way GU16 ..36 C1
Parsons Cl
  Arborfield Garrison RG2 ..15 E8
  Fleet GU52 ....74 F5
  Newbury RG14 ....1 E4
Parsons Down Inf & Jun Schs
  RG19 ....2 E3
Parsons Field GU47 ....34 F8
Parsons La GU26 ......167 B6
Part La RG7 ....14 C4
Partridge Ave GU46 ....33 F6
Partridge Cl
  Barton Stacey SO21 ...130 D7
  Basingstoke RG22 .....90 F7
  Ewshot GU10 ....98 B8
  Frimley GU16 ....25 D1
Partridge Down SO22 .197 B3

Partridge Gn GU34 ....139 F5
Paschal Rd GU15 ....36 D8
Passfield Ent Ctr GU30 .187 B8
Passfield Mill Bsns Pk
  GU30 ....165 B1
Passfield Rd
  Liphook GU30 ....187 C8
  Passfield GU30 ....165 C1
Pastures The
  Cheriton SO24 ....201 C6
  Kings Worthy SO23 ...154 B1
Paternoster Ho **4** SO23 .209 E5
Paternoster Row **5**
  SO23 ....209 E5
Paterson Cl RG22 ......91 C7
Paterson Rd GU33 ....186 C2
Pathfinders The GU14 ..55 A3
Patrick's Cl GU33 .....208 A4
Patrick's Copse Rd
  GU33 ....208 A4
Patten Ave GU46 ....34 A5
Pattison Cres SP11 ...105 A7
Paul Cl GU11 ....99 C8
Paul's Field RG27 ......33 C8
Paulet Pl Old Basing RG24 .70 B6
  Winchester SO22 ......209 C3
Pavilion Rd
  Aldershot GU11 ....76 C1
  Farnborough GU14 .....76 B7
Pavilions End The GU15 .36 B3
Paviors GU9 ....99 A3
Pawley Cl GU10 ....100 D7
Pawmers Mead GU52 ..74 F3
Pax Hill GU10 ....119 F4
Paxton Cl RG22 ....91 B7
Payne's Mdw RG24 ....70 A8
Paynes Cl
  Broughton SO20 ......170 B7
  Headley RG19 ....24 C8
Paynes Hay Rd SO51 .194 C1
Paynes La SO20 ....170 B7
Paynesdown Rd RG19 ..2 F4
Peabody Rd GU14 ....77 B8
Peach Gr SP11 ....124 E5
Peach Tree Cl GU14 ....55 E7
Peacock Pl **4** SO23 ...198 C8
Peake Cl RG24 ....69 F7
Peakfield GU10 ....144 A7
Pear Tree Ave **4** GU51 .53 F2
Pear Tree Cl GU35 ....164 F4
Pear Tree Ct GU15 .....36 F8
Pear Tree Hts GU35 ...164 F4
Pear Tree La
  Newbury RG14 ....2 A5
  Rowledge GU10 ....121 D3
Pear Tree Rd GU35 ....164 F4
Pearces Pl RG20 ....24 D1
Pearl Ho SP11 ....57 A2
Pearman Dr SO20 .....106 D8
Peatmoor Cl GU51 .....53 E2
Pecche Pl RG24 ....49 A2
Peckmoor Dr RG19 .....6 A7
Peddlars Gr GU46 ......34 C6
Peel Ave GU16 ....56 E7
Peel Ct Farnborough GU14 .77 A8
  Hartley Wintney RG27 ..52 C6
Peel Gdns RG20 ....24 C3
Pegasus Ave GU12 .....77 C2
Pegasus Cl
  Haslemere GU27 ......189 B5
  Thatcham RG19 ....2 E4
Pegasus Ct
  Aldershot GU12 ....77 C1
  Farnborough GU14 .....56 C1
  Fleet GU51 ....53 F2
  Whitchurch RG28 ......86 C6
Pegasus Rd GU14 ......55 D7
Peked Mede RG27 ......51 D1
Pelham St Bordon GU35 .164 D1
  Old Basing RG24 ......70 B5
Pelham Pl GU10 ....142 C1
Pelican Ct SP10 ....83 B1
Pelican La RG14 ....1 E4
Pelican Rd RG26 ....10 C2
Pelton Rd RG21 ....68 F6
Pembroke Bwy GU15 ...36 A5
Pembroke Ct SP10 ....106 A7
Pembroke Rd
  Basingstoke RG23 .....68 B5
  Newbury RG14 ....1 D3
Pembury Pl GU12 ......77 A1
Pemerton Rd
  Basingstoke RG22 .....69 C7
  Winchester SO22 .....175 D3
Pen Cl SP10 ....106 C7
Pendennis Cl RG23 ....68 B6
Pendle Gn SO51 ....191 F1
Penfold Croft GU9 .....99 D4
Pengilly Rd GU9 ....98 F1
Peninsula Rd SO22 ...209 C5
Peninsula Sq SO23 ...209 D5
Peninsular Cl GU15 ....36 F7
Penn Rd RG14 ....1 B5
Pennefather's Rd GU11 .76 D3
Pennine Cl GU14 ....56 A3
Pennine Way
  Basingstoke RG22 .....68 B3
  Farnborough GU14 .....55 C7
Pennings Rd SP9 ......78 F6
Penns Wood GU14 .....56 B1
Penns Yd GU12 ....98 F2
Penny Hill Cvn Site GU17 .34 A2
Penny La SO20 ....150 A1
Penny's Hatch RG25 ...24 E2
Penrhyn Cl GU12 ....76 F1
Penrith Rd GU15 ....69 A4
Penrose Cl RG14 ....1 D5
Penrose Gdns GU12 ....77 E6

Penrose Way GU34 ....160 A2
Penryn Dr GU35 ....166 A5
Penshurst Rise GU16 ..56 D8
Pentangle The RG14 ....1 E4
Pentland Cl RG22 ......68 B3
Pentland Pl GU14 .....105 B7
Penton La
  Penton Grafton SP11 ...81 F5
  Penton Mewsey SP11 ..82 A3
Penton Pl **8** SO23 ....209 F4
Penwith Dr GU27 .....189 C5
Penwood Hts RG20 ....21 E8
Penwood Rd RG20 ......5 A3
Peregrins GU12 ....77 E2
Perham Cres SP11 .....97 E2
Perins Cl SO24 ....179 B4
Perins Sch SO24 ......179 C5
Periwinkle Cl GU35 ...165 A5
Perowne St GU11 ......76 D2
Perring Ave GU14 ......55 D8
Perring Rd GU14 ....55 D8
Perry Dr GU51 ....53 D1
Perry Way Farnham GU9 .98 F7
  Headley GU35 ....165 D4
Perryfield RG24 ....48 B3
Perth Rd SP11 ....79 D7
Peshawar Cl SP9 ......78 D7
Pest Hos GU12 ....203 C1
Peter Symonds Coll
  SO22 ....209 D7
Petersfield RG23 ......90 B8
Petersfield Cl RG24 ...49 B4
Petersfield Gn SP9 ...178 E5
Petersfield Rd
  Bordon GU33,GU35 ...186 B6
  Bramdean SO24 ......202 B5
  Cheriton SO24 ....201 D4
  Chilcomb SO21 ......198 D7
  East Tisted GU34,SO24 .182 D2
  Greatham GU33 ....185 F2
  Ropley SO24 ....181 D3
  Winchester SO23 ....198 C7
Petrel Croft RG22 ......90 F8
Petty's Brook Rd RG24 .49 A4
Petunia Cl RG22 ....91 A8
Petworth Cl
  Basingstoke RG22 .....91 B6
  Camberley GU15 ......56 D8
Petworth Ct GU15 .....56 D8
Pevensey Way GU16 ..56 E8
Peveral Way RG22 .....68 D3
Peveral Wlk RG22 .....68 D3
Peverel Cl SP10 ......187 F5
Pewsey Ho **4** SP9 .....78 F6
Pexalls Cl RG27 ....51 D1
Phaleron Cotts RG20 ..24 D1
Pheaben's Field RG26 .28 E3
Pheasant Cl
  Barton Stacey SO21 ..130 E7
  Basingstoke RG22 .....90 F8
Pheasant Copse GU51 ..53 E2
Pheasant La RG20 ......6 D3
Pheasantry Dr RG27 ...32 B4
Pheby Rd RG22 ....68 D2
Philips Ho GU26 ......166 F3
Phillips Cl Headley GU35 .165 D5
  Tongham GU10 ....100 C8
Phillips Cres GU35 ...165 D5
Phoenix Ct
  8 Aldershot GU11 .....76 E1
  Hartley Wintney RG27 ..52 B4
  Kingsclere RG20 ....42 B3
Phoenix Park Terr RG21 .69 B6
Phoenix Terr RG27 ....52 B4
Phoenix Wlk RG14 ......5 A6
Pickaxe La RG29 ....118 A4
Picket Twenty SP11 ...106 E7
Picketts Hill GU35 ....143 B2
Pickford St GU11 ......76 F2
Pickwick Gdns GU15 ..36 F4
Picton Cl SP10 ....36 F7
Picton Rd SP10 ....106 A5
Pierrefondes Ave GU14 .55 F5
Pigeon Cl RG26 ....29 F5
Pigeonhouse Cotts
  SO21 ....131 C4
Pigeonhouse Field
  SO21 ....131 C4
Pigeonhouse Yd SO21 .131 C4
Pigeons Farm Rd RG19 .6 B8
Pike Cl GU11 ....77 A2
Pike St RG14 ....1 C4
Pilcot Rd GU51,RG27 ..74 C6
Pilgrims Cl GU9 ......121 E8
Pilgrims Gate SO23 ..209 C7
Pilgrims Sch The SO23 .209 E5
Pilgrims Way
  Andover SP10 ....83 C1
  Headley GU35 ....165 C5
Pilgrims' Way Sch The
  GU9 ....121 F8
Pimpernel Way RG24 ..90 D5
Pinchington La RG14,RG19 .5 F7
Pindar Pl RG14 ....2 C5
Pine Ave GU15 ....36 B3
Pine Bank GU26 ......167 C4
Pine Cl Ash Vale GU12 ..77 E6
  Sandhurst GU15 ....35 C7
  South Wonston SO21 ..153 C4
  Winchester SO22 .....197 B3
Pine Cotts GU33 ......208 A1
Pine Dr Blackwater GU17 ..35 C3
  Finchampstead RG40 ...16 E7
  Mortimer RG7 ....11 D6
Pine Gr Farnham GU10 .122 C6
  Fleet GU51 ....75 B6
Pine Mount Rd GU15 ..36 B4
Pine Rd GU34 ....160 C3

Pine Ridge RG14 ....2 A5
Pine Ridge Dr GU10 ..122 A6
Pine View GU35 ....166 A6
Pine View Cl GU9 ......99 E5
Pine Wlk
  8 Andover SP10 .....105 D6
  Liss GU33 ....208 A6
Pinecrest GU17 ....35 C1
Pinefields GU35 ......164 D2
Pinehill Rise GU47 .....35 A8
Pinehurst RG26 ....26 F7
Pinehurst Ave GU14 ...55 F2
Pinehurst Cotts GU14 .55 F2
Pinehurst Rd GU14 ....55 F2
Pinelands Cvn Pk RG7 .10 A4
Pines The Fleet GU51 ..53 F2
  Liphook GU30 ....187 C4
Pines The Ho GU51 ...105 F8
  Camberley GU15 ......36 D7
Pinetree Ho **8** SP9 .....79 A7
Pineview GU14 ....55 E4
Pinewood GU14 ....48 E3
Pinewood Cl
  Pamber Heath RG26 ....9 B1
  Sandhurst GU47 ....34 D8
Pinewood Cres GU14 ..55 A5
Pinewood Ct **2** GU51 ..54 A2
Pinewood Dr RG20 .....5 E2
Pinewood Hill GU51 ...54 A2
Pinewood Pk GU14 .....55 A7
Pinkerton Rd RG22 ....68 D2
Pinks La RG26 ....9 C1
Pinnell Cl RG22 ....91 A6
Pintail Cl RG22 ....90 F7
Pipers Croft GU52 .....75 A4
Pipers Patch **1** GU14 ..55 F4
Pipit Cl GU52 ....2 F3
Pipsons Cl GU46 ....34 B6
Pirbright Rd GU14 .....56 A3
Pit Wlk SP4 ....123 D7
Pitcairn Cl RG24 ....48 D2
Pitfield La Mortimer RG7 ..11 F3
  Stratfield Mortimer RG7 .12 A4
Pitfold Ave GU27 .....189 B6
Pitfold Cl GU27 ....189 C6
Pither Rd RG29 ....95 C8
Pithouse La RG19 ......25 D6
Pittman Cl RG22 ....68 B2
Pitt Hall Cotts RG26 ..45 F5
Pitt La GU10 ....143 E6
Pitt Rdbt SO22 ....197 B5
Pitt Way GU14 ....55 C1
Pittard Rd RG21 ....68 F3
Pitter Cl SO22 ....175 B5
Pitts La SP10 ....106 A6
Pitts Rd GU11 ....76 F4
Place Ct GU11 ....100 A7
Plantation Farm Cotts
  RG26 ....45 A7
Plantation Rd
  Andover SP10 ....105 E7
  Mill Brow GU33 ......208 B2
  Pamber Heath RG26 ...29 A1
  South Tidworth SP9 ...78 F5
Plantation Row GU15 ..35 F5
Plantation The RG27 ..49 D8
Plantation Way GU35 .164 A1
Plassey Rd SP9 ....78 E7
Pleasant Hill RG26 ....26 F8
Plough Gdns GU14 .....55 D7
Plough La RG27 ....32 A6
Plough Rd GU34 ......142 C7
Plough Way SO22 ....209 B7
Plover Cl Andover SP10 .83 B2
  Basingstoke RG22 .....68 A1
Plover La GU27 ....15 C1
Plovers Down SO22 ..197 B3
Plovers Way GU34 ....140 A5
Plum Fell La GU34 ....184 E7
Plumer Rd GU33 ......186 C3
Plumpton Rd RG14 .....2 A1
Plumpton Way GU34 .160 C3
Poachers Field RG29 ..95 A3
Pococks La GU33 .....206 F7
Poets Way SO22 ......209 B6
Poland La RG29 ....72 F6
Polden Cl GU14 ....56 A3
Polecat Cnr RG24 ......70 B1
Polkerris Way GU52 ...75 B4
Pollards The GU10 ....120 A4
Pollen's Almshouses
  SP10 ....106 A8
Polmear Cl GU52 ......75 B4
Pomlingbroke RG27 ...51 D1
Pond Cl Newbury RG14 ..5 B7
  Overton RG25 ....92 E3
Pond Croft GU46 ....34 C6
Pond La Churt GU10 ..144 B4
  Grateley SP11,SO20 ...125 B7
Pond Rd Bramley RG26 .29 A2
  Farnborough GU14 .....55 F2
  Headley GU35 ....165 D6
Pondpenny La GU51 ...54 E1
Pondtail Cl GU51 ......75 C8
Pondtail Gdns GU51 ...75 C8
Pondtail Rd GU51 .....75 C8
Pondview Cl GU51 .....54 C2
Pool Rd Aldershot GU11 .100 A7
  Hartley Wintney RG27 ..52 B4
Poors Farm Rd RG26 ..70 E8
Popes Hill RG20 ....24 C7
Popham La RG25 ......112 F8
Poplar Cl Baughurst RG26 .26 B8
  Mytchett GU16 ....75 F8
  Sherfield on L RG27 ...29 D1
  Thatcham RG19 ....7 E6
Poplar Cotts GU16 .....56 D6

Poplar Pl RG14 ....1 E5
Poplar Wlk GU9 ....99 B7
Poplars Cl GU15 ....55 A5
Popley Way RG24 ......48 B1
Poppy Cl SP10 ....105 C7
Poppy Fields RG24 .....70 A8
Poppyhills Rd GU15 ...36 D8
Porchester Cl SP10 ....82 D3
Porchester Rd GU14 ....1 E1
Porchester Sq **12** RG21 .69 B5
Port La
  Standon SO21,SO22 ..196 E1
  Winchester SO22 .....197 A2
Portacre Rise RG21 ....68 F3
Portal Cl SP10 ....105 B7
Portal Rd SO23 ....209 F4
Portal Ct RG29 ....95 C8
Porter End RG14 ....5 F8
Porter Rd RG22 ....68 F1
Porters Cl Andover SP10 .82 D1
  Dummer RG25 ....90 D1
Portesbery Hill Dr GU15 .36 C6
Portesbery Rd GU15 ...36 B6
Portesbery Sch GU15 ..36 B6
Portiswood Cl RG20 ...27 B8
Portland Dr GU52 ......74 F4
Portland Gr SP10 .....106 A8
Portland Sq **5** GU33 .207 F4
Portsmouth Cl GU34 .139 D1
Portsmouth Cres GU32 .68 D2
Portsmouth Rd
  Frimley GU16 ....36 D4
  Hindhead GU8 ....167 F6
  Hindhead,Nutcombe GU26 .167 C2
  Liphook GU30 ....187 F2
Portsmouth Way RG22 .68 D2
Portsmouth Wlk RG22 .68 D2
Portway Pamber Heath RG26 .9 C1
  Riseley RG7 ....14 A2
Portway Cl SP10 ......105 D8
Portway Ind Est SP10 ..82 B1
Portway Inf Sch SP10 .105 D8
Portway Jun Sch SP10 .105 C8
Portway RG23 ....68 B5
Post Horn La RG27 .....50 D5
Post Office La RG25 ...90 D1
Posting House Mews
  RG14 ....1 C4
Pot La GU34 ....70 F8
Potbridge Rd RG29 ....72 F7
Potley Hill Prim Sch
  GU46 ....34 E5
Potley Hill Rd GU46 ...34 D5
Potter's Cross GU14 ..101 F4
Potter's Rise **3** RG21 ..69 B5
Potteries La GU14 ......55 B6
Potteries The GU14 ....55 B6
Potters Cres GU12 .....77 F2
Potters Field GU33 ...208 A4
Potters Gate GU9 ......98 E2
Potters Gate CE Prim Sch
  GU9 ....98 E2
Potters La GU27 ....75 C5
Potters Lt RG27 ....29 F3
Pottery Ct GU10 ......121 D6
Pottery La GU10 ......121 D6
Poultons Cl RG25 ......88 A7
Poultons Rd RG25 .....88 A7
Pound Cl Bramley RG26 .28 E3
  Headley GU35 ....165 D5
  Over Wallop SO20 ....125 C2
  Upper Wield SO24 ...137 A2
Pound Farm Barns
  GU34 ....161 D8
Pound Gate GU34 .....140 A5
Pound Hill SO24 ......179 D6
Pound La Burghclere RG20 .22 C6
  Newbury RG14 ....1 C3
  Thatcham RG19 ....2 E3
Pound Mdw
  Sherfield on L RG27 ...49 E8
  Whitchurch RG28 ......86 D5
Pound Rd
  8 Aldershot GU12 .....77 A1
  Kings Worthy SO23 ..175 C2
  Over Wallop SO20 ....125 C2
  Overton RG25 ....88 B7
Pound St RG14 ....1 D2
Pound The SO20 ......170 B6
Pound View SP11 ......83 C7
Poveys Mead RG20 ....24 E1
Power Ho RG14 ....70 B7
Poyle Rd GU10 ....100 C7
Poynings Cres RG21 ..69 C7
Poynters Ct SP10 ......82 F2
Poyntz Rd RG25 ....88 A8
Pragnells Cotts SP5 ..169 A1
Premier Ct RG27 ....29 D1
Prentice Cl GU14 ......55 F8
  Headley GU35 ....165 C5
Prescelly Cl RG22 .....68 B3
Preston Candover CE Prim
  Sch RG25 ....136 B8
Preston Pl RG14 ....2 B5
Pretoria Cl RG23 .....186 D2
Pretoria Rd SP11 ....57 B1
Preymead Ind Est GU11 .99 F7
Priest Down RG22 .....68 B3
Priestley Rd RG21,RG24 .68 E8
Primrose Ct **8** SP10 ..105 D6
Primrose Dr RG27 .....52 D7
Primrose Gdns
  Basingstoke RG22 .....91 B5
  Farnborough GU14 ....55 C3
Primrose La GU33 ....208 D4

Primrose Wlk
3 Fleet GU51 . . . . .53 F2
Yateley GU46 . . . . .33 F6
Primula Rd GU35 . . . . .164 E3
Prince Albert Gdns **1**
SP10 .106 A7
Prince Charles Cres
GU14 .56 A7
Prince Cl SP10 . . . . .83 D2
Prince Hold Rd RG19 . . . . . . .2 E3
Prince of Wales Wlk **4**
GU15 . . . . .36 A6
Prince's Ave GU11 . . . . .77 A5
Prince's Bldgs **21** SO23 . .209 E6
Prince's Mead Sch
SO21 .176 E6
Princes Cl GU15 . . . . .164 C1
Princes Ct SP9 . . . . .78 F7
Princes Mead GU14 . . . . . . .55 F3
Princes Pl SO22 . . . . .209 C3
Princes Way GU14 . . . . .76 E2
Princes' Cres RG22 . . . . .68 E3
Princess Ct
2 Farnborough GU14 . . . . . . .77 A8
11 Winchester SO23 . . . . . .209 E6
Princess Dr GU34 . . . . .139 D3
Princess Louise Sq
GU34 .139 D1
Princess Marina Dr
Arborfield Garrison RG2 . . . . .15 D8
Arborfield Garrison RG2,
RG40 .15 F8
Princess Way GU15 . . . . . . .36 A6
Prinstead Cl **5** SO23 . . . .209 F4
Printers Row **13** SO23 . .209 D6
Prior Croft Cl GU15 . . . . . . .36 E4
Prior End GU15 . . . . .36 E5
Prior Heath Com Inf Sch
GU15 . . . . .36 E5
Prior Place Cross Rds
GU15 .36 F4
Prior Rd GU15 . . . . .36 E5
Prior's La GU17 . . . . .34 E5
Priors Barton SO23 . . . . . .209 D4
Priors Cl
Farnborough GU14 . . . . .55 F8
Kingsclere RG20 . . . . .24 D2
Priors Ct GU12 . . . . .77 C1
Priors Dean Rd SO22 . . . . .175 D4
Priors Keep GU52 . . . . .75 B8
Priors Rd RG26 . . . . .9 E1
Priors Row RG29 . . . . .72 C4
Priors Way The SO24 . . . . . .182 B1
Priors Wood GU27 . . . . . . .189 D6
Priory Cl GU51 . . . . .74 D8
Priory Cotts RG7 . . . . .13 A4
Priory Ct Farnham GU9 . . . .122 A8
Sandhurst GU15 . . . . .35 D5
Priory Gdns
Old Basing RG24 . . . . .70 B7
18 Winchester SO23 . . . . .209 E6
Priory La Frensham GU10 .144 C8
Hartley Wintney RG27 . . . . . . .52 C4
Laverstoke RG28 . . . . .87 A6
Priory Pl RG19 . . . . .5 F6
Priory Prim Sch The
RG26 . . . . .27 B1
Priory Rd RG14 . . . . .1 C6
Priory St GU14 . . . . .56 B4
Pritchard Cl RG19 . . . . .6 B7
Privet La SP11 . . . . .80 F5
Privet Rd GU35 . . . . .165 A5
Privett Cl RG24 . . . . .70 A8
Privett Rd GU32 . . . . .205 E2
Project Workshops
SP11 .103 A5
Propeller Rd GU14 . . . . .55 F2
Prospect Ave GU14 . . . . . . .55 F6
Prospect Bsns Ctr SO24 .179 C4
Prospect Cotts GU12 . . . . . .77 E4
Prospect Hill GU35 . . . . . .165 C8
Prospect Pl RG14 . . . . .1 E1
Prospect Rd
Ash Vale GU12 . . . . .77 E5
Farnborough GU14 . . . . .55 E5
New Alresford SO24 . . . . .179 C4
Rowledge GU10 . . . . .121 C3
Providence Pl **6** GU9 . . . . .99 A2
Pruetts La GU31 . . . . .207 F1
Puckridge Gate Rd GU11 .76 C6
Pudding La SO23 . . . . .176 B5
Puffers Way **1** RG14 . . . . . .1 C2
Puffin Cl RG22 . . . . .90 F6
Pug's Hole SP5 . . . . .191 B7
Punsholt La SO24 . . . . .203 F5
Purbrook Rd RG26 . . . . .26 E8
Purcell Cl RG22 . . . . .68 F1
Purley Way GU16 . . . . .56 C8
Purmerend Cl **1** GU14 . . .55 A5
Puttenham Rd
Chineham RG24 . . . . .49 A3
Seale GU10 . . . . .100 F4
Puttocks Cl GU27 . . . . .189 B5
Pyestock Cres GU14 . . . . . . .55 A4
Pyle Hill RG14 . . . . .1 F1
Pyotts Copse RG24 . . . . . . .49 A1
Pyotts Ct RG24 . . . . .49 A1
Pyotts Hill RG24 . . . . .49 A1

Q

Quadrangle The RG27 . . . . .32 B4
Quadrant The GU14 . . . . . . .77 E4
Quantock Cl RG22 . . . . .68 B3
Quarry Cotts RG20 . . . . .43 B8
Quarry La GU46 . . . . .34 C5
Quarry Rd SO23 . . . . .198 C7
Quebec Cl GU30 . . . . .188 A3
Quebec Gdns GU17 . . . . . . .35 B4
Queen Anne's Sq **18**
RG21 .69 B5
Queen Anne's Wlk **2**
RG21 .69 B5
Queen Annes Gate GU9 . . .99 B7
Queen Elizabeth Cl GU12 .77 E2
Queen Elizabeth Dr
GU11 .76 D2
Queen Mary Ave
Basingstoke RG21 . . . . .69 B6
Camberley GU15 . . . . .35 E5
Queen Mary Cl GU51 . . . . . .53 F3
Queen Mary's Coll RG21 . . .69 B3
Queen St GU11 . . . . .77 B2
Queen Victoria Cross Roads
GU15 .35 E6
Queen Victoria Ct GU15 . . .55 F5
Queen Victoria's Wlk
GU15 .35 D6
Queen's Cl GU14 . . . . .76 F8
Queen's Ct GU14 . . . . .77 A8
Queen's Gate Rd GU14 . . . .76 F8
Queen's Par RG21 . . . . .69 B4
Queen's Rd Alton GU34 . . .139 E3
Basingstoke RG21 . . . . .68 F5
Newbury RG14 . . . . .1 F2
Winchester SO22 . . . . .209 B5
Queen's Rdbt GU11,GU14 . .76 F7
Queens Ave
Aldershot GU11 . . . . .76 F4
Andover SP10 . . . . .106 A8
Queens Cotts SP11 . . . . .61 E2
Queens Ct Farnham GU9 . . .98 F7
Newbury RG14 . . . . .1 E1
17 Winchester SO23 . . . . .209 D5
Queens Keep **5** GU35 . . . .36 B5
Queens La GU9 . . . . .98 F7
Queens Mead SO22 . . . . . .209 A4
Queens Mead Gdns
RG29 .72 D3
Queens Rd
Aldershot GU11 . . . . .76 D2
Camberley GU15 . . . . .35 F4
Farnborough GU14 . . . . .77 B8
Farnham GU9 . . . . .99 A6
Fleet GU52 . . . . .75 A7
Kingsclere RG20 . . . . .24 E1
Liphook GU30 . . . . .187 A3
North Warnborough RG29 . . .72 C3
Whitchurch RG28 . . . . .86 D3
Queensbury Pl GU17 . . . . . .35 A3
Queensdale Ct RG21 . . . . . . .69 A3
Queensfield RG25 . . . . .90 D1
Queensgate GU14 . . . . .55 F3
Queensmead GU14 . . . . .55 F3
Queensway Andover SP10 . .83 D2
Camberley GU15 . . . . .36 E7
Queenwood Rd SO20 . . . . .170 B6
Queenwood Rise SO20 . . . .170 B6
Quennells Hill GU10 . . . . . .121 D5
Quetta Pk GU10 . . . . .75 B2
Quilter Rd RG22 . . . . .68 C1
Quince Tree Way RG27 . . . .51 B1
Quinnettes GU10 . . . . .144 D1
Quinneys GU14 . . . . .34 D6
Quorn Terr GU33 . . . . .186 C3

R

Race Course Rd RG14 . . . . . .1 F1
Racedown Cotts SP11 . . . .102 F6
Raceview Bsns Ctr RG14 . . .1 F2
Rack & Manger Cotts
SO21 .174 A8
Rack Cl SP10 . . . . .106 B8
Rack Close Rd GU34 . . . . . .139 E3
Rackfield GU27 . . . . .189 B7
Rackstraw Rd GU47 . . . . . . .35 B8
Radar Rd GU14 . . . . .55 B1
Radcliffe Cl GU16 . . . . .56 E7
Radford Cl GU9 . . . . .99 C5
Radford Gdns RG21 . . . . . . .68 F7
Radical Ride RG40 . . . . .16 D7
Rae Rd GU14 . . . . .55 F1
Raeburn Cl SO24 . . . . .201 D5
Raeburn Way GU47 . . . . . . .35 B6
RAF Gate Rd GU14 . . . . .55 B5
Raghill RG7 . . . . .10 B6
Raglan Cl Aldershot GU12 .77 A1
Camberley GU16 . . . . .56 E8
Raglan Ct RG22 . . . . .91 C8
Ragmore La GU33 . . . . .205 E5
Railton **2** GU15 . . . . .36 B6
Railway Cotts
Bordon GU35 . . . . .164 A5
East Tisted GU34 . . . . .183 D5
West Dean SP5 . . . . .190 D3
West Tisted GU34 . . . . .204 C6
Railway Rd
Greatham GU33 . . . . .186 D3
Newbury RG14 . . . . .1 E1
Railway Terr RG7 . . . . .12 C5
Rainbow Cl RG24 . . . . .90 C7
Rainham Cl RG22 . . . . .90 F7
Rake Bsns Pk GU33 . . . . . .208 E4
Rake CE Fst Sch GU33 . . .208 F5
Rake Rd GU33 . . . . .208 B4
Rakemakers GU34 . . . . . . .140 D7
Raleigh Way GU16 . . . . .36 D5
Ralph Ct GU10 . . . . .97 D5
Ram Alley Ashford Hill RG19 .8 B1

Ram Alley continued
Fair Oak RG19 . . . . .25 A8
Ramillies Cl GU11 . . . . .77 C7
Ramillies Rd GU11 . . . . .77 B5
Ramparts The SP10 . . . . . .105 E5
Rampton Rd RG28 . . . . .86 D4
Ramptons La RG7 . . . . .10 F6
Ramridge Ho SP11 . . . . .81 C4
Ramsay Cl GU15 . . . . .36 D7
Ramsay Rd SO23 . . . . .176 C8
Ramsdell Cl RG21 . . . . .69 A2
Ramsdell Rd Fleet GU51 . . .53 D4
Pamber End RG26 . . . . .27 B1
Wolverton RG26 . . . . .25 D1
Ramsholt Cl RG25 . . . . .89 E1
Rances Way SO22 . . . . .209 C3
Randell Cl GU17 . . . . .35 A1
Randolph Dr GU14 . . . . .55 A3
Ranelagh Rd SO23 . . . . . . .209 D4
Range Rd
Farnborough GU14 . . . . .55 C1
Finchampstead RG40 . . . . . . .16 F7
Range Ride GU15 . . . . .35 D7
Range View GU47 . . . . .35 C8
Rank The Fyfield SP11 . . . . .80 E2
Hurstbourne Tarrant SP11 . . .60 F7
Penton Grafton SP11 . . . . . . .81 D2
Rankine Cl GU9 . . . . .99 E6
Rankine Rd RG24 . . . . .69 D8
Rapallo Cl GU14 . . . . .56 A4
Raphael Cl RG21 . . . . .69 D3
Rapley Cl GU15 . . . . .36 C8
Rashleigh Ct GU52 . . . . .75 B4
Rasset Mead GU52 . . . . .74 E3
Ratcliffe Rd GU14 . . . . .55 D8
Ravel Cl RG22 . . . . .68 E1
Ravelin Cl GU10 . . . . .97 D5
Raven Cl **6** GU46 . . . . .33 F6
Raven Rd RG27 . . . . .51 A1
Raven Sq GU34 . . . . .139 C6
Ravenscote Com Jun Sch
GU16 .36 E3
Ravenscroft RG22 . . . . .68 A1
Ravensdale Cotts RG26 . . .167 A1
Ravenswing Pk RG7 . . . . . . .10 B2
Ravenswood Dr GU15 . . . . .36 C5
Ravensworth Rd RG7 . . . . . .11 C5
Rawdon Rise GU15 . . . . .36 F5
Rawlings Rd RG27 . . . . .72 B8
Rawlinson Rd
Farnborough GU11 . . . . .77 A5
Sandhurst GU15 . . . . .35 D6
Raygnoldes GU52 . . . . .74 E3
Rayleigh Rd RG21 . . . . .69 A5
Rayner Dr RG2 . . . . .15 E7
Rays Cl RG26 . . . . .27 A8
Read's Field GU34 . . . . .160 B2
Reading Dr N RG27 . . . . . . .32 B4
Reading Dr S RG27 . . . . . . .32 B4
Reading Rd
Aldermaston RG7 . . . . .10 D5
Chineham RG24 . . . . .48 F2
Eversley Centre RG27 . . . . . . .33 B8
Farnborough GU14 . . . . .56 A1
Hook RG27 . . . . .51 A2
Padworth RG7 . . . . .11 D8
Rotherwick RG27 . . . . .51 D5
Sherfield on L RG27 . . . . .49 D8
Yateley GU46 . . . . .34 D6
Reading Rd N GU51 . . . . . . .53 E1
Reading Rd S GU52 . . . . . . .75 A6
Rebecca Cl GU52 . . . . .74 E3
Recreation Cl GU14 . . . . . . .35 D1
Recreation Rd
Andover SP10 . . . . .106 B8
Odiham RG29 . . . . .72 D2
Rowledge GU10 . . . . .121 C3
Rectory Cl Newbury RG14 . .1 D2
Tadley RG26 . . . . .34 D8
Rectory Hill
West Dean SP5 . . . . .190 D3
West Tytherley SP5 . . . . .169 A1
Rectory La Bentley GU10 .120 B4
Bramshott GU30 . . . . .188 B7
Broughton SO20 . . . . .170 B7
Hannington RG26 . . . . .45 A8
Itchen Abbas SO21 . . . . .178 A7
Rectory Pl SP11 . . . . .81 D2
Rectory Rd
Farnborough GU14 . . . . .56 A4
Hook RG27 . . . . .72 A8
Oakley RG23 . . . . .66 F1
Padworth RG7 . . . . .10 D7
Rectory Row RG25 . . . . .92 A7
Reculver Way SP10 . . . . .82 D3
Red Deer Ct **4** SO22 . . . .209 C6
Red Hill
Ashmansworth RG20 . . . . . . .41 B7
Four Marks GU34 . . . . .160 B5
Mattingley RG27 . . . . .31 E2
Red La Aldermaston RG7 . . .10 B5
Ellisfield RG25 . . . . .115 C4
Headley GU35 . . . . .165 F7
West Tytherley SP5 . . . . .191 A7
Red Lion La
Basingstoke RG21 . . . . .69 B4
Farnham GU9 . . . . .98 F1
Overton RG25 . . . . .88 A8
Red Lion Mews RG29 . . . . . .72 E3
Red Oaks GU10 . . . . .121 D3
Red Post Bridge SP11 . . . .104 F7
Red Post La SP11 . . . . .104 F7
Red Rice Rd SP10 . . . . .105 C2
Red Villas SP9 . . . . .101 E8
Redan Gdns **1** GU12 . . . . . .77 A1

Redan Hill Est GU12 . . . . . . .77 A2
Redan Rd GU12 . . . . .77 A2
Redbridge Dr SP10 . . . . . . .105 F6
Redbridge La
Old Basing RG24 . . . . .69 F5
Ropley SO24 . . . . .182 A4
Redcrest Gdns GU15 . . . . . . .36 D5
Rede Ct **5** GU14 . . . . .56 A1
Redenham Dro SP11 . . . . . . .81 A8
Redes Ct RG27 . . . . .51 D1
Redfield Ct RG14 . . . . .2 B4
Redfields La GU10,GU52 . . .74 E2
Redfields Pk GU52 . . . . .74 E2
Redgauntlet RG40 . . . . .16 C6
Redgrave Ct GU12 . . . . .77 D2
Redhearne Fields GU10 . .144 C1
Redhouse Mews GU30 . . . .188 A2
Redlands La
Crondall GU10 . . . . .97 E7
Ewshot GU10 . . . . .98 A7
Redlane Hill RG7 . . . . .10 A6
Redon Way SP10 . . . . .82 F1
Redshank Ct RG19 . . . . .2 E3
Redvers Buller Rd GU11 . . .77 B7
Redwing Rd RG22 . . . . .90 F7
Redwood Ct GU34 . . . . .160 A8
Redwoods Way GU52 . . . . . .74 F5
Reed Cl GU11 . . . . .77 B5
Reed Wlk RG14 . . . . .2 A4
Reeds La GU35 . . . . .208 D6
Reeds Rd The GU10 . . . . . .122 D3
Rees Rd SO21 . . . . .153 C2
Reeves Rd GU12 . . . . .77 A1
Regal Ct **8** RG14 . . . . .1 C6
Regal Cl GU52 . . . . .75 A8
Regent Ct
7 Aldershot GU11 . . . . .76 F2
Basingstoke RG21 . . . . .69 C6
Fleet GU51 . . . . .74 F8
18 Winchester SO23 . . . . .209 E8
Regent St GU15 . . . . .55 D5
Regent Way GU16 . . . . .56 B7
Regents Ct Andover SP10 . .83 E1
Newbury RG14 . . . . .1 D3
Newbury RG14 . . . . .1 F3
Regents Pl GU47 . . . . .35 A8
Regiment Cl GU14 . . . . .55 A3
Regnum Dr RG14 . . . . .1 A6
Reith Way SP10 . . . . .82 E7
Rembrandt Cl RG21 . . . . . . .69 B1
REME Mus* RG2 . . . . .15 E8
Remembrance Gdns
RG24 .48 F2
Remembrance Rd RG14 . . . .1 D4
Rennie Ct RG14 . . . . .1 D4
Renoir Cl RG27 . . . . .69 D3
Renown Way RG24 . . . . .48 F2
Reservoir Rd GU14 . . . . .55 B1
Restormel Cl RG23 . . . . .68 B6
Reuben's Cres RG26 . . . . . . .26 F7
Revelstoke Ave GU14 . . . . . .55 F6
Rewlands Dr SO22 . . . . . . .175 C4
Rex Ct GU27 . . . . .189 D6
Reynards Cl RG26 . . . . .26 F8
Reynolds Cl RG21 . . . . .69 D4
Reynolds Ct SP10 . . . . .82 F1
Reynolds Gn GU47 . . . . .35 B6
Reynolds Ho RG22 . . . . .68 C2
Reyntiens View RG29 . . . . .72 E2
Rhine Banks GU14 . . . . .55 B5
Rhodes Sq SP10 . . . . .82 F1
Rhododendron Cnr RG40 . .16 E4
Rhododendron Rd
Camberley GU16 . . . . .56 F8
Frimley GU16 . . . . .36 F1
Rhododendron Wlk RG19 . . .7 F5
Rhyll Gdns GU11 . . . . .76 D1
Ribble Cl **34** SP10 . . . . .83 C2
Ribble Pl GU14 . . . . .55 C6
Ribble Way RG21 . . . . .69 D5
Richard Cl GU51 . . . . .74 E7
Richard Way **17** RG21 . . . . .69 D5
Richardson Cl RG26 . . . . . . .28 F7
Richborough Dr SP10 . . . . .82 C3
Richmond Ave RG19 . . . . .2 E3
Richmond Cl
Bordon GU35 . . . . .164 D2
Farnborough GU14 . . . . .55 B3
Fleet GU52 . . . . .74 F6
Frimley GU16 . . . . .36 D1
Richmond Cres SP9 . . . . .79 A6
Richmond Ho
Basingstoke RG21 . . . . .69 B4
Sandhurst GU47 . . . . .35 C8
Richmond Rd
Basingstoke RG21 . . . . .69 B4
3 Winchester SO22 . . . . .209 D6
Riddings La RG19 . . . . .8 A2
Rideway Cl GU15 . . . . .35 F4
Ridge Cl RG22 . . . . .91 C5
Ridge Ct RG27 . . . . .72 B8
Ridgemoor Cl GU10 . . . . . .167 C5
Ridges Cl SP11 . . . . .83 D8
Ridges View GU35 . . . . .83 D8
Ridgeway SO22 . . . . .209 B6
Ridgeway Com Sch The
GU9 . . . . .122 A7
Ridgeway Hill Rd GU9 . . . .122 A8
Ridgeway Par GU52 . . . . . . .75 A8
Ridgeway The GU34 . . . . . .139 F2
Ridgway Rd GU9 . . . . .122 A8
Ridings The Frimley GU16 . .36 F2
Liss GU33 . . . . .208 B4
Ridley Cl GU21 . . . . .51 D1
Ridleys Piece RG29 . . . . . . .95 A4

Rifle Way GU14 . . . . .55 A3
Riley La RG24 . . . . .70 B7
Riley Rd SO21 . . . . .153 F3
Rimbault Cl GU14 . . . . .77 B7
Rimes's La RG26 . . . . .26 D6
Rindle Cl **4** GU14 . . . . .55 A4
Ringlet Way **5** SO23 . . . . .198 C8
Ringshall Gdns RG26 . . . . . .28 F7
Ringway Ctr The RG21 . . . . .68 F7
Ringway E RG21 . . . . .69 E6
Ringway N RG21 . . . . .69 B8
Ringway S RG21 . . . . .69 B3
Ringway W RG21,RG22,
RG23 .68 E5
Ringwood Rd
Blackwater GU17 . . . . .35 A6
Farnborough GU14 . . . . .56 A7
Ripon Rd GU17 . . . . .34 D1
Ripplesmore Cl GU47 . . . . . .34 F8
Rise The RG40 . . . . .15 E2
Riseley Bsns Ctr RG7 . . . . .14 A3
Rivendell Ct GU15 . . . . .55 C4
River Cl GU34 . . . . .160 B2
River Gn GU12 . . . . .121 C7
River Park Ind Est RG14 . . .1 E1
River Rd GU46 . . . . .33 F8
River Row Cotts GU10 . . . .121 D8
River View GU34 . . . . .128 F3
River View GU34 . . . . .140 A4
River Way SP10 . . . . .83 C2
River Wlk RG14 . . . . .2 A4
Riverdale GU10 . . . . .121 C7
Riverdale Ct RG14 . . . . .2 A3
Riverhead SO24 . . . . .180 C4
Rivermead Rd GU15 . . . . . . .35 F2
Rivermede GU35 . . . . .164 E4
Rivers Cl GU52 . . . . .56 C1
Riverside Bsns Pk GU9 . . .99 B3
Riverside Cl
Basingstoke RG21 . . . . .55 D5
Liss GU33 . . . . .207 F4
Old Basing RG24 . . . . .70 B8
Overton RG25 . . . . .88 B8
Riverside Cotts RG28 . . . . . .86 B2
Riverside Ct GU9 . . . . .99 A3
Riverside Gn SO20 . . . . . . .172 A3
Riverside Ind Pk GU9 . . . . .99 B3
Riverside Way GU15 . . . . . . .35 E3
Riverwey Ind Est GU34 . . .140 B4
Robert May's Sch RG29 . . .72 C3
Robert Mays Rd RG29 . . . . .72 C2
Robert Sandilands Prim Sch
RG14 . . . . .1 C4
Robert Way GU16 . . . . .56 D3
Roberts Cl SO23 . . . . .154 B1
Roberts Rd
Aldershot GU12 . . . . .77 B1
Barton Stacey SO21 . . . . . . .130 E8
Greatham GU33 . . . . .186 C2
Sandhurst GU15 . . . . .35 E6
Robertsfield RG19 . . . . .2 D3
Robertson Cl Alton GU34 .139 D1
Liss GU33 . . . . .5 F8
Robertson Rd SO24 . . . . . .179 C4
Robertson Way GU12 . . . . .140 A1
Robin Cl Alton GU34 . . . . . .140 A1
Ash Vale GU12 . . . . .77 E6
Basingstoke RG22 . . . . .91 A8
Robin Hill Dr GU15 . . . . .36 E3
Robin Hood Cl GU14 . . . . . .55 E7
Robin La
Bishop's Green RG20 . . . . .6 D3
Sandhurst GU47 . . . . .34 F8
Robin Way SP10 . . . . .83 B2
Robins Cl GU51 . . . . .74 E7
Robins Gr GU51 . . . . .75 A8
Robins Grove Cres GU46 . . .33 F6
Robins Nest GU34 . . . . .139 F4
Robinson Crusoe Pk
RG40 .15 F6
Robinson Way GU35 . . . . . .164 E2
Rochester Cl RG22 . . . . .91 B8
Rochester Gr GU51 . . . . .75 A8
Rochford Rd RG21 . . . . .69 A5
Rock Gdns GU11 . . . . .76 D1
Rock La GU10 . . . . .121 C5
Rockbourne Rd SO22 . . . . .175 D4
Rockdale **6** GU26 . . . . .167 B3
Rockdale Dr GU26 . . . . .167 B3
Rockdale Ho **6** GU26 . . . .167 B3
Rockery The GU14 . . . . .55 C3
Rocket Rd GU14 . . . . .55 B1
Rockfield Way **7** GU47 . . . .35 B8
Rockingham Rd RG14 . . . . . .1 D2
Rockmoor La SP11 . . . . .18 D2
Rockpit Cotts GU33 . . . . . .208 B4
Rodfield La SO21,SO24 . . .200 C5
Roding Cl RG21 . . . . .69 D5
Rodmel Ct GU14 . . . . .56 C1
Rodney Ct SP10 . . . . .83 D1
Roe Downs Rd GU34 . . . . .160 A5
Roebuts Cl RG14 . . . . .5 D8
Roedeer Copse GU27 . . . . .189 C6
Roentgen Rd RG24 . . . . .69 F7
Rogers Ct **1** GU34 . . . . . . .139 F3
Roke La RG29 . . . . .96 B8
Rokeby Cl RG14 . . . . .5 F7
Rokes Pl GU46 . . . . .33 E6
Rolston Ho GU47 . . . . .189 D6
Roman Rd
Basingstoke RG23 . . . . .68 B6
Stockbridge SO20 . . . . .149 D3
Roman Way Andover SP10 .83 B3
Barton Stacey SO21 . . . . . . .130 E8
Basingstoke RG23 . . . . .68 A5
Farnham GU9 . . . . .99 C4

Roman Way continued
Thatcham RG18 . . . . .2 F4
Roman Way Prim Sch
SP10 . . . . .83 B4
Romano Ct 2 RG14 . . . . .1 F2
Romans Bsns Pk GU9 . . . . . .99 B3
Romans Field RG7 . . . . .10 F1
Romans Gate RG26 . . . . .10 D1
Romans Ind Pk GU9 . . . . .99 B3
Romans' Rd SO23 . . . . .209 D4
Romany The GU51 . . . . .54 E1
Romayne Cl GU14 . . . . .55 E5
Romley Ct GU9 . . . . .99 B1
Romney Rd GU14 . . . . .55 C1
Romsey Cl
Aldershot GU11 . . . . .100 A6
Basingstoke RG24 . . . . .48 A1
Blackwater GU17 . . . . .35 A6
Romsey Rd
Broughton SO20 . . . . .170 B5
King's Somborne SO20 . . . . . . .171 F1
Nether Wallop SO20 . . . . .147 E6
Wherwell SP11,SO20 . . . . .128 D6
Winchester SO22,SO23 . . . . . .209 A4
Ronald Bowker Ct 1
SO22 . . . . .209 C6
Rook La SO21 . . . . .133 A3
Rooke's Way RG18 . . . . .2 C4
Rookery Cl GU14 . . . . .15 E6
Rookery La SO20 . . . . .170 D6
Rookery The
West Dean SP5 . . . . .190 D3
Whitchurch RG28 . . . . .86 C5
Rooks Down Rd SO22 . . . . . .209 B3
Rooksbury Rd SP10 . . . . .105 B6
Rooksdown Ave RG24 . . . . . . .68 C8
Rooksdown La RG24 . . . . .47 C1
Rooksfield RG20 . . . . .6 E2
Rookswood GU34 . . . . .139 F5
Rookswood Cl RG27 . . . . .51 B1
Rookwood La GU34 . . . . .159 C1
Rookwood Sch SP10 . . . . .105 F7
Room Cotts SO20 . . . . .129 A5
Ropewalk Ho 7 SO23 . . . . . .209 A5
Ropley CE Prim Sch
SO24 . . . . .181 G4
Ropley Ct RG26 . . . . .26 E7
Ropley Rd GU34 . . . . .183 A4
Ropley Sta* SO24 . . . . .180 F5
Rorkes Drift GU16 . . . . .56 E4
Rosa Ct SP10 . . . . .105 D7
Rosalind Hill Ho SO20 . . . . .149 F3
Rosary Gdns GU46 . . . . .34 B6
Rose Cl RG22 . . . . .91 B8
Rose Cotts GU12 . . . . .77 E2
Rose Est The RG27 . . . . .72 B8
Rose Gdns GU14 . . . . .55 C3
Rose Hodson Pl RG23 . . . . . . .68 C7
Rose Wlk GU51 . . . . .53 F2
Rosebank Cl 6 RG26 . . . . .26 F8
Rosebay Gdns RG27 . . . . .51 C1
Roseberry Rd RG22 . . . . .91 B5
Rosebery Rd SO24 . . . . .179 C5
Rosedale GU12 . . . . .77 A2
Rosedene Gdns GU51 . . . . . . .53 F2
Rosedene La 8 GU47 . . . . .63 F8
Rosefield Ct RG27 . . . . .52 D7
Rosehip Way RG24 . . . . .69 F7
Rosemary Ave GU12 . . . . .77 E8
Rosemary Cl GU14 . . . . .55 B4
Rosemary Dr RG26 . . . . .26 F6
Rosemary Gdns GU17 . . . . . . .35 B5
Rosemary La
Blackwater GU17 . . . . .35 B5
Rowledge GU10 . . . . .121 C4
Rosemary Terr RG14 . . . . .1 C2
Rosemoor Gdns RG14 . . . . .2 A4
Rosetree Cotts GU34 . . . . . . .140 A4
Rosewarne Ct 9 SO23 . . . . . .209 E7
Rosewood Chineham RG24 . . . .48 F3
Mytchett GU16 . . . . .56 E4
Rosewood Ct 5 SP9 . . . . .79 A7
Rosewood Rd GU35 . . . . .165 A5
Ross Cl RG21 . . . . .69 A2
Ross Terr 2 RG14 . . . . .1 D1
Rossini Cl RG22 . . . . .91 E8
Rossmore Gdns GU11 . . . . . . .76 D1
Rothay Ct 18 RG21 . . . . .69 D5
Rother Cl GU47 . . . . .35 A8
Rother Ho GU33 . . . . .207 F3
Rother Rd GU14 . . . . .55 C7
Rotherbank Farm La
GU33 . . . . .208 A6
Rotherwick Ct GU14 . . . . .77 A8
Rotherwick Ho GU51 . . . . .53 D4
Rotherwick La RG27 . . . . .50 D8
Rotherwick Rd RG26 . . . . .27 A7
Rotten Green Rd RG27 . . . . . .53 E6
Rotten Hill RG25,RG28 . . . . . . .87 E6
Rotunda Est The 11 GU11 . . . .76 F2
Round Cl GU34 . . . . .34 D5
Round End RG14 . . . . .2 B5
Roundabouts The GU33 . . . .208 A5
Roundaway La SP11 . . . . .58 F3
Roundhuts Rise 3
SO23 . . . . .198 C8
Roundmead Rd RG21 . . . . .69 A4
Roundway Ct SP10 . . . . .105 B8
Rounton Rd GU52 . . . . .75 A5
Row The SO21 . . . . .177 E5
Rowan Chase GU10 . . . . .121 B6
Rowan Cl Camberley GU15 . . . .58 D8
Fleet GU51 . . . . .54 C1
South Wonston SO21 . . . . .153 E4
Tadley RG26 . . . . .27 A8
Rowan Ct 9 SP9 . . . . .78 F7
Rowan Dale GU52 . . . . .74 F5
Rowan Dr RG14 . . . . .1 E5

Rowan Rd RG26 . . . . .27 B8
Rowan Tree Cl GU33 . . . . . . .208 A4
Rowans Cl GU14 . . . . .55 C8
Rowans The Andover SP10 . . .82 E1
Grayshott GU26 . . . . .167 B2
Rowanside Cl GU35 . . . . .166 A4
Rowanwood RG40 . . . . .15 E6
Rowcroft Cl GU12 . . . . .77 E6
Rowcroft Rd RG12 . . . . .15 D7
Rowdell Cotts SO24 . . . . .181 C5
Rowhill Ave GU11 . . . . .99 D8
Rowhill Cl 5 GU14 . . . . .55 A4
Rowhill Cres GU11 . . . . .99 D8
Rowhill Nature Trail* . . . .
. . . . .99 B8
Rowhills GU9 . . . . .99 B8
Rowhills Cl GU9 . . . . .99 D7
Rowland's Cl RG7 . . . . .11 A5
Rowledge CE Prim Sch
GU10 . . . . .121 C3
Rowlings Rd SO22 . . . . .175 D3
Roxbee Cox Rd GU51 . . . . . . .54 E1
Roxburghe Cl GU35 . . . . .164 D2
Royal Cescent The 8
SP9 . . . . .79 A7
Royal Cl RG22 . . . . .91 A5
Royal Greenjackets Mus*
SO23 . . . . .209 D5
Royal Hampshire Cty Hospl
SO22 . . . . .209 C5
Royal Hampshire Regiment
Mus* SO23 . . . . .209 D5
Royal Nuts Ave GU26 . . . . . . .167 D4
Royal Jun Sch The
GU26 . . . . .167 C2
Royal Military Academy
Hospl GU15 . . . . .35 E8
Royal Military Ct The 2
GU11 . . . . .76 F2
Royal Oak Cl GU46 . . . . .34 C6
Royal Par GU26 . . . . .167 D4
Royal The GU47 . . . . .64 F7
Royal Winchester Mews
SO22 . . . . .209 A5
Royale Cl GU11 . . . . .100 A8
Royce Cl SP10 . . . . .82 B1
Roycroft La RG40 . . . . .16 C8
Roydon Cl SO22 . . . . .209 A5
Royston Ctr GU12 . . . . .77 D8
Rozeldene GU26 . . . . .167 C3
Rozelle Cl SO22 . . . . .175 A5
Rubens Cl RG21 . . . . .69 D2
Rucstall Ctr RG21 . . . . .69 D3
Rucstall Prim Sch RG21 . . . . . .69 D3
Rudd Hall Rise GU15 . . . . .36 B3
Ruffield Cl SO22 . . . . .209 A8
Rufford Cl GU52 . . . . .75 A6
Rune Dr SP10 . . . . .82 F4
Runfold-St George GU10 . . . . .99 F5
Runnymede Ct 1 GU14 . . . . . .55 E7
Runnymede Ho 5 SP10 . . . .106 D7
Runwick La GU10 . . . . .98 B1
Rupert Rd RG14 . . . . .5 D7
Rural Cl GU9 . . . . .121 D6
Rural Life Ctr Mus*
GU10 . . . . .122 D3
Rushden Way GU9 . . . . .99 B7
Rushes The 12 RG21 . . . . .69 D5
Rushfield Rd GU33 . . . . .207 F3
Rushmoor Cl GU52 . . . . .75 A7
Rushmoor Ct GU14 . . . . .77 A8
Rushmoor Ind Sch GU14 . . . . .56 A1
Ruskin Rd RG21 . . . . .91 A4
Ruskin Cl RG21 . . . . .69 E3
Russell Ct
Blackwater GU17 . . . . .35 B5
Hindhead GU26 . . . . .167 D4
Russell Dr SO51 . . . . .192 D1
Russell Rd
Basingstoke RG21 . . . . .69 B3
Newbury RG14 . . . . .1 C2
Winchester SO23 . . . . .209 E8
Russet Cl
New Alresford SO24 . . . . .179 C4
Tongham GU10 . . . . .100 C7
Russet Gdns GU15 . . . . .36 B3
Russet Glade GU11 . . . . .99 C8
Russet Rd GU34 . . . . .140 A3
Russetts Dr GU51 . . . . .75 A8
Rustic Glen GU52 . . . . .74 F5
Ruth Cl GU14 . . . . .55 A5
Rutherford Cl RG20 . . . . .21 D5
Rutherford Rd RG24 . . . . .69 D8
Rutland Cl GU11 . . . . .76 E3
Ryan Mount GU47 . . . . .34 E8
Rycroft Mdw RG22 . . . . .91 A4
Rydal Cl Basingstoke RG22 . . . .91 B6
Bordon GU35 . . . . .164 D5
Farnborough GU14 . . . . .55 B3
Rydal Dr
Crookham Village GU52 . . . . . . .74 E5
Thatcham RG19 . . . . .2 E3
Ryde Ct 10 GU11 . . . . .77 A1
Ryde Gdns GU46 . . . . .33 F6
Rye Cl Farnborough GU14 . . . . .55 C7
Fleet GU51 . . . . .54 C5
Rye Croft 6 GU52 . . . . .74 E4
Ryecroft Gdns GU17 . . . . .35 C4
Ryeland Cl GU51 . . . . .54 C5
Ryes The GU52 . . . . .75 A5
Ryle Rd GU9 . . . . .121 F8
Ryon Cl SP10 . . . . .83 A4
Ryves Ave GU46 . . . . .33 E5

S

Sabre Ct 3 GU11 . . . . .76 C2
Saddleback Rd GU15 . . . . .36 C8
Saddleback Way GU51 . . . . . . .54 B4
Saddler Cnr GU47 . . . . .34 F7
Saddlers Cl SO21 . . . . .131 C4
Saddlers Ct RG14 . . . . .13 C4
Saddlers Scarp GU26 . . . . . . .166 E4
Saddlewood GU15 . . . . .36 A4
Saffron Cl Chineham RG24 . . . .49 A4
Newbury RG14 . . . . .1 D3
Saffron Ct 1 GU14 . . . . .55 A4
Sages La GU34 . . . . .204 D5
Sainfoin La RG23 . . . . .90 B8
Sainsbury Cl SP10 . . . . .105 B6
Saint Lucia Pk RG35 . . . . .164 E5
St Albans Rdbt GU14 . . . . .77 A8
St Alphege Gdns SP10 . . . . . . .82 F2
St Andrew's CE Inf Sch
GU9 . . . . .98 F2
St Andrew's Ct 4 GU9 . . . . . . .99 A2
St Andrew's Rd RG22 . . . . .68 D3
St Andrew's Way GU16 . . . . . . .56 D7
St Andrews Rd
Bordon GU35 . . . . .164 B2
North Tidworth SP9 . . . . .78 E6
St Ann's Cl SP10 . . . . .105 F7
St Anne's RC Prim Sch
RG22 . . . . .68 D3
St Annes Cl
Goodworth Clatford SP11 . . . . .106 A1
Winchester SO22 . . . . .209 A2
St Aubins Cl GU34 . . . . .160 B2
St Augustine's Cl GU12 . . . . . .77 B1
St Augustine's RC Prim Sch
GU12 . . . . .36 D2
St Barbara's Cl RG26 . . . . .29 B2
St Bartholomew Sch RG14 . . . .1 C1
St Bede CE Prim Sch
SO23 . . . . .209 E6
St Bede's Ct 8 SO23 . . . . . . .209 E7
St Bede's RC Prim Sch
RG24 . . . . .48 B1
St Benedict's Convent Sch
SP11 . . . . .82 A3
St Benedicts Cl GU11 . . . . .76 D2
St Bernadette RC Prim Sch
GU14 . . . . .55 E5
St Birinus Gdns SP10 . . . . .82 F3
St Birstan Gdns SP10 . . . . .82 F2
St Catherine's Hill RG7 . . . . . .11 C6
St Catherine's Rd SO23 . . . . .209 F4
St Catherines Rd
Camberley GU16 . . . . .56 E8
Frimley GU16 . . . . .36 D1
St Catherines Wood
GU15 . . . . .36 A4
St Christopher's Gn
GU27 . . . . .189 E6
St Christopher's Rd
Farnborough GU14 . . . . .55 E3
Haslemere GU27 . . . . .189 E6
St Christophers Cl
Aldershot GU12 . . . . .77 B2
Basingstoke RG22 . . . . .68 C3
Haslemere GU27 . . . . .189 E6
St Christophers Pl GU14 . . . . . .55 D3
St Christophers Rd GU14 . . . . .55 D3
St Clement St 2 SO23 . . . . . . .209 D3
St Clements Cl GU14 . . . . .55 F7
St Cross Ct 3 SO23 . . . . .209 D3
St Cross Hospl* SO22 . . . . . .209 D2
St Cross Mede SO23 . . . . . . .209 C2
St Cross Rd
Camberley GU16 . . . . .56 F7
Crondall GU10 . . . . .97 D5
Farnham GU9 . . . . .99 A3
Winchester SO23 . . . . .209 D3
St David's Cl
Farnborough GU14 . . . . .55 D8
Farnham GU9 . . . . .99 C7
St David's Ct GU11 . . . . .76 F1
St David's Rd
Basingstoke RG22 . . . . .68 E3
Newbury RG14 . . . . .1 E4
St Davids Cl RG29 . . . . .72 C2
St Donats Pl RG14 . . . . .1 E2
St Edmund's Sch GU26 . . . . . .167 B3
St Faith Cl GU34 . . . . .160 B2
St Faith's CE Prim Sch
SO23 . . . . .209 D3
St Faith's Rd SO23 . . . . .209 D3
St Gabriel's Sch RG20 . . . . . . .25 F5
St Gabriel's Ct GU11 . . . . .76 E1
St Gabriels La RG24 . . . . .49 A3
St George's Ave RG14 . . . . .1 C2
St George's Cl GU9 . . . . .99 F6
St George's Cl SP9 . . . . .78 E5
St George's Ho 16 SO23 . . . .209 E6
St George's Rd
Aldershot GU11 . . . . .76 F1
Camberley GU15 . . . . .36 B6
Farnham GU9 . . . . .99 B1
St George's Rd E GU12 . . . . . .76 F1
St Georges Ave SP9 . . . . .78 E5
St Georges Cl SO23 . . . . .209 E6
St Georges Ind Est GU15 . . . . .35 F3
St Georges Mews GU9 . . . . . . .99 A3
St Georges Rd
Farnham GU9 . . . . .99 F5
North Tidworth SP9 . . . . .78 E6
St Georges Yd GU9 . . . . .99 A2
St Giles Cl SO23 . . . . .209 F5
St Giles Hill SO23 . . . . .209 F5
St Helens Cres GU47 . . . . .34 F8

St Hubert Rd SP10 . . . . .105 E7
St James Cl RG26 . . . . .29 B1
St James Ct Farnham GU9 . . . .99 A3
Fleet GU51 . . . . .74 F8
St James Rd
Finchampstead RG40 . . . . .16 C8
Fleet GU51 . . . . .74 F8
St James' Ave GU9 . . . . .99 A3
St James' La SO22,SO23 . . . .209 D5
St James' Terr
Farnham GU9 . . . . .99 A3
Winchester SO22,SO23 . . . . . .209 D5
St James' Villas SO23 . . . . . .209 D5
St John Cl RG26 . . . . .29 A2
St John the Baptist RC Prim
Sch SP10 . . . . .105 D7
St John the Evangelist CE Inf
Sch RG14 . . . . .1 D1
St John's CE Inf Sch
GU10 . . . . .144 C1
St John's CE Prim Sch
RG21 . . . . .69 A3
St John's Cotts RG27 . . . . .71 E8
St John's Cross SP11 . . . . . . .105 A2
St John's Ctr
Farnborough GU14 . . . . .55 B5
12 Petersfield GU31 . . . . .54 A1
St John's Gdns 1 RG14 . . . . . . .1 D1
St John's Hospital
(Almshouses)(N) **1**
SO23 . . . . .209 F5
St John's Hospital
(Almshouses)(S) **3**
SO23 . . . . .209 F5
St John's Piece RG23 . . . . .90 B8
St John's Rd
Andover SP10 . . . . .106 B8
Farnborough GU14 . . . . .55 C5
Farnham GU9 . . . . .121 F8
Mortimer RG7 . . . . .11 E5
Newbury RG14 . . . . .1 E1
Oakley RG23 . . . . .67 C2
Sandhurst GU47 . . . . .34 F7
Winchester SO23 . . . . .209 F6
St John's St SO23 . . . . .209 F5
St Johns Cl RG21 . . . . .51 B1
St Johns Gr GU9 . . . . .121 F8
St Johns Rd RG27 . . . . .25 D6
St Joseph's Cres RG24 . . . . . . .48 F2
St Joseph's RC Prim Sch
RG14 . . . . .1 E4
St Joseph's Rd GU12 . . . . .76 E1
St Josephs Ct RG14 . . . . .1 F4
St Josephs RC Prim Sch
GU11 . . . . .99 E8
St Just Cl SP4 . . . . .123 B5
St Lawrence CE Prim Sch
GU34 . . . . .139 F4
St Lawrence Rd GU34 . . . . . . .139 F4
St Leger Ct RG41 . . . . .1 C4
St Leonard's Ave RG24 . . . . . . .49 A3
St Leonard's Rd SO23 . . . . . .198 C6
St Leonards Cl SO21 . . . . .153 C4
St Lukes Cl RG22 . . . . .68 C3
St Margarets SP11 . . . . .81 E8
St Mark's CE Prim Sch
Basingstoke RG22 . . . . .91 B6
Farnborough GU14 . . . . .77 B8
St Marks Cl Bramley RG26 . . . .29 A2
Farnborough GU14 . . . . .56 A1
St Martin's Cl SO23 . . . . .209 F6
St Martin's East Woodhay CE
Prim Sch RG20 . . . . .20 E7
St Martins Trad Pk
SO23 . . . . .209 D5
St Mary Bourne Prim Sch
SP11 . . . . .61 F2
St Mary Magdalen
Almshouses **2** SO23 . . . . . . .209 F5
St Mary St SO22 . . . . .209 B3
St Mary's Almshouses 13
RG14 . . . . .1 D2
St Mary's Ave RG26 . . . . .10 A4
St Mary's CE Inf Sch
GU10 . . . . .144 B7
St Mary's CE Jun Sch
Old Basing RG24 . . . . .70 B6
Stratfield Mortimer RG7 . . . . . . .12 B5
St Mary's Cl
Kings Worthy SO23 . . . . .176 C5
Old Basing RG24 . . . . .70 B6
St Mary's Cotts GU10 . . . . . . .144 A7
St Mary's Ct
Basingstoke RG21 . . . . .69 C5
Bramley RG26 . . . . .29 B2
1 Newbury RG14 . . . . .1 D2
St Mary's Mdw SP11 . . . . .105 A4
St Mary's Pl Farnham GU9 . . . .99 A3
Newbury RG14 . . . . .1 E4
St Mary's Rd
Ash Vale GU12 . . . . .77 E5
Camberley GU15 . . . . .36 A6
Hartley Wintney RG27 . . . . .52 C5
Kingsclere RG20 . . . . .24 D2
Liss GU33 . . . . .207 F4
Mortimer RG7 . . . . .11 E5
Newbury RG14 . . . . .1 D2
St Marys Bentworth CE Prim
Sch GU34 . . . . .138 B5
St Marys Cl Alton GU34 . . . . .139 F3
Sandhurst GU47 . . . . .35 A8
St Mathews Rd SO23 . . . . . . .209 F5
St Matthew's CE Prim Sch
GU33 . . . . .186 A8
St Michael's CE Inf Sch
GU11 . . . . .99 E8

St Michael's CE Jun Sch
GU11 . . . . .100 A8
St Michael's CE Prim Sch
GU47 . . . . .34 D8
St Michael's Rd 2 RG25 . . . . . .89 E1
St Michael's Gdns 8
SO23 . . . . .209 D5
St Michael's Hall GU11 . . . . . . .99 F8
St Michael's Pas SO23 . . . . . .209 E4
St Michael's Pl 2 GU15 . . . . . . .35 F5
St Michael's Rd
Aldershot GU11 . . . . .76 F1
Basingstoke RG22 . . . . .68 C3
Farnborough GU14 . . . . .55 F6
Newbury RG14 . . . . .1 E4
Sandhurst GU47 . . . . .34 D8
Winchester SO23 . . . . .209 D5
St Michael's Sch RG20 . . . . . . .22 D6
St Michaels Ave SP9 . . . . .78 E5
St Michaels Cl GU51 . . . . .75 C8
St Michaels Gn SP9 . . . . .78 E5
St Michaels Rd GU15 . . . . .35 F5
St Michaels View SP9 . . . . . . .78 E7
St Neot's Rd RG27 . . . . .32 D8
St Neot's Sch RG27 . . . . .32 C8
St Nicholas Cl Fleet GU51 . . . .53 F1
Ludgershall SP11 . . . . .57 B2
St Nicholas Ct RG14 . . . . .1 D2
St Nicholas Rd RG14 . . . . .1 D2
St Nicholas Rise 3 SO23 . . . .176 B6
St Nicholas Sch GU52 . . . . . . .74 E2
St Nicholas' Rd RG14 . . . . .1 D2
St Nicolas CE Jun Sch
RG14 . . . . .1 E1
St Patrick's La GU33 . . . . .208 D5
St Patrick's RC Prim Sch
GU14 . . . . .54 F2
St Patrick's Rd RG22 . . . . .68 E3
St Patricks Ave SP9 . . . . .78 E5
St Paul's CE Inf Sch
GU11 . . . . .100 E7
St Paul's Hill SO22 . . . . .209 D6
St Paul's Rd RG22 . . . . .68 E3
St Pauls Cl GU10 . . . . .100 D7
St Pauls Ct 15 SO22 . . . . .209 D6
St Pauls Pl RG22 . . . . .209 D6
St Peter St SO23 . . . . .209 E6
St Peter's CE Jun Sch
Farnborough GU14 . . . . .56 A4
Yateley GU46 . . . . .34 C6
St Peter's CE Prim Sch
Appleshaw SP11 . . . . .81 B7
Farnham GU9 . . . . .121 E6
St Peter's Cl RG7 . . . . .8 C5
St Peter's Ct
Goodworth Clatford SP11 . . . . .106 B2
Tadley RG26 . . . . .26 F7
St Peter's Gdns
Farnham GU10 . . . . .121 D6
Yateley GU46 . . . . .34 B6
St Peter's RC Prim Sch
SO22 . . . . .197 B5
St Peter's Rd RG22 . . . . .68 D4
St Peter's Way GU16 . . . . .56 D7
St Peters Cl Headley RG19 . . . . .7 B1
Shipton Bellinger SP9 . . . . .101 E7
St Peters Mead GU12 . . . . . . .77 F2
St Peters Pk GU11 . . . . .99 C8
St Philips Ct 3 GU51 . . . . .54 A2
St Polycarp's RC Prim Sch
GU9 . . . . .99 B1
St Richards Rd RG14 . . . . .1 F5
St Stephen's Cl RG27 . . . . .71 B5
St Stephen's Rd SO22 . . . . . .209 B8
St Stephens Cl GU27 . . . . . . .189 D6
St Swithin Way SP10 . . . . .82 F2
St Swithun St SO23 . . . . .209 D3
St Swithun's Sch SO21 . . . . .198 D8
St Swithun's Sch GU14 . . . . . . .1 D2
St Thomas Cl SP10 . . . . .82 E3
St Thomas Mews 3
SO23 . . . . .209 D5
St Thomas SO23 . . . . .209 D5
St Thomas' CE Inf Sch
RG20 . . . . .21 B8
St Thomas Cl RG21 . . . . .69 A4
Salamander Ct 8 SP9 . . . . . . .78 F7
Salcombe Rd RG14 . . . . .1 C1
Salcot Rd SO23 . . . . .209 E8
Salerno Cl GU11 . . . . .76 E2
Sales Ct 3 GU34 . . . . .139 E6
Salesian Gdns GU14 . . . . .56 B1
Salesian View GU14 . . . . .77 C8
Salisbury Cl Alton GU34 . . . . .140 A2
Odiham RG29 . . . . .72 F2
Salisbury Gdns RG22 . . . . .68 E3
Salisbury Gr GU16 . . . . .56 E3
Salisbury Ho 1 SO20 . . . . . . .147 C8
Salisbury Rd
Abbotts Ann SP11 . . . . .105 B3
Andover SP10 . . . . .105 E6
Ash GU12 . . . . .77 E2
Blackwater GU17 . . . . .35 A5
Broughton SO20 . . . . .169 F8
Farnborough GU14 . . . . .56 A3
New Alresford SO24 . . . . .179 D5
Over Wallop SP11 . . . . .124 F6
Shipton Bellinger SP9 . . . . .101 E6
Salisbury Terr GU16 . . . . .56 E3
Salmon Rd GU12 . . . . .77 A3
Salmond Rd SP11 . . . . .57 A2
Salmons Rd RG29 . . . . .72 C2
Salters Gardens GU14 . . . . .1 D2
Salters Heath Rd RG26 . . . . . . .47 B7
Salters La SO22 . . . . .175 B2

Saltram Rd GU14 . . . . .56 C2
Sam Whites Hill SP11 . . .105 E4
Samarkand Cl GU15 . . . . .36 F4
Sampson Bsns Pk GU15 . .35 F3
Sampson's Almshouses **3**
GU9 .98 E1
Samuel Cody Ho GU12 . . .77 D7
Samuel Cody Sch The
GU14 . . . . .76 F7
San Carlos App GU11 . . . .77 A2
Sand Hill GU14 . . . . .55 F7
Sand Hill Ct GU14 . . . . . . .55 F7
Sandbanks Dr RG22 . . . . .91 B7
Sandford Cl RG20 . . . . . . .24 F2
Sandford Ct GU11 . . . . . . .76 D1
Sandford Ho RG20 . . . . . .24 F4
Sandford Rd
Aldershot GU11 . . . . .76 D1
Farnham GU9 . . . . .98 F7
Tadley RG26 . . . . .26 E8
Sandham Meml Chapel*
RG20 . . . . .22 C6
Sandheath Rd GU26 . . . .167 A7
Sandhurst GU10 . . . . . . .100 A4
Sandhurst La GU17 . . . . . .34 F6
Sandhurst Rd
Finchampstead RG40 . . . . .16 F8
Sandhurst GU46 . . . . .34 D7
Sandhurst Royal Military
Acad GU15 . . . . .35 E7
Sandhurst Sch GU47 . . . . .35 B8
Sandhurst Sta GU47 . . . . .34 E7
Sandleford Lodge Pk
RG19 . . . . .5 F6
Sandown Cl Alton GU34 . .140 A2
Blackwater GU17 . . . . .35 B5
Sandown Cres GU11 . . . . .99 F7
Sandown Dr GU16 . . . . . . .36 C2
Sandown Way RG14 . . . . . .2 A1
Sandpiper Way RG22 . . . . .90 F7
Sandpit Cotts GU10 . . . . .75 B1
Sandpit Hill RG20 . . . . .5 A4
Sandpit La RG7 . . . . .14 F5
Sandringham Cl GU34 . . .139 D3
Sandringham Ct RG22 . . . .68 D3
Sandringham Ho **5**
SP10 . . . . .83 A3
Sandringham Sch GU16 . .56 D7
Sandringham Way GU16 . .56 D7
Sandrock Hill Rd GU10 . .121 E5
Sands Cl GU10 . . . . .100 C2
Sands Rd GU10 . . . . .100 B2
Sands The GU35 . . . . .164 A2
Sandy Cross GU10 . . . . . .100 D4
Sandy Hill Rd GU9 . . . . . . .98 F7
Sandy La Camberley GU15 . .36 C6
Farnborough GU14 . . . . . . .55 B7
Fleet GU52 . . . . .75 B4
Hartley Wintney RG27 . . . .52 D5
Haslemere,Nutcombe
GU26 . . . . .167 D2
Haslemere,Woolmer Hill
GU27 . . . . .189 A7
Rake GU33 . . . . .208 E4
Rushmoor GU10 . . . . .144 F5
Shortfield Common GU10 .122 A1
Tadley RG26 . . . . .27 B7
Sandydown Cotts SO20 . .150 F3
Sandys Cl RG22 . . . . .68 E3
Sandys Rd RG22 . . . . .68 E3
Sandys Road Rdbt RG22 . .68 E4
Sankey La GU51 . . . . .54 D4
Santina Cl GU9 . . . . .99 B8
Saor Mews **3** SP10 . . .105 F8
Sapley La RG25 . . . . .88 A7
Sarah Way GU14 . . . . .55 F4
Sarisbury Cl RG26 . . . . . . .26 E8
Sarson Cl SP11 . . . . .104 B6
Sarson La Amport SP11 . .104 B7
Weyhill SP11 . . . . .104 C5
Sarsons Barns SP11 . . . .104 C5
Sarum Cl
Over Wallop SO20 . . . . . .147 D8
Shipton Bellinger SP9 . . .101 D8
Winchester SO22 . . . . . . .209 A5
Sarum Ct SO22 . . . . .209 B5
Sarum Hill RG21 . . . . . . .209 A6
Sarum Ho **6** SP10 . . . .106 A7
Sarum Rd
Pamber Heath RG26 . . . . . .9 E1
Winchester SO22 . . . . . . .197 B7
SO22 . . . . .209 A5
Sarum Road Hospl
SO22 . . . . .209 A5
Sarum View SO22 . . . . . .197 B7
Saturn Ho **9** RG7 . . . . . .9 C2
Saunders Gdns **7** RG26 . .26 F8
Saunders Gdns GU14 . . . .55 E6
Savernake Ho **3** SP9 . . .78 F6
Savile Cres GU35 . . . . . . .164 D3
Saville Gdns GU15 . . . . . .36 F5
Savoy Cl SP10 . . . . .106 B7
Savoy Ct GU15 . . . . .36 A5
Savoy Rd GU17 . . . . .35 B3
Sawyer Cl SO22 . . . . .175 B1
Sawyers Ley RG7 . . . . .12 B8
Saxon Croft GU9 . . . . .99 A1
Saxon Cl **3** Andover SP10 . .83 A3
North Tidworth SP9 . . . . . .78 F6
Thatcham RG19 . . . . .2 E3
17 Winchester SO23 . . .209 E6
Saxon Ho **2** GU34 . . . .139 F3
Saxon Leas SP5 . . . . .168 B6
Saxon Mews **2** GU34 . .139 F3
Saxon Rd SO23 . . . . .209 E7
Saxon Way Andover SP10 . .82 F3

Saxon Way continued
Old Basing RG24 . . . . .69 F7
Saxon Wood Sch RG24 . . .68 B8
Saxony Cres SO21 . . . . . .174 B4
Saxony Way GU46 . . . . . . .34 A4
Sayers Cl Camberley GU16 . .56 C7
Newbury RG14 . . . . .5 F8
Sbac TK GU11 . . . . .76 C6
Scamblers Mead SP11 . . .81 F3
Scarlatti Rd RG22 . . . . . . .91 F8
Scarlet Oaks GU15 . . . . . .36 C3
Scarlett's Rd GU11 . . . . . .76 B3
School Cl SP11 . . . . .38 C5
School Fields GU35 . . . . .142 B1
School Hill
Farnham GU10 . . . . .121 D6
Seale GU10 . . . . .100 F4
School La Bentley GU10 .120 B5
Bishop's Sutton SO24 . . . .180 B4
Broughton SO20 . . . . .170 B7
Ewshot GU10 . . . . .98 B8
Farnham GU10 . . . . .122 B6
Itchen Abbas SO21 . . . . . .177 F7
Kings Worthy SO23 . . . . . .176 B4
3 Liss GU33 . . . . .207 F4
Middle Wallop SO20 . . . . .147 F8
Riseley RG7 . . . . .14 C3
Ropley SO24 . . . . .181 C4
Silchester RG7 . . . . .10 F1
Yateley GU46 . . . . .33 F6
School Lane Cotts SO20 .147 F8
School Rd Bordon GU35 . .164 D4
Grayshott GU26 . . . . .166 F4
Haslemere GU27 . . . . .189 D5
Riseley RG7 . . . . .14 C1
Rowledge GU10 . . . . .121 C3
Schroeder Cl RG21 . . . . . .69 A2
Schubert Rd RG22 . . . . . .91 E8
Scotland Cl GU12 . . . . . . .77 E5
Scotland Farm Rd GU12 . .77 E5
Scotland Hill GU47 . . . . . .34 E8
Scotland La GU27 . . . . . .189 F5
Scotlands Cl GU27 . . . . . .189 F5
Scotlands Dr GU27 . . . . .189 F5
Scotney Rd RG21 . . . . .69 B7
Scots Ct RG27 . . . . .51 C4
Scott Cl Andover SP10 . . . .83 E1
King's Somborne SO20 . . .172 A2
Scott's Ct GU14 . . . . .55 F7
Scrubbs La SO24 . . . . . . .180 A3
Scures Rd RG24 . . . . .49 A7
Scylla Ind Est SO23 . . . . .198 C8
Seafire Way GU11 . . . . . . .76 C7
Seagull Cl RG22 . . . . .90 F8
Seal Rd RG21 . . . . .69 B5
Seale La GU10 . . . . .100 D4
Searing Way RG26 . . . . . . .9 E1
Searl's La Hook RG27 . . . . .51 B4
Hook RG27 . . . . .51 C2
Searle Rd GU9 . . . . .122 A8
Searles Cl SO24 . . . . .179 D5
Sebastopol Rd GU11 . . . . .76 F2
Second Ave GU14 . . . . .10 A2
Second St E RG19 . . . . .6 E5
Second St W RG19 . . . . . . .6 E4
Sedgefield Rd RG14 . . . . . .6 A8
Sedgemoor GU14 . . . . .55 F7
Seebys Oak GU47 . . . . . . .35 B6
Seevour's Ct RG26 . . . . . . .86 C5
Sefton Hi **11** GU11 . . . . .76 E2
Sek Kong Cl SO20 . . . . . .126 A4
Selborne Ave GU11 . . . . .100 A6
Selborne CE Prim Sch
GU34 . . . . .184 D8
Selborne Cl
Blackwater GU17 . . . . .35 A6
Hook RG27 . . . . .51 B1
Selborne Gdns GU34 . . . .121 E8
Selborne Pl SO22 . . . . . . .209 B3
Selborne Rd Alton GU34 . .139 C1
Hartley Mauditt GU34 . . . .162 D5
Selborne Way GU35 . . . . .164 A2
Selborne Wlk RG26 . . . . . .26 F8
Seldon Cl SO22 . . . . .48 B1
Seldon Cl SO22 . . . . .197 B4
Selwyn Dr GU46 . . . . .33 F6
Sepen Meade **8** GU52 . .74 E4
Seremban Cl SO20 . . . . .126 A5
Sermon Rd SO22 . . . . . . .209 A7
Seton Dr RG27 . . . . .71 F8
Sett The GU46 . . . . .33 F5
Seventh St RG19 . . . . .6 D5
Severals The RG24 . . . . . .47 E3
Severn Cl Sandhurst GU47 . .35 A8
Thatcham RG18 . . . . .2 F5
Severn Ct SO17 . . . . .83 C2
Severn Gdns RG23 . . . . . .67 B1
Severn Rd GU14 . . . . .55 C6
Severn Way **21** RG26 . . . .69 D5
Seville Cres SP10 . . . . . . .83 C1
Seymour Ct GU51 . . . . . . .54 A2
Seymour Dr GU15 . . . . . . .36 F8
Seymour Pl RG29 . . . . .72 E3
Seymour Rd
Basingstoke RG22 . . . . . . .68 C2
Headley GU35 . . . . .166 A4
Shackleton Cl GU12 . . . . .77 D6
Shackleton Sq **11** SP10 . .83 C2
Shady Nook GU9 . . . . .98 F6
Shafer Ct RG14 . . . . .1 E1
Shaftesbury Ct
3 Bordon GU35 . . . . . .164 D2
Farnborough GU14 . . . . . . .77 A8
Shaftesbury Mount **1** GU17 . .34 F4
Shakespeare Ave SP10 . . .82 D1
Shakespeare Gdns GU14 . .55 B5
Shakespeare Rd GU9 . . . .69 C8

Shalbourne Rise GU15 . . .36 B5
Shalden La GU34 . . . . . . .138 F7
Shalden Rd GU12 . . . . . . .100 B8
Shaldon Way GU51 . . . . . .74 D8
Shamrock Cl GU16 . . . . . .56 B8
Shanklin Ct GU12 . . . . .77 A1
Shannon Ct **3** SP10 . . . . .83 C2
Shapley Heath RG27 . . . . .52 B2
Shapley Hill GU12 . . . . . . .52 C2
Shapley Hill RG27 . . . . . . .52 C2
Shapley Ho RG27 . . . . .52 A3
Shaw Cl SP10 . . . . .105 C8
Shaw Farm Rd RG14 . . . . . .1 F6
Shaw Hill RG14 . . . . .1 F5
Shaw Ho SP11 . . . . .81 B6
Shaw La RG26 . . . . .26 D7
Shaw Mill RG14 . . . . .1 F5
Shaw Pightle RG27 . . . . . .50 F1
Shaw Rd RG14 . . . . .1 F4
Shaw-cum-Donnington CE
Prim Sch RG14 . . . . .1 E6
Shawfield La GU12 . . . . . .77 D2
Shawfield Prim Sch
GU12 . . . . .77 E3
Sheddon Pl SO21 . . . . . . .174 D2
Sheep Dro SO20 . . . . . . .147 D4
Sheep Fair SP10 . . . . .106 C7
Sheep Fair Ct SP10 . . . . .106 C8
Sheephatch La GU10 . . . .122 F5
Sheephouse GU9 . . . . . . .122 A8
Sheepmoor Dr GU51 . . . . .53 F3
Sheepwash La
Burghclere RG20 . . . . .5 E2
Ramsdell RG26 . . . . .46 D7
Sheerlands Rd RG2,RG40 . .15 C4
Sheffield Cl GU14 . . . . . . .55 D4
Shefford Lodge **6** RG14 . . .1 E2
Sheldon's Ca RG27 . . . . . .51 A1
Sheldon's Rd RG27 . . . . . .51 A1
Shell La GU14 . . . . .183 B2
Shelley Cl
Basingstoke RG24 . . . . . . .69 C8
Fleet GU51 . . . . .75 A8
Itchen Abbas SO21 . . . . . .177 E6
Winchester SO22 . . . . . . .209 B6
Shelley Ct GU15 . . . . .36 A5
Shelley Rise GU14 . . . . . . .55 D6
Shelleys La GU34 . . . . . . .140 F1
Shenstone Cl RG40 . . . . . .16 E8
Shepherd & Flock Rdbt
GU9 . . . . .99 C4
Shepherd Lodge SP10 . . . .83 A1
Shepherds Cl SP10 . . . . . .83 A1
Shepherds Cl GU9 . . . . . .122 A8
Shepherds Down SO24 . .179 C4
Shepherds Rd SO23 . . . .198 C8
Shepherds Rise SP10 . . . .38 C6
Shepherds Row SP10 . . . .106 C7
Shepherds Spring Inf Sch
SP10 . . . . .83 B3
Shepherds Spring Jun Sch
SP10 . . . . .83 B3
Shepherds Spring La
SP10 . . . . .83 B1
Shepherds Way GU30 . . .188 B3
Shepherds Wlk GU14 . . . .55 C7
Sheppard Almshouses
SP11 . . . . .104 A5
Sheppard Cl RG28 . . . . . . .86 C4
Sheppard Rd RG21 . . . . . .69 A2
Sheppard Sq **3** SP10 . . .83 C2
Sheraton Ave RG22 . . . . . .91 B2
Sheraton Cl GU17 . . . . . . .35 C4
Sherborne Rd
Basingstoke RG21 . . . . . . .69 A7
Sherborne St John RG24 . .47 F1
Sherborne St John CE Prim
Sch RG24 . . . . .47 E3
Sherbrooke Cl SO23 . . . .176 C8
Sherfield Rd RG26 . . . . . . .29 B2
Sherfield St RG27 . . . . . . .49 E6
Sheridan Cl
Aldershot GU11 . . . . .99 E8
Winchester SO22 . . . . . . .209 A3
Sheridan Cres RG26 . . . . . .9 C1
Sheridan Ct
Camberley GU15 . . . . .56 B8
Newbury RG14 . . . . .2 A3
Sheridan Rd GU16 . . . . . . .56 B8
Sherington Cl GU14 . . . . .55 F6
Sherlock Lea RG27 . . . . . .33 C7
Sherrardmead RG14 . . . . . .1 F7
Sherrington Way RG22 . . .68 F2
Sherwin Cres GU14 . . . . . .55 F8
Sherwood Cl
Basingstoke RG22 . . . . . . .91 C6
Liss GU33 . . . . .208 A7
Sherwood Terr GU34 . . . .140 A3
Shetland Rd RG24 . . . . . . .48 D1
Shetland Way GU51 . . . . . .54 B4
Ship Alley GU14 . . . . .56 A6
Ship La GU14 . . . . .56 A6
Shipley Cl GU34 . . . . .140 A5
Shipley Ct **1** GU30 . . . .188 A3
Shipton Bellinger Prim Sch
SP9 . . . . .101 D8
Shipton Way RG22 . . . . . . .68 C2
Shire Ave GU51 . . . . .54 C4
Shire Ct **2** GU51 . . . . . . .76 C2
Shires Way GU46 . . . . .34 B2
Shoddesden La SP11 . . . . .80 C7
Shoe La GU11,GU14 . . . . .76 E6
Shooters Way RG21 . . . . . .69 C6
Shop La RG14 . . . . .1 C7
Short La SP11 . . . . .82 A1
Short St Aldershot GU12 . .76 E2
Ludgershall SP11 . . . . .57 A2
Shortdale Rd GU11 . . . . . .100 A6

Shortfield Rd GU10 . . . . .122 A1
Shortheath Crest GU9 . . .121 D6
Shortheath Rd GU9 . . . . .121 E6
Shortwood Copse La
RG23 . . . . .90 F5
Shotter's La GU34 . . . . . .183 F6
Shottermill Inf Sch
GU27 . . . . .189 D7
Shottermill Jun Sch
GU27 . . . . .189 D7
Shottermill Pk GU27 . . . .189 C7
Shottermill Rd GU27 . . . .189 C5
Shrave The GU14 . . . . . . .160 E4
Shrewsbury Terr RG14 . . . .1 D1
Shrivenham Cl GU47 . . . . .35 B8
Shrubbery The GU14 . . . . .55 B3
Shrubs La GU10 . . . . .121 D4
Shyshack La RG26 . . . . .9 D1
Sian Cl GU52 . . . . .75 B5
Sibelius Cl RG22 . . . . .91 E7
Sickle Mill Cl GU27 . . . . .189 D6
Sickle Rd GU27 . . . . .189 D5
Sickles La GU35 . . . . .142 B2
Sidbury Circular Rd SP9 . .78 C7
Sidbury Hill Ave SP9 . . . . .78 E8
Sidestrand Rd
Farnborough GU11 . . . . . . .76 C7
Newbury RG14 . . . . .5 C7
Sidings The GU11 . . . . . . .77 A3
Sidlaw Cl RG22 . . . . .68 A3
Sidlaws Rd GU14 . . . . .55 A2
Sidmouth Rd SP10 . . . . . .106 C8
Silchester CE Prim Sch
RG7 . . . . .10 F1
Silchester Cl SP10 . . . . . .82 E2
Silchester Dr **3** GU51 . . . .53 D3
Silchester Pl **11** SO23 . . .209 E7
Silchester Rd
Bramley RG26 . . . . .28 C3
Little London RG26 . . . . . . .27 E4
Pamber Heath RG7,RG26 . .10 D2
Silk Mill La RG25 . . . . .87 F8
Silkstead La SO21,SO22 .197 A1
Silkweavers Rd SP10 . . . .106 B8
Silver Birch Ct GU52 . . . . .74 F5
Silver Birch Rd SP10 . . . . .82 E1
Silver Hill Sandhurst GU47 . .35 C8
Winchester SO23 . . . . . . .209 E5
Silver La RG7 . . . . .10 F8
Silver Park Cl GU52 . . . . . .75 B6
Silverdale GU52 . . . . .75 A6
Silverdale Rd RG26 . . . . . . .9 F1
Silverglades GU46 . . . . . . .34 A4
Silverwood Cl GU52 . . . . .209 B3
Silverwood Dr GU15 . . . . .36 E7
Silvester Cl RG21 . . . . .69 C7
Silvester Way GU52 . . . . . .74 F4
Silwood Ct SO22 . . . . . . .209 C7
Simmondstone La GU10 .144 B2
Simmons Wlk **27** RG21 . . .69 D5
Simms Farm La RG7 . . . . .11 D5
Simonds Ct **3** SO23 . . . . .209 B8
Simons Cl RG22 . . . . .48 F2
Simons Rd RG24 . . . . .48 F2
Sims Cl RG26 . . . . .29 B2
Sine Ct SP11 . . . . .55 F8
Sinhurst Rd GU15 . . . . . . .35 F4
Sixth Form Coll Farnborough
GU14 . . . . .55 F6
Sixth St RG19 . . . . .6 E5
Skates La RG26 . . . . .27 B5
Skew Rd SP11 . . . . .103 B3
Skinners Green La RG14 . .16 A7
Skippetts La E RG21 . . . . .69 C2
Skippetts La W RG21 . . . . .69 B2
Skippons Cl RG14 . . . . .5 A6
Skylark Cl RG22 . . . . .90 F6
Skylark Rise RG28 . . . . . . .86 B2
Skylings RG14 . . . . .2 A4
Slade Hill Gdns RG20 . . . . .4 D2
Slade The GU32 . . . . .205 F2
Sladen Cnr SP11 . . . . .61 F8
Sleeper's Hill SO22 . . . . .209 B4
Sleeper's Hill Ho SO22 . .209 B4
SO22 . . . . .209 C4
Sleepers Hill Gdns
SO22 . . . . .209 B4
Sleepy Hollow (Cvn Pk)
RG26 . . . . .27 B7
Slessor Cl SP11 . . . . .105 B7
Slim Cl GU11 . . . . .77 C7
Slim Rd GU15 . . . . .36 A7
Smallfield Dr RG27 . . . . . .51 C1
Smallridge RG26 . . . . .28 B1
Smannell & Enham CE Prim
Sch SP11 . . . . .83 E7
Smannell Rd SP10,SP11 . .83 D4
Smay Down La SN8 . . . . . .17 B3
Smeaton Ct RG14 . . . . .1 D4
Smeaton Rd SP10 . . . . . . .82 B1
Smith's Field RG25 . . . . . .88 B7
Smithfield La GU10,
GU35 . . . . .143 E1
Smiths Mead RG25 . . . . . .89 F1
Smithy Cl GU34 . . . . .140 D7
Smithy La GU10 . . . . .143 C2
Smithy Rd RG26 . . . . .28 F3
Smugglers La GU34 . . . . .182 A2
Smugglers' Way GU10 . . .100 C1
Snailing La GU33 . . . . . . .207 C8
Snailslynch GU9 . . . . .99 B2
Snipe La
Bishop's Green RG20 . . . . . .6 D2
Marley Heights GU27 . . . .189 E1

Snoddington Rd
Kimpton SP11 . . . . .80 E1
Shipton Bellinger SP11 . . .102 F8
Snode Hill GU34 . . . . .139 A3
Snowdon Rd GU14 . . . . . . .55 C7
Snowdrop Cl RG22 . . . . . . .91 A8
Snowdrop Wlk **2** GU32 . .205 F2
Soalwood La GU32 . . . . . .205 F1
Soame's La SO24 . . . . . . .181 E2
Sobers Sq **7** SP10 . . . . . .83 C2
Soke Hill GU34 . . . . .159 F1
Soke Rd RG7 . . . . .10 D3
Soke The SO24 . . . . .179 D6
Solartron Rd GU14 . . . . . . .55 F3
Solartron Retail Pk GU14 . .55 E3
Solby's Rd **3** RG21 . . . . . .69 A5
Soldridge Rd GU34 . . . . .159 F4
Solent Dr RG22 . . . . .91 B7
Somborne Park Rd
SO20 . . . . .172 D7
Somers Cl SO22 . . . . .209 B3
Somerset Ave GU35 . . . . .164 D3
Somerset Ct **3** GU14 . . . .56 A1
Somerset Ho RG22 . . . . . .68 D8
Somerset Rd GU14 . . . . . .56 A1
Somerville Cres GU46 . . . .34 C6
Somerville Rd SP10 . . . . . .83 D1
Somerville Rd SO23 . . . . .176 C8
Somme SP11 . . . . .79 D7
Sonning Cl RG22 . . . . .90 F7
Sonninge Cl GU47 . . . . . . .35 B8
Soper Gr RG21 . . . . .44 A4
Sopwith Cl SO20 . . . . . . .172 A2
Sopwith Pk SP10 . . . . .82 B1
Sorrel Cl
2 Farnborough GU14 . . . .55 A5
Newbury RG14 . . . . .2 B5
Sorrell's Cl GU24 . . . . .48 F3
Sotherington La GU33,
GU34 . . . . .185 C6
South Atlantic Dr GU11 . . .77 A3
South Ave GU10 . . . . .99 B6
South Cl SO24 . . . . .179 B5
South Dr Littleton SO22 . .175 B4
Sherfield on L RG27 . . . . . .49 D7
South Tidworth SP9 . . . . . .78 E4
South End Rd SP10 . . . . .106 B6
South Farnborough Inf Sch
GU14 . . . . .55 B3
South Farnborough Jun Sch
GU14 . . . . .99 B1
South Gr GU51 . . . . .54 C4
South Ham Rd RG22 . . . . .68 E4
South Hill GU25 . . . . .94 C5
South Hurst SO23 . . . . . .164 D1
South La GU12 . . . . .77 F1
South Rd Ash Vale GU12 . .77 E4
Broughton SO20 . . . . .170 C5
Kingsclere RG20 . . . . .24 E2
Liphook GU30 . . . . .188 B1
New Alresford SO24 . . . . .179 B5
South Ridge RG9 . . . . .72 E2
South Side GU10 . . . . . . .100 D7
South St Andover SP10 . .106 A7
Farnborough GU14 . . . . . . .56 C1
Farnham GU9 . . . . .99 A2
Ropley SO24 . . . . .181 C4
South Town Rd GU34 . . . .159 F6
South View SO22 . . . . . . .209 C6
South View Cl SO21 . . . . .131 D3
South View Cotts
Bentley GU10 . . . . .120 A4
Hook RG27 . . . . .72 A8
South View Gdns
Andover SP10 . . . . .106 B7
4 Newbury RG14 . . . . .1 F4
South View Jun Sch SP10 . .106 B7
South View Jun Sch
RG21 . . . . .69 C7
South View Park Homes
SO22 . . . . .209 A1
South View Rd SO22 . . . .197 B4
South View Terr SP11 . . . . .85 B8
South Way SP10 . . . . .83 E1
South Wlk GU12 . . . . .77 B2
South Wonston Prim Sch
SO21 . . . . .153 D4
Southampton Cl GU17 . . . .35 A6
Southampton St GU14 . . . .76 F8
Southbrook Cotts SO21 . .133 D3
Southbrook Pl SO21 . . . . .133 A3
Southby Dr GU51 . . . . .54 B1
Southcote Dr GU15 . . . . . .36 E5
Southdown Rd
Tadley RG26 . . . . .26 E8
Thatcham RG19 . . . . .2 D4
Southdowns SO24 . . . . . .157 C1
Southend Rd RG23 . . . . . .69 A5
Southern Haye RG27 . . . . .52 C5
Southern Rd
Basingstoke RG21 . . . . . . .69 B4
Bordon GU35 . . . . .164 D5
Camberley GU15 . . . . .36 A6
Southern Way
Farnborough GU14 . . . . . . .55 C3
Farnham GU9 . . . . .99 A1
Southgate St SO23 . . . . . .209 D5
Southgate Villas SO23 . . .209 D4
Southington Cl RG25 . . . . .87 F7
Southington La RG25 . . . . .87 F8
Southlands RG24 . . . . .48 E3
Southlands Cl GU12 . . . . . .77 E1
Southlands Ct GU12 . . . . . .77 E1
Southlands Rd GU12 . . . . .77 E1
Southlea RG25 . . . . .92 A8
Southmead Rd GU11 . . . . .99 F8

Southrope Gn RG25 ....116 C7
Southside Rd SP11 ....108 B4
Southview Cotts GU10 ....122 B1
Southview Rd GU35 ....165 F5
Southview Rise GU34 .....139 E5
Southwark Cl
  North Tidworth SP9 ......79 A6
  Yateley GU46 ....34 A6
Southway GU15 ....35 C4
Southwell Park Rd GU15 ..36 A5
Southwick Cl SO22 ....175 D4
Southwood Cres GU14 .....55 B4
Southwood Inf Sch GU14 ..55 B3
Southwood La
  Farnborough GU51 ....54 E3
  Farnborough,Southwood
  GU14 ....55 B3
Southwood Rd
  Farnborough GU14 ....55 C4
  Hawley GU17 ....34 D1
  Shalden GU34 ....139 B7
Sovereign Ct 8 GU51 .....53 F1
Sovereign Dr GU15 ....36 F7
Sowcroft La RG29 ....118 A5
Sovereign Rd GU19 ....6 A8
Spain La GU34 ....115 E3
Sparkford Cl SO22 ....209 C4
Sparkford Rd SO22 ....209 C5
Sparrowhawk Cl GU10 .....98 B8
Sparsholt CE Prim Sch
  SO21 ....174 D3
Sparsholt Coll Hampshire
  SO21 ....174 A4
Sparsholt Rd SO22 ....196 C3
Sparvell Way GU15 ....36 A6
Sparvells RG27 ....33 C8
Spats La GU35 ....165 D8
Spearywell Wood Woodland
  Wlk* SO51 ....192 C4
Speckled Wood Rd RG24 ..48 B1
Speen Hill Cl GU14 ....1 C4
Speen La RG14 ....1 B4
Speen Lodge Ct RG14 .....1 C4
Speen Pl RG14 ....1 B4
Speenhamland Ct 3 RG14 ..1 D4
Speenhamland Prim Sch
  RG14 ....1 D4
Spencer Cl
  Camberley GU16 ....56 C6
  Fleet GU52 ....75 C5
  Four Marks GU34 ....160 B3
  Pamber Heath RG26 ....10 C1
Spencer Rd RG14 ....5 B6
Spencers Ct GU35 ....164 D1
Spenser Cl GU34 ....140 A5
Sperrin Cl RG22 ....68 B3
Spey Ct 8 RG21 ....83 C2
Spicers GU34 ....140 A3
Spicers Ct 2 SO22 ......209 D6
Spiers Cl RG26 ....27 A8
Spiers La SO24 ....135 E3
Spindle Ho 1 SP10 ......106 B8
Spindlewood RG24 ....48 E4
Spinney Cvn Pk The
  SO24 ....179 C6
Spinney The
  Bramdean SO24 ....202 C5
  Finchampstead RG40 ......16 D8
  Fleet GU51 ....74 D8
  Grayshott GU26 ....166 E4
  Hook RG27 ....51 A2
  Yateley GU46 ....34 A4
Spitalfields Rd GU34 ....139 F4
Spitalhatch GU34 ....140 B4
Spitfire End 2 SO23 ....198 D8
Spitfire La SO20 ....148 F3
Spitfire Way GU14 ....76 C7
Spoil La GU10 ....100 D7
Spokane Cl GU11 ....99 D8
Sportsmans Ct 3 GU11 ....1 F7
Sprat's Hatch La RG27 ...73 E7
Spray Leaze SP11 ....57 B2
Spreadbury Dr GU51 ......53 F3
Sprents La RG25 ....88 B7
Spring Cl
  Sherborne St John RG24 ..47 D3
  Sherborne St John RG24 ..47 E4
Spring Gdns
  Enborne Row RG20 ....4 F3
  Farnborough GU14 ....55 E7
  Frimley GU15 ....36 E5
  New Alresford SO24 .....179 C4
Spring Hill La SP11 .....62 A2
Spring Ho 9 RG21 ....69 A4
Spring La
  Aldermaston RG7 ....10 A6
  Burghclere RG20 ....22 D5
  Farnham GU9 ....98 E7
  Mortimer RG7 ....11 E6
  Swallowfield RG7 ....13 F5
  Swallowfield,Stanford End
  RG7 ....13 E4
Spring La W GU9 ....98 E6
Spring Leaze SP11 ....61 C4
Spring Mews SP10 ....83 B1
Spring Way SO24 ....179 C4
Spring Woods GU52 ....74 F7
Springcross Ave GU17 ....35 B4
Springdale RG40 ....16 C8
Springfarm Rd GU27 .....189 F5
Springfield 2 Liss GU33 .207 F4
  Oakley RG23 ....67 C2
Springfield Ave RG27 ....52 C7
Springfield Cl SP10 ....106 D8
Springfield La Fleet GU51 .53 E1
  Newbury RG14 ....5 F8
Springfield Rd
  Ash Vale GU12 ....77 E5
Springfield Rd continued
  Frimley GU15 ....36 F5
  Pamber Heath RG26 ....10 C1
Springholm Cl GU9 ....99 F6
Springlakes Est GU12 ....77 C3
Springmead Ct GU27 .....189 B5
Springs The RG7 ....29 B8
Springvale Ave SO23 ....176 B6
Springvale Rd SO23 .....176 B7
Springwell La RG27 ......52 E8
Spruce Ave GU35 ....164 B3
Spruce Cl 1 Andover SP10 .105 C7
  South Wonston SO21 ....153 E4
Spruce Way GU51 ....54 D1
Spurs Ct 11 GU11 ....76 C2
Spybush La GU34 ....135 C2
Square Dr GU27 ....189 F1
Square The
  Bishop's Green RG20 ......6 E3
  3 Grayshott GU26 ......167 B3
  Greenham RG19 ....6 E4
  Hurstbourne Tarrant SP11 .60 D7
  Liphook GU30 ....187 F4
  Nether Wallop SO20 .....148 A6
  Rowledge GU10 ....121 C3
  Sutton Scotney SO21 ....131 C4
  Upper Froyle GU34 ......119 A2
  Winchester SO23 ....209 E5
Squarefield Gdns RG27 ...51 C2
Squires Ct GU15 ....36 A3
Squirrel Cl GU47 ....34 F8
Squirrel Dr RG23 ....90 F3
Squirrel La GU14 ....55 E5
Sqush Court Gate Rd
  GU14 ....55 F1
Stable Cl RG27 ....50 F1
Stable Ct RG14 ....1 E6
Stable Rd GU35 ....164 D6
Stable View GU46 ....34 B7
Stables Rd SP9 ....78 E4
Stables The RG26 ....29 C4
Staddlestones Cotts
  SP11 ....82 A4
Staff Coll GU15 ....36 A6
Staff College Rd GU15 ...35 F6
Staff Rd Aldershot GU12 ..77 A2
  Michelmersh SO51 ......193 B3
Stag Hill RG22 ....68 D2
Stag Oak La RG24 ....48 E4
Stainers La SO23 ....153 C4
Stake La GU14 ....55 E4
Stamford Ave GU16 ....36 D1
Stanbury Cl SP11 ....103 E8
Stanbury Rd SP11 ....106 B8
Stancomb Broad La
  GU34 ....159 C2
Stancombe La
  Medstead GU34 ....159 D3
  Shalden GU34 ....117 D1
Standford Hill GU35 ....165 A1
Standford La GU35 ......165 A3
Standing Hill SP5 ......190 F8
Stanfield RG26 ....9 F1
Stanford Rd RG22 ....91 C8
Stanham Cl SO21 ....153 D2
Stanhope Rd GU15 ....35 D4
Stanley Dr GU14 ....55 A3
Stanley Rd RG14 ....1 F2
Stanmore Gdns RG7 ......11 D5
Stanmore La SO22 ......209 B3
Stanmore Prim Sch
  SO22 ....209 C3
Stanton Dr GU51 ....74 E8
Staple Gdns 31 SO23 ...209 D6
Stapleton Cl RG14 ....5 A6
Stapley La SO34 ....181 D2
Star Hill Churt GU10 ...144 B2
  Hartley Wintney RG27 ....32 F1
Star Hill Dr GU10 ....144 B3
Star La Ash GU12 ....77 D2
  Highclere RG20 ....21 D6
Star Post Rd GU15 ....36 D8
Starling Cl RG22 ....90 F8
Starting Gates RG14 ......2 A1
Statham Sq SP11 ....83 C3
Station App
  Andover SP10 ....105 F8
  Ash Vale GU12 ....77 E7
  Blackwater GU17 ....35 C4
  Four Marks GU34 ....160 B3
  Grateley SP11 ....124 F7
  Haslemere GU27 ....189 F6
  New Alresford SO24 ....179 D5
  Overton RG25 ....65 B2
Station Cl SO21 ....209 F7
Station Hill Farnham GU9 .99 A2
  Itchen Abbas SO21 .....177 E6
  Ropley SO24 ....180 F5
  Winchester SO23 ....209 D6
Station Ind Est GU51 ....54 A3
Station Mall 16 RG21 ....69 B5
Station Rd Aldershot GU11 .77 A4
  Alton GU34 ....140 A4
  Bentley GU10,GU34 .....120 B3
  Bordon GU35 ....164 C5
  Camberley GU16 ....56 A8
  Chilbolton SO20 ....128 F3
  Cliddesden RG25 ....92 B7
  East Tisted GU34 ......183 C5
  Enborne Row RG20 ....4 E3
  Farnborough GU14 ....55 F4
  Frimley GU16 ....36 A1
  Grateley SP11 ....125 A8
  Hook RG27 ....72 A8
  Liphook GU30 ....188 A2
  Liss GU33 ....207 F4
  New Alresford SO24 ....179 D6
Station Rd continued
  Newbury,Speen RG14 ......1 E2
  Newbury,Speen RG14 ......1 B5
  Oakley RG23 ....66 F2
  Over Wallop SO20 ......125 C1
  Overton RG25 ....65 B1
  South Tidworth SP9 .....78 F5
  Stratfield Mortimer RG7 ..12 C5
  Whitchurch RG28 ....86 C6
  2 Winchester SO23 ....209 D6
  Winchfield RG27 ....52 E8
Station Rd E GU12 ....77 E7
Station Rd W GU12 ....77 D8
Station View GU12 ....77 E8
Stavedown Rd SO21 .....153 E4
Steeles Rd GU11 ....76 F4
Steeple Dr GU34 ....139 F4
Steepways GU26 ....166 F6
Stephury Dr RG25 ......136 B8
Step Terr SO22 ....209 C6
Stephen Gould Ho GU14 ..76 F8
Stephen's Cl RG7 ....11 D5
Stephen's Rd RG7 ....11 D6
Stephendale Rd GU9 .....99 B4
Stephens Firs RG7 ....11 D6
Stephens Rd RG26 ....27 A8
Stephenson Cl SP10 .....82 C1
Stephenson Ct
  Farnham GU9 ....121 D8
  Newbury RG14 ....5 F8
Stephenson Rd
  Arborfield Garrison RG2 ..15 C7
  Basingstoke RG21 ....68 E6
Stepping Stones Sch
  GU26 ....167 D4
Sterling Gdns GU47 ......35 C8
Sterling Pk SP10 ....82 C1
Stevens Dro SO20 ....171 C5
Stevens Gn SP11 ....62 A1
Stevens Hill GU46 ....34 C5
Steventon Rd RG25 ......89 E2
Stewards Rise GU27 ....121 D7
Stewart Rd RG24 ....69 E8
Stile Gdns GU27 ....189 D6
Stiles Dr SP10 ....106 D8
Stillions Cl GU34 ......140 A3
Stilwell Cl GU46 ....34 C6
Stirling Cl Ash Vale GU12 .77 D5
  Farnborough GU14 ....55 E3
  Frimley GU16 ....36 C2
  Stirling East RG14 ......6 B4
Stirling Way GU11 ....76 C7
Stirrup Cl RG14 ....5 F7
Stoatley Hollow GU27 ...189 B8
Stoatley Rise GU27 ....189 E8
Stockbridge Cl RG24 ....49 B4
Stockbridge Dr GU11 ...100 A6
Stockbridge Prim Sch
  SO20 ....149 F3
Stockbridge Rd
  Fleet GU51 ....53 D4
  Goodworth Clatford SP11 .127 A5
  King's Somborne SO20 ..172 A3
  Sutton Scotney SO21 ....131 C4
  Winchester SO22 ....209 A6
  Winchester SO22 ....209 C6
Stockbridge Way GU46 ....34 B4
Stocker Cl RG21 ....69 A2
Stockers Rd SO22 ......209 B7
Stocks La GU34 ....204 B2
Stockton Ave GU51 ......53 F2
Stockton Pk GU51 ....53 F2
Stockwell Pl SO21 .....174 E2
Stockwood Rise GU35 ....36 D5
Stockwood Way GU9 ......99 D7
Stodham La
  Hill Brow GU33 ....208 A2
  Liss GU33 ....207 F1
Stoke Charity Rd SO21,
  SO23 ....154 B2
Stoke Gate SP11 ....61 C5
Stoke Hill SP11 ....61 B3
Stoke Hills GU9 ....99 A3
Stoke Ho RG26 ....26 F8
Stoke La SP11 ....61 B5
Stoke Rd
  Hurstbourne Tarrant SP11 .60 D7
  Smannell SP11 ....83 C7
  Stoke SP11 ....61 A2
  Winchester SO23 ....176 A3
Stoken La RG27 ....51 F8
Stokes La RG26 ....9 A1
Stone Cl Andover SP10 ..105 E6
  Middle Winterslow SP5 ..168 A6
Stone Copse RG18 ....2 C7
Stone Gdns GU34 ......160 D8
Stonedene Cl GU35 .....165 F4
Stonehill Pk GU35 .....165 F4
Stonehill Rd GU35 .....166 A4
Stonehills RG25 ....89 B5
Stonehouse Rd GU30 ....188 B4
Stonehouse Rise GU16 ...36 C1
Stonelea Gr RG29 ....72 C6
Stoneleigh Ct GU16 .....36 B1
Stoner Hill Rd GU32 ....206 B1
Stoney Bottom GU26 ....167 A3
Stoney Cl GU46 ....34 B4
Stoney Ct SO22 ....209 C6
Stoney La
  Four Marks GU34 ....160 B4
  Newbury RG18 ....2 C7
  Winchester SO23 ......209 C8
Stoneycroft 7 GU11 .....76 D1
Stoneyfields GU9 ....99 C1
Stookes Way GU46 ....33 F4
Stour Rd RG23 ....67 B1
Stourhead Cl
  Basingstoke RG21 ......105 E7
  Farnborough GU14 ....54 F7
Stovid's Way GU11 ....99 D8
Stowe Cl GU35 ....142 B3
Straits The GU35 ....142 B3
Stratfield Ave RG26 .....26 F7
Stratfield Cl RG26 ......27 A8
Stratfield Ho 4 RG21 ....11 F6
Stratfield Rd RG21 ......69 A8
Stratfield Saye Ho* RG7 .30 C8
Stratfield Saye Rd RG7,
  RG26 ....29 A5
Stratford Ct
  Farnborough GU14 ....56 A4
  Farnham GU9 ....99 A1
  10 Winchester SO23 ...209 E8
Stratton Ho 11 GU34 ...139 F3
Stratton Rd GU12 ....77 D8
Strathfield Rd SP10 ...106 A5
Strathmore Ct 1 RG21 ...36 B6
Stratton Cl SO21 ......134 A4
Stratton La SO21 ......134 B3
Stratton Rd
  Basingstoke RG21 ....68 F2
  Winchester SO23 ....198 C7
Stratton Wlk GU14 ....55 E7
Strauss Rd RG22 ....90 B1
Stravinsky Rd RG22 .....90 B1
Strawberry Fields RG26 ..28 F3
Strawberry Hill RG14 .....1 D4
Stream Farm Cl GU10 ...122 B7
Stream Valley Rd GU10 .122 A6
Streamside GU51 ....75 A8
Street End RG27 ....33 C8
Street The Aldermaston RG7 .9 F7
  Binsted GU34 ....141 E7
  Bramley RG26 ....28 D3
  Crookham Village GU51 ..74 D5
  Dockenfield GU10 ......143 C6
  Farnham GU10 ....121 D6
  Frensham GU10 ....144 A7
  Greywell RG29 ....71 F3
  Long Sutton RG29 ....95 D2
  Old Basing RG24 ....70 B7
  Rotherwick RG27 ....50 E5
  Stratfield Mortimer RG7 ..12 B5
  Swallowfield RG7 ....14 A6
  Tongham GU10 ....100 D6
Streetway Rd SP11 .....124 E7
Strokins Rd RG20 ....24 D3
Stroller Cl RG19 ....2 C8
Stroud Cl Chineham RG24 .48 F2
  Pamber Heath RG26 ......10 C1
Stroud La
  Blackwater GU17 ....34 E4
  Crookham Village GU51 ..74 C5
Stroudley Rd RG24 ......69 E8
Stuart Cl GU14 ....55 D5
Stuart Cres SO23 ......209 C3
Stuart Ct 2 SP10 ....83 A3
Stuart Jones Ho GU11 ...77 C5
Stuart Rd RG14 ....5 B6
Stubbington Ave GU35 ..164 C1
Stubbs Cl SP10 ....82 F1
Stubbs Folly GU47 ......35 E8
Stubbs Ind Site GU11 ...77 C5
Stubbs Moor Rd GU14 ....55 D5
Stubbs Rd RG22 ....69 C2
Stud Offices The SP11 ...80 E7
Stukeley Rd RG21 ....69 A4
Sturdee Cl GU16 ....36 C1
Sturt Ave GU27 ....189 D5
Sturt Rd Camberley GU16 .56 A8
  Farnham GU9 ....98 F7
  Haslemere GU27 ....189 D5
Stymies GU35 ....164 B1
Suddern Cotts SO20 ....147 C8
Suffolk Rd SP10 ....106 A7
Sullivan Cl GU14 ....55 E4
Sullivan Rd
  Basingstoke RG22 ....68 F1
  Camberley GU15 ....35 E5
  Basingstoke RG22 ....68 D1
Sulzers Rdbt GU14 ......55 F3
Summer Down La RG23,
  RG26 ....66 C6
Summerdown Cotts
  GU26 ....167 B3
Summerfield La GU10 ...121 F2
Summerfields RG24 ......49 A4
Summerhouse Ct 11
  GU26 ....167 B3
Summerlea Ct GU35 .....116 C6
Summersfield GU33 ....207 F3
Summit Ave GU14,GU51 ..55 A4
Summit Cl RG40 ....16 C7
Summit Ctr GU14 ....55 A3
Sumner Gdns GU9 ....99 A3
Sumner Rd GU9 ....99 A3
Sun Brow GU27 ....189 E5
Sun Hill Cres SO24 ....179 D4
Sun Hill Inf & Jun Sch
  SO24 ....179 D5
Sun La
  New Alresford SO24 ....179 D5
  Swallowfield RG7 ....13 F2
Sun Ray Est GU47 ....34 D8
Sun Valley Bsns Pk
  SO23 ....176 C1
Sunbury Cl GU35 ....164 E3
Sunderland Gdns RG14 ...1 B2
Sunflower Cl RG22 ......91 A7
Sunley Cl RG14 ....76 B2
Sunny Hill Rd GU11 .....76 B2
Sunny Mead RG23 ....90 B8
Sunny View Cl 7 SP11 ...77 A1
Sunnybank SP11 ....104 E6
Sunnybank Rd GU14 ......55 B6
Sunnydell La GU10 .....121 E6
Sunnybown Rd SO22 ....197 A3
Sunnyside Donnington RG14 .1 C6
  Fleet GU51 ....53 E2
  Kingsley GU35 ....142 C1
Sunnyside Cl SP10 ......82 E2
Sunnyside Cotts RG20 ...24 C1
Sunnyside Rd GU35 .....166 A4
Sunvale Ave GU27 ......189 B6
Sunvale Cl GU27 ....189 B6
Surrey Ave GU15 ....35 C4
Surrey Heath Mus*
  ....36 B6
Surrey Ho RG24 ....48 F5
Surrey Inst of Art & Design
  Coll The GU9 ....98 E2
Sussex Gdns GU51 ....54 B4
Sussex St SO23 ....209 D6
Sutcliffe Sq SP10 ......83 C3
Sutherland Cl GU35 ....164 D1
Sutherland Ct SP10 ....83 A1
Sutherlands RG14 ....5 C7
Sutton Field GU35 .....164 C1
Sutton Gdns SO23 .....209 E6
Sutton Rd
  Basingstoke RG21 ....69 B7
  2 Camberley GU15 ......36 E8
  Newbury RG14 ....1 B5
Suttonwood La SO24 ....180 F7
Swains Cl RG26 ....26 F8
Swains Rd RG26 ....26 F8
Swale Rd GU14 ....55 C6
Swaledale Gdns GU51 ...54 B4
Swallow Cl Alton GU34 ..140 A6
  Basingstoke RG22 ....90 F8
  North Tidworth SP9 .....78 F6
  Yateley GU46 ....33 F6
Swallowfield Rd
  Arborfield Garrison RG2,
  RG7 ....14 E8
  Swallowfield RG7 ....14 E6
Swallowfield St RG7 ....14 A7
Swallowfields SP10 .....83 B2
Swan Ct 4 Andover SP10 .106 B8
  Hartley Wintney RG27 ....52 D6
  Newbury RG14 ....1 D3
Swan Ho GU47 ....34 F7
Swan La Sandhurst GU47 ..34 F7
  Winchester SO23 ....209 E6
Swan Mews RG29 ....72 C4
Swan St RG20 ....24 C1
Swan Way RG14 ....74 D7
Swanmore Cl SO22 .....175 D4
Swansdown Wlk RG19 .....2 F3
Swanwick Wlk 4 RG26 ...26 F8
Swedish Hos RG26 ....27 A7
Sweetzer's Piece RG7 ...11 C6
Swelling Hill SO24 ....182 A6
Swift Cl Andover SP10 ...83 B2
  Winchester SO22 ....209 B3
Swift Ct 10 GU51 ....54 A1
Swift Way GU51 ....99 F1
Swift's Cl GU10 ....99 F1
Swindon Ho 8 SP9 ....78 F7
Swing Swang La GU14 ...69 E7
Swingate Rd GU14 .....122 B8
Swiss Cl GU10 ....121 E4
Swiss St GU17 ....35 A4
Switchback La
  Rowledge GU10 ....121 D4
  Rowledge GU10 ....121 E3
Swordfish Way GU14 .....76 C7
Sycamore Cl Frimley GU16 .36 C1
  North Tidworth SP9 .....79 A7
  Sandhurst GU47 ....34 F8
Sycamore Cres GU51 ....74 E6
Sycamore Dr
  Ash Vale GU12 ....77 E7
  Farnham GU10 ....121 E6
  Frimley GU16 ....36 C1
  Kings Worthy SO23 ....176 B8
Sycamore Ho RG24 ......49 A3
Sycamore Pk GU34 .....140 B4
Sycamore Rise GU12 ....56 B2
Sycamore Wlk RG23 .....68 D7
Sycamore Wlk SP10 ....105 D6
Sycamores The
  Blackwater GU17 ....34 F5
  Farnborough GU14 ....56 B3
Sydings The RG14 ....1 B5
Sydney Loader Pl GU17 ..34 E5
Sydney Rd GU35 ....164 D3
Sydney Villas GU12 .....77 E8
Syers Cl GU32 ....207 F4
Syers Rd GU34 ....140 C8
Sylvan Cl GU14 ....77 B8
Sylvan Way GU52 ....74 F5
Sylvaner Ct RG21 ....69 B6
Sylvester Cl RG14 ....1 C5
Sylvia Cl RG21 ....69 A3
Symonds St SO23 ......209 D6
Syon Pl GU14 ....56 B4
Tadley Cl GU51 ....53 D4
Tadley Com Prim Sch
  RG26 ....27 A6
Tadley Common Rd
  RG26 ....10 A1
Tadley Hill RG26 ....27 A7
Tadpole La GU10 ....75 B1

Taiping Rd SO20 ....126 A5
Talavera Inf & Jun Sch GU11 ....76 F3
Talbot Cl Mytchett GU16 ..56 E4
  Newbury RG14 ....1 C5
Talbot Rd GU9 ....121 F8
Talgarth Dr GU14 ....56 B2
Tall Pines GU52 ....74 D5
Tallis Gdns RG22 ....68 E1
Tally-Ho Lodge RG21 ..69 A6
Talmey Cl RG24 ....48 E3
Tamar Dr RG23 ....67 B2
Tamarisk Cl RG22 ....91 C5
Tamworth Dr GU51 ..54 B4
Tangier Cl GU11 ....76 D2
Tanglewood RG40 ....16 E7
Tangway RG24 ....48 F4
Tanhouse La GU34 ..139 F3
Tank Rd GU15 ....35 D5
Tanker Rd GU14 ....55 F1
Tanner Ct RG14 ....1 E4
Tanner St SO23 ....209 E5
Tanners Way RG23 ....64 F2
Taplin's Farm La RG27 ..52 E3
Taplings Cl SO22 ....175 D3
Taplings Rd SO22 ....175 D3
Tarbat Ct GU47 ....35 B8
Tarn Cl GU14 ....55 C2
Tarn Howes Cl RG19 ....2 E3
Tarn La RG14 ....15 C5
Tarn Rd GU26 ....167 C3
Tarragon Cl GU14 ....55 A4
Tarrant Gdns RG27 ....52 C4
Taskers Dr SP11 ....105 C4
Tasmania Cl RG24 ....48 C2
Tate Sq SP10 ....83 C3
Taverner Rd RG21 ....69 D7
Tavistock Gdns GU14 ..55 F7
Tavistock Inf Sch GU51 ..74 D8
Tavistock Rd GU51 ....74 D8
Tawny Gr GU34 ....160 A2
Tay Cl GU14 ....55 C6
Taylor Dr RG26 ....29 B2
Taylor Rd GU11 ....77 B7
Taylors Cl GU35 ....164 F5
Taylors Cnr SO23 ....176 B5
Taylors La GU35 ....164 F5
Teachers Terr GU33 ....207 F4
Teal Cres RG22 ....90 F7
Tedder Cl SP11 ....105 B7
Tees Cl GU14 ....55 C6
Teg Down Meads SO22 ..209 A7
Tegg Down Rd SO24 ..180 F3
Tekels Ave GU15 ....36 B4
Tekels Ct GU15 ....36 C4
Tekels Way GU15 ....36 D3
Telconia Cl GU35 ....166 A4
Telegraph La GU34 ..160 D2
Telegraph Way SO21 ..199 B7
Telford Ct RG14 ....1 D4
Telford Gate
  Andover SP10 ....82 B1
  Andover SP10 ....82 B2
Telford Rd RG21 ....68 E7
Templar Cl GU47 ....34 E8
Templar Lodge GU12 ..77 A1
Temple Gdns GU35 ..208 A6
Temple Twrs RG21 ....69 A6
Temple's Cl GU10 ..100 A1
Templer Ave GU14 ....55 A8
Templeton Ho SP10 ..106 A8
Ten Acre Wlk GU10 ..121 D4
Tenby Rd GU14 ....56 E8
Tennyson Way RG22 ..68 E2
Tern Cl RG22 ....90 F7
Terra Cotta Ct GU10 ..121 D6
Terrace The
  Camberley GU15 ....35 E5
  Chawton GU34 ....161 D8
Terry Cl RG22 ....90 F4
Terrys Cotts RG29 ....72 B3
Tesimond Dr GU46 ....33 E5
Texas Dr SO22 ....197 B3
Test Ct SP10 ....83 D2
Test Ho SO23 ....209 F4
Test House Gate Rd GU14 ..55 F2
Test Mews RG28 ....86 C4
Test Rd RG28 ....86 C4
Test Rise SO20 ....129 A3
Test Valley Sch SO20 ..149 D2
Test Way RG21 ....69 D5
Testbourne Com Sch RG28 ....86 D3
Tewkesbury Cl RG24 ..48 B1
Thackham's La
  Hartley Wintney RG27 ..52 A5
  West Green RG27 ....51 F5
Thames Cl GU14 ....55 C6
Thames Ct Andover SP10 ..82 D2
  Basingstoke RG21 ....69 D5
Thames Rd RG18 ....2 F5
Thatcham Nature Discovery Ctr* RG19 ....2 F2
Theal Cl GU47 ....35 B8
Theatre Rd GU14 ....76 F8
Thibet Rd GU47 ....35 A8
Third Ave RG7 ....10 A2
Third Street E RG19 ....6 E5
Thirlestane Ct GU26 ..167 D5
Thirlmere Cl
  Bordon GU35 ....164 D5
  Farnborough GU14 ....55 C4
Thirlmere Cres GU52 ..74 E5
Thirsk Ct GU12 ....77 B2

Thirt Way SO20 ....129 C1
Thistledown Cl SP10 ..82 E1
Thomas Askew Ho RG14 ..1 C1
Thomas La RG40 ....16 C8
Thomas Merriman Ct RG14 ....1 E2
Thomas Rd GU11 ....77 B7
Thorburn Chase GU47 ..35 C6
Thorlands GU27 ....189 E7
Thorn Ct Farnham GU10 ..121 E4
  Four Marks GU34 ....160 C3
Thorn Cres GU34 ....160 B2
Thorn La GU34 ....160 C2
Thorn Rd GU10 ....121 E5
Thorneley Rd RG20 ....24 D2
Thornfield RG19 ....7 B3
Thornfield Gn GU17 ..161 A4
Thornford Rd
  Greenham,Head's Hill RG19 ..7 B5
  Headley, Nr Greenham RG19 ..7 C3
Thorngate SP5 ....169 B1
Thorngrove Sch RG20 ..21 C7
Thornhill Cres GU11 ..77 A3
Thornhill Rd GU11 ....77 A4
Thornhill Way RG24 ..49 B4
Thornton Cl GU34 ....29 B2
Thornton End GU34 ..140 C6
Thornycroft Cl RG14 ..1 F3
Thornycroft Ind Est RG21 ..68 F5
Thornycroft Rdbt RG22 ..68 E5
Thornyhurst Rd GU16 ..56 E4
Thorold Rd GU9 ....99 A3
Thorpe Gdns GU34 ..139 E4
Threadgill Way SP9 ..101 D7
Threadneedle Ho SP10 ....106 B8
Three Acre Rd RG14 ....5 D8
Three Horse Shoes La SO24 ....203 E2
Three Stiles Rd GU9 ....98 D3
Three Ways GU10 ....143 B6
Threshers Cnr GU51 ..54 C4
Throakmead GU34 ..120 A2
Throgmorton Rd GU46 ..33 C5
Thrush Cl RG22 ....67 F1
Thruxton Ind Est SP11 ..113 C7
Thumwood RG24 ....48 F3
Thundery Hill GU10 ..100 D8
Thurbans Rd GU9 ....121 E7
Thurmond Cres SO22 ..209 A4
Thurmond Rd SO22 ..209 A4
Thursley Ho GU27 ....167 F1
Thurstons GU34 ....141 E7
Thyme Cl RG24 ....49 A4
Thyme Ct GU14 ....55 A5
Tibb's Mdw SP11 ....57 F8
Tiberius Cl RG22 ....68 C7
Tiberius Rd SP10 ....83 B3
Tichborne Cl GU47 ....35 B5
Tichborne Down SO24 ..179 D3
Tichborne Pl GU12 ..100 B8
Tichbourne Cl GU16 ..36 D3
Tickenor Dr GU46 ....16 D7
Tidbury Cotts SP11 ..109 B1
Tides End Ct GU16 ....36 D4
Tidworth Rd SP9 ....101 A8
Tigwells Field RG29 ..95 A4
Tilbury's Cl GU35 ....164 D3
Tile Barn Cl GU14 ....55 E5
Tile Barn Row RG20 ....4 C1
Tilford Rd
  Beacon Hill GU26 ....167 B6
  Hindhead GU26 ....167 D4
  Tilford GU10 ....122 D6
Tilling Cotts GU34 ..141 B1
Tilney Cl GU34 ....139 E4
Timber Bank GU16 ....56 E6
Timber Cl GU9 ....98 F2
Timbercroft Cl GU34 ..160 B4
Timberlake Rd RG21 ..69 A5
Timbermill Ct GU27 ..189 D6
Times Ho GU11 ....76 E2
Timor Ct RG24 ....48 C1
Timothy's Field SP11 ..104 F3
Timson Ct RG14 ....1 F3
Tindal Cl GU46 ....34 B6
Tindle Ent Ctr GU35 ..164 C1
Tinker's Cnr RG20 ....3 B8
Tinley Gdns RG29 ....72 F3
Tintagel Cl Andover SP10 ..83 A3
  Basingstoke RG23 ....68 C6
Tintagel Dr GU16 ....36 D1
Tintagel Rd RG40 ....16 E8
Tintern Cl RG24 ....68 F8
Tippett Gdns RG21 ..69 F7
Tisbury Cl GU51 ....53 E3
Titan Ho RG7 ....9 C2
Titchfield Cl RG40 ....27 A7
Tithe Mdw RG22 ....91 C5
Tithelands La GU34 ..202 F4
Tittymouse La SP11 ..81 C2
Tiverton Rd RG23 ....68 B5
Tiverton Way GU16 ..36 D6
Toad La GU17 ....35 C4
Tobago Cl RG24 ....48 B1
Tobruk Cl SP11 ....83 B7
Tockington Ct GU46 ..34 B6
Todmore GU33 ....185 F3
Toledo Gr Andover SP10 ..83 C1
  Andover SP10 ....83 C1
Tollgate Rd GU35 ....82 E1
Tollgate The SO23 ..209 E7
Tollway RG24 ....49 A3
Tolpuddle Way GU46 ..34 D5
Tomlins Ave GU16 ....36 D2
Tomlins Cl RG26 ....26 F7

Tomlinscote Sch & Sixth Form Coll GU16 ....36 E2
Tomlinscote Way GU16 ..36 E2
Tomlinson Dr RG40 ....16 E7
Tongham Mdws GU10 ..100 D7
Tongham Rd
  Aldershot GU10 ....100 B5
  Runfold GU10 ....100 A4
Top Terrace Rd GU14 ..76 C8
Topaz Dr SP10 ....105 D8
Tope Cres RG2 ....15 C7
Tope Rd RG2 ....15 D8
Topiary The
  Farnborough GU14 ....55 C3
  Old Basing RG24 ....70 A8
Toplady Pl GU9 ....99 A7
Tor Rd GU9 ....98 D2
Torridon Ct GU30 ..187 F6
Torrington Cl GU35 ..165 A5
Tothill RG20 ....22 C8
Totland Cl GU14 ....55 E6
Tottenham Ct RG26 ....28 F4
Totters La
  Murrell Green RG27 ....51 F2
  Winchfield RG27 ....72 F8
Tournai Cl GU11 ....77 C7
Tovey Ct SP10 ....83 D1
Tovey Pl RG31 ....176 C7
Tower Cl Andover SP10 ..82 D3
  Hindhead GU26 ....167 C4
  Liphook GU30 ....187 F4
Tower Cl SO22 ....209 D6
Tower Hill GU14 ....55 C3
Tower Hill Prim Sch GU14 ....209 D6
Tower Rd Hindhead GU26 ..167 C4
  Liphook GU30 ....187 F4
  Winchester SO23 ....209 D6
Tower St Alton GU34 ..139 F2
  Winchester SO23 ....209 D6
Town Cl SO24 ....181 D5
Town Hall Rd GU14 ....86 C5
Town Mill RG25 ....88 B8
Town Mill La RG28 ....86 D5
Town Mills RG14 ....1 D3
Town Sq GU15 ....36 A6
Townsend Ct RG21 ....68 F4
Townside Pl GU15 ....36 B6
Trade St RG20 ....21 B8
Trafalgar Ct GU9 ....99 A1
Trafalgar St SO23 ..209 D6
Trafalgar Way
  Camberley GU15 ....35 D4
  Stockbridge SO20 ..149 F2
Trafford Rd GU16 ....56 B8
Trajan Wlk SP10 ....83 B3
Transport Rd GU14 ....55 F1
Travis La GU47 ....35 A7
Treasury Ct SO23 ..209 D6
Treble Cl SO22 ....197 B4
Trebor Ave GU9 ....99 B1
Tredenham Cl GU14 ....77 A8
Tree Tops Ave GU15 ..36 F8
Treeside Cl RG22 ....90 F8
Trefoil Cl RG27 ....52 C7
Tregenna Ho GU30 ..187 F5
Tregolls Dr GU14 ....56 A4
Trellis Dr RG24 ....70 A8
Treloar Coll GU34 ..140 B6
Treloar Sch GU34 ..119 B2
Trenchard Pk GU35 ..164 D4
Trenchard Rd SP11 ..105 B7
Trendham Gdns RG24 ..68 C8
Trent Cl GU14 ....55 C6
Trent Cres RG18 ....2 F5
Trent Ct RG21 ....83 C2
Trent Way RG21 ....69 D5
Trenton Cl GU16 ....36 D1
Tresham Cres GU46 ..33 E6
Triangle The RG45 ....7 B1
Trilakes Ctry Pk* GU46, GU47 ....34 D7
Trimmer's Almshouses GU9 ....98 E1
Trimmers Cl GU9 ....99 A7
Trimmers Field GU9 ..99 C1
Trimmers Wood GU26 ..167 C6
Trinidad Cl RG24 ....48 B1
Trinity Fields GU9 ..98 E6
Trinity Gdns SO23 ..209 E6
Trinity Hill Farnham GU9 ..98 E6
  Medstead GU34 ....159 E8
Trinity Ho
  Andover SP10 ....106 A8
  North Tidworth SP9 ....78 E7
Trinity Rise GU11 ..137 E1
Trinity Rise SP11 ....81 F4
Trinity Sch RG14 ....1 F5
Trooper Bottom GU32 ..206 B3
Trotsford Mdw GU17 ..35 A4
Trout Rd GU27 ....189 C6
Trout Wlk RG14 ....1 F4
Trowbridge Cl SO23 ..209 E6
Trowbridge Ho SP9 ..78 F7
Trowe's La Beech Hill RG7 ..13 B3
  Swallowfield RG7 ....14 B5
Trueman Sq SP10 ....83 C3
Trunk Rd GU14 ....55 B1
Truro Pl RG22 ....91 B8
Trussell Cl SO22 ....175 D3
Trussell Cres SO22 ..175 D3
Tryplets GU32 ....74 E3
Tubb's La Highclere RG20 ..21 D6
  Monk Sherborne RG26 ..47 A7
Tudor Ct Bramley RG26 ..28 C2
  Grayshott GU26 ....167 B2
Tudor Ct Andover SP10 ..83 A3

Tudor Ct continued
  Basingstoke RG21 ....69 B3
  Baughurst RG26 ....26 F8
  Fleet GU51 ....54 C4
Tudor Dr GU46 ....34 B4
Tudor Hall GU15 ....36 D6
Tudor Rd RG14 ....1 E1
Tudor Way Fleet GU52 ..75 A4
  Kings Worthy SO23 ..176 B8
Tufton Warren Cotts RG28 ....109 E6
Tulip Cl RG22 ....91 A7
Tull Way RG18 ....2 C1
Tulls La GU35 ....165 B2
Tumber Cl GU34 ....77 E2
Tunball La SN8 ....37 D8
Tunbridge Cres GU30 ..187 F5
Tunbridge La GU30 ..187 F6
Tunnel La RG29 ....72 B4
Tunnel Rd GU14 ....55 C1
Tunworth Cl GU51 ....53 E4
Tunworth Ct RG26 ....27 A8
Tunworth Mews RG26 ..27 A8
Tunworth Rd RG25 ....70 E2
Turbary Gdns RG26 ..26 F7
Turf Hill Rd GU35 ....36 D8
Turgis Rd GU51 ....53 E4
Turin Ct SP10 ....83 B4
Turk St GU34 ....139 F3
Turk's La RG7 ....11 D4
Turnberry Dr RG22 ....91 A5
Turner Cl RG21 ....69 E4
Turner Ct SP10 ....82 F1
Turner Pl GU47 ....35 B6
Turner's Green La
  Elvetham RG27 ....53 C5
  Elvetham RG27 ....53 D5
Turners Ave GU51 ....53 E4
Turners Way GU51 ....53 D3
Turnhill Way GU11 ....83 B7
Turnpike Cotts RG25 ..88 B8
Turnpike Down SO21 ..198 C8
Turnpike Ind Est RG14 ..2 B5
Turnpike Rd RG14 ....2 B5
Turnpike Way RG23 ..67 A2
Turnstone End GU46 ..33 F6
Tuscam Way GU15 ....54 C6
Tuscany Way GU46 ....34 A4
Tweed Cl GU14 ....55 C6
Tweedsmuir Cl
  Basingstoke RG22 ....68 B4
  Farnborough GU14 ....55 A3
Twelve Acre Cres GU14 ..55 A5
Tweseldown Inf Sch GU52 ....75 B4
Tweseldown Rd GU52 ..75 B4
Twinley La
  Laverstoke RG28 ....87 B7
  Whitchurch RG28 ....64 B2
Twisell Thorne GU52 ..74 E4
Two Gate La GU27 ....187 E4
Two Gate Mdw RG25 ..88 B8
Two Rivers Way RG14 ....2 C3
Twoways Ct GU35 ....164 C1
Twyford Cl GU51 ....53 E4
Twyford Ct SO23 ..209 E8
Twyford La GU10 ....121 F6
Tydehams RG14 ....5 D7
Tyfield RG22 ....47 E3
Tyler Dr RG2 ....15 C7
Tylney La RG27 ....50 D1
Tylney Wood GU26 ..166 D7
Tylston Mdw GU30 ..187 F5
Tyndalls GU26 ....167 D4
Tyne Cl GU14 ....55 C6
Tyne Ct SP10 ....83 D2
Tyne Way RG18 ....2 F5
Tyrells Croft SP10 ..106 C8
Tytherley Rd SP5 ....168 C5

U

Ullswater Ave GU14 ..55 C3
Ullswater Cl
  Bordon GU35 ....164 D5
  Farnham GU9 ....98 E6
  Thatcham RG19 ....2 E3
Ullswater Ct GU12 ....77 D5
Ullswater Gr SO24 ..179 D4
Underhill La GU10 ..121 F7
Underwood Ave GU12 ..77 D1
Underwood Rd GU27 ..189 D7
Unicorn Trad Est The GU27 ....189 F6
Union Rd GU30 ....24 D5
Union Rd GU9 ....99 A2
Union Rise GU33 ....186 D2
Union St Aldershot GU11 ..76 E2
  Andover SP10 ....106 A7
  Farnborough GU14 ....55 C4
  Winchester SO23 ..209 F6
Union Terr GU11 ....76 E2
Unity Ho RG19 ....6 E4
Univ of Winchester SO22 ....209 C5
Up St Dummer RG25 ..113 C8
  North Waltham RG25 ..89 E1
Upfallow RG24 ....70 A8
Uphill Rd GU27 ....175 C5
Upland La GU33 ....207 D5
Upland Rd GU33 ....36 B7
Uplands Cl GU47 ....34 H8
Uplands La GU34 ....160 A1
Uplands Prim Sch GU47 ..34 F8
Uplands Rd Farnham GU9 ..99 C1
  Winchester SO22 ..209 A6
Upnor Cl SP11 ....79 D7

Upper Bourne La GU10 ..121 F5
Upper Bourne Vale GU10 ....121 E5
Upper Brook St SO23 ..209 E6
Upper Charles St GU15 ..36 A6
Upper Chestnut Dr RG21 ..68 F3
Upper Chobham Rd GU15 ....36 F3
Upper Church La GU9 ..98 F2
Upper College Ride RG28 ....109 E6
Upper Dro SP10 ....82 C1
Upper Elms Rd GU11 ..76 E1
Upper Farm Rd RG21 ..90 B8
Upper Froyle Dr GU51 ..53 D3
Upper Gn GU33 ....206 E7
Upper Gordon Rd GU15 ..36 B5
Upper Grove Rd GU34 ..139 F2
Upper Hale Rd GU9 ....99 A6
Upper High St SO23 ..209 D6
Upper House Farm SO24 ....203 D2
Upper Lanham La SO24 ..158 D7
Upper Mead SO20 ....126 B4
Upper Mount GU33 ....207 E3
Upper Mount St GU51 ..53 D3
Upper Neatham Mill La GU34 ....140 C6
Upper Old Park La GU9 ..98 E5
Upper Park Rd GU15 ....36 C6
Upper Raymond Almshouses RG14 ....1 D7
Upper School Dr GU27 ..189 D5
Upper Sherborne Rd RG21 ....69 A7
Upper Soldridge Rd GU34 ....159 D2
Upper South View GU9 ..99 A3
Upper St GU51 ....53 F1
Upper St Michael's Rd GU11 ....99 F8
Upper Stroud Cl RG24 ..48 E2
Upper Terrace Rd GU14 ..76 E8
Upper Union St GU11 ..76 E2
Upper Union Terr GU11 ..76 E2
Upper Verran Rd GU15 ..36 B3
Upper Way GU10 ....121 F8
Upper Weybourne La GU9 ....99 C7
Upper Wield Dr GU51 ..53 E4
Upron Field Ct RG22 ..91 B7
Upton Cl GU14 ....56 B3
Upton Cres RG21 ....69 A7
Upton Grey Cl SO22 ..175 D3
Upton Grey Dr GU51 ..53 E3
Upton Grey Rd RG25, RG29 ....71 E1
Urchfont Ho SP9 ....79 A6

V

Valdean Home Pk SO24 ..179 D6
Vale Cl GU10 ....122 A4
Vale Ct GU12 ....77 E7
Vale Rd Ash Vale GU12 ..77 E5
  Camberley GU15 ....35 E4
  Winchester SO23 ..198 C6
Vale The RG23 ....67 B1
Vale View Dr RG7 ....13 B5
Vale Way SO23 ....134 B1
Vale Wood Dr GU10 ..122 B4
Vale Wood La GU26 ..167 A4
Valencia Way SO23 ....83 B1
Valiant Way GU14 ....76 B8
Valley Ct The SO22 ..209 B4
Valley La GU10 ....122 A7
Valley Mead SP11 ....105 C4
Valley Rd Camberley GU16 ..56 F8
  Littleton SO22 ....175 B5
  Newbury RG14 ....5 C8
Valley Rise SO22 ....105 E4
Valley Side GU30 ....187 F5
Valley The SO22 ....209 B4
Valley View GU47 ....34 E2
Valmeade Cl RG27 ....51 B1
Valon Rd RG2 ....15 D8
Valour Cl GU15 ....36 B6
Vampire Way GU11,GU14 ..76 D8
Van Dyck Cl RG2 ....69 E4
Vanburgh Gdns RG22 ..91 B7
Vanners La RG20 ....4 B5
Varna Rd GU35 ....164 E3
Varndell Rd RG22 ....50 F1
Varney Cl GU14 ....55 A5
Vaughans GU34 ....140 A3
Vectis Cl GU34 ....160 B2
Velmead Cl GU52 ....75 B7
Velmead Jun Sch GU52 ..75 B7
Velmead Rd GU52 ....75 B7
Venice Ct SP10 ....83 C3
Venison Terr SO20 ..170 B7
Venning Rd RG22 ....51 B8
Ventnor Terr GU12 ....77 A1
Verden Way SP10 ....82 F3
Verdi Cl RG22 ....91 C7
Verge Wlk GU11 ....99 F7
Verica Gdns RG26 ....10 C2
Verity Sq SP10 ....83 D3
Verlynch Cotts SO20 ..149 F7
Vermont Woods RG40 ..16 C7
Verne The GU32 ....75 A5
Verner Cl GU35 ....164 E3
Vernham Dean Gillum's CE Prim Sch SP11 ....38 C5
Vernham Rd SO22 ....209 C8

Vernham Row SP11 ....38 A7
Vernon Ct GU9 ....98 E1
Veronica Cl RG22 ....91 A7
Veronica Dr GU51 ....74 D5
Verran Rd GU15 ....36 B3
Vesey Cl GU14 ....55 E6
Vespasian Gdns RG24 ....68 C8
Vespasian Rd SP10 ....83 B3
Vestry Ct SP10 ....105 F8
Vetch Fields RG27 ....51 C1
Viables Ind Est RG22 ....69 A1
Viables La RG22 ....69 B1
Viables Rdbt RG21,RG22 ....68 F1
Vian Pl SO23 ....176 C8
Vicarage Cl
  Farnham GU9 ....122 B7
  Finchampstead RG40 ....16 D6
Vicarage Gdns Fleet GU52 ....74 F4
  Grayshott GU26 ....167 A3
Vicarage Hill Alton GU34 ....139 F3
  Farnham GU9,GU10 ....122 C7
  Hartley Wintney RG27 ....52 D5
Vicarage La Farnham GU9 ....98 F2
  Farnham,Lower Bourne
  GU9 ....122 B7
  Farnham,Upper Hale GU9 ....99 F7
  Haslemere GU27 ....189 D6
  Mattingley RG27 ....31 A2
  Ropley SO24 ....181 B4
  Yateley GU46 ....34 A7
Vicarage Rd Alton GU34 ....139 E2
  Blackwater GU17 ....35 C4
  Yateley GU46 ....33 F7
  Yateley GU46 ....34 A7
Vickers Bsns Ctr RG24 ....68 E8
Victor Way GU14 ....76 B8
Victoria Ave GU15 ....35 E5
Victoria Cotts RG22 ....20 E7
Victoria Ct Andover SP10 ....105 F7
  Camberley GU15 ....35 B5
  [10] Fleet GU51 ....53 F1
Victoria Dr GU17 ....35 A4
Victoria Gdns
  Farnborough GU14 ....55 B4
  [6] Fleet GU51 ....53 F1
  Newbury RG14 ....1 E4
Victoria Gr GU14 ....1 E2
Victoria Hill Rd GU51 ....53 E1
Victoria Ho SO23 ....209 D6
Victoria Pl
  Basingstoke RG22 ....68 B4
  Hurstbourne Tarrant SP11 ....60 E7
Victoria Rd
  Aldershot GU11 ....76 F2
  Alton GU34 ....139 F4
  Farnborough GU14 ....55 E4
  Farnham GU9 ....99 F2
  Fleet GU51 ....53 A1
  Mortimer RG7 ....11 E6
  Winchester SO23 ....209 D7
Victoria Rd E GU34 ....140 A4
Victoria St RG21 ....69 B4
Victoria Terr GU34 ....167 A3
Victoria Tk GU11 ....76 C7
Victoria Way GU30 ....187 F4
Victory Rdbt RG21 ....69 A5
Vidlers Farm RG24 ....47 F3
Vienna Ct GU14 ....55 E6
Vigo Inf Sch SP10 ....83 C1
Vigo La GU46 ....34 A4
Vigo Rd SP10 ....106 B8
Viking Way SP10 ....83 B4
Villa Pl RG7 ....14 A6
Village St
  Bentworth GU34 ....138 B5
  Chilbolton SO20 ....129 A4
Village The
  Finchampstead RG40 ....16 C3
  Litchfield RG28 ....63 C8
  West Tytherley SP5 ....169 B1
Village Way GU46 ....34 B7
Villiers Ct SO23 ....209 D5
Villiers Way GU14 ....5 A6
Villiers Wlk RG14 ....5 A6
Vincent Ct [8] GU51 ....54 A1
Vincent Dr SP10 ....106 B7
Vindomis Cl GU34 ....140 D7
Vine Cl Farnborough GU11 ....76 E6
  Farnham GU10 ....121 E4
  Mytchett GU16 ....56 D1
Vine Ct RG14 ....1 F1
Vine House Cl GU16 ....56 E3
Vine La GU10 ....121 E5
Vine St GU11 ....76 E1
Vine Tree Ct RG26 ....27 B7
Vine Way GU10 ....121 E5
Vinns La RG29 ....87 F7
Vinson Rd GU33 ....208 A4
Violet Cl RG22 ....91 A7
Violet La RG26 ....26 B6
Virginia Gdns GU14 ....56 A2
Viscount Cl GU12 ....77 D5
Viscounts Ct SP10 ....83 E1
Vitellius Gdns RG22 ....68 C8
Vivaldi Cl RG22 ....91 E7
Vivian Cl GU52 ....75 B6
Vivian Rd GU21 ....69 C7
Vockins Cl GU9 ....78 E8
Vokes Cotts SO23 ....176 A5
Vulcan Cl GU47 ....34 E7
Vulcan Ho [3] RG7 ....9 C2
Vulcan Way GU47 ....34 E7
Vyne Cl GU34 ....139 F4
Vyne Com Sch The RG21 ....69 B7
Vyne Mdw RG24 ....47 F4

Vyne Rd Basingstoke RG21 ....69 B6
  Bramley RG26 ....28 C1
  Sherborne St John RG24 ....48 B6
Vyne The* RG24 ....48 B6

W

Wade Rd RG24 ....69 E8
Wadwick Bottom SP11 ....62 B5
Waggoners Way GU26 ....166 E4
Waggoners Wells Rd
  GU26 ....166 E2
Wagner Cl RG22 ....91 E8
Wagon La RG27 ....51 B2
Wakeford Cl RG26 ....10 C1
Wakeford Ct RG26 ....10 C2
Wakefords Cl GU11 ....77 B6
Wakefords Copse GU52 ....75 B3
Wakefords Pk GU52 ....75 B3
Wakes Cotts GU34 ....184 E8
Walburton Ho RG27 ....52 D6
Walcote Pl [30] SO23 ....209 D6
Waldegrave Pl RG14 ....1 E3
Waldorf Hts GU17 ....35 B3
Wales St SO23 ....209 F6
Walk The RG27 ....49 E7
Walker's Ridge GU15 ....36 C5
Walkers Rise SO20 ....147 F8
Wall La RG7 ....11 B2
Wallace Way GU11 ....76 D3
Walldown Rd GU35 ....164 E1
Walled Gdn The RG47 ....13 C5
Walled Mdw
  Andover SP10 ....106 B8
  Andover SP10 ....106 A7
Waller Dr RG25 ....2 C5
Wallins Copse RG24 ....48 F2
Wallis Ct RG23 ....68 D6
Wallis Dr RG23 ....29 B2
Wallis Rd RG23 ....69 B3
Wallop Dr RG22 ....91 A6
Wallop Dro SO20 ....147 D3
Wallop Prim Sch SO20 ....147 F8
Wallop Rd SO20,SP11 ....125 A4
Walls Cvn Pk RG27 ....51 D2
Walmer Ct GU16 ....56 E7
Walnut Cl Aldershot GU11 ....99 E8
  Camberley GU15 ....35 E1
  Yateley GU46 ....34 B4
Walnut Gr SO20 ....209 B7
Walnut Tree Cl SO21 ....153 D4
Walnut Tree Ground
  SP11 ....80 F2
Walnut Tree Rd SP10 ....105 F7
  Whitchurch RG28 ....86 C5
Walpole Gdns RG22 ....54 B3
Walpole Ho [3] GU51 ....76 F2
Walpole Rd SO22 ....209 A3
Walrus Rd GU14 ....76 B8
Walsh Cle Jun Sch GU47 ....77 E1
Walsh Meml CE Inf Sch
  GU12 ....77 D1
Waltham La
  North Waltham RG25 ....89 C2
  Overton RG25 ....88 C7
Waltham Rd RG25 ....88 B7
Walton Ct GU51 ....74 F8
Walton Pl SO22 ....209 B3
Walton Way RG14 ....4 B3
Walworth Ent Ctr SP10 ....83 D1
Walworth Ind Est SP10 ....83 E1
Walworth Rd
  Andover SP10 ....83 E2
  Picket Piece SP10 ....84 C4
Wandle Ct GU47 ....77 E1
Wandsdyke Cl GU16 ....56 D8
Wansey Gdns RG14 ....2 B5
Wantage Rd GU47 ....35 B8
Wapiti Way GU14 ....76 B8
Warbleton Rd RG24 ....49 A2
Warblington Cl RG26 ....27 A7
Warbrook La RG27 ....32 E8
Ward Cl SP10 ....83 D2
Warehouse Rd RG19 ....6 D5
Wargrove Dr GU47 ....34 E4
Warmister Ho [6] SP9 ....78 F7
Warner Ct
  [7] Andover SP10 ....105 F8
  [3] Sandhurst GU47 ....35 B7
  [12] Winchester SO23 ....209 E8
Warren Cl Bordon GU35 ....164 A2
  Finchampstead RG40 ....16 D6
  Fleet GU52 ....75 B7
  Hartley Wintney RG27 ....52 E7
  Sandhurst GU47 ....34 E8
Warren Cnr GU10 ....98 A7
Warren Dr SP11 ....104 F3
Warren Ho GU11 ....76 D1
Warren La
  Finchampstead RG40 ....16 C5
  Warren Corner GU10 ....206 B5
  Winchester SO21 ....199 E1
Warren Rd
  Greatham GU33 ....186 D2
  Liss GU33 ....208 B7
  Newbury RG14 ....1 C7
  Winchester SO23 ....198 C8
Warren Rise GU16 ....56 D1
Warren The
  Aldershot GU11 ....76 D1
  Farnham GU9 ....99 C8
  North Tidworth SP11 ....79 D6
  Tadley RG26 ....11 A1
Warren Way RG22 ....68 C3
Warrington Mews GU11 ....99 C8
Warton Rd RG21 ....69 C6

Warwick Cl
  Aldershot GU11 ....100 A8
  Frimley GU15 ....36 F3
  Whitchurch RG28 ....86 C5
  [14] Winchester SO23 ....209 E8
Warwick Ct [15] SO23 ....209 E8
Warwick Dr RG14 ....1 F1
Warwick Rd
  Ash Vale GU12 ....77 E8
  Basingstoke RG23 ....68 C6
  Farnborough GU14 ....76 B8
Wash Brook RG27 ....51 A2
Wash Water RG20 ....4 F3
Washbury Ho RG14 ....5 C7
Washford Cl GU35 ....164 F4
Washford La GU35 ....164 F4
Washington Dr RG19 ....2 E3
Washington Gdns RG40 ....16 E8
Wasing Cnr RG7 ....9 F6
Wasing La RG7 ....9 C7
Watchetts Lake Cl GU15 ....36 A3
Watchetts Rd GU15 ....35 F4
Watchmoor Pk [4] GU15 ....35 F4
Watchmoor Rd GU15 ....35 E4
Watchmoor Trad Ctr
  GU15 ....35 E3
Water Cl SO23 ....209 E6
Water End La RG20 ....71 A7
Water End Mobile Home Pk
  RG24 ....71 A7
Water La
  Bishop's Sutton SO24 ....180 C4
  Farnborough GU14 ....55 E7
  Farnham GU9 ....99 D7
  Greenham RG19 ....6 A8
  Upper Clatford SP11 ....105 F5
  Winchester SO23 ....209 F5
Water Mdws The [1] GU14 ....1 F4
Water Rede GU52 ....74 E3
Water Ridges RG23 ....90 B8
Water Way [1] RG21 ....209 A3
Waterbrook Rd GU34 ....140 B4
Watercress Ct GU34 ....140 A4
Watercress Mdw SO24 ....179 B4
Waterfront Bsns Pk
  GU14 ....1 F4
Waterhouse Mead GU47 ....35 B7
Wateridge Rd RG21 ....69 C8
Waterloo Cl RG21 ....69 D5
Waterloo Ave RG23 ....68 C7
Waterloo Cotts
  Fleet GU51 ....74 E7
  Sandhurst GU47 ....35 A8
Waterloo Ct
  Andover SP10 ....106 A7
  Basingstoke RG23 ....86 C5
Waterloo Rd GU12 ....77 A1
Waterman Cl GU15 ....164 F2
Watermeadows Small
  Industries Pk GU33 ....165 A4
Watermeadows The
  SP10 ....105 F5
Waterside Cl GU35 ....164 E4
Waterside Ct Alton GU34 ....140 A4
  Fleet GU51 ....74 E7
  Newbury RG14 ....1 F3
Waterside Mews GU51 ....54 B3
Watersmead SO23 ....209 D3
Watersmeet [5] SO23 ....209 F5
Watery La Andover SP10 ....83 B1
  Crookham Village GU52 ....74 E3
  Hamstead Marshall RG20 ....2 C3
Watkins Cl RG40 ....16 C7
Watley La SO21 ....174 D4
Watling End RG22 ....91 B7
Watson Acre SP10 ....105 E8
Watson Way RG23 ....68 D6
Watt Cl SP10 ....82 C1
Watts Common Rd GU11 ....76 C7
Watts Rd GU14 ....55 D5
Wavell Cl RG22 ....91 C7
Wavell Ct [11] GU12 ....77 A1
Wavell Rd SO22 ....209 B3
Wavell Sch The GU14 ....76 F7
Wavell Way SO22 ....209 A3
Waverley Abbey* GU9 ....122 F7
Waverley Ave
  Basingstoke RG22 ....69 A2
  Fleet GU51 ....74 E7
  Frimley GU15 ....36 D4
  Odiham RG29 ....72 F3
Waverley Dr
  Ash Vale GU12 ....77 E6
  Camberley GU15 ....35 D5
  South Wonston SO21 ....153 E4
Waverley La GU9 ....99 C1
Waverley La GU9 ....56 B3
Waverley Rd GU14 ....16 D8
Wayfarers GU34 ....140 A4
Wayman Rd GU14 ....36 C6
Waynflete La GU9 ....98 D2
Waynflete Pl SO22 ....209 A4
Ways End GU15 ....36 C4
Waysend Ho GU11 ....36 C4
Wayside Cotts GU10 ....144 C3
Wayside Rd GU33 ....208 B5
Weale Ct RG21 ....69 B6
Weatherby Gdns RG27 ....52 D6
Weathermore La GU34 ....140 D2
Weaver Moss GU47 ....34 F7
Weaver's Wlk RG14 ....1 E3
Weavers Cl
  Andover SP10 ....106 B8

Weavers Cl continued
  Middle Winterslow SP5 ....168 A4
Weavers Gdns GU34 ....121 D7
Webb Cl RG22 ....48 F2
Webbs Farm Cl RG28 ....86 C3
Webster Rd SO22 ....209 A7
Wedderburn Ave RG22 ....91 B5
Wedman's La RG27 ....50 F6
Wedman's Pl RG27 ....50 F6
Wedmore Cl SO22 ....197 A3
Weeke Manor Cl SO22 ....209 B8
Weeke Prim Sch SO22 ....209 B8
Weir Ave GU14 ....55 E3
Weir Cl GU14 ....55 E3
Weir Cotts RG20 ....42 E8
Weir Rd Farnborough GU51 ....54 E2
  Hartley Wintney RG27 ....52 B4
Weir The [3] SO23 ....209 F4
Weirs The [3] SO23 ....209 F4
Welbeck Cl GU14 ....55 D3
Weldon Cl GU52 ....75 B5
Well Cl Camberley GU15 ....35 F4
  North Waltham RG25 ....89 E1
  Wootton St Lawrence RG23 ....67 E7
Well House La
  Kings Worthy SO22 ....175 E5
  Lower Common RG7 ....14 F3
Well La GU34 ....119 B7
Well Mdw RG14 ....1 F5
Well Rd GU10 ....97 C6
Well St RG20 ....22 E5
Wella Rd RG22 ....68 F2
Wellburn Cl GU47 ....34 F7
Weller Dr
  Arborfield Garrison RG40 ....15 E6
  Camberley GU15 ....36 A3
Wellesley Cl GU12 ....77 D7
Wellesley Ct GU15 ....106 A5
Wellesley Gate [3] GU12 ....76 F1
Wellesley Gdn [3] GU9 ....99 A7
Wellesley Rd
  Aldershot GU11 ....76 C2
  Camberley GU15 ....106 A6
  Andover SP10 ....106 A6
  Rushmoor GU10 ....144 F6
Wellhouse Rd GU34 ....139 A2
Wellington Ave
  Aldershot GU11 ....76 D2
  Bordon GU35 ....164 D2
  Fleet GU51 ....54 B2
Wellington Cl
  Newbury RG14 ....2 A5
  Sandhurst GU47 ....35 A8
Wellington Cotts RG20 ....3 F2
Wellington Cres RG26 ....9 B1
Wellington Ctr The [9]
  GU11 ....76 E2
Wellington Ctry Pk* RG7 ....14 C1
Wellington Gdns [4]
  GU11 ....76 D1
Wellington La GU9 ....99 B7
Wellington Pl GU12 ....77 D4
Wellington Rd
  Andover SP10 ....82 F1
  Sandhurst GU47 ....35 A8
Wellington Rdbt GU11 ....76 C2
Wellington Terr
  Basingstoke RG23 ....68 C7
  Sandhurst GU47 ....35 A8
Wellington Way GU11, ...76 B7
Wellingtonia Cotts RG27 ....31 A7
Wellow Cl GU11 ....53 C4
Wells Cotts GU15 ....121 E7
Wells La RG29 ....86 B4
Wellspring Ho RG22 ....68 C2
Wellum Ct [8] SP10 ....106 A7
Wells La RG27,RG29 ....11 D5
Welshman's Rd RG14 ....10 E5
Welton Ct RG21 ....69 A5
Wendan Rd RG14 ....5 D8
Wensley Dr GU51 ....54 A3
Wentworth Cl
  Ash Vale GU12 ....77 E7
  Farnham GU9 ....99 D6
Wentworth Cres
  Ash Vale GU12 ....77 E6
  Basingstoke RG22 ....91 A5
Wentworth Ct RG14 ....1 F1
Wentworth Gdns GU34 ....139 E4
Wentworth Grange
  SO22 ....209 C4
Wentworth Lodge [5]
  RG14 ....1 C2
Wesley Cl SP10 ....105 F8
Wesley Dr Odiham RG22 ....72 D1
  Winchester SO23 ....209 C4
Wesley Ho [15] SO23 ....209 E6
Wesley Wlk [11] RG14 ....1 E2
Wessex Ave RG22 ....72 D1
Wessex Cl RG21 ....69 A3
Wessex Cres SP10 ....91 B7
Wessex Ct [22] SO23 ....209 D6
Wessex Dr Odiham RG22 ....72 D1
  Winchester SO23 ....209 C4
Wessex Pl GU9 ....99 A1
Wessex Rd GU9 ....55 C2
West Ave GU9 ....99 B6

West Berkshire Com Hospl
  RG18 ....2 C4
West Berkshire Mus*
  RG14 ....1 E3
West Cl GU9 ....99 B7
West Cotts GU26 ....167 A6
West Downs Student Village
  SO22 ....209 B5
West End Rd RG24 ....47 D4
West End Cl SO22 ....209 C6
West End Gr GU9 ....98 E2
West End Ho RG14 ....1 F5
West End La
  Medstead GU34 ....159 B4
  Rowledge GU10 ....121 E1
West End Rd RG7 ....11 C5
West End Terr SO22 ....209 C6
West Field Cl RG26 ....27 B8
West Field Rd GU35 ....154 C1
West Fryerne GU46 ....34 B8
West Gn GU46 ....34 B8
West Green House Gdn*
  RG27 ....51 E5
West Green Rd
  Hartley Wintney RG27 ....52 B6
  West Green RG27 ....51 F6
West Ham Cl RG22 ....68 D4
West Ham Ct RG22 ....68 C4
West Ham Est RG22 ....68 E4
West Ham La
  Basingstoke RG22 ....68 D5
  Basingstoke,Worting RG22 ....68 B4
West Hayes SO22 ....209 B5
West Heath Rd GU14 ....55 D4
West Hill Dr SO22 ....209 C6
West Hill Gdns GU51 ....53 F2
West Hill Pk SO22 ....209 B6
West Hill Rd N SO21 ....153 E5
West Hill Rd S SO21 ....153 E4
West Hundreds The
  [2] Fleet GU51 ....53 D3
  [1] Fleet GU51 ....53 D3
West Mills RG14 ....1 D3
West Mills Yd RG14 ....1 D3
West Portway SP11 ....81 B6
West Portway SP11 ....82 C2
West Rd Est
  Barton Stacey SO21 ....130 D7
  Camberley GU15 ....36 A5
  Farnborough GU14 ....55 F7
West St Andover SP10 ....105 F7
  Burgclere RG20 ....22 C4
  Farnham GU9 ....98 E1
  New Alresford SO24 ....179 D6
  Newbury RG14 ....1 D3
  Odiham RG29 ....72 C2
  Tadley RG26 ....27 B8
West Street Cl RG26 ....27 A8
West Tisted Cl SO23 ....53 E3
West Tytherley CE Prim Sch
  SP5 ....191 A8
West View Andover SP10 ....106 A2
  Bordon GU35 ....164 B1
West View Dr GU35 ....129 A3
West View Rd GU35 ....86 D4
West Way SP10 ....83 D1
Westbourne Rd GU47 ....35 C7
Westbourne Terr [3] RG14 ....1 E4
Westbrook Cl RG23 ....90 B8
Westbrook Ct RG22 ....68 A4
Westbrook Wlk [10] GU34 ....139 F3
Westbrooke Cl [4] SP10 ....106 A7
Westbrooke Rd GU34 ....139 E3
Westburn Fields GU34 ....139 E3
Westbury Gdns GU51 ....75 D8
Westbury Gr GU51 ....75 D8
Westbury Gdns
  Farnham GU9 ....99 C4
  Fleet GU51 ....75 D8
Westbury Ho [5] SP9 ....78 F6
Westbury Way GU12 ....77 B2
Westdeane Ct RG21 ....68 F4
Westdeane Dr GU16 ....56 F3
Western Ave
  Andover SP10 ....106 A8
  Newbury RG14 ....1 D1
Western CE Prim Sch
  SO22 ....209 B6
Western Cross RG29 ....72 D2
Western End [2] RG14 ....1 E2
Western La RG22 ....72 D3
Western Rd
  Aldershot GU11 ....76 F2
  Bordon GU35 ....164 B1
  Liss GU33 ....207 F4
  Winchester SO22 ....209 B6
Western Way RG22 ....68 D3
Westfield CE
  [8] Andover SP10 ....106 B7
  [11] Fleet GU51 ....54 A1
Westfield Dro SO24 ....201 B1
Westfield La GU10 ....121 C6
Westfield Rd
  Basingstoke RG22 ....69 C3
  Camberley GU15 ....35 F2
  Littleton SO22 ....175 B5
  Thatcham RG19 ....2 E4
Westfield Way [3] RG14 ....1 C2
Westfields Inf Sch GU46 ....33 F5
Westfields Jun Sch GU46 ....33 F5

Westgate CI RG23 . . . . **68** B5
Westgate Ct RG14 . . . . .1 C1
Westgate Mus* SO23 . . . . . **209** D6
Westgate Rd RG14 . . . . .1 C2
Westgate Sch The SO22 . . . **209** C7
Westglade GU14 . . . .**55** B4
Westland RG18 . . . . .2 F4
Westlands Ho **7** RG22 . . . . .**69** A4
Westlands Rd RG14 . . . . .5 F8
Westley CI SO22 . . . .**209** B7
Westley Court Rd SO21 . .**174** A4
Westley La SO21 . . . .**174** C4
Westlyn Rd RG26 . . . . .10 C1
Westman Rd SO22 . . . .**175** D3
Westmarch Bsns Ctr
   SP10 . . . .**83** B2
Westmead
   Farnborough GU14 . . . .**55** F3
   Farnborough GU14 . . . .**55** F4
   3 Farnham GU9 . . . .**98** F2
Westmead Dr RG14 . . . . .5 D8
Westminster CI
   Basingstoke RG22 . . . .**91** B7
   1 Fleet GU51 . . . .**54** A2
Westminster Gate SO22 .**197** B5
Westminster Ho **3** RG21 . .**69** B5
Westmorland Dr GU16 . . . .**36** F3
Weston CI RG25 . . . .**94** B5
Weston Colley Cotts
   SO21 . . . .**132** D3
Weston Ct SP11 . . . .**83** B8
Weston Down Rd SO21 . . .**132** E5
Weston Ho RG27 . . . .**29** D1
Weston La SP5 . . . .**168** A5
Weston Rd RG25 . . . .**94** B4
Westover Rd GU51 . . . .**54** C1
Westpoint **3** GU15 . . . .**36** B6
Westray CI RG21 . . . .**69** D7
Westridge RG20 . . . .**21** C1
Westside CI RG22 . . . .**68** D3
Westview Rd SO22 . . . .**175** A2
Westwood Rd RG14 . . . . .6 A8
Westwood View SO24 . . . .**201** E1
Wetherby Gdns
   Andover SP10 . . . .**82** E2
   11 Farnborough GU14 . . .**56** A1
Wetherby Ho GU15 . . . .**36** B7
Wey CI Ash GU12 . . . .**77** F7
   Camberley GU15 . . . .**35** F5
Wey Hill GU27 . . . .**189** E6
Wey Lodge CI GU30 . . . . . .**188** B4
Weybank GU10 . . . .**120** C3
Weybank CI GU9 . . . .**99** A3
Weybourne Inf Sch GU9 . .**99** C6
Weybourne Rd GU9 . . . .**99** C6
Weybridge Mead GU46 . . .**34** C7
Weybrook Ct RG24 . . . .**47** D4
Weydon Farm Cotts
   GU9 . . . .**121** F8
Weydon Farm La GU9 . . . .**121** F8
Weydon Hill CI GU9 . . . . . .**121** F8
Weydon Hill Rd GU9 . . . . .**121** F8
Weydon La GU9 . . . .**121** E8
Weydon Mill La GU9 . . . . . .**98** F1
Weydon Sch GU9 . . . .**121** D7
Weydown Ct GU27 . . . .**189** F7
Weydown Rd GU27 . . . .**189** F7
Weyford Jun & Inf Schs
   GU35 . . . .**164** F4
Weyhill Bsns Pk SP11 . . . . .**81** B2
Weyhill CI RG26 . . . . .26 F7
Weyhill Gdns SP11 . . . . .81 D2
Weyhill Lodge SP11 . . . . . . .81 D2
Weyhill Rd Andover SP10 .**105** D8
   Penton Corner SP10,SP11 .**82** A1
   Penton Grafton SP11 . . . . .**81** E2
Weyland CI GU30 . . . .**188** A5
Weyside GU9 . . . .**99** A2
Weysprings GU27 . . . .**189** E6
Weysprings CI **3** RG21 . . . .**69** D5
Weywood CI GU9 . . . .**99** D7
Weywood La GU9 . . . .**99** C7
Wharf CI RG23 . . . .**209** F4
Wharf Mill **1** SO23 . . . . . .**209** F4
Wharf Rd Ash Vale GU12 . . .7 F4
   Camberley GU16 . . . .**56** E6
   Newbury RG14 . . . . .1 E3
Wharf St RG14 . . . . .1 E3
Wharf The Newbury RG14 . .1 E3
   Odiham RG29 . . . .**170** D7
Wharf Way GU16 . . . .**56** E6
Wharfenden Way GU16 . . . .**56** D6
Wheatland CI SO22 . . . .**209** B3
Wheatlands La RG14 . . . . .4 F6
Wheatley Ho GU51 . . . .**53** E4
Wheatley La GU35,GU34 .**142** A6
Wheatley Rd GU11 . . . .**76** D3
Wheatleys CI RG25 . . . .**89** B4
Wheatsheaf Cotts GU35 .**165** D6
Wheatsheaf La RG14 . . . . . . .1 C4
Wheeler CI RG26 . . . .**86** D4
Wheeler Hill RG27 . . . .**51** C1
Wheelers St SO21 . . . .**131** C4
Wheelside GU16 . . . .**56** B4
Wheelwright Ho **6** GU12 .**77** A1
Wheelwrights La GU26 . . .**166** A4
Wherwell Dr **12** GU51 . . . . .**53** D3
Wherwell Prim Sch
   SP11 . . . .**129** B7
Whetstone Rd GU14 . . . .**55** A4
Whin Holt GU52 . . . .**74** A7
Whinchat CI RG27 . . . .**52** C7
Whins CI **2** GU15 . . . .**35** F4
Whins Dr GU15 . . . .**35** F4

Whistler CI RG21 . . . . .69 D3
Whistler Gr GU47 . . . . .35 B6
Whistlers La RG7 . . . . .10 F1
Whitaker Ct GU18 . . . . .2 F4
Whitby CI GU14 . . . . .56 C1
Whitchurch CE Prim Sch
   RG28 . . . . .86 D4
Whitchurch CI GU11 . . . . . .100 B6
Whitchurch Rd GU51 . . . . . .53 E3
Whitchurch Silk Mill*
   RG28 . . . . .86 C4
Whitchurch Sta RG28 . . . . . .86 C6
White Acres Rd GU16 . . . . . .56 D4
White Ave GU33 . . . . .186 C2
White Cottage CI GU9 . . . . .99 B6
White Hart Ho GU17 . . . . . . .35 C4
White Hart Ind Est GU17 . .35 C4
White Hart La
   Basingstoke RG21 . . . . .69 C4
   Charter Alley RG26 . . . . . . .46 E8
White Hill
   Basingstoke RG20 . . . . .22 B2
   Ecchinswell RG20 . . . . .23 D3
   Kingsclere RG20 . . . . .44 B6
   Long Sutton RG29 . . . . .96 B2
White Ho The SP9 . . . . .78 F6
White Horse La RG40 . . . . . .16 B5
White House CI RG22 . . . . . .68 E2
White House Farm RG7 . . . .10 B2
White House Gdns GU46 . . .34 A7
White House La RG7 . . . . . . .13 D8
White House Wlk GU9 . . . . .99 B7
White La Deane RG26 . . . . . .44 F3
   Greywell RG27 . . . . .71 D2
White Lion Way GU46 . . . . . .34 B7
White Oak Way SP11 . . . . .105 C4
White Post La GU10 . . . . . . .121 E4
White Rd GU15 . . . . .35 D6
White Rose La GU10 . . . . . .121 F7
White Swan Ct SO21 . . . . . .131 C3
Whitebeam Gdns GU14 . . . .55 A3
Whitebines GU9 . . . . .99 E2
Whitedown GU34 . . . . .139 E2
Whitedown Cotts **1**
   GU34 . . . . .139 E3
Whitedown La GU34 . . . . . .139 D2
Whitedown Rd RG26 . . . . . . .26 D8
Whitedown Sch GU34 . . . . . .1 D7
Whitefield Cotts RG14 . . . . . .1 D7
Whitehall Rd RG2 . . . . .15 D8
Whitehall Rd SO20 . . . . .172 F7
Whitehead CI RG24 . . . . .69 F7
Whitehill CI GU15 . . . . .36 B7
Whitehill Pk GU35 . . . . .186 E8
Whitehill
   Bordon GU35 . . . . .164 F1
   Bordon GU35 . . . . .165 A1
Whitehouse CI GU46 . . . . . . .55 F6
Whites CI RG27 . . . . .50 F1
Whites Rd GU14 . . . . .56 C1
Whiteshoot SO20 . . . . .170 B6
Whiteshute La SO23 . . . . . .209 C3
Whitestones RG22 . . . . .91 C6
Whitethorn CI GU22 . . . . . . .77 F1
Whitewater CE Prim Sch
   RG27 . . . . .50 E5
Whitewater Rd RG29 . . . . . . .72 C4
Whitewater Rise RG27 . . . . .51 C2
Whiteways End GU10 . . . . .100 B4
Whitewood RG24 . . . . .48 F3
Whitgift CI RG22 . . . . .91 B5
Whitley CI GU12 . . . . .98 F1
Whitley Rd GU46 . . . . .34 B4
Whitmarsh La RG24 . . . . .49 B3
Whitmoor Vale Rd
   GU26 . . . . .166 E6
Whitmore CI **2** GU47 . . . . . .35 B8
Whitmore Gn GU9 . . . . .99 C6
Whitmore Hill Cotts
   GU26 . . . . .167 A4
Whitmore Vale GU26 . . . . .166 D6
Whitmore Vale Rd
   Grayshott GU26 . . . . .166 F4
   Headley GU26 . . . . .166 C7
Whitney Rd RG24 . . . . .69 E7
Whitsbury Ho GU51 . . . . . . .53 E4
Whittle CI Ash Vale GU12 . . .77 D5
   Finchampstead RG40 . . . . . .16 C7
Whittle Cres GU14 . . . . .55 D7
Whittle Rd SP10 . . . . .82 B1
Whittle Rdbt GU11 . . . . .55 A1
Whitworth Rd RG2 . . . . .15 E7
Whynot La SP10 . . . . .105 E8
Whyte Ave GU12 . . . . .100 B7
Wick Hill La
   Finchampstead RG40 . . . . . .16 E5
   Finchampstead RG40 . . . . . .16 E6
Wicket Hill GU10 . . . . .121 E6
Wickham CI Alton GU34 . .139 D2
   Crookham Village GU52 . . .74 E5
   Tadley RG26 . . . . .26 F8
Wickham Ct GU52 . . . . .74 E6
Wickham PI GU52 . . . . .74 E6
Wickham Rd
   Camberley GU15 . . . . .36 C8
   Fleet GU52 . . . . .74 E6
Wicklow Ct GU22 . . . . .68 B3
Widgeons GU34 . . . . .139 F5
Widmore Rd RG22 . . . . .68 C2
Wield Industries SO24 . . . .137 A4
Wield Rd Medstead GU34 . .159 D7
   Upper Wield GU34 . . . . . . .137 C2
Wigan Rd GU14 . . . . .76 B8
Wights Wlk RG22 . . . . .91 B7
Wigmore Rd RG26 . . . . .9 D1
Wilberforce CI **2** SO22 . .209 A4
Wild Briar RG40 . . . . .16 D7

Wild Herons RG27 . . . . .51 C1
Wilderness Rd GU16 . . . . . . .36 C2
Wilders Ct GU15 . . . . .36 B3
Wildmoor La
   Church End RG2 . . . . .49 D5
   Sherfield on L RG27 . . . . . . .49 D7
   Sherfield on L RG27 . . . . . . .49 F7
Wildwood Dr RG26 . . . . .9 B1
Wildwood Gdns GU46 . . . . . .34 A4
Wilfred Way GU34 . . . . .139 D3
Will Hall CI GU34 . . . . .139 D3
Will Hall Farm GU34 . . . . . .139 D3
Willems Ave GU11 . . . . .76 D2
Willems Rdbt GU11 . . . . .76 D2
William Cobbett Jun Sch
   GU9 .99 C6
William Ct
   Farnborough GU14 . . . . . . .55 F4
   3 Farnborough,South
   Farnborough GU14 . . . . . . .56 A1
William Farthing CI **7**
   GU11 . . . . .76 E2
William Hitchcock Ho **3**
   GU14 . . . . .55 F4
William Ho SP11 . . . . .83 B8
William Way GU34 . . . . .140 A5
Williams Way GU51 . . . . .54 C1
Willian PI GU35 . . . . .167 C6
Willington CI GU15 . . . . .35 F6
Willis Ct GU34 . . . . .160 E1
Willis Way* RG21 . . . . .69 B4
Willis Waye SO23 . . . . .176 C6
Willoughby CI GU34 . . . . . . .139 E2
Willoughby Way RG23 . . . . . .68 D6
Willow CI Bordon GU35 . . . .164 E3
   Liphook GU30 . . . . .188 B3
   Mytchett GU16 . . . . .56 C4
   Newbury RG14 . . . . .1 D1
Willow Cres GU14 . . . . .55 F7
Willow Ct Alton GU34 . . . . .139 E3
   Ash Vale GU12 . . . . .17 E7
   Frimley GU16 . . . . .36 E7
Willow Fields GU17 . . . . .77 F1
Willow Gdns GU30 . . . . .188 B3
Willow Gr GU51 . . . . .105 F7
Willow Ho RG24 . . . . .49 A3
Willow La GU17 . . . . .35 B4
Willow Mews **2** SP9 . . . . . .79 A7
Willow Pk GU12 . . . . .77 D2
Willow Rd
   Bishop's Green RG20 . . . . . . .6 D2
   Liss GU33 . . . . .208 A4
   Tadley RG26 . . . . .26 F8
Willow Way
   Aldershot GU12 . . . . .100 C8
   Basingstoke RG23 . . . . .68 D7
   Farnham GU9 . . . . .99 B6
   Sherfield on L RG27 . . . . . . .49 D7
Willowdale RG40 . . . . .16 D8
Willowford GU46 . . . . .34 B6
Willowmead CI RG14 . . . . . . .5 A5
Willows End GU47 . . . . .34 F8
Willows The
   Andover SP10 . . . . .105 F6
   North Warnborough RG29 . .72 C4
   Runfold GU10 . . . . .100 A4
Wilmot CI **10** GU34 . . . . . .139 E2
Wilmot Way
   Basingstoke RG23 . . . . .68 D6
   Frimley GU15 . . . . .36 D3
Wilmot Wlk RG14 . . . . .5 A6
Wilsom CI GU34 . . . . .140 A3
Wilsom Rd GU34 . . . . .140 A3
Wilson CI SO20 . . . . .126 A4
Wilson Ho SP9 . . . . .78 E8
Wilson Rd Aldershot GU12 . .77 B1
   Farnborough GU14 . . . . . . .55 D3
Wilson Valkenburg Ct
   RG14 .1 C4
Wilsons Rd GU35 . . . . .165 F5
Wilton Ct GU14 . . . . .56 B3
Wilton PI RG21 . . . . .68 F4
Wilton Rd GU15 . . . . .35 F3
Wilton Terr SP9 . . . . .101 E7
Wiltshire Ho RG24 . . . . .68 D8
Wimborne Ho RG40 . . . . .16 B2
Wimbushes RG40 . . . . .16 B6
Wincanton Ct GU34 . . . . . . .140 A2
Winchcombe CI GU51 . . . . . .75 A8
Winchcombe Rd
   Basingstoke RG22 . . . . .69 A4
   Newbury RG14 . . . . .1 E2
Winchester By Pass
   SO23 . . . . .176 C2
Winchester Cath* . . . .
   SO23 . . . . .209 E5
Winchester Christian Sch
   SO23 . . . . .209 B3
Winchester City Mill*
   SO23 . . . . .209 F5
Winchester Coll SO23 . . . . .209 E4
Winchester Ct **9** RG14 . . . .1 E2
Winchester City Mus*
   SO23 . . . . .209 E5
Winchester Gdns SP10 . . . .106 B6
Winchester Hill SO21 . . . . .131 C3
Winchester Rd
   Alton GU34 . . . . .139 E1
   Ash GU34 . . . . .77 E3
   Basingstoke RG22,RG23 . . .91 A7
   Chawton GU34 . . . . .161 D8
   Chilbolton SO20,SP11 . . . .129 B6
   Four Marks GU34 . . . . .160 F8
   King's Somborne SO20 . . . .172 B3
   Kingsclere RG20 . . . . .24 C1
   Micheldever SO21 . . . . .133 B2
   New Alresford SO24 . . . . . .179 B5
   North Street SO24 . . . . .181 C7
   Rushmoor GU10 . . . . .144 F7

Winchester Rd continued
   Upper Clatford SP11 . . . . .106 A4
   Wherwell SP11 . . . . .128 E2
   Whitchurch RG28 . . . . .86 C3
Winchester Road Rdbt
   RG21 . . . . .68 F3
Winchester Sch of Art
   SO23 . . . . .209 E6
Winchester St
   5 Andover SP10 . . . . . . .106 A7
   7 Basingstoke RG21 . . . .69 B4
   Chilbolton SO20 . . . . .129 B5
   Farnborough GU14 . . . . . . .77 A8
   Overton RG25 . . . . .88 B7
   Whitchurch RG28 . . . . .86 C4
Winchester Sta SO23 . . . . .209 D7
Winchester Trad Pk
   SO23 . . . . .176 C1
Winchester Way GU17 . . . . .35 A6
Winchfield CI RG27 . . . . .53 A1
Winchfield Ct RG27 . . . . .52 A7
Winchfield Sta RG27 . . . . . . .52 C1
Windermere Ave RG22 . . . . .68 F4
Windermere CI GU14 . . . . . .55 C3
Windermere Ct GU12 . . . . . .77 D4
Windermere Gdns
   SO24 . . . . .179 D4
Windermere Rd GU35 . . . . .164 D5
Windermere Way
   Farnham GU9 . . . . .98 E6
   Thatcham RG19 . . . . .2 E3
Winding Wood Dr GU15 . . .36 F3
Windmill Cnr RG7 . . . . .11 E6
Windmill Ct
   6 Aldershot GU12 . . . . . .77 A1
   Alton GU34 . . . . .139 F2
   Mortimer RG7 . . . . .11 E6
Windmill Dr GU35 . . . . .165 F6
Windmill Fields
   East Worldham GU34 . . . . .141 A1
   Selborne GU34 . . . . .160 C3
Windmill Hill GU34 . . . . . . .140 B2
Windmill Hill La Alton GU34 .140 B2
   Anna Valley SP11 . . . . .105 E4
   Hurstbourne Tarrant SP11 . .60 C7
Windmill Rd
   Aldershot GU12 . . . . .77 A1
   Mortimer RG7 . . . . .11 E6
Windmills The **14** GU34 .139 F3
Windrush CI **28** RG21 . . . . .69 D5
Windrush Hts GU47 . . . . .34 F8
Windsor CI Alton GU34 . . . .139 D3
   Farnborough GU14 . . . . . . .55 F4
   Farnborough GU14 . . . . . . .98 E6
Windsor Ct
   Camberley GU15 . . . . .36 A1
   8 Fleet GU51 . . . . .54 A1
   Newbury RG14 . . . . .1 F2
Windsor Gdns Ash GU12 . . .77 D1
Windsor Ho **1** SO23 . . . . .209 F6
Windsor Pk GU22 . . . . .68 B3
Windsor Rd
   Andover SP10 . . . . .105 F8
   Farnborough GU14 . . . . . . .76 B8
   Farnborough,South Farnborough
   GU14 . . . . .56 B1
   Four Marks GU34 . . . . .160 B4
   Lindford GU35 . . . . .164 F5
   New Alresford SO24 . . . . . .179 C4
Windsor Ride
   Finchampstead RG40 . . . . . .16 E7
   Finchampstead RG40 . . . . . .35 E8
Windsor Rise RG14 . . . . .6 A8
Windsor Way
   Aldershot GU11 . . . . .99 E4
   Camberley GU16 . . . . .56 D8
Windsor Wlk GU35 . . . . .164 E4
Wingate CI GU11 . . . . .76 D2
Wingate La RG29 . . . . .99 F5
Wings CI GU9 . . . . .98 F6
Wings Rd GU9 . . . . .98 F6
Winklebury CI RG23 . . . . . . .68 C5
Winklebury Inf Sch RG23 . .68 D6
Winklebury Jun Sch
   RG23 . . . . .68 D6
Winklebury Way RG23 . . . . .68 D5
Winkworth La RG7,RG26 . . .9 A3
Winkworth PI GU9 . . . . .99 A3
Winnall CI SO23 . . . . .176 C1
Winnall Manor Rd SO23 .198 C1
Winnall Prim Sch SO23 . . .198 C1
Winnall Trad Est
   Winchester SO23 . . . . .176 C1
   Winchester SO23 . . . . .198 C6
Winnall Valley Rd SO23 . .198 C1
Winnipeg CI GU30 . . . . .188 C3
Winslade La RG25 . . . . .115 D8
Winslade Rd SO23 . . . . .175 C4
Winston Ave RG26 . . . . .27 B6
Winston CI GU16 . . . . .56 D6
Winston Rise GU34 . . . . . . .160 B3
Winston Way RG19 . . . . .2 D4
Winston Wlk GU10 . . . . .122 A4
Winter CI GU22 . . . . .77 E8
Winterbourne Ho RG22 . . . .68 C2
Winterbourne Wlk GU16 . .56 D8
Winterdyne Mews SP9 . . . .105 F7
Winterthur Way RG21 . . . . . .69 A5
Winterton Dr RG14 . . . . .1 B5
Wintney St GU51 . . . . .53 D3
Winton Chase SP10 . . . . . . .106 D8
Winton Cl
   South Tidworth SP9 . . . . . . .78 F4
   Winchester SO22 . . . . .209 D8
Winton Cres GU46 . . . . .34 B5
Winton Hill SO20 . . . . .150 A3
Winton Rd **11** GU34 . . . . . .76 E1

Winton Sch SP10 . . . . .106 D8
Winton Sq RG21 . . . . .69 B4
Wiremead La SP11 . . . . .103 F7
Wishanger La GU10 . . . . . . .143 F2
Wishmoor CI GU15 . . . . .36 C8
Wishmoor Rd GU15 . . . . .36 C8
Wisley Gdns GU14 . . . . .55 B2
Wisley Rd SP10 . . . . .105 E7
Wistaria Ct SP10 . . . . .105 F7
Wistaria La GU46 . . . . .34 A5
Wisteria Ct GU51 . . . . .99 A3
Wisteria Dr **11** GU35 . . . .164 D2
Wisteria Mews GU34 . . . . . .140 D6
Witan CI SP10 . . . . .83 B4
Witan Ct RG28 . . . . .86 B6
Wither Rise RG23 . . . . .67 A2
Witherslack Cl GU35 . . . . . .166 A4
Withies The
   Crondall GU10 . . . . .97 D6
   Longparish SP11 . . . . .108 F3
Witt Rd SP5 . . . . .168 B5
Wittcomb Terr GU34 . . . . . .164 C1
Wittmead Rd GU16 . . . . .56 D4
Witton Hill SO24 . . . . .178 D4
Wivelrod Rd GU34 . . . . .138 C1
Woburn Ave GU14 . . . . .56 B3
Woburn CI GU16 . . . . .36 E1
Woburn Gdns RG22 . . . . .68 C3
Wokefield Row RG7 . . . . .12 B8
Wolds The RG22 . . . . .68 B3
Wolf's La GU34 . . . . .161 E8
Wolfe CI SO22 . . . . .209 A3
Wolfe Rd GU12 . . . . .77 A2
Wolfmere La GU33 . . . . .186 A6
Wolmer Cotts GU33 . . . . . . .186 B6
Wolmer Terr GU33 . . . . .186 A4
Wolseley Rd GU11 . . . . .76 E1
Wolverdene Specl Sch
   SP10 . . . . .106 B7
Wolverdene CI SP10 . . . . . .106 C7
Wolverdene Gdns
   SP10 . . . . .106 C7
Wolverdene Rd SP10 . . . . . .106 C7
Wolverton La RG26 . . . . .25 D1
Wolverton Rd
   Baughurst RG26 . . . . .26 B7
   Wolverton Common RG26 . .25 E5
Wolverton Towns End
   RG26 . . . . .25 E2
Wolsesey Castle (Old
   Bishop's Palace)*
   SO23 . . . . .209 E5
Wolvesey Terr **3** SO23 . . .209 F4
Wonston CI SO21 . . . . .131 D3
Wonston La SO21 . . . . .131 D2
Wood End RG24 . . . . .48 E2
Wood Hill La RG29 . . . . .95 B6
Wood La Beech Hill RG7 . . .13 C5
   Bramdean SO24 . . . . .202 E6
   Farnborough GU14 . . . . . . .55 E3
   Fleet GU51 . . . . .54 C1
   Seale GU10 . . . . .100 F5
Wood Moor RG40 . . . . .16 D2
Wood Pk SP11 . . . . .57 A2
Wood Rd
   Beacon Hill GU26 . . . . .167 B6
   Camberley GU15 . . . . .35 F2
   Farnham GU9 . . . . .99 A7
Wood Ridge RG14 . . . . .5 C7
Wood St GU12 . . . . .99 A1
Woodbarn The GU9 . . . . .99 A1
Woodbine CI GU47 . . . . .35 A7
Woodbine La GU10 . . . . .5 D1
Woodbourne Gr GU9 . . . . . .99 C7
Woodbourne CI
   Liss GU33 . . . . .208 A4
   Yateley GU46 . . . . .34 B6
Woodbridge Dr GU15 . . . . . .36 B7
Woodbridge Rd GU17 . . . . . .34 F5
Woodbury Ct RG7 . . . . .15 B4
Woodbury Rd RG22 . . . . .91 B7
Woodcot Gdns GU14 . . . . . . .55 B4
Woodcote Cotts
   Bramdean SO24 . . . . .202 E4
   Sutton Scotney SO21 . . . . .131 C4
Woodcote Gn GU51 . . . . .74 D8
Woodcote Rd SN8 . . . . .18 A7
Woodcott Ho
   1 Tadley RG26 . . . . .26 F8
   5 Pamber Heath RG26 . . .9 E1
Woodcott Terr GU12 . . . . . .100 B8
Woodcroft RG23 . . . . .90 B8
Woodcut Rd GU10 . . . . .121 D6
Woodend
   1 Camberley GU15 . . . . . .36 E7
   Farnborough GU14 . . . . . . .56 B3
Woodfalls Ho GU51 . . . . .53 E4
Woodfield RG35 . . . . .142 B1
Woodfield Cotts GU32 . . . .206 B3
Woodfield Dr SO22 . . . . . . .197 B6
Woodgarston Dr RG22 . . . . .91 A3
Woodgate GU51 . . . . .54 C2
Woodgreen Rd GU10 . . . . . .122 C4
Woodhouse La RG19 . . . . .2 C3
Woodland Cres GU14 . . . . . .56 A6
Woodland Dr
   Bramley RG26 . . . . .29 B2
   Farnham GU10 . . . . .121 F6
Woodland Rise GU51 . . . . . .74 F5
Woodland Wlk GU12 . . . . . . .77 D4
Woodlands
   Andover SP10 . . . . .106 C8
   Chineham RG24 . . . . .49 A4
   Fleet GU51 . . . . .53 F2
   Overton RG25 . . . . .88 A8
   Penwood RG20 . . . . .21 E7

Woodlands continued
Runfold GU10 ....100 B4
Yateley GU46 ....34 B4
Woodlands Ave GU9 ......99 D7
Woodlands Bsns Village
RG21 ....69 D6
Woodlands Cl
Ash Vale GU12 ....77 E5
Farnborough GU17 ....35 C1
Woodlands Cotts SO24 ..203 D2
Woodlands Ct
Alton GU34 ....139 D1
1 Winchester,Hyde SO23 ..209 E7
Winchester,Weeke SO22 ..209 A8
Woodlands La
Haslemere GU27 ....189 D7
Hill Brow GU33 ....208 B3
Woodlands Pk GU12 ....77 D1
Woodlands Rd
Camberley GU15 ....35 F5
Farnborough GU14 ....55 B6
Pamber Heath RG26 ......9 B1
Woodlands The
Bordon GU35 ....186 D8
Kings Worthy SO23 ....176 C6
Woodlands Way SP10 ..106 C8
Woodlands Wlk GU17 ..35 C1
Woodlane Cl SO24 ....202 D5
Woodlark Glade GU15 ..36 B7
Woodlarks Camp Site
GU10 ....122 D7
Woodlea Cl SO22 ......209 C8
Woodlea Prim Sch
GU35 ....164 D1
Woodleigh GU51 ......75 A8
Woodleys RG20 ....23 D4
Woodman Cl GU51 ....174 D2
Woodman Ct GU51 ....74 F8
Woodman La SO21 ....174 C2
Woodmanfield RG25 ....94 C6
Woodmere Croft RG22 ..90 F7
Woodpecker Cl
Basingstoke RG22 ......90 F8
Bordon GU35 ....164 D2
Ewshot GU10 ....98 B8
Woodpeckers
3 Andover SP10 ......106 A8
Winchester SO23 ......209 E8
Woodpeckers Dr SO22 ..209 A8
Woodridge Ho RG14 ....5 C7
Woodridge Manor GU15 ..36 B7
Woodroffe Dr RG22 ....68 C1
Woods La RG25 ....91 F7
Woodside
Blackwater GU17 ......35 A3
Farnborough GU14 ......55 F7
Newbury RG14 ....5 B7
Sandhurst GU15 ....35 D7
Vernham Dean SP11 ....38 A5

Woodside Cl
Bordon GU35 ....164 D3
Finchampstead RG40 ....16 C8
Mortimer RG7 ....11 E6
Woodside Cotts RG25 ..112 E7
Woodside Cres GU35 ..164 D3
Woodside Gdns
Chineham RG24 ....49 A4
Fleet GU51 ....54 C1
Woodside La GU34 ....161 B4
Woodside Pk GU35 ....164 D3
Woodside Rd
Farnborough GU14 ......76 D7
Farnham GU9 ....99 C7
Woodstock Mead RG22 ..91 B6
Woodstocks GU14 ......56 B6
Woodville Cl
Blackwater GU17 ......34 F5
Chineham RG24 ....48 F2
Woodville Rise RG24 ..48 F2
Woodway GU15 ....35 F5
Wool Gr SP10 ....106 C8
Wooland Ct 1 GU52 ..74 E4
Woodlings Farm Vineyard *
RG28 ....63 F1
Wooldridge Cres RG29 ..95 C8
Woolfield La GU32,GU34 ..205 B3
Woolford Cl 1 SO22 ..209 A4
Woolford Way RG23 ....68 D6
Woollards Rd GU12 ....77 F4
Woolley Sq SP10 ......83 C3
Woolmead Ct GU9 ......99 A3
Woolmead Rd GU9 ......99 A3
Woolmead The GU9 ....99 A3
Woolmead Wlk GU9 ....99 A3
Woolmer Hill Ho GU27 ..189 A6
Woolmer Hill Rd GU27 ..189 B7
Woolmer Hill Tech Coll
GU27 ....189 B7
Woolmer La GU30 ....188 A7
Woolmer Rd GU33 ....186 B3
Woolmer Trad Est
GU35 ....164 C3
Woolmer View 12 GU26 ..167 B3
Woolmer Way GU35 ....164 C2
Woolton Hill Jun Sch
RG20 ....21 C8
Woolton Lodge Gdns
RG20 ....4 D2
Woolverston SO22 ....209 C7
Wootey Inf Sch GU34 ..139 F6
Wootey Jun Sch GU34 ..139 F6
Wooteys Way GU34 ....139 F6
Worcester Ave RG25 ....91 B8
Worcester Cl GU14 ....55 F7
Worcester Ct 18 GU51 ..53 E3
Worcester Ho RG24 ....68 D8
Wordsworth Ave GU46 ..33 F4

Wordsworth Cl
Basingstoke RG24 ......69 C8
Winchester SO22 ......209 B6
Worldham Hill GU34 ..141 A1
Worldham Ho GU51 ....53 E4
Wormersley Rd RG19 ....6 B7
Worrell Sq SP10 ......83 C3
Worsam Ct RG22 ......68 B4
Worsley Rd GU16 ......56 D7
Worthy La SO23 ......209 E7
Worthy Rd SO23 ......209 E8
Worting Rd
Basingstoke,Buckskin RG22 ..68 B4
Basingstoke,West Ham
RG22 ....68 E4
Worting Road Rdbt RG22 ..68 C4
Wote St RG21 ....69 B4
Wouldham Cl SP11 ....79 D7
Wrecclesham Hill GU10 ..121 C5
Wrecclesham Rd GU10 ..121 D8
Wrekin Cl RG22 ......68 B3
Wrekin The GU14 ......56 C1
Wren Cl Alton GU34 ..140 A5
Winchester SO22 ......209 B3
Yateley GU46 ....33 F6
Wren Ct GU12 ....77 F3
Wren Way GU14 ......55 D7
Wrights Cl SO21 ....153 D4
Wrights Way SO21 ....153 D4
Wyatt Ct 5 GU47 ....35 B7
Wychwood Cl GU12 ....77 D2
Wychwood Pl GU15 ....36 F8
Wyck La Binsted GU34 ..141 E6
Binsted,Wyck GU34 ....141 B3
Wye Ct SP10 ....83 D2
Wyke Mark SO22 ......209 A8
Wykeham Pk SO21 ....199 A7
Wykeham Dr RG23 ......68 A4
Wykeham Pl SO22 ....209 B4
Wykeham Terr 7 SO23 ..209 F4
Wykeham Ind Est The
SO23 ....176 C2
Wylde Green La GU33 ..208 B5
Wylye Rd SP9 ....78 F7
Wymering Ct GU14 ....56 B3
Wyndham Cl GU46 ....34 B7
Wyndham Rd
Andover SP10 ....105 F6
Newbury RG14 ....2 B5
Wyndham St GU12 ....77 A1
Wynfields GU16 ......56 D3
Wynne Gdns GU52 ....75 B5
Wyvern Cl GU12 ......77 D5

Y
Yarnhams Cl GU34 ....160 B2
Yateley Common Ctry Pk *
GU46,GU17 ....34 D3
Yateley Inds GU46 ....34 B7
Yateley Inf Sch GU46 ..34 B6
Yateley Manor Sch GU46 ..34 B6
Yateley Rd GU47 ......34 D8
Yateley Sch GU46 ......34 A6
Yates Copse RG14 ......2 C5
Yatesbury Cl GU9 ....121 D7
Yellowhammer Rd RG22 ..90 F6
Yellowhammers GU34 ..139 F5
Yeomans RG27 ....33 C7
Yeomans Cl
Farnborough GU14 ......55 E5
Tongham GU10 ....100 D8
Yeomans La
Burghclere RG20 ......5 E1
Liphook GU30 ....187 E4
Yeomans Pl GU35 ....165 C5
Yeomans Way GU15 ....36 C5
Yeosfield RG7 ....14 A3
Yeovil Cl GU14 ....56 B1
Yeovil Rd GU14 ......56 C1
Yetminster Rd GU14 ..56 B1
Yew Cl RG20 ....24 E2
Yew Gate RG14 ....1 D6
Yew Tree Cl
Bramley RG26 ....29 A2
Farnborough GU14 ......55 A3
Goodworth Clatford SP11 ..106 A1
Oakley RG23 ....90 B8
Yew Tree La
North Waltham RG25 ....89 E1
West Tytherley SP5 ..169 B4
Yew Tree Pl GU33 ....208 A4
Yew Tree Wlk GU16 ....36 D1
Yolland Cl GU9 ......99 A7
York Cl Basingstoke RG22 ..91 B8
York Ct 4 SP10 ......83 A3
York Ho
5 Aldershot GU11 ....76 D1
Basingstoke RG22 ......68 E3
20 Winchester SO23 ..209 E8
York La RG27 ....52 C5
York Lodge 4 GU12 ..77 A1
York Mews GU34 ....140 A4
York Pl GU15 ....36 B7
York Rd Aldershot GU11 ..76 D1
Ash GU12 ....77 E3
Camberley GU15 ......36 B7
Farnborough GU14 ......55 D1
Farnborough GU14 ......76 C8

York Rd continued
Farnborough,South Farnborough
GU14 ....56 A1
· Farnham GU9 ....99 A1
Newbury RG14 ....1 F2
York Terrace La GU15 ..35 E5
York Town Ind Est GU15 ..35 E4
York Way GU47 ....34 F8
Yorktown Rd
Sandhurst,College Town
GU47 ....35 C7
Sandhurst,Little Sandhurst
GU47 ....34 F7
Yorkwood GU33 ......207 F4
Youlden Cl GU15 ......36 E5
Youlden Dr GU15 ......36 F6
Young Cres RG19 ......6 B8
Young's Ind Est RG7 ....9 D4
Youngs Dr GU12 ......77 D2
Youngs Paddock SP5 ..168 A6
Youngs Rd GU34 ....139 F4

Z
Zephyr Ho 11 RG7 ......9 C2
Zinnia Cl RG22 ....91 A7
Zion Rd SP11 ....124 D5
Zodiac Ho 12 RG7 ......9 C2
Zouch Ave SP9 ....78 E7
Zouch Cl SP9 ....78 E7
Zouch Farm Rd SP9 ....78 E7
Zouch Mkt SP9 ....78 E7
Zouch Prim Sch SP9 ..78 D8

Addresses

Name and Address	Telephone	Page	Grid reference